THE ROOTS OF PSYCHOLOGY

© 1974 by Basic Books, Inc.
Library of Congress Catalog Card Number: 72–76919
SBN 465–06740–9
Manufactured in the United States of America
DESIGNED BY VINCENT TORRE
74 75 76 77   10 9 8 7 6 5 4 3 2 1

The Roots of Psychology

A Sourcebook in the History of Ideas

EDITED BY

Solomon Diamond

Basic Books, Inc., Publishers

NEW YORK

PREFACE

A countryside which is ravishingly beautiful when viewed from a hilltop or from a small plane may lose much of its charm as seen by the modern jet traveler from an altitude of five or six miles. It is thus with history. Seen remotely it may be dull, but there is a favorable distance from which its patterns can be discerned without excessive loss of those details which give it distinctive charm. The purpose of a source book is to help see history close up. Even so, the glimpses it can give are like those caught when flying above a broken cloud cover which hides more than it discloses. In the end, whoever wants to see all the beauty of the countryside must walk. The justification for anthologies is that no one has the time to walk on all roads.

Most previous source books for psychology seem to be imbued with the spirit of Ebbinghaus's famous epigram, that "psychology has a long past but a short history." As one of the great pioneers of modern experimental psychology, Ebbinghaus felt the need to emphasize the independence of the new discipline from speculative philosophy. Today, with that issue long resolved, we feel the contrary need to trace the beginnings of psychological thought before the experimental era. One important lesson to be learned from studying the history of psychology is that the fundamental viewpoints on many controversial issues were formulated independently of all experimental evidence in the modern sense of that phrase and that most men continue to take sides on them without regard to such evidence. Regrettable perhaps, but true. The experiments of psychologists have settled only minor issues in psychology, and too often, like dreams, they are wish-fulfilling. Meanwhile, advances in other sciences, and major changes in social structure, have often exercised decisive influence on the building of psychological theories. It is a major purpose of this book to make such influences apparent.

There are presently four source books in English which try to cover the full historical range of psychology. Each has important merits, and I would like to point these out before saying how this source book differs from them. The oldest is Benjamin Rand's Classical Psychologists (1912). Its content reflects its compiler's predominantly philosophic interest, and when it appeared—in the same year with John B. Watson's *Behavior*—it was already out of tune with the spirit of American psychology. However, Rand's own translations from Beneke, Drobisch, Maine de Biran, Weber, Stumpf, and Carl Lange provided important materials not elsewhere available in English.

Thirty-six years went by before Wayne Dennis (1948) provided a set of readings more to the modern taste. Emphasis was shifted from the speculative to the experimental, and coverage was extended well into the twentieth century, but at the price of including only a dozen authors prior to the nineteenth.

Both Rand and Dennis used a purely chronological arrangement which later source books have abandoned. Herrnstein and Boring (1965) group their selections into 15 topical chapters. Seven of these deal with aspects of sensation and perception; none deals with motivation, emotion, personality, developmental, abnormal, or social psychology. The selection is therefore representative (as is Dennis) of the interests of experimental psychologists, and not of the full spectrum of psychology either today or in the past. The value to the student is increased by editorial comments which give an historical context for each selection.

Sahakian (1968) groups his selections by schools, and hence largely by nationality of authorship. Several chapters are devoted to clinical psychology, and some attention is given to child and social psychology and to theories of personality. However, this increased breadth is attained for the most part in twentieth-century selections. If it is true, as Sahakian states, that "a reading of the leading current source books devoted to the history of psychology would imply the absence of important areas in psychology, such as, personality theory, abnormal psychology, psychotherapy, and social psychology," then the reading of Sahakian's sources would seem to imply that there were no noteworthy contributors to any of these areas before the late nineteenth century.

Dennis, Herrnstein and Boring, and Sahakian agree in this: selections from earliest times through the eighteenth century are allocated less than one third of the space given to the nineteenth century. Psychology's "long past" is thus compressed into a short introduction, and as a consequence the historical beginnings of psychology in most problem areas are omitted. This method of selection tends to foster the sort of prejudice which was once expressed in Condillac's disdainful phrase that "after Aristotle came Locke." Such prejudice has far less justification today than it had in the eighteenth century, because in fact a careful reading of history will show that twentieth-century theory is often following eighteenth-century models.

If this is a situation which calls for remedy, then a new source book is needed. In my effort to meet that need, I have tried to supplement existing source books rather than to supplant them and to avoid reprinting of the same sources which are already conveniently available when other materials can serve to fill out the historical picture in a representative way. My admiration for Hunter and Macalpine's Three Hundred Years of Psychiatry (1963) has led me to give less space to the description of mental illness than would otherwise have been the case and has permitted me to give other areas proportionately better coverage.

The selections are grouped into 28 chapters, each of which is intended to illustrate the historical development of views in a problem area. There can be no logical linear progression for these chapters. I have tried to give them a convenient order, but where interrelationships are so complex, inconsistencies and non sequiturs are unavoidable. Occasionally deficiencies in one chapter are remedied by cross-references to selections in other chapters, but the work as a whole must be illustrative rather than exhaustive, since it is obvious that a fat source book could be compiled under almost any of our chapter headings.

I am sure that my chief motivation in compiling this new collection of source materials has been the compulsion we all feel to share a good book with our friends. If the reader will feel some of the same delight which I have felt in "discovering" these selections for myself, I shall be rewarded.

Translations which are not otherwise credited are the work of the editor. Most footnotes, subheads, and marginal glosses have been dropped without notice, and internal parenthetic references were either omitted or shortened. Nor do subheads always follow the source in style and capitalization. Otherwise I have been faithful to the original texts, except for such minimal changes as substituting u's for archaic v's, and correcting vagaries of spelling and punctuation which would have been acknowledged as typographical errors in their own time. Words enclosed in square brackets [thus] are explications provided by translators; my own comments of a similar nature (where I am not the translator) are enclosed in braces {thus}.

Since my introductory comments are intended only to provide a minimal scaffolding and not to offer scholarly interpretation, I have dispensed with any further apparatus of notes.

Grateful acknowledgement is made to the many learned societies and publishers who have permitted the reprinting of copyrighted materials. Each such instance is noted in its proper place. I owe special thanks to my very patient friends, Professors Stanley Burstein and Kenneth J. Pratt, both of the Department of History, California State University, Los Angeles, who have guided me through difficulties arising because I am blind in Greek and halt in Latin. Professor Giovanni Cecchetti, of the University of California at Los Angeles, gave indispensable aid with a difficult early Italian text. For errors in which I persist despite this generous aid, I am alone responsible.

ADVISORY NOTE

For some of the deficiencies which the reader will inevitably discover in this source book, he may seek remedy in the following:

Clarke, E., and O'Malley, C. D. *The Human Brain and Spinal Cord. A Historical Study Illustrated by Writings from Antiquity to the Twentieth Century.* Berkeley: University of California Press, 1968.

Dennis, W. *Readings in the History of Psychology.* New York: Appleton-Century-Crofts, 1948.

Ellis, W. D. *A Source Book of Gestalt Psychology.* London: Routledge & Kegan Paul, 1938.

Herrnstein, R. J., and Boring, E. G. *A Source Book in the History of Psychology.* Cambridge, Mass.: Harvard University Press, 1965.

Hunter, R., and Macalpine, Ida. *Three Hundred Years of Psychiatry, 1535–1860. A History Presented in Selected English Texts.* London: Oxford University Press, 1963.

Rand, B. *The Classical Psychologists. Selections Illustrating Psychology from Anaxagoras to Wundt.* Boston: Houghton Mifflin Company, 1912.

Rapaport, D. *Organization and Pathology of Thought. Selected Sources.* New York: Columbia University Press, 1951.

Sahakian, W. S. *History of Psychology. A Source Book in Systematic Psychology.* Itasca, Ill.: Peacock Press, 1968.

Shipley, T. *Classics in Psychology.* New York: Philosophical Library, 1961.

CONTENTS

Contents

Contents

ILLUSTRATIONS

THE ROOTS OF PSYCHOLOGY

 # Chapter 1

THE CONCEPT
OF MAN

In the larger sense, all human psychology has as its topic "the concept of man." Every bit of significant psychological thought and research contributes toward shaping and coloring this concept in its own time, and each of the selections included in this volume, under whatever heading, is chosen either because it made an especially noteworthy contribution of this sort, or because it is representative of a point of view which was conditioned by a contemporary concept of man. I say "a" contemporary concept because, at most times in the history of western culture, men are bitterly at odds in their views of human nature. The history of psychology is no smooth evolution of a modern viewpoint which replaces its predecessors; it is a struggle between opposing views which were defined relatively early and which have been in continual conflict. Let us begin, then, with three gemlike reminders of early attitudes which persist, in various modifications, down to the present time.

Man is the measure of all things, of things that are that they are, and of things that are not that they are not.   —Protagoras, 5th century B.C.

Man is a political animal.   —Aristotle, 4th century B.C.

God created man in his own image.   —*Genesis*, 1:27.

3

1.1

Plato

(427?–347 B.C.)

*The Timaeus has special historical interest because, for many centuries
after the close of the classical period, it was almost the only work of Plato
which was known to western Europe. The references to an immortal soul
earned the respect of Christian theologians who were made receptive by
Augustine's favorable comments on Platonism (which actually referred to
what we now call Neoplatonism), and they were prepared to interpret the
pagan elements in Plato's thought as allegorical. The final portion of this
selection can be read as supporting the ideals of a monastic life.*

Again, it is reasonable and proper to set forth in turn the subject complementary to the foregoing {discussion of sickness}, namely the remedial
treatment of body and mind, and the causes which conserve this. For
what is good merits description more than what is evil. All that is good
is fair, and the fair is not void of due measure; wherefore also the living
creature that is to be fair must be symmetrical. Of symmetries we distinguish and reason about such as are small, but of the most important
and the greatest we have no rational comprehension. For with respect to
health and disease, virtue and vice, there is no symmetry or want of
symmetry greater than that which exists between the soul itself and the
body itself. But as regards these, we wholly fail to perceive or reflect that,
whenever a weaker and inferior type of body is the vehicle of a soul that
is strong and in all ways great,—or conversely, when each of these two is
of the opposite kind,—then the creature as a whole is not fair, seeing that
it is unsymmetrical in respect of the greatest of symmetries; whereas a
creature in the opposite condition is of all sights, for him who has eyes to
see, the fairest and most admirable. A body, for example, which is too
long in the legs, or otherwise disproportioned owing to some excess, is
not only ugly, but, when joint effort is required, it is also the source of
much fatigue and many sprains and falls by reason of its clumsy motion,
whereby it causes itself countless evils. So likewise we must conceive of
that compound of soul and body which we call the "living creature."
Whenever the soul within it is stronger than the body and is in a very
passionate state, it shakes up the whole body from within and fills it with
maladies; and whenever the soul ardently pursues some study or investi-

Timaeus. Translated by R. G. Bury. In *Plato, with an English translation, Vol. VII.*
Cambridge, Mass.: Harvard University Press (Loeb Classical Library), 1929. Pp. 1–253.
[87C–88C, 89D–90D.] Reprinted by permission of the publisher and the Loeb
Classical Library.

gation, it wastes the body; and again, when the soul engages, in public or in private, in teachings and battles of words carried on with controversy and contention, it makes the body inflamed and shakes it to pieces, and induces catarrhs; and thereby it deceives the majority of so-called physicians and makes them ascribe the malady to the wrong cause.

And, on the other hand, when a large and overbearing body is united to a small and weak intellect, inasmuch as two desires naturally exist among men,—the desire of food for the body's sake, and the desire of wisdom for the sake of the most divine part we have,—the motions of the stronger part prevail and augment their own power, but they make that of the soul obtuse and dull of wit and forgetful, and thereby they produce within it that greatest of diseases, ignorance.

From both these evils the one means of salvation is this—neither to exercise the soul without the body nor the body without the soul, so that they may be evenly matched and sound of health. . . .

Concerning both the composite living creature and the bodily part of it, how a man should both guide and be guided by himself so as to live a most rational life, let our statement stand thus. But first and with special care we must make ready the part which is to be the guide to the best of our power, so that it may be as fair and good as possible for the work of guidance. Now to expand this subject alone in accurate detail would in itself be a sufficient task. But treating it merely as a side-issue, if we follow on the lines of our previous exposition, we may consider the matter and state our conclusions not inaptly in the following terms. We have frequently asserted that there are housed within us in three regions three kinds of soul, and that each of these has its own motions; so now likewise we must repeat, as briefly as possible, that the kind which remains in idleness and stays with its own motions in repose necessarily becomes weakest, whereas the kind which exercises itself becomes strongest; wherefore care must be taken that they have their motions relatively to one another in due proportion. And as regards the most lordly kind of our soul, we must conceive of it in this wise: we declare that God has given to each of us, as his daemon, that kind of soul which is housed in the top of our body and which raises us—seeing that we are not an earthly but a heavenly plant—up from earth towards our kindred in the heaven. And herein we speak most truly; for it is by suspending our head and root from that region whence the substance of our soul first came that the Divine Power keeps upright our whole body.

Whoso, then, indulges in lusts or in contentions and devotes himself overmuch thereto must of necessity be filled with opinions that are wholly mortal, and altogether, so far as it is possible to become mortal, fall not short of this in even a small degree, inasmuch as he has made great his mortal part. But he who has seriously devoted himself to learning and to true thoughts, and has exercised these qualities above all his others, must necessarily and inevitably think thoughts that are immortal

5

and divine, if so be that he lays hold on truth, and in so far as it is possible for human nature to partake of immortality, he must fall short thereof in no degree; and inasmuch as he is for ever tending his divine part and duly magnifying that daemon who dwells along with him, he must be supremely blessed. And the way of tendance of every part by every man is one—namely, to supply each with its own congenial food and motion; and for the divine part within us the congenial motions are the intellections and revolutions of the Universe. These each one of us should follow, rectifying the revolutions within our head, which were distorted at our birth, by learning the harmonies and revolutions of the Universe, and thereby making the part that thinks like unto the object of its thought, in accordance with its original nature, and having achieved this likeness attain finally to that goal of life which is set before men by the gods as the most good both for the present and for the time to come.

1.2

Pliny

(23–79)

Plinius Secundus, called the Elder to distinguish him from a nephew who also attained literary fame, died in the destruction of Pompei. His massive Historia mundi, *or Natural history of the world, may be likened to an intellectual lava flow which has indiscriminately preserved for posterity much of the science and superstition of his time. He shows by modern standards an astonishing credulity about such things as a race of men with feet big enough to serve them as umbrellas, but he also expresses a sophisticated disbelief in notions about human immortality. Of course, such realistic resignation to death comes more easily to the aristocrat who has enjoyed life fully than to the plebeian, who hopes that a future life, if it does not reward him, will at least punish his persecutor.*

In Pliny's time, as will appear in later selections, it was generally accepted that the pneuma, or air, was the source of all life. The distinction which he makes between soul and shadow (or "shade") may be compared with these statements by his contemporary, the apostle Paul:

"May your spirit and soul and body be preserved entire, without blame at the coming of Christ" (I Thessalonians, 4:23).

"For the word of God is living and active, and sharper than any two-

The historie of the world, commonly called, The naturall historie of C. Plinius Secundus. Translated into English by Philemon Holland, Doctor of Physicke. London, 1601. [Book 7, Proeme, pp. 152–153, and Ch. 55, p. 187.]

edged sword, piercing even to the dividing of soul and spirit, of both joints and marrow, and quick to discern the thoughts and intents of the heart" (Epistle to the Hebrews, 4:12).

This translation is one of the earliest in which the literary treasures of the ancient world were made accessible to those not schooled in Latin and Greek. The appearance of such translations responded to the demand of a new class of educated men—men of some wealth, privilege, and leisure, who were not trained to theology, law, or medicine.

Thus as you see, we have in the former bookes sufficiently treated of the Universall world, of the Lands, Regions, Nations, Seas, Ilands and re-nowned Cities therein contained. It remaineth now to discourse of the living creatures comprised within the same, and their natures: a point doubtlesse that would require as deepe a speculation, as any part else thereof whatsoever, if so be the spirit and mind of man were able to comprehend and compasse all things in the world. And to make a good entrance into this treatise and historie, me thinkes of right wee ought to begin at Man, for whose sake it should seeme that Nature made and produced all other creatures besides: though this great favour of hers, so bountifull and beneficiall in that respect, hath cost them full deere. In so much, as it is hard to iudge, whether in so doing she hath done the part of a kind mother, or a hard and cruell step-dame. For first and formost, of all other living creatures, man she hath brought forth all naked, and cloathed him with the good and riches of others. To all the rest, given she hath sufficient to clad them everie one according to their kind: as namely, shells, cods, hard hides, prickes, shagge, bristles, haire, downe feathers, quils, skailes, and fleeces of wooll. The very trunkes and stemmes of trees and plants, shee hath defended with barke and rind, yea and the same sometime double, against the iniuries both of heat and cold: man alone, poore wretch, she hath laid all naked upon the bare earth, even on his birth-day, to cry and wraule presently from the very first houre that he is borne into this world: in such sort, as among so many living creatures, there is none subiect to shed teares and weepe like him. And verily to no babe or infant is it given once to laugh before he be fortie daies old, and that is counted verie early and with the soonest. Moreover, so soone as he is entred in this manner to enioy the light of the sunne, see how he is immediatly tyed and bound fast, and hath no member at libertie; a thing that is not practised upon the young whelpes of any beast among us, be he never so wild. The child of man thus untowardly borne, and who another day is to rule and commaund all other, loe how he lyeth bound hand and foot, weeping and crying, and beginning his life with miserie, as if he were to make amends and satisfaction by his punishment unto Nature, for this onely fault and trespasse, that he is borne alive. O follie of all follies, ever to think (considering this simple beginning of ours) that we were sent into this world to live in pride and carrie our head aloft! The first hope that wee conceive of our strength, the first gift that Time affourdeth us, maketh us no better yet than four-footed beasts. How long is it ere we can goe alone? how long before we can prattle and speake, feed our selves, and chew our meat strongly? what a while continueth the mould and crowne of our heads to beat and pant, before our braine is well setled; the undoubted marke and token that bewrayeth our exceeding great weaknesse above all other creatures? What should I say of the infirmities and sicknesses that soone seaze upon our feeble bodies? what need I speake of so many medicines and remedies devised against these maladies: besides the new diseases that come everie day, able to check and frustrate all our provision of Physicke whatsoever? As for all other living creatures, there is not one, but by a secret instinct of nature knoweth his owne good, and whereto he is made able: some make use of their swift feet, others of their flight wings: some are strong of limme; others are apt to swimme, and practise the same: man onely knoweth nothing unlesse hee be taught; he can neither speake, nor goe, nor eat, otherwise than he is trained to it: and to be short, apt and good at nothing he is naturally, but to pule and crie. And hereupon it is, that some have been of this opinion, That better it had been, and simply best for a man, never to have been borne, or else speedily to die. None but we doe sorrow and waile, none but we are given to excesse and superfluitie infinitely in everything, and shew the same in every member that we have. Who but we again are ambitious and vainglorious? who but we are covetous and greedie of gathering good? wee and none but we desire to live long and never to die, are superstitious, carefull of our sepulture and buriall, yea, and what shall betide us when we are gone. Mans life is most fraile of all others, and in least securitie he liveth: no creature lusteth more after every thing than he: none feareth like unto him, and is more troubled and amazed in his fright: and if he be set once upon anger, none more raging and wood than he. To conclude, all other living creatures live orderly and well, after their owne kind: we see them flocke and gather together, and readie to make head and stand against all others of a contrarie kind: the lyons as fell and savage as they be, fight not one with another: serpents sting not serpents, nor bite one another with their venimous teeth: nay the verie monsters and huge fishes of the sea, warre not amongst themselves in their owne kind: but beleeve me, Man at mans hand receiveth most harme and mischiefe. . . .

Of the Ghosts and Spirits of Men Departed

After men are buried, great diversitie there is in opinion, what is become of their souls and ghosts, wandering some this way, and others that. But this is generally held, that in what estate they were before men were borne, in the same they remain when they are dead. For neither body nor soul hath any more sence after our dying day, than they had before the day of our nativitie. But such is the follie and vanitie of men, that it extendeth still even to the future time, yea, and in the very time of death flattereth it selfe with fond imaginations, and dreaming of I wot not what life after this. For some attribute immortalitie to the soule: others devise a certain transfiguration thereof. And there be againe who suppose, that the ghosts sequestred from the bodie, have sence: whereupon they do them honour and worship, making a god of him that is not so much as a man. As if the manner of mens breathing differed from that in other living creatures: or as if there were not to bee found many other things in the world, that live much longer than men, and yet no man judgeth in them the like immortalitie. But shew mee what is the substance and bodie as it were of the soule by it selfe? what kind of matter is it apart from the bodie? where lieth her cogitation that she hath? how is her seeing, how is her hearing performed? what toucheth she? nay, what doth she at all? How is she emploied? or if there bee in her none of all this, what goodness can there be without the same? But I would know where she setleth and hath her abiding place after her departure from the bodie? and what an infinite multitude of souls like shaddowes would there be, in so many ages, as well past as to come? now surely these be but fantasticall, foolish, and childish toies: devised by men that would fain live alwaies, and never make an end. The like foolerie there is in preserving the bodies of dead men. And the vanity of *Democritus* is no lesse, who promised a resurrection thereof, and yet himselfe could never rise againe. And what a follie is this of all follies to thinke (in a mischeefe) that death should bee the way to a second life? what repose and rest should ever men have that are borne of a woman, if their soules should remaine in heaven above with sence, while their shaddowes tarried beneath among the internall wights? Certes, these sweet inducements and pleasing persuasions, this foolish credulitie and light-beleefe, marreth the benefite of the best gift of Nature, to wit, Death: it doubleth besides the paine of a man that is to die, if he happen to thinke and consider what shall betide him the time to come. For if it bee sweet and pleasant to live, what pleasure and contentment can one have, that hath once lived, and now doth not. But how much more ease and greater securitie were it for each man to beleeve himselfe in this point, to gather reasons, and to ground his resolution and assurance upon the experience that hee had before hee was borne?

1.3

Lactantius

(*c.* 260–c. 340)

Lactantius was a third-century Christian apologist whose literary eloquence earned him the title of "the Christian Cicero." His principal work is the Divine institutions, but of this he himself prepared an Epitome, from which we take two brief passages. They represent the completely anthropocentric view which is to remain characteristic of Christian thinking until it is shaken by the Copernican theory.

[Ch. 69] . . . God made the world for man: anyone who fails to recognize this fact is little better than an animal. Who gazes heavenward but man? who marvels to behold sun, and stars, and all the works of the Creator but man? who tills the earth and takes the fruit therefrom? who sails the ocean, who has dominion over fishes, and flying creatures, and four-footed things, but man? It was for man's sake that God made all things, because they have served man's advantage. Philosophers have observed this, but its sequel, that God made man for His own sake, this they have not seen. Hence it was right and necessary (since God accomplished such mighty works for man, when he bestowed upon him such glory and power as to be lord of the world) that man should acknowledge God, the Author of all these blessings, who made the world itself on his account, and should moreover pay Him the worship and honor that is due to him. . . .

[Ch. 70] Pleasure belongs to all living creatures, virtue to man alone; the one is faulty, the other honorable; the one is in harmony with nature, the other contrary—unless the soul is immortal. . . . Here lies the supreme proof of immortality, that man alone has a knowledge of God. In dumb brutes there is no idea of religion, for they are creatures of earth and are bent earthward. Man, who stands upright, gazes to heaven that he may seek after God. . . . Lastly, only man employs the celestial element, which is fire. For if light comes to us through fire, and life through light, clearly he that employs fire is not mortal, since this is closely connected with Him apart from whom there is neither life nor light.

Epitome of the divine institutes. Translated by E. H. Blakeney. London: S.P.C.K., 1950. [Pp. 118–119.]

1.4

Moses Maimonides

(1135–1204)

An ancient concept very popular in the Middle Ages was that of the parallel between man, the microcosm, and the universe at large, or macrocosm. Later, in the Renaissance, the occult bond between specific bodily parts and certain heavenly bodies played a large part in astrology, and hence in chiromancy and physiognomy. In this passage Maimonides, a Spanish Jew who served as physician to the Sultan of Cairo, and doubtless the most prominent of the Jewish scholars whose writings helped to bridge the gulf between the Mohammedan and Christian worlds, stresses that this parallel would be meaningless if intellect were not also common to both man and the universe.

. . . Bear in mind, however, that in all that we have noticed about the similarity between the Universe and the human being, nothing would warrant us to assert that man is a microcosm; for although the comparison in all its parts applies to the Universe and any living being in its normal state, we never heard that any ancient author called the ass or the horse a microcosm. This attribute has been given to man alone on account of his peculiar faculty of thinking, I mean the intellect, viz., the hylic intellect which appertains to no other living being. This may be explained as follows. An animal does not require for its sustenance any plan, thought or scheme; each animal moves and acts by its nature, eats as much as it can find of suitable things, it makes its resting-place wherever it happens to be, cohabits with any mate it meets while in heat in the periods of its sexual excitement. In this manner does each individual conserve itself for a certain time, and perpetuates the existence of its species without requiring for its maintenance the assistance or support of any of its fellow creatures; for all the things to which it has to attend it performs by itself. With man it is different; if an individual had a solitary existence, and were, like an animal, left without guidance, he would soon perish, he would not endure even one day, unless it were by mere chance, unless he happened to find something upon which he might feed. For the food which man requires for his subsistence demands much work and preparation, which can only be accomplished by reflection and by plan; many vessels must be used, and many individuals,

The guide for the perplexed. Translated from the original Arabic text by M. Friedländer. Second edition. London: Routledge and Kegan Paul, 1904. [Part I, Ch. 72, pp. 117–118.]

each in his peculiar work, must be employed. It is therefore necessary that one person should organize the work and direct men in such a manner that they should properly cooperate, and that they should assist each other. The protection from heat in summer and from cold in winter, and shelter from rain, snow, and wind, require in the same manner the preparation of many things, none of which can properly be done without design and thought. For this reason man has been endowed with intellectual faculties, which enable him to think, consider, and act, and by various labours to prepare and procure for himself food, dwelling and clothing, and to control every organ of his body, causing both the principal and the secondary organs to perform their respective functions. Consequently, if a man, being deprived of his intellectual faculties, only possessed vitality, he would in a short time be lost. The intellect is the highest of all faculties of living creatures; it is very difficult to comprehend, and its true character cannot be understood as easily as man's other faculties.

There also exists in the Universe a certain force which controls the whole, which sets in motion the chief and principal parts, and gives them the motive power for governing the rest. Without that force, the existence of this sphere, with its principal and secondary parts, would be impossible. That force is God; blessed be His name! It is on account of this force that man is called microcosm; for he likewise possesses a certain principle which governs all the forces of the body, and on account of this comparison God is called "the life of the Universe"; comp. "and he swore by the life of the Universe" (Dan. xii. 7).

1.5

Pierre Charron

(1541–1603)

During the sixteenth century, men in the western world learned a new independence in thinking. At the opening of the seventeenth century, Shakespeare reflects the new self-respect which men have attained, quite different from the former childlike identification with an all-powerful Father figure:

> What a piece of work is man! how noble in reason! how infinite in faculty! in form and moving how express and admirable! in action how like an angel!

[*De la sagesse, trois livres* (Of wisdom, three books). Bourdeaux, 1601. Second edition, revised, Paris, 1603.] *De la sagesse, suivant la vraye copie de Bourdeaux, en trois livres.* Paris, 1657. [Ch. 16, pp. 120–132.]

in apprehension how like a god! the beauty of the world! the paragon of animals! (*Hamlet*, Act 2, Scene 2.)

In the same year appeared Charron's work Of wisdom. Charron has been called "Montaigne's secretary," and this book is both a systematization and elaboration of Montaigne's views about man and society. It is strongly at variance with the author's own earlier pietistic writings, and it became at once the target of hostile criticism. Charron softened it somewhat for a second edition, but he died before that was in print, never to fill the lucrative post which apparently had been offered to him if he would make this concession to orthodoxy. Man's pride in the power of his own mind is forcefully expressed in these portions of the chapter on the human spirit.

There is a 1658 translation by Samson Lennard and a 1697 translation by George Stanhope. Both are based on the revised version in which this was the fourteenth chapter. Lennard's is awkward, inaccurate in detail, but faithful in spirit; Stanhope's has better syntax but less authenticity. What follows is a free revision of the Lennard translation, brought into conformity with the original French text.

The human mind and its economy—this great and lofty intellectual part of the soul—are a depth of obscurity, full of crevices and hidden corners, a confused and involved labyrinth and bottomless pit, which consists of many parts, faculties, actions, and divers motions, which have as many names, all harboring doubts and difficulties. . . .

I'd stop no man who sings and sets forth the praises and greatness of the mind of man; its capacity, vivacity, and quickness. Let it be called the image of the living God, a celestial ray to which God has given reason and an animated helm to move it by rule and measure; that it is an instrument of perfect harmony; that by it there is a kind of kindred between God and man, and that to be reminded of this, man's roots are turned towards the heavens, so that he shall always look toward the place of his birth; in short, that there is nothing great on earth but man, nothing great in man but his mind, and if a man rises to it, he rises above the heavens. These are all plausible words, with which the schools and pulpits ring.

But I desire that after all this we should fathom the mind and study how to know it, for we shall find that it is a dangerous instrument both to itself and others, a little troublemaker, a ferret which is to be feared, an annoying and importunate parasite, which, like a juggler playing at sleight of hand, under the guise of some gentle motion, subtle and smiling, forges, invents, and causes all the mischief in the world; for without it, there would be none. . . .

First, the mind is perpetually active; it cannot be without action, and rather than that will forge for itself false and fantastical subjects, deceiving itself in earnest and to its own discredit. . . . If it is not occupied with some subject, it will run riot in imagination. There is no folly nor vanity

that it will not produce, and if it has no set limit, it will lose itself in wandering. . . .

It is also universal, meddling in everything, . . . subjects vain and of no account as well as those noble and weighty, those we can understand as well as those we cannot. . . .

Thirdly, it is prompt and speedy, running in a moment from one end of the world to another, busying itself without stay or rest, penetrating everywhere. . . .

Because of these three conditions—because it is perpetually active, swift, and universal—it has been regarded as immortal, and as having in itself some spark of divinity.

The action of the mind is to search, ferret, and endlessly twist about, like one that is famished for want of knowledge, to seek and inquire. . . . There is no end to our inquiries: the pursuits of the human mind are without form or end; its food is doubt and ambiguity; it is perpetually in movement, without rest or bound; the world is a school of investigation; the chase and its excitement are our proper meat, but whether we catch the prey or miss it is another matter. . . .

1.5 Pierre Charron

It has two ends in view, of which the first is common and natural: this is the Truth, which it seeks and pursues, for there is no desire more natural than to know the truth. We try every means we can to attain it, but in the end all our endeavours fall short, for truth is not an ordinary booty, nothing to be seized in the hand, and still less something to be possessed by the human mind. . . .

Its second end, less natural but more ambitious, is Invention, and it aspires to this as to the point of highest honor, by which it may prove its worth; this receives the highest praise, and seems like an image of divinity. It is this abundance of inventiveness which has produced all those works which have captured the admiration of the world, while those which have some public value have deified their authors. . . .

It is easy to see, from all of this, how rash and dangerous the mind of man may be, especially when it is lively and vigorous; for being so eager, so free and universal, so unrestrained in its movements, using its liberty so boldly in all things, without bowing to any, it may easily shake off common opinions and all the rules by which one tries to bind and restrain it, as being an unjust tyranny. It will examine everything, and judging most of those things which the world views as plausible to be ridiculous and absurd, but finding some likelihood everywhere, it will make excuses for everything. In so doing, it is to be feared that it will wander and lose its way, and in fact we see that those who have extraordinary vivacity and rare excellence {of mind} are usually disordered in their opinions and in their conduct. . . .

That is why there is good reason to give the mind strict limits, to bridle and bind it with religions, laws, customs, sciences, precepts, threats, promises mortal and immortal, yet still we see that in its unruly manner it escapes and makes itself free of all restrictions, for it is by nature stubborn, fierce and proud, and if it is to be led it must be by deception, and not by force.

1.6

Baruch Spinoza

(1632–1677)

Charron's breach of orthodoxy was mild compared to what was soon to follow. Later in the seventeenth century, Spinoza points to the need for honest, unprejudiced evaluation of human nature, and in this pursuit he applies the "geometric method" of Descartes more ruthlessly than Descartes ever did. The modernity of Spinoza's views is such that in 1826 Johannes Müller declared (see 7.11) that the treatment of the passions in Spinoza's Ethics is a model of the method to be pursued in developing a scientific physiological psychology.

Philosophers conceive of the passions which harass us as vices into which men fall by their own fault, and, therefore, generally deride, bewail, or blame them, or execrate them, if they wish to seem unusually pious. And so they think they are doing something wonderful, and reaching the pinnacle of learning, when they are clever enough to bestow manifold praise on such human nature, as is nowhere to be found, and to make verbal attacks on that which, in fact, exists. For they conceive of men, not as they are, but as they themselves would like them to be. Whence it has come to pass that, instead of ethics, they have generally written satire, and that they have never conceived a theory of politics, which could be turned to use, but such as might be taken for a chimera, or might have been formed in Utopia, or in that golden age of the poets when, to be sure, there was least need of it. Accordingly, as in all sciences, which have a useful application, so especially in that of politics, theory is supposed to be at variance with practice; and no men are esteemed less fit to direct public affairs than theorists or philosophers.

2. But statesmen, on the other hand, are suspected of plotting against mankind, rather than consulting their interests, and are esteemed more crafty than learned. No doubt, nature has taught them, that vices will exist, while men do. And so, while they study to anticipate human wickedness, and that by arts, which experience and long practice have taught, and which men generally use under the guidance more of fear than of reason, they are thought to be enemies of religion, especially by divines, who believe that supreme authorities should handle public affairs in accordance with the same rules of piety, as bind a private individual. Yet there can be no doubt, that statesmen have written about politics far

A political treatise [1678]. In *The chief works of Benedict de Spinoza.* Translated from the Latin, by R. H. M. Elwes. London: G. Bell and Sons, 1883. 2 vols. Vol. I, pp. 279–387. [Pp. 287–289.]

more happily than philosophers. For as they had experience for their mistress, they taught nothing that was inconsistent with practice. . . .

4. Therefore, on applying my mind to politics, I have resolved to demonstrate by a certain and undoubted course of argument, or to deduce from the very condition of human nature, not what is new and unheard of, but only such things as agree best with practice. And that I might investigate the subject-matter of this science with the same freedom of spirit as we generally use in mathematics, I have laboured carefully, not to mock, lament, or execrate, but to understand human actions; and to this end I have looked upon passions such as love, hatred, anger, envy, ambition, pity, and the other perturbations of the mind not in the light of vices of human nature, but as properties, just as pertinent to it, as are heat, cold, storm, thunder, and the like to the nature of the atmosphere, which phenomena, though inconvenient, are yet necessary, and have fixed causes by means of which we endeavour to understand their nature, and the mind has just as much pleasure in viewing them aright, as in knowing such things as flatter the senses.

5. For this is certain, and we have proved its truth in our Ethics, that men are of necessity liable to passions, and so constituted as to pity those who are ill, and envy those who are well off; and to be prone to vengeance more than to mercy; and moreover, that every individual wishes the rest to live after his own mind, and to approve what he approves, and reject what he rejects. And so it comes to pass, that, as all are equally eager to be first, they fall to strife, and do their utmost mutually to oppress one another; and he who comes out conqueror is more proud of the harm he has done to the other, than of the good he has done to himself. And although all are persuaded, that religion, on the contrary, teaches every man to love his neighbour as himself, that is to defend another's right just as much as his own, yet we showed that this persuasion has too little power over the passions. It avails, indeed, in the hour of death, when disease has subdued the very passions, and man lies inert, or in temples, where men hold no traffic, but least of all, where it is most needed, in the law-court or the palace. We showed, too, that reason can indeed, do much to restrain and moderate the passions, but we saw at the same time, that the road which reason herself points out, is very steep; so that such as persuade themselves, that the multitude or men distracted by politics can ever be induced to live according to the bare dictate of reason, must be dreaming of the poetic golden age, or of a stage-play.

1.7

Mathew Hale

(1609–1676)

Mathew Hale, lord chief justice of England, took time from his onerous public duties to prepare a painstakingly thorough brief for a very conservative, pious view of man's nature. The argument that man's better mind brings him dread, not happiness, is a foretaste of Kierkegaard and of his existentialist followers in our own day.

Although in the lower World there are various accommodations of things one to another, yet the chief and ultimate accommodation of things seems principally to terminate in Man. . . . The accommodation of Brutes to Men is an accommodation of an Inferior to a Superior; the accommodation of Man to Brutes is an accommodation of a Superior to an Inferior, an accommodation of Regiment and Protection. . . .

It is true, that some things Man hath in common with the rest of created visible Beings, as that he is a corporeal Being, hath Life and Sensation, and is a beautiful Piece of the Furniture of this lower World. In these things, therefore, or by them, we are not to seek that special End for which man was made; because under these and the like Considerations he seems to have a common parity with the other created Beings.

But our search must be, 1. Whether there be not some peculiarities in the Humane Nature, some Faculties and Powers, something in his Constitution, and some adaptations and appropriate accommodations therein peculiar to his nature, and of a far more advanced use and perfection than those of the best of other inferior Animals. . . .

. . . As we find in the Sensitive Nature certain congenit or connatural Instincts, whereby they are secretly and powerfully biassed, and inclined, and carried to their proper sensitive Good, either individual or specifical; such as are their inclination to that Food which is suitable for them, their *Appetitus procreativus,* their care for their Young, and infinite more; so there seems to be lodged in the Intellective and Rational Nature certain Rudiments and Tendencies, whereby they are carried to the good of an intellectual Life, certain *communes notitiae,* lodged and connaturally implanted in the Intellect, which serve as a kind of connatural inward stock for the Understanding to work upon, and also as a secret biass and inclination to carry him on to the good of an intellectual Life: Such as are a secret inscribed Notion that there is a God, that he is to be wor-

The primitive origination of mankind, considered and examined according to the light of nature. London, 1677. [Pp. 360–361, 365, 374–375.]

shipped, honoured, served, and obeyed; and certain inscribed common Notices of Moral Good and Evil, that make him propense to Justice, Honesty, to do as he would be done by, and the like. . . .

Again, it is apparent that the very excellency and preference of the Intellectual Nature doth render the fruition of the Good of Sense less good, less satisfactory, than it is to the Brutes: the Good of Sense is so far from being the specifical or peculiar end of Man, that the very Make, Texture, and Order of his nobler Faculties renders it not only incomplete, but deficient, and less competent to him, than if he had not this excellency of Faculties which are specifical to his Nature. . .

The fruition of the delights of Sense in the Beasts are more entire, simple, and unallayed than they are in Men; because it is apparent, that in the Intellective Nature there is something that checks, controls, and sowrs the fruition of Sense, namely the Conscience, which hath oftentimes a contrary motion, and checks the inferior Faculties of Sense, even when it oftentimes cannot control it, it chides and allays the contentation of sensual Delights; so that even in Laughter the Heart is sorrowful: but the Brutes have no such correction of their Delights in fruition of Sense, but are entire in their enjoyments.

Again, it is a great perfection of the Human Nature, that it hath a more fixed, strong, and compact memory of things past than the Brutes have: A Brute forgets his fruitions when they are past, hath not the sense, much less the memory of any faults or follies committed by him; and therefore his present fruitions are not sowred with the remembrance of those better seasons of delight that he once had: But Man hath ever a remembrance of what is past, he remembers his faults and follies, and what sensible advantages he lost by this or that inadvertence, oversight, or folly; if his prosperity or fruition were formerly greater, it depreciates his present enjoyment: so that the excellence of his memorative Faculties makes his present enjoyment faint, weak, and tastless. . . .

Again, and most principally of all the rest, the Brutes have little prospect to the future, if any at all. . . . And hence it is, that they have no consideration or fear of death till they feel it; and if they have a good Pasture at present, they are not solicitous how long it will last, or what they shall do after: they are not tormented with fears of what may come, because they have no anticipation or suspitions of what may be in the future; and by this means their enjoyments are sincere, unallayed with fears or suspitions, they fear not death, because they are not sensible of their own mortality till they feel themselves dying: But the case is quite otherwise with Man, the excellency of his Faculties, and the impression of Experience and Observation gives him a foresight of many things that will come, and a strong suspition of many more that may come; and by this means he anticipates Miseries, and becomes twice miserable: first, in fears, pre-apprehensions, and anticipation, and then again in the actual undergoing of it; and if those suspected and feared evils never overtake him, yet he is equally if not more miserable than if they did: For his pre-apprehensions and suspitions renders them as sharp as if they were felt, and many times sharper, by the apposition of the most hideous and aggravating circumstances that his thoughts and fears can fashion. And this very anticipation and foresight, which is a perfection and excellence in Man above the Brutes, saddens his Joy, galls and frets his sensual Contentment, and upon the very account of his own excellency and perfection renders the fruition of a sensible good utterly incompetible to be that end of fruition which the wise God designed for him: Thus when he hath Wealth and Plenty he is under a thousand cares and fears, sometimes of false Accusers, sometimes of Thieves and Robbers, sometimes of Fire and Casualty; and while he is rich and plentiful in fruition, he is poor and miserable by anticipation; If he be in Health and Strength, whereby sensual Goods have their proper gust and relish with him, yet he is under the fear of Sickness, Pain, and Discomposure, which fear renders the Disease in a manner present before it comes, and so gives a distast and disrelish to even his present fruition.

1.8

Julien Offray de la Mettrie

(1709–1751)

Approximately a century after Descartes, La Mettrie drew the full dire consequence of scientific advance in his declaration that "man is a machine"—but one capable of pleasure. His argument included a review of current advances in physiology and statements about the power of education which have a strong behavioristic flavor (see 13.6). Having lost a post as army physician because of an outcry against his first and milder statement (L'Histoire naturelle de l'ame, 1745), La Mettrie took what he thought was safe refuge in the Netherlands and pulled out all the stops. He proved that even Dutch tolerance had limits. L'Homme machine was publicly burned, and its author found a new refuge at the court of the free-thinking Frederick of Prussia. There he is said to have met an Epicurean demise from overeating. As one of history's most outspoken materialists, La Mettrie has always been fair game for slander.

The bracketed sentence is omitted from Miss Bussey's somewhat sanitized translation.

[*L'Homme machine,* 1748.] Translated by Gertrude C. Bussey, as *Man a machine.* La Salle, Ill.: Open Court Publishing Co., 1912. (Includes the complete French text.) [Pp. 121, 143–144, 148–149.]

We were not originally made to be learned; we have become so perhaps by a sort of abuse of our organic faculties, and at the expense of the State, which nourishes a host of sluggards whom vanity has adorned with the name of philosophers. Nature made us all solely to be happy— yes, all of us from the crawling worm to the eagle lost in the clouds. For this she has given all animals some share of natural law, a share greater or less according to the needs of each animal's organs when in normal condition. . . .

To be a machine, to feel, to think, to know how to distinguish good from bad, as well as blue from yellow, in a word, to be born with an intelligence and a sure moral instinct, and to be but an animal, are therefore characters which are no more contradictory, than to be an ape or a parrot and to be able to give oneself pleasure. {For (we take this opportunity to point out) who would have imagined *a priori* that a drop of liquid discharged during the sexual act could cause one to feel such divine pleasures, and that from it there might be born a little creature who might one day, given certain conditions, enjoy the same delights?} I believe that thought is so little incompatible with organized matter that it seems to be one of its properties on a par with electricity, the faculty of motion, impenetrability, extension, etc. . . .

Let us then conclude boldly that man is a machine, and that in the whole universe there is but a single substance differently modified. . . .

Such is my system, or rather the truth, unless I am much deceived. It is short and simple. Dispute it now who will.

1.9

Condorcet

(1743–1794)

Marie Jean Antoine Nicolas Caritat, Marquis de Condorcet, mathematician by profession and fellow-traveler of the French revolution, composed this book while in hiding during the revolutionary terror. Imprisoned as an unidentified vagrant, he took poison only a few weeks before the fall of Robespierre, and his book was published posthumously at the expense of the republic. No document gives clearer expression to the eighteenth-century dream of the infinite perfectibility of man, which is here based on a view of human nature deriving chiefly from Condillac (16.6).

Esquisse d'un tableau historique des progrès de l'esprit humain. Paris, 1794. Translated anonymously, as *Outlines of an historical view of the progress of the human mind.* London, 1795. [Pp. 1–4, 15–16.]

Man is born with the faculty of receiving sensations. In those which he receives, he is capable of perceiving and of distinguishing the simple sensations of which they are composed. He can retain, recognise, combine them. He can preserve or recal them to his memory; he can compare their different combinations; he can ascertain what they possess in common, and what characterises each; lastly, he can affix signs to all these objects, the better to know them, and the more easily to form from them new combinations. . . .

Sensations are accompanied with pleasure or pain, and man has the further faculty of converting these momentary impressions into durable sentiments of a corresponding nature, and of experiencing these sentiments either at the sight or recollection of the pleasure or pain of beings sensitive like himself. And from this faculty, united with that of forming and combining ideas, arise, between him and his fellow creatures, the ties of interest and duty, to which nature has affixed the most exquisite portion of our felicity, and the most poignant of our sufferings.

Were we to confine our observations to an enquiry into the general facts and unvarying laws which the development of these faculties presents to us, in what is common to the different individuals of the human species, our enquiry would bear the name of metaphysics.

But if we consider this development in its results, relative to the mass of individuals co-existing at the same time on a given space, and follow it from generation to generation, it then exhibits a picture of the progress of human intellect. This progress is subject to the same general laws, observable in the individual developement of our faculties; being the result of that very developement considered at once in a great number of individuals united in society. . . .

. . . From these observations on what man has heretofore been, and what he is at present, we shall be led to the means of securing and of accelerating the still further progress, of which, from his nature, we may indulge the hope.

Such is the object of the work I have undertaken; the result of which will be to show, from reasoning and from facts, that no bounds have been fixed to the improvement of the human faculties; that the perfectibility of man is absolutely indefinite; that the progress of this perfectibility, henceforth above the control of every power that would impede it, has no other limit than the duration of the globe upon which nature has placed us. . . .

We shall expose the origin and trace the history of general errors, which have more or less contributed to retard or suspend the advance of reason, and sometimes even, as much as political events, have been the cause of man's taking a retrograde course towards ignorance.

Those operations of the mind that lead to or retain us in error . . . belong equally . . . to the theory of the developement of our individual faculties. . . . Like truths which improve and enlighten [the human mind], they are the consequences of its activity, and of the disproportion that always exists between what it actually knows, what it has the desire to know, and what it conceives there is a necessity of acquiring.

1.10

Thomas Huxley

(1825–1895)

Darwinian evolution provided a new basis for understanding man's relation to other animals. Huxley was the chief public advocate for the new viewpoint in the early years when it was under severe attack. He tells us that in 1860 he "delivered six Lectures to the Working Men" on the subject of this essay.

The allusion to "the pitiful tenderness of human affections" as one claimed mark of difference from animals reminds us sharply of the recent experimental work of Harlow on monkey-love.

The question of questions for mankind—the problem which underlies all others, and is more deeply interesting than any other—is the ascertainment of the place which Man occupies in nature and of his relations to the universe of things. Whence our race has come; what are the limits of our power over nature, and of nature's power over us; to what goal we are tending; are the problems which present themselves anew and with undiminished interest to every man born into the world. . . .

It is quite certain that the Ape which most nearly approaches man, in the totality of his organization, is either the Chimpanzee or the Gorilla; and as it makes no practical difference, for the purposes of my present argument, which is selected for comparison, on the one hand, with Man, and on the other hand, with the rest of the Primates, I shall select the latter (so far as its organization is known)—as a brute now so celebrated in prose and verse, that all must have heard of him, and have formed some conception of his appearance. I shall take up as many of the most important points of difference between man and this remarkable creature, as the space at my disposal will allow me to discuss, and the necessities of the argument demand; and I shall inquire into the value and the magnitude of these differences, when placed side by side with those which separate the Gorilla from other animals of the same order. . . .

"On the relations of man to the lower animals." In *Evidence as to man's place in nature* [London, 1863]. New York: Appleton, 1877. [Pp. 71, 86–87, 123–124, 129–130, 132.]

Thus, whatever system of organs be studied, the comparison of their modifications in the ape series leads to one and the same result—that the structural differences which separate Man from the Gorilla and the Chimpanzee are not so great as those which separate the Gorilla from the lower apes.

But in enunciating this important truth I must guard myself against a form of misunderstanding, which is very prevalent. I find, in fact, that those who endeavour to teach what nature so clearly shows us in this matter, are liable to have their opinions misrepresented and their phraseology garbled, until they seem to say that the structural differences between man and even the highest apes are small and insignificant. Let me take this opportunity then of distinctly asserting, on the contrary, that they are great and significant; that every bone of a Gorilla bears marks by which it might be distinguished from the corresponding bone of a Man; and that, in the present creation, at any rate, no intermediate link bridges over the gap between *Homo* and *Troglodytes*.

It would be no less wrong than absurd to deny the existence of this chasm; but it is at least equally wrong and absurd to exaggerate its magnitude, and, resting on the admitted fact of its existence, to refuse to inquire whether it is wide or narrow. Remember, if you will, that there is no existing link between Man and the Gorilla, but do not forget that there is a no less sharp line of demarcation, a no less complete absence of any transitional form, between the Gorilla and the Orang, or the Orang and the Gibbon. I say, not less sharp, though it is somewhat narrower. The structural differences between Man and the Man-like apes certainly justify our regarding him as a family apart from them; though, inasmuch as he differs less from them than they do from other families of the same order, there can be no justification for placing him in a distinct order. . . .

On all sides I shall hear the cry—"We are men and women, and not a mere better sort of apes, a little longer in the leg, more compact in the foot, and bigger in brain than your brutal Chimpanzees and Gorillas. The power of knowledge—the conscience of good and evil—the pitiful tenderness of human affections, raise us out of all real fellowship with the brutes, however closely they may seem to approximate us."

To this I can only reply that the exclamation would be most just and would have my entire sympathy, if it were only relevant. But it is not I who seek to base Man's dignity upon his great toe, or insinuate that we are lost if an Ape has a hippocampus minor. On the contrary, I have done my best to sweep away this vanity. I have endeavoured to show that no absolute structural line of demarcation, wider than that between the animals which immediately succeed us in the scale, can be drawn between the animal world and ourselves; and I may add the expression of my belief that the attempt to draw a psychical distinction is equally futile, and that even the highest faculties of feeling and of intellect begin to germinate in lower forms of life. At the same time no one is more strongly convinced than I of the vastness of the gulf between civilized man and the brutes; or is more certain that whether *from* them or not, he is assuredly not *of* them. . . .

. . . Our reverence for the nobility of manhood will not be lessened by the knowledge, that Man is, in substance and in structure, one with the brutes; for, he alone possesses the marvellous endowment of intelligible and rational speech, whereby, in the secular period of his existence, he has slowly accumulated and organized the experience which is almost wholly lost with the cessation of every individual life in other animals; so that now he stands raised upon it as on a mountain top, far above the level of his humble fellows, and transfigured from his grosser nature by reflecting, here and there, a ray from the infinite source of truth.

1.11

Herbert Spencer Jennings

(1868–1947)

After evolution came genetics, which offered, in place of the yearned-for immortality of the individual soul, a quasi-immortality of the hereditary substance. Jennings gives poignant expression to this biologist's conclusion, with its implication that the personality, like the body that houses it, is no more than a short-lived fruit that "hangs on the great netted vine" of interlaced genetic strands.

To biological science, any species, any group of related organisms, presents itself as a series of successive and interwoven generations. Taken together, the generations constitute a great web or network. This network extends indefinitely forward and backward in time. It is formed by innumerable strands, the genes, which pass continuously through the net; which interweave, and at intervals are gathered into knots, that we call individuals. From the knots, the strands again issue, separate, interweave with other strands, and form new knots, individuals of a new generation.

Thus any individual—you or I—is a knot of strands, of genes, that extend backward into the remote past, there forming other individuals, and that will extend forward into the future, forming still others. Every knot, every individual, is a new combination of strands, diverse from the combination forming any other, but containing strands that have been

The biological basis of human nature. New York: W. W. Norton & Co., 1930. [Pp. 290–296.]

part of many earlier individuals. The personal peculiarities of any individual, his characteristics, depend in large measure on what combinaton of strands has entered into him.

As material organisms potentially visible, you and I have been in existence ever since the race that developed into human beings began. This is literal truth. An unlimited microscopist could have followed with his eyes your course and my course down through countless ages, never losing sight of the material organisms for an instant; as the experimenter follows day by day his thousands of generations of infusoria. You and I were in material existence as living organisms, and indeed millions of years old, when the pyramids were built, and the unlimited microscopist could give our history from that time to this, without a break.

But as he followed us, we would not maintain our unity, our personal identity. Tracing the strands from you and from me backward in time, they diverge, into hundreds, into thousands of earlier individuals, with different characteristics. And if they are traced forward into the future, they again diverge, uniting with those from other individuals, to form a multitude of new personalities. The strands that make you have come from a hundred other individuals, and will later pass to other hundreds. Of your store of genes you may say, as Iago said of his purse, " 'Twas mine, 'tis his, and has been slave to thousands."

As a feeling, experiencing, knowing self, I, the ego, am identified with only one of the great number of knots into which the living strands are tied; my experiences cling to one of these exclusively. This fact arouses questions. Why should my experience not embrace the entire network, the entire organism, instead of merely one knot of its interlaced strands? What is the relation of my self to the other knots existing at the same time? And what is the relation of my self to the knots that came earlier and will follow later?

Playing a most important role for these questions is a further fact of biology. When the genes become knotted together to form an individual, the knot grows, develops, produces a fruit that hangs on the great netted vine. That fruit—the body of the individual—though all its parts can be traced back in unbroken genetic continuity to remote past ages, does not as a whole continue forward into the future. It carries within itself, besides the genes that have developed and transformed to produce the body, sets of genes that have remained in the unchanged, undeveloped condition. And it is these unchanged genes that continue into the future. The rest of the fruit drops from the vine and disappears.

The individual self appears, from straightforward biological observation, to be identified with the developed body rather than with the undeveloped genes that it contains. Its experiences as a self seem to cease with the disappearance of that body, even though the genes that made it continue to exist and produce other bodies. . . .

What is the relation of my self, identified as it is with one particular knot in the great network that constitutes humanity, to the other knots now existing? Why should I be identified with one only? To an observer standing apart from the net, it will not appear surprising that the different knots, since they are formed of diverse combinations of strands, should have different peculiarities, different characteristics. But that the observer himself—his total possibility of experience, that without which the universe for him would be non-existent—that he himself should be tied in relations of identity to a single one of the millions of knots in the net of strands that have come down from the unbeginning past—this to the observer appears astonishing, perplexing. Through the operation of what determining causes is my self, my entire possibility of experiencing the universe, bound to this particular one of the combination of strands, to the exclusion of some millions of others? Would *I* never have been, would *I* have lost my chance to participate in experience, would the universe never have existed for me, if this particular combination had not been made? . . .

And what about the selves that would have come into existence if other combinations of genes had been made? If each diverse combination yields a different *self,* then there existed in the two parents the potentialities, the actual beginnings, of thousands of billions of selves, or personalities, as distinct as you and I. Each of these existed in a form as real as your existence and my existence before our component germ cells had united. Of these thousands of billions, but four or five come to fruition. What has become of the others? A thousand earths might have been populated with these personalities now consigned to the limbo of nothingness. Or if we include in our thoughts the combinations that might have been formed by union of other persons, and by previous generations, what must we conclude? An infinity of potential, inchoate, selves is cancelled in each generation, a potential and inchoate population sufficient to people all the regions that mythology has invented, all the worlds that astronomy has discovered. Our instincts and education impel us to regard a human personality as the highest and most real of entities, having attributes of worth possessed by nothing else. What are we to say of this infinite number of personalities whose existence was foreshadowed and prepared in exactly the way that gave origin to you and to me; who depended only on a chance meeting of particular germ cells for their full fruition, yet never advanced further? Nature, it appears, plays in the same infinitely wasteful way, whether with the spores of fungi and the eggs of fish, or with the potencies and beginnings of human personalities.

Chapter 2

THE RIDDLE OF LIFE

Before men thought about thinking, they thought about life, and changing ideas about it have exerted continuing influence upon ideas about man and his behavior. Successive steps in understanding life processes have gradually narrowed the range of phenomena presumed subject to influence by the soul, or mind.

In the sixth century B.C., Anaximenes taught that "as our soul, being air, holds us together, so breath and air encompass the universe." This pneumatic doctrine is consistent with the theory of life which is found in the earliest Hebrew writings, for the Yahvist source in Genesis states: "And the Lord Yahveh formed man of the dust of the earth, and breathed into his nostrils the breath of life [2: 7]." On the other hand, the later Priestly source in Genesis conforms to the Babylonian tradition in referring the source of life to the blood: "But flesh and the life thereof, which is the blood thereof, shall ye not eat [9: 4]." Both doctrines have survived in western thought, but it is the pneuma theory which has been most influential in psychology. Phrenes and psyche were two other breath-related terms in Homeric Greek, and, along with pneuma, they gave rise to three words—phrenology, psychology, pneumatology—which in the nineteenth century were all used in the same sense, to designate the science of mind.

2.1

Aristotle

(384–322 B.C.)

Aristotle, writing as naturalist and not as "philosopher" in the modern sense, defined all living things including plants as "be-souled." He considered it a part of the naturalist's task to study this soul, as the form-giving principle, and not to confine his attention to "efficient causes." However, he excludes one part of this soul, "the intellectual part" which is found in men only, from the province of natural science.

It is not enough to state simply the substances out of which they {man and the animals and their parts} are made, as "Out of fire," or "Out of earth." If we were describing a bed or any other like article, we should endeavour to describe the form of it rather than the matter (bronze, or wood)—or, at any rate, the matter, if described, would be described as belonging to the concrete whole. For example, "a bed" is a certain form in certain matter, or, alternatively, certain matter that has a certain form; so we should have to include its shape and the manner of its form in our description of it—because the "formal" nature is of more fundamental importance than the "material" nature.

If, then, each animal and each of its parts is what it is in virtue of its shape and its colour, what Democritus says will be correct, since that was apparently his view, if one understands him aright when he says that it is evident to everyone what "man" is like as touching his shape, for it is by his shape and his colour that a man may be told. Now a corpse has the same shape and fashion as a living body; and yet it is not a man. Again, a hand constituted in any and every manner, *e.g.*, a bronze or wooden one, is not a hand except in name; and the same applies to a physician depicted on canvas, or a flute carved in stone. None of these can perform the functions appropriate to the things that bear those names. Likewise, the eye or the hand (or any other part) of a corpse is not really an eye or a hand. . . .

It must now be evident that the statements of the physiologers are unsatisfactory. We have to state how the animal is characterized, *i.e.*, what is the essence and character of the animal itself, as well as describing each of its parts; just as with the bed we have to state its Form.

Now it may be that the Form of any living creature is Soul, or some part of Soul, or something that involves Soul. At any rate, when its Soul

Parts of animals. With an English translation by A. L. Peck. Cambridge, Mass.: Harvard University Press (Loeb Classical Library), 1955. [640b–641b.] Reprinted by permission of the publisher and the Loeb Classical Library.

is gone, it is no longer a living creature, and none of its parts remains the same, except only in shape, just like the animals in the story that were turned into stone. If, then, this is really so, it is the business of the student of Natural science to inform himself concerning Soul, and to treat of it in his exposition; not, perhaps, in its entirety, but of that special part of it which causes the living creature to be such as it is. He must say what Soul, or that special part of Soul, is; and when he has said what its essence is, he must treat of the attributes which are attached to an essence of that character. This is especially necessary, because the term "nature' 'is used—rightly—in two senses: (a) meaning "matter," and (b) meaning "essence" (the latter including both the "Efficient" Cause and the "End"). It is, of course, in this latter sense that the entire Soul or some part of it is the "nature" of a living creature. Hence on this score especially it should be the duty of the student of Natural science to deal with Soul in preference to matter, inasmuch as it is the Soul that enables the matter to "be the nature" of an animal (that is, *potentially*, in the same way as a piece of wood "is" a bed or a stool) rather than the matter which enables the Soul to do so.

In view of what we have just said, one may well ask whether it is the business of Natural science to treat of Soul in its entirety or of some part of it only; since if it must treat of Soul in its entirety (*i.e.* including intellect) there will be no room left for any other study beside Natural science—it will include even the objects that the intellect apprehends. For consider: wherever there is a pair of interrelated things, such as sensation and the objects of sensation, it is the business of one science, and one only, to study them both. Now intellect and the objects of the intellect are such a pair; hence, the same science will study both of them, which means that there will be nothing whatever left outside the purview of Natural science. All the same, it may be that it is neither Soul in its entirety that is the source of motion, nor yet all its parts taken together; it may be that one part of Soul, (a), viz. that which plants have, is the source of growth; another part, (b), the "sensory" part, is the source of change; and yet another part, (c), the source of locomotion. That even this last cannot be the intellectual part is proved, because animals other than man have the power of locomotion, although none of them has intellect. I take it, then, as evident that we need not concern ourselves with Soul in its entirety; because it is not Soul in its entirety that is an animal's "nature," but some part or parts of it.

2.2

Saint Augustine

(354–430)

If there is no life without soul, and the soul is indivisible, how can life,
or at least some of its phenomena, persist in parts of the body separated
from animals? This problem is stated here by Augustine, and will also
be dealt with in the two following selections. Augustine acknowledges the
question to be unanswerable on the available facts, and has recourse to
faith.

The other participant in the dialogue is named Evodius.

(62) E. I would have nothing more to add, if I did not now remember
how much we used to marvel, when we were boys, that the tails of
lizards would quiver after we had cut them off from the rest of the body.
That this movement can take place without a soul I am unable to convince myself. And it is also beyond me to understand how it can be that
the soul has no material extension, when it can be cut off also with the
body.

A. I might answer that air and fire, which are retained in a body of
earth and moisture by the presence of the soul, so that a blending of all
four elements is formed, in making their way to the upper region, when
the soul departs, and in freeing themselves, start a vibration of those little
bodies, more or less rapid in proportion to the freshness of the wound
from which they make their hasty exodus; then the movement grows
weak and finally ceases, while the escaping elements become less and
less, and finally issue forth in their entirety. But, an incident recalls me
from this explanation, an incident which I saw with my own eyes so
recently that it deserves credence. A short while ago when we were in
Liguria, these boys of ours who were with me for the sake of studies,
noticed lying on the ground in a shady spot a manyfooted creeping
animal, a long worm, I would say. The worm is well known but I had
never experienced what I am telling. One of the boys cut the animal in
half with the edge of the stylus that he carried, and both parts of the
body then moved in opposite directions away from the cut with as much
speed and energy as if they had been two living animals. Frightened at
this novel sight, and eager to know the reason, they brought the living
parts to me and to Alypius where we were sitting. We, too, were aston-

The magnitude of the soul. Translated by John J. McMahon, in *The Fathers of the*
Church, Vol. IV. New York: Fathers of the Church, 1947. Pp. 49–149. [Pp. 128–131,
133]. Reprinted by permission of the Catholic University of America Press, Wash-
ington, D.C.

ished to see the two parts running over the tablet wherever they could. One of them, touched by the stylus, would turn itself toward the place of the pain, while the other, feeling nothing, moved freely on its way. And, more surprising yet, when we tried to find how far this could go, and we cut the worm, or worms, in many sections, these would also move, so that if we had not cut them at all and if the fresh wounds were not visible, we would have believed that each section had been separately born and was living its own life.

(63) But, what I said to the boys when they looked at me, eager for an explanation, I am afraid to say to you now, for we have already gone so far that, unless I give you a different answer to support my case, our attention, after weathering the barrage of so many words, may appear to have succumbed to the bite of a single worm. I advised the boys to continue their studies, as they had begun, and thus they would come at the right time to search out and learn the answer to these problems, if they warranted an answer. But what I said to Alypius, as the boys went away, and both of us, each in his own way, fell to sifting and spinning out hypotheses in our search for an answer, if I wished to explain all this, it would call for more words than we have used in this dialogue from its start, with all its meanderings and digressions. But, what I really think, I will not keep a secret from you. If I had not been well versed in questions about the nature of a body, the form that is in the body, about place, time and motion—questions that succeed in arousing sharp and learned clashes of wits because of their connection with our present topic —I should be inclined to bestow the palm of victory on the proponents of the doctrine that the soul is a body. Wherefore, as far as I can, I warn you not to allow yourself to be swept along in your reading or discussion by the torrent of words that pour out of men who rely too much on the senses of the body, until you make straight and steady the steps that lead the soul up to God. My counsel is given you lest you be turned away from that unseen and silent haven to which the soul, while here on earth, is a stranger, lest you be turned away more readily by the turmoil of study than the repose of lethargy.

(64) Now as a reply to this difficulty, which, I see, terribly upsets you; here is one that is the quickest if not the best of many, and it is the best suited to you and not the easiest proof for myself that I can select. . . .

First I say this: If the reason for this phenomenon that results from the cutting of certain bodies is elusive, we should not be so upset by this one fact, therefore, as to reverse our judgment on many things which before you saw to be true more clearly than light. For, it may be that the cause of this phenomenon is hidden from us because it is beyond the comprehension of human nature, or, if known to some one, it is not possible for us to question him, or, possibly, even if we could question him, our minds might be too dull to grasp his explanation. Does it become us, therefore, to skip and allow the truth to be wrenched from our hold, the truth of the opposite conclusion which we arrived at by most certain reasons and which we acknowledge to be indubitably correct? If the replies you made to my questions retain this full force of their truth and certainty, there is no reason for our childish fear of this little worm, even though we cannot establish the cause of its many lives.

For, if you had ascertained beyond the shadow of a doubt that a certain person is a man of honor, and if you had discovered him among a gang of thieves whom you had pursued, and if by some chance he were to drop dead before you could question him, you would think up any reason whatever to explain his association with criminals, even though it remained a perpetual enigma, rather than attribute it to a desire of crime and evil fellowship. Since, therefore, from the many arguments set forth earlier, which you accepted as most certain, it was made clear to you that the soul is not contained in place and for that reason lacks that quantity which we notice in bodies, why do you not take it for granted that there is some cause why a certain animal, when cut up, continues to live in each segment and that the cause is not that the soul can be divided with the body? If it is beyond our power to discover that cause, is it not better to continue our search for the true cause, rather than accept one that is false? ...

(68) ... Even though a part, just because it is a part, lives in a smaller space after the body has been cut, we should not conclude that the soul has been cut or that it is smaller in a smaller space, despite the fact that in the undivided living worm the soul was the equal possession of all the parts and the parts occupied a larger space. For, the soul did not occupy a place, but held the body which was moved by it. Just as the meaning of a word, without being extended in time, gave life, so to speak, and filled out all the letters that take up slight intervals of time [to pronounce]. With this illustration I ask you for the present to be content.

2.3

Ignace Gaston Pardies

(1636?–1673)

The question whether vital phenomena may have their basis in a corporeal soul is examined anew by this Jesuit scholar, a professor of mathematics. We shall cite the slender book from which this selection comes in other connections as well. (See 7.6 on sensory qualities and 16.2 on perception

Discours de la connoissance des bestes [Discourse on the knowledge of beasts]. Paris, 1672. [Arts. 34–36.]

without consciousness.) The same issue reappears in several selections of the chapter on control of movement (Perrault, Whytt, and Pflüger).

. . . If the soul of animals resides in some particular place, that no doubt would be in the brain, as most of the moderns maintain, or in the heart, as Aristotle believed. But it cannot be in either one or the other, for we have seen that after the head of an animal has been cut off, and after its heart has been removed, the rest of the body continues to live for some time, and to give all the same signs of feeling. I had a kind of maybug, which I kept for more than a month after I had cut off its head, but which nevertheless lived for all that time, and whenever it was touched or pricked it became excited, moved its wings, and flew just as if it had been intact. Ducks and bustards also live for some time after beheading; and even the most perfect animals perform some movements after their heads have been cut off. But to confine ourselves to what I just said about the maybug: all its excitement clearly shows either that it is without any sensitive or perceptive principle or at least that this principle cannot reside in the head, since the animal that has been thus mutilated shows the same signs of life and feeling as before.

In the same way, one cannot say that this principle resides in the heart. . . . It is a commonplace occurrence, which I have seen myself on a number of occasions when making dissections of live dogs, that after the heart has been removed they continue to struggle vigorously, as if they felt great pain. Therefore this sensitive principle cannot reside either in the head or in the heart; but on the contrary, if there is such a principle, one must say that it is spread throughout the body.

And indeed, if we cut a snake in two, each half goes on living for a long time; it moves, and if one pricks it after it has been quiet for a while, it will become excited again just as if it felt pain. Thus each of the parts into which it has been divided gives the same signs of life, feeling, and pain as when they were joined together in the intact snake. Therefore this sensitive and perceptive principle is not collected in one part of the snake, but is spread throughout the body. It is not unique and indivisible, since now we find it in two separate places.

2.4

Francesco Redi

(1626–1697)

What might be the origin of this sensitive soul in animals? Must God in-
fuse a soul into each insect, as into each human embryo? In the seventeenth century, the discovery of the uncountable living creatures in the
microscopic world made it easier to suppose that some of the less perfect
creatures, at least, might come into being spontaneously, from the putrefaction of organic wastes. Redi proved that this was not so in one of the
earliest examples of a controlled experiment. The fact that many learned
men continued to believe in spontaneous generation for more than a
century afterward demonstrates the attractiveness of that idea. Before
condemning the diehards out of hand, consider that a belief in spontaneous
generation was consistent with the idea that certain conditions of warmth,
temperature, and chemistry were all that was necessary for the lower forms
of life; rejecting the idea seemed to imply that life even of the lowliest sort
was more than physical in nature. And if a soul were involved, the implication of Redi's discovery was that this soul must be capable of multiplication.

Marzolino, ricotta, and ravegiolo are varieties of cheese.

In a large glass bottle, which I left with the mouth open, I had placed
half a marzolino, very fresh, and the best I could find late in June. After
a few days some worms appeared on it, and these, when carefully examined, were seen to be of two kinds: the larger ones were exactly like
all the other worms that are born on meat; the smaller ones were of the
same shape, but their movements were quick and bizarre, moving about
the glass with agility, bringing head and tail together to form a circle
and then suddenly jumping this way or that, so that sometimes they even
succeeded in jumping out of the bottle in which they had been born.
Three or four days after they had appeared, both kinds hardened and
wrinkled into eggs, which differed only in size. I collected these and
placed them separately in two different pots. After one week there
emerged from the larger eggs so many ordinary flies, while from the
smaller ones there were born, after 12 days, a kind of black midges, somewhat like winged ants, which had scarcely been born when they took to
leaping about and flying with incredible speed, in what might be called
perpetual motion. Meanwhile the males all coupled with their females,
performing those acts through which they might naturally hope to

Esperienze intorno alla generazione degl'insetti [Experiments on the generation of insects. 1668]. Third edition. Florence, 1674. [Pp. 75–78.]

propagate themselves, but, having nothing to eat, they died in a very short time.

While I was making these observations, I had the good fortune to find another marzelino which had started to become wormy, and I was able to separate the wormy part from the healthy part, and place them in different jars. No more grubs were born from the healthy half, and from those grubs which had already been born on the wormy half there appeared many of those black midges which I have described above, but no ordinary flies. On the other hand, in a ricotta which had started to become wormy, the worms, after turning into eggs, produced only ordinary flies. And from a ravegiolo which became wormy in September, there were born both ordinary flies and a few small midges of the sort which are attracted to wine and vinegar.

I know it is hard to believe that all these cheeses do not spontaneously produce grubs, since we know that when we open one of our delicious Lucardo marzolini, we often find grubs in the very middle of it. But one can answer that the seeds of these grubs were deposited in the milk by the flies at the time when it was being stirred, or when the peasants poured it into pots for congealing, being surrounded by innumerable flies. . . .

This reply would seem to have some value, although it does not altogether satisfy me. I have observed that before they have grubs, the marzolini crack and split in places. I think that the flies deposit their eggs on these cracks and openings, and the grubs, which always seek the softest and most delicate nourishment, follow them down into the middle of the cheese, and stay there feeding until their proper time to come out and to turn, for a few days, into eggs, from which they will emerge as different kinds of winged animals, corresponding to the differences among the fathers who first generated the grubs. . . .

Take note also that just as it is true that worms are not born on meats, fish, and cheese which are kept in a closed place, so likewise is it true that fruits and raw or cooked vegetables which are kept in the same manner do not become wormy. On the other hand, if they are left in an open place they produce different kinds of insects, now of one species and now of another, according to the differences among the animals which deposit their seed on them. However, I have noticed that some prefer one kind of herb or fruit rather than another, although sometimes I have seen seven or eight tribes of animalcules born at the same time on a single plant.

2.5

Abraham Trembley

(1710–1784)

*Another experimental observation which forced reexamination of tradi-
tional ideas about the soul as the life-giving entity was the discovery that
fresh-water polyps have so great a regenerative power that any fragment
of one can reconstitute itself into a complete animal. By Trembley's time,
the continuing activity of a portion of a divided animal was indeed interpreted as due to a residual portion of "animal spirits," rather than as due
to a "soul," but more than animal spirit was needed to explain the building
of a head from a foot. One may say that the pursuit of this problem has
been the central task of experimental embryology to this day. Trembley's
findings were even more startling to his contemporaries than, in our day,
the somewhat analogous report that effects of practice are retained in
flatworms regenerated from the tails of trained animals. Earlier letters in
this volume of the Transactions testify to the astonishment with which
learned men received the first reports of this finding by a still unnamed
young man, and the eagerness with which they awaited further news. As
stated in one of those letters: "Some of our Friends, who are firmly attached to the general Metaphysical Notions we have formerly learned,
reason strongly against the very Possibility of such a Fact." Trembley
stays clear of metaphysics, but his facts are clear.*

There is not on the Body of a *Polypus* any distinguished Place, by which
they bring forth their Young. I have some of them, that have greatly
multiplied under my Eyes, and of which I might almost say, that they
have produced young ones, from all the exterior Parts of their Body. . . .

If the Body of a *Polypus* is cut into two Parts transversly, each of
those Parts becomes a complete *Polypus*. On the very Day of the Operation, the first Part, or anterior End of the *Polypus*, that is, the Head, the
Mouth, and the Arms; this Part, I say, lengthens itself, it creeps, and eats.

The second Part, which has no Head, gets one; a Mouth forms itself,
at the anterior End; and shoots forth Arms. This Reproduction comes
about more or less quickly, according as the Weather is more or less
warm. In Summer, I have seen Arms begin to sprout out 24 Hours after
the Operation, and the new Head perfected in every respect in a few
Days.

Each of those Parts, thus become a perfect *Polypus*, performs abso-

Observations and experiments upon the fresh-water polypus. *Philosophical Transactions*, 42 (1743), No. 467, iii–xi. [Pp. vi–x.]

lutely all its Functions. It creeps, it eats, it grows, and it multiplies; and all that as much as a *Polypus* which never had been cut.

In whatever Place the Body of a *Polypus* is cut, whether in the Middle, or more or less near the Head, or the posterior Part, the Experiment has always the same Success.

If a *Polypus* is cut transversly, at the same Moment, into three or four Parts, they all equally become so many complete ones.

The Animal is too small to be cut at the same time into a great Number of Parts; I therefore did it successively. I first cut a *Polypus* into four Parts, and let them grow; next, I cut those Quarters again; and at this rate I proceeded, till I had made 50 out of one single one: And here I stopp'd, for there would have been no End of the Experiment. . . .

A *Polypus* may also be cut in two, lengthways. Beginning by the Head, one first splits the said Head, and afterwards the Stomach: The *Polypus* being in the Form of a Pipe, each Half of what is thus cut lengthways forms a Half-pipe; the anterior Extremity of which is terminated by the half of the Head, the half of the Mouth, and Part of the Arms. It is not long before the two Edges of those Half-pipes close, after the Operation: They generally begin at the posterior Part, and close up by degrees to the anterior Part. Then, each Half-pipe becomes a Whole-one, complete: A Stomach is formed, in which nothing is wanting; and out of each Half-mouth a Whole-one is formed also. . . .

If a *Polypus* is cut lengthways, beginning at the Head, and the Section is not carried quite through; the Result is, a *Polypus* with two Bodies, two Heads, and one Tail. Some of those Bodies and Heads may again be cut, lengthways, soon after. In this manner I have produced a *Polypus* that had seven Bodies, as many Heads, and one Tail. I afterwards, at once, cut off the seven Heads of this new *Hydra:* Seven others grew again; and the Heads, that were cut off, became each a complete *Polypus.*

2.6

Pierre Jean Georges Cabanis

(1757–1808)

In the ritual of execution, aristocracy has often been privileged to die by the executioner's sword or ax, rather than to be strangled by a noose. Technological progress enabled the French Revolution to extend the same

Note sur le supplice de la guillotine [A note on execution by the guillotine. *Magasin encyclopédique,* 1795.] *Oeuvres complètes,* 1823, Vol. 2, pp. 163–183.

privilege to innumerable victims without regard to class. But was death by the guillotine truly quick and painless? Or did the human victim still suffer in parts, like Augustine's worm? The controversy found the German writer Oelsner on one side, claiming the support of the distinguished neurologist Sömmering, and Cabanis on the other. As late as 1838, a group of German physicians performed gruesome experiments on an executed criminal, including shouting "Pardon" into one ear moments after the beheading, in an attempt to test the theory of a lingering consciousness. (Bischoff, Archiv fur Anatomie, Physiologie und wissenschaftliche Medicin, pp. 486–502).

Cabanis displays the positive approach which is characteristic of all his writing. He speaks of known effects of known lesions, and refuses to enter into metaphysical speculation. This "defense" [!] of the guillotine has often been cited, but of course not quoted, to link its author's name with the terror which he abhorred. In his major work, Rapports du physique et du moral de l'homme (see 10.3 and 15.11), this gentle man wrote on the responsibility of the physician to study the manner of death at different ages and from different diseases, so that he might lessen the suffering which sometimes but not always attends it.

Ever since the liberty of speech and of the press was restored to us on the tenth of Thermidor [July 28, 1794], everyone in whose heart there is some feeling of humanity has spoken out strongly against the judicial assassinations which the tyranny of the magistrates had spread over all of France. Recently, some writers have tried to turn the public indignation against the method of execution as such. They see it as very painful, and it is from this point of view that they request its suppression. . . .

To prove that heads severed from their trunks by the guillotine can feel intense pain, Mm. Oelsner and Sömmering cite the convulsive movements of the temporal and masseter muscles, leading to clenching of the teeth, as well as the facial muscles and those moving the eyes, which often give them a frightful appearance. They report some analogous facts taken from the literature of physiology, and they conclude that since these heads—in which, according to them, the soul is concentrated in its entirety—have no other way to show their feelings outwardly, they express their intense pain and suffering in this manner: a cruel condition which should be measured by its violence rather than its duration in point of time. Among the facts which they consider as supporting this conclusion, they offer above all the account about Charlotte Corday, who is supposed to have blushed with shame or indignation at the moment when the executioner, in a cowardly atrocity, slapped her cheek as he held up her bleeding head to the public view; they regard this blush as a moral action which could not have taken place without full consciousness.

Citizen Sue enunciates almost the same opinion, cites the same or similar facts, and repeats the tale of Charlotte Corday with much conviction; but in opposition to the two German writers he maintains that one can suffer in the trunk as well as in the head, and that a man who has been cut into several parts can feel pain in all of them. . . .

But a little reflection on the animal economy will show that [they] start from a false principle. The movement of a part of the body does not presuppose sensation, nor does the faculty of producing these movements presuppose that of feeling. In certain paralytic ailments, the motive powers are still intact, although the sensitive powers are abolished, that is, an organ may be insensible and yet quite capable of moving. Practitioners see this every day. I saw a man who walked wonderfully well, moved all the joints of his legs, his feet, and his toes, and who felt not the slightest pain when long pins were plunged into his flesh. In the convulsive ailments, on the contrary, even when there is not the slightest defect of sensibility, one limb or the whole body will often undergo the most violent agitation without the patient experiencing the slightest sensation from it; or, if he does feel pain, it is from the very violence of the movements. . . . These patients sometimes lose all consciousness for a period, and ordinarily that is when the convulsions are most frightful. At such a time the patient can be pinched, pricked, pulled, cauterized, without giving the least sign of feeling. When he comes to himself again, he will often remember nothing of what happened during the attack, when the consciousness of *self* was completely suspended, and he must return to the moment of loss of consciousness to pick up the thread of his sensations and of his existence. . . .

It was already known to the ancients that to kill the most furious animal at once, as by lightning, it suffices to plunge a dagger between the first and second ventricles of the neck. . . .

A simple concussion of the cerebellum or of the medulla oblongata, a violent blow to the occiput or the cervical vertebrae, is enough to cause death. If the blow does no more than interrupt consciousness momentarily, the patient, when he comes to himself, has no memory of it. He did not feel it.

Any practicing physician can verify this, each day. This was the experience of the celebrated Franklin, when he received a shock from an electric battery, with the effects of which he was as yet little acquainted. He fell to the ground in a mass; and when he had recovered his senses, others had to tell him what had happened. . . .

. . . It follows that a man who is guillotined suffers pain neither in his limbs nor in his head; that his death is as swift as the blow which strikes it; and if certain movements, whether regular or convulsive, are noticed in the muscles of the arms, legs, and face, they prove neither pain nor sensibility. They depend solely on a residue of the vital faculty which is not instantly abolished in the muscles and the nerves by the death of the individual, the destruction of the *self*. . . .

I shall not talk about what Citizen Sue says regarding the nature, origin and end of the vital principle. I have absolutely no ideas about that, and I do not see that, in four thousand years, the greatest geniuses have had a single idea which can stand up under the examination of reason. I believe nothing, I deny nothing, I don't even examine it; I am absolutely ignorant; but I ignore this, I must admit, as a man who does not have much respect for conjurors, and still less for assertions or for absolute denials about matters to which we are absolutely unable to apply the true instruments of our intelligence. . . .

As to the tale they tell about Charlotte Corday, I say flatly that I don't believe it. I know too well how easily these marvels are seen in times of agitation and misfortune. Since the general public enlightenment no longer permits us to see miracles, we find them instead in new natural phenomena. I was not present at the execution of Charlotte Corday, nor at any other. My gaze could not withstand such a spectacle. But several persons of my acquaintance did follow [her] cart from the prison to the scaffold. . . . One of my friends, a doctor, did not lose sight of her for a moment. He told me that her grace and simple serenity was always unchanged; that at the foot of the scaffold, she paled for a moment, but soon her beautiful face took on even a brighter glow. As to that fresh blush which is supposed to have covered her cheeks after the decapitation, he saw nothing of it, although he is a very sharp observer, and he was at the time a very attentive observer. Others to whom I have spoken did not see it either.

2.7

Julian Jean César Le Gallois

(1770–1814)

To paraphrase Aristotle, perhaps it is not the whole head, or the whole brain, which is necessary for life. After Fontana's experiments (described in this selection), Le Gallois showed that life can maintain itself in a decapitated animal when the spine is severed above the origin of the pneumogastric nerve. If this is injured, death follows immediately when the lungs are not artificially aërated. Le Gallois' important conclusion was that life does not depend on the "highest" parts of the brain, but on spinal structures.

Experiments on the principle of life, and particularly on the principle of the motions of the heart, and on the seat of this principle [1812]. Translated by N. C. and J. G. Nancrede. Philadelphia, 1813. [Pp. 23–26, 37–38, 44–49, 51–52.]

41

Of the faculties peculiar to animals, those by which they are eminently characterized are sensation and motion; and it may be said, that the real end of organization in an animal, is to produce and maintain these two faculties. . . .

It might be imagined that the principle of sensation and motion resided in every part of the body, as all seem more or less to participate in these two faculties. But observation having shown that the section of a nerve, in any part of its course, instantly deprives of sensation and motion all the parts to which the inferior portion of the divided nerve is distributed, · it necessarily follows that the sentient principle does not reside in the part which receives the impression, and likewise that the power causing motion, exists not in the part which moves; but to discover its seat, it is necessary to recur to the origin of the nerves. Now as all nerves derive from the brain and the spinal marrow, the source of life has been supposed to be derived from the brain and spinal marrow. . . . Moreover, the spinal marrow has been considered by anatomists only as a large nerve arising from the brain. . . . The brain therefore was considered as a center of the nervous power, and consequently as the only seat of the principle of life.

This opinion was carried still further. The unity of *self*, the metaphysical ideas referred to it, and the observation, that certain parts of the brain might be wounded, and even destroyed with impunity, led to the conclusion, that this viscus in its entire capacity was not the seat of this principle, and that there must be a defined spot where all sensation terminated, and whence all motion received its impulse; and this place, designated under the name of *sensorium commune*, or the seat of the soul, was for a long time an object of inquiry among physiologists. . . .

The theory of irritability produced no change in the state of the question, and the difficulties which I have mentioned, continued in full force from the time of Haller and the authors of his school referred the sources of nervous power to the brain. Among the experiments of these authors, one was nevertheless well calculated to make them renounce this opinion. I mean that made by the celebrated Fontana {in 1787}. After having decapitated rabbits and guinea-pigs, and prevented the hemorrhage by the ligature of the vessels of the neck, he had maintained the life of those animals for a long space of time by blowing air into their lungs. This experiment proved clearly that even in the mammiferous adult as well as in reptiles, the life of the trunk does not depend immediately on the brain. After this, only one step remained to be taken; to inquire what was the true source of that life, and to ascertain this source by real experiments. But Fontana did not pursue his experiments further, because he thought he understood the *rationale*. Strongly prepossessed by the doctrine of Haller, which he extended much farther than that great man, he placed the source and the principle of life and of all animal motion in irritability. The inflation of the lungs was only, in his estimation, one mean of prolonging life in a decapitated animal, only because it contributed to the maintaining of irritability by keeping up the circulation, which was, as he pretended, independent of the nervous power. . . .

My first experiments were made upon rabbits at the time that the foetuses, separated from their mothers, can live without breathing; and on the same animals, I continued the investigation of the phenomena accompanying decapitation. I remarked first, that, after the decapitation of a rabbit, life continues in the trunk, and that sensation and voluntary motion continue during a period which is constantly the same, as when a rabbit of the same age is reduced to a state of asphyxia. . . . Thus, in a new born rabbit, sensation and voluntary motion are only extinguished after an asphyxia of fifteen minutes; whilst they are extinguished in two minutes in a rabbit thirty days old. . . .

From the connection of these facts, I conclude that the decapitated animal is only in a state of asphyxia, and that he is so because he can no longer perform the motions necessary to introduce air into his lungs. Substituting the artificial inflation of the lungs instead of natural respiration, affords a ready means of ascertaining the correctness of this conclusion. Accordingly I made the experiment, and the success was complete. . . . In a word, a decapitated animal may in this manner be kept perfectly alive, during a time varying according to the age and the species, and which in very young rabbits is at least several hours.

It evidently results from these facts that the principle of sensation and voluntary motion does not reside in the brain, according to the usually received opinion, or at least, that the brain is not its exclusive seat. But where then is the seat of this principle? Is it peculiar and circumscribed, or is it disseminated over every part of the body? The following experiment soon convinced me that it resides only in the spinal marrow. Thus if in a decapitated rabbit, which has been most completely revived, and which is kept alive by the inflation of the lungs, the medulla spinalis be destroyed, by pushing an iron rod through the whole length of the vertebral canal, all the phenomena of life instantly disappear, nor is it possible to restore them by any means; only those of irritability are left, which it is known always continue some time after death. If another rabbit be taken, and instead of decapitating it, a simple incision be made in the vertebral canal near the occiput, and an iron wire be introduced through this opening, destroying the spinal marrow, although in this case the brain continues untouched as well as all its nervous connections with the trunk, life will nevertheless instantly and irrevocably disappear in the trunk; it only continues in the head, as is indicated by the gapings. —Finally, if another rabbit be cut in two, each portion as well as the head in the preceding experiment, remains alive for several minutes, varying according to the age of the animal which I shall point out hereafter. If immediately after the division has been made, the whole medulla spinalis is destroyed, in either of these portions, life instantly disappears in it, whilst it continues in the other, and if this portion of the spinal marrow be destroyed, all the parts which receive their nerves from this portion, are struck with death at the same time, whilst the remainder of this same portion continues alive.

These experiments prove not only that the life of the trunk is dependent upon the medulla spinalis; but they also prove that the life of each part is specially dependent upon the portion of the spinal marrow, from which it receives its nerves. . . .

It is not upon the whole of the brain that respiration depends, but upon a particular and small part of the *medulla oblongata* situated at a small distance from the occipital foramen, and near the origin of the nerves of the eighth pair (or *pneumo-gastric*). . . .

Hence an animal might be decapitated in such a manner, that it should continue to live by its inherent powers, without recourse being had to the artificial inflation of the lungs. For this purpose, our instruments are to be so managed in removing the cranium and the brain, as to spare that particular portion of the medulla oblongata in which the primum mobile or respiration resides, preserving at the same time its continuity with the spinal marrow.

2.8

Johannes Müller

(1801–1858)

After physiologists generally had rejected the vitalist view that an immaterial soul must knowingly direct bodily processes, they postulated instead a "life force" without which vital phenomena could not take place. Since the interchangeability of various forms of physical energy was not yet known, it seemed within the bounds of science to postulate one more "imponderable substance"—a phrase commonly applied to light, heat, magnetism and electricity—to meet this need. In accepting this view, Müller also specifically rejects the hypothesis which J. C. Reil had advanced (in 1795, in the first issue of his journal, Archiv für Physiologie) that a combination of physical factors might suffice to support life.

The manner in which their elements are combined, is not the only difference between organic and inorganic bodies; there is in living organic

Handbuch der Physiologie des Menschen [Handbook of human physiology]. Coblenz, 1833–1840. Translated by W. Baly as *Elements of physiology* [London, 1838–1842]. Philadelphia, 1843. [Pp. 27, 32, 33–35.]

matter a principle constantly in action, the operations of which are in accordance with a rational plan, so that the individual parts which it creates in the body, are adapted to the design of the whole; and this it is which distinguishes organism. Kant says, "The cause of the particular mode of existence of each part of a living body resides in the whole, while in dead masses each part contains this cause within itself.". . .

It is only in very simple animals or plants which possess a certain number of similar parts, or where the dissimilar parts are repeated in each successive segment of the individual, that the body can be divided, and the two portions, each still possessing all the essential parts of the whole, though in smaller number, continue to live. . . .

. . . Stahl's contemporaries and followers have partly misunderstood this great man, in believing that, according to his view, the soul, which forms mental conceptions, also conducts with consciousness, and designedly, the organisation of the body. The *soul* (*anima*) spoken of by Stahl is the organising power or principle which manifests itself in conformity with a rational law. But Stahl has gone too far in placing the manifestations of a soul, combined with consciousness, on a level with the organising principle; the operations of which, though in accordance with design, obey a blind necessity. The organising principle, which according to an eternal law creates the different essential organs of the body, and animates them, is not itself seated in one particular organ. . . .

The existence of the organic principle in the germ, and its apparent independence of any special organ in the adult, as well as the fact that it is manifested in plants, in which both nervous system and consciousness are wanting, prove that this principle cannot be compared with mental consciousness, which is an after product of development, and has its seat in one particular organ. Mind can generate no organic products, it can merely form conceptions; our ideas of the organised being are mere conscious conceptions of the mind. The formative or organising principle, on the contrary, is a creative power modifying matter, blindly and unconsciously, according to the laws of adaptation. . . .

The unity resulting from the combination of the organising force with organic matter could be better conceived, if it were possible to prove that the organising force and the phenomena of life are the result, manifestation, or property of a certain combination of elements. . . . Reil has stated this bold theory in his famous treatise on the "vital energy." . . .

Reil refers organic phenomena to original difference in the composition and form of organic bodies. Differences in composition and form are, according to his theory, the cause of all the variety in organised bodies, and in their endowments. But if these two principles be admitted, still the problem remains unsolved; it may still be asked, how the elementary combination acquired its form, and how the form acquired its elementary combination. Into the composition of the organic matter of the living body there must enter an unknown (according to Reil's theory, subtile material) principle, or the organic matter must retain its properties by the operation of some unknown forces. Whether this principle is to be regarded as an imponderable matter, or as a force or energy, is just as uncertain as the same question is in reference to several important phenomena in physics; physiology in this case is not behind the other natural sciences, for the properties of this principle, as displayed in the functions of the nerves, are nearly as well known as those of light, caloric, and electricity, in physics. . . .

We have thus seen that organic bodies consist of matters which present a peculiar combination of their component elements—a combination of three, four, or more to form one compound, which is observed only in organic bodies, and in them only during life. Organised bodies moreover are constituted of organs,—that is, of essential members of one whole,—each member having a separate function, and each deriving its existence from the whole: and they not merely consist of these organs, but by virtue of an innate power they form them within themselves. Life, therefore, is not simply the result of the harmony and reciprocal action of these parts; but it is first manifested in a principle, or imponderable matter which is in action in the substance of the germ, enters into the composition of the matter of this germ, and imparts to organic combinations properties which cease at death.

2.9

John Tyndall

(1820–1893)

The middle of the nineteenth century witnessed a vigorous materialist movement, in which the outstanding names, in Germany, were Ludwig Büchner (Force and matter), Carl Vogt (Physiological letters) and Jacob Moleschott (Circle of life). In England there was George Henry Lewes (Physiology of common life). But in the war of science with theology, these men were outriders, not generals. The armies were engaged in earnest when John Tyndall, a physicist, proclaimed in his presidential address to the British Association of Science, in 1874, that there were no problems sheltered by sanctity from scientific experimental investigation, and that life must be studied as a manifestation of matter.

. . . Believing, as I do, in the continuity of nature, I cannot stop abruptly where our microscopes cease to be of use. Here the vision of the mind

The Belfast address. In *Fragments of science*. New York: Appleton, 1898. Vol. 2, pp. 135–201. [Pp. 191, 197–198, 200.]

authoritatively supplements the vision of the eye. By a necessity engendered and justified by science I cross the boundary of the experimental evidence, and discern in that Matter which we, in our ignorance of its latent powers, and notwithstanding our professed reverence for its Creator, have hitherto covered with opprobrium, the promise and potency of all terrestrial Life. . . .

The impregnable position of science may be described in a few words. We claim, and we shall wrest from theology, the entire domain of cosmological theory. All schemes and systems which thus infringe upon the domain of science must, in so far as they do this, submit to its control, and relinquish all thought of controlling it. Acting otherwise proved always disastrous in the past, and it is simply fatuous to-day. Every system which would escape the fate of an organism too rigid to adjust itself to its environment, must be plastic to the extent that the growth of knowledge demands. When this truth has been thoroughly taken in, rigidity will be relaxed, exclusiveness diminished, things now deemed essential will be dropped, and elements now rejected will be assimilated. The lifting of the life is the essential point; and as long as dogmatism, fanaticism, and intolerance are kept out, various modes of leverage may be employed to raise life to a higher level. . . .

. . . I thought you ought to know the environment which, with or without your consent, is rapidly surrounding you, and in relation to which some adjustment on your part may be necessary. A hint of Hamlet's, however, teaches us how the troubles of common life may be ended; and it is perfectly possible for you and me to purchase intellectual peace at the price of intellectual death. The world is not without refuges of this description; nor is it wanting in persons who seek their shelter, and try to persuade others to do the same. The unstable and the weak have yielded and will yield to this persuasion, and they to whom repose is sweeter than the truth. But I would exhort you to refuse the offered shelter, and to scorn the base repose—to accept, if the choice be forced upon you, commotion before stagnation, the breezy leap of the torrent before the foetid stillness of the swamp. In the course of this Address I have touched on debatable questions, and led you over what will be deemed dangerous ground—and this partly with the view of telling you that, as regards these questions, science claims unrestricted right of search.

2.10

Jacques Loeb

(1859–1924)

One of the boldest spirits to answer Tyndall's call was a German biologist who, having been brought to America by the Rockefeller-endowed University of Chicago, later became the most distinguished member of the Rockefeller Institute for Medical Research. His experiments on artificial stimulation of development in the unfertilized eggs of sea urchins were a dramatic episode in the still-continuing twentieth-century effort to create life in a test tube.

The nature of life and of death are questions which occupy the interest of the layman to a greater extent than possibly any other purely theoretical problem; and we can well understand that humanity did not wait for experimental biology to furnish an answer. The answer assumed the anthropomorphic form characteristic of all explanations of nature in the prescientific period. Life was assumed to begin with the entrance of a "life principle" into the body; that individual life begins wth the egg was of course unknown to primitive or prescientific man. Death was assumed to be due to the departure of this "life principle" from the body.

Scientifically, however, individual life begins (in the case of the sea-urchin and possibly in general) with the acceleration of the rate of oxidation in the egg, and this acceleration begins after the destruction of its cortical layer. Life of warm-blooded animals—man included—ends with the cessation of oxidation in the body. As soon as oxidations have ceased for some time, the surface films of the cells, if they contain enough water and if the temperature is sufficiently high, become permeable for bacteria, and the body is destroyed by micro-organisms. The problem of the beginnning and the end of individual life is physico-chemically clear. It is, therefore, unwarranted to continue the statement that in addition to the acceleration of oxidations the beginning of individual life is determined by the entrance of a metaphysical "life principle" into the egg; and that death is determined, aside from the cessation of oxidation, by the departure of this "principle" from the body. In the case of the evaporation of water we are satisfied with the explanation given by the kinetic theory of gases and do not demand that—to repeat a well-known jest of Huxley—the disappearance of the "aquosity" be also taken into consideration. . . .

That in the case of our inner life a physico-chemical explanation is

The mechanistic conception of life. Chicago: University of Chicago Press, 1912. [Pp. 14–15, 26, 30.]

not beyond the realm of possibility is proved by the fact that it is already possible for us to explain cases of simple manifestations of animal instinct and will on a physico-chemical basis; namely, the phenomena which I have discussed in former papers under the name of animal tropisms. As the most simple example we may mention the tendency of certain animals to fly or creep to the light. . . .

Our wishes and hopes, disappointments and sufferings have their source in instincts which are comparable to the light instinct of the heliotropic animals. The need of and the struggle for food, the sexual instinct with its poetry and its chain of consequences, the maternal instincts with the felicity and the suffering caused by them, the instinct of workmanship, and some other instincts are the roots from which our inner life develops. For some of these instincts the chemical basis is at least sufficiently indicated to arouse the hope that their analysis, from the mechanistic point of view, is only a question of time.

2.11

J. D. Watson   AND   F. H. C. Crick

(born 1928)   (born 1916)

For unriddling the molecular structure of DNA, James D. Watson and Francis Crick shared a Nobel prize with M. F. H. Wilkins, whose x-ray diffraction pictures provided the basis for their work. They gave the gene substantive reality and established the basic similarity of all known forms of life from the simplest virus to man. Many details of the genetic code that they envisaged have since been filled in, and its efficiency is such that the genetic information which can thus be carried in a single cell of the human body is enough to fill a thousand textbooks!

Closely related to the DNA molecule is RNA. (See 11:10 for work relating RNA to learning, which is of course another problem of information storage.)

The importance of deoxyribonucleic acid (DNA) within living cells is undisputed. It is found in all dividing cells, largely if not entirely in the nucleus, where it is an essential constituent of the chromosomes. Many lines of evidence indicate that it is a carrier of a part of (if not all) the genetic specificity of the chromosomes and thus of the gene itself. Until now, however, no evidence has been presented to show how it might

Genetical implications of the structure of deoxyribonucleic acid. *Nature,* 171 (1953): 964–967.

carry out the essential operation required of a genetic material, that of self-duplication.

We have recently proposed a structure for the salt of [DNA] which, if correct, immediately suggests a mechanism for its self-duplication. . . .

The chemical formula of [DNA] is now well established. The molecule is a very long chain, the backbone of which consists of a regular alternation of sugar and phosphate groups. . . . To each sugar is attached a nitrogenous base. . . . Two of the possible bases—adenine and guanine— are purines, and the other two—thymine and cytosine—are pyrimidines. So far as is known, the sequence of bases along the chain is irregular. The monomer unit, consisting of phosphate, sugar and base, is known as a nucleotide.

The first feature of our structure which is of biological interest is that it consists not of one chain, but of two. These two chains are both coiled around a common fibre axis. . . .

The other biologically important feature is the manner in which the two chains are held together. This is done by hydrogen bonds between the bases. . . . The bases are joined together in pairs, a single base from one chain being hydrogen-bonded to a single base from the other. The important point is that only certain pairs of bases will fit into the structure. One member of a pair must be a purine, and the other a pyrimidine in order to bridge between the two chains. If a pair consisted of two purines, for example, there would not be room for it.

We believe that the bases will be present almost entirely in their most probable tautomeric forms. If this is true, the conditions for forming hydrogen bonds are more restrictive, and the only pairs of bases possible are: adenine with thymine; guanine with cytosine. . . . The phosphate-sugar backbone of our model is completely regular, but any sequence of the pairs of bases can fit into the structure. It follows that in a long molecule many different permutations are possible, and it therefore seems likely that the precise sequence of the bases is the code which carries the genetical information. If the actual order of the bases on one of the pair of chains were given, one could write down the exact order of the bases on the other one, because of the specific pairing. Thus one chain is, as it were, the complement of the other, and it is this feature which suggests how the [DNA] molecule might duplicate itself.

Previous discussions of self-duplication have usually involved the concept of a template, or mould. Either the template was supposed to copy itself directly or it was to produce a 'negative,' which in its turn was to act as a template and produce the original 'positive' once again. In no case has it been explained in detail how it would do this in terms of atoms and molecules.

Now our model for [DNA] is, in effect, a *pair* of templates, each of which is complementary to the other. We imagine that prior to duplication the hydrogen bonds are broken, and the two chains unwind and separate. Each chain then acts as a template for the formation on to itself of a new companion chain, so that eventually we shall have *two* pairs of chains, where we only had one before. Moreover, the sequence of the pairs of bases will have been duplicated exactly. . . .

. . . Our proposed structure for [DNA] may help to solve one of the fundamental biological problems—the molecular basis of the template needed for genetic replication. The hypothesis we are suggesting is that the template is the pattern of bases formed by one chain of the [DNA] and that the gene contains a complementary pair of such templates.

Chapter 3

THE INNER MAN

Though life is mystery enough, men have often felt that a still greater mystery marks them off from other living things. A supposedly undeniable sign of this special human nature is the quality of self-consciousness—not merely to have sensation, but to have awareness of sensation; not merely to have a knowing mind, but to have a mind that turns round upon itself and becomes aware that it knows. Is this the key to "human nature"? Is it an evidence of incorporeality? Is it the essential matter of psychological science? Or is it a deception, and must we resolutely close our eyes to this pretended special vision before we can have a scientific knowledge of ourselves?

3.1

Saint Augustine

(354–430)

Three times in the history of psychology, apparently independently, a closely similar argument has been advanced to prove the existence of an incorporeal self. This passage from The city of God is only one of several in which Augustine deals with this matter. The statement is blurred some-

Of the city of God: with the learned comments of J. Ludovicus Vives. Englished by J. H[ealey]. 2nd ed. London, 1620. [Book XI, Ch. 26.]

what by his doctrinal concern with man's triple nature, as evidence that man is made in God's image, but the essential point—certainty of one's own existence as a thinking being, independent of all sensory information —is clear enough.

This seventeenth-century translation is based on an edition which had been annotated by Luis Vives in the previous century, and dedicated by him to King Henry VIII, who fancied himself somewhat of a scholar. One of his glosses on this passage is included. Writing a century before Descartes, he seems to miss the point.

Of the Image of the Trinity which is in some sort in every man's nature, even before his glorification.

And we have in our selves an image of that holy Trinity which shal be perfected by reformation, and made very like it: though it bee farre un-equall, and far distant from it, briefly neither coeternall with God, nor of his substance, yet is it the nearest it of any creature; for we both have a being, know it, and love both our being and knowledge. And in these three no false apparance ever can deceive us. For we do not discern them as things visible, by sence, as we see colours, heare sounds, sent smels, tast savours, and touch things hard and soft; the abstracts[a] of which sensibles we conceive, remember, and desire in incorporeall forms most like to these other: in those three it is not so; I know without all fantasticall imagination that I am my selfe, that this I know and love. I fear not the Λοαδεmike arguments in these truths, that say: *What if you erre?* If I erre, I am. For he that hath no being cannot erre, and therefore mine error proves my being: which being so, how can I erre in holding my being? For though I bee one that may erre, yet doubt-lesse in that I know my being, I erre not: and consequently, if I know that I know my being: and loving these two, I adioyne this love as a third of equall esteeme with the two. For I do not erre in that I love, knowing the two things I love, without error: if they were false, it were true that I loved false things. For how could I be iustly checked for loving false things if it were false that I loved them? But seeing the

---

[a] {Note by Vives:} For shut our eyes and taste, our thoughts tell us what a thing whitenesse and sweetnesse is, whereupon our dreames are fraught with such things; and we are able to iudge of them without their presence. But these are in our exterior senses, our imagination, our common sense, and our memory, all which beasts have as well as we; and in these many things are rashly observed, which if wee assent unto, wee erre: for the senses are their weake, dull, and unsure teachers, teaching those other to apprehend things often false, for true. But the reasonable minde, being proper onely to man, pondereth all, and useth all diligence to avoid falsehoods for truth, warning us to observe well ere we iudge.

things loved, are true and sure, how can the love of them be but true and sure? And there is no man that desireth not to be, as there is none that desires not to be happy: for how can hee have happinesse, and no being?

3.2

Avicenna

(980–1037)

Avicenna's psychology, which occupies the sixth book of his Art of healing, leans heavily on Aristotle, but his argument for the incorporeality of the human soul is original. It occurs near the start of the book, and is restated near the end. The reference to "length, width and depth" makes this a closer parallel to Descartes' argument than the statement by Augustine which Descartes was accused of plagiarising.

Let a man suppose that he has been created all at one stroke, in finished form, but that his sight is veiled, so that he is without any sensory awareness of external things, and that he was created falling through the air or in the void, so that the constitution of the air did not affect him so as to make him feel, and his limbs were separated so that they did not meet or feel one another. Let him then consider: can he affirm the existence of his being without having any doubt of the affirmation that he exists, and despite this not affirm either the existence of his limbs, nor of his heart, or brain, or of any external object? Better, he will affirm his being, but he will not affirm that it has any length, or width, or depth. And if in this state it were possible for him to imagine a hand or another member, he would not imagine it as a part of his being or as a condition of his being. . . . Therefore, the being whose existence has been affirmed possesses the quality of being something other than his body and the limbs which were not affirmed. Therefore he who affirms has a means for affirming it, by virtue of the existence of the soul as something different from the body, or, better said, without a body. Assuredly, he will know and perceive this fact. And if he has forgotten it, he needs to have it drawn to his attention. . . .

For I am myself, even if I am unaware that I possess a hand, a foot, or any other member of those that have been enumerated above. Or rather, I think that these members depend on myself, and I believe that they are instruments which belong to me, which I employ for my needs; if these needs did not exist, I would have no need to possess them, but would still be myself, though they would not exist.

Psychologie d'Ibn Sīnā (Avicenne) d'après son oeuvre Aš-Šifā. Editée et traduite en français par Ján Bakoš. Prague, 1956. 2 vols. [VI, 1; VI, 4(3).]

3.3

René Descartes

(1596–1650)

For Descartes, the independent existence of a thinking substance was the first indubitable fact, which became the foundation of his philosophy. His first statement of this principle was in the epoch-making Discourse on method. The principle was restated within a few years in the more ponderous Meditations, written in Latin as was then more usual for a serious work inviting the attention of the learned world. The Second Meditation is subtitled, "Of the nature of the human mind, and that it is more easily known than the body." Our selections are taken from the first English editions of these works. Twenty years later, Molyneux would translate Locke's Essay into Latin, for the benefit of continental scholars. One might say that in the battle between rationalism and empiricism, he carried ammunition for both armies!

[A]

. . . I had long since observed that as for manners, it was sometimes necessary to follow those opinions which we know to be very uncertain, as much as if they were indubitable, as is beforesaid: But because that then I desired onely to intend the search of truth, I thought I ought to doe the contrary, and reject as absolutely false all wherein I could imagine the least doubt, to the end I might see if afterwards anything might remain in my belief, not at all subject to doubt. Thus because our senses sometimes deceive us, I would suppose that there was nothing which was such as they represented it to us. And because there are men who mistake themselves in reasoning, even in the most simple matters of Geometry, and make therein Paralogismes, judging that I was as subject to fail as any other Man, I rejected as false all those reasons, which I had before taken for Demonstrations. And considering, that the same thoughts which we have waking, may also happen to us sleeping, when as not any one of them is true. I resolv'd to faign, that all those things which ever entred into my Minde, were no more true, then the illusions of my dreams. But presently after I observ'd, that whilst I would think

[A] *Discours de la methode pour bien conduire sa raison . . .* [Leyden, 1637]. Translated as *A discourse of a method for the well guiding of reason, and the discovery of truth in the sciences.* London, 1649. [Part III, pp. 50–53.]
[B] *Meditationes de prima philosophia . . .* [Paris, 1641]. Translated by William Molyneux, as *Six metaphysical meditations; wherein it is proved . . . that mans mind is really distinct from his body.* London, 1680. [Med. II; pp. 16–22, 25–26.]

that all was false, it must necessarily follow, that I who thought it, must be something. And perceiving that this Truth, *I think*, therefore, *I am*, was so firm and certain, that all the most extravagant suppositions of the scepticks was not able to shake it, I judg'd that I might receive it without scruple for the first principle of the Philosophy I sought.

Examining carefully afterwards what I was; and seeing that I could suppose that I had no *body*, and that there was no *World*, nor any *place* where I was: but for all this, I could not feign that I *was not;* and that even contrary thereto, thinking to doubt the truth of other things, it most evidently and certainly followed, That *I was:* whereas, if I had ceas'd to *think*, although all the rest of whatever I had imagined were true, I had no reason to beleeve that *I had been.* I knew then that I was a substance, whose whole essence or nature is, but to *think*, and who to *be*, hath need of no place, nor depends on any materiall thing. So that this *Me*, to wit, my soul, by which I am what I am, is wholly distinct from the Body, and more easie to be known then *it;* and although *that* were not, it would not therefore cease to be what it is.

After this I considered in generall what is requisite in a Proposition to make it true and certain: for since I had found out one which I knew to be so, I thought I ought also to consider wherein that certainty consisted: and having observed, That there is nothing at all in this, *I think*, therefore *I am*, which assures me that I speak the truth, except this, that I see most cleerly, That to *think*, one must have a *being;* I judg'd that I might take for a generall rule, That those things which we conceive cleerly and distinctly, are all true; and that the onely difficulty is punctually to observe what those are which we distinctly conceive.

[B]

But am I nothing besides? I will consider—I am not that *structure* of *parts*, which is called a Mans *Body*, neither am I any sort of *thin Air* infused into those Parts, nor a *Wind*, nor *Fire*, nor *Vapour*, nor *Breath*, nor whatever I my self can feign, for all these things I have supposed *not to Be.* Yet my Position stands firm, *Nevertheless I am something.* . . . I am sure that I exist, I ask who I am whom I thus know, certainly, the knowledge, of *Me* (precisely taken) depends not on those things, whose existence I am yet ignorant of; and therefore not on any other things that I can *feign* by my *imagination.*

. . . Which things Consider'd I should be no less foolish in saying, *I will imagine that I may more thoroughly understand what I am*, then if I should say, *at Present I am awake and perceive something true*, *but because it appears not evidently enough, I shall endeavour to sleep*, *that in a Dream I may perceive it more evidently and truely.* . . .

Let me ask therefore *What I am, A Thinking Thing*, but What is That?

3.3 René Descartes

That is a thing, *doubting, understanding, affirming, denying, willing, nilling, imagining* also, and *sensitive.* These truely are not a few *Properties,* if they all belong to Me. And Why should they Not belong to me? For am not I the very same who at present *doubt* almost of All things; yet *understand* something, which thing onely I *affirm* to be true, I *deny* all other things, I am *willing* to know more, I *would not* be deceived, *imagine* many things *unwillingly,* and *consider* many things as coming to me by my *senses.* Which of all these faculties is it, which is not as *true* as that I *exist,* tho I should *sleep,* or my *Creator* should as much as in him lay, strive to *deceive* me? which of them is it that is *distinct* from my *thought?* which of them is it that can be *seperated* from *me?* For that I am the same that *doubt, understand,* and *will* is so *evident,* that I know not how to explain it more manifestly, and that I also am the same that *imagine,* for tho perhaps (as I have supposed) no thing that can be *imagined* is *true,* yet the *imaginative Power* it self is *really* existent, and makes up a part of my *Thought;* and last of all that I am the same that am *sensitive,* or *perceive corporeal* things as by my *senses,* yet that I now *see* light, *hear* a noise, *feel* heat, these things are false, for I suppose my self *asleep,* but I *know* that I *see, hear,* and am *heated,* that cannot be *false;* and this it is that in me is *properly* called Sense, and this strictly taken is the same with *thought.*

By these Considerations I begin a little better to *understand My self* what I am; But yet it *seems,* and I cannot but *think* that *Corporeal Things* (whose *Images* are formed in my *thought,* and which by my *senses,* I perceive) are much more *distinctly known* then that *confused Notion* of *My Self* which *imagination* cannot afford me. And yet 'tis strange that things *doubtful, unknown, distinct from Me,* should be *apprehended* more *clearly* by *Me,* then a Thing that is *True,* then a thing that is *known,* or then *I my self.* . . .

Let me consider those things, which of all Things I formerly conceived most *evident,* that is to say, *Bodies* which we touch, which we see. . . .

Let us chuse for example this piece of *Bees-wax,* it was lately taken from the *Comb,* it has not yet lost all the *tast* of the *Honey,* it retains something of the *smell* of the *Flowers* from whence 'twas gather'd, its *colour, shape,* and *bigness* are manifest, 'tis *hard,* 'tis *cold,* 'tis *easily felt,* and if you will knock it with your finger, 'twill *make a noise:* In fine, it hath all things requisite to the most perfect notion of a *Body.*

But behold whilst I am speaking, 'tis put to the Fire, its *tast* is purged away, the *smell* is vanish'd, the *colour* is changed, the *shape* is alter'd, its *bulk* is increased, its become *soft,* 'tis *hot,* it can scarce be *felt,* and now (though you strike it) it makes no *noise.* Does it yet continue the same Wax? surely it does, this all confess, no one denies it, no one doubts it. What therefore was there in it that was so evidently known? surely none of those things which I *perceived* by my *senses* . . . and yet the *Wax remains.* . . . It remains therefore for me only to confess, that I cannot

57

imagine what this Wax is, but that I *perceive* with my *Mind* what it is. . . .

But what shall I now say as to my *mind,* or my *self?* (for as yet I admit nothing as belonging to me but a *mind.*) Why (shall I say?) should not I, who seem to perceive this Wax so *distinctly,* know my *self* not only more *truly* and more *certainly,* but more *distinctly* and *evidently?*

And now behold of my own accord am I come to the place I would be in; for seeing I have now discover'd that *Bodies themselves* are not *properly perceived* by our *senses* or *imagination,* but only by our *understanding,* and are not therefore *perceived,* because they are *felt* or *seen,* but because they are *understood;* it plainly appears to me, that nothing can possibly be *perceived* by me *easier,* or more *evidently,* than my *Mind.*

3.4

Mathew Hale

(1609–1676)

If Descartes' argument were sound, psychology conducted along these lines should be less open to error than the natural sciences. This claim was to be made many times, for more than two centuries to come, but it sounded increasingly more hollow as physics first, then chemistry, then zoology, swept from triumph to triumph, while psychologists failed to agree on first principles. But Mathew Hale, following close upon Descartes, was still persuaded that the mind is more accessible to study than the body.

. . . But Man is an Object of greatest vicinity to himself, and hath thereby, and by other contributions, the best opportunity to know and understand himself with the greatest certainty and evidence. . . .

But though this vicinity of our selves to our selves, cannot give us the full prospect of all the Intrigues of our Nature, yet we have thereby, and by other opportunities, much more advantage to know our selves, than to know other things without us. . . .

1. We have hereby an opportunity to know the Constitutions, Frame and Order of our Bodies. . . .

2. We have hereby an opportunity to know much more of the Nature, Operations and other things relating to our Souls, than we can touching other things or Natures. There hath been much Dispute among Learned men, concerning the manner of the Intellection of Spirits and Intelligences; and by others, touching the knowledge of Brutes, touching their

The primitive origination of mankind, considered and examined according to the light of nature. London, 1677. [Pp. 20–22, 24–25.]

remembring Faculty, whether they have a kind of Discursive Faculty, which some call Reason; whether they do prescind or abstract touching their Voyces; how far they are significant, and whether they intentionally signifie by them, how far their Animal motions are spontaneous, or meerly mechanical, and which are of one kind, which of another; or whether, as *Des Cartes* would have it, all are purely mechanical.

Many vain things have been asserted by men that would be counted eminent Wits; but without debating in this place the truth of any of these things, it is no marvel if we are to seek what are the manner of these operations of abstract Spirits or Brutes; we cannot know them, unless we were in them, so as to be acquainted with their inward motions, or at least, unless they had some such way of communicating their Perceptions and Phantasms unto us, as we have to our selves, or one to another: But whatever can be known of them, we may easily by inspecting and observing our selves, know much concerning our own Souls and the operations of them: We may know that we have a principle within, which we do, as it were, feel distinct from our Bodies, whereby we think, and we know we think. . . .

. . . But there is yet a farther opportunity of very much certainty in that knowledge that a man may have of himself, and of those things concerning himself; by that conversation, by the help of speech or signs that he hath, or may have with other men. Man only, of all visible Creatures, having this priviledge of communicating his thoughts and conceptions by instituted signs of speech or writing; and by this a man acquires a threefold superadded certainty of what he may or doth know concerning himself: Namely,

1. He thereby knows that there is a special Identity between him and other men, and that they agree in one common rational Nature . . .

2. He likewise knows that as they concenter in one common rational Nature, so every one of that *Species*, hath yet an individual Principle of his own, that individuates, and personally discriminates one from another: For till we mutually communicate our thoughts by instituted signs, he knows not what I think or purpose, nor I what he thinks or purposeth.

3. This adds a certainty to me that I am not deceived in those reflections that I make upon my self, and the collections I make from them; for as I do find I think, I reason, abstract, divide, define, purpose, so I find by the help of Speech and Signs that he hath the very like internal operations; and as I do find that those do arise from a principle different and distinct from that *moles Corporea* which I have, so I find that he hath the same perception of the original of these internal operations, and attributes them to a Principle in him distinct from the Body: So that if I might have any imaginable doubt of those reflexed perceptions which I have touching those appropriate operations of my own Mind, I am confirmed in them, because I find all the like perceptions in all the men I converse with.

3.5

David Hume

(1711–1776)

Someone had to challenge the presumably unquestionable thinking ego. Hume became the ogre by declaring that personal identity is a fiction and an illusion. His dissolution of mind into a "bundle of perceptions" is the culminating expression of a pessimistic scepticism. One can compare it with the optimistic "stream of consciousness" of William James, who had similar difficulty in finding the "self" apart from the flow of perceptions, and thought perhaps he had isolated it for himself in the muscle sensations of his head and throat (Principles of psychology, 1890, vol. I, p. 391). We will return to Hume's sceptical challenge of reality in Chapter 5, and there we shall see also how it was answered first by Reid and then by Kant. But Hume had his own answer, as stated in the second part of this selection, which became the direct target of Reid's satire.

Of Personal Identity

There are some philosophers, who imagine we are every moment conscious of what we may call our SELF; that we feel its existence and its continuance in existence; and are certain, beyond the evidence of a demonstration, both of its perfect identity and simplicity. . . .

. . . For my part, when I enter most intimately into what I call *myself*, I always stumble on some particular perception or other, of heat or cold, light or shade, love or hatred, pain or pleasure. I never can catch *myself* at any time without a perception, and never can observe any thing but the perception. When my perceptions are remov'd for any time, as by sound sleep, so long am I insensible of *myself*, and may truly be said not to exist. And were all my perfections remov'd by death, and cou'd I neither think, nor feel, nor see, nor love, nor hate after the dissolution of my body, I shou'd be entirely annihilated, nor do I conceive what is further requisite to make me a perfect non-entity. If any one upon serious and unprejudic'd reflection, thinks he has a different notion of *himself*, I must confess I can reason no longer with him. All I can allow him is, that he may be in the right as well as I, and that we are essentially different in this particular. He may, perhaps, perceive something simple and continu'd, which he calls *himself*; tho' I am certain there is no such principle in me.

A treatise of human nature, being an attempt to introduce the experimental method of reasoning into moral subjects. 3 vols. London, 1739–1740. [Vol. I, pp. 436, 438–440, 466–468.]

But setting aside some metaphysicians of this kind, I may venture to affirm of the rest of mankind, that they are nothing but a bundle or collection of different perceptions, which succeed each other with an inconceivable rapidity, and are in a perpetual flux and movement. Our eyes cannot turn in their sockets without varying our perceptions. Our thought is still more variable than our sight; and all our other senses and faculties contribute to this change; nor is there any single power of the soul, which remains unalterably the same, perhaps for one moment. The mind is a kind of theatre, where several perceptions successively make their appearance; pass, re-pass, glide away, and mingle in an infinite variety of postures and situations. There is properly no *simplicity* in it at one time, nor *identity* in different, whatever natural propension we may have to imagine that simplicity and identity. The comparison of the theatre must not mislead us. They are the successive perceptions only, that constitute the mind; nor have we the most distant notion of the place, where these scenes are represented, or of the materials, of which it is compos'd. . . .

*   *   *

But what have I here said, that reflections very refin'd and metaphysical have little or no influence upon us? This opinion I can scarce forbear retracting, and condemning from my present feeling and experience. The *intense* view of these manifold contradictions and imperfections in human reason has so wrought upon me, and heated my brain, that I am ready to reject all belief and reasoning, and can look upon no opinion as more probable or likely than another. Where am I, or what? From what cause do I derive my existence, and to what condition shall I return? Whose favour shall I court, and whose anger must I dread? What beings surround me? and on whom have I any influence, or who have any influence on me? I am confounded with all these questions, and begin to fancy myself in the most deplorable condition imaginable, inviron'd with the deepest darkness, and utterly depriv'd of the use of every member and faculty.

Most fortunately it happens, that since reason is incapable of dispelling these clouds, nature herself suffices to that purpose, and cures me of this philosophical melancholy and delirium, either by relaxing this bent of mind, or by some avocation, and lively impression of my senses, which obliterate all these chimeras. I dine, I play a game of back-gammon, I converse, and am merry with my friends; and when after three or four hour's amusement, I wou'd return to these speculations, they appear so cold, and strain'd, and ridiculous, that I cannot find in my heart to enter into them any farther.

Here then I find myself absolutely and necessarily determin'd to live, and talk, and act like other people in the common affairs of life. But notwithstanding that my natural propensity, and the course of my animal spirits and passions reduce me to this indolent belief in the general maxims of the world, I still feel such remains of my former disposition, that I am ready to throw all my books and papers into the fire, and resolve never more to renounce the pleasures of life for the sake of reasoning and philosophy. For those are my sentiments in that splenetic humour which governs me at present. I may, nay I must yield to the current of nature, in submitting to my senses and understanding; and in this blind submission I shew most perfectly my sceptical disposition and principles.

3.6

Auguste Comte

(1798–1857)

In the long run, it was not metaphysical reasoning, but the rich fruits of inductive science which would discredit a psychology based on the analysis of inner experience. However, about 100 years after Hume, Comte challenged the right to construct a science of man on such a flimsy foundation, and his positivism points toward the behaviorism of the twentieth century. At the time, however, he placed his faith in phrenology!

. . . In any case, in order better to show the true general spirit of phrenological psychology by an illuminating contrast, it will not be without value to analyse very briefly the fundamental faults in the pretended psychological method. However, we shall look only at as much of it as is common to all the principal contemporary schools—that is to say, what are called the French school, the German school, and finally, least consistent but also least absurd of all, the Scottish school—insofar at least as one can conceive of any true school in a philosophy which must, by its nature, engender as many irreconcilable opinions as it has imaginatively gifted adepts. One can always fully rely on these various sects for the mutual refutation of their most profound differences.

As to their fruitless fundamental principle of *interior observation,* it would certainly be superfluous to add anything to what was already sufficiently indicated at the start of this treatise, to show the profound absurdity of the mere supposition, so obviously contradictory, of a man who watches himself thinking. A few years ago, in a work which provided a happy response to the deplorable psychological mania which a famous sophist had momentarily succeeded in inducing in French youth,

Cours de philosophie positive [Course of positive philosophy]. Volume 3, 1838. [Lesson 45; pp. 772–776, 778–781.]

3.6 Auguste Comte

M. Broussais very judiciously remarked in this regard that even if such a method were possible, it must tend to greatly restrict the study of intelligence, by necessarily limiting it to the single case of the healthy human adult, with no hope of ever throwing light on this very difficult problem either by comparison of different ages or by consideration of various pathological states, although both of these are unanimously recognized as indispensable auxiliaries for the simplest researches on man. Taking the same thought further, we must be struck by the absolute interdiction which is thus inevitably imposed on all intellectual or moral study of animals, for psychologists no doubt do not expect any *interior observation* from them. . . .

Coming back to the elementary notions of philosophical good sense, it is obvious that no function can be studied without reference to that organ which performs it, or to the phenomena which it accomplishes; and that in the second place, by their very nature the affective and above all the intellectual functions present in this regard this special characteristic, that they cannot be directly observed at the time of their actual accomplishment, but only in their results, which are more or less remote and more or less lasting. Therefore there are only two distinct ways of really considering functions of this kind: either by determining with all possible precision the various organic conditions on which they depend, and this constitutes the principal purpose of phrenological psychology, or by directly observing the effective consequences of intellectual and moral actions. . . . Thus envisaged, this important study would be indissolubly linked, on the one hand, to all earlier parts of natural philosophy, and most especially to the fundamental doctrine of biology, and on the other hand, to all of actual history, including that of animals, of men, and even of mankind. . . .

Psychology or ideology—considered now not with respect to its method, which we have already examined, but directly with respect to its doctrine—presents us at once with a fundamental distortion which is essentially common to all sects, in a false assessment of the relationship existing between affective and intellectual functions. The preponderance given to the latter has no doubt been conceived in different ways by different theories, but all metaphysicians agree in taking it as their principal point of departure. The *intellect* has been the almost exclusive subject of their speculations, and the various affective faculties have been almost entirely neglected, and always subordinated to the intelligence. Now this conception represents precisely the reverse of reality, not only for animals, but also for man. Daily experience shows us in the most unequivocal manner that, on the contrary, the feelings, penchants, emotions, constitute the principal motive forces of human life; and that far from being the effects of intelligence, their spontaneous and independent impulsion is indispensable to the first awakening and continued development of the various intellectual faculties. . . . It can be easily shown that two purely philosophical causes . . . have essentially led all metaphysicians to this hypothetical supremacy of intelligence. The first consists in the fruitless fundamental distinction which, as we have said, metaphysicians were forced to establish between animals and man. . . . In second place, a cause of this distortion which is more direct, more intimate, and more general results from the strict obligation which all metaphysicians are under, to conserve, as a unique or at least sovereign principle, what they call the unity of the *ego*. This corresponds to the rigorous unity of the *soul* which was necessarily imposed on them by theological philosophy, for, if we wish to really understand the historic progress of the human mind, we must never forget that metaphysical philosophy is nothing but a simple final transformation of theological philosophy.

3.7

Henry Maudsley

(1834–1918)

Comte was too disdainful of psychology to make his attack more than superficial, but his influence appears clearly in the vigorous and exhaustive catalogue of introspection's failings given by the English psychiatrist Henry Maudsley.

But the method of interrogating self-consciousness may be employed, and is largely employed, without carrying it to a metaphysical extreme. Empirical psychology, founded on *direct* consciousness as distinguished from the *transcendental* consciousness on which metaphysics is based, claims to give a faithful record of our different states of mind and their mutual relations, and has been extravagantly lauded, by the Scotch School, as an inductive science. Its value as a science must plainly rest upon the sufficiency and reliability of consciousness as a witness of that which takes place in the mind. Is the foundation then sufficiently secure? It may well be doubted; and for the following reasons:

(a.) There are but few individuals who are capable of attending to the succession of phenomena in their own minds; such introspection demanding a particular cultivation, and being practised with success by those only who have learned the terms, and been imbued with the theories, of the system of psychology supposed to be thereby established.

(b.) There is no agreement between those who have acquired the power of introspection: and men of apparently equal cultivation and

The physiology and pathology of mind. London, 1867. [Pp. 9–11, 13–17, 20, 22–25.]

capacity will, with the utmost sincerity and confidence, lay down directly contradictory propositions. . . .

(c.) To direct consciousness inwardly to the observation of a particular state of mind is to isolate that activity for the time, to cut it off from its relations, and, therefore, to render it unnatural. In order to observe its own action, it is necessary that the mind pause from activity; and yet it is the train of activity that is to be observed. . . .

(d.) The madman's delusion is of itself sufficient to excite profound distrust, not only in the objective truth, but in the subjective worth, of the testimony of an individual's self-consciousness. Descartes laid it down as the fundamental proposition of philosophy that whatever the mind could clearly and distinctly conceive, was true: if there is one thing more clearly and distinctly conceived than another, it is commonly the madman's delusion. . . .

It is not merely a charge against self-consciousness that it is not reliable in that of which it does give information; but it is a provable charge against it that it does not give any account of a large and important part of our mental activity: its light reaches only to states of consciousness, and not to states of mind. . . . May we not then justly say that self-consciousness is utterly incompetent to supply the facts for the building up of a truly inductive psychology? Let the following reasons further warrant the assertion:

1. It is the fundamental maxim of the inductive philosophy that observation should begin with simple instances. . . . [Introspection] is a method which is applicable only to mind at a high degree of development, so that it perforce begins with those most complex instances which give the least certain information; while it passes completely by mind in its lower stages of development, so that it ignores those simpler instances which give the best or securest information. . . .

2. Consciousness given no account of the essential material conditions which underlie every mental manifestation, and determine the character of it: let the function of an individual's optic ganglia be abolished by disease or otherwise, and he would not be conscious that he was blind until experience had convinced him of it. . . .

3. There is an appropriation of external impressions by the mind or brain, which regularly takes place without any, or only with a very obscure, affection of consciousness. . . . It is a truth which cannot be too distinctly borne in mind, that consciousness is not co-extensive with mind. . . .

. . . The preconscious action of the mind, as certain metaphysical psychologists in Germany have called it, and the unconscious action of the mind, which is now established beyond all rational doubt, are assuredly facts of which the most ardent psychologist must admit that self-consciousness can give us no account.

4. Everything which has existed with any completeness in conscious-

ness is preserved, after its disappearance therefrom, in the mind or brain, and may reappear in consciousness at some future time. . . . Consciousness is not able to give any account of the manner in which these various residua are perpetuated, and how they exist latent in the mind. . . .

5. Consciousness reveals nothing of the process by which one idea calls another into activity, and has no control whatever over the manner of the reproduction; it is only when the idea is made active by virtue of some association, when the *effect* solicits or extorts attention, that we are conscious of it; and there is no power in the mind to call up ideas indifferently. If we would recollect something which at the moment escapes us, the best way of succeeding confessedly is to permit the mind to work unconsciously; and while the consciousness is otherwise occupied, the forgotten name or circumstance will oftentimes flash into the memory. . . .

6. The brain not only receives impressions unconsciously, registers impressions without the co-operation of consciousness, elaborates material unconsciously, calls latent residua again into activity without consciousness, but it responds also as an organ of organic life to the internal stimuli which it receives unconsciously from other organs of the body. . . .

To what has been before said of unconscious mental action this more may now be added—that the deep basis of all mental action lies in the organic life of the brain, the characteristic of which in health is, that it proceeds without consciousness. He whose brain makes him conscious that he has a brain is not well, but ill; and thought that is conscious of itself is not natural and healthy thought. . . .

Such are the charges against self-consciousness whereon is founded the conclusion as to its incompetency: they show that he who thinks to illuminate the whole range of mental action by the light of his own consciousness is not unlike one who should go about to illuminate the universe with a rushlight. . . .

Is it not supremely ridiculous that while we cannot trust consciousness in so simple a matter as whether we are hot or cold, we should be content to rely entirely on its evidence in the complex phenomena of our highest mental activity? The truth is, that what has very often happened before has happened here: the quality or attribute has been abstracted from the concrete, and the abstraction then converted into an entity; the attribute, consciousness, has miraculously got rid of its substance, and with a wonderful assurance assumed the office of passing judgment upon its nature. Descartes was in this case the clever architect; and his success has fully justified his art: while the metaphysical stage of human development lasts, his work will doubtless endure.

3.8

Edward Bradford Titchener

(1867–1927)

Whatever the limits of introspection, Titchener probably came closer to attaining them than any other man. The subtlety of his observation, sharpened in the Wundtian school, is far above the ken of Augustine, Avicenna, or Descartes. "What is a thinking being?" asked Descartes, and answered that "it is a thing that doubts, understands, affirms, denies. . . ." Now Titchener tells us that when he turns round upon consciousness in moments of "doubt, hesitations, belief, assent . . ." he always finds imaginal content as the vehicle for these mental states. Painstakingly exact introspection has indeed turned the "self" into a bundle of sensations! Far from contending for a supersensory metaphysical self (which is where it all started), Titchener rejects the allegation that thinking is possible in other than imaginal terms.

The "context theory of meaning" which is included in this selection was advanced by Titchener as an answer to the arguments for imageless thinking put forth by Woodworth (26.5) and the Würzburg school (16.9).

My mind, then, is of the imaginal sort,—I wish that we had a better adjective!—and my ideational type is of the sort described in the psychologies as mixed. I have always had, and I have always used, a wide range and a great variety of imagery; and my furniture of images is, perhaps, in better than average condition, because—fearing that, as one gets older, one tends also to become more and more verbal in type—I have made a point of renewing it by practice. I am able now, for instance, as I was able when I entered the class-room nearly twenty years ago, to lecture from any one of the three main cues. I can read off what I have to say from a memory manuscript; or I can follow the lead of my voice; or I can trust to the guidance of kinesthesis, the anticipatory feel of the movements of articulation. I use these three methods under different circumstances. . . .

When I am working for myself, reading or writing or thinking, I experience a complex interlacing of imagery which it is difficult to describe, or at any rate to describe with just emphasis. . . . If I may venture on a very sweeping statement, I should say that I never sit down to read a book or to write a paragraph, or to think out a problem, without a musical accompaniment. . . .

My visual imagery, voluntarily aroused as for Galton's breakfast-table

Lectures on the experimental psychology of the thought-processes. New York: Macmillan, 1909. [Pp. 7–9, 13–14, 16–19, 175–176, 180, 182, 193–194.]

test, is extremely vivid, though it seems bodiless and papery when compared with direct perception. . . . My mind, in its ordinary operations, is a fairly complete picture gallery,—not of finished paintings, but of impressionist notes. Whenever I read or hear that somebody has done something modestly, or gravely, or proudly, or humbly, or courteously, I see a visual hint of the modesty or gravity or pride or humility or courtesy. The stately heroine gives me a flash of a tall figure, the only clear part of which is a hand holding up a steely grey skirt; the humble suitor gives me a flash of a bent figure, the only clear part of which is the bowed back, though at times there are hands held deprecatingly before the absent face. A great many of these sketches are irrelevant and accessory; but they often are, and they always may be, the vehicles of a logical meaning. The stately form that steps through the French window to the lawn may be clothed in all the colours of the rainbow; but its stateliness is the hand on the grey skirt. I shall not multiply instances. All this description must be either self-evident or as unreal as a fairy-tale.

It leads us, however, to a very important question,—the old question of the possibility of abstract or general ideas. . . .

The issue, in its psychological formulation, is an issue of fact. Is wordless imagery, under any circumstances, the mental representative of meaning? And if it is, do we find a correlation of vague imagery with abstract and of definite imagery with particular meaning?

The first of these questions I have already answered, for my own case, in the affirmative. In large measure I think, that is, I mean and I understand, in visual pictures. The second question I cannot answer in the affirmative. . . . In my own experience, attentional clearness seems to be the one thing needful to qualify a process for meaning. Whether the picture as picture is sharply outlined and highly coloured is a matter of indifference.

Come back now to the authorities: to Locke's triangle and Huxley's composite animal. My own picture of the triangle, the image that means triangle to me, is usually a fairly definite outline of the little triangular figure that stands for the word 'triangle' in the geometries. . . . Horse is to me, a double curve and a rampant posture with a touch of mane about it; cow is a longish rectangle with a certain facial expression, a sort of exaggerated pout. Again, however, these things mean horse and cow, are the psychological vehicles of those logical meanings.

And what holds of triangle and horse and cow holds of all the "unpicturable notions of intelligence [Hamilton]." No one of them is unpicturable, if you do but have the imaginal mind. "It is impossible," remarks a recent writer [T. H. Huxley], to ideate a meaning; one can only know it." Impossible? But I have been ideating meanings all my life. And not only meanings, but meaning also. Meaning in general is represented in my consciousness by another of these impressionist pictures. I see meaning as the blue-grey tip of a kind of scoop, which has a bit of yellow above it (probably a part of the handle), and which is just digging into a dark mass of what appears to be plastic material. I was educated on classical lines; and it is conceivable that this picture is an echo of the oft-repeated admonition to 'dig out the meaning' of some passage of Greek or Latin. I do not know; but I am sure of the image. . . .

I hold that, from the psychological or existential point of view, meaning—so far as it finds representation in consciousness at all—is always context. An idea means another idea, is psychologically the meaning of that other idea, if it is that idea's context. And I understand by context simply the mental process or complex of mental processes which accrues to the original idea through the situation in which the organism finds itself,—primitively, the natural situation; later, either the natural or the mental. . . . Meaning is, originally, kinesthesis, the organism faces the situation by some bodily attitude, and the characteristic sensations which the attitude involves give meaning to the process that stands at the conscious focus, are psychologically the meaning of that process. Afterwards, when differentiation has taken place, context may be mainly a matter of sensations of the special senses, or of images, or of kinesthetic and other organic sensations, as the situation demands. The particular form that meaning assumes is then a question to be answered by descriptive psychology. . . .

What, then, of the imageless thoughts, the awarenesses, the *Bewusstseinslagen* of meaning and the rest? . . . What I have personally found out does not, so far, shake my faith in sensationalism. . . .

I have turned round, time and time again, upon consciousnesses like doubt, hesitation, belief, assent, trying to remember, having a thing on my tongue's tip, and I have not been able to discover the imageless processes. No doubt, the analysis has been rough and uncontrolled; but it has been attempted at the suggestion of the imageless psychologists, and with the reports of their introspections echoing in my mind. . . .

My task has been to persuade you that there is no need, as things are, to swell the number of the mental elements; that the psychology of thought, so far as we have it, may be interpreted from the sensationalistic standpoint, and so far as we still await it, may be approached by sensationalistic methods. What the future will bring forth, no one can foresee. . . . In any event, I see less prospect of gain from a revolution than from persistent work under the existing regime.

3.9

John B. Watson

(1878–1958)

In 1905 William McDougall defined psychology as "the positive science of the conduct of living creatures" (28.4). In 1912 he called it "the positive science of behavior." However, he had no intention to exclude consciousness as an object of study. Watson coined the word "behaviorist" to initiate a new epoch. "Psychology as the behaviorist views it" appeared in the Psychological Review bearing the obvious marks of Watson's vigorous platform manner. (That article appears, unabridged, in Dennis's Readings.) It was slightly altered, with the belligerent I's changed to half-conciliatory we's, to become the opening chapter of Behavior, here condensed.

On thinking as implicit speech, see Ferrier (16.8).

Psychology as the behaviorist views it is a purely objective experimental branch of natural science. Its theoretical goal is the prediction and control of behavior. Introspection forms no essential part of its methods, nor is the scientific value of its data dependent upon the readiness with which they lend themselves to interpretation in terms of consciousness. The behaviorist attempts to get a unitary scheme of animal response. He recognizes no dividing line between man and brute. . . .

It has been maintained by its followers generally that psychology is a study of the science of the phenomena of consciousness. . . . It is agreed that introspection is the method *par excellence* by means of which mental states may be manipulated for purposes of psychology. On this assumption, behavior data (including under this term everything which goes under the name of comparative psychology) have no value *per se*. They possess significance only in so far as they may throw light upon conscious states. . . .

. . . More than one student of behavior has attempted to frame criteria of the psychic—to devise a set of objective, structural, and functional criteria which, when applied to the particular instance, will enable him to decide whether such and such responses are positively conscious, merely indicative of consciousness, or whether they are purely "physiological." Such problems as these can no longer satisfy behavior men. It would be better to give up the province altogether and admit frankly that the study of the behavior of animals has no justification, than to admit that the search is of such a "will o' the wisp" character. One can assume either the presence or the absence of consciousness anywhere in

Behavior: an introduction to comparative psychology. New York: Holt, 1914. [Pp. 1–2, 4–5, 7–9, 16–17, 19–21, 26.]

the phylogenetic scale without affecting the problems of behavior by one jot or tittle; and without influencing in any way the mode of experimental attack upon them. . . .

The time seems to have come when psychology must discard all reference to consciousness; when it need no longer delude itself into thinking that it is making mental states the object of observation. We have become so enmeshed in speculative questions concerning the elements of mind, the nature of conscious content (e.g., imageless thought, attitudes, and Bewusstseinslage, etc.), that experimental students are beginning to feel that something is wrong with the premises and the types of problems which develop from them. . . . While it is admitted that every growing science is full of unanswered questions, surely only those who are wedded to the system as we now have it . . . can confidently believe that there will ever be any greater uniformity than there is now in the answers we have to such questions. One must believe that two hundred years from now, unless the introspection method is discarded, psychology will still be divided on the question as to whether auditory sensations have the quality of "extension," whether intensity is an attribute which can be applied to color, whether there is a difference in "texture" between image and sensation; and upon many hundreds of others of like character. . . .

The most serious problem in the way of a free passage from structuralism to behaviorism is the "centrally aroused sensation" or "image." If thoughts go on in terms of centrally aroused sensations, as is maintained by the majority of both structural and functional psychologists, we should have to admit that there is a serious limitation on the side of method in behaviorism. Imagery from Galton on has been the inner stronghold of a psychology based upon introspection. . . .

Feeling so, it seems wisest, even at the cost of exposing the weakness of our position, to attack rather than to remain upon the defensive. . . .

When the stimulus produces either an *immediate overt response* . . . or a *delayed overt response* . . . we have examples of what we may call *explicit behavior*. In contrast to behavior of this type, which involves the larger musculature in a way plainly apparent to direct observation, we have behavior involving only the speech mechanisms (or the larger musculature in a minimal way; e.g., bodily attitudes or sets). This form of behavior, for lack of a better name, we may call *implicit behavior*. Where explicit behavior is delayed (i.e., where deliberation ensues), the intervening time between stimulus and response is given over to implicit behavior (to "thought processes").

Now it is this type of implicit behavior that the introspectionist claims as his own and denies to us because its neural seat is cortical and because it goes on without adequate bodily portrayal. Why in psychology the stage for the neural drama was ever transferred from periphery to cortex must remain somewhat of a mystery. The old idea of strict localization of brain function is in part responsible. . . . When the psychologist threw away the soul he compromised with his conscience by setting up a "mind" which was to remain always hidden and difficult of access. . . .

It is implied in these words that there exists or ought to exist a method of observing implicit behavior. There is none at present. The larynx and tongue, we believe, are the loci of most of the phenomena. If their movements could be adequately portrayed we should obtain a record similar to that of the phonogram. . . .

Now it is admitted by all of us that words spoken or faintly articulated belong really in the realm of behavior as do movements of the arms and legs. If implicit behavior can be shown to consist of nothing but word movements (or expressive movements of the word-type) the behavior of the human being as a whole is as open to objective control as the behavior of the lowest organism. . . .

Will there be left over in psychology a world of pure psychics, to use Yerkes' term? The plans which we most favor for psychology lead practically to the ignoring of consciousness in the sense in which the term is used by psychologists today. . . . If you will grant the behaviorist the right to use consciousness in the same way that other natural scientists employ it—i.e., without making consciousness a special object of observation—you have granted all that our thesis requires.

 # Chapter 4

PURPOSE IN NATURE: THE HUMAN HAND

Men have often expressed chagrin that one animal or another excels over us in fleetness of foot, acuity of the senses, general bodily strength, ability to withstand heat or cold, and the like. Some, like birds, can perform feats of which men can only dream. Metaphysical advantages aside, among nature's gifts we can point only to the hand as evidence of superiority or of the special favor of providence. As man gets a more objective view of his place in the general scheme of things, he gets a better understanding of the hand.

4.1

Aristotle

(384–322 B.C.)

A teleologist as always, in his discussion of the human hand, Aristotle gives, as so often, many arguments that will be echoed for centuries. Compare his discussion of the hand's structure with that by Napier, which closes the chapter.

Parts of animals. With an English translation by A. L. Peck. Cambridge, Mass.: Harvard University Press (Loeb Classical Library), 1937. [687a–687b.] Reprinted by permission of the Publisher and the Loeb Classical Library.

We have now stated why it is that some animals have two feet, some many, some none at all; why some creatures are plants and some animals; and why man is the only one of the animals that stands upright. And since man stands upright, he has no need of legs in front; instead of them Nature has given him arms and hands. Anaxagoras indeed asserts that it is his possession of hands that makes man the most intelligent of the animals; but surely the reasonable point of view is that it is because he is the most intelligent animal that he has got hands. Hands are an instrument; and Nature, like a sensible human being, always assigns an organ to the animal that can use it (as it is more in keeping to give flutes to a man who is already a flute-player than to provide a man who possesses flutes with the skill to play them); thus Nature has provided that which is less as an addition to that which is greater and superior; not *vice versa*. We may conclude, then, that, if this is the *better* way, and if Nature always does the *best* she can in the circumstances, it is not true to say that man is the most intelligent animal because he possesses hands, but he has hands because he is the most intelligent animal. We should expect the most intelligent to be able to employ the greatest number of organs or instruments to good purpose; now the hand would appear to be not one single instrument but many, as it were an instrument that represents many instruments. Thus it is to that animal (viz. man) which has the capability for acquiring the greatest number of crafts that Nature has given that instrument (viz. the hand) whose range of uses is the most extensive.

Now it must be wrong to say, as some do, that the structure of man is not good, in fact, that it is worse than that of any other animal. Their grounds are: that man is barefoot, unclothed, and void of any weapon of force. Against this we may say that all the other animals have just one method of defence and cannot change it for another: they are forced to sleep and perform all their actions with their shoes on the whole time, as one might say; they can never take off this defensive equipment of theirs, nor can they change their weapon, whatever it may be. For man, on the other hand, many means of defence are available, and he can change them at any time, and above all he can choose what weapon he will have and where. Take the hand: this is as good as a talon, or a claw, or a horn, or again, a spear or a sword, or any other weapon or tool: it can be all of these, because it can seize and hold them all. And Nature has admirably contrived the actual shape of the hand so as to fit in with this arrangement. It is not all of one piece, but it branches into several pieces; which gives the possibility of its coming together into one solid piece, whereas the reverse order of events would be impossible. Also, it is possible to use them singly, or two at a time, or in various ways. Again, the joints of the fingers are well constructed for taking hold of things and for exerting pressure. One finger is placed sideways: this is short and thick, not long like the others. It would be as impossible to get a hold if this were not placed sideways as if no hand were there at all. It exerts its pressure upwards from below, whereas the others act downwards from above; and this is essential for a strong tight grip (like that of a strong clamp), so that it may exert a pressure equivalent to that of the other four. It is short, then, first for strength, but also because it would be no good if it were long. (The end finger also is small—and the middle one is long like an oar amidships, because any object which is being grasped for active use has to be grasped right around the middle.) And on this account it is called "big" although it is small, because the other fingers are practically useless without it. The nails, too, are a good piece of planning. In man they serve as coverings: a guard, in fact, for the tips of the fingers. In animals they serve for practical use as well.

4.2

Galen

(131–200)

Sherrington called this work "the earliest separate treatise dealing with human physiology." It seeks to show that nature has made each of the body's parts ideally for its purpose. It is not at all surprising that to prove this thesis Galen devotes the entire first book to the human hand.

2. . . . Now to man—for he is an intelligent animal and, alone of all creatures on earth, godlike—in place of any and every defensive weapon she {Nature} gave hands, instruments necessary for every art and useful in peace no less than in war. . . . If he were born with a horn or some other defensive weapon of the kind growing upon his hands, he could not use them at all to build a house or a tower, or to make a spear or corslet or other similar things. With these hands of his, a man weaves himself a cloak and fashions hunting-nets, fish-nets and traps, and fine-meshed bird-nets, so that he is lord not only of animals upon the earth, but of those in the sea and the air also. Such is the hand of man as an instrument of defense. But, being also a peaceful and social animal, with his hands he writes laws for himself, raises altars and statues to the gods, builds ships, makes flutes, lyres, knives, fire-tongs, and all the other instruments of the arts, and in his writings leaves behind him commentaries on the theories of them. . . .

On the usefulness of the parts of the body. Translated by Margaret Tallmadge May. Ithaca, N.Y.: Cornell University Press, 1968. 2 vols. [Vol. 1, pp. 68–72.] Copyright © 1968 by Cornell University. Used by permission of Cornell University Press.

3. Thus man is the most intelligent of the animals and so, also, hands are the instruments most suitable for an intelligent animal. For it is not because he has hands that he is the most intelligent, as Anaxagoras says, but because he is the most intelligent that he has hands, as Aristotle says, judging more correctly. Indeed, not by his hands, but by his reason has man been instructed in the arts. Hands are an instrument, as the lyre is the instrument of the musician, and tongs of the smith. Hence just as the lyre does not teach the musician or tongs the smith but each of them is a craftsman by virtue of the reason there is in him although he is unable to work at his trade without the aid of his instruments, so every soul has through its very essence certain faculties, but without the aid of instruments is helpless to accomplish what it is by Nature disposed to accomplish. . . . {The omitted passage is given as selection 14.2.}

4. Now, just as man's body is bare of weapons, so is his soul destitute of skills. Therefore, to compensate for the nakedness of his body, he received hands, and for his soul's lack of skill, reason, by means of which he arms and guards his body in every way and equips his soul with all the arts. . . . For though the hand is no one particular instrument, it is the instrument for all instruments because it is formed by Nature to receive them all, and similarly, although reason is no one of the arts in particular, it would be an art for the arts because it is naturally disposed to take them all unto itself. Hence man, the only one of all the animals having an art for arts in his soul, should logically have an instrument for instruments in his body.

5. Come now, let us investigate this very important part of man's body, examining it to determine not simply whether it is useful or whether it is suitable for an intelligent animal, but whether it is in every respect so constituted that it would not have been better had it been made differently. . . .

4·3

Gregory of Nyssa

(335?–395?)

Nowhere, perhaps, does the Christian derogation of merely bodily activity appear more clearly than in this declaration that the hand is a specifically human instrument, not for what it can do, but because by taking over the

On the making of man. Translated by H. A. Wilson. In *A select library of Nicene and post-Nicene Fathers of the Christian Church.* Second series, Vol. V: *Gregory of Nyssa.* London, 1893. Pp. 387–427. [Pp. 393–395.]

task of food-gathering (why not also fighting?) it freed the mouth for development as the organ of speech. This view is consistent with the general position on the incorporeality of the soul and its independence of any particular organs, as stated in another selection from this work (8.3).

In the same spirit is the statement of Richard de Bury (1287–1345) that "We do not read of the Son of God that he sowed or plowed, wove or digged; nor did any other of the mechanic arts befit the divine wisdom incarnate except to trace letters in writing {John, 8:6}, that every gentleman and sciolist may know that fingers are given by God to men for the task of writing rather than for war." (Philobiblon, trans. by E. C. Thomas; Oxford, 1960.)

[VIII.] 1. But man's form is upright, and extends aloft towards heaven, and looks upwards: and these are marks of sovereignty which show his royal dignity. For the fact that man alone among existing things is such as this, while all others bow their bodies downwards, clearly points to the difference of dignity between those which stoop beneath his sway and that power which rises above them: for all the rest have the foremost limbs of their bodies in the form of feet, because that which stoops needs something to support it: but in the formation of man these limbs were made hands, for the upright body found one base, supporting its position securely on two feet, sufficient for its needs.

2. Especially do these ministering hands adapt themselves to the requirements of the reason: indeed if one were to say that the ministration of hands is a special property of the rational nature, he would not be entirely wrong; and that not only because his thought turns to the common and obvious fact that we signify our reasoning by means of the natural employment of our hands in written characters. It is true that this fact, that we speak by writing, and, in a certain way, converse by the aid of our hands, preserving sounds by the forms of the alphabet, is not unconnected with the endowment of reason; but I am referring to something else when I say that the hands co-operate with the bidding of reason. . . .

8. Now since man is a rational animal, the instrument of his body must be made suitable for the use of reason; as you may see musicians producing their music according to the form of their instruments, and not piping with harps nor harping upon flutes, so it must needs be that the organization of these instruments of ours should be adapted for reason, that when struck by the vocal organs it might be able to sound properly for the use of words. For this reason the hands were attached to the body; for though we can count up very many uses in daily life for which these skillfully contrived and helpful instruments, our hands, that easily follow every art and every operation, alike in war and peace, are serviceable, yet nature added them to our body pre-eminently for the sake of reason. For

if man were destitute of hands, the various parts of his face would certainly have been arranged like those of the quadrupeds, to suit the purpose of his feeding: so that its form would have been lengthened out and pointed towards the nostrils, and his lips would have projected from his mouth, lumpy, and stiff, and thick, fitted for taking up the grass, and his tongue would either have lain between his teeth, of a kind to match his lips, fleshy, and hard, and rough, assisting his teeth to deal with what came under his grinder, or it would have been moist and hanging out at the side like that of dogs and other carnivorous beasts, projecting through the gaps in his jagged row of teeth. If, then, our body had no hands, how could articulate sounds have been implanted in it, seeing that the form of the parts of the mouth would not have had the configuration proper for the use of speech, so that man must of necessity have either bleated, or "baaed," or barked, or neighed, or bellowed like oxen or asses, or uttered some bestial sound? but now, as the hand is made part of the body, the mouth is at leisure for the service of the reason. Thus the hands are shown to be the property of the rational nature, the Creator having thus devised by their means a special advantage for reason.

4·4

Claude Helvetius

(1715–1771)

The spirit of Anaxagoras is revived in the eighteenth century: Helvetius regards the hand as a fortunate accident rather than as a necessary part of Nature's plan. The original edition of De l'esprit appeared in 1758, and had an enormous vogue in the fashionable world after it had been officially thrown to the flames along with some other overly enlightened books. The subtitle of the translation is not really faithful to Helvetius's thought, since he did not subscribe to a faculty psychology, although he does use the word at times.

If nature, instead of hands and flexible fingers, had terminated our wrist with the foot of a horse, mankind would doubtless have been totally destitute of art, habitation, and defence against other animals. Wholly employed in the care of procuring food, and avoiding the beasts of prey,

De l'esprit [Paris, 1758]. Translated anonymously, as *De l'esprit; or essays on the mind, and its several faculties.* London, 1759. [Pp. 1–3.]

they would have still continued wandering in the forests, like fugitive flocks.[a]

It is therefore evident, that according to this supposition, the police {civilization} would never have been carried in any society to that degree of perfection, to which it is now arrived. There is not a nation now existing, but with regard to the action of the Mind, must not have continued very inferior to certain savage nations, who have not two hundred different ideas, nor two hundred words to express those ideas; and whose language must consequently be reduced, like that of animals, to five or six different sounds or cries, if we take from it, the words Bow, Arrow, Nets, &c. which suppose the use of hands. From whence I conclude, that without a certain exterior organisation, Sensibility and Memory in us would prove two steril faculties. We ought to examine if these two faculties, by the assistance of this organisation, have in reality produced all our thoughts.

[a] . . . But some may ask why monkeys, whose paws are nearly as dexterous as our hands, do not make a progress equal to that of Man? Because they are inferior to him in several respects; because men are more multiplied upon the earth; because among the different species of monkeys, there are but few whose strength can be compared to that of man; because the monkeys being frugiverous, have fewer wants, and therefore less invention than man, because their life is shorter, and they form only a fugitive society with regard to man, and such animals as the tyger, the lion, &c. and finally because the organical disposition of their body, keeps them like children, in perpetual motion, even after their desires are satisfied. Monkeys are not susceptible of lassitude {see 21.8}, which ought to be considered . . . as one of the principles of the perfection of the human mind.

By combining all these differences between the nature of man and beast, we may understand, why sensibility and memory, though faculties common to man and other animals, are in the latter only steril faculties.

4.5

Charles Bell

(1774–1842)

Charles Bell, a skilled and insightful anatomist, is aware of the relation of the human hand to analogous structures in all other vertebrate animals. He recognizes that in all of these a principle of "adaptation" is at work, but he falls short of seeing how this principle had determined evolutionary change in the series. This volume is the most distinguished of the "Bridgewater Treatises" financed by a special bequest to the Royal Society of Lon-

The hand: Its mechanism and vital endowments as evincing design. London, 1833. [Pp. 21–24, 37.]

don for publication of a work "On the Power, Wisdom, and Goodness of God, as manifested in the Creation; illustrating such work by all reasonable arguments, as for instance the variety and formation of God's creatures in the animal, vegetable, and mineral kingdoms." It is thus a relatively late expression of "natural theology," which had developed with the accumulation of scientific knowledge and consequent distrust in the older doctrinal foundations of religious belief. The work of Reimarus on instinct (15.8) was an earlier expression of that movement.

We recognize the bones which form the upper extremity of man, in the fin of the whale, in the paddle of the turtle, and in the wing of the bird. We see the same bones, perfectly suited to their purpose, in the paw of the lion or the bear, and equally fitted for motion in the hoof of the horse, or in the foot of the camel, or adjusted for climbing or digging in the long clawed feet of the sloth or bear.

It is obvious, then, that we should be occupied with too limited a view of our subject, were we to consider the human hand in any other light than as presenting the most perfect combination of parts: as exhibiting the bones and muscles which in different animals are suited to particular purposes, so combined in the hand, as to perform actions the most minute and complicated, consistently with powerful exertion.

The wonder still is, that whether we examine this system in man, or in any of the inferior species of animals, nothing can be more curiously adjusted or appropriated; and we should be inclined to say, whatever instance occupied our thoughts for the time, that to this particular object the system had been framed. . . .

There is not only a scheme or system of animal structure pervading all the classes of animals which inhabit the earth, but that the principle of this great plan of creation was in operation, and governed the formation of those animals which existed previous to the revolutions that the earth itself has undergone: that the excellence of form now seen in the skeleton of man, was in the scheme of animal existence long previous to the formation of man, and before the surface of the earth was prepared for him or suited to his constitution, structure, or capacities. . . .

The principle, then, in the application of which we shall be borne out, is, that there is an adaptation, an established and universal relation between the instincts, organization, and instruments of animals on the one hand, and the element in which they are to live, the position which they are to hold, and their means of obtaining food on the other;—and this holds good with respect to the animals which have existed, as well as those which now exist.

4.6

Charles Darwin

(1809–1882)

Darwin brought to full clarity the insight of which Bell had a glimmering. His formulation of the problem of evolution (in The origin of species, 1859) had previously removed the need for a teleological orientation in science, which had been variously expressed in Aristotle's "final cause," in Galen's emphasis on design in nature, and in the movement of natural theology.

Although the intellectual powers and social habits of man are of paramount importance to him, we must not underrate the importance of his bodily structure. . . .

Even to hammer with precision is no easy matter, as every one who has tried to learn carpentry will admit. To throw a stone with as true an aim as can a Fuegian in defending himself, or in killing birds, requires the most consummate perfection in the correlated action of the muscles of the hand, arm, and shoulder, not to mention a fine sense of touch. . . . To chip a flint into the rudest tool, or to form a barbed spear or hook from a bone, demands the use of a perfect hand. . . . A man-like animal who possessed a hand and arm sufficiently perfect to throw a stone with precision or to form a flint into a rude tool, could, it can hardly be doubted, with sufficient practice make almost anything, as far as mechanical skill alone is concerned, which a civilised man can make. The structure of the hand in this respect may be compared with that of the vocal organs, which in the apes are used for uttering various signal-cries, or, as in one species, musical cadences; but in man closely similar vocal organs have become adapted through the inherited effects of use for the utterance of articulate language. . . .

It seems to me far from true that because "objects are grasped clumsily" by monkeys, "a much less specialised organ or prehension" would have served them as well as their present hands. On the contrary, I see no reason to doubt that a more perfectly constructed hand would have been an advantage to them, provided, and it is important to note this, that their hands had not thus been rendered less well adapted for climbing trees. We may suspect that a perfect hand would have been disadvantageous for climbing; as the most arboreal monkeys in the world . . . either have their thumbs much reduced in size and even rudimentary, or

The descent of man, and selection in relation to sex. London, 1871. 2 vols. [Vol. I, pp. 138–141.]

their fingers partially coherent, so that their hands are converted into mere grasping-hooks.

As soon as some ancient member in the great series of the Primates came, owing to a change in its manner of procuring subsistence, or to a change in the conditions of its native country, to live somewhat less on trees and more on the ground, its manner of progression would have been modified; and in this case it would have had to become either more strictly quadrupedal or bipedal. . . . Man alone has become a biped; and we can, I think, partly see how he has come to assume his erect attitude, which forms one of the most conspicuous differences between him and his nearest allies. Man could not have attained his present dominant position in the world without the use of his hands which are so admirably adapted to act in obedience to his will. As Sir C. Bell insists "the hand supplies all instruments, and by its correspondence with the intellect gives him universal dominion." But the hands and arms could hardly have become perfect enough to have manufactured weapons, or to have hurled stones and spears with a true aim, as long as they were habitually used for locomotion and for supporting the whole weight of the body, or as long as they were especially well adapted, as previously remarked, for climbing trees.

4·7

John Napier

(born 1917)

Darwin's speculations are both supported and modified by the most recent evidence on the antecedents of man. At Olduvai Gorge in Tanganyika, Leakey discovered the million-year-old man-ape which he named Zinjan-thropus. Napier discusses the significance of some hand bones later discovered at the same site. He concludes that hands capable of toolmaking existed before man as we now know him.

In *Nature* of December 17, 1960, Dr. L. S. B. Leakey reported on the discovery of a number of fossil bones of the hand and the foot on a living floor some 20 ft below the uppermost limit of Bed I, Olduvai. . . .

Fifteen of the hand bones pertaining to at least two individuals, an adult and a juvenile, have been identified and examined. . . .

While morphologically the precise affinities of the Olduvai hand are

Fossil hand bones from Olduvai Gorge. *Nature,* 196 (1962): 409–411.

indistinct, functionally there seems little reason to doubt that the hand is that of a hominid.

The hand of modern man is capable of two basic prehensile movements that have been termed precision grip and power grip. . . . In the power grip the object is held as in a clamp between the flexed fingers and the palm, reinforcement and counter-pressure being supported by the adducted thumb. The precision grip, nevertheless, is used by man where a delicate touch and a precise control of movement is required and is achieved by means of a grip between the palmar aspect of the terminal phalanx of the fully opposed thumb and the terminal phalanges of the fingers. . . . It would seem . . . that the Olduvai hand was capable of power grip equal in performance, but, in view of the evidence of the attachment of the flexor tendons, comparatively greater in strength than in modern man. There is less certainty with regard to precision grip, which, while undoubtedly possible, may not have been as effective as in modern man. The overall picture presented by this assemblage is of a short powerful hand with strong, curved digits, surmounted by broad, flat nails and held in marked flexion. The thumb is strong and opposable, though possibly rather short.

At a recent conference . . . organized by the Wenner-Gren Foundation for Anthropological Research, an attempt was made to produce a diagnosis for the genus *Homo*. It was agreed that such a diagnosis could not be made unless certain characters and character complexes were present in combination. Included in these characters . . . was the criterion that "the hand is capable of making tools of a recognizable culture." If one assumes that the artifacts of an early Oldowan culture found on the living floor were the work of the species the remains of which are found there, then this criterion is fulfilled and, in addition, an interesting conclusion is possible: that toolmaking was established in the human lineage long before the hand had assumed its modern human form. . . .

Given the intellectual ability, the construction of the crude, rather small pebble-tools of the type found on the living floor, is well within the physical capacity of the Olduvai hand. Precision grip, which is imperfectly evolved in the fossil hand, is not an essential requirement at this level of craftsmanship as personal experiments in the construction of "Oldowan" pebble-tools and "Chellean" hand-axes have shown.

Chapter 5

KNOWLEDGE AND ILLUSION

Can man know the world truly? How much reliance should he place on the information obtained through the senses, how much on the intuitions independent of them, how much on the reasoning of his mind? These intertwined problems have been a battleground for psychological theorists through the ages, and only in the very recent period have they been put to experimental test.

5.1

Aristotle

(384–322 B.C.)

Aristotle believed that the senses could not be false to that aspect of reality to which they were attuned, and that error in perception was due to our mistaken interpretation of sensory data which are in themselves correct.

On the soul. In *Aristotle: On the soul; Parva naturalia; On breath.* With an English translation by W. S. Hett. Cambridge, Mass.: Harvard University Press (Loeb Classical Library), 1957. Pp. 1–203. [Book III, Ch. 3; 427a–429a.] Reprinted by permission of the publisher and the Loeb Classical Library.

5.1 Aristotle

This opinion exercised more influence over later philosophers than on those nearer to him in time.

. . . Indeed the older philosophers assert that thinking and perceiving are identical. . . . And yet they ought to have made some mention of error at the same time; for error seems to be more natural to living creatures, and the soul spends more time in it. . . . Now it is quite clear that perceiving and practical thinking are not the same; for all living creatures have a share in the former, but only a few in the latter. Nor again is speculative thinking, which involves being right or wrong . . . the same thing as perceiving; for the perception of proper objects is always true, and is a characteristic of all living creatures, but it is possible to think falsely, and thought belongs to no animal which has not reasoning power; for imagination is different from both perception and thought; imagination always implies perception, and is itself implied by judgement. . . .

If imagination is (apart from any metaphorical sense of the word) the process by which we say that an image is presented to us, it is one of those faculties or states of mind by which we judge and are either right or wrong. Such are sensation, opinion, knowledge and intelligence. It is clear from the following considerations that imagination is not sensation. Sensation is either actual or potential, *e.g.*, either sight or seeing, but imagination occurs when neither of these is present, as when objects are seen in dreams. Secondly, sensation is always present but imagination is not. If sensation and imagination were identical in actuality, then imagination would be possible for all creatures; but this appears not to be the case; for instance it is not true of the ant, the bee, or the grub. Again, all sensations are true, but most imaginations are false. . . .

But since when a particular thing is moved another thing may be moved by it, and since imagination seems to be some kind of movement, and not to occur apart from sensation, but only to men when perceiving, and in connexion with what is perceptible, and since movement may be caused by actual sensation, and this movement must be similar to the sensation, this movement cannot exist without sensation, or when we are not perceiving; in virtue of it the possessor may act and be acted upon in various ways; and the movement may be true or false. The reason for this last fact is as follows. The perception of proper objects is true, or is only capable of error to the least possible degree. Next comes perception that they are attributes, and here a possibility of error at once arises; for perception does not err in perceiving that an object is white, but only as to whether the white object is one thing or another. Thirdly comes perception of the common attributes which accompany the concomitants to which the proper sensibles belong (I mean, *e.g.*, motion and magnitude); it is about these that error is most likely to occur. But the movement produced by the sense-activity will differ from the actual sensation in each of these three modes of perception. The first is true whenever the sensation is present, but the others may be false both when it is present and when it is absent, and especially when the sensible object is at a distance. If, then, imagination involves nothing else than we have stated, and is as we have described it, then imagination must be a movement produced by sensation actively operating. . . . Again, because imaginations persist in us and resemble sensations, living creatures frequently act in accordance with them, some, *viz.*, the brutes, because they have no mind, and some, *viz.*, men, because the mind is temporarily clouded over by emotion, or disease, or sleep. Let this suffice about the nature and cause of imagination.

5.2

Sextus Empiricus

(flourished A.D. 200–250)

Pyrrho of Elis, the founder of scepticism, died in 270 B.C., having lived to the age of 90 despite, we are told, an utter disregard for such sensory facts as cliffs, chariots, or dogs. His doctrines also proved hardy. The arguments of the sceptics were summed up by a Greek physician, Sextus the Empiric, six centuries later. Since the ultimate thrust of scepticism must be against any established system of beliefs, the anonymous translator of this work into French is duly apologetic, and cautiously disclaims agreeing with the author. But the eighteenth century was very much an age of scepticism, as seen especially in the writings of Hume (3.5) and La Mettrie (1.7).

Ch. IV. *What Scepticism Is*

Scepticism is a faculty or a method of examination, which compares apparent and sensible things, as well as those which are perceived by the understanding, and sets them one against the other in all possible ways. By this means—because of the equal weight which exists in opposed things or arguments—we first reach the state of *Epoch*, or suspension of judgment, and thereafter the state of *Ataraxy*, that is, freedom from concern, or tranquility of the soul. . . .

Les hipotiposes, ou institutions pirroniens. Paris, 1725. [Pp. 4, 12–13, 15, 17–18, 20–21, 31, 50–51.]

Ch. X. *Whether Sceptics Destroy Sensory Phenomena*

Those who say that Sceptics deny or destroy the obvious phenomena of the senses, seem not to understand what we are saying. We do not turn things upside down, for indeed the passivity of our imagination compels us, willy-nilly, to give our assent to all things; thus we say: These things are appearances of the senses. When we seek to discover if an object is what it appears to be, we accept its appearance. We do not doubt or question concerning what a thing seems to be, but only concerning what is said about this thing which appears. This is quite another thing from disputing the appearance. For example, it seems to us that honey tastes sweet; in that we agree, because we feel the sweetness, but we doubt whether honey *is* sweet, if one were to make a judgment by reason and intellect. This intellectual judgment is not about an appearance, but it is a conclusion based on the appearance. If we raise difficulties concerning certain sensory appearances, it is not to overturn the appearances. Our intention is only to point out the temerity of the Dogmatists. For if reason sometimes deceives us to the point that it almost prevents us from perceiving the sensory appearances, and what is before our very eyes, how much must we not distrust it in uncertain things, if we wish to avoid falling into foolhardy judgments, as we shall do by following it?

Ch. XII. *What Is the Goal of Scepticism?*

. . . The goal of the sceptical philosopher is to attain *Ataraxy,* or freedom from concern with regard to opinions, and *Metriopathy,* or moderation in the emotions and sufferings resulting from necessary, enforced perceptions. . . .

Nevertheless, we do not believe that the Sceptic will always be tranquil, and exempt from every annoyance; he will be affected by necessary sufferings, which arise from the impact or action of certain external objects, and we admit that sometimes he will suffer from cold, or thirst, or other similar discomforts.

But we should take note, with respect to these discomforts, that most men suffer doubly: first by being tormented by them, and again because they think that these things are real evils, inherently so. The sceptic does not regard any of the things which inconvenience him as inherently evil in themselves, and he suffers from them with more moderation than other men. . . .

Ch. XIV. *The Ten Methods for Attaining Epoch*

The ancient Sceptics left us ten methods, by the use of which we are able to suspend and withhold our judgment. . . .

The first is concerned with the diversity of animals; the second, with differences among men; the third, with the instruments or organs of sense, compared with one another; the fourth, with circumstances; the fifth, with situations, distances, and places; the sixth, with mixtures; the seventh, with quantities and the constitution or composition of objects; the eighth, with relations, that is to say, with how one thing is related to another; the ninth, with the frequency or rarity of certain events; the tenth, with laws, customs, institutions, mythical beliefs, and the opinions of the Dogmatists. . . .

{With respect to the first method} . . . If the same things which are agreeable to some animals are disagreeable to others, and if being agreeable or disagreeable depends on the perception or imagination, it follows necessarily that the same objects produce different perceptions in different animals. And if the same things appear differently because of the diversity among animals, it is true that we can say how an object appears to us, but we must hold our judgment in suspense, and decide nothing, with respect to its true nature. . . .

{With respect to the second method} . . . Since some men seek what others avoid, it is easy to see that they are not affected by the same objects in the same way, because otherwise they would all seek or avoid the same objects in the same degree. . . .

Those who say that we should agree with the opinions of the majority talk like children. No one can survey the opinions of all men, and discover what pleases most of them; for it is possible that among nations unknown to us, there are certain things quite common, which are rare among us, and other things which happen frequently to us, are rare to them. For example, some of these people feel no pain from the bite of a spider, and suffer no discomfort whatever from it, and one may say the same with regard to other special temperaments. . . .

{With respect to the third method} . . . One might also say that an apple has qualities which are not apparent to us, and for this reason. Imagine a man who from birth has been possessed of touch, smell, and taste, but was deprived of sight and hearing. Such a man would believe that there is nothing that can be perceived by sight and by hearing, and that there are only three kinds of qualities, which can be perceived by his three senses. Therefore it is possible that since we have five senses, we do not perceive some other qualities which the apple really possesses, but which our senses do not permit us to perceive, and that there are other qualities which would be perceived by other organs of sense which we do not possess, for we can only perceive those things which are sensible by means of our organs.

{With respect to the fourth method} . . . This method consists in considering the sensations and perceptions of a person in a natural or unnatural state, asleep or awake, at different ages, in rest or in motion, in love or in hate, when hungry or satiated, when drunk or sober, when he has certain dispositions or habits, when he is happy or sad.

For example, objects appear differently to us according to whether we are in a natural or unnatural state. Frenetics, for example, and those who believe that they are inspired by some god, imagine that they hear spirits, while we hear nothing. These same enthusiasts often say that they smell stirax or incense or some other odor, while we neither perceive these nor many other things which they believe they perceive. Water which seems tepid to us will seem boiling hot when it is poured on a part of the body which is enflamed. A cloth which will seem red to someone whose eyes are bloodshot will not seem so to us. And honey, which seems sweet to us, will seem bitter to those who have jaundice.

5.3

Lucretius (Titus Lucretius Carus)

(† 55 B.C.)

Although Lucretius wrote about 250 years before Sextus, his statement reads almost like a direct answer, for the basic arguments had been well rehearsed in the earlier history of Greek philosophy. Lucretius propounds the views of Epicurus (341–270), who asserts faith in sensory data as the foundation of scientific knowledge. Nevertheless, Pyrrhonism and Epicureanism are not irreconcilable opposites, and both streams of thought merge in early modern anti-fideism, as for example in La Mettrie. It is the "thing in itself," as Kant would say in due time, which is unknowable, and this conviction is not inconsistent with the view that we must abandon the quest for ultimate causes of events, and live on the plane of sensory phenomena.

Our shadow likewise seems to move in the sunshine and to follow our steps and mimic our action; if you think forsooth that air deprived of life can step, imitating the motions and the actions of men; for that which we are wont to term shadow can be nothing but air devoid of light. Sure enough because the earth in certain spots successively is deprived of light wherever we intercept it in moving about, while that part of it which we have quitted is filled with light, therefore that which was the shadow of our body, seems to have always followed us unchanged in a direct line with us. . . .

On the nature of things (*De rerum natura*). Translated by H. A. J. Munro. Fourth revised edition. Cambridge, 1886. [Book IV, lines 364–512.]

And yet in all this we do not admit that the eyes are cheated one whit. For it is their province to observe in what spot soever light and shade are; but whether the lights are still the same or not, and whether it is the same shadow which was in this spot that is now passing to that, or whether what we said a little before is not rather the fact, this the reason of the mind, and only it, has to determine; nor can the eyes know the nature of things. Do not then fasten upon the eyes this frailty of the mind. The ship in which we are sailing, moves on while seeming to stand still; that one which remains at its moorings, is believed to be passing by. . . . When children have stopped turning round themselves, the halls apppear to them to whirl about and the pillars to course round to such a degree, that they can scarce believe that the whole roof is not threatening to tumble down upon them. . . . Then a puddle of water not more than a finger-breadth deep, which stands between the stones in the streets, offers a prospect beneath the earth of a reach as vast, as that with which the high yawning maw of heaven opens out above the earth; so that you seem to discern clouds and see the bodies of birds far withdrawn into that wondrous sky beneath the earth. . . . Again although a portico runs in parallel lines from one end to the other and stands supported by equal columns along its whole extent, yet when from the top of it it is seen in its entire length, it gradually forms the contracted top of a narrowing cone, until uniting roof with floor and all the right side with the left it has brought them together into the vanishing point of a cone. . . . Then if our hand chance to be placed beneath one eye and press it below, through a certain sensation all things which we look at appear then to become double as we look; the light of lamps brilliant with flames to be double, double too the furniture through the whole house, double men's faces and men's bodies. Again when sleep has chained down our limbs in sweet slumber and the whole body is sunk in profound repose, yet then we seem to ourselves to be awake and to be moving our limbs, and mid the thick darkness of night we think we see the sun and the daylight; and though in a confined room, we seem to be passing to new climates seas rivers and mountains and to be crossing plains on foot and to hear noises, though the austere silence of night prevails all round, and to be uttering speech though quite silent. Many are the other marvels of this sort we see, which all seek to shake as it were the credit of the senses: quite in vain, since the greatest part of these cases cheats us on account of the mental suppositions which we add of ourselves, taking those things as seen which have not been seen by the senses. For nothing is harder than to separate manifest facts from doubtful which straightway the mind adds on of itself.

Again if a man believe that nothing is known, he knows not whether this even can be known, since he admits he knows nothing. I will therefore decline to argue the case against him who places himself with head where his feet should be. And yet granting that he knows this, I would still put this question, since he has never yet seen any truth in things, whence he knows what knowing and not knowing severally are, and what it is that has produced the knowledge of the true and the false and what has proved the doubtful to differ from the certain. You will find that from the senses first has proceeded the knowledge of the true and that the sense cannot be refuted. For that which is of itself to be able to refute things false by true things must from the nature of the case be proved to have the higher certainty. Well then what must fairly be accounted of higher certainty than sense? Shall reason founded on false sense be able to contradict them, wholly founded as it is on the senses? and if they are not true, then all reason as well is rendered false. Or shall the ears be able to take the eyes to task, or the touch the ears? Again shall the taste call in question this touch, or the nostrils refute or the eyes controvert it? Not so, I guess; for each apart has its own distinct office, each its own power; and therefore we must perceive what is soft and cold or hot by one distinct faculty, by another perceive the different colours of things and thus see all objects which are conjoined with colour. Taste too has its faculty apart; smells spring from one source, sounds from another. It must follow therefore that any one sense cannot confute any other. No nor can any sense take itself to task, since equal credit must be assigned to it at all times. What therefore has at any time appeared true to each sense, is true. And if reason shall be unable to explain away the cause why things which close at hand were square, at a distance looked round, it yet is better, if you are at a loss for the reason, to state erroneously the causes of each shape, than to let slip from your grasp on any side things manifest and ruin the groundwork of belief and wrench up all the foundations on which rest life and existence. For not only would all reason give way, life itself would at once fall to the ground, unless you choose to trust the senses and shun precipices and all things else of this sort that are to be avoided, and to pursue the opposite things. All that host of words then be sure is quite unmeaning, which has been drawn out in array against the senses.

5.4

David Hume

(1711–1776)

In the eighteenth century, the collapse of old institutions and the explora-
tion of new worlds with their strange customs and values fostered the re-
birth of scepticism. We saw one expression of Hume's scepticism in his
discussion of personal identity (3.5). Here, in expressing doubts regarding
the reality of the external world, he forms a bridge between the radical
idealism of Berkeley and the transcendental idealism of Kant. By extend-
ing his scepticism to embrace the so-called primary qualities of the external
world, Hume poses the question which was to awaken Kant from his "dog-
matic slumbers."

It seems evident, that Men are carry'd, by a natural Instinct or Prepossession, to repose Faith in their Senses; and that, without any Reasoning,
or even almost before the Use of Reason, we always suppose an external
Universe, which depends not on our Perception, but would exist, tho' we
and every sensible Creature were absent or annihilated. . . .

It seems also evident, that, when Men follow this blind and powerful
Instinct of Nature, they always suppose the very Images, presented by
the Senses, to be the external Objects, and never entertain any Suspicion,
that the one are nothing but Representations of the other. . . .

But this universal and primary Opinion of all Men is soon destroy'd
by the slightest Philosophy, which teaches us, that nothing can ever be
present to the Mind but an Image or Perception, and that the Senses are
only the Inlets, thro' which these Images are receiv'd, without being ever
able to produce any immediate Intercourse betwixt the Mind and the
Object. . . .

So far, then, are we necessitated by Reasoning to depart from, or contradict the primary Instincts of Nature, and embrace a new System with
regard to the Evidence of our Senses. But here Philosophy finds itself
extremely embarrass'd, when it would justify this new System, and ob-
viate the Cavils and Objections of the Sceptics. It can no longer plead the
infallible and irresistible Instinct of Nature: For that led us to a quite
different System, which is acknowledg'd fallible and even erroneous. And
to justify this pretended philosophical System, by a Chain of clear and
convincing Argument, or even any Appearance of Argument, exceeds the
Power of all human Capacity.

By what Argument can it be prov'd, that the Perceptions of the Mind

Philosophical essays concerning human understanding. London, 1748. (Later editions
are entitled *An Enquiry,* etc.) [Pp. 234–241, 243.]

must be caus'd by external Objects, entirely different from them, tho' resembling them (if that be possible) and could not arise either from the Energy of the Mind itself, or from the Suggestion of some invisible and unknown Spirit, or from some other Cause still more unknown to us? 'Tis acknowledg'd, that, in fact, many of these Perceptions arise not from any thing external, as in Dreams, Madness, and other Diseases. And nothing can be more inexplicable than the Manner, in which Body should so operate upon Mind as ever to convey an Image of itself to a Substance suppos'd of so different, and even contrary a Nature.

'Tis a Question of Fact, whether the Perceptions of the Senses be produc'd by external Objects, resembling them: How shall this Question be determin'd? By Experience surely, as all other Questions of a like Nature. But here Experience is, and must be entirely silent. The Mind has never any thing present to it but the Perceptions, and cannot possibly reach any Experience of their Connexion with Objects. The Supposition of such a Connexion is, therefore, without any Foundation in Reasoning.

To have recourse to the Veracity of the supreme Being, in order to prove the Veracity of our Senses, is surely making a very unexpected Circuit. If his Veracity were at all concern'd in this Matter, our Senses would be entirely infallible; because it is not possible he can ever deceive. Not to mention, that if the external World be once call'd in doubt, we shall be at a loss to find Arguments, by which we may prove the Existence of that Being or any of his Attributes.

This therefore is a Topic, in which the profounder and more philosophical Sceptics will always triumph, when they endeavour to introduce an universal Doubt into all Subjects of human Knowledge and Enquiry. Do you follow the Instincts and Propensities of Nature, may they say, in assenting to the Veracity of Sense? But these lead you to believe, that the very Perception or sensible Image is the external Object. Do you disclaim this, in order to embrace a more rational Principle, that the Perceptions are only Representations of something external? You here depart from your natural Propensities and more obvious Sentiments; and yet are not able to satisfy your Reason, which can never find any convincing Argument from Experience to prove, that the Perceptions are connected with any external Objects.

There is another Sceptical Topic of a like Nature, deriv'd from the most profound Philosophy; which might merit our Attention were it requisite to dive so deep, in order to discover Arguments and Reasonings, that can serve so little any serious Purpose or Intention. 'Tis universally allow'd by modern Enquirers, that all the sensible Qualities of Objects, such as hard, soft, hot, cold, white, black, &c. are merely secondary, and exist not in the Objects themselves, but are Perceptions in the Mind, without any external Archetype or Model, which they represent. If this be allow'd, with regard to secondary Qualities, it must also follow with regard to the suppos'd primary Qualities of Extension and Solidity; nor can the latter be any more entitled to that Denomination than the former. The Idea of Extension is entirely acquir'd from the Senses of Sight and Feeling; and if all the Qualities, perceiv'd by the Senses, be in the Mind, not in the Object, the same Conclusion must reach the Idea of Extension, which is wholly dependent on the sensible Ideas or the Ideas of secondary Qualities. Nothing can save us from this Conclusion, but the asserting, that the Ideas of those primary Qualities are attain'd by *Abstraction;* which, if we examine accurately, we shall find to be unintelligible, and even absurd. An Extension, that is neither tangible nor visible, cannot possibly be conceiv'd: and a tangible or visible Extension, which is neither hard nor soft, black nor white, is equally beyond the Reach of human Conception. Let any Man try to conceive a Triangle in general, which is neither *Isoceles,* nor *Scalenum,* nor has any particular Length nor Proportion of Sides; and he will soon perceive the Absurdity of all the scholastic Notions with regard to Abstraction and general Ideas. . . .

The chief Objection against all *abstract* Reasonings is deriv'd from the Nature of Space and Time, which, in common Life and to a careless View, seem very clear and intelligible, but when they pass thro' the Scrutiny of the profound Sciences . . . afford Principles and Notions full of Absurdity and Contradiction. No priestly *Dogmas,* invented on purpose to tame and subdue the rebellious Reason of Mankind, ever shock'd common Sense more than the Doctrine of the infinite Divisibility of Extension, with all its Consequences; as they are pompously display'd by all Geometricians and Metaphysicians, with a kind of Triumph and Exultation. . . .

The Absurdity of these bold Determinations of the abstract Sciences becomes, if possible, still more palpable with regard to Time than Extension. An infinite Number of real Parts of Time, passing in Succession, and exhausted one after another, is so evident a Contradiction, that no Man, one should think, whose Judgment is not corrupted, instead of being improv'd, by the Sciences, would ever be able to admit of it.

5.5

Thomas Reid

(1710–1796)

Reid's reply to Hume is perhaps no more than an underlining of what Hume had conceded: that our natural disposition runs counter to philosophic scepticism. In doing this, however, he laid the foundation not only for the vigorous Scottish school but also for the nativist approach in modern psychology.

Too much emphasis is often placed on Reid's piety, as in his statement that "If we are deceived, (it is) by him that made us." But in fact his appeal is as much to biological disposition as to divine fiat. His argument is a biological one which is even stronger today, in the light of evolutionary theory.

[Ch. V, Sec. II] Here then is a phenomenon of human nature, which comes to be resolved. Hardness of bodies is a thing which we conceive as distinctly, and believe as firmly, as any thing in nature. We have no way of coming at this conception and belief, but by means of a certain sensation of touch, to which hardness hath not the least similitude; nor can we, by any rules of reasoning, infer the one from the other. The question is, How we come by this conception and belief? . . .

Is it self-evident, from comparing the ideas, that such a sensation could not be felt, unless such a quality of bodies existed. No. Can it be proved by probable or certain arguments? No, it cannot. Have we got this belief then by tradition, by education, or by experience? No, it is not got in any of these ways. Shall we then throw off this belief, as having no foundation in reason? Alas! it is not in our power; it triumphs over reason, and laughs at all the arguments of a philosopher. Even the author of the *Treatise of human nature*, though he saw no reason for this belief, but many against it, could hardly conquer it in his speculative and solitary moments; at other times he fairly yielded to it, and confesses that he found himself under a necessity to do so.

What shall we say then of this conception, and this belief, which are so unaccountable and untractable? I see nothing left, but to conclude, that, by an original principle of our constitution, a certain sensation of touch both suggests to the mind the conception of hardness, and creates the belief of it: or, in other words, that this sensation is a natural sign of hardness. And this I shall endeavour more fully to explain. . . .

[Sec. V] Let a man press his hand against the table: *he feels it hard.*

An inquiry into the human mind, on the principles of common sense. Edinburgh, 1764. [Pp. 120–122, 136–138, 143–147, 153–157.]

But what is the meaning of this? The meaning undoubtedly is, that he hath a certain feeling of touch, from which he concludes, without any reasoning, or comparing ideas, that there is something external really existing, whose parts stick so firmly together, that they cannot be displaced without considerable force.

. . . The hardness of the table is the conclusion, the feeling is the medium by which we are led to that conclusion. Let a man attend distinctly to this medium, and to the conclusion, and he will perceive them to be as unlike as any two things in nature. The one is a sensation of the mind, which can have no existence but in a sentient being; nor can it exist one moment longer than it is felt: the other is in the table, and we conclude without any difficulty, that it was in the table before it was felt, and continues after the feeling is over. . . .

And as the feeling hath no similitude to hardness, so neither can our reason perceive the least tie or connection between them; nor will the logician ever be able to show a reason why we should conclude hardness from this feeling, rather than softness, or any other quality whatsoever. But in reality all mankind are led by their constitution to conclude hardness from this feeling. . . .

[Sec. VI] Upon the whole, it appears, that our philosophers have imposed upon themselves, and upon us, in pretending to deduce from sensation the first origin of our notions of external existences, of space, motion, and extension, and all the primary qualities of body, that is, the qualities whereof we have the most clear and distinct conception. These qualities do not at all tally with any system of the human faculties that hath been advanced. They have no resemblance to any sensation, or to any operation of our minds; and therefore they cannot be ideas either of sensation, or of reflection. The very conception of them is irreconcilable to the principles of all our philosophic systems of the understanding. The belief of them is no less so.

[Sec. VII] It is beyond our power to say, when or in what order we came by our notions of these qualities. When we trace the operations of our minds as far back as memory and reflection can carry us, we find them already in possession of our imagination and belief, and quite familiar to the mind: but how they came first into its acquaintance, or what has given them so strong a hold of our belief, and what regard they deserve, are no doubt very important questions in the philosophy of human nature.

Shall we, with the Bishop of Cloyne [Berkeley], serve them with a *Quo Warranto,* and have them tried at the bar of philosophy, upon the statute of the ideal system? Indeed, in this trial they seem to have come off very pitifully. For although they had very able counsel, learned in the law, *viz.* DesCartes, Malebranch, and Locke, who said every thing they could for their clients; the Bishop of Cloyne, believing them to be aiders and abettors of heresy and schism, prosecuted them with great vigour, fully answered all that had been pleaded in their defence, and silenced their ablest advoctaes; who seem for half a century past to decline the argument, and to trust to the favour of the jury rather than to the strength of their pleadings.

Thus, the wisdom of *philosophy* is set in opposition to the *common sense* of mankind. The first pretends to demonstrate *a priori*, that there can be no such thing as a material world; that sun, moon, stars, and earth, vegetable and animal bodies, are, and can be nothing else, but sensations in the mind, or images of those sensations in the memory and imagination; that, like pain and joy, they can have no existence when they are not thought of. The last can conceive no otherwise of this opinion, than as a kind of metaphysical lunacy; and concludes, that too much learning is apt to make men mad; and that the man who seriously entertains this belief, though in other respects he may be a very good man, as a man may be who believes that he is made of glass; yet surely he hath a soft place in his understanding, and hath been hurt by much thinking.

This opposition betwixt philosophy and common sense, is apt to have a very unhappy influence upon the philosopher himself. He sees human nature in an odd, unamiable, and mortifying light. He considers himself, and the rest of his species, as born under a necessity of believing ten thousand absurdities and contradictions, and endowed with such a pittance of reason, as is just sufficient to make this unhappy discovery: and this is all the fruit of his speculations. Such notions of human nature tend to slacken every nerve of the soul, to put every noble purpose and sentiment out of countenance, and spread a melancholy gloom over the whole face of things.

If this be wisdom let me be deluded with the vulgar. . . .

All reasoning must be from first principles; and for first principles no other reason can be given but this, that, by the constitution of our nature, we are under a necessity of assenting to them. Such principles are parts of our constitution, no less than the power of thinking: reason can neither make nor destroy them; nor can it do any thing without them: it is like a telescope, which may help a man to see farther, who hath eyes; but without eyes, a telescope shews nothing at all. . . .

How or when I got such first principles, upon which I build all my reasoning, I know not; for I had them before I can remember: but I am sure they are parts of my constitution, and that I cannot throw them off. That our thoughts and sensations must have a subject, which we call *ourself*, is not therefore an opinion got by reasoning, but a natural principle. That our sensations of touch indicate something external, extended, figured, hard or soft, is not a deduction of reason, but a natural principle. The belief of it, and the very conception of it, are equally parts of our constitution. If we are deceived in it, we are deceived by him that made us, and there is no remedy.

5.6

Immanuel Kant

(1724–1804)

Kant's insistence that space and time do not inhere in reality, but are the subjectively determined conditions which make experience possible for us, was the most important factor in determining the nativist tendency of most subsequent German psychology. The "new philosophy" of the Cartesians had emphasized the subjective nature of much perception; Locke had formalized this in the distinction between primary and secondary qualities; Hume indeed asked whether this distinction was really fundamental; but it was left for Kant, with German thoroughness, to reduce the primary qualities also to mere subjective phenomena. We shall see later how this Kantian flavor makes Johannes Müller's statement of the doctrine of specific energies (7.11) utterly different from Bell's (7.10).

These paragraphs from the "transcendental doctrine of elements" are taken from the first English translation of the Critique.

[II.] By means of the external sense (a property of our mind) we represent to ourselves objects as external to us, and these all in space. Therein is determined, or is determinable, their shape, quantity, and relationship towards each other. The internal sense, by means of which the mind envisages itself or its internal state, gives indeed no intuiton of the soul itself as an object; but there is still a determinate form, under which the intuition of its internal state alone is possible, so that all which belongs to the internal determinations is represented in relationships of Time. Externally, Time can be viewed as little as Space, as something in us. Now what are Time and Space? Are they real beings? Are they in fact only determinations, or likewise relations of things, but still such as would belong to these things in themselves, though they should not be envisaged; or are they such, that they cleave only to the form of the intuition and consequently to the subjective property of our mind, without which these predicates could not be attributed even to anything? . . .

1st. Space is no empirical conception which has been derived from external experiences. For in order that certain sensations may be referred to something external to me, (that is, to something in another part of space to that in which I am,) and likewise in order that I may be able to represent them as without of and near 'to each other, consequently not merely different, but as in different places, the representation of space for this purpose must already lie at the foundation. The representation of

Kritik der reinen Vernunft [Riga, 1781]. Translated by Francis Haywood, as *Critick of pure reason*. Second edition. London, 1848. [Pp. 23–24, 29, 34–35, 38–39.]

space cannot therefore be borrowed from the relations of the external phenomenon by experience, but this external experience is itself first only possible by the stated representation.

2nd. Space is a necessary representation à priori, which lies at the foundation of all external intuitions. We can never make to ourselves a representation of this,—that there is no space,—although we may very readily think that no objects therein are to be met with. It is therefore regarded as the condition of the possibility of phenomena, and not as a determination depending upon them, and it is a representation à priori, which necessarily lies at the foundation of all external phenomena. . . .

[IV.] 1. Time is no empirical conception, which can be deduced from an experience. For simultaneousness or succession would not even come into the perception, if the representation of time did not à priori, lie at the foundation. Only under this pre-supposition can we represent to ourselves that something can be in one and the same time, (contemporaneously,) or in different times (successively).

2. Time is a necessary representation, which lies at the foundation of all intuitions. We cannot, in respect of phenomena in general, do away with time itself, although, we may indeed very well take away from time, phenomena. Time is therefore given à priori. In it alone is all reality of phenomena possible. These may all disappear, but it itself, (as the general condition of their possibility,) cannot be annihilated. . . .

[VII. *Explanation.*] Against this theory which accords to Time empirical, but contends against absolute and transcendental reality, I have heard from perspicacious men so concurring an objection, that I have collected from it, that such naturally presents itself to every reader who is unaccustomed to these considerations. It runs thus:—changes are real (the alternation of our own representations shows this, although we should deny all external phenomena together with their changes). Now these changes are only possible in time, consequently time is something real. The answer presents no difficulty. I concede the whole argument. Time is certainly something real, that is to say, it is the real form of the internal intuition. It has, therefore, subjective reality in regard of internal experience; that is, I have really the representation of time, and of my determinations in it. It is therefore not to be looked at really as object, but as the mode of representation of myself as object. But if I could envisage myself, or if any other creature could envisage me, without this condition of sensibility, the self-same determinations which we represent to ourselves, now, as changes, would then afford us a cognition, in which the representation of time, and consequently also of change would not at all occur. Its empirical reality remains, therefore, as condition of all our experiences. Only absolute reality can, according to what is above advanced, not be granted to it. It is nothing but the form of our internal intuition. If we take away from it the particular condition of our sensibility, then the conception of time vanishes also, and it adheres not to the objects themselves, but simply to the subject which envisages them. . . .

[VIII.] . . . We have therefore intended to say, that all our intuition is nothing but the representation of phenomenon,—that the things which we envisage are not that in themselves for which we envisage them; neither are their relationships in themselves so constituted as they appear to us, and that if we do away with our subject, or even only the subjective quality of the senses in general, every quality, all relationships of objects in space and time, nay, even space and time themselves would disappear, and cannot exist as phenomena in themselves, but only in us. It remains wholly unknown to us, what may be the nature of the objects in themselves, separated from all this conception of our sensibility. . . . If we could carry this our intuition even to the highest degree of clearness, yet should we not thereby come nearer to the quality of objects in themselves. We should still, in any case, only know completely our own mode of intuition, that is, our sensibility, and this always only under the conditions of space and time, originally inherent in the subject. What the objects may be in themselves would still never be known by the clearest cognition of their phenomenon, which phenomenon alone is given to us.

5.7

Hermann von Helmholtz

(1821–1894)

By insisting on the learned components in optical illusions, and excluding all native influences, Helmholtz returns to the position of Aristotle, that the senses do not err although we may err in interpreting the data derived through them. This selection is from the final volume of the Optics, first published in 1866. It may be compared with Helmholtz's earliest statement of this view, in 1855 (see 6.8).

The general rule determining the ideas of vision that are formed whenever an impression is made on the eye, with or without the aid of optical instruments, is that *such objects are always imagined as being present in the field of vision as would have to be there in order to produce the same*

Handbuch der physiologischen Optik. [1856–1866.] Translated as *Treatise on physiological optics.* Edited by J. P. C. Southall. New York: Dover Publications, Inc. and Optical Society of America, 1924–1925. 3 vols. (The translator for the portion from which the selection is taken was William Kunerth.) [Vol. III, pp. 2–5.] Reprinted through permission of Dover Publications, Inc.

*impression on the nervous mechanism, the eyes being used under or-
dinary normal conditions.* To employ an illustration which has been
mentioned before, suppose that the eyeball is mechanically stimulated
at the outer corner of the eye. Then we imagine that we see an appearance of light in front of us somewhere in the direction of the bridge of
the nose. Under ordinary conditions of vision, when our eyes are stimulated by light coming from outside, if the region of the retina in the
outer corner of the eye is to be stimulated, the light actually has to enter
the eye from the direction of the bridge of the nose. Thus, in accordance
with the above rule, in a case of this kind we substitute a luminous object
at the place mentioned in the field of view, although as a matter of fact
the mechanical stimulus does not act on the eye from in front of the field
of view nor from the nasal side of the eye, but, on the contrary, is exerted
on the outer surface of the eyeball and more from behind. . . .

Thus it happens, that when the modes of stimulation of the organs of
sense are unusual, incorrect ideas of objects are apt to be formed; which
used to be described, therefore, as *illusions of the senses.* Obviously, in
these cases there is nothing wrong with the activity of the organ of sense
and its corresponding nervous mechanism which produces the illusion.
Both of them have to act according to the laws that govern their activity
once for all. It is rather simply an illusion in the judgment of the material
presented to the senses, resulting in a false idea of it.

The psychic activities that lead us to infer that there in front of us at a
certain place there is a certain object of a certain character, are generally not conscious activities, but unconscious ones. In their result they
are equivalent to a *conclusion,* to the extent that the observed action on
our senses enables us to form an idea as to the possible cause of this
action; although, as a matter of fact, it is invariably simply the nervous
stimulations that are perceived directly, that is, the actions, but never the
external objects themselves. But what seems to differentiate them from a
conclusion, in the ordinary sense of that word, is that a conclusion is an
act of conscious thought. An astronomer, for example, comes to real
conscious conclusions of this sort, when he computes the positions of the
stars in space, their distances, etc., from the perspective images he has
had of them at various times and as they are seen from different parts of
the orbit of the earth. His conclusions are based on a conscious knowledge of the laws of optics. In the ordinary acts of vision this knowledge
of optics is lacking. Still it may be permissible to speak of the psychic
acts of ordinary perception as *unconscious conclusions,* thereby making a
distinction of some sort between them and the common so-called conscious conclusions. And while it is true that there has been, and probably
always will be, a measure of doubt as to the similarity of the psychic
activity in the two cases, there can be no doubt as to the similarity between the results of such unconscious conclusions and those of conscious
conclusions.

These unconscious conclusions derived from sensation are equivalent in their consequences to the so-called *conclusions from analogy*. Inasmuch as in an overwhelming majority of cases, whenever the parts of the retina in the outer corner of the eye are stimulated, it has been found to be due to external light coming into the eye from the direction of the bridge of the nose, the inference that we make is that it is so in every new case whenever this part of the retina is stimulated; just as we assert that every single individual now living will die, because all previous experience has shown that all men who were formerly alive have died.

But, moreover, just because they are not free acts of conscious thought, these unconscious conclusions from analogy are irresistible, and the effect of them cannot be overcome by a better understanding of the real relations. It may be ever so clear how we get an idea of a luminous phenomenon in the field of vision when pressure is exerted on the eye; and yet we cannot get rid of the conviction that this appearance of light is actually there at the given place in the visual field; and we cannot seem to comprehend that there is a luminous phenomenon at the place where the retina is stimulated. It is the same way in the case of all the images that we see in optical instruments.

On the other hand, there are numerous illustrations of fixed and inevitable associations of ideas due to frequent repetition, even when they have no natural connection, but are dependent merely on some conventional arrangement, as, for example, the connection between the written letters of a word and its sound and meaning. Still to many physiologists and psychologists the connection between the sensation and the conception of the object usually appears to be so rigid and obligatory that they are not much disposed to admit that, to a considerable extent at least, it depends on acquired experience, that is, on psychic activity. On the contrary, they have endeavoured to find some mechanical mode of origin for this connection through the agency of imaginary organic structures. With regard to this question, all those experiences are of much significance which show how the judgment of the senses may be modified by experience and by training derived under various circumstances. . . .

But how far this influence does extend, it would perhaps be impossible to say precisely at present.

5.8

Ewald Hering

(1834–1918)

Empiricists are fond of saying that nativism discourages efforts to investigate the true causes of behavioral phenomena. In fact, however, nativists have often been excellent experimenters, and this is particularly true of Hering. Empiricists reasoned that simultaneous contrast must be a central phenomenon, because they assumed that it was influenced by our experience with colors. Hering refutes this theory with an ingenious experiment, which exposes the fallacy of the Aristotle-Helmholtz dictum that the senses in themselves do not err.

For this experiment, the subject looks through two differently colored transparent glass sheets, one for each eye, toward a black stripe on a white ground, but he fixates on a suspended button, so that the stripe is seen doubled, but on a uniform ground resulting from binocular fusion.

If a small gray field of suitable brightness is placed on a larger, whitish-violet background, it does not of course appear colorless, but as a result of contrast it seems more or less distinctly tinted with the complementary color, that is, yellow-green. The whitish-violet background may also be obtained by binocular fusion, if, for example, a whitish-red surface visible only to the left eye is brought into binocular coincidence with a whitish-blue surface visible only to the right eye. If now two small gray fields of the same brightness are so placed on these surfaces that they also coincide in the binocular mixture, then once again we see a simple yellow-green field. According to the psychological theory of simultaneous contrast, which is now current, the violet color of the background is the cause of the approximately complementary coloring of the objectively gray field. But if the two small gray fields are so placed that binocular fusion of them is no longer possible, but instead they are seen side by side at a short distance from each other against the background (which because of color-mixing appears to be whitish-violet), then their color is no longer yellow-green, as would be expected under that theory. Instead, the two fields seem to be strikingly different in color, that on the left seeming blue-green [assuming spectral red, not pure red, is used], and that on the right, yellow. With appropriate choice of colors for the background, and brightness of the two gray fields, they seem even more

Beitrag zur Lehre von Simultankontrast [A contribution to the theory of simultaneous contrast]. *Zeitschrift für Psychologie und Physiologie der Sinnesorgane,* 1 (1890): 18–28. [Pp. 23–24.]

saturated than the background color. This is a proof that it is not the color of the background, as we *see* it, which is decisive for the nature of the color contrast, but the composition of the light which stimulates the two eyes. The left eye receives yellowish-red light, and its image of the small colorless field therefore appears blue-green, despite the violet color of the background; the other eye receives blue light, and its image of the gray field is therefore yellow, hence likewise not yellow-green, as the psychological theory would lead us to expect because of the violet ground.

5.9

Wolfgang Köhler

(1887–1967)

The experimental study of illusions has been a prominent theme in Gestalt psychology, starting with Wertheimer's investigation of illusory visual movement in 1912. (Extensive portions of his report are given by Shipley; smaller portions by Herrnstein and Boring and by Sahakian.) Köhler, who was well grounded in theoretical physics, developed Wertheimer's speculation about a possible correspondence between cortical and phenomenal events. (His book, Die physischen Gestalten in Ruhe und im stationären Zustand [Physical configurations at rest and in steady state, 1920], is condensed in paraphrase by Ellis.) Here the core of that theory is restated in brief. It attracted fresh attention when Köhler and Wallach published their study of "figural aftereffects" in 1944. Their supposition that electro-cortical fields might be involved in pattern recognition did not stand up under experimental tests by Lashley, Chow and Semmes (1951) or by Sperry and Miner (1955). Nevertheless, the Wertheimer-Köhler concept that isomorphism exists between subjective and cortical processes remains an important approach to the problems of thinking generally. (Compare also Craik, 16.11.)

Every system to which the second law of thermodynamics can be applied sooner or later reaches an equilibrium for the given conditions, either at rest or in a steady state. Processes taking place in the nervous system have often been considered from this point of view, but the necessary consequences have certainly not been drawn. What properties must

Gestaltprobleme und Anfänge einer Gestalttheorie [Gestalt problems and beginnings of a Gestalt theory]. *Jahresbericht über die gesammte Physiologie*, 3 (1925): 512–539. [Pp. 527, 529–531.]

the end state exhibit, if the separate regions of the system are not functionally isolated from each other, but are to a certain degree in functional communication? Physics can easily inform us about this. . . .

Theoretical physics deals with problems of this sort as problems of "boundary values." It investigates what the internal spontaneous equilibrium distribution must be in a system of known material properties, when certain conditions are specified for the boundaries. . . .

This simple principle of a stationary distribution which comes about through internal dynamics, and which is characterized by the fact that the state of each region of the system *codetermines* events in every other region—as opposed to the mechanistic distribution that results from being bound together—represents the single general conceptual basis which the theory of physical Gestalten employs. . . .

Now, since the modern psychology of human perception shows, ever more clearly, that a mere geometry of externally arranged elementary excitations is quite incapable of making the observed phenomena intelligible, and since the recalcitrant phenomena strike us as having properties just like those which appear in the physical structure of spontaneous distributions, the following hypothesis suggests itself: The somatic processes which are the basis of visual fields at rest are stationary equilibrium distributions, which develop of themselves from the inner dynamics of the optical system; the spatial ordering and articulation of a visual field corresponds to the actual physical structure of this stationary process. . . .

Herewith there collapses an assumption which many of us will not willingly surrender: The spontaneous distribution of the somatic processes which now must provide the foundation for our vision can no longer be an almost perfect representation of the retinal stimulus geometry. But we would have had to give up this somewhat reassuring idea in any event, because of properties of our spatial perception which we discussed earlier. I repeat: representation on each separate *retinal* region takes place almost independently of all others, but the *visual field* is spontaneously articulated into "visual objects"; thus there is a discrepancy from the mere geometry of the stimuli, and one which has enormous positive biological significance. The opposition of "figure" and "ground" likewise does not have its parallel in the stimulus geometry, which is indeed totally lacking in Gestalt properties. A physical correlate for the latter is attained for the first time through the principle of real dynamic structures. Finally, the well-known geometric optical illusions, so numerous in all their variations, demonstrate that our visual field constantly exhibits discrepancies from the relationships which exist in retinal geometry. There is of course an endless number of these discrepancies which we do not detect, because we are not incessantly undertaking the relevant objective measurements on stimulating objects. How far such discrepancy extends in these respects—in distortions of shape, change of size, displacements of direction, etc.—cannot be established a priori from the general principle now introduced, but it depends greatly on that special sort of process which occurs particularly in the optical sector of the nervous system. . . .

Finally, the very nature of the discrepancies between the articulation of the visual field at any moment and the geometry of the retinal stimuli reveals another striking resemblance to the spontaneously arising equilibrium structures of physics. The spontaneous distributions in physical systems come about because the internal energies of these systems are constantly tending as a whole toward *equalization* among themselves and with external conditions, and therefore equilibrium distributions in physics are generally distinguished from other distributions—such as those which have not yet reached equilibrium—by their simplicity and regularity (Mach). If optical structures are formed according to the same principle, we should expect the same tendency to simplicity and regularity in them. Before any connection had been discussed between such physical considerations and psychological problems, Wertheimer did in fact find in perceptual structures a tendency toward "pregnancy of configuration" which is now known through many examples, and which leads to the same simplification, emphasis on symmetry, etc., which characterize the physical equilibrium distributions.

There is as yet no completed theory of the perceptual process based on this new general principle. . . . But we can already see some profit in the fact that this no longer questionable rejection of purely mechanistic theory construction offers new possibilities for understanding the phenomena of perception, which have hitherto been so puzzling, through scientific procedures.

Chapter 6

SPACE PERCEPTION

Size and shape were among the "common sensibles" for Aristotle (see 7.1) because they were perceived by either sight or touch. This chapter deals only with certain limited aspects of the visual perception of shape and distance. There are in general three ways to explain such perception: (1) as the function of bodily mechanisms which are innately adequate to the task; (2) as a function of reason or intelligence, which must interpret visual data not inherently meaningful; (3) as a skill which is attained in hit-and-miss fashion, as a child (perhaps) learns how far to stretch its arm for a rattle, or as a chick (perhaps) learns how to strike a grain when pecking.

Lucretius states a theory of the first type: crude indeed, but with the virtue that it is equally applicable to all creatures that have eyes. Plotinus makes the judgment of size and distance an act of intellect, and such intellectual activity remains uppermost, despite empirical elements, in the theories of Roger Bacon, Descartes, and Malebranche. Berkeley shifted the emphasis to learning, and his view became dogma for the next 250 years. What we have recently learned about the visual apparatus of frogs and salamanders as well as the performance of birds and mammals in the "visual cliff" apparatus (6.10) surely indicates that Lucretius was right to seek an answer in terms of innate mechanism rather than of intellect.

6.1

Lucretius (Titus Lucretius Carus)

(†55 B.C.)

Lucretius, who says that his purpose is only to set in stately Latin verse the otherwise forbidding philosophy of Epicurus, sees the basis of vision in a succession of infinitesimally thin films (variously called species, images, or idols by different translators) which are cast off by objects in all directions. In effect, this atomistic theory is a forerunner of the corpuscular theory of light. It is characteristic of this thoroughly materialistic philosophy that the perception of distance is made to depend on an external aspect of this process, rather than on the understanding of the viewer. It is also characteristic that in stating his theory of vision he seizes the opportunity to combat superstition, which he does by giving an objective explanation of the appearance of ghosts.

The reference to recognition of squareness by both touch and vision states a problem which will be given a very different turn by Berkeley (6.6) in the eighteenth century, and again by the Gestalt psychologists in the twentieth.

And now that I have taught what the nature of the mind is . . . I will attempt to lay before you a truth which most nearly concerns these questions, the existence of things which we call idols of things: these, like films peeled off from the surface of things, fly to and fro through the air, and do likewise frighten our minds when they present themselves to us awake as well as in sleep, what time we behold strange shapes and idols of the light-bereaved, which have often startled us in appalling wise as we lay relaxed in sleep: this I will essay, that ye may not haply believe that souls break loose from Acheron or that shades fly about among the living or that something of us is left behind after death, when the body and the nature of the mind destroyed together have taken their departure into their several first-beginnings.

I say then that pictures of things and thin shapes are emitted from things off their surface, to which an image serves as a kind of film, or name it if you like a rind, because such image bears an appearance and form like to the thing whatever it is from whose body it is shed and wanders forth. . . .

Smells too incessantly stream from certain things; as does cold from rivers, heat from the sun, spray from the waves of the sea, that eater into

On the nature of things (De rerum natura). Translated by H. A. J. Munro. Fourth revised edition. Cambridge, 1886. [Book IV, lines 26–53, 222–255, 353–363.]

6.1 Lucretius

walls near the shore. Various sounds also cease not to fly through the air. Then too a moist salt flavour often comes into the mouth, when we are moving about beside the sea; and when we look on at the mixing of a decoction of wormwood, its bitterness affects us. In such a constant stream from all things the several qualities are carried and are transmitted in all directions round, and no delay, no respite in the flow is ever granted, since we constantly have feeling, and may at any time see smell and hear the sound of anything.

Again since a particular figure felt by the hands in the dark is known to be the same which is seen in the bright light of day, touch and sight must be excited by a quite similar cause. Well then if we handle a square thing and it excites our attention in the dark, in the daylight what square thing will be able to fall on our sight, except the image of that thing? Therefore the cause of seeing it is plain lies in images and no thing can be perceived without them. Well the idols of things I speak of are borne along all round and are discharged and transmitted in all directions; but because we can see with the eyes alone, the consequence is that, to whatever point we turn our sight, there all the several things meet and strike it with their shape and colour. And the image gives the power to see and the means to distinguish how far each thing is distant from us; for as soon as ever it is discharged, it pushes before it and impels all the air which lies between it and the eyes; and thus that air all streams through our eyes and brushes so to say the pupils and so passes through. The consequence is that we see how far distant each thing is. And the greater the quantity of air which is driven on before it and the larger the current which brushes our eyes, the more distant each different thing is seen to be. You must know these processes go on with extreme rapidity, so that at one and the same moment we see what like a thing is and how far distant it is. . . .

Again when we descry far off the square towers of a town, they often appear to be round for this reason: all the angles are seen from a distance to look obtuse, or rather are not seen at all, and their blow is lost and their stroke never makes its way to our sight, because while the idols are borne on through much air, the air by repeated collisions blunts the stroke perforce. When in this way all the angles have together eluded the sense, the stone structures are rounded off as if by the lathe; yet they do not look like the things which are close before us and really round, but somewhat resembling them as in shadowy outline.

6.2

Plotinus

(205–270)

For Plotinus, the Neoplatonist, the appreciation of distance is an act of
intellect, and is not to be explained by mechanical aspects of the process
of vision.

Why Distant Objects Appear Small

1. Seen from a distance, objects appear reduced and close together, however far apart they be: within easy range, their sizes and the distances
that separate them are observed correctly.

Distant objects show in this reduction because they must be drawn
together for vision and the light must be concentrated to suit the size of
the pupil; besides, as we are placed farther and farther away from the
material mass under observation, it is more and more the bare form that
reaches us, stripped, so to speak, of magnitude as of all other quality.

Or it may be that we appreciate the magnitude of an object by observing the salience and recession of its several parts, so that to perceive its
true size we must have it close at hand.

Or again, it may be that magnitude is known incidentally (as a deduction) from the observation of colour. With an object at hand we know
how much space is covered by the colour; at a distance, only that something is coloured, for the parts, quantitatively distinct among themselves,
do not give us the precise knowledge of that quantity, the colours themselves reaching us only in a blurred impression.

What wonder, then, if size be like sound—reduced when the form
reaches us but faintly—for in sounds the hearing is concerned only about
the form; magnitude is not discerned except incidentally.

Well, in hearing magnitude is known incidentally; but how? Touch
conveys a direct impression of a visible object; what gives us the same
direct impression of an object of hearing?

The magnitude of a sound is known not by actual quantity but by
degree of impact, by intensity—and this in no indirect knowledge; the
ear appreciates a certain degree of force, exactly as the palate perceives,

by an indirect knowledge, a certain degree of sweetness. But the true magnitude of a sound is its extension; this the hearing may define to itself incidentally by deduction from the degree of intensity but not to the point of precision. The intensity is merely the definite effect at a particular spot; the magnitude is a matter of totality, the sum of space occupied.

Still (it will be objected) the colours seen from a distance are faint; but they are not small as the masses are.

True; but there is the common fact of diminution. There is colour with its diminution, faintness; there is magnitude with its diminution, smallness; and magnitude follows colour diminishing stage by stage with it.

But, as the phenomenon is more easily explained by the example of things of wide variety. Take mountains with dotted houses, woods, and other landmarks; the observation of each detail gives us the means of calculating, by the single objects noted, the total extent covered: but, where no such detail of form reaches us, our vision, which deals with detail, has not the means towards the knowledge of the whole by measurement of any one clearly discerned magnitude. This applies even to objects of vision close at hand: where there is variety and the eye sweeps over all at one glance so that the forms are not all caught, the total appears the less in proportion to the detail which has escaped the eye; observe each single point and then you can estimate the volume precisely. Again, magnitudes of one colour and unbroken form trick the sense of quantity: the vision can no longer estimate by the particular; it slips away, not finding the stand-by of the difference between part and part.

It was the detail that prevented a near object deceiving our sense of magnitude: in the case of the distant object, because the eye does not pass stage by stage through the stretch of intervening space so as to note its forms, therefore it cannot report the magnitude of that space.

2. The explanation by lesser angle of vision has been elsewhere dismissed; one point, however, we may urge here.

Those attributing the reduced appearance to the lesser angle occupied allow by their very theory that the unoccupied portion of the eye still sees something beyond or something quite apart from the object of vision, if only air-space.

Now consider some very large object of vision, that mountain for example. No part of the eye is unoccupied; the mountain adequately fills it so that it can take in nothing beyond, for the mountain as seen either corresponds exactly to the eye-space or stretches away out of range to right and to left. How does the explanation by lesser angle of vision hold good in this case, where the object still appears smaller, far, than it is and yet occupies the eye entire?

Or look up to the sky and no hesitation can remain. Of course we cannot take in the entire hemisphere at one glance; the eye directed to it could not cover so vast an expanse. But suppose the possibility: the entire eye, then, embraces the hemisphere entire; but the expanse of the heavens is far greater than it appears; how can its appearing far less than it is be explained by a lessening of the angle of vision?

6.3

Roger Bacon

(*c.* 1214–1292)

Roger Bacon was an assiduous student of the Arabian philosophers, as appears clearly from a more extensive reading of the chapter on Optics from which this selection is taken. Even more important, his treatment of space perception shows the empirical tendency which makes him a forerunner of the scientific movement.

Of those things that are perceived through reasoning likewise notable examples can be given. First among these is distance or remoteness. In regard to this the first consideration is that excessive distance hinders vision, because the same object at a distance makes a small angle, which near would make a large one. . . . Since from the small size of the angle it results that a small part of the pupil is occupied, the object cannot sensibly be distinguished as it should in the eye, and for this reason the object is imperfectly perceived because of excessive distance. Distance is perceived and determined, if it is moderate by a continuous series of sensible objects lying between the eye and the remote object. As, for example, when a person is near a wall and sees another wall beyond the first more elevated than it and quite a distance from it, he cannot judge of the distance between them because there are no bodies in a continuous series between them, or he cannot perceive these bodies because of the interposition of the first wall beneath which he is standing.

Hence it happens that when we are not near high mountains, but are in level country, we cannot judge of the height of clouds; nay, we reckon that they are more remote from us than they are, because there are not sensible bodies lying between us and them, but the air only, which is not sensible to us, and for this reason we cannot judge of the height of the clouds under these circumstances. But when we are near high mountains, although mountains are not very high with a maximum height of about

The opus majus. Translated by R. B. Burke. 2 vols. Philadelphia: University of Pennsylvania Press, 1928. [Pp. 523–525.]

eight miles, we shall see clouds on the tops of the mountains and the summits higher than the clouds. . . .

Distance, then, is judged when there is a series of objects between the eye and the object of vision, and this is true in the case of moderate distance, and when the eye has viewed those objects and has made certain of their measurements. But if any one of these conditions is not fulfilled, distance will not be determined. Moreover, a moderate distance with respect to vision, that is, one whose extent is determined by vision, is a distance at the end of which no part with an extent sensible with respect to the whole distance is hidden from vision. . . . But a distance which is excessive with respect to vision is that at the end of which an extent bearing a sensible proportional relationship to that whole distance is hidden from vision. And a distance excessive with reference to the object of vision is one that hides from vision parts in proportional relationship sensible with reference to the whole. Therefore an error is made in the determination of distance owing to excessive remoteness of objects from the eye. For in this way trees at a great distance, although they are quite far apart, appear continuous or to be near one another. For this reason also the planets will be judged to be in the same surface as fixed stars because of the immense distance of the stars from the eye, although the planets are a very great distance from the fixed stars. Moreover, a figure of many equal sides placed directly opposite the eye looks like a circular figure, and the circle looks like a straight line, and a sphere will be judged to be a plane figure. For owing to excessive distance the angles of the figure, although they are sensible with respect to the whole at the required distance, yet when they are at an excessive distance will be hidden from vision with respect to the whole, and therefore an angular object will be judged to be round, because when such an angle is hidden, the figure appears round. Likewise when the gibbosity of the arc of a circle is presented to the sight, although the middle of the gibbosity of the circle is nearer the sight than the ends of the arc at the diameter, yet this nearness is not apparent to the sight because of the excessive distance; and for this reason the approach of the part nearer the sight is hidden, and the gibbosity itself is removed in the judgment of vision; wherefore the curved line will appear straight. . . . A sphere will appear as a plane surface for the same reason. The nearness of its convex surface exceeds imperceptibly the nearness of the limits of that convex surface because of the excessive distance. Therefore both sun and moon appear to be plane surfaces although they are spheres.

6.4

René Descartes

(1596–1650)

Descartes, the inventor of descriptive geometry, was justifiably proud of his accomplishments in the field of optics. He solved the problem of space perception in part by giving to all men a full share of his own geometric genius. Berkeley will refer to this theory of a "natural geometry" as still, in his time, "the received opinion." However, Descartes also mentions changes in shape of the lens, differences in clearness of vision, and judgments based on knowledge of size, as additional cues in distance perception.

This account was written about 1634. There is a fuller treatment of the problem in the sixth discourse of La Dioptrique (1637). It is given at length by Sahakian; about half of it appears in Herrnstein and Boring.

It only remains for me to tell you what gives the soul the means for sensing position, shape, distance, size, and other similar qualities which

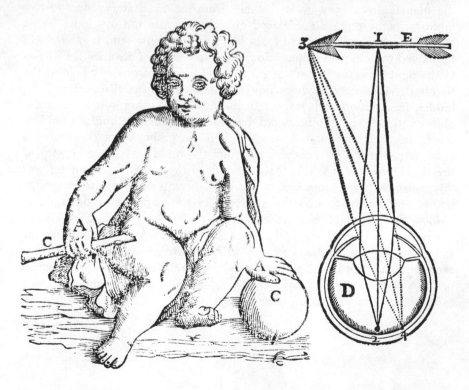

De l'homme [On man]. Paris, 1664. [Art. 48: pp. 47–50.]

do not relate to any single sense in particular, like those of which I have seen speaking until now, but are common to both touch and vision, and in some fashion also to the other senses.

Therefore take note first that if the hand A, for example, touches the object C, the parts of the brain B, from which the little fibers of its nerves come, will be differently disposed than if it touched an object of a different shape, or a different size, or situated in a different place, and thus the soul will be able to know through them the position of this object, its shape and its size, and all other similar qualities. And in the same fashion, if the eye D is turned toward the object E, the soul will know the position of this object, inasmuch as the nerves of the eye will be differently disposed than if it were turned elsewhere; and it will be able to know its shape, inasmuch as the rays from point 1 are brought together at point 2, against what is called the optic nerve, and those from point 3 at point 4, and so with the others, tracing on it a shape exactly like their own; and that it will be able to know the distance of point 1, for example, inasmuch as the disposition of the crystalline humor, in order to make all the rays from this point converge at the back of the eye exactly on point 2, which I suppose to be their focus, will be of a different shape than it would be if this point were nearer or more distant, as I have

already said just now. And furthermore it will know the distance of point 3, and of all the other points whose rays are entering the eye at the same time, because when the crystalline humor is disposed in this manner, the rays from point 3 do not converge so exactly at point 4 as do those from point 1 at point 2, and similarly with the others, so that their action will be proportionably less strong, as has also just been stated. And finally, that the soul will be able to know the size of visual objects, and all other similar qualities, solely from the knowledge it has of their distance and of the position of points on them, and reciprocally, it will sometimes judge their distance from the opinion which it has about their size.

Let us also take note that if the two hands, F and G, each holds a rod, I and H, with which they touch an object K, even though the soul does not know the length of these rods, as long as it does know the distance between the two points F and G, and the size of the angles, FGH and GFI, it will be able to know, by a sort of natural geometry, where the object K is situated. And in the same manner, if the two eyes, L and M, are turned toward an object N, the magnitude of the line LM and of the angles LMN and MLN enable it to know where the point N is situated.

6.5

Nicholas Malebranche

(1638–1715)

As a committed Cartesian, Malebranche starts with aspects of distance perception which Descartes had mentioned, but he goes beyond these, and more important, he is deeply psychological in his entire treatment. He appeals to experimental evidence on one point, and he draws attention to the part played by feelings of tension in the eye muscles (whose function he misinterprets). The controversy over the moon-size illusion is still not resolved today, but it is a curious fact that Berkeley rejected Malebranche's quite plausible explanation in favor of one put forward by another Cartesian, Sylvain Régis, based on the effects of vapor in the evening air.

The entire discussion supports Malebranche's general thesis that all judgments based on the senses are "Precarious and Uncertain."

De la recherche de la vérité, où l'on traite de la nature de l'esprit de l'homme, et de l'usage qu'il en doit faire pour éviter l'erreur dans les sciences [The search for truth, in which the nature of man's mind is considered, and the use which he should make of it to avoid error in the sciences]. Paris, 1674–1675. Translated by T. Taylor, as *Father Malebranche his Treatise concerning the search after truth* [1694]. Second edition. London, 1700. [Pp. 22–24.]

6.5   Nicholas Malebranche

The first, the most universal, and sometimes the safest way we have, whereby to judge of the distance of Objects, is the Angle made by the Rays of our Eyes, whereof the Object is the Vertical Point, that is, the Object is the Point, where the two Rays meet. When this Angle is very large, the Object appears near at hand, on the contrary when it is very acute, we see the Object a great way off. And the change which happens in the situation of our Eyes, according to the changes of this Angle, is the means the Soul employs to judge concerning the Distance or Nighness of Objects. For just as a Blind Man having two strait Sticks in his hands, the length whereof he did not know, may by a kind of *Natural Geometry* give a tolerable conjecture concerning the distance of any Body, in touching it with the end of his two Sticks, by reason of the Disposition and Distance he finds his hands in, with respect to one another; so it may be said that the Soul judges of the Distance of an Object by the Disposition of her Eyes, which is different according as the Angle, whereby she sees, is great or little, that is, as the Object is nearer or farther off.

A Man could easily be convinc'd of what I say, if he should be at the trouble of making a very easie Experiment: As, let him hang a Ring at the end of a thread, so plac'd that the hoop being turn'd directly towards him, the aperture of it may not appear; or if he please let him drive a Stick in the ground, and take another in his hand, that is curv'd at the end; let him retreat three or four steps from the Ring or the Stick, and shutting one Eye with one hand, let him try to hit the aperture of the Ring, or with the bent end of the Stick in his hand to touch the other across, at an height that is much upon a level with the Eye; and he will be surpriz'd to find himself incapable of doing it at an hundred tryals, though nothing in the world seems easier: Nay, though he should lay aside the Stick, and only endeavour to direct his finger cross ways into the concavity of the Ring, he would find it difficult enough to be done, though he stood very near it. . . .

The Disposition then of the Eyes, which accompanies the Angle made of the *Visual* Rays which cut each other and centre in the Object, is one of the best and most universal means the Soul imploys whereby to judge of the Distance of things. If then that Angle receives no sensible alteration upon a little removal of the Object, whether it approaches nearer us, or recedes from us, it will then follow that it is a fallacious means, and unserviceable to the Soul whereby to judge of the true distance of that Object.

Now 'tis plain that this Angle is notably chang'd, when an Object at about a foot distance from our sight is translated four foot off: but if it be only translated from four to eight, the Alteration is much less discernible; if from eight to twelve, less yet; if from a thousand to an hundred thousand, hardly at all: Lastly, in carrying the Object farther on, even to the imaginary spaces, the changes of the Angle grows imperceptible, and is quite lost. . . .

This is the Reason why we see the Sun and Moon, as if they were involv'd in Clouds, tho' they are vastly distant from them; and that we naturally think all the Stars rang'd in an equal distance from us; that we imagine the *Comets* are fixt, and almost motionless, at the end of their course. . . .

The second *Medium* the Soul imploys to judge concerning the Distance of Objects, consists in a Disposition of the Eyes different from that I have been speaking of. In order to explain it, we must know that it is absolutely necessary that the figure of the Eye be different according to the different Distance of Objects which we see: For when a man sees an Object near him, there is a necessity of his Eyes being longer, than if the Object were farther off; Because to the end the Rays of this Object may be collected in the Optick Nerve, which is necessary to its being seen, the distance between the Nerve and the Crystalline ought to be greater.

It is true, If the Crystalline became more convex when the Object were near, that would effect the same thing as the Elongation of the Eye. But 'tis not credible that the Crystalline can easily change its convexity; and on the other side, we have a most evident Experiment for the Elongation of the Eye: for *Anatomy* informs us there are Muscles that surround the middle of the Eye; and we are sensible of the Effort these Muscles make to compress it, and lengthen it, when we have a mind to see any thing very near.

But it is not at all necessary, we should know here, by what way this is done; it is enough that there happens a *Change* in the Eye, whether it proceeds from the Pressure of the Muscles, that surround it; or whether the little Nerves, which answer to the *Ciliary* Ligaments which hold the *Crystalline,* suspended betwixt the other Humours of the Eye, become relax'd, to augment the convexity of the Crystalline; or intense, to diminish it.

For this Change which happens, whatever it be, is only to collect and unite the Rays of Objects, with an exact justness, upon the Optick Nerve. But it is certain that when the Object is five hundred Paces, or ten thousand Leagues distant, we behold it with the same Disposition of Eyes, without any sensible Change in the Muscles which surround the Eye, or in the Nerves which answer to the *Ciliary* Ligaments of the Crystalline: And the Rays of Objects are very exactly collected upon the *Retina,* or the Optick Nerve. Thus the Soul judges, that Objects at ten thousand or an hundred thousand Leagues distance, are no more than five or six hundred Paces off; when she judges of their Distance, only by the Disposition of the Eyes, which I have been speaking of.

However, it is certain this Medium is of use to the Soul, when the Object is nigh at hand. If, for instance, an Object is only at half a foot Distance, we discern its Distance well enough, through the Disposition of the Muscles which constringe our Eyes, in order to make them somewhat longer: And this Disposition is moreover painful. If the Object be remov'd two foot, we can still discern the Distance, because the Disposition of the Muscles is somewhat sensible still, although no longer painful. But if the Object is remov'd still some feet farther, this Disposition of our Muscles, grows so imperceptible, that it is altogether useless to us in judging of the Distance of the Object. . . .

The third *Medium* consists in the Greatness of the Image painted on the fund of the Eye, and that makes the Representation of the Objects which we see. 'Tis confess'd that this Image grows less in proportion as the Object is remov'd to a greater Distance, but this Disposition grows so much less discernible, as the Object which changes its Distance is more remote. . . . Thus the third *Medium* has the same defect as the other two, of which we have been speaking.

It is farther to be observ'd, That the Soul does not judge those Objects the remotest, that have the least Images painted on the *Retina*. When I see, for instance, a Man and a Tree at an hundred Paces Distance, or suppose many Stars in the Heaven, I do not judge the Man to be more remote than the Tree, and the Little Stars farther distant than the Greater; though the Images of the Man, and the little Stars, that are pictur'd on the *Retina*, are less than the images of the Tree and the Greater Stars. Besides it is necessary to know the greatness of an Object, to be able to judge nearly of its Distance, and because I know an House is bigger than a Man, tho' the Image of the House be bigger than that of a Man, I do not judge the House to be nearest upon that account. . . .

We judge farther of the remoteness of an Object by the *Force* wherewith it acts upon our Eyes, because a remote Object acts more languishing and weakly than another; and again, by the *Distinctness* and *Clearness* of the Image, which is form'd in the Eye; because when an Object is remote, the Pupil of the Eye must needs be more open and Capacious, and Consequently the Rays must be collected somewhat confusedly. . . . It is plain enough, that these last *Means* are too fallible whereby to judge with any kind of Certainty concerning the distance of Objects: and I shall not any longer insist upon them, but come to the last of all, as being that which helps the Imagination most, and inclines the Soul more easily to judge that Objects are very remote.

The sixth then and the Principal *Medium* of all, consists in this, *viz.*, that the Eye exhibits not to the Soul a single Object separate from others, but gives her View at once of all those which lye, betwixt us and the Principal Object of our actual Consideration.

When for instance, we behold a Steeple at a considerable Distance, we usually see a great many interjacent Lands and Houses at the same time: and because we judge of the Remoteness of these Lands, and Houses, and in the mean time see the Steeple beyond them, we judge likewise, that it is not only more remote, but a great deal larger and taller, than if we saw it all alone: Notwithstanding the Image which is projected in the Fund of the Eye, is always of an equal Bigness, whether there are Lands and Houses lying betwixt us and it, or whether there are none, provided we see it from a place equally Distant, which is suppos'd. Thus we judge of the Bigness of Objects, according as we believe them remote from us; and the Bodies which we see betwixt us and the Objects, assist the Imagination mightily in judging of their Remoteness: just as we judge of the Extent of our Duration, or of the time that has pass'd since we have done any Action by the confus'd Remembrance of the things we have done, or of the Thoughts we have had successively since that Action. . . .

Hence it is easy to assign the true Reason of the Moon's appearing larger at her Rising, than when considerably elevated above the Horizon. For at her Rising she appears many Leagues distant, and even beyond the sensible Horizon, or the Lands which terminate our Sight. Whereas we judge her but at half a Leagues Distance, or seven or eight times higher than our Houses when she is ascended above our Horizon. Thus we judge her far greater when she is near the Horizon, than when at a great distance from it; because we judge her to be far more remote from us, when she rises, than when mounted very high above our Horizon. . . .

These then are all the Means we have to judge of the Distance of Objects; in which, since we have found considerable Imperfections we cannot but conclude, that the Judgments that are grounded upon them, must needs be very *Precarious* and Uncertain.

6.6

George Berkeley

(1685–1753)

The essay from which this selection is taken has been called (by Brett) "the most significant contribution to psychology produced in the eighteenth century." It was certainly one of the most influential, since its thesis went almost unchallenged for more than 200 years. It is also a colossal blunder, a prime example of that absurdity which only astute philosophers can attain. Even today, many psychologists still subscribe to the view that humans must learn their depth perceptions, while admitting that chicks and frogs have them built in at birth.

Berkeley follows Locke in using idea to mean any conscious content. It is consistent with his radical empiricism to insist that only conscious content can influence judgment. In tracing this influence, he takes a significant

An essay towards a new theory of vision. Dublin, 1709. [Pp. 1–3, 7, 9–13, 15–16, 51–52, 89–90, 117, 125, 138–140, 147–148, 154–157.]

6.6 George Berkeley

step beyond *Locke* by making a positive use of associative learning, although he does not use the word association.

[I.] My Design is to shew the manner, wherein we perceive by Sight the Distance, Magnitude, and Situation of *Objects*. Also to consider the Difference there is betwixt the *Ideas* of Sight and Touch, and whether there be any *Idea* common to both Senses. In treating of all which, it seems to me, the Writers of *Optics* have proceeded on wrong Principles.

[II.] It is, I think, agreed by all that *Distance* of itself, and immediately cannot be seen. . . .

[III.] I find it also acknowledg'd, that the Estimate we make of the Distance of *Objects* considerably remote, is rather an Act of Judgment grounded on *Experience*, than of *Sense*. . . .

[IV.] But when an *Object* is placed at so near a Distance, as that the Interval between the Eyes bears any sensible Proportion to it. It is the receiv'd Opinion that the two *Optic Axes* . . . concurring at the *Object* do there make an *Angle*, by means of which, according as it is Greater or Lesser, the *Object* is perceiv'd to be nearer or farther off. . . .

[XII.] But those *Lines* and *Angles*, by means whereof Mathematicians pretend to explain the Perception of Distance, are themselves not at all perceiv'd, nor are they in Truth, ever thought of by those unskilful in *Optics*. . . . In vain shall all the *Mathematicians* in the World tell me, that I perceive certain *Lines* and *Angles* which introduce into my Mind the various *Ideas* of *Distance;* so long as I my self am conscious of no such thing. . . .

[XVI.] . . . It remains that we enquire what *Ideas*, or *Sensations* there be that attend *Vision*, unto which we may suppose the *Ideas* of Distance are connected, and by which they are introduced into the Mind. And *First*, It is certain by Experience, that when we look at a near *Object* with both Eyes, according as it approaches, or recedes from us, we alter the Disposition of our Eyes, by lessening or widening the Interval between the *Pupils*. This Disposition or Turn of the Eyes is attended with a Sensation, which seems to me, to be that which in this Case brings the *Idea* of greater, or lesser Distance into the mind.

[XVII.] Not, that their is any natural or necessary Connexion between the Sensation we perceive by the Turn of the Eyes, and greater or lesser Distance. But because the Mind has by constant *Experience* found the different Sensations corresponding to the different Dispositions of the Eyes, to be attended each, with a Different Degree of Distance in the *Object:* There has grown an Habitual or Customary Connexion, between those two sorts of *Ideas*. So that the Mind no sooner perceives the Sensation arising from the different Turn it gives the Eyes, in order to bring the *Pupils* nearer, or farther asunder; but it withal perceives the different *Idea* of Distance which was wont to be connected with that Sensation.

Just as upon hearing a certain Sound, the *Idea* is immediately suggested to the Understanding, which Custom had united with it.

[XVIII.] Nor do I see, how I can easily be mistaken in this Matter. I know evidently that Distance is not perceived of it self. That by consequence, it must be perceived by means of some other *Idea* which is immediately perceiv'd, and varies with the different Degrees of Distance. I know also that the Sensation arising from the Turn of the Eyes is of it self, immediately perceiv'd, and various Degrees thereof are connected with different Distances; which never fail to accompany them into my Mind, when I view an *Object* distinctly with both Eyes, whose Distance is so small that in respect of it, the Interval between the Eyes has any considerable Magnitude. . . .

[XX.] From all which it plainly follows, that the Judgment we make of the Distance of an *Object,* view'd with both Eyes, is entirely the *Result of Experience.* If we had not constantly found certain Sensations arising from the various Disposition of the Eyes, attended with certain degrees of Distance. We shou'd never make those sudden Judgments from them, concerning the Distance of *Objects;* no more than we wou'd pretend to judge of a Man's Thoughts, by his pronouncing Words we had never heard before.

[XXI.] *Secondly,* An *Object* placed at a Certain distance from the Eye, to which the breadth of the *Pupil* bears a considerable Proportion, being made to approach, is seen more confusedly. And the nearer it is brought, the more confused Appearance it makes. And this being found constantly to be so, there arises in the Mind an *Habitual* Connexion between the several Degrees of Confusion and Distance. . . .

[XXV.] That one *Idea* may suggest another to the Mind, it will suffice that they have been observ'd to go together; without any demonstration of the necessity of their Coexistence, or without so much as knowing what it is that makes them so to Coexist. Of this there are innumerable Instances, of which no one can be Ignorant. . . .

[XLVI.] From what we have shewn it is a manifest Consequence, that the *Ideas* of Space, Outness, and things placed at a Distance are not, strictly speaking the *Object* of Sight. They are no otherwise perceived by the Eye than by the Ear. Sitting in my Study I hear a Coach drive along the Streets. I look through the Casement and see it. I walk out and enter into it. Thus, common Speech wou'd incline one to think, I heard, saw, and touch'd the same Thing, viz. the Coach. It is, nevertheless, certain, the *Ideas* intromitted by each Sense are widely different, and distinct from each other; but having been observed constantly to go together, they are spoken of as one and the same thing. By the variation of the Noise, I perceive the different Distances of the Coach, and know that it approaches before I look out. Thus by the Ear I perceive Distance, just after the same manner, as I do by the Eye. . . .

[LXXIX.] From what has been said we may safely deduce this consequence, viz. That a Man born Blind, and made to See, wou'd, at first opening of his Eyes, make a very different Judgment of the Magnitude of *Objects* intromitted by them, from what others do. He wou'd not consider the *Ideas* of Sight with reference to, or as having any Connexion with the Ideas of Touch. His view of them being intirely terminated within themselves, he can no otherwise judge them *Great* or *Small*, than as they contain a greater or lesser Number of Visible Points. . . .

[CIII.] That which I see is only variety of Light and Colours. That which I feel is Hard or Soft, Hot or Cold, Rough or Smooth. What Similitude, what Connexion have those *Ideas* with these? Or how is it possible, that any one should see reason to give one and the same Name, to combinations of *Ideas* so very different, before even he had experienced their Coexistence? . . .

[CX.] Hence it follows, that a Man Born Blind, and afterwards, when grown up, made to see, wou'd not in the first act of Vision, parcel out the *Ideas* of Sight, into the same distinct Collections that others do, who have experienced which do regularly coexist and are proper to be bundled up together under one name. . . .

[CXXI.] We have shewn the way wherein the Mind by Mediation of Visible *Ideas* doth perceive or apprehend the *Distance, Magnitude* and *Situation* of Tangible Objects. I come now to enquire more particularly, concerning the Difference betwixt the *Ideas* of *Sight* and *Touch,* which are call'd by the same Names; and see whether there be any *Idea* common to both Senses. From what we have at large set forth and demonstrated in the foregoing part of this Treatise, 'tis plain there's no one self-same numerical Extension, perceiv'd both by Sight and Touch. But that the particular Figures and Extensions perceiv'd by Sight, however they may be called by the same Names, and reputed the same Things with those perceived by Touch, are nevertheless different, and have an Existence very distinct and Separate from them. So that the Question is not now concerning the same numerical Ideas, but whether there be any one and the same sort or Species of Ideas equally perceivable to both Senses? Or, in other Words, whether Extension, Figure, and Motion perceiv'd by Sight, are not specifically distinct from Extension, Figure and Motion perceived by Touch. . . .

[CXXVII.] . . . In answer to which I shall venture to lay down the following Proposition, *viz. The Extension, Figures, and Motions perceiv'd by Sight are specifically Distinct from the* Ideas *of touch, called by the same Names; nor is there any such thing as one* Idea, *or* Kind *of* Idea, *common to both Senses.* . . .

[CXXXII.] A further Confirmation of our Tenent may be drawn from the solution of Mr. *Molyneux's* Problem, publish'd by Mr. *Locke* in his *Essay.* Which I shall set down as it there lies, together with Mr. *Locke's* Opinion of it. '*Suppose a Man Born Blind, and now Adult, and taught by his Touch to distinguish between a Cube and a Sphere of the same Metal,*

*and nighly of the same Bigness, so as to tell, when he felt one and t'other,
which is the Cube, and which the Sphere. Suppose then the Cube and
Sphere placed on a Table, and the Blind Man to be made to see: Quare,
Whether by his Sight, before he Touch'd them, he could now distinguish,
and tell, which is the Globe, which the Cube.* To which the acute and judicious Proposer {*i.e.* Molyneux} Answers: *Not. For though he has obtain'd the experience of, how a Globe, how a Cube affects his Touch; yet
he has not yet attained the Experience, that what affects his Touch so or
so, must affect his Sight so or so: Or that a protuberant Angle in the Cube,
that pressed his Hand unequally, shall appear to his Eye, as it doth in the
cube.* I {this is Locke!} agree with this thinking Gentleman, whom I am
proud to call my Friend, in his Answer to this his Problem; and am of
opinion, that the blind man, at first sight, would not be able with certainty
to say, which was the Globe, which the Cube, whilst he only saw them.'
Essay on Human Understand. b. ii. c. 9. § 8.

[CXXXIII.] . . . We must therefore allow, either that Visible Extension
and figures are specifically distinct, from Tangible Extension and Figures,
or else, that the Solution of this Problem, given by those two very thought-
ful and ingenious Men, is wrong.

6.7

Rudolph Hermann Lotze

(1817–1881)

*We must look upon the title of this book as an approach toward the phrase
"physiological psychology," which had not yet been coined; the subtitle
by itself would have implied at that time no more than a descriptive analysis of mental phenomena. Lotze was a young physiologist evolving into a
philosopher (somewhat as William James did later in the century) and
seeking to apply his medical knowledge to philosophic problems. Almost
one-fourth of the book is devoted to the theory of local signs, in which
he uses the "medical" fact of reflex orientation to stimuli as the key to
reconciling the concept of the soul as an unextended entity with the
Kantian concept of space as an a priori form of thought (see 5.6). This
theory gives a nativistic explanation of two-dimensional visual space, and
Lotze specifically rejects the hypothesis that learned associations play any
part in it. But the Berkeleian influence is not to be denied, and Lotze
concedes (in the last paragraph of our selection) that distance perception,*

Medizinische Psychologie: oder Physiologie der Seele [Medical psychology, or physiology of the soul]. Leipzig, 1852.

the third dimension, must be acquired by experience. Later he introduced an empirical element into the statement of the local signs theory proper, and it is the latter form (based on an abstract of lectures near the end of his career) which is usually seen in translation.

286. . . . Nature has employed such skill and pains in the eye, that the light rays coming from an object strike the retina in such an orderly fashion that after passing through it, or being reflected from it, they can still provide a clear picture of the object to another eye. But although the spatial position of points on the object was in itself an external matter of indifference to the soul, the image on the retina is a summation of our own *living responses,* cast into a similar spatial pattern. . . .

287. The prejudgment that the spatial form in which a number of neural *excitations* simultaneously take place, side by side, provides the immediate basis for a similar spatial disposition of *sensations,* is an error which occurs again and again, in the most varied forms, and which everywhere vitiates the explanation of our sensory perception of the outer world. . . . There must infallibly be some point, in the process of transition to the soul, when this whole geometric configuration is dissolved without trace, and is replaced by a *sum of intensive excitations,* which, like many tones sounding together, no longer contains any indication of spatial extension or position. Therefore if we are to attain any perception of the true positions of external objects, this cannot be done by *grasping* those spatial relationships, but rather by *reproducing* them. . . .

289. . . . If we find arrangements anywhere such that a number of external stimuli shall take effect on the nervous system in a regular geometric relationship, we must look upon this as an important indication that nature means to take something out of those spatial relationships, for consciousness. But in themselves they explain nothing, and it is necessary simultaneously to look everywhere in the sensory apparatus for that other means, by which the position of the excited points may exert an effect on the soul, in addition to that of their qualitative excitation. Now, since the subsequent localization of a sensation element in the spatial perception of things is independent of its qualitative content, so that very different sensations can occupy the same places in our spatial picture at different moments, it follows that each excitation must receive a characteristic coloration by virtue of the point in the nervous system where it takes place. We shall call this its *local sign.* . . .

292. . . . Supposing it agreed that the soul does receive such a local sign along with every qualitative sensation, . . . is it not nevertheless a deception to assert that it is *able,* and is *compelled,* by this means alone, not only to *distinguish* its sensations from one another, but also to separate them from each other *spatially?* . . . Nor was it at all our intention to derive from the local signs either the capacity of the soul to perceive

space at all, or the necessity that it should apprehend its sensations in a spatial manner. . . . But if it is assumed, and agreed to as a fact to be recognized in advance, that the soul *can* form spatial percepts and *wishes* to do so, the question still remains as to what principles of choice it uses, in assigning one sensation to this spot and another to that spot within the overall spatial perception which it constructs, or how it comes to regard sensations a and b as adjacent, a and c as remote from each other. . . .

310. If three differently colored rays of light strike three different points on the retina, one might suppose that the qualitative differences among these excitations would offer sufficient basis to differentiate their sensations spatially as well. But a glance at the simultaneous sensation of several tones teaches us that this basis is inadequate. Still less would it be the case, if three rays of light of exactly the same color were to strike three points of the retina, that the soul should thereby be compelled to have the resulting qualitative sensation, blue for example, three times instead of once, and to place these three samples of it at *different points in space*. A deception is already contained in the tacit assumption that the resulting color sensation is itself punctiform, so that it easily lends itself to being localized at a particular place in the visual field. There is no more reason why a sensation of color should be experienced as a point sensation, if we do not postulate a special adaptation of the soul for this, than that this should happen for a tone. Since there is nothing at all extended about it, it cannot even be experienced as a point, that is, as the spatial negation of extension, but only as a quality, which has neither a positive nor an expressly negative relationship to spatial extension. Some special reason is needed why similar sensations should be differentiated from one another at all, to exist side by side, as well as why they should assume definite spatial positions in contrast to one another. This can only consist in the fact that local side-effects which are linked with the response of each point on the retina prevent the collapse of the several sensations into one, and that in addition these local signs form such a structured system that the sensations are arranged by them according to graded differences and relationships. The latter appear in spatial perception as equal units of distance separating the sensory points from one another, and as relationships within it, independent of quality. . . .

311. If the image of a luminous point falls on a *peripheral portion of the retina*, it tends at once to produce a movement of the eye, by means of which this image is brought to the point of clearest vision. . . . If v is the point of clearest vision, while a, b, and c are other points on the retina, then an image falling on a requires a different combination, direction, and magnitude of eye movements than b or c, in order to reach v; and in general the group of movements which must be initiated in order to bring the point of clearest vision beneath the image

will be quite specific for each part of the retina, and it can never coincide with the group which any other point must evoke for the same purpose. . . . If we let s stand for the sum of all these movements, then this is a specific and invariable combination for each point of the retina, and therefore we believe that in it we have found the local sign which differentiates the excitation of each point from that of any other point.

312. This distinctive character of s at each point makes it very difficult to explain its *origin through association*. For even if we had learned, with respect to sensation at point a, as a result of accidentally turning the eye from any cause whatever, that the sensation became clearer when the eye performed this particular turn, we would still not be able to conclude by analogy that images at all the other points $[a, b, \ldots z]$ would undergo the same improvement in clarity as a result of analogous turns $[av, bv, \ldots zv]$, which however would be quite different in direction and magnitude. We would rather have to learn this for each point of the retina, and we would therefore have to assume that the movement required for thus sharpening the image had been once *accidentally* associated with the stimulation of each of the innumerable points of the retina. Although this is quite possible, in view of the eye's mobility, it seems to me very improbable that a function which is so essential for vision should develop by this long path, through innumerable associations, particularly since it is already present, as much as might be expected, in early childhood. . . . We are therefore fully convinced that what we see here is a *physiological mechanism* by which the stimulation of each point of the retina is so transferred to the different fibers of the motor nerves of the eye, according to the principle of reflex movemont, that a special and invariable movement group results for each. . . .

313. . . . We do not trace the ordering of points in the visual field to the actual movements, nor to the conscious sensations of those movements. Rather, we look upon the observable fact of this involuntary turning of the eye upon its axis as no more than a phenomenon from which we can infer that even the first localization of sensory elements, which takes place quite unconsciously, is based on the same connection between sensory and motor nerves, and that it is the excitation of the latter at their central terminations which gives a local character to each color sensation.

6.8

Hermann von Helmholtz

(1821–1894)

Berkeley had refused to acknowledge the influence of any factor which did not show itself in consciousness. Both he and Malebranche had pointed to the conscious sensations from eye muscles as clues to the perception of distance, although Malebranche thought of them as arising directly from the process of focusing in a single eye, while Berkeley correctly derived them from the convergence of the two eyes. In the mid-eighteenth century, Condillac spoke of "touch instructing vision," and early in the nineteenth century, Thomas Brown invoked the kinesthesis of the arm in building a learned concept of space. Lotze appealed to kinesthetic clues derived from reflex organization of the visual apparatus, but these are utilized unconsciously, not unlike the petites perceptions of Leibnitz. Now Helmholtz again emphasizes the empirical element, but without insisting on consciousness. His earliest statement of the theory of "unconscious inference" was in this popular lecture delivered in 1855. (See 5.7 for his later, more explicit statement of the theory.)

I have always said that our perception judges, draws conclusions, considers, and so forth, but I have always guarded myself against saying that we judge, conclude, consider. For I have recognized that these acts take place without our knowledge, nor can they be changed by our will and our better convictions. Should we therefore designate as a process of thinking what takes place here: this thinking without self-consciousness and free from the control of self-conscious intelligence? . . .

. . . In young children we can clearly see that they have quite false perceptions of the distance of objects which they see, and perhaps many of you will still be able to recall from your childhood events in which there was a gross deception regarding distance. I myself still clearly remember the moment when the law of perspective, that distant objects appear small, first occurred to me. I was passing a high tower, on the topmost gallery of which there were some people, and I asked my mother to take the cute little dolls down for me, for I was quite of the opinion that if she were to stretch out her arm she could reach the gallery of the tower. I have often since looked at that tower in

Ueber das Sehen von Menschen [On human vision]. In *Vorträge und Reden* [Lectures and addresses]. Fourth edition. 2 vols. Braunschweig, 1896. Vol. I, pp. 85–117. [Pp. 110, 114.]

passing by, when people were standing on it, but for my more practised eye they would no longer turn into cute little dolls.

The assurance and the exactness of spatial construction by the eye
is also explained by the principle of practice, by the education of our
sense organs. . . . We are all skilled performers with our eyes, whose
skill stirs no astonishment because every one else can do all the same
tricks.

6.9

George Malcolm Stratton

(1865–1957)

*Stratton's rather heroic experiments with inverting lenses were published
in 1897, and those with mirrors in 1899. (Herrnstein and Boring give
lengthy excerpts from the former, with descriptions of first-day and seventh-
day experiences.) Here Stratton states what he believes his experiments
proved about the empirical nature of eye-hand coordination, if not space-
perception per se.*

*Stratton's work inspired that by Ivo Kohler, among others, reported in
his article, "Experiments with goggles," in the Scientific American for
May, 1962.*

But now as to the harmony which the senses show in reporting the
more exact direction and position of things. For centuries a puzzling
problem has been to explain how we can see things right side up, although the image by which we see them is upside down like the picture
on the ground glass of a photographic camera. Some, however, have
taken the bull by the horns, and declared that . . . upright vision . . .
is dependent on there being in the eye an inverted image of the outer
world.

Recent experiments, however, are decidedly against this conclusion. In
order to see whether the inversion of the image was really so necessary
as the advocates of this view supposed, an observer wore a set of lenses
that turned the retinal image into an upright position for a considerable
length of time. The results showed that an experience coming from
such an upright image would in time be indistinguishable from our
normal experience. The first effect was to make things, as seen, appear
to be in a totally different place from that in which they were felt. But

Experimental psychology and its bearing upon culture. New York: Macmillan, 1903.
[Pp. 145–149.]

this discord between visual and tactual positions tended gradually to disappear; not that the visual scene finally turned to the position it had before the inversion, but rather the tactual feeling of things tended to swing into line with the altered sight of them. The observer came more and more to refer his touch impressions to the place where he saw the object to be; so that it was clearly a mere matter of time when a complete agreement of touch and sight would be secured under these unusual conditions. And when once the sight of things and the feeling of them accord perfectly, then all that we mean by upright vision has been attained.

A later experiment of a somewhat similar kind has shown that the agreement of touch and sight can surmount even greater obstacles than these. A set of mirrors was attached to the body by a light frame so that the observer viewed himself as from above his own head. By means of screens on this frame, vision was confined as nearly as possible to the view which the mirrors gave, and these mirrors reflected things not only out of their proper direction, but gave them, as well, a false distance from the observer. Here again the result was, at first, an utter discord in the spatial reports of the two senses. The whole body was seen in a different place from where it was felt; it was in fact projected at a right angle to the front and several feet away. . . . But the constant sight of the feet and hands, for instance, tended to pull the feeling of these members over into the place where they were seen, so that, on the third day, there were occasions, especially during rapid walking, when no conflict was felt as to the place of the various impressions. Such a harmony, it must be confessed, was only occasional; but that it could come at all, and particularly that it came more forcibly the longer the experiment was tried, shows clearly what the harmony of the tactual and visual space-world consists in. The experiment indicates that if we were to see a thing long enough in any given place, we should, sooner or later, also feel it there. If the world had been so constructed that we always saw our bodies a hundred yards away from our point of view, our touch sensations would undoubtedly have taken this same position. The reason for it is this: there is no place in the visual field where we can say beforehand we ought to see something that we happen to be touching. Experience alone can teach us where it will appear. And similarly, before experience has guided us, there is no way of telling where we shall feel an object that we are looking at. This is why those who are born blind and are suddenly given sight make such work of touching the things they see. They grope and fumble and seem to hit the mark solely by chance. But once a person has noted the kind of arm movement that will bring his hand to what he sees, then, when the visual experience is repeated, he naturally expects that if he repeats his former movement he will again touch the object. If he actually finds the thing there, he feels that touch and sight are in accord; if he finds it elsewhere, they seem to disagree. The agreement is, therefore, a matter of training and expectation. One can learn to expect anything that has been regularly experienced. So that a harmony of touch and sight can grow up under the greatest variety of circumstances, provided merely that the experience remains uniform long enough to develop fixed expectations.

6.10

Richard D. Walk   Eleanor Gibson
(born 1920)   (born 1910)

AND

Thomas J. Tighe
(born 1928)

The experiment described here has also been carried out, with suitable modifications of the apparatus, on chicks, goats, and human infants, and the results were summarized by Gibson and Walk in Scientific American (April 1960). They arrive at the conclusion that in all animals, ability to judge distance matures by the time when they are able to move freely in the environment. Rarely has a long-standing problem in psychology received such a clear experimental answer.

A technique of testing for visual depth perception which involves no pretraining at all—the "visual cliff"—was developed. It is based on the assumption that, given a choice, an animal will avoid descending over a vertical edge to a surface which appears to be far away. The apparatus was constructed of two thicknesses of glass (24 in. by 32 in.), parallel to the floor and held by metal supports 53 in. above it. A board (4 in. wide, 24 in. long, and 3 in. high) extended across the glass, dividing it into two equal fields. On one side (the "near" side), patterned wallpaper was inserted between the two sheets of glass. Through the clear glass of the other side (the "far" side) the same pattern was visible on the floor and also on the walls below the glass surface.

Optically speaking, the edge on one side of the board dropped away

Behavior of light- and dark-reared rats on a visual cliff. *Science,* 126 (1957): 80–81.

for a distance of 53 in. (making the simulated cliff), while on the other side the edge dropped away for only 3 in. Thus, two visual fields existed, both filled with patterned wallpaper, but the pattern of the "far" field was optically much smaller and denser than that of the other and elicited more motion parallax. . . .

Subjects for the experimental condition were 19 dark-reared, hooded rats, 90 days old, and 29 light-reared litter mates. Twenty minutes after coming into the light, the dark-reared rats were placed on the apparatus. An animal was placed on the center board in a box, to avoid any handling bias. It was then observed for 5 minutes. . . . Of the light-reared rats, 23 descended on the near side, three descended on the far side, and three remained on the board for all 5 minutes. Of the dark-reared rats, 14 descended on the near side, three descended on the far side, and two remained on the board. . . .

These results suggest two conclusions. First, hooded rats, 90 days of age, do discriminate visual depth or distance. They avoid a visual cliff as compared with a short visual drop-off, and this preference is eliminated when the visual cliff is eliminated. Second, such discrimination seems to be independent of previous visual experience, since dark-reared adult animals behaved like their light-reared litter mates only 20 minutes after being exposed to the light.

Chapter 7

SENSE QUALITIES

Through the senses we learn about the external world. That this information, or interpretations based on it, might be false was recognized early,
but that it could be a projection of our own dispositions rather than a
reflection of real qualities in external objects is a realization which has
come to man slowly by many stages. This idea has been so difficult to
grasp in its full import that it is less than a century since the distinction
has been made between "warm" and "cold" as two senses rather than as
two qualities detected by a single "temperature sense."

7.1

Aristotle

(384–322 B.C.)

For Aristotle the qualities perceived by the senses are intrinsic in external
things, and the five senses are adequate to perceive all these qualities.
However, such aspects of reality as shape and number are "common sensibles" which are detectable through more than one sense.

On the soul. In *Aristotle: On the soul; Parva naturalia; On breath*. With an English
translation by W. S. Hett. Cambridge, Mass.: Harvard University Press (Loeb Classical Library), 1957. [418a, 422b, 424b–425a.] Reprinted by permission of the publishers and the Loeb Classical Library.

[Book II] VI. In discussing the several senses we must speak first of their respective objects. The term "object of sense" is used of three types; two of them we say that we perceive directly, and one indirectly. Of the first two, one is an object proper to a given sense, and the other is an object perceptible by all the senses. By proper object I mean that which cannot be perceived by any other sense, and concerning which error is impossible; *e.g.*, sight is concerned with colour, hearing with sound, and taste with flavour. Touch of course has many varieties of objects. Each sense has its proper sphere, nor is it deceived as to the fact of colour or sound, but only as to the nature and position of the coloured object or the thing that makes the sound. Such objects we call proper to a particular sense, but perception of movement, rest, number, shape and size are shared by several senses. For things of this kind are not proper to any one sense, but are common to all; for instance, some kinds of movement are perceptible both by touch and by sight. I call an object indirectly perceived if, for instance, the white thing seen is the son of Diares; this is an indirect perception, because that which is perceived (the son of Diares) only belongs incidentally to the whiteness. . . .

XI. . . . It is difficult to say whether touch is one sense or more than one, and also what the organ is which is perceptive of the object of touch; whether it is flesh, and whatever is analogous to this in creatures without flesh, or whether this is only the medium, and the primary sense organ is something distinct and internal. For every sensation appears to be concerned with one pair of contraries, *e.g.*, vision is of white and black, hearing of high and low pitch, and taste of bitter and sweet; but in the tangible there are many pairs of contraries, hot and cold, dry and wet, hard and soft, and all other like qualities. Some solution may be found to this difficulty in the fact that the other senses too are conscious of more than one pair of contraries: so in sound there is not merely high and low pitch, but also loud and soft, smooth and rough, and so on. There are similarly other differences in colour. But what in the case of touch is the single substrate corresponding to sound in hearing is not obvious. . . .

[Book III] I. One may be satisfied that there are no other senses apart from the five (I mean vision, hearing, smell, taste and touch) from the following arguments. We may assume that we actually have perception of everything which is apprehended by touch (for by touch we perceive all those things which are qualities of the tangible object, *qua* tangible). Again, if we lack some sense, we must lack some sense organ; and, again, all the things which we perceive by direct contact are perceptible by touch, a sense which we in fact possess; but all those things which are perceived through media, and not by direct contact, are perceptible by means of the elements, *viz.*, air and water. . . . But sense organs are composed of only two of these elements, air and water (for the pupil of the eye is composed of water, and the hearing organ of air, while the organ of smell is composed of one or other of these). But fire is the medium of no perception, or else is common to them all (for there is no possibility of perception without heat), and earth is the medium of no sense perception, or else is connected in a special way with the sense of touch. So we are left to suppose that there is no sense organ apart from water and air; and some animals actually have organs composed of these. The conclusion is that all the senses are possessed by all such animals as are neither undeveloped nor maimed; even the mole, we find, has eyes under the skin. If then there is no other body, and no property other than those which belong to the bodies of this world, there can be no sense perception omitted from our list.

7.2

Nemesius

(flourished c. 350 A.D.)

In De Sensu (Ch. 2) Aristotle specifically rejects the theory advanced by certain "modern thinkers" who relate each of the senses to one of the elements, but are embarrassed because there are five senses and but four elements. But Nemesius takes this simpler view of the situation, and finds a reason for the fifth sense, while still excluding the possibility of a sixth.

Little is known of Nemesius. He was apparently a physician who, late in life, turned to a career in the Church and became the bishop of Emesa, a thriving Near East city.

[VI] 2. There are five *seats* for the *senses;* but all are properly but one *sense,* which is the SOUL it self, who, by the seats of the *senses,* discernes all such things as fall out in them. It discernes, or taketh knowledge of an *Earthy* nature, by that *sense,* which is most *Earthie* and *Bodily,* namely the *Touching:* It perceiveth perspicuous (or bright shining things) by that sense which is most perspicuous, that is to say, the *sight:* It judgeth such things as are pertinent to *aire* by that seat which is ordained for the *aire;* for the very substance of the *voice* is *aire,* or the smiting of the aire: and it receiveth every *tast* by a certaine quality of the instrument of the *sense* of *tasting;* which attracts, by its waterish and spongy nature.

The nature of man [Peri physios anthropon]. *A learned and useful tract written in Greek by Nemesius, surnamed the Philosopher.* . . . English'd by George Wither. London, 1636. [Pp. 274–275.]

For it is the nature of every *sensible thing*, to be discerned by some thing which hath a nature like unto it: and by this reason it should seeme that their being onely foure *Elements* there should bee no more but foure *senses*.

But, because there is a kinde ov *vapour*, and certaine smells which have a middle-nature betweene *aire* and *water;* the parts whereof are somewhat thicker then *aire*, & thinner then *water* (which appeares by them who are sick of a heavinesse in the head, by rhumes, and stoppings; for they drawing the aire by respiration, have no feeling of the vapour, by reason the fatnesse of the odour is hindered by obstructions, from approaching the sense) therefore, a *fifthe seat* of the *sense*, namely, *smelling*, was provided by nature, that no such thing as may bee brought unto our knowledge, should be hidden from the *sense*.

7·3

Boethius

(*c.* 480–524)

In an age when learning had become rare in the western world, Boethius stands out as one who is still master of the ancient sciences. He enjoyed distinction as an official under the emperor Theodoric, but fell under suspicion of treason. Several years of imprisonment which preceded his execution gave him the opportunity to be "consoled" by philosophy, which appears before him in truly pagan fashion as a divinely beautiful woman. It is she who speaks in this selection, in which the emphasis on the subjective limitation of all knowledge includes a hint of the future doctrine of the specific energies of the senses.

[V, iv, *fin.*] . . . Men think that all knowledge is cognized purely by the nature and efficacy of the thing known. Whereas the case is the very reverse: all that is known is grasped not conformably to its own efficacy, but rather conformably to the faculty of the knower. An example will make this clear: the roundness of a body is recognised in one way by sight, in another by touch. Sight looks upon it from a distance as a whole by a simultaneous reflection of rays; touch grasps the roundness piecemeal, by contact and attachment to the surface, and by actual movement round the periphery itself. Man himself, likewise, is viewed in one way by Sense, in another by Imagination, in another way, again, by Thought, in another by pure Intelligence. Sense judges figure clothed

The consolation of philosophy [Philosophiae consolationis]. Translated by H. R. James. London, 1897. [Pp. 247–249.]

in material substance, Imagination figure alone without matter. Thought transcends this again, and by its contemplation of universals considers the type itself which is contained in the individual. The eye of Intelligence is yet more exalted; for overpassing the sphere of the universal, it will behold absolute form itself by the pure force of the mind's vision. Wherein the main point to be considered is this: the higher faculty of comprehension embraces the lower, while the lower cannot rise to the higher. For Sense has no efficacy beyond matter, nor can Imagination behold universal ideas, nor Thought embrace pure form; but Intelligence, looking down, as it were, from its higher standpoint in its intuition of form, discriminates also the several elements which underlie it; but it comprehends them in the same way as it comprehends that form itself, which could be cognized by no other than itself. For it cognizes the universal of Thought, the figure of Imagination, and the matter of Sense, without employing Thought, Imagination, or Sense, but surveying all things, so to speak, under the aspect of pure form by a single flash of intuition. Thought also, in considering the universal, embraces images and sense-impressions without resorting to Imagination or Sense. For it is Thought which has thus defined the universal from its conceptual point of view: "Man is a two-legged animal endowed with reason." This is indeed a universal notion, yet no one is ignorant that the *thing* is imaginable and presentable to Sense, because Thought considers it not by Imagination or Sense, but by means of rational conception. Imagination, too, though its faculty of viewing and forming representations is founded upon the senses, nevertheless surveys sense-impressions without calling in Sense, not in the way of Sense-perception, but of Imagination. See'st thou, then, how all things in cognizing use rather their own faculty than the faculty of the things which they cognize? Nor is this strange; for since every judgment is the act of a judge, it is necessary that each should accomplish its task by its own, not by another's power.

7.4

Kenelm Digby

(1603–1665)

Here the educability of the senses is recognized, for Digby argues that men could smell as well as dogs if they had the need to do so. The passage is also of interest for its account of one of those "wild" children who became

Two treatises, in the one of which, the nature of bodies; in the other, the nature of mans soule; is looked into. Paris, 1644. [First treatise, Ch. 27; pp. 246–248.]

the objects of still greater interest in the eighteenth century, as subjects of educational speculation and experiment. (Cf. Itard, 17.5.)

6. . . . And experience teacheth us in all beastes, that the smell is given unto living creatures, to know what meates are good for them, and what are not. . . .

7. And doubtlessely, the like use men would make of this sense, had they not on the one side better meanes then it to know the qualities of meates: and therefore, this is not much reflected upon. And on the other side, were they not continually stuffed and clogged with grosse vapours of steamy meates, which are dayly reeking from the table and their stomakes; and permitt not purer atomes of bodies, to be discerned; which require cleare and uninfected organes to take notice of them. As we see it fare with dogges; who have not so true and sensible noses, when they are high fed, and lye in the kitchin amiddest the steames of meate; as when they are kept in their kennell, with a more spare diett fitt for hunting.

One full example, this age affordeth us in this kind, of a man whose extremity of feare, wrought upon him to give us this experiment. He was borne in some village of the country of Liege: and therefore among strangers he is knowne by the name of Iohn of Liege. I have beene informed of this story by severall (whom I dare confidently beleeve) that have had it from his owne mouth; and have questioned him with great curiosity, particularly about it.

When he was a little boy, there being warres in the country . . . the village of whence he was, had notice of some unruly scattered troopes that were coming to pillage them: which made all the people of the village fly hastily with what they could carry with them, to hide themselves in the woods: which were spacious enough to afford them shelter, for they ioyned upon the forest of Ardenne. There they lay, till some of their scoutes brought them word, that the souldiers of whom they were in such apprehension, had fired their towne and quitted it. Then all of them returned home, excepting this boy; who, it seemeth, being of a very timorous nature, had images of feare so strong in his fansie; that first, he ranne further into the wood then any of the rest; and afterwardes apprehended that every body he saw through the thickets, and every voyce he heard was the souldiers: and so hidd himselfe from his parents, that were in much distresse seeking him all about, and calling his name as loud as they could. When they had spent a day or two in vaine, they returned home without him, and he lived many yeares in the woods, feeding upon rootes, and wild fruites, and maste.

He said that after he had beene some time in this wild habitation, he could by the smell iudge of the tast of any thing that was to be eaten: and that he could att a great distance wind by his nose, where wholesome fruites or rootes did grow. In this state he continued (still shun-

ning men with so great feare as when he first ranne away; so strong
the impression was, and so litle could his litle reason master it) untill
in a very sharpe winter, that many beastes of the forest perished for
want of foode; necessity brought him to so much confidence, that leaving the wild places of the forest, remote from all peoples dwellings, he
would in the eveninges steale among cattle that were fothered; especially the swine, and among them, gleane that which served to sus-
taine wretchedly his miserable life. He could not do this so cunningly,
but that returning often to it, he was upon a time espyed: and they
who saw a beast of so strange a shape (for such they tooke him to be;
he being naked and all over growne with haire) beleeving him to be
a satyre, or some such prodigious creature as the recounters of rare
accidents tell us of; layed wayte to apprehend him. But he that winded
them as farre off, as any beast could do, still avoyded them, till att the
length, they layed snares for him; and tooke the wind so advantagiously
of him, that they caught him: and then, soone perceived he was a man;
though he had quite forgotten the use of all language: but by his gestures and cryes, he expressed the greatest affrightednesse that might be.
Which afterwardes, he said (when he had learned anew to speake)
was because he thought, those were the souldiers he had hidden himselfe to avoyde, when he first betooke himselfe to the wood; and were
alwayes lively in his fansie, through his feares continually reducing
them thither.

This man within a little while after he came to good keeping and
full feeding, quite lost that acutenesse of smelling which formerly governed him in his taste; and grew to be in that particular as other ordinary men were. But att his first living with other people, a woman that
had compassion of him to see a man so neere like a beast; and that
had no language to call for what he wished or needed to have; tooke
particular care of him; and was always very sollicitous to see him furnished with what he wanted: which made him so apply himselfe unto
her in all his occurrents, that whensoever he stoode in neede of ought,
if she were out of the way, and were gone abroad into the fieldes, or
to any other village neare by, he would hunt her out presently by his
sent, in such sort as with us those dogges use to do which are taught
to draw dry foote. I imagine he is yet alive to tell a better story of himselfe then I have done; and to confirme what I have here said of him:
for I have from them who saw him but few yeares agone, that he was
an able strong man, and likely to last yet a good while longer.

7.5

Thomas Hobbes

(1588–1679)

This book had been completed by 1640, the date of the dedicatory epistle, but in that year Hobbes commenced an exile of eleven years, because of his royalist affiliations. But Hobbes had spent most of a year, several years earlier, in Paris, in close communication with Mersenne's circle of philosophic friends, and it may well have been from them that he caught his hint of the principle that sense qualities are not inherent in the objects to which we attach them, but are forms of response characteristic of the sensitive percipient.

The bracketed words were added in the second (1651) edition.

9. As Colour is not inherent in the Object, but an effect thereof upon us, caused by such motion in the Object as hath been described: so neither is *Sound* in the thing we hear, but in our selves. . . . Nothing can make any thing which is not in it self: the *Clapper* hath no *sound* in it, but *motion,* and maketh motion in the internal parts of the Bell; so the Bell hath motion, and not sound; that imparteth *motion* to the *Air;* and the *Air* hath motion, but not sound; the *Air imparteth motion* by the *Ear* and *Nerve* unto the *Brain;* and the Brain hath motion, but not sound: from the *Brain,* it reboundeth back into the Nerves *outward,* and thence it becometh an *apparition without,* which we call *Sound.* And to proceed to the *rest* of the *Senses,* it is apparent enough, that the *Smell* and *Taste* of the *same thing,* are *not* the *same* to *every Man;* and therefore are *not* in the thing *smelt* or *tasted,* but in the *men.* So likewise the *heat* we feel from the fire is manifestly in *us,* and is quite *different* from the heat [which] is in the *fire:* for *our* heat is *pleasure* or *pain,* according as it is *great* or *moderate;* but in the *coal* there is no such thing. By this the Fourth and last Proposition is proved, *viz.* That as in [vision, so also in] Conceptions that arise from *other* Senses, the Subject of their Inherence is not in the Object, but [in] the Sentient.

10. And from hence also it followeth, that *whatsoever accidents* or qualities our Senses make us think there be in the *world,* they be *not* there, but are *seeming* and *apparitions* onely: the things that really *are* in the world without us, are those *motions* by which these seemings are

Humane nature: or, the fundamental elements of policie. Being a discoverie of the faculties, acts, and passions of the soul of man, from their original causes; according to such philosophical principles as are not commonly known or asserted. London, 1650. [Pp. 16–18.]

caused. And this is the *great deception of Sense,* which also is to be by Sense *corrected:* for as Sense telleth me, when I see *directly,* that the Colour seemeth to *be* in the Object; so also Sense telleth me, when I see by *reflection,* that Colour is not in the Object.

7.6

Ignace Gaston Pardies

(1636?–1673)

In a charming introduction to his main topic (the animal mind), this Jesuit author presents a series of paradoxes of the "new philosophy," that is, the developing Cartesian movement. This particular paradox was of course the inevitable outcome of Descartes' distinction between extended matter and unextended mind. The traditional so-called Aristotelian philosophy of the period distinguished between "substance" and "accidents," but now all the "accidents" are seen to be qualities of mind rather than of matter. See Descartes' discussion of the changing appearance of a piece of wax (in 3.3).

Here is something which is still more surprising. Until now, our senses were [thought to be] capable of judging sensible things. Their judgment of these was absolute, and no one would contest their jurisdiction; in any matter that concerned colors, or sounds, or tastes, and things of that sort, one would turn to the eyes, to the ears, to the tongue, and not expect to be deceived. There are even some philosophers who will acknowledge no other rule by which one can judge the truth infallibly, and who think that we can never have greater certainty than when our different senses join in the representation of the same object. Whether this is a good rule or not, it is certain that there is nothing which we are less disposed to doubt than those things which we, and all other men with us, have experienced by our senses since our birth. Thus we do not have the slightest doubt that the light which we see is spread throughout the world, or that the sound of the words which we hear has been produced in the mouth of the person who is talking, and that it is carried through the air until it strikes our ears. We firmly believe that a diamond is hard, that snow is white, that fire is hot. But they want us to think that we deceive ourselves in all this and that it is only an illusion of our senses, and some prejudice acquired in childhood,

Discours de la connoissance des bestes [Discourse on animal knowledge]. Paris, 1662. [Art. 7: pp. 11–15.]

which leads us to imagine colors and other qualities where they do not exist. That in effect there is no hardness in the diamond, nor sweetness in the milk, nor weight in stones. That all these things are in us, and not in the objects and that, in a word, everything that is referred to as *sensible quality* in everyday philosophy does not consist in accidents of the bodies, but in states of our own mind—that is to say, that they are in truth thoughts which we have when those objects are presented to our senses. The ordinary philosophers are therefore far afield when they take such pains to determine whether the heat of fire is substance or accident. They just don't understand: it is neither substance nor accident, because it is an illusion, which never existed except in our mistaken imaginations, for there is no other heat except that in our own minds. After that, we no longer see how we can ever be sure of anything, since we deceive ourselves so mightily in those things which seem so clear.

7·7

John Locke

(1632–1704)

Locke is often credited with introducing the distinction between primary and secondary qualities, but it would be more correct to say that he promoted a general awareness of it. We have seen it stated by Hobbes, and A. C. Fraser points out in his edition of the Essay that Locke's friend Robert Boyle wrote of "secondary qualities" in 1666. Locke's statement of it was complete, as to its essentials, in the first edition, but the question of "powers" gave him unending trouble, leading to revisions and additions in the second edition (1694) and again in the fourth, from which we take this selection.

The short Section 11, given entire, was somewhat longer in the earlier editions. Then Locke had said that impulse was the only way one body can act on another, "it being impossible to conceive, that Body should operate on what it does not touch." The shorter, less sweeping statement is in deference to Newton's law of gravity.

§7. To discover the nature of our *Ideas* the better, and to discourse of them intelligibly, it will be convenient to distinguish them, as they are *Ideas* or Perceptions in our Minds; and as they are modifications of matter in the Bodies that cause such Perceptions in us; that so we *may*

An essay concerning humane understanding [1690]. Fourth edition. London, 1700. [Book II, Ch. VIII; pp. 60–61.]

not think (as perhaps usually is done) that they are exactly the Images and *Resemblances* of something inherent in the subject; most of those of Sensation being in the Mind no more the likeness of something existing without us, than the Names, that stand for them are the likeness of our *Ideas*, which yet upon hearing, they are apt to excite in us.

§8. Whatever the Mind perceives in it self, or is the immeditae object of Perception, Thought, or Understanding, that I call *Idea;* and the Power to produce any *Idea* in our mind, I call *Quality* of the Subject wherein that power is. Thus a Snow-ball having the power to produce in us the *Ideas* of *White, Cold,* and *Round,* the powers to produce those *Ideas* in us, as they are in the Snow-ball, I call *Qualities;* and as they are Sensations, or Perceptions, in our Understandings, I call them *Ideas;* which Ideas, if I speak of sometimes, as in the things themselves, I would be understood to mean those Qualities in the Objects which produce them in us.

§9. Qualities thus considered in Bodies are, First such as are utterly inseperable from the Body, in what estate soever it be; such as in all the alterations and changes it suffers, all the force can be used upon it, it constantly keeps; and such as Sense constantly finds in every particle of Matter, which has bulk enough to be perceived, and the Mind finds inseparable from every particle of Matter, though less than to make it self singly be perceived by our Senses. *v.g.* Take a Grain of Wheat, divide it into two parts, each part has still *Solidity, Extension, Figure,* and *Mobility;* divide it again, and it retains still the same qualities; and so divide it on, till the parts become insensible, they must retain still each of them all those qualities. . . . These I call *original* or *primary Qualities* of Body, which I think we may observe to produce simple *Ideas* in us, *viz.* Solidity, Extension, Figure, Motion, or Rest and Number.

§10. *2dly.* Such *Qualities,* which in truth are nothing in the Objects themselves, but Powers to produce various Sensations in us by their *primary Qualities, i.e.* by the Bulk, Figure, Texture, and Motion of their insensible parts, as Colours, Sounds, Tasts, *&c.* These I call *secondary Qualities.* To these might be added a third sort which are allowed to be barely Powers, though they are as much real Qualities in the Subject, as those which I to comply with the common way of speaking call *Qualities,* but for distinction *secondary Qualities.* For the power in Fire to produce a new Colour, or consistency in Wax or Clay by its primary Qualities, is as much a Quality in Fire, as the power it has to produce in me a new *Idea* or Sensation of warmth or burning, which I felt not before, by the same primary Qualities, *viz.* The Bulk, Texture and Motion of its insensible parts.

§11. The next thing to be consider'd, is how *Bodies* produce *Ideas* in us, and that is manifestly *by impulse,* the only way which we can conceive Bodies operate in.

7.8

Isaac Newton

(1642–1727)

Newton's experimental analysis of the spectrum, which established a solid basis for the development of color theory, was reported to the Royal Society in 1672 (Philosophical Transactions, No. 80; reprinted in Dennis). At that time he spoke of color as a characteristic of light, or even used the terms interchangeably, as in stating that "if any of the prismatick Colours, supposed Red, be intercepted . . . 'tis necessary, either that the colours be very well separated before the red be intercepted," etc. But later, in our selection, he is precise in adopting the position which had been stated so much earlier by Hobbes, that light does not possess color, but a power to evoke color sensation in us. Hobbes had been virtually ignored, but as Locke was attentive to Newton, so Newton was attentive to Locke. There was mutual respect between these men whom their contemporaries revered as the world's greatest thinkers.

All homogeneal Light has its proper Colour answering to its Degree of refrangibility, and that Colour cannot be changed by reflexions and refractions.

In the Experiments of the 4th Proposition of the first Book, when I had separated the heterogeneous rays from one another, the Spectrum pt formed by the separated rays, did in the progress from its end p, on which the most refrangible rays fell, unto its other end t, on which the least refrangible rays fell, appear tinged with this Series of Colours, violet, indico, blue, green, yellow, orange, red, together with all their intermediate degrees in a continual succession perpetually varying: So that there appeared as many degrees of Colours, as there were sorts of rays differing in refrangibility.

Exper. V.

Now that these Colours could not be changed by refraction, I knew by refracting with a Prism sometime one very little part of this Light, sometimes another very little part, as is described in the 12th Experiment of

Opticks: or, a treatise of the reflexions, refractions, inflexions and colours of light. London, 1704. [Book I, Part II, Prop. II, Theor. II; pp. 87–91.]

the first Book. For by this refraction the Colour of the Light was never changed in the least. . . .

Exper. VI.

And as these Colours were not changeable by refractions, so neither were they by reflexions. For all white, grey, red, yellow, green, blue, violet Bodies . . . in red homogeneal Light appeared totally red, in blue Light totally blue, in green Light totally green, and so of other Colours. . . .

From all which it is manifest, that if the Sun's Light consisted of but one sort of rays, there would be but one Colour in the whole World, nor would it be possible to produce any new Colour by reflexions and refractions, and by consequence that the variety of Colours depends upon the composition of Light.

Definition

The homogeneal light and rays which appear red, or rather make Objects appear so, I call rubrific or red-making; those which make Objects appear yellow, green, blue, and violet, I call yellow-making, green-making, blue-making, violet-making, and so of the rest. And if at any time I speak of light and rays as coloured or endued with Colours I would be understood to speak not philosophically and properly, but grosly, and according to such conceptions as vulgar People in seeing all these Experiments would be apt to frame. For the rays to speak properly are not coloured. In them there is nothing else than a certain power and disposition to stir up a sensation of this or that Colour. For as sound in a Bell or musical String, or other sounding Body, is nothing but a trembling Motion, and in the Air nothing but that Motion propagated from the Object, and in the Sensorium 'tis a Sense of that Motion under the form of sound; so Colours in the Object are nothing but a disposition to reflect this or that sort of rays more copiously than the rest; in the rays they are nothing but their dispositions to propagate this or that Motion into the Sensorium, and in the Sensorium they are Sensations of these Motions under the forms of Colours.

7·9

Denis Diderot

(1713–1784)

Diderot emphasizes the subjectivity of the senses by pointing out how they shape our outlook on the world. His Letter on the blind, for the use of those who see (1749) made this point in part by hinting that a blind man could not be made to believe in a God he could not touch. For this irreverence he was comfortably lodged for some weeks in the Bastille by a reluctant censor yielding to strong clerical pressures. The Letter on the deaf and mute is on the whole less interesting, but it has a special historical interest because this passage is said to have induced Buffon, Condillac, and Bonnet to write, in that order, about the gradual development of mental faculties in a statue endowed at first only with sensibility.

My idea would be to decompose a person, as it were, and to consider what he obtains from each of his senses. I recall that I once engaged in this sort of metaphysical anatomizing, and I thought that of all the senses the eye was most superficial, the ear most arrogant, smell most voluptuous, taste most superstitious and inconstant, touch most profound and most the philosopher. It would make, I think, an interesting gathering, to have five such persons, each of whom had but one sense; there can be no doubt that each would regard all the others as out of their senses, and I leave it to you to consider with what justification. Nevertheless, this is a picture of what is happening in the world all the time: each of us has but one sense, and passes judgment on all. Besides, there is a peculiar observation which might be made on this gathering of five persons, each of whom possesses but one sense; namely, that by means of their faculty of abstraction they could all become mathematicians and understand each other very well, but only in mathematics.

Lettre sur les sourds et muets, à l'usage de ceux qui entendent & qui parlent [A letter on the deaf and mute, for the use of those who hear and speak]. Paris, 1751. [Pp. 22–25.]

7.10

Charles Bell

(1774–1842)

Bell points to the brain, not the sense organ, as the seat of the special qualities of sensation. The Idea was privately printed in only 100 copies, of which only nine can now be found. It failed to arouse the interest which its author had anticipated, and though he invited comments from the "friends" to whom he sent it, he received not one. Chapter 9 gives another selection from it, and there we will speak of the controversy which surrounded, and perhaps still surrounds, this book. The full text is reprinted in the Journal of Anatomy and Physiology, 1868; also in Dennis, except for the doubtless accidental omission of one short paragraph (see below, starting "But there is an occurrence"). It has recently been reprinted in facsimile.

See Battie (24.7, par. 3) for what may well have been the hint which started Bell on this train of thought. When Bell started the work which finally led to writing the Idea, he wrote to his brother that he thought he might write something "on madness," so it is reasonable to suppose that he would have given Battie's treatise a close reading.

The prevailing doctrine of the anatomical schools is, that the whole brain is a common sensorium; that the extremities of the nerves are organized, so that each is fitted to receive a peculiar impression; or that they are distinguished from each other only by delicacy of structure, and by a corresponding delicacy of sensation; that the nerve of the eye, for example, differs from the nerves of touch only in the degree of its sensibility.

It is imagined that impressions, thus differing in kind, are carried along the nerves to the sensorium, and presented to the mind; and that the mind, by the same nerves which receive sensation, sends out the mandate of the will to the moving parts of the body. . . .

In opposition to these opinions, I have to offer reasons for believing . . .

That the external organs of the senses have the matter of the nerves adapted to receive certain impressions, while the corresponding organs of the brain are put in activity by the external excitement: That the idea or perception is according to the part of the brain to which the nerve is attached, and that each organ has a certain limited number of changes to be wrought upon it by the external impression: That the nerves of sense, the nerves of motion, and the vital nerves, are distinct

Idea for a new anatomy of the brain. London, 1811. [Pp. 4–6, 8–12.]

through their whole course, though they seem sometimes united in one bundle; and that they depend for their attributes on the organs of the brain to which they are severally attached. . . .

It is admitted that neither bodies nor the images of bodies enter the brain. It is indeed impossible to believe that colour can be conveyed along a nerve; or the vibration in which we suppose sound to consist can be retained in the brain: but we can conceive, and have reason to believe, that an impression is made upon the organs of the outward senses when we see, or hear, or taste.

In this inquiry it is most essential to observe, that while each organ of sense is provided with a capacity of receiving certain changes to be played upon it, as it were, yet each is utterly incapable of receiving the impressions destined for another organ of sensation.

It is also very remarkable that an impression made on two different nerves of sense, though with the same instrument, will produce two distinct sensations; and the ideas resulting will only have relation to the organ affected. . . .

There are four kinds of Papillae on the tongue. . . . Of these, the Papillae of one kind form the seat of the sense of taste . . . [and another] are the organs of touch in the tongue. When I take a sharp steel point, and touch one of *these* Papillae, I feel the sharpness. The sense of *touch* informs me of the shape of the instrument. When I touch a Papilla of taste, I have no sensation similar to the former. I do not know that a point touches the tongue, but I am sensible of a metallic taste. . . .

In the operation of couching the cataract, the pain of piercing the retina with a needle is not so great as that which proceeds from a grain of sand under the eyelid. And although the derangement of the stomach sometimes marks the injury of an organ so delicate, yet the pain is occasioned by piercing the outward coat, not by the affection of the expanded nerve of vision. . . .

But there is an occurrence during this operation on the eye, which will direct us to the truth: when the needle pierces the eye, the patient has the sensation of a spark of fire before the eye.

. . . Indeed the mere effect of a blow on the head might inform us, that sensation depends on the exercise of the organ affected, not on the impression conveyed to the external organ; for by the vibration caused by the blow, the ears ring, and the eye flashes light, while there is neither light nor sound present.

It may be said, that there is here no proof of the sensation being in the brain more than in the external organ of sense. But when the nerve of a stump is touched, the pain is as if in the amputated extremity. If it be still said that this is no proper example of a peculiar sense existing without its external organ, I offer the following example: when the glans penis is eaten away by an ulcer, and nothing but the base remains, sensation nevertheless remains in the endings of the genital nerve, and an exquisite sense of pleasure. [In the original, this example is given in Latin.]

If light, pressure, galvanism, or electricity produce vision, we must conclude that the idea in the mind is the result of an action excited in the eye or in the brain, not of any thing received, though caused by an impression from without. The operations of the mind are confined not by the limited nature of things created, but by the limited number of our organs of sense.

7.11

Johannes Müller

(1801–1858)

This is Müller's first statement of the doctrine of specific energies, twelve years before the publication of that portion of his Handbuch der Physiologie des Menschen, which dealt with the topic at length. It is clear (despite some confusion which has developed on this subject) that he attributes specificity to the portions of the brain involved in vision (the inner part of the "visual substance") and not merely to the nerves, so that the passage also has implications for study of brain localization. This selection should be compared with the one immediately preceding.

Max Verworn pointed out in his Silliman Lectures (Irritability, 1911) that Müller's doctrine of specific energies was a natural extension of Haller's principle of irritability (see 9.7).

The present investigation is to be regarded as a continuation of the author's previous physiological work on vision. . . . It deals with the higher forms of relationship between the sense of vision and those organs whose vital activity we designate as psychic, or mental. To the author, the soul is only one special form of life among the many which are objects of physiological research. He is therefore convinced that physiological investigation must itself become psychological in its ultimate outcome. Therefore the science of the life of the soul, as a special form of life, is only one part of physiology, in the broad sense of this word. When contrasted to physiology in the narrow sense, this part is called psychology. However, what we ordinarily call psychology is related to the future science of the life of the soul, in the same way that the ordinary physiology of bodily apparatus and functions is related to true physiological

Ueber die phantastischen Gesichtserscheinungen [On visual fantasy phenomena]. Coblenz, 1826. [Pp. iii–iv, 4–7, 16, 33–35.]

science. If the author were to explain in brief what he regards as a scientific treatment of psychology, then—while defending himself against any suspicion of Spinozism—he would find no objection to setting up as an example the last three books of Spinoza's *Ethics*, which deal with the emotions, and in which the psychological content can be regarded as independent of his other doctrines. Even though Spinoza may not be correct in what he says about the emotions, even though his explanation of this aspect of life may not be the *true* one, still there can be no doubt that in method and content they do constitute a real explanation of life, and this is more than can be said for most psychological investigations.

[4] . . . There are in nature some instances of change in which the causal object neither transfers its own potency onto the object which is altered (as in mechanical change), nor does it combine with the potency of the latter object so that a different sort of activity results (as in chemical change), but it serves instead only to bring into expression some quality inherent in the thing which changes, and which is quite independent of the nature of the cause.

[5] Things which behave in this manner, so that causal influences acting on them serve only as *stimuli,* are *organic.* All effects into which causal factors enter only insofar as they are stimuli can be called organic, and the concept of the stimulus should be reserved for this type of causal action. It is all the same whether a muscle is stimulated by galvanism, by chemical agents, by mechanical irritation, or by internal organic stimuli which are transmitted to it sympathetically from other organs. The muscle reacts with movement to anything which stimulates it, to whatever affects it; movement is therefore both the muscle's energy and the way in which it is affected. It is all the same how the eye is stimulated—by pushing or pulling, by galvanism, by pressure, or by stimuli which are sympathetically communicated to it from other organs—the optic nerve will react indifferently to all these different causes, simply as to stimuli, feeling the affect always as a sensation of brightness, and having a sense of darkness when it is at rest. The kind of stimulus is therefore a matter of indifference, so far as the brightness sensation is concerned; it can only *alter* that sensation. The visual substance can have no other states except sensation of brightness and of color when it is active, and of darkness when it is at rest.

[6] This is the situation with respect to all organic reactions. Suppose that something which is chemically active burns the skin destructively. It combines chemically only with the burned, dead tissue, but along the edges of this area the organic substance reacts against the chemical agent in an organic manner, by inflammation. Thus, absolutely nothing has been gained by all the explanations of how nerves act by means of electrical currents: instead, the essential energies of the organ have been overlooked. A sensory nerve reacts to any stimulus, of whatever sort, with its own inherent energy. Pressure, friction, galvanism, and internal

organic stimulation, acting on the optic nerve, produce the sensation of brightness which is proper to it; acting on the auditory nerve, they produce a sensation of tone, which is proper to it; in tactual nerves, they produce feelings of touch. On the other hand, anything that can have any effect on a secretory gland, will produce changes in secretion; if it can have any effect on a muscle, it will produce movement. There is nothing special about galvanism in this regard; like all stimuli, of whatever sort, it can do nothing but stimulate.

[7] We want to discuss this truth further, only insofar as it concerns the optic nerve. Darkness is its state of rest, light and color are its affections. Darkness also is something positive, which can only be experienced where there is an optic nerve. The eye sees brightness and color when stimulated by a mechanical blow or by a galvanic current; stimuli which are communicated to it from other organs are experienced by it as brightness; it sees flashes if pressure is exerted on the brain, or if the brain is filled with an excess of blood (as in a person who is hanged); its vision is misted in ailments of the abdominal organs, which are sympathetically communicated to it; all pathological states of the visual substance find expression in subjective phenomena of brightness and of color.

[8] The only share which can be allowed to external factors, in regard to this specific sensation, is to set up different states of excitation in the visual substance, by virtue of their own variety and their different effects. However, these different states appear only as light, or as colors that are brighter or darker. Among various stimuli, one will cause a sensation that is more yellowish, another one that is more blue, because they set up different states of excitation. One and the same stimulus, like mechanical irritation by pressure, can at different times produce different color phenomena, or degrees of brightness, depending on the intensity of its effect. The visual substance of the eye can have no other states, no other manifestations of life, other than the sensation of darkness, of color, and of brightness. . . .

[24] For purposes of our investigation, we may accept as an established fact that when in the course of its activity any organ of the brain—regardless of whether the proper energy of this organ in itself is sensory, motor, imaginal, or concerned with any other animal function—propagates its own excitation to the visual substance, there will arise in the latter a sympathetic excitation of brightness and color phenomena. This is because any excitatory state of the visual substance, whether aroused sympathetically or immediately, can only express itself as light, color, or darkness.

[25] The theory of visual fantasy phenomena which we now offer is only a consequence of what has been said. If states of excitation in those organs which are concerned with ideation and imagination can be sympathetically propagated to the visual substance . . . the only effect which they can evoke in that substance is of a sort specific to it, that is,

phenomena of light. Therefore if the organ which produces fantasy exerts an influence on the visual substance, because its own activity is very strong, this must be expressed as a light phenomenon. Fantasy, like any other stimulus, can produce no other effect but brightness and color when it acts upon the organ of sensation for brightness and color. . . .

[60] The few observations which have been made concerning the optical delusions of blind persons in a state of madness are extremely important. . . .

Esquirol treated a businessman who was blinded by amaurosis in the forty-first year of a very active life. A few years later he became maniacal, was extremely excitable, and spoke aloud with persons whom he thought he could see and hear. He saw very extraordinary things, which produced facial expressions of lively rapture.

[61] In the Salpêtrière, in 1816, there was a 38-year-old Jewess who was blind and raving mad. She saw the strangest things, and persons whom she knew. After her sudden death, Esquirol found that the optic nerves were atrophied all the distance from the eye to the chiasma. . . .

[63] We make bold to assert: As long as the sensation of darkness has not disappeared, as long as a blind person can still see darkness, *hallucinatory* internal brightness phenomena are still possible. I have never heard of a blind person who could not see darkness. And yet darkness is something positive, and it is only experienced where the visual substance exists, for it is impossible for us to have the experience of darkness in back of ourselves. . . .

[66] . . . The occurrence of fantasy images after destruction of the eyes proves that they have their seat in the deeper immovable portions of the visual substance. . . .

7.12

Hermann von Helmholtz

(1821–1894)

After stating the cochlear or place theory of tone discrimination, Helmholtz goes on in this passage to discuss the general significance of that theory, as well as his three-process theory of color vision. The doctrine of specific energies is given a further logical extension. Compare paragraph 8 in the previous selection.

Die Lehre von den Tonempfindungen als physiologischer Grundlage für die Theorie der Musik [Braunschweig, 1863]. Translated by A. J. Ellis, from the German edition of 1870, as *On the sensations of tone as a physiological basis for the theory of music.* London, 1875. [Pp. 222–224.]

[Ch. VI] Physiologically it should be observed that the present assumption reduces sensations which differ qualitatively according to pitch and quality of tone, to a difference in the nerve fibres which are excited. This is a step similar to that taken in a wider field by Johannes Müller in his theory of the specific energies of sense. He has shewn that the difference in the sensations due to various senses, does not depend on the actions which excite them, but upon the various nervous arrangements which receive them. We can convince ourselves experimentally that in whatever manner the optic nerve and its expansion, the retina of the eye, may be excited, by light, by twitching, by pressure, or by electricity, the result is never anything but a sensation of light, and that the tactual nerves on the contrary never give us sensations of light or of hearing or of taste. The same solar rays which are felt as light by the eye, are felt by the nerves of the hand as heat; the same agitations which are felt by the hand as flutters, are tone to the ear.

Just as the ear apprehends vibrations of different periodic time as tones of different pitch, so does the eye perceive luminiferous vibrations of different periodic time, as different colours, the quickest giving violet and blue, the slowest red. The laws of the mixture of colours led Thomas Young to the hypothesis that there were three kinds of nerve fibres in the eye, for feeling red, for feeling green, and for feeling violet. In reality this assumption gives a very simple and perfectly consistent explanation of all the optical phenomena depending on colour. And by this means the qualitative differences of the sensations of sight are reduced to differences in the nerves which receive the sensations. For the sensations of each individual fibre of the optic nerve there remain only the quantitative difference of greater or less irritation.

The same result is obtained for hearing by the hypothesis to which our investigation of quality of tone has led us. The qualitative difference of pitch and quality of tone is reduced to a difference in the fibres of the nerve receiving the sensation, and for each individual fibre of the nerve there remains only the quantitative differences in the amount of excitement.

. . . The two hypotheses just explained really reduce the processes in the nerves of man's two principal senses, notwithstanding their apparently involved qualitative differences of sensations, to the same simple scheme with which we are familiar in the nerves of motion. Nerves have been often and not unsuitably compared to telegraph wires. Such a wire conducts one kind of electric current and no other; it may be stronger, it may be weaker, it may move in either direction; it has no other qualitative differences. Nevertheless, according to the different kinds of apparatus with which we provide its terminations, we can send telegraphic dispatches, ring bells, explode mines, decompose water, move magnets, magnetise iron, develop light, and so on. So with the nerves. The condition of excitement which can be produced in them and is conducted by them, is, so far as it can be recognised in isolated fibres of a nerve, everywhere the same, but when it is brought to various parts of the brain, or the body, it produces motion, secretions of glands, increase and decrease of the quantity of blood, of redness and of warmth of individual organs, and also sensations of light, of hearing, and so forth. Supposing that every qualitatively different action is produced in an organ of a different kind, to which also separate fibres of nerve must proceed, then the actual process of irritation in individual nerves may always be precisely the same, just as the electrical current in the telegraph wires remains one and the same notwithstanding the various kinds of effects which it produces at its extremities. On the other hand, if we assume that the same fibre of a nerve is capable of conducting different kinds of sensation, we should have to assume that it admits of various kinds of processes of irritation, and this we have been hitherto unable to establish.

In this respect then the view here proposed, like Young's hypothesis for the difference of colours, has a still wider signification for the physiology of the nerves in general.

7.13

Magnus Blix

(1849–1904)

This article is a translation of a paper published two years earlier in a Swedish medical journal. Goldscheider in Germany and Donaldson in the United States independently made the same discovery. Then in 1895, von Frey discovered that very warm objects serve as inadequate stimuli for cold-spots, releasing "paradoxical cold," and the distinctive sensation of "heat" was explained as a summation of response from warm- and cold-spots. However, Blix's quite reasonable expectation that easily identifiable specific end-organs would be found corresponding to spots of differential sensitivity has thus far proved mistaken—a fact which only serves to further emphasize that it is not the end-organ, but the "specific energy" of the nerve (or of its central terminus) which determines the quality of sensation.

The experiments to be discussed take their starting point from Johannes Müller's law of the specific energy of nerves. This law states that an ex-

Experimentelle Beiträge zur Lösung der Frage über die specifische Energie der Hautnerven [Experimental contributions toward solution of the question of the specific energy of the cutaneous nerves]. *Zeitschrift für Biologie,* 20 (1884): 141–156.

cited sensory nerve evokes only one kind of sensation, regardless of the nature of the means of stimulation. . . .

The skin is the seat of several kinds of nerve end-organs. This is apparent not only from its anatomy, but also from the variety of stimuli which are effective on it, and of the resulting sensations. These sensations are usually divided into three classes: sensations of pressure, of temperature, and of pain. . . .

The question arises whether there are different kinds of specific end-organs for pressure and for temperature, or whether these sensations are mediated by the same end-organs. . . .

Guided by these thoughts, I undertook faradic stimulation of the skin, with the strictest possible localization. One pole of a duBois-Reymond induction coil formed a moist conductor, which was spread wide on the skin. The other, on the contrary, was a fine metal point. With this arrangement the induction current goes deep enough to evoke excitation only at the latter pole, assuming that one does not use too strong a current.

It turned out that stimulation did indeed evoke different sensations at different points, and with different intensities of current. . . .

I found it most advantageous to select a strength of current which did not cause pain when the point-electrode touched the skin without noticeable pressure, but did so when it was pressed somewhat more firmly against it. . . .

. . . One thing is plain, that electrical stimulation can produce different sensations at different points of the skin. At one point there is only pain, at another a sensation of cold, at a third a sensation of warmth, at a fourth perhaps a sensation of pressure. Thus it is confirmed that the kind of sensation is not bound to the sort of stimulus used, but depends rather on the specific energy of the activated end-organs. . . .

On the basis of these experiments I venture to state that cold sensations can be released only from certain relatively scattered, sharply limited points, lying more or less deep beneath the surface, which contain nervous end-organs possessing the specific capacity to excite the nerve fiber when they are being cooled. . . .

No great difficulties now stand in the way of answering the question whether the same end-organs can also be excited by being warmed, and whether they will then release a sensation of warmth.

. . . Two brass tubes were fitted into the base of a thin-walled cone made of German silver, the tip of which was somewhat blunted; one of the tubes continued inside the cone almost to its tip. . . . [Using rubber and glass tubing, one of these is connected to a hot water boiler, the other to a bottle of cold water.] By raising or lowering the flask a stream of either hot or cold water can be introduced through the rubber tubes. . . .

With this apparatus one can not only seek out the cold-spots which occur in a given area of the skin . . . but also in the same way demonstrate the existence of analogous warm-spots, that is, isolated small portions of the skin from which sensations of warmth can be released, although the intervening parts of the skin are not sensitive to this form of stimulation.

A decisive test of the main question can now be carried out in the following manner. One can begin by raising the bottle containing the cold water, so that a cooling stream flows through the metal cone. With the tip of the cool cone one finds a cold-spot, and marks its position exactly. Then the bottle is lowered far enough so that hot water from the boiler flows into the cone, until it reaches a temperature of about 50° C., so that it is quite warm to the fingers holding the cone, but not hot. The tip of the cone is then placed on the previously discovered cold-spot. According to Hering's hypothesis, a sensation of warmth should occur. However, experience shows that in general this is not so. The experimentum crucis, which consists in first finding a warm-spot and then trying to release a cold sensation from it, leads to the same negative result. Only exceptionally do warm- and cold-spots lie so near one another that the two opposite temperature sensations can be released from the same point. . . .

On the basis of the facts so established, I venture to state the view that *the different sensations of cold and warmth arise from excitation of separate, specific end-organs in the skin.* Thus it appears that the temperature sense also, as well as the performance of its peripheral organs and nerves, is in perfect harmony with the law of the specific energy of the nerves.

7.14

John Paul Nafe

(1888–1970)

We should have said, in our comment on Blix, that it is perhaps the specific energy of the nerve (or of its central termination) which determines the quality of sensation. Nafe questions such specificity and wishes to narrow the concept of quality. The specific energies issue is still far from resolved, but the reader is invited to consider, for example, the implications of "pleasure zones" in the brain (see 21.13).

An earlier statement of this theory will be found in Nafe's chapter on

The pressure, pain, and temperature senses. In C. Murchison, Ed., *Handbook of general experimental psychology.* Worcester, Mass.: Clark University Press, 1934. Pp. 1037–1087. [Pp. 1037, 1077–78.]

7.14 John Paul Nafe

"The sense of feeling" in what is essentially an earlier edition of this hand-book: The foundations of experimental psychology, *ed. by Carl Murchison,* 1929.

It is often stated that the skin is sensitive to mechanical, chemical, electrical, and thermal stimuli. The most usual stimulus is tension which is brought about in the muscles, both plain and striated, by contraction or by movement caused by direct stimulation such as external pressure. In the viscera tension is usually brought about by distension and in the skin by the establishment of a gradient. The peculiarity of such an experience as hunger lies in the manner of arousal rather than in any distinctive activity of the individual nerve fibers. The activity of the muscle in contraction is accompanied by a pattern of discharge over large numbers of end-organs, a pattern that is not set up in any other manner, and the feelings of hunger depend upon this pattern and not upon specific properties of individual nerves. That particular series of events in a group of end-organs and their nerves results in feelings of hunger. The same nerves and end-organs also are capable of being activated in other patterns, e.g., from external pressure, and when so excited produce a series of discharges that do not arouse an experience of hunger but an experience of pressure. . . .

The patterns of discharges set up in the end-organs involved in sensitivity to warmth and cold evidently are impossible to attain within striated muscle as are the patterns for hunger and nausea in structures other than the musculature of the stomach but this does not involve specificity of the end-organs and nerves. It may well be that the hair-bulb and its nerve termination are incapable of setting up the pattern for pain and the capsulated endings may lie too deep in the tissue of the skin to be involved in a pattern of cutaneous tickle. If the end-organs for hearing were exactly like those of the retina we would never see anything with them, not because they would be specific but because of their location. . . . If thermal effects are mediated by the muscles of the blood vessels [as above contended], there would seem to be only two real modes of stimulation: tension and injury, and, for the end-organs, only tension. With only one type of stimulation possible what room is left for specificity and what need for it? For every different type of stimulus object a different pattern of excitation is set up. What difference would it make if the end-organs were specific? If all pains were alike and all pressures alike, we could perhaps deal with specific fibers but no two pains are alike and no two pressures, so if we grant specificity we must still invoke differences in the pattern of excitation to account for the differences in experience.

This theory has been called "quantitative" to distinguish it from theories which posit difference in experience which are not due to variables capable of quantitative expression and which are incorrectly called "qualities," incorrectly because they are given the attributes of different modalities or different senses, in that different end-organs, nerves, and cortical areas, all specific to the particular type of experience, are posited. As to differences in intensities, extensities, etc., and in mixtures and fusions of qualities, there has been little or no disagreement with the proposition that they are correlated with neurological differences which may be quantitatively expressed. It is the concept of "quality" as defined above that is here challenged for lack of sufficient evidence. The experimental evidence as it now exists forces the hypothesis that all differences in common sensation depend upon quantitative, i.e., temporal and spatial, differences in the patterns of a single fundament, the nervous impulse which, for purposes of analysis, must be taken as the basis of nerve action and psychological experience alike.

Auditory stimuli furnish an analogy: all variations are variations of one element, the air wave and, except for intensity, the temporal patterns in which the waves occur account for every difference from the merest squeak to the most elaborate musical recital. . . .

In sensory feeling, specificity of the pattern of discharge, and hence of the quality (in its proper meaning) of experience, depends upon change in the tissues in which it is aroused. A certain wave of muscular tissue is felt as hunger and is not aroused in any other part of the body, not because of a specific end-organ or nerve that has been excited. In just such a manner, warmth is aroused only by certain movements of vascular muscle, but such a specificity is a concept entirely apart from that of end-organs specific for certain types of stimuli. A cut nerve may set up a feeling of pain without any end-organ whatever, but not without the special conditions existing at the severed end. The result for our theories is to make experience, not a matter of the addition of impulses from certain types of nerves, but a matter of the arrangement of impulses in a system of nerves.

Chapter 8

BRAIN AND SPIRITS

We have already quoted Maudsley's remark (see 3.7) that "he whose brain makes him conscious that he has a brain is not well, but ill." It is therefore not surprising that men should have placed the seat of mind, or soul, in the pounding heart or in the heaving chest before seeking it inside the head. Genesis (6:5) placed man's thought and imagination in the heart, and Aristotle held the same view, considering that the function of the brain was to keep the blood from overheating. Our chapter begins, however, with the earlier statement by Hippocrates on the importance of the brain. Greek medicine transmuted the pneuma of the philosophers into physiological pneumas or spirits, and Galen's formulation of this doctrine exercised a dominating influence over medical and psychological thinking for 1,500 years. Weakened but not vanquished by Harvey's discovery of the circulation of the blood, the animal spirits did not finally evaporate from medical theory until the advance in the knowledge of electricity provided a plausible alternative.

This chapter includes a sampling of hypotheses regarding "the seat of the soul," although the localization of specific functions is reserved for Chapter 10.

8.1

Hippocrates

(*c.* 460–*c.* 377 B.C.)

It was a widespread belief in ancient times that any trance state represents a form of divine visitation which brings with it a gift of prophecy. Even in our own day, the occult medium ostensibly enters a trance, speaks and acts without voluntary control, and professedly retains no memory of what transpires. It is therefore easily understandable that epilepsy should have been regarded as a "sacred disease." Hippocrates speaks out against this superstition in one of the most important of all the Hippocratic writings, and one which is usually considered to be authentic, and in any event not a later invention. He attributes the disease to brain pathology, and in stating his case, he explains the importance of the brain for behavior generally. The brain, however, is in its turn dependent for its healthy state on a proper balance of the humors, and a proper supply of air, or pneuma.

Thus is this disease formed and prevails from those things which enter into and go out of the body, and it is not more divine than other diseases. And men ought to know that from nothing else but thence (*from the brain*) come joys, delights, laughter and sports, and sorrows, griefs, despondency, and lamentations. And by this, in an especial manner, we acquire wisdom and knowledge, and see and hear, and know what are foul and what are fair, what are bad and what are good, what are sweet, and what unsavory; some we discriminate by habit, and some we perceive by their utility. By this we distinguish objects of relish and disrelish, according to the seasons; and the same things do not always please us. And by the same organ we become mad and delirious, and fears and terrors assail us, some by night, and some by day, and dreams and untimely wanderings, and cares that are not suitable, and ignorance of present circumstances, desuetude, and unskilfulness. All these things we endure from the brain, when it is not healthy, but is more hot, more cold, more moist, or more dry than natural, or when it suffers from any other preternatural and unusual affection. And we become mad from humidity (*of the brain*). For when it is more moist than natural, it is necessarily put into motion, and the affection being moved, neither the sight nor hearing can be at rest, and the tongue speaks in accordance with the sight and hearing. As long as the brain is at rest, the man enjoys

On the sacred disease. In *The genuine works of Hippocrates.* Translated from the Greek by Francis Adams. Baltimore: Williams & Wilkins, 1939. Pp. 347–360. [Pp. 357–360.] First published by the Sydenham Society in 1849.

8.1 Hippocrates

his reason, but the depravement of the brain arises from phlegm and bile, either of which you may recognize in this manner: Those who are mad from phlegm are quiet, and do not cry out nor make a noise; but those from bile are vociferous, malignant, and will not be quiet, but are always doing something improper. If the madness be constant, these are the causes thereof. But if terrors and fears assail, they are connected with derangement of the brain and derangement is owing to its being heated. And it is heated by bile when it is determined to the brain along the blood-vessels running from the trunk; and fear is present until it returns again to the veins and trunk, when it ceases. He is grieved and troubled when the brain is unseasonably cooled and contracted beyond its wont. This it suffers from phlegm, and from the same affection the patient becomes oblivious. He calls out and screams at night when the brain is suddenly heated. The bilious endure this. But the phlegmatic are not heated, except when much blood goes to the brain, and creates an ebullition. Much blood passes along the aforesaid veins. But when the man happens to see a frightful dream and is in fear as if awake, then his face is in a greater glow, and the eyes are red when the patient is in fear. And the understanding meditates doing some mischief, and thus it is affected in sleep. But if, when awakened, he returns to himself, and the blood is again distributed along the aforesaid veins, it ceases. In these ways I am of opinion that the brain exercises the greatest power in the man. This is the interpreter to us of those things which emanate from the air, when it (*the brain*) happens to be in a sound state. But the air supplies sense to it. And the eyes, the ears, the tongue and the feet, administer such things as the brain cogitates. For inasmuch as it is supplied with air, does it impart sense to the body. It is the brain which is the messenger to the understanding. For when the man draws the breath (*pneuma*) into himself, it passes first to the brain, and thus the air is distributed to the rest of the body, leaving in the brain its acme, and whatever has sense and understanding. For if it passed first to the body and last to the brain, then having left in the flesh and veins the judgment, when it reached the brain it would be hot, and not at all pure, but mixed with the humidity from the fleshy parts and the blood, so as to be no longer pure. Wherefore, I say, that it is the brain which interprets the understanding. But the diaphragm has obtained its name {*phrenes*} from accident and usage, and not from reality or nature, for I know no power which it possesses, either as to sense or understanding, except that when the man is affected with unexpected joy or sorrow, it throbs and produces palpitations, owing to its thinness, and as having no belly to receive anything good or bad that may present themselves to it, but it is thrown into commotion by both these, from its natural weakness. It then perceives beforehand none of those things which occur in the body, but has received its name vaguely and without any proper reason, like the parts about the heart, which are called auricles, but which contribute nothing towards hearing. Some say that we think with the heart, and that this is the part which is grieved, and experiences care. But it is not so; only it contracts like the diaphragm, and still more so for the same causes. For veins from all parts of the body run to it, and it has valves, so as to perceive if any pain or pleasurable emotion befall the man. For when grieved the body necessarily shudders, and is contracted, and from excessive joy it is affected in like manner. Wherefore the heart and the diaphragm are particularly sensitive, they have nothing to do, however, with the operations of the understanding, but of all these the brain is the cause.

8.2

Galen

(131–200)

Galen states that the psychic pneuma or animal spirits are generated from a mixture of air which has been introduced by way of the anterior ventricles and vital pneuma, already in the blood, which has been further refined in the rete mirabile. (This is a network of blood vessels found in ungulates or hoofed animals, such as pigs and goats, which he used extensively in dissection, but not in men. It is not known whether Galen ever dissected a man, though he did dissect some apes.) Given the importance of pneuma, it is natural that the ventricles should seem the most important structures in the brain. This account continued to be influential even into early modern times. This selection also gives Galen's unfavorable judgment on a theory that the pineal gland regulates the flow of spirits into the fourth ventricle—a theory oddly like that which Descartes would advance in the sixteenth century. The parencephalis is of course the cerebellum.

{Book VIII} 10. Now let me explain first about the ventricles of the encephalon, about the size, location, and shape of each, about the channels that connect them with one another, and the total number of ventricles; afterwards I shall speak of the parts lying upon and beside them. The two anterior [lateral] ventricles perform inspiration, expiration, and the blowing out of the breath from the encephalon. I have demonstrated this elsewhere. I have also shown that they elaborate and prepare the psychic pneuma for it. . . .

On the usefulness of the parts of the body. Translated from the Greek by Margaret Tallmadge May. Ithaca, N.Y.: Cornell University Press, 1968. [Pp. 412–414, 416–420, 430–433.] Copyright © 1968 by Cornell University Press. Used by permission of the publisher.

11. Now since all the nerves distributed to parts of the body below the head grow out either from the *parencephalis* or from the spinal medulla, the ventricle of the *parencephalis* had to be of considerable size and had to receive the psychic pneuma already elaborated in the anterior [*lateral*] ventricles. Hence a canal had to be formed leading from these two into the ventricle of the *parencephalis,* which is indeed seen to be large. The canal entering it from the anterior ventricles is also very large and forms the only connection between the encephalon [here the cerebrum] and *parencephalis.* . . .

12. This is enough to have said about the shape of the ventricles. As regards their size, I may say that not only here but also throughout the body the cavities receiving the more turbid substances are properly larger and those receiving substances that are more potent, as one might say, are smaller. . . . Hence the ventricle of the parencephalis [the fourth ventricle] too has with good reason been made smaller than the anterior [lateral] ventricles, and even if the space [the third ventricle] common to the anterior ventricles should be counted separately and reckoned as a fourth ventricle of the encephalon, the ventricle of the *parencephalis* [the fourth ventricle] is also smaller than that one. . . .

14. Coming back, then, to the subject of the parts behind the middle [third] ventricle, let us examine the body [the pineal body] which lies at the beginning of the canal connecting the middle ventricle with the posterior encephalon and which is called κωνάριον (little pine cone) by those versed in anatomy, to see for what usefulness it was formed. This body is a gland to judge by its substance, but in shape it very closely resembles a pine cone, and from this it takes its name. Some think it has the same usefulness as the pylorus of the stomach; for they say that the pylorus too is a gland and prevents the nutriment from being taken over from the stomach into the thin intestine before it is concocted, and that this gland, the pineal body, standing at the beginning of the canal that transmits the pneuma from the middle [third] ventricle to the one in the *parencephalis* [the fourth ventricle] is a guardian and housekeeper, as it were, regulating the quantity that is transmitted. . . .

The notion that the pineal gland is what regulates the passage of the pneuma is the opinion of those who are ignorant of the action of the vermiform epiphysis [*vermis superior cerebelli*] and who give more than due credit to the gland. Now if the pineal body were a part of the encephalon itself, as the pylorus is part of the stomach, its favorable location would enable it alternately to open and close the canal because it would move in harmony with the contractions and expansions of the encephalon. Since this gland, however, is by no means a part of the encephalon and is attached not to the inside but to the outside of the ventricle, how could it, having no motion of its own, have so great an effect on the canal? But perhaps some will say, "What is to prevent it from having a motion of its own?" What, indeed, other than that if it had, the gland on account of its faculty and worth would have been assigned to us as an encephalon, and the encephalon itself would be only a body divided by many canals and would be like an instrument that was suited to be of service to a part formed by Nature to move and capable of doing so? Why need I mention how ignorant and stupid these opinions are? . . .

{Book IX} 4. The plexus called retiform [*rete mirabile*] by anatomists . . . encircles the gland [the hypophysis] itself and extends far to the rear; for nearly the whole base of the encephalon has this plexus lying beneath it. . . .

Well, what is this wonderful thing, and for what purpose has it been made by a Nature who does nothing in vain? If you remember what I said and demonstrated when I was explaining the teachings of Hippocrates and Plato, you will derive from it no small assurance in answering these questions, and you will easily find the usefulness of this plexus. For wherever Nature wishes material to be completely elaborated, she arranges for it to spend a long time in the instruments concocting it. Now I have already pointed this out in several other places, but for our present needs it will be enough for me to cite one example of the arrangement in question by reminding you of the varicose convolutions in which the blood and pneuma are rendered suitable to form the semen. For the veins and arteries there are intricately coiled and in the first part of the coils contain pure blood; in the last part, however, near the testes, the humor contained in them is no longer perfectly red but is already whitish and needs little to complete the change into the substance of the semen, a change which is added by the testes themselves. But the retiform plexus is as much more intricately coiled than the varicose plexus as the elaboration needed by the psychic pneuma in the encephalon is more perfect than that needed by the semen. I was right, then, when I showed . . . that the vital pneuma passing up through the arteries is used as the proper material for the generation of psychic pneuma in the encephalon. . . .

In those commentaries I have given the demonstrations proving that the rational soul is lodged in the encephalon; that this is the part with which we reason; that a very large quantity of psychic pneuma is contained in it; and that this pneuma acquires its own special quality from elaboration in the encephalon. Here we see that both the retiform plexus and other features of its construction are in wonderful harmony with those correct demonstrations. . . .

. . . Hence, remaining for a very long time in the arteries, the pneuma is elaborated, but when its elaboration is complete, it falls at once into the ventricles of the encephalon; for it ought not to be delayed longer, nor should it escape before it has been elaborated.

8.3

Gregory of Nyssa

(c. 335–c. 395)

The early Christian apologists faced the task of reconciling the accepted medical views of their own time with the doctrine of an immaterial and immortal soul. One of the most effective was Gregory of Nyssa, a father of the Eastern Church, who played a prominent part in the council of Constantinople. He explains the apparent dependence of the mind on the body by arguing that the body is an imperfect instrument which limits the expression of the mind. (Compare his discussion of the hand, 4.3.) This selection gives most of Chapter 12 and a portion of Chapter 14; for parts of the intervening chapter, dealing with dreams, see 19.4.

{XII} 1. Let there be an end, then, of all the vain and conjectural discussion of those who confine the intelligible energy to certain bodily organs; of whom some lay it down that the ruling principle is in the heart, while others say that the mind resides in the brain, strengthening such opinions by some plausible superficialities. For he who ascribes the principal authority to the heart makes its local position evidence of his argument (because it seems that it somehow occupies the middle position in the body), on the ground that the motion of the will is easily distributed from the centre to the whole body, and so proceeds to operation; and he makes the troublesome and passionate disposition of man a testimony for his argument, because such affections seem to move this part sympathetically. Those, on the other hand, who consecrate the brain to reasoning, say that the head has been built by nature as a kind of citadel of the whole body, and that in it the mind dwells like a king, with a body-guard of senses surrounding it like messengers and shield-bearers. And these find a sign of their opinion in the fact that the reasoning of those who have suffered some injury to the membrane of the brain is abnormally distorted, and that those whose heads are heavy with intoxication ignore what is seemly.

2. Each of those who uphold these views puts forward some reasons of a more physical character on behalf of his opinion concerning the ruling principle. One declares that the motion which proceeds from the understanding is in some way akin to the nature of fire, because fire and the understanding are alike in perpetual motion; and since heat is allowed to have its source in the region of the heart, he says on this ground that the motion of mind is compounded with the mobility of

On the making of man (for details, see 4.3). [Pp. 397–398, 402–403.]

heat, and asserts that the heart, in which heat is enclosed, is the receptacle of the intelligent nature. The other declares that the cerebral membrane (for so they call the tissue that surrounds the brain) is as it were a foundation or root of all the senses, and hereby makes good his own argument, on the ground that the intellectual energy cannot have its seat save in that part where the ear, connected with it, comes into concussion with the sounds that fall upon it, and the sight (which naturally belongs to the hollow of the place where the eyes are situated) makes its internal representation by means of the images that fall upon the pupils, while the qualities of scents are discerned in it by being drawn in through the nose, and the sense of taste is tried by the test of the cerebral membrane, which sends down from itself, by the vertebrae of the neck, sensitive nerve-processes to the isthmoidal passage, and unites them with the muscles there.

3. I admit it to be true that the intellectual part of the soul is often disturbed by prevalence of passions; and that the reason is blunted by some bodily accident so as to hinder its natural operation; and that the heart is a sort of source of the fiery element in the body, and is moved in correspondence with the impulses of passion; and moreover, in addition to this, I do not reject (as I hear very much the same account from those who spend their time on anatomical researches) the statement that the cerebral membrane (according to the theory of those who take such a physiological view), enfolding in itself the brain, and steeped in the vapours that issue from it, forms a foundation for the senses; yet I do not hold this for a proof that the incorporeal nature is bounded by any limits of place.

4. Certainly we are aware that mental aberrations do not arise from heaviness of head alone, but skilled physicians declare that our intellect is also weakened by the membranes that underlie the sides being affected by disease, when they call the disease frenzy, since the name given to those membranes is {phrenes}. And the sensation resulting from sorrow is mistakenly supposed to arise at the heart; for while it is not the heart, but the entrance of the belly that is pained, people ignorantly refer the affection to the heart. . . .

5. Furthermore, the opposite affection, that, I mean, of mirth and laughter, contributes to establish the argument; for the pores of the body, in the case of those who are dissolved in mirth by hearing something pleasant, are also somehow dissolved and relaxed. . . . {Consequently} some air is drawn in through them into the interior, and thence again expelled by nature through the passage of the mouth, while all the viscera (and especially, as they say, the liver) join in expelling this air by a certain agitation and throbbing motion; whence it comes that nature, contriving to give facility for the exit of the air, widens the passage of the mouth, extending the cheeks on either side round about the breath; and the result is called laughter.

6. We must not, then, on this account ascribe the ruling principle any more to the liver than we must think, because of the heated state of the blood about the heart in wrathful dispositions, that the seat of the mind is in the heart; but we must refer these matters to the character of our bodily organization, and consider that the mind is equally in contact with each of the parts according to a kind of combination which is indescribable. . . .

8. And although I am aware that the intellectual energies are blunted, or even made altogether ineffective in a certain condition of the body, I do not hold this a sufficient evidence for limiting the faculty of the mind by any particular place, so that it should be forced out of its proper amount of free space by any inflammations that may arise in the neighbouring parts of the body (for such an opinion is a corporeal one, that when the receptacle is already occupied by something placed in it, nothing else can find place there); for the intelligible nature neither dwells in the empty spaces of bodies, nor is extruded by encroachments of the flesh; but since the whole body is made like some musical instrument, just as it often happens in the case of those who know how to play, but are unable, because the unfitness of the instrument does not admit of their art, to show their skill (for that which is destroyed by time, or broken by a fall, or rendered useless by rust or decay, is mute and inefficient, even if it be breathed upon by one who may be an excellent artist in flute-playing); so too the mind, passing over the whole instrument, and touching each of the parts in a mode corresponding to its intellectual activities, according to its nature, produces its proper effect on those parts which are in a natural condition, but remains inoperative and ineffective upon those which are unable to admit the movement of its art, for the mind is somehow naturally adapted to be in close relation with that which is in a natural condition, but to be alien from that which is removed from nature.

{XIV} 1. But we have wandered far from our subject, for the purpose of our argument was to show that the mind is not restricted to any part of the body, but is equally in touch with the whole, producing its motion according to the nature of the part which is under its influence. There are cases, however, in which the mind even follows the bodily impulses, and becomes, as it were, their servant; for often the bodily nature takes the lead by introducing either the sense of that which gives pain or the desire for that which gives pleasure, so that it may be said to furnish the first beginnings, by producing in us the desire for food, or, generally, the impulse towards some pleasant thing; while the mind, receiving such an impulse, furnishes the body by its own intelligence with the proper means towards the desired object. Such a condition, indeed, does not occur in all, save in those of a somewhat slavish disposition, who bring the reason into bondage to the pleasures of sense by allowing them the alliance of their mind; but in the case of more perfect men this does not happen; for the mind takes the lead, and chooses the expedient course by reason and not by passion, while their nature follows in the tracks of its leader.

2. But since our argument discovered in our vital faculty three different varieties—one which receives nourishment without perception, another which at once receives nourishment and is capable of perception, but is without the reasoning activity, and a third rational, perfect, and co-extensive with the whole faculty—so that among these varieties the advantage belongs to the intellectual,—let no one suppose on this account that in the compound nature of man there are three souls welded together, contemplated each in its own limits, so that one should think man's nature to be a sort of conglomeration of several souls. The true and perfect nature is naturally one, the intellectual and immaterial, which mingles without material nature by the agency of the senses; but all that is of material nature, being subject to mutation and alteration, will, if it should partake of the animating power, move by way of growth: if, on the contrary, it should fall away from the vital energy, it will reduce its motion to destruction.

3. Thus, neither is there perception without material substance, nor does the act of perception take place without the intellectual faculty.

8.4

Andreas Vesalius

(1514–1564)

Vesalius—a Belgian who studied at Paris, became professor at Padua, and later physician to emperor Charles V—personifies the resurgence of anatomical knowledge based on dissection. Although he rejected many of Galen's errors in anatomy, Vesalius accepted the Galenic doctrine of spirits and of the brain's role in their concoction. Certainly he shows more respect for Galen than for many of his own contemporaries who assign higher mental faculties to parts of the brain. He seems not only to question their theories, but the very possibility of relating human reason to the brain. His De humani corporis fabrica [On the structure of the human body] is prized especially for its magnificent woodblocks, including the famous frontispiece which shows Vesalius proudly conducting a dissection before a great throng

De humani corporis fabrica [On the structure of the human body, 1543]. Portions translated by Charles Singer, as *Vesalius on the human brain*. London: Oxford University Press, 1952. [Pp. 1–7, 39–40.]

of spectators, instead of merely lecturing while leaving the dissection to butchers.

The belief in "animal spirits" as the controlling force of all behavior which men have in common with animals, along with faith in an incorporeal reason which man alone possesses, provided both theologians and physicians with the basis for a dual psychology permitting emphasis on one aspect or the other.

There is in the substance of the heart the power of the *vital spirit*. In the liver is the faculty of the *natural spirit*. The liver produces thick dark blood and from that the natural spirit; while the heart produces [thin light] blood which impetuously rushes through the body with the vital spirit, from which the inner organs draw their proper substances, by channels appropriate to all the bodily parts. So too the brain—containing a matter appropriate to its own function—produces, at the proper places and by those instruments which serve its function, the finest and subtlest of all [the three spirits, namely] the *animal spirit*. This it uses partly for the divine operations of the Reigning Soul, partly however it distributes it continuously to the organs of sense and motion through the nerves, as through little tubes. These organs are thus never without the spirit which is the chief author of their function, just as liver and heart supply all parts with their own proper substances (so long as man is in good health), though not always in identical amounts and quality.

We have shown in Book IV that the nerves originate in the brain. . . . They deliver the spirit, which the brain has prepared, to those instruments to which it is to be conveyed. . . . The vital spirit supplies matter for the animal spirit, for it inundates by numerous arteries the two membranes of the brain with things that it carries and further with that air which, as we have explained, is drawn to the brain by breathing.

. . . Moreover, the air which we inhale is passed through very narrow, very curved, and very winding vessels in the membranes of the brain. It is refined by this arduous passage and, being so prepared, is sent up the brain where it finds entrance, penetrating into the right, left, and middle [= third] ventricles. Thus the vital spirit, which abounds in all the vessels or ducts of the cerebral membranes, is also very plentiful in the ventricles. . . .

From the air which has entered the brain, and from that vital spirit which, by its devious course, becomes progressively more assimilated in the ventricles to the action of the brain, the animal spirit is elaborated by the cerebral power (*virtus*). We believe that this power depends on the opportune balancing of the elements of the brain substance.

Further, in the third ventricle a portion of this animal spirit is carried . . . into that ventricle [= fourth ventricle] which is formed partly by the cavity of the cerebellum and partly by that of the dorsal marrow. From this a portion of the animal spirit is distributed to the dorsal marrow and thus to the nerves which spring therefrom. But from the other ventricles, so we believe, the spirit is distributed into the nerves which arise in their proximity [= cranial nerves] and so into the organs of sensation and voluntary motion. . . .

I can in some degree follow the brain's functions in dissections of living animals, with sufficient probability and truth, but I am unable to understand how the brain can perform its office of imagining, meditating, thinking, and remembering. . . .

If by accurate and painstaking examination of the parts of the brain, and from an observation of the other parts of the body, the use of which is obvious even to one little practised in dissection, some analogy were traceable, or if I could reach any probable conclusion, I would set it out, if I could do so without injury to our Most Holy Religion (*fidei*). For who—O, Immortal God—can fail to be astonished at the host of contemporary philosophers and even theologians who detract ridiculously from the divine and most wonderful contrivances of man's brain. For they fabricate . . . some image of the brain, while they refuse to see that structure which the Maker of Nature has wrought, with incredible foresight, to accommodate it to the actions of the body. . . . {Here Vesalius recalls his experience as a student with the *Margarita Philosophica* (see 10.1)}.

Such are the inventions of those who never look into our Maker's ingenuity in the building of the human body! . . .

But what impiety can such a description of the uses of the ventricles (as it concerns the powers of the Reigning Soul) produce in ignorant minds not yet confirmed in our Most Holy Religion! For such [ignorant ones] will examine carefully (even though I myself were silent) the brains of quadrupeds. These closely resemble those of men in all their parts. Should we on that account ascribe to these [beasts] every power of reason, and even a rational soul, on the basis of such doctrines of the theologians?

Certainly in the brain of sheep, goat, ox, cat, ape, dog, and of such birds as I have dissected, there is a shaping of the parts corresponding to that of the human brain, and specifically is this so of the ventricles. There is hardly any difference that we have detected in bulk, [though] the brains do vary according to the intelligence with which the animals are endowed. For to man has been given the largest brain; next after him the ape, the dog, and so on, according to the order that we have learned of the power of reason in animals. And to man's lot falls a brain not only bigger in proportion to his bulk of body, but actually bigger than the brain of any other animal. The brain of man surpasses two brains of oxen, horses, or donkeys. . . .

Now I do not deny that the ventricles bring the animal spirit into being, but I hold that this explains nothing about the faculties of the Reigning Soul. Yet those men who glory in the name of theologians, believing themselves thereby immune from censure, so assign them. [This last sentence omitted in second edition.] All our contemporaries, so far as I can understand them, deny to apes, dogs, horses, sheep, cattle, and other animals, the main powers of the Reigning Soul—not to speak of other [powers]—and attribute to man alone the faculty of reasoning; and ascribe this faculty in equal degree to all men. And yet we clearly see in dissecting that men do not excel those animals by [possessing] any special cavity [in the brain]. Not only is the number [of ventricles] the same, but also all the other things [in the brain] are similar, except only in size and in the complete consonance [of the parts] for virtue.

8.5

René Descartes

(1596–1650)

A century after Vesalius, the influence of the Galenic system was still strong in the speculations of Descartes. He attributed the brain's effects (which for him included governance of all vital and voluntary movements, but not truly "mental" phenomena) to the movement of spirits into the neural tubes. Movements of the pineal gland direct these spirits (see 9.4). This function of the gland had been stated earlier in De l'homme, but that work was not published until a dozen years after Descartes' death, and the first clear statement of it was in his little book on the passions.

This is a supreme example of rationalistic argument, but not too different from Lotze's argument two centuries later (6.7) that since mind is unextended, our perception of space must be founded on some quality of experience which is independent of spatial extension.

[31] It is also necessary to know, that although the soul be joyned to all the body, yet there is some part in that body wherein shee exercises her functions more peculiarly than all the rest; and it is commonly believed that this part is the brain, or, it may bee, the heart: the brain, because thither tend the organs of the senses; and the heart, because therein the Passions are felt; but having searched this businesse care-

Les passions de l'âme. Amsterdam, 1649. Translated anonymously, as The passions of the soule. London, 1650. [Pp. 25–27.]

fully, me thinks I have plainly found out, that that part of the body wherein the soul immediately exercises her functions is not a jot of the heart; nor yet all the brain, but only the most interiour part of it, which is a certain very small kernell, situated in the middle of the substance of it, and so hung on the top of the conduit by which the spirits of its anteriour cavities have communication with those of the posteriour, whose least motions in it cause the course of the spirits very much to change, and reciprocally, the least alterations befalling the course of the spirits, cause the motions of the kernell very much to alter.

[32] The reason which perswades me that the soul can have no other place in the whole body but this kernell, where shee immediately exercises for {her} functions is, for that I see: all the other parts of our brain are paired, as also we have two eyes, two hands, two ears: lastly, all the organs of our exteriour senses are double: and forasmuch as we have but one onely, and single thought of one very thing at one and the same time, it must necessarily be that there is some place where the two images that come from the two eyes, or the two other impressions that come from any single object through the double organs of the other senses, have some where to meet in one, before they come to the soul, that they may not represent two objects in stead of one; and it

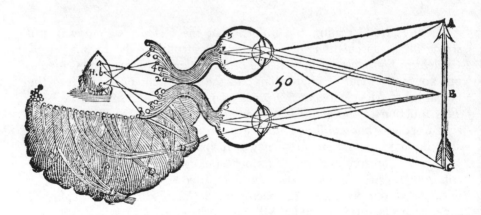

may bee easily conceived, that these images, or other impressions joyn together in this kernell by intercourse of the spirits that fill the cavities of the brain; but there is no other place in the body where they can be so united, unless it be granted that they are in this kernell.

8.6

Niels Steno

(1648–1686)

At the time when Descartes' De l'homme was published, the absurdity of
some of its anatomical assumptions had already become apparent to all
informed persons. The facts were clearly set forth by Niels Steno, a Danish
naturalist whose most important contribution was to pioneer the science
of paleontology, in a notable lecture delivered at Paris in 1665.

The Ventricles or Cavities of the Brain are no less unknown than its
Substance. They who place the Animal Spirits there, think they are as
much in the right as they who make them the Receptacles of the Excrements; but they are both equally puzzled, when they are desired to
explain the Origin of these Spirits and Excrements. . . .

Among those who place the Animal Spirits in the Ventricles, some
make them pass from the anterior to the posterior Ventricles, there to
meet with the Entries of the Nerves, while others affirm that these Entries are in the anterior Ventricles. . . .

We are still more uncertain about what relates to the Animal Spirits.
Are they Blood, or a particular Substance separated from the Chyle by
the Glands of the Mesentery? Or may they not be derived from a Lym-
phatic Serum? Some compare them to Spirit of Wine, and it may be
doubted whether they are not the Matter of Light. Our common dissections cannot clear up any of these difficulties. . . .

M. Descartes knew too well how imperfect an History we have of
the Human Body, to attempt an Exposition of its true Structure; and
accordingly in his *Tractatus de Homine*, his Design is only to explain
a Machine capable of performing all the Functions done by Man. Some
of his Friends have indeed expressed themselves on this Subject differently from him; but it is evident from the beginning of that Work, that
he intended no more than what I have said; and in this sense, it may
justly be said that *M. Descartes* has gone beyond all the other Philosophers. He is the only Person who has explained mechanically all the
human Actions, and especially those of the Brain. The other Philosophers describe to us the Human Body itself. *M. Descartes* speaks only
of a Machine, but in such a manner, as to convince us of the insufficiency
of all that had been said before him, and to teach us a Method of

Discours sur l'anatomie du cerveau [1669]. Reprinted in facsimile, along with a 1733
English translation by G. Douglas, as Nicolaus Steno: *A dissertation on the anatomy
of the brain.* Copenhagen, 1950. [Pp. 4–5, 9–11, 16.]

inquiring into the uses of the Parts with the same evidence with which he demonstrates the Parts of his Machine called a Man, which none had done before him.

We must not therefore condemn *M. Descartes*, though his System of the Brain should not be found altogether agreeable to experience; his excellent Genius which shines no where more than in his *Tractatus de Homine* casts a Veil over the Mistakes of his Hypotheses, especially since even Vesalius himself and other Anatomists of the first rank, are not altogether free from such Mistakes. And since we can forgive these great Men their Errors, who passed the greatest part of their lives in dissecting, why should not *Descartes* meet with the same Indulgence, who has happily imployed his time in other Speculations?

The respect which I and all the World owe to such superior Geniuses, would have inclined me to continue only to admire this Treatise as containing the Description of a fine Machine invented by the Author, if I had not met with several Persons who would make us believe that it is a faithful relation of the most secret Springs of the real Human Body. Since these Persons are not convinced by *Silvius*'s repeated Demonstrations that *M. Descartes*'s Descriptions do not agree with what appears in dissecting the Human Body, I find myself obliged to point out some Parts of his System, without relating the whole, in which they must see, if they have a mind to be instructed, the vast difference there is between *Descartes*'s imaginary Machine, and the real Machine of the Human Body. . . .

Such of *M. Descartes*'s Friends who look upon his Man only as a Machine, will be so good as to believe that I do not here speak against his Machine, the contrivance of which I have always admired; but as for those who pretend to demonstrate that *M. Descartes*'s Man is made like other Men; Anatomical Observations may easily convince them that this is a fruitless attempt.

8.7

Thomas Willis

(1621–1675)

Willis, who coined the word "neurology," devoted himself singlemindedly to study of the nervous system, and he runs the gamut from pioneering contributions to comparative neuroanatomy to equally decisive contribu-

[*De anima brutorum*, etc., 1672.] *Two discourses concerning the soul of brutes, which is that of the vital and sensitive of man.* Englished by S. Pordage. London, 1683. [Pp. 24–25, 27.]

tions to psychiatry. *Willis represents the highest point reached by the medical psychologists of the renaissance before John Locke, who had studied medicine under him at Oxford, started a new era by expressly excluding physiological considerations from his* Essay on Human Understanding. (16.4). *With Willis (and his French contemporary Vieussens), the brain's complex structure begins to receive the attention it deserves. The spirits are still there, but they are not concocted or stored in the ventricles, which have become mere sinks for waste; they are produced in the cortex, stored in gray matter there and elsewhere. Despite the formal and doubtless sincerely intended exclusion of matters relating to the incorporeal soul, all behavior is in practice governed by this corporeal soul which men share with animals.*

Most readers would more readily recognize the "streaked bodies" and "callous body" of the translation if they were allowed to retain their Latin names: corpora striata *and* corpus callosum.

Therefore the Animal Spirits . . . are most subtil Bodies, and highly active, instilled from the inkindled Blood into the Brain, and its Appendix, which partly of their own nature, for as much as they are lucid and aerial, and partly from the agreeable furniture of the Organs, for that they are shut up within Passages, as it were Pipes and other Machines, abound with both an objective Virtue, by which many rays of Light promptly meet together in the Images of all sensible things, and effect the sension of every Kind, and also, an Active {virtue}, by which the loco-motive powers, and also the acts of the Spasmodic Affections, are performed, beyond the forces or Instincts of wind, or any blast shut up in machines. . . .

. . . In the Animal Government, altho the Spirits are disposed, as it were an Army spread abroad thorow the whole Field, yet we say, that they obtain Orders and Offices, one thing in this part, and something different in that. In every one of these we have noted, as it were a double Aspect or Gesture, in the Provinces in the Medullary shanks of the Head, in the Nerves and also nervous Fibres, to wit, one of Begetting and Dispensing, and another of Exercise and Government.

As to the first, we have shown, that the animal spirits being procreated wholly in the Cortical or Barky substances of the Brain and Cerebel, do descend by and by into the middle or marrowy parts, and there are kept in great plenty, for the businesses of the Superiour Soul; in the mean time, a sufficient stock of these, gently flowing from this highest Province into the oblong and Spinal Marrow, and thence into the Nerves & Nervous Shoots, actuates all these passages, and blows them up into a certain Tensity. Lastly, a sufficient plenty of Spirits, distilling forth from the ends of the Nerves, enter into the nervous Fibres, planted in the Muscles, Membranes, and Viscera, and so constitute them, the proper and immediate Organs of the Sence and Motion. After this manner, the Region of the whole Sensitive Soul being viewed, if we would describe its *Idea* or Image, we must altogether represent the same Figure and Dimension, and the whole Head with its System and Appendix; so that as we may behold all these parts, shadowed in the same image, we ought to frame at once, the *Hypostasis* of this Soul, adequate and Co-extended to them.

As to the several sorts of Offices and Exercises of the Spirits, so planted in distinct Provinces, First, we deservedly attribute to them a two-fold Aspect, to wit, inward for Sense, and outward for Motion: But more particularly, we may conceive the middle or Marrow part of the brain, as it were the inferiour Chamber of the Soul, glased with dioptric Looking-Glasses; in the Penetralia or inmost parts of which, the Images or Pictures of all sensible things, being sent or intromitted by the Passages of the Nerves, as it were by Pipes or strait holes, pass first of all thorow the streaked Bodyes, as it were an objective Glass, and then they are represented upon the Callous Body, as it were upon a white Wall; and so induce a Perception, and a certain Imagination of the thing felt: Which Images or Pictures there expressed, as often as they import nothing besides the mere Knowledg of the Object, then by and by further progressing, as it were by another waving, from the Callous Body towards the Cortix or shell of the Brain, and entring into its folds, the phantasie vanishing, they Constitute the memory or remembrance of a Thing: But if the sensible species being impressed on the Imagination, promises anything of Good or Evil, presently the spirits being Excited, respect or look back upon the Object, by whose appulse they were moved, and for the sake of embracing or removing it away, by other spirits flowing within the Passages of the Nerves, and successively by others implanted in the Members and moving Parts, they swiftly give their Commands of performing the respective motions. So the Sense brings in the Imagination; this the Memory or the Appetite, or both at once, and at length the appetite stirs up local motions, performing the prosecution or driving away of the appearing Good or Evil. For the several Kinds of these sort of Animal Functions, yea for the Various Acts of either Kind to be performed, the Animal Spirits, who are the immediate Instruments of them all, obtain peculiar and distinct tracts or paths; within which, if there be any let or bar to hinder, presently some function is hindred, or some member of the sensitive Soul, being as it were cut off, becomes impotent. . . .

As to the Offices and Uses of the streaked Bodies, though we can discern nothing with our eyes, or handle with our hands, of these things that are done within the secret Conclave or Closset of the Brain; yet, by the effects, and by comparing rationally the Faculties, and Acts, with the Workmanship of the Machine, we may at least conjecture, what sort of works of the Animal Function, are performed in these or those, or within some other parts of the Head; especially because it plainly appears, that the Offices of the Interior Motions, and Senses, as well as the Exterior, are acted by the help of the Animal Spirits, ordained within certain and distinct Paths, or as it were small little Pipes.

As therefore it appears from what we have said, that the chamfered or streaked Bodies are so placed, between the Brain and Cerebel, and the whole nervous Appendix, that nothing can be carried from these into that, or on the contrary be brought back hither, but it must pass thorow these Bodies; and as peculiar passages lead into these most ample Diversories, from the several Organs of Motions, Sense, and the other Functions; and further, as Passages lie open from these into the Callous Body, and into all the Marrowy Tracts of the Brain, nothing seems more probable, than that these parts are that common Sensory, that receives and distinguishes the Species, and all Impressions, transferrs them, being ordained into fit Series, to the Callous Body, and represents them to the Imagination there presiding; that also transmitts the Force and Instincts of all spontaneous motions, begun in the Brain, to the nervous Appendix, to be performed by the motive Organs. By reason of these manifold and diverse offices, so many Marrowy streakes or internal Nerves are produced within the streaked Bodies, for the Various Tendences and Beamings forth of the Animal Spirits, it may very well be concluded that the Sensitive Soul, as to all its Powers and Exercises of them, is truly within the Head, as well as in the nervous System, meerly Organical, and so extended, and after a manner Corporeal.

8.8

Claude Perrault

(1613–1688)

In another reaction against the growing popularity of Cartesianism, Perrault questions whether even the behavior of a decerebrate snake can be explained mechanistically. The content of this selection is relevant to the following chapter, and also to Chapter 14 on "animal mind." The answer given here is decidedly vitalistic, although it was published several years before the earliest work of Stahl (1660–1734). But it also includes a strong element of empiricism—and provides in any event a fascinating look into the mind of a seventeenth–century natural philosopher.

Du bruit [On sound], 1680. In Oeuvres diverses de physique et de méchanique. 2 vols. Leyden, 1721. Vol. I, pp. 153–283. [Pp. 265–267, 270–271, 273–274, 277, 279–280.]

It is the common opinion that the soul . . . has its principal seat in the most important parts, and that it presides over the functions of the internal senses in the brain, to which all the organs of the external senses are connected by nerves. . . . Everybody feels quite secure about these general principles, and they are uncertain only about the particular spot which nature has chosen as the court where the soul passes judgment on everything brought to it by the senses. . . . But I confess that I am not so advanced in my understanding of this matter as to have surmounted the difficulties which prevent me from considering what seat the soul has chosen for judgment or for memory. I am still concerned with understanding how the motion and vibration which are caused by a sensation can be propagated all the way into the brain. For if this is done by spirits, I cannot conceive how the movement which objects have imprinted on the organ can at the same time be carried by one spirit to the brain, while the nerve is filled with other spirits which the brain is sending in the opposite direction, to give the organ its required sensitivity; or how a single spirit can perform these contrary actions at the same time. . . .

That is why I think one may question whether these images do necessarily enter the brain . . . and this is the basis of the new system which I propose for the external senses. The reason for this hypothesis is that the soul, which is united to all parts of the living body, has no need to go to the brain to contemplate these images. It can do so just as well in the organs where they are imprinted by the sensation. It has no need to seek in the brain or in any other part of the body for instruments with which to judge these objects, or to perform any of the other actions of the internal senses, which we may with greater reason suppose to be incorporeal. According to my hypothesis, the function which the brain performs with regard to the senses is only to prepare the spirits which are necessary to dispose each organ of the external senses so that it shall be readily moved by objects. . . .

As for those who want to explain all natural things by mechanics, and who say that we should not seek any other principle for the actions of the internal senses of animals than that which moves inanimate bodies, I cannot believe that they are speaking in good faith, and that they are really satisfied with the way in which they explain the acts of imagination, judgment and memory by saying that they are only the necessary consequences of corporeal effects which we understand. . . .

I saw a snake dissected at the Royal Library which, after its head had been cut off and its heart and all the other entrails removed, crawled off in its usual manner, went from the courtyard into a garden, found a pile of rocks and hid itself among them. It is impossible to assert that memory had any part in this action, which showed that the animal not only had the power of locomotion, but could also, by using the sense of touch which was the only one remaining to him, select the sort of place which he formerly would have known to be a suitable refuge. This could not have been done by a pretended renewal of old traces that had been imprinted in the brain, since it no longer had a brain; nor can one say that the spinal medulla . . . performed the functions of the brain except in the way that I understand [the brain to work], that is, by furnishing the nerves that go to the muscles with the spirits they need for motion. It is easier to conceive how each part of the brain is capable of furnishing these spirits, than to understand how each part can conserve all the images needed for the representations of memory. . . .

These examples, and a hundred others of the same sort . . . lead us to believe that animal functions include something which cannot be explained by what we know about the properties of corporeal things. . . . Put a match to a cannon, and the impulsion of the ignited powder, the movement of the ball, the crashing of the wall which it strikes, and the resulting fall of rocks, are operations which have a necessary consequence, because they depend on one another in a natural manner. But to perform the operations of memory we must find a means of joining together things which do not have a disposition to do that according to the order and sequence by which corporeal things are naturally related. . . .

Those who find it at first strange to grant to a horse or a dog a kind of understanding which they do not even see in the actions of men, most of whom do not know what it means to reason, will agree, if they stop to consider the matter, that it is not necessary to know what thinking and reasoning are in order to think and to reason. Even the most stupid man thinks incessantly, and reasons in his slightest acts, without knowing or believing that he is thinking. Long habit has the power of making us insensible to the acts of thinking, although they always accompany all the other acts of every animal.

For if it is true that our soul does not reside in the body as in a house, but is united with it, then it must be considered as active in all our actions; and since thinking is certainly inseparable from all actions of the soul, it follows that thought partakes of all our acts. To understand how this may be, although we are not aware of it, we must remember that we think in two different ways. There is a kind of thinking which is distinct and explicit, for those matters to which we apply ourselves with care, and a kind of thinking which is confused and negligent, for things which long practice has rendered so easy that exact and explicit thinking is not necessary. . . .

Now we are almost always thinking in these two different ways at once, especially when we are awake, because we are always busy with acts which habit has made easy, and at the same time with others to which we must apply ourselves with care, either from some immediate need or from our own choice. If it were true that we do not think except when we believe that we are thinking, then we would not think at all when we sleep without dreaming, which is false; because it is only the explicit thinking which stops, and the soul is still occupied with natural functions for which negligent and confused thinking suffice. But this is nevertheless less confused and less negligent than when we are awake, for then our explicit thoughts sometimes make the thoughts attached to the natural faculties a little too negligent. That is why, often enough, long and profound meditation interferes with digestion, or causes headaches, because the soul cannot apply itself energetically to explicit thinking without neglecting to tend as it should, with confused thoughts, to the process of digestion and the secretion of humors. And on the contrary, these functions usually proceed better during sleep. If during sleep we must work hard at the natural functions, we scarcely have any dreams. . . .

Now the power which habit has to increase the facility with which we perform all acts not only leads to our performing them perfectly without the need to apply any explicit thinking to them, but it also leads to their performance against our explicit thought and will. The conduct of the heart's movement, as I understand it, seems to be a proof of this power of habit: for although this movement is performed by muscles, which are organs of voluntary action, the animal's long habit of exercising this movement, which is the first and oldest function in life, along with the great value which the soul has from the start attached to this movement, has led it, so to say, to take a resolve that it shall never be interrupted. . . .

The anatomy of the eye and the infallible laws of optics do not permit us to doubt that at birth all animals see objects upside down. The Gospel story of the man blind from birth attests to it [see *Mark* 8:22–25]. It tells us that when our Lord first touched him, to cure him, he saw trees upside down, and that He touched him another time to perform another miracle, and accomplish in an instant what long habit and education ordinarily do for all animals. . . . After having so often corrected this error by touch or some other indication, and so often concluded that what seems above is really below, habit makes this persuasion a necessity . . . which the imagination can no longer overcome.

When we force our eyes out of the balanced position which they ought to have with regard to each other, we see objects doubled; nevertheless, cross-eyed persons, whose eyes are always in this position, do not see them doubled. This is due to a faculty which they must have acquired by long habit in childhood, by accustoming themselves to grasp the two objects they saw as only one.

Nevertheless, no one remembers the trouble we had in working out all these corrections. . . .

Anyone who makes astronomical observations, and who uses a telescope which has two convex lenses, which causes objects to appear in positions opposite to their real positions, will readily understand how habit not only can make difficult acts become easy, but can even erase the memory of the difficulty they once caused. If he just thinks of the ease he has acquired in using that sort of telescope . . . he will have no difficulty in understanding how we can have forgotten all the trouble we had in the period just after we were born, in conducting all the actions required for the maintenance of life, and are now not even aware of the attention which our soul continually gives to them.

I think that this hypothesis about the attention which the soul gives to directing all the animal functions, of which we are not aware, seems a paradox to us only because we have not thought about it. I think that the more astonishing this direction is, which is so wonderful even in the smallest animal, the more reason there is to attribute it to the soul, for there is no other power which could be capable of it.

8.9

Isaac Newton

(1642–1727)

The publication of Newton's Principia mathematica in 1687 helped to encourage speculative mechanistic explanations for all sorts of phenomena. Newton himself, despite the claim (in the first paragraph of our selection) that he did not deal in hypotheses, could not resist the temptation. Others had already speculated, in defiance of anatomy, that the nerves were "taut strings" for the transmission of vibrations. In the last paragraph of the "general scholium" which Newton added in 1713, he suggested that the vibrations were in fact carried by that "elastic Spirit" which fills all space to make action at a distance possible. This provided a substitute for the outdated animal spirits. The suggestion will be taken up by Cheyne in the next selection, and by Hartley later (13.8).

Hitherto we have explained the phaenomena of the heavens and of our sea, by the power of Gravity, but have not yet assign'd the cause of this power. . . . But hitherto I have not been able to discover the cause of those properties of gravity from phaenomena, and I frame no hypotheses. For whatever is not deduc'd from the phaenomena, is to be called an hypothesis; and hypotheses, whether metaphysical or physical, whether of occult qualities or mechanical, have no place in experimental

The mathematical principles of natural philosophy. Translated into English by Andrew Motte. 2 vols. London, 1729. [Vol. 2, pp. 392–393.]

philosophy. In this philosophy particular propositions are inferr'd from the phaenomena, and afterwards render'd general by induction. . . . And to us it is enough, that gravity does really exist, and act according to the laws which we have explained, and abundantly serves to account for all the motions of the celestial bodies, and of our sea.

And now we might add something concerning a certain most subtle Spirit, which pervades and lies in all gross bodies; by the force and action of which Spirit, the particles of bodies mutually attract one another at near distances, and others, if contiguous; and electric bodies operate to greater distances, as well repelling as attracting the neighbouring corpuscles; and light is emitted, reflected, refracted, inflected, and heats bodies; and all sensation is excited, and the members of animal bodies move at the command of the will, namely, by the vibrations of this Spirit, mutually propagated along the solid filaments of the nerves, from the outward organs of sense to the brain, and from the brain into the muscles. But these are things that cannot be explain'd in few words, nor are we furnish'd with that sufficiency of experiments which is required to an accurate determination and demonstration of the laws by which this electric and elastic spirit operates.

8.10

George Cheyne

(1671–1743)

Cheyne, a "solidist," complains that belief in the animal spirits leads to ineffectual therapies for what we now call neuroses. He is ready to accept Newton's "elastick Spirit" as an alternative.

[Ch. VIII] § V. The most difficult Problem in all the Animal Oeconomy, is to give any tolerable Account of *Muscular Action,* or *Animal Motion.* The Similitude of a Machine put into Action and Motion by the Force of Water convey'd in Pipes, was the readiest Resemblance the *Lazy* could find to explain *Muscular Motion* by. It was easy, from this Resemblance, to forge a thin, imperceptible Fluid, passing and repassing through the Nerves, to blow up the Muscles, and thereby to lengthen one of their Dimensions, in order to shorten the other. On such a slender and imaginary Similitude, the precarious *Hypothesis* of

The English malady: or, A treatise of nervous diseases of all kinds: as, spleen, vapours, lowness of spirits, hypochondriacal, and hysterical distempers, &c. London, 1733. [Pp. 74–76, 88–89.]

Animal Spirits seems to be built. But as their Existence is, I fear, precarious, so, were it real, they are not sufficient to solve the Appearances, as shall be more particularly consider'd hereafter. All I shall further say here, is, that this and the other abstruse Appearances in the Animal and Vegetable Kingdoms, particularly *Vegetation, Elasticity, Cohesion,* the Emission, Reflexions and Refractions of Light, *Attraction* in the greater and lesser Bodies, and all the other secret and internal Actions of the Parts of Matter upon one another, are, with some shew of Possibility suspected, and by some Observations (not otherwise to be accounted for) made not improbable by the late *sagacious* and *learned Sir* Isaac Newton, to be owing to an infinitely subtil, elastick Fluid, or Spirit, (as he strongly expresses that subtil Matter) distended thro' this whole *System,* penetrating all Bodies with the greatest Facility, infinitely active and volatile, but more condens'd in *Vacuo,* or Spaces void of grosser Matter, than towards the Surfaces of Bodies, or in them: And by this *Aether, Spirit,* or most subtile Fluid, the Parts of Bodies are driven forcibly together, and their mutual attractive Virtue arises, and the other beforemention'd Appearances are produced. The Existence of this *subtil Fluid* or Spirit, is made probable by what he has observ'd of Liquors, *heating* and *cooling,* Mercury rising and continuing rais'd, and smooth Bodies clinging together, and requiring an equal Force to separate them in *Vacuo,* or in an exhausted Receiver, as in Air: And a great many other Experiments have been suggested, not otherwise to be so readily accounted for. And it is probable, that those other mention'd Appearances may be owing to the same Cause; since we find always *similar* Effects have *similar* Causes, and that Nature is frugal in *Causes,* but various and manifold in *Effects:* But Sir *Isaac* not having been able to make a sufficient Number of Experiments to determin all the laws of this Fluid, nor indeed sufficient absolutely to prove its Existence, he leaves it to the Sagacity of future Ages to determin them, and to apply them to the Appearances; and finding nothing in the Writings of other *Philosophers, Mathematicians,* or *Physicians,* of equal Probability with this, tho' imperfect Account of these Difficulties, I will offer the Reader no other.

[Ch. IX] § VIII. To conclude this dark Subject of *animal Spirits;* if they must be suppos'd, we may affirm, they cannot be of the Nature of any Fluid we have a Notion of, from what we see or know. Indeed, the large Size, the wonderful Texture, and the great Care and Security Nature has employ'd about the *Brain,* makes it probable it has been design'd for the *noblest* Uses, *viz.* to be the Temple or *Sensorium* of the *sentient and intelligent Principle.* And its Resemblances, in many Circumstances, to the other *Glands,* which certainly separate Liquors, makes it not improbable that it may have Uses *analogous* to those. But how to assign them, explain, or accord them with what has been suggested above, I know not. May not the *sentient Principle* have its Seat in some Place in the Brain, where the Nerves terminate, like the *Musician* shut up in his Organ-Room? May not the infinite Windings, Convolutions, and Complications of the Beginnings of the Nerves which constitute the Brain, serve to determin their particular Tone, Tension, and consequently the Intestine Vibrations of their Parts? May they not have interwoven Blood Vessels and Glands to separate a milky Liquor, to soften, moisten, and continue their *Elasticity,* and innate Mechanick Powers, through the whole *nervous System?* And also to keep them in a proper Condition to play off the *Vibrations, Tremors,* and *Undulations* made on them by Bodies, or their *Effluvia?* May not these *Vibrations* be propagated through their Lengths, by a subtile, spiritous, and infinitely elastick Fluid, which is the *Medium* of the Intelligent Principle? As sound is convey'd thro' Air to the *Tympanum,* and by it to this *Medium* or *Aether,* and from the *Medium* to the *Intelligent Principle,* and as *Sight* is perform'd thro' or by Light. And is not the *Analogy* of Nature and Things thus, in some measure, preserv'd? I own, it is much easier to confuse than establish; and I should not be very *sanguine* about the Non-existence of animal Spirits, but that I have observ'd the dwelling so much upon them, has led *Physicians* too much to neglect the mending of Juices, the opening Obstructions, and the strengthening the Solids, wherein only the proper and solid Cure of Nervous Distempers consists; and apply to *Volatiles, Foetids,* and *Stimulants:* which, at best, are but a Reprieve, and is not unlike blowing up the Fire, but at the same time forcing it to spend faster, and go out sooner; for *Volatiles, Aromaticks,* and *Cordials,* are much of one and the same Nature, and all but Whips, Spurs, and pointed Instruments to drive on the *resty and unwilling Jade.*

8.11

Luigi Galvani

(1737–1798)

At the time when Newton hypothesized an "electric and elastick spirit" as the basis for nervous action, knowledge of electricity was still very vague. In 1745 the Leyden jar was invented, and in 1752 Franklin demonstrated that lightning is electricity. Galvani's experiments, which utilized both at-

De viribus electricitatis in motu musculari. **Commentarius.** Bologna, 1791. Translated by Margaret Glover Foley as *Commentary on the effects of electricity on muscular motion.* Norwalk, Conn.: Burndy Library, 1953. (This publication includes a facsimile of the original work.) [Pp. 57, 59–60, 73–74, 78–79.]

mospheric and friction-created electrical charges, opened the era of electro-physiology, and his surmise that the muscle fiber might be "something like a small Leyden jar" anticipated much later understanding of the polariza-tion of muscle and nerve membranes. But soon Volta's invention of bat-tery "piles" suggested that Galvani might have been deceived by an artifact and "animal electricity" became a subject of controversy. The analogy with Mesmer's discredited animal magnetism did not encourage belief by critical thinkers. Nevertheless, the hypothesis of an electric current in the nerves offered an attractive alternative to both animal spirits and vibrations. Hence-forth, the problem of spirits became the problem of nervous "currents."

Part II.   The Effects of Atmospheric Electricity on Muscular Motion

Having already set forth our discoveries on the effects of artificial elec-tricity on muscular contractions, we wanted nothing better than to in-vestigate whether so-called atmospheric electricity produces the same phenomena or not, or more precisely whether lightning flashes like dis-charged sparks excite muscular contractions when the same techniques are used.

Therefore in the open air, we set up and insulated a long conductor, appropriately made of iron . . . and fastened one end of it to a high part of the house. When a thunderstorm arose we fastened the nerves of prepared frogs or the prepared limbs of warmblooded animals to the other end. . . . Then we attached to their feet another similar conductor of the greatest possible length so that it might reach down to the water of the well. . . . As we hoped, the result completely paralleled that in the experiment with artificial electricity. Whenever lightning flashed, all the muscles simultaneously fell into numerous violent contractions. . . .

Part III.   The Effects of Animal Electricity on Muscular Motion

After we had assessed the effects of atmospheric electricity present in storms, I was extremely eager also to investigate the strength of ordi-nary quiescent electricity.

Since I had upon occasion remarked that prepared frogs, which were fastened by brass hooks in their spinal cord to an iron railing which sur-rounded a certain hanging garden of my home, fell into the usual con-tractions not only when lightning flashed but even at times when the sky was quiet and serene, I surmised that these contractions had their origin in changes which occur during the day in the electricity of the atmosphere. . . . Therefore at different hours and for a span of many days I observed the animals which were appropriately arranged for this purpose, but scarcely any motion was evident in their muscles. . . .

Now since I had observed these contractions only in the open air and had not yet carried out the experiment elsewhere, I was on the point of postulating that such contractions result from atmospheric electricity slowly insinuating itself in the animal, accumulating there, and then being rapidly discharged when the hook comes in contact with the iron railing. For in experimenting, it is easy to be deceived and to think we have seen and detected things which we wish to see and detect.

But when I brought the animal into a closed room, placed it on an iron plate, and began to press the hook which was fastened in the spinal cord against the plate, behold! the same contractions and movements occurred as before. I immediately repeated the experiment in different places with different metals and at different hours of the day. The results were the same except that the contractions varied with the metals used; that is, they were more violent with some and weaker with others. Then it occurred to me to experiment with other substances that were either non-conductors or very poor conductors of electricity, like glass, gum, resin, stones, and dry wood. Nothing of the kind happened and no muscular contractions or movements were evident. These results surprised us greatly and led us to suspect that the electricity was inherent in the animal itself. An observation that a kind of circuit of a delicate nerve fluid is made from the nerves to the muscles when the phenomenon of contractions is produced, similar to the electric circuit which is completed in a Leyden jar, strengthened this suspicion and our surprise.

Furthermore, while I held in one hand a prepared frog with a hook fastened in its spinal cord in such a way that it stood on its feet on a silver box, with the other hand I struck the top of the box on which the frog's feet rested, or its side, using some metallic instrument. Contrary to expectation, I saw the frog react in violent contractions as often as I used this technique.

After making these observations I asked . . . {a friend, Rialpus} to offer a helping hand in this experiment just as he had very kindly done in other experiments. I suggested that he hold the frog as I myself had done before, not only for the sake of convenience, but also that I might alter the method of experiment a little, while I struck the box again. Contrary to expectation, however, the contractions were absent. . . .

This result led me to hold the animal in one hand, as I had done before, and Rialpus' hand in the other and to ask him either to touch or strike the box with his free hand so as to form a kind of electrical chain. To our joy and surprise, contractions immediately took place, only to disappear if we separated our hands. . . .

8.11   Luigi Galvani

Part IV.   *The Effects of Animal Electricity on Muscular Motion, Conjectures and Some Conclusions*

From the things that have been ascertained and investigated thus far, I believe it has been sufficiently well established that there is present in animals an electricity which we, together with Bartholonius and others are wont to designate with the general term, "animal." This electricity is present, if not in all, at least in many parts of animals. It is seen most clearly, however, in the muscles and nerves. Its special characteristic, not recognized before, seems to be that it courses strongly from the muscles to the nerves or rather from the latter to the former, and directly enters an arc, a chain of men, or other conducting bodies which lead from the nerves to the muscles by the shortest and most direct course possible, and passes in all haste from one to the other through them. . . .

. . . Perhaps the hypothesis is not absurd and wholly speculative which compares a muscle fibre to something like a small Leyden jar or to some other similar electrical body charged with a twofold and opposite electricity, and by comparing a nerve in some measure to the conductor of the jar; in this way one likens the whole muscle, as it were, to a large group of Leyden jars. . . .

So much for the innate character and capacity of animal electricity. Now a few words about its source. I should think this would be identical with that indicated by physiologists as being the source of animal spirits, namely the cerebrum. For although we have stated that electricity is inherent in the muscles, we are not of the opinion, however, that it emanates from them as from its proper and natural source.

For since all nerves, not only those which extend to the muscles, but also those which project to other parts of the body, seem to be identical in appearance and in their natural qualities, who will rightly deny that all carry a fluid of a like nature? Now inasmuch as we have already shown that electric fluid is carried through the nerves of the muscles, it must therefore be transmitted through all of the nerves. . . .

We believe, therefore, that the electric fluid is produced by the activity of the cerebrum, that it is extracted in all probability from the blood, and that it enters the nerves and circulates within them in the event that they are hollow and empty, or, as seems more likely, they are carriers for a fine lymph or other similarly subtle fluid which is secreted from the cortical substance of the brain, as many believe. If this be the case, perhaps at last the nature of animal spirits, which has been hidden and vainly sought after for so long will be brought to light with clarity.

8.12

Pierre Jean Georges Cabanis

(1757–1808)

In 1796, Year IV of the revolutionary calendar, Cabanis began a series of memoirs presented to joint meetings of the two chambers of the National Academy, emphasizing the need to combine the natural sciences and the social sciences in the study of man. After the sixth memoir, ill health prevented him from continuing, and the completed work, published in 1802, includes six more which are longer because they are no longer limited by the conditions of a lecture. The first part of this selection is from the second memoir, and includes the famous metaphor which is often misquoted (and usually attributed to Carl Vogt, who used it later) as "the brain secretes thoughts as the liver secretes bile." The last two paragraphs, from the eleventh memoir, sum up Cabanis' consideration of the converse problem, the influence of mind on body. Cabanis is refreshingly positive in method, and cuts through metaphysical knots by simply sticking to the facts, without resorting to hypothetical mechanistic explanations.

[II: vii] In order to form a correct idea of the operations which give rise to thought, one must look upon the brain as a special organ, which is particularly designed to produce it, in the same way that the stomach and the intestines are designed for performing digestion, the liver for filtering the bile, the parotid and maxillary and sublingual glands for producing salivary juices. Impressions, when they reach the brain, stimulate it to activity, just as foods, when they fall into the stomach, excite it to a more abundant secretion of gastric juice and to movements which are favorable to their proper dissolution. The proper function of one is to perceive each individual impression, to attach signs to it, to compare them with each other, to draw judgments from them and to arrive at determinations, just as the function of the other is to act on the nutritive substances whose presence stimulates it, to dissolve them and to assimilate their juices into our nature.

Does one object that the organic movements by which the functions of the brain are performed are unknown to us? But the action by which the nerves of the stomach determine the different operations which constitute digestion, and the manner in which they impregnate the gastric juice with the most active power of dissolution, have no less eluded our

Rapports du physique et du morale de l'homme [Relations between the body and the mind of man]. In *Oeuvres Complètes de Cabanis*, vols III & IV. Paris, 1824. [Vol. III, pp. 159–161, vol. IV, pp. 425–426.]

research. We see the foods drop into this viscus, having certain qualities of their own; we see them emerge from it with new qualities, and we conclude that it has in fact changed them in this manner. We see equally that impressions reach the brain by the intermediary of the nerves; they are at that time, isolated, disorganized. The viscus enters into action; it acts on them, and soon they reappear metamorphosed into ideas which the language of facial expression and of gesture, or the signs of speech and writing, manifest outwardly. We conclude with the same certainty that the brain in some sense digests the impressions; that it organically produces the secretion of thought.

This completely resolves the difficulty raised by those who look upon sensibility as a passive faculty, and therefore cannot understand how judging, reasoning, imagining, can ever be anything other than sensing. The difficulty no longer exists when we recognize, in these different operations, the activity of the brain on the impressions which are transmitted to it. . . .

[XI: viii] If, therefore, we now bring together under a single point of view the various circumstances which determine the nature and power of the influence which one organ exerts on specific other organs, or on the system as a whole, we see that they all combine to favor the cerebral organ; that is to say, no other organ, according to the laws of the vital economy, can exercise a total action which is more constant, more vigorous, and more general. . . .

Therefore we can no longer be uncertain in deciding on the true meaning of this expression, *the influence of the mind on the body.* We clearly see that it designates this very influence of the cerebral system, as the organ of thinking and volition, over other organs, which by its sympathetic action it is capable of exciting, suspending, and even perverting in all their functions. It is that; it can be nothing more than that.

8.13

Hans Berger

(1873–1941)

Considerations of space compel us to forego the tempting task of tracing through the nineteenth and early twentieth centuries the swift development of knowledge on the nature of the nervous impulse, leading to our present, still imperfect understanding of the role of chemical transmitters

Ueber das Elektrenkephalogramm des Menschen [On the human electroencephalogram]. *Archiv für Psychiatrie,* 87 (1929): 527–570. [Pp. 527, 537, 552–553, 567–570.]

at synapses. *Prominent in such a survey would be the contributions of du Bois-Reymond, Helmholtz, Bernstein, Sherrington, Adrian, Dale, and a "full hand" of contemporary Nobel laureates still at work. However, we close this chapter with a selection from the article which introduced a new technique, as useful to the experimental psychologist as to the clinician, for investigating the correspondence between cortical events and other bodily and environmental conditions. "Brain waves" are far from being the substance of thought but, as Berger suggests, they do permit us to keep track of the thinking process in much the same way that an electrocardiogram permits a physician to observe the action of the heart.*

As early as 1874, Caton published researches on the brains of rabbits and apes, in which non-polarizing electrodes were placed either on the surface of both hemispheres, or one electrode was placed on the cortex and the other on the outer surface of the skull. . . . There were distinct fluctuations of current, which became stronger especially on awakening from sleep and as death approached, becoming weaker after death and then disappearing completely. He was able to show that strong current fluctuations took place on the cortex when the eye was illumined, and he already expressed the opinion that under some circumstances these cortical currents might be useful for localization. . . .

. . . After a number of vain attempts I succeeded, on July 6, 1924, in making the first observations of this kind on a young man, 17 years of age, who had undergone palliative trepanation over the left hemisphere, because of a suspected tumor. . . . This was the first result which indicated that constant electrical currents might be recorded from the surface of the intact cerebral cortex in man, just as in rabbit, dog and ape. . . . [Work with other patients having skull openings is described at length.]

I recorded 73 curves during 14 sessions with my son Klaus, who was 15 to 17 years old during these investigations. . . . Zinc-plated needle electrodes were placed subcutaneously on the midline of the skull, just inside the hairline over the forehead and about the width of two fingers above the external occipital prominence. . . .

I have also had a whole series of curves taken from my own scalp, both with needle electrodes and other kinds, and with the most varied placement of the electrodes. . . .

Thus I believe that I have indeed discovered the electroencephalogram in man, and published it here for the first time.

The electroencephalogram is a continuous curve with constant fluctuations, in which, as I have pointed out repeatedly, one can distinguish large waves of a first type, which have an average duration of 90 σ, and smaller waves of a second type, averaging 35 σ. The larger deviations have a maximal value of 0.00015–0.0002 volts.

If we now turn to the question of how the electroencephalogram comes about at all, I would like again to point out that these fluctuating currents can be taken not only from the dura of the cerebrum, but also from that of the cerebellum. Therefore the electroencephalogram certainly does not represent a special characteristic of the cerebrum, even though the cerebellar electroencephalogram shows a somewhat different form and fewer large bursts of current. Whether the current arises in the cortex of the cerebrum and cerebellum or in deeper parts we are completely unable to decide. . . .

We regard the electroencephalogram as an attendant phenomenon, which accompanies the constant neural processes which take place in the brain, exactly as the electrocardiogram is an attendant phenomenon to the contractions of the separate segments of the heart.

Naturally many questions forced themselves upon me during these investigations, for example, whether changes take place in the human electroencephalogram under the influence of peripheral stimulation, as has been shown to be the case in animal experiments; also the question whether a difference in the electroencephalogram could be demonstrated in sleeping and waking states, how it would behave under narcosis, and other such questions. Above all, what about the question which had already occurred to Fleischl von Marxow when he wrote [about 1890] that we might be able to observe the electrical phenomena accompanying the processes in our own brains? Is it possible to demonstrate an influence of intellectual work on the human encephalogram, as it has been described here? We should not build too great hopes in advance, for, as I have already stated, mental work only increases by a little the cortical work which is constantly going on, and not only in the waking state. However, it is quite possible that this increase might be recognizable in the electroencephalogram which accompanies the constant activity of the brain. Naturally I have performed numerous experiments of this sort, but I have reached no *unambiguous* answer. I am inclined toward the view that during strenuous mental work the longer waves, averaging about 90 σ in duration, that is, those of the first type, become less prominent and the smaller, 35 σ waves of the second type become more frequent. The best encephalograms, in which both kinds of waves appear in rather regular arrangement, are obtained in complete rest, with closed eyes, in the dark. These statements are based primarily on investigations of healthy persons, having no skull openings, and hence with the use of lead-foil electrodes attached to the scalp. . . . Especially in experiments with my son Klaus I gained the impression that during strenuous intellectual work, and even during strong attentive concentration, the smaller and shorter waves predominate. However, this can by no means be regarded as a final determination, but rather as one which needs much more investigation, so that I do not wish to fix on a definite answer at present. . . . Predominantly practical points of view have led me to work on this problem again and again for many years, particularly *the* question whether it might perhaps be possible to discover an objective means for investigation of *pathological* changes in the activity of the central nervous system, similar to the electrocardiogram in regard to heart ailments—something which naturally would be of the greatest importance diagnostically.

Chapter 9

THE CONTROL OF MOVEMENT

Aristotle mentions that earlier Greek philosophers had looked upon the soul as the source of movement. The belief that body, as matter, is inert and must owe all movement to a spiritual agent died very hard. Even in the eighteenth century, we will find Whytt arguing that movement must have its basis in an incorporeal principle. Leibnitz, shortly before, had recognized movement as inseparable from all existence, but this was only a way of altogether denying the existence of matter independent of mind. Self-moving matter has sometimes seemed as heretical as matter that thinks!

Nevertheless, the gradual growth of understanding about the nature of involuntary movements, first the "vital" movements and later of adaptive movements of a reflex nature, inevitably led to acceptance of bodily movement as a purely physical phenomenon. This chapter begins with Galen's distinction between voluntary and involuntary movements, in which he explains ambiguous instances by a fleeting and obscure consciousness. The chapter ends with a reminder (we have no space for more!) of Sherrington's brilliant experimental analysis of posture and locomotion. If the story were carried forward, it would be highlighted by discoveries pinpointing areas for the release and arrest of specific movements. However, these will find their place in the latter part of the next chapter.

9.1

Galen

(131–200)

Galen establishes a criterion for "voluntary" actions, by which respiration and other actions subject to a degree of control are called voluntary. He also makes the important distinction between clear and unclear perception and uses it to explain why some voluntary acts are not remembered as such.

The translation has also been compared with Greek and Latin texts of the Opera omnia edited by C. G. Kühn (Leipzig, 1821–1833).

[I, 1] All the muscles have important connections with the brain and the spinal marrow, because from the brain or the spinal marrow they must receive a nerve which is small to the eye, but which has a force that is far from being small. You will recognize this in lesions of the nerve. Indeed, if the nerve is cut, or compressed, or contused, tied, or suffering from decay or from a tumor, this takes away all movement and feeling from the muscle. . . . Therefore there exists in the nerves a considerable force which flows down from above, from the great source, for this faculty is not innate in them nor do they get it by themselves. You will recognize this above all in the following fact: if you cut any nerve you please, or indeed the spinal marrow, the part [of the nerve] situated above the incision and remaining connected with the brain will still keep the energies which come from that source, while the part that is below will not be able to communicate either feeling or movement to any organ.

Thus the nerves play the part of conduits which bring to the muscles the energies which they draw from the brain. . . .

[II, 5] There is therefore little basis for the opinion according to which all the actions of people who are asleep, and who have fallen into a lethargic slumber, are physical. Such a statement is not completely true. Indeed, why do they move about and move their limbs in all sorts of ways? Why do they talk in their sleep? Will anyone maintain that these also are physical actions? But perhaps someone will say that these actions are not performed consciously! Indeed, neither do you reflect upon the movements of all your parts during the continual movement of your eyelids, or in speaking, either in an oration or in a conversation, nor do you, when you walk from Piraeus to Athens on foot, reflect on all the separate movements of your legs. . . . Is walking therefore not an action of the soul which is voluntarily performed? . . .

Du mouvement des muscles [On the movement of the muscles]. In *Oeuvres anatomiques, physiologiques et médicales de Galien*. Translated (into French) by Ch. Daremberg. 2 vols. Paris, 1854–1856. Vol. II, 321–375. [Pp. 362–367.]

. . . What then is the criterion by which we judge actions to be voluntary? I will give you not one sign but many, all of which agree with one another. In effect, if you can at wish stop the execution of actions that have been started and carry out those that have not been started, this is by the effect of the will. If, further, you have the power to do the action faster or slower, more or less frequently, is it not altogether clear that the action is subordinate to the will? The will cannot check the movement of an artery or of the heart, or excite it, nor make it more frequent or more rare, or speed it up [nor slow it down]. Therefore we do not say that such actions are actions of the soul, but of nature. . . .

[6] To arrive at truths, we start from the principle, that many people often do many things they have totally forgotten a moment later, like those who through fear or drunkenness or from some similar cause do not have the least memory of what they did in those conditions. The cause of this forgetfulness is, I believe, that they did not apply the full attention of their mind to these actions. In effect, the imaginative part of the soul, whatever it is, is the part which is endowed with memory. If this part of the soul receives clear impressions of objects in its perceptions, it conserves them permanently, and that constitutes memory. If, on the contrary, it receives them in an obscure and quite superficial manner, it does not conserve them and that constitutes forgetting. Thus in anger, in deep meditation, drunkenness, madness, fear, and in general in all strong affections of the soul, one cannot later recall anything of what one did while in those states. Why then should it be so surprising if, in sleep, when the soul acts in an obscure manner, perceptions also are obscure and therefore they do not persist? Why is it surprising if even when awake, when the spirit is occupied in meditation and almost entirely absorbed in its reflections, an extremely small part of the spirit, which concerns itself with walking, receives an obscure impression of the action and consequently forgets it immediately, not even remembering if the action was done voluntarily?

9.2

Gregor Reisch

(?–1525)

The Margarita philosophica, a one-volume encyclopedia in the form of a dialogue between teacher and pupil, gives us compact statements of the traditional views from which Renaissance and early modern empirical

Margarita philosophica, cum additionibus novi ab auctore suo studiossima revisione quarto super additis [The pearl of philosophy, with new additions, carefully revised by the author]. Basle, 1517. [Book X, Tract II, Ch. 31.]

writers start out. Its author was a Carthusian prior, confessor to the Emperor Maximilian I. The first edition is thought to have been in 1496, and it still seemed contemporary enough to merit an Italian translation (albeit somewhat amended and expanded) in 1594.

Note in this selection the distinction between motor and sensory nerves, which had already been made by Galen. The introduction to the next selection will discuss this point more fully.

Student: Now you must briefly touch upon the motive powers which execute what has been commanded.

Master: The motive power is divided in three ways, for there is a natural sort, a vital sort, and an animal sort. . . . The animal [faculty] is in the brain. Thence, through nerves which leave the brain, it brings vigor to the senses and motion to the other members. The brain, which is located beneath the cranium, is wrapped in two membranes, of which the outer one next to the cranium is firmer, and is called the dura mater; the inner which is more delicate is called the pia mater. From the former arise those nerves which are the instruments of voluntary motion, and which extend from the back of the head. From the latter arise those nerves which go from the front of the head to the separate sense organs of which we have spoken above. The nerves from the dura mater spread out through the body of the animal, flowing into the muscles and the arms. When the motive power flows through these the animal moves, which takes place as follows. The object which is apprehended by the perceptive power is either desired or rejected by the appetitive power; this commands the motive power into the nerves, the muscles and the arms, so that it shall move the body to obtain what is desired or flee from the contrary, which command is swiftly obeyed. The members are extended or relaxed by the ligaments, moving first those which are near and then the others in turn, either to obtain what is desired or to flee what has been rejected.

S: Thus it is clear that the arm moves the hand, the hand the finger, and the finger touches the object.

M: In the same way for legs, feet, and toes. . . .

S: All these things are clear, but it is still not clear what the motive power is.

M: The motive power is a certain substance which arises in the heart, and which is given form in different parts to perform different things. Thus, for the operations of nutrition it receives its form in the liver; for vital operations, in the heart; but for the operations of sense and motion it receives its form in the brain. This substance, which we also call spirit, is animated by the sensitive soul . . . and cannot be joined to a body without blood. For as Augustine said, spirits cannot dwell in dry places. Therefore men have another kind of motion which is not organic, which does not move one part after the other but all at once, and [Duns] Scotus adds that this is of the same essence as the intellect, which moves the heavenly bodies.

S: Then the organic force is a body, which we call a spirit because of its subtlety and swiftness; but that of which you have just spoken is not a body, but is thought to be the intellectual soul itself.

M: You have summed it up clearly.

9·3

Simone di San Paolo

(?–1622)

The need for separate afferent and efferent nerves was often overlooked before the work of Bell [7.10] and Magendie. Hunter and Macalpine credit Walter Charleton, in 1690, followed by Malcolm Flemyng, in 1740, with pioneering the view (in Flemyng's words) that "some nerves are sensory and others motor, there being no good reason why one and the same nerve should perform both functions." It is however wrong to suppose that Galen's distinction had been completely forgotten. It is explicit in the previous selection, and implicit in the selection we shall give from Glisson. It might be objected that Reisch spoke only of sensory nerves serving the principal sense organs in the head. In this selection from the writing of a barefoot Carmelite monk, who had studied medicine at Siena before taking holy orders, it is specified that both sets of nerves "spread themselves through the body." The context from which this is taken is a discussion of the physical basis of the passions.

. . . And leaving aside for the present the vital spirits, which the soul makes use of for the nutrition and growth of the body, which have nothing to do with our problem, we must take note that there are also other spirits, which are called animal, and that these are of two kinds, of which one serves to give movement to the limbs, and the other sensibility, and the avenues through which they run and spread themselves through the body are two different [sets of] nerves, some to carry those which cause movement, and others those which give sensibility. These spirits are like very subtle rays of light, as one can see from the fact that, when one receives a strong blow on the head, or when one rubs the eyes after sleeping well, one sees rays of light coming out, and these are nothing but these spirits; for just as the heavens are the cause of all the move-

Il riforma dell'huomo. Opera spirituale. [The reform of man; a spiritual work. 1623.] Venice, 1671. [P. 246.]

ments and changes which take place in this lower world, by means of the rays of the sun, and the planets, so the brain, which is like the heaven in this small world of man, causes all the movements and sensations in our body, by means of the rays of this light.

9.4

René Descartes

(1596–1650)

Descartes' purely mechanical man serves as a foil to his purely intellectual, unextended mind. This man-machine has the ability to make appropriate responses to external sensory stimulation without conscious direction, as the action initiated by an external stimulus is reflected back from the center to the muscles. It is interesting that this first description of a "reflex" act is not an instance of vital action but concerns instead an adaptive response to an environmental object, of the sort that would ordinarily be regarded as requiring volitional control. Descartes solved the problems of two-way communication between brain and peripheral organs by tugging at filaments inside the nerve to deliver a message to the brain, but dispatching animal spirits through the remaining hollow space in the nerve to regulate the muscular response.

Because Descartes' drawings were lost, the rival French and Latin editions have different illustrations. Those in the Latin edition were prepared by a better anatomist.

After this, in order to understand how it [the machine] can be incited by external objects which strike the sense organs, so as to move all its members in a thousand other ways, remember that the little threads which I have so often told you come from the inmost part of the brain, and which compose the marrow of the nerves, are so distributed to all the parts which serve as organs that they can very easily be moved by objects of the senses; and when they are moved ever so slightly, they pull at the same instant at the parts of the brain from which they come, and by this means they open the entries of certain pores which are on the internal surface of the brain. Through these the animal spirits which are in the cavities immediately begin to take their course, passing through them into the nerves, and into the muscles, which serve in this machine to per-

De l'homme [On man]. Paris, 1664. [Art. 26.]
De homine, figuris, et latinate donatus a Florentio Schuyl [Leyden, 1662]. Second edition, Leyden, 1664. [Fig. 12.]

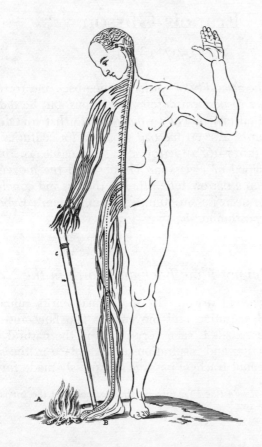

form movements entirely similar to those to which we are naturally incited when our senses are touched in the same manner.

For example, if the fire A is close to the foot B, the small particles of fire, which as you know move very swiftly, are able to move as well the part of the skin which they touch on the foot. In this way, by pulling at the little thread cc, which you see attached there, they at the same instant open e, which is the entry for the pore d, which is where this small thread terminates; just as, by pulling one end of a cord, you ring a bell which hangs at the other end.

Now when the entry of the pore, or the little tube, de, has thus been opened, the animal spirits flow into it from the cavity F, and through it they are carried partly into the muscles which serve to pull the foot back from the fire, partly into those which serve to turn the eyes and the head to look at it, and partly into those which serve to move the hands forward and to turn the whole body for its defense.

9·5

Francis Glisson

(1597–1677)

Glisson recognized the absurdity of spirits running back and forth through the same narrow tubes to perform different functions, but he did not stop there. He performed an experiment to demonstrate that muscles are not inflated by animal spirits, as everyone had supposed for centuries.

Jan Swammerdam (1637–1680) performed a comparable experiment with a frog's muscle contained in a glass jar. He observed the movement of a drop of water placed in a narrow tube fitted to the jar, and concluded that the shortened muscle decreases in volume. Swammerdam's Bybel der natuure was published posthumously, 1737–1738.

That Spirits Cannot Flow Back and Forth in the Nerves

I come now to the second reason why the animal spirits cannot be the immediate source of sensation and movement. The flow and reflux of material in the same vessels is seen very rarely in the natural economy. In respiration, expiration and inspiration do take place in the same vessels but the cartilagenous tracheal passage is expressly made for this, and

Tractatus de ventricule et intestine [Treatise on the stomach and the intestines]. Amsterdam, 1677. [Pp. 190–192.]

the thorax likewise alternately contracts and expands organically. The flow and reflux of chyle in the intestines must be conceded: but the peristaltic motion is doubtless designed for that purpose, that is, to turn the chyle over repeatedly. In the nerves, however, there is hardly a sufficient reason why the spirits should be carried sometimes outwards, sometimes inwards; unless we also assume a peristaltic motion in the nerves, or suppose that the animal spirits run up and down like playful little animals, wilfully flowing now this way, now that. But they run outward in order to nourish the parts, and to make the sense organs suited for their function. This I embrace with both arms. But nevertheless they must run back, to inform the common sense about what is happening in the peripheral organ. In what language they report, or how they transmit the idea in a peripheral organ to a point distant from it, I do not understand. The idea in the peripheral and internal organs is one continuous representation, so that the object is sensed as one thing. But the sensation of the same object sometimes lasts for several hours. During all that time, do the animal spirits simultaneously run up and down in the same nerve, in order that the sensation of the object shall persist in both the internal and the peripheral organs? These riddles are inexplicable. But in addition these spirits run outward in order to flow into the fibers of motion, so that, being swollen and distended in width, shortened in length, they pull on the bones to which their tendons are attached. However, this explosion of the spirits and inflation of the muscles have now for some time been silenced by experimental proof. Prepare a long glass tube, sufficiently large and suitably shaped, into which another little tube is inserted on the outside and top, near its mouth, like a funnel. Into the mouth of the larger tube a robust, brawny man inserts his naked arm entirely, and then the opening is stuffed on all sides around the shoulder so that no water can flow out. Then water is poured in through the funnel, enough to fill the tube and have some rising also into the funnel. This done, the workman is ordered by turns now to strongly tense all the muscles of his arm at once, now to relax them. During the period of tension the water in the tube subsides, and during the period of relaxation it rises higher. Whence it is evident that the tensed or invigorated muscle is not inflated or swollen during that time, but rather grows smaller, contracts and is detumescent. For if it were inflated, the water would ascend higher in the tube, and surely not descend. And thus it is to be inferred that the fibers are shortened by their own vital motion, nor do they have any need for a copious influx of spirits, either vital or animal, by which they are inflated in order to shorten them, to execute movements at the command of the brain. I fear that this digression concerning the animal spirits may have been quite irksome to the reader. In truth, it was not possible simply to avoid it, nor to say more concisely what seemed necessary.

9.6

Giovanni Alfonso Borelli

(1608–1679)

Borelli's analysis of animal movement as a physical problem, treating the bones as levers and calculating the force needed to obtain the observed effects, represented a step of major importance in the scientific approach to life phenomena. He also recognized mechanical problems inherent in the doctrine of animal spirits: the nerves can neither permit the passage of that large volume of spirits needed to inflate the muscles, nor can they, imbedded as they are in other tissues, transmit vibrations. His solution was to propose a "nervous juice" which, as he conceived it, could be squeezed out at either end in an instantaneous response to pressure at the other end. Although his conjecture about a fermentation in the muscles was wrong and based on the misleading notion that the muscles actually inflate, he was correct in assuming that the nerve does introduce some substance (now called a chemical transmitter) to initiate a chemical reaction in the muscle fiber.

Concerning the Probable Cause of the
Vital Contraction of Muscles

It appears from what has been said above that the *vital action of the muscles,* that is, their contraction and their *turgidity,* depend on causes quite different from an admixture of an effluent from the blood, or on a motive force of the blood itself, or on ambient pressure of air, or on an impulsive force from the heart, or on the weight and motion of the blood itself, as a means of making the moist fibers contract. We shall try to indicate to the extent of our powers the true cause of this wonderful operation, and show by what organs and mechanical means it is performed.

Prop. XXII.   *Two Causes Are Required for the Vital
Contraction of Muscles, One Existing in the Muscle
Itself, the Other Entering from Without*

Since all the muscles, with few exceptions, do not perform their vital motion except when we will, and since the volitional command from the

De motu animalium [On the movement of animals]. Rome, 1680–1681. [Second Part, Ch. 3. Vol. II, pp. 55–59.]

brain, which is the ruler of the sensitive and animal soul, is not transmitted by any other paths than through the nerves—as all acknowledge, and has been shown by the clearest experiments—and since we have already rejected the supposition that this is an act of the incorporeal faculty or of an aerial spirit; therefore it follows that some corporeal substance is transmitted through the nerves to the muscles, or a vibration is communicated to them, which can effect the real inflation which is evident to our eyes.

But this inflation, firmness, and contraction does not take place in the pathways by which this substance is diffused and where the motive faculty itself exists, that is, not in the nerves themselves, but outside of them, which is to say in the muscles. Therefore this substance or faculty which the nerves transmit is not sufficient to effect the inflation by itself. It is necessary that something else be added, which is to be found in the muscles; something waiting there in abundance, and from which something like a fermentation or ebullition can be produced, to cause that swift inflation of the muscles. . . .

Prop. XXIII. *The Structure of the Fibers and the Nerves, Their Power and Operations*

We must still ask what it is that is introduced by the nerves, how and with what force it is impelled, and by which canals.

First we must inquire about the structure of the nervous fibers. It is clear that the nerve is a bundle or strand made up of many fine threads, like hairs, fastened together by some membranous envelope. And these fibers may be hollow, like the blood vessels or like reeds, notwithstanding that they appear to be solid and full to the simple vision. . . . Therefore it is not impossible that the nerves are hollow fistulas . . . that is to say, tubes which are filled with some moist and spongy substance, like the marrow of sumach twigs. . . .

We may suppose that the spongy hollows of the nerve fibers are always moist and filled to swelling with a juice or spirit which is received from the brain. And just as we see in an intestine, when it is filled with water and closed at both ends, that if one end is compressed and lightly struck, the motion is quickly communicated through the turgid intestine to the other end; so it would seem that a light compression or irritation made at one end of the canal, where it ends in the brain itself, would cause the discharge of a small amount of that spongy substance or juice into the meat of the muscle itself.

9.7

Albrecht von Haller

(1708–1777)

The old view of muscular action had been that the muscles are passively inflated by animal spirits. Borelli had emphasized that something within the muscle must contribute to this response. Now Haller says that contractility is altogether an intrinsic characteristic of muscular tissue which responds to any irritation with its own inherent force. He called this characteristic irritability, taking the word from Glisson, who had advanced a somewhat similar concept. Within two years after publication of these lectures, they had been translated into French, German, Italian, Swedish, and English.

There is no basis for Haller's charge that La Mettrie had put himself forward as the originator of this concept. L'Homme machine had been dedicated to Haller without permission, and it is understandable that Haller wished to disassociate himself from that "impious system." However, irritability was already no secret, and La Mettrie needed no secret information from a "young Swiss." There is in fact a dissertation, De irritabilitate, published at Leyden in 1748 (by the very publisher of La Mettrie's book) and written by a certain Johannes Lups who is described as a Muscovite Russian. Lups gave credit to Haller and wrote that "Irritability is the principle of movement in the human body, as the pendulum is in a clock."

I call that part of the human body irritable, which becomes shorter upon being touched; very irritable if it contracts upon a slight touch, and the contrary if by a violent touch it contracts but little.

I call that a sensible part of the human body, which upon being touched transmits the impression of it to the soul; and in brutes, in whom the existence of a soul is not so clear, I call those parts sensible, the Irritation of which occasions evident signs of pain and disquiet in the animal. . . .

We have seen that the sensible parts of the body are the *nerves* themselves, and those to which they are distributed in the greatest abundance; for by intercepting the communication between any part and its nerve, either by compression, tying, or cutting, it is thereby immediately deprived of sensation. . . . Wherefore the nerves alone are sensible of themselves, and their whole sensibility resides in their medullary part, which

[*De partibus corporis humanis sensibilibus et irritabilibus*. Göttingen, 1753.] *A dissertation on the sensible and irritable parts of animals*. London, 1755. [Pp. 4, 31–32, 34–38, 57, 66–67.]

is a production of the internal substance of the brain, to which the *pia mater* furnishes a coat. . . .

[II] I proceed now to irritability, which is so different from sensibility, that the most irritable parts are not at all sensible, and *vice versa,* the most sensible are not irritable. I shall prove both these propositions by facts, and at the same time I shall demonstrate, that irritability does not depend upon the nerves, but on the original fabric of the parts which are susceptible to it. . . .

Farther, we must not conclude that a part is sensible, because it is irritable; for the tying or cutting of a nerve, which destroys the sensibility of that part to which it is sent, does by no means destroy its irritability. . . .

I have tried experiments of the same kind upon parts separate from the body. The intestines in this state after being deprived of all communication with the brain, preserve their peristaltic motion; and if you touch them with a knife or corrosives, they put on the same appearances, as if they were in their natural situation, and still preserved their connexion with the nerves and brain. The same thing is to be observed in the heart, and in any other muscle cut off from the body. . . .

If therefore we say that an animal only feels, when any external impression is represented to the mind, certainly that part of the body must be void of sensation, whose communication with the brain is destroyed by the nerve being cut, or the part being taken quite out of the body. In asserting that there was no motion of our body but by the soul, Dr. Whytt has found himself obliged to admit the divisibility of the soul, which he believes to be separable into as many parts as the body. . . .

The soul is a being which is conscious of itself, represents to itself the body to which it belongs, and by means of that body the whole universe. I am myself, and not another, because that which is called I, is changed by every thing that happens to my body and the parts belonging to it. If there is a muscle, or an intestine, whose suffering makes impressions upon another soul, and not upon mine, the soul of that muscle or intestine is not mine, it does not belong to me. But a finger cut off from my hand, or a bit of flesh from my leg, has no connexion with me, I am not sensible of any of its changes, they can neither communicate to me idea nor sensation; wherefore it is not inhabited by my soul nor by any part of it; if it was, I should certainly be sensible of its changes. I am therefore not at all in that part that is cut off, it is intirely separated both from my soul, which remains as entire as ever, and from those of all other men. The amputation of it has not occasioned the least harm to my will, which remains quite entire, and my soul has lost nothing at all of its force, but it has no more command over that amputated part, which in the mean while continues still to be irritable. Irritability therefore is independent of the soul and the will. . . .

From all these experiments collected together it appears, that there is nothing irritable in the animal body but the muscular fibre, and that the faculty of endeavouring to shorten itself when we touch it is proper to this fibre. From the same experiments it likewise follows, that the vital parts are the most irritable; the diaphragm frequently moves after all the other muscles have ceased, the intestines and stomach move still longer, and lastly the heart continues its motions after all the other parts are quiet. This furnishes us with a distinct character between the vital organs and the others, *viz.* the first, being extremely irritable, require only a weak stimulus to put them in motion, whereas the others, which are endowed with very little Irritability, are not to be moved but by the determinations of the will, or by very strong irritations, the application of which is capable of producing in them violent commotions, known by the name of convulsions. . . .

The deceased M. De La Mettrie has made irritability the basis of the system which he advanced against the spirituality of the soul; and after saying that Stahl and Boerhaave knew nothing of it, he has the modesty to assume the invention to himself, without ever having made the least experiment about it. But I am certainly informed, that he learnt all he knew about it of a young Swiss with whom I am not acquainted: who never was my pupil, nor is he a physician, but he had read my works, and seen some of the famous Albinus's experiments, and upon these La Mettrie founded his impious system, which my experiments totally refute. For if Irritability subsists in parts separate from the body, and not subject to the command of the soul, if it resides every where in the muscular fibres, and is independent of the nerves, which are the *satellites* of the soul, it is evident, that it has nothing in common with the soul, and it is absolutely different from it; in a word, that neither irritability depends upon the soul, nor is the soul what we call Irritability in the body.

9.8

Robert Whytt

(1714–1766)

The principal opponent of Haller's views was Robert Whytt, who held the vitalistic position that mind must be involved in all forms of activity, including the vital functions. In the long run, the experimental evidence

[A] *An essay on the vital and other involuntary motions of animals.* Edinburgh, 1751. [Pp. 229–230, 239–240, 380–382, 384, 389–390.]
[B] *Observations on the nature, causes, and cure of those disorders which have been commonly called nervous, hypochondriac, or hysteric: to which are prefixed some remarks on the sympathy of the nerves.* Edinburgh, 1765. [Pp. 29–31, 37–39, 42–44, 50–51.]

he used to support this position fostered the understanding of reflex phenomena as responses free from control of mind.

[A]

[Sec. X] The muscular fibres of animals are so framed, as to contract whenever a cause proper to excite their action is applied to them, or, in defect of this, always to remain at rest. This cause is either an effort of the will, or a *stimulus* of some kind or other: to the former are owing the voluntary motions; and to the latter all such as we call vital and spontaneous.

How or in what manner the will acts upon the voluntary muscles, so as to bring them into contraction, is a question wholly beyond the reach of our faculties; and indeed, were it otherwise, the answer would be of no great importance, it being sufficient that experience convinces us the will is really possessed of this power. But, in this our endeavour to trace the vital and other involuntary motions up to their first source, it seems to be a matter of no small moment, to investigate the cause or causes which enable *stimuli* of various kinds to excite the muscles of living animals into contraction. . . .

4. Several physiological writers have supposed some latent power or property in the muscular fibres of animals, to which their motions, in consequence of an irritation are to be referred.

But this opinion seems to be no more than a refuge of ignorance, which nothing, but the despair of success in their inquiries into this matter, can have driven them into. For, if they here mean some unknown active powers resulting from the peculiar constitution or mechanical structure of a muscular fibre, it may be sufficient reason with us for denying there are any such latent causes, that the assertors of them have hitherto been as unable to vindicate their existence by *phaenomena,* which cannot be explained without them, as to specify their true nature; besides that it must appear greatly unphilosophical to attribute active powers to what, however modified or arranged, is yet no more than a system of pure matter; powers, I say, which are not only confessedly superior to the utmost efforts of mechanism, but contrary to all the known properties of matter. . . .

[Sec. XIII] 28. . . . Whoever considers the structure and *phaenomena* of the animal frame, will soon be convinced that the soul is not confined to an indivisible point, but must be present at one and the same time, if not in all the parts of the body, yet, at least, where-ever the nerves have their origin; *i.e.* it must be, at least, diffused along a great part of the brain and spinal marrow. . . .

But if the soul, without extension, be present at one and the same time in different places of the brain; and if in many animals it can act along the spinal marrow for a great while after the head is cut off, why may not it also actuate parts separated from the body, without being extended? On the other hand, if we allow the soul to occupy space, I don't see why it may not continue to be present with the parts of its body after they are separated, as well as when they were united. And with respect to the divisibility of the soul, which is generally thought to follow from the supposition of its being extended; why may it not be a substance so perfectly and essentially one, as that a division or separation of its parts would necessarily infer a destruction of its essence? . . .

But, not to perplex ourselves any longer with metaphysical difficulties, we shall recite a few experiments and observations, from which we are led, by the most obvious analogy, to conclude, that the motions of the separated parts of animals are owing to the soul or sentient principle still continuing to act in them.

29. A frog lives, and moves its members, for half an hour after its head is cut off; nay, when the body of a frog is divided in two, both the anterior and posterior extremities preserve life and a power of motion for a considerable time. . . .

[Other accounts of movement by mutilated animals are given, included a beheaded cock, a beheaded snake (see Perrault, 8.8), Redi's tortoise, etc.]

35. To sum up all in a few words; from what has been said, it appears undeniable, that the involuntary motions of living animals, and the alternate contractions of their muscles, after the general death of the body, or their being separated from it, are owing to one and the same cause; *viz.* an irritation of their fibres or membranes, or of such parts as are nearly connected with them. If then, as we have shewn, the motions of animal fibres, from a *stimulus*, must certainly bespeak a feeling, and cannot be explained unless we admit it; and if feeling be not a property of matter, but owing to a superior principle, it must follow, by necessary consequence, that the motions of the heart, and other muscles of animals, after being separated from their bodies, are to be ascribed to this principle; and that any difficulties, which may appear in this matter, are owing to our ignorance of the nature of the soul, of the manner of its existence, and of its wonderful union with, and action upon the body.

[B]

[Ch. I] 12. All *sympathy* or *consent* supposes feeling, and therefore must be owing to the nerves, which are the sole instruments of sensation. The truth of this seems to be fully evinced by the following experiment. When the hinder toes of a frog are wounded, immediately after cutting off its head, there is either no motion at all excited in the muscles of the legs, or a very inconsiderable one. But if the toes of this animal be pinched, or wounded with a pen-knife, ten or fifteen minutes after decollation, the muscles, not only of the legs and thighs, but also of the trunk of the body, are, for the most part, strongly convulsed, and the frog sometimes moves from one place to another. In this case, is not the irritation of the toes, immediately after decollation, rendered ineffectual to produce any motion in the muscles of the legs and thighs, by the greater pain occasioned by cutting off the head? And are not the muscles of the posterior extremities, as well as of the trunk of the body, brought into action by wounding the toes fifteen minutes after decollation, because the pain produced by cutting off the head, is now so much lessened, as not to prevent the animal from feeling very sensibly, when its toes are hurt?

But farther, that all *sympathy* is owing to feeling, and consequently proceeds from the nerves, appears evident, because the changes in the body, occasioned by the sympathy of the parts, are stopt by whatever affects the nervous system so strongly, as to overcome the sensations that produced those changes.—Thus the hiccup is stopt by terror, fear, surprise, or other strong passions.—An irritation of the nose will not occasion sneezing, when the first effort to sneeze is attended with an acute pain, in some of the muscles of the back or sides from a rheumatic cause. . . .

The prevailing opinion has been, that these *sympathies* are owing to the communications between the nerves, and particularly to the connexion which the intercostals have with the fifth, sixth, and eighth pairs, and with almost all those which proceed from the spinal marrow. Upon this principle, it has been thought easy to trace the various *sympathies*, not only between the several parts of the *abdomen*, but also between them and the head, neck, *thorax*, and extremities. But however plausible this theory may appear at first view, and how readily soever it may seem to explain many remarkable instances of *consent*, yet a more strict examination will shew it to be liable to insuperable difficulties.

(*a*) Since every individual nerve, appears to be quite distinct from every other, not only in its rise from the medullary substance of the brain or spinal marrow, but also in its progress to that part where it terminates, it follows, that the various instances of *sympathy*, observed between the different parts of the body, cannot be owing to any communication or *anastomosis* of their nerves. . . .

(*d*) We observe a remarkable sympathy between many parts, whose nerves have certainly not the smallest communication with one another. Thus the dimness of sight occasioned by a disorder of the stomach, the *nausea* upon seeing others vomit, and the flux of *saliva* into the mouth of a hungry person, at the sight of savoury food, are proofs, that the stomach and salivary glands *sympathize* with the *retina*, tho there is no communication between the optic nerves and any other.—A shudder is excited by particular sounds, and yet the *portio mollis* of the auditory nerve, after it leaves the brain, does not appear to communicate with the *portio dura,* nor any other nerve.—Altho' the optic nerves unite at the *cella Turcica,* yet it has been shewn, that their fibres do not cross, intermix, or truly communicate with each other; nevertheless, there is a considerable sympathy between the two eyes.—Altho' the nerves of the two kidneys, do not appear to have any connection with each other, yet, when one of these glands is inflamed, or irritated by a stone, the secretion from the other is frequently much diminished.—We know for certain, that the different size of the pupil in different lights, is owing to a *consent* between the *retina* and *uvea,* and yet the optic nerves, and those belonging to the *uvea,* have no communication, in their course from the brain to the eye. Nor can any sympathy be supposed to arise from the nerves of the *uvea,* passing between the *retina* and *tunica choroidea,* as there is no *anastomosis,* nor any other kind of union between them. The nerves, with which the *uvea* of the two eyes are furnished, have no connection, and yet we find a most remarkable sympathy between the motions of the two pupils. . . .

15. If, therefore, the various instances of sympathy cannot be accounted for, from any union or *anastomosis* of the nerves, in their way from the brain to the several organs; and if there are many remarkable influences of *consent,* between parts whose nerves have no connexion at all; it follows, that all sympathy must be referred to the brain itself and spinal marrow, the source of all the nerves.

9·9

Charles Bell

(1774–1842)

The discovery that each spinal nerve includes sensory fibers which enter the spinal column by the nerve's posterior root and motor fibers which leave it by the anterior root was a decisive step toward understanding motor control.. However, when Bell discovered the distinction between the roots he did not interpret it in this manner, and what he says in the first selection below should not be read with preconceptions based on present knowledge. He wrote to his brother, in March 1810, that "It is almost superfluous to say that the part of the spinal marrow having sensibility is what comes from the cerebrum; the posterior and insensible part belongs to the cerebellum." His error was in part due to the fact that he worked

[A] *Idea for a new anatomy of the brain.* London, 1811. [Pp. 17–23.]
[B] On the nervous circle which connects the voluntary muscles with the brain. *Philosophical Transactions,* 116 (1826), Part II, 163–173. [163–168, 170.]

with stunned animals. After Magendie (1783–1835) demonstrated the correct distinction in 1822, Bell's friends claimed priority for him. However, Bell did then develop the implications of this distinction, as seen in the second selection.

[A]

On examining the grand divisions of the brain we are forced to admit that there are four brains. For the brain is divided longitudinally by a deep fissure; and the line of distinction can even be traced where the sides are united in substance. . . .

I speak of the lateral divisions of the brain being distinct brains combined in function, in order the more strongly to mark the distinction betwixt the anterior and posterior grand divisions. Betwixt the lateral parts there is a strict resemblance in form and substance: each principal part is united by transverse tracts of medullary matter; and there is every provision for their acting with perfect sympathy. On the contrary, the *cerebrum,* the anterior grand division, and the *cerebellum,* the posterior grand division, have slight and indirect connection. In form and division of parts, and arrangement of white and grey matter, there is no resemblance. There is here nothing of that symmetry and correspondence of parts which is so remarkable betwixt the right and left portions. . . .

From these facts . . . we are entitled to conclude, that in the operations excited in the brain there cannot be such sympathy or corresponding movement in the cerebrum and cerebellum as there is betwixt the lateral portions of the cerebrum; that the anterior and posterior grand divisions of the brain perform distinct offices. . . .

. . . We can trace down the crura of the cerebrum into the anterior fasciculus of the spinal marrow, and the crura of the *cerebellum* into the posterior fasciculus. I thought that here I might have an opportunity of touching the *cerebellum,* as it were, through the posterior portion of the spinal marrow, and the cerebrum by the anterior portion. To this end I made experiments which, though they were not conclusive, encourage me in the view I had taken.

I found that injury done to the anterior portion of the spinal marrow convulsed the animal more certainly than injury done to the posterior portion; but I found it difficult to make the experiment without injuring both portions.

Next considering that the spinal nerves have a double root, and being of opinion that the properties of the nerves are derived from their connections with the parts of the brain, I thought that I had an opportunity of putting my opinion to the test of experiment, and of proving at the same time that nerves of different endowments were in the same cord, and held together by the same sheath.

On laying bare the roots of the spinal nerves, I found that I could cut across the posterior fasciculus of nerves, which took its origin from the posterior portion of the spinal marrow without convulsing the muscles of the back; but that on touching the anterior fasciculus with the point of the knife, the muscles of the back were immediately convulsed.

Such were my reasons for concluding that the cerebrum and the cerebellum were parts distinct in function, and that every nerve possessing a double function obtained that by having a double root.

[B]

But having satisfied myself that the roots of the spinal nerves had distinct powers, I followed up the columns of the spinal marrow; and with a knowledge of the composition of those nerves as a key, I examined the different properties of the nerves of the encephalon. . . . I hope now to demonstrate—*that where nerves of different functions take their origin apart and run a different course: two nerves must unite in the muscles, in order to perfect the relations betwixt the brain and these muscles.* . . .

Having in a former Paper demonstrated that the portio dura of the seventh nerve was the motor of the face, and that it ran distinct from the sensitive nerve, the fifth, and observing that they joined at their extremities, or plunged together into the muscles, I . . . therefore cast about for other examples of the distribution of the muscular nerves. It was easy to find motor nerves in combination with sensitive nerves, for all the spinal nerves are thus composed; but we wanted a muscular nerve clear in its course, to see what alliance it would form in its ultimate distribution in the muscle. I found in the lower maxillary nerve the example I required.

The fifth pair, from which this lower maxillary nerve comes . . . arises in two roots; one of these is the muscular nerve, the other the sensible nerve: on this last division the Gasserian ganglion is formed. But we can trace the motor nerve clear of the ganglion and onward in its course to the muscles of the jaws and so it enters the temporal masseter pterygoid and buccinator muscles.

If all that is necessary to the action of a muscle be a nerve to excite to contraction, these branches should have been unaccompanied; but on the contrary, I found that before these motor nerves entered the several muscles, they were joined by branches of the nerves which came through the Gasserian ganglion, and which were sensitive nerves.

I found the same result on tracing motor nerves into the orbit, and that the sensitive division of the fifth pair of nerves was transmitted to the muscles of the eye, although these muscles were supplied by the third, fourth, and sixth nerves. . . .

. . . The question therefore may thus be stated: why are nerves, whose office it is to convey sensation, profusely given to muscles in addition to those motor nerves which are given to excite their motions? and why do both classes of muscular nerves form plexus? . . .

I shall first inquire, if it be necessary to the governance of the muscular frame, that there be a consciousness of the state or degree of action of the muscles? That we have a sense of the condition of the muscles, appears from this: that we feel the effects of over exertion and weariness, and are excruciated by spasms, and feel the irksomeness of continued position. We possess a power of weighing in the hand:—what is this but estimating the muscular force? We are sensible of the most minute changes of muscular exertion, by which we know the position of the body and limbs, when there is no other means of knowledge open to us. . . .

If it be granted that there must be a sense of the condition of the muscle, we have next to show that a motor nerve is not a conductor towards the brain, and that it cannot perform the office of a sensitive nerve. . . .

Expose the two nerves of a muscle; irritate one of them, and the muscle will act; irritate the other, and the muscle remains at rest. Cut across the nerve which had the power of exciting the muscle, and stimulate the one which is undivided—the animal will give indication of pain; but although the nerve be injured so as to cause universal agitation, the muscle with which it is directly connected does not move. Both nerves being cut across, we shall still find that by exciting one nerve the muscle is made to act, even days after the nerve has been divided; but the other nerve has no influence at all. . . .

Between the brain and the muscles there is a circle of nerves; one nerve conveys the influence from the brain to the muscle, another gives the sense of the condition of the muscle to the brain. If the circle be broken by the division of the motor nerve, motion ceases; if it be broken by division of the other nerve, there is no longer a sense of the condition of the muscle, and therefore no regulation of its activity.

9.10

Eduard Pflüger

(1829–1910)

One hundred years after Whytt, Pflüger took up again the defense of what Lotze, in a famous controversy, derided as a "spinal soul." Pflüger contends that conscious purpose, as well as sensibility, must guide the adaptive behavior he describes in decerebrate frogs.

Die sensorischen Functionen des Rückenmarks der Wirbelthiere [The sensory function of the spinal medulla in vertebrates]. Berlin, 1853. [Pp. 125–129.]

We behead a frog in the manner described, lay it on its back, and wait a little while until the exhaustion which usually occurs after decapitation is over. If then the hind legs are drawn up to the body with such force that the frog pulls them in if we try to stretch them, or even pushes defensively against the fingers, the animal is suitable for the experiment.

We then dip a wire or a glass rod in acetic acid, and place a small drop on the skin above the inner condyle of the femur. The consequence is that the frog bends the irritated leg while stretching the other, so that its body is pulled down somewhat over the limb that is stretched. The foot belonging to the irritated thigh is now brought up so that the back of its toes touches the irritated spot, and it brushes off the corrosive substance by rubbing back and forth, by alternate abduction and adduction of the foot.

To explain this movement in the fashion that is usually accepted we would have to say that the particular point of the skin is connected, by way of nerves which terminate there, with a special motor group in the spinal medulla, and by this means a stimulus to this particular spot produces this particular movement. Especially so, since it always occurs in this same way, as I have witnessed on 40 or 50 occasions.

But now we shall see whether particular motor mechanisms are innervated from this particular spot, as in a reflex, so that this wiping action is merely the necessary consequence of a reflex mechanism running its course, or whether the act of wiping is the end to be attained, so that the innervation of particular motor elements is only a means to this end. We will cut away the shank in another frog which has been prepared in the same way, and see what will happen now that the former movement no longer can achieve the wiping action, when we irritate the same spot as before. If we are dealing with a machine, the same thing will happen as before, particular motor elements will be innervated from this same particular spot of the skin, just because it is a machine by virtue of which these particular skin nerves are connected in the spinal medulla with particular motor elements, or yoked to them. But if all this is not the case, if the earlier action was voluntary, then the frog will now take other measures to achieve its purpose, and quite other movements will take place than before.

The reflex mechanism has all the same conditions for appearing as before. But the wiping effect will not be achieved!—Now what happens? —Since the frog must suppose that it still has its shank, because of the . . . phenomena going on in the sensitive fibers, it will try to use its old method again. And in fact, when we stimulate the little spot of skin over the inner condyle of the femur, the irritated thigh does bend, the leg which is not stimulated does stretch, and the stump of the shank moves in a manner which leaves no doubt that up to this point we have the same phenomenon as before. But then the scene changes. The animal's movements become very restless, and give an appearance as if it were seeking a new means to remove the source of pain. And after it has carried out various purposeless movements, it does rather often find the suitable means.

Now we see that the leg which has been stimulated, and the stump of which is amputated, is extended, and the one which had not been stimulated is rather strongly bent and adducted, so that . . . it becomes possible to wipe off the acid irritant with the sole of the opposite foot. As we see, these movements are completely different from the previous ones. Previously we had flexion of the stimulated leg, and extension of the one not stimulated. Now, although only one piece of skin was stimulated in both cases, we see quite the opposite: extension of the stimulated leg and flexion of the one not stimulated. Thus we see that if the frog is denied the use of one foot, he quite simply makes use of the other, and thus it makes a choice between different means. . . .

Take the head off a frog, lay it on its stomach, and stimulate the skin of the back on either the right side or the left. If we stimulate the right side, it reaches toward its back with the toes of the right foot and wipes away the corrosive acid, which is made possible by flexion and abduction of the femur. If we stimulate on the left side, it uses the left foot. We know too well what the generally accepted explanation of this action is.

Now cut off one leg of the decapitated frog, for example the right leg, and apply acid to the right side of the back. Now it is the left leg which takes over the task of wiping away the acid that is on the right side. . . .

One can devise many variations of this basic experiment, all of which come down to this fact, that after we apply an irritant to the animal it is not a matter of having certain motor elements innervated, but of achieving a certain purpose. It is not the attainment of the purpose which is sidetracked, to carry out the reflex process, but it is the innervation of specific motor elements which is sidetracked, if the purpose can no longer be attained through them. And since the movement which is aroused by an irritant, even though it is always the same spot on the skin that is irritated, may take many different forms, as may be required for the attainment of a specific purpose, it is irrefutably demonstrated that the fragmented animals with which we are dealing are endowed with sensation and volition.

9.11

Ivan Sechenov

(1829–1905)

Sechenov found that by stimulating certain points in the brain stem of a decapitated frog it is possible to inhibit lower spinal reflexes. Thus he discovered a neurological basis for the sort of variability in response which Pflüger had regarded as evidence of conscious purpose. Sechenov applied the result boldly to the solution of a problem which he had expressed six years earlier: "the outstanding feature of the normal activity of the brain . . . is the disproportion between excitation and effect." The result was a theoretical model in which the mechanism for control of movement became the very substance of thought. He called it "An attempt to establish the physiological basis of mental processes." The czarist censor objected both to the title and to the work's planned appearance in Sovremenik (The contemporary), a liberal journal of opinion edited by Chernyshevsky. It was permitted to appear serially in a medical weekly, with a title which has, to our ears, a more revolutionary sound: The reflexes of the brain. The book passed through intermittent periods of suppression, and it was influential on the student generation which included Pavlov and Bekhterev.

§11. . . . *All psychical acts without exception, if they are not complicated by elements of emotion . . . develop by way of reflex. Hence, all conscious movements resulting from these acts and usually described as voluntary, are reflex movements in the strict sense of the word.*

§12. Thus, the question whether voluntary movements are based on stimulation of sensory nerves has been answered in the affirmative. . . .

Now I shall pass to the second question: Does the mechanism of inhibition, already known to us from the study of reflexes, play any role in originating voluntary movements? . . .

Are there any phenomena in man's conscious life which show that movements are inhibited? These phenomena are so numerous and so pronounced that it is because of them that all movements effected with full consciousness are called voluntary movements. On what is the usual concept of these movements based? It is based on the fact that man, influenced by one and the same external and moral conditions, can perform a definite series of movements, exhibit no movement at all, or, finally,

Reflexes of the brain [Refleksii mozga, 1863]. In *Selected physiological and psychological works.* Edited by K. Koshtoyants, translated by S. Belsky. Moscow: Foreign Languages Publishing House, n.d. Pp. 31–139. [Pp. 110–113, 116.]

can perform movements of an altogether reverse nature. As is known, people of strong will can suppress the most irresistible, seemingly involuntary movements; for example, one man screams and struggles when suffering acute pain, another endures it silently without making the slightest movement, while a third performs movements which are utterly incompatible with pain, for example, he jokes and laughs.

Consequently in conscious life there are cases of inhibition both of movements generally regarded as involuntary, and of those known as voluntary. Since, however, voluntary movements develop in accordance with the basic laws of reflexes, we may, naturally, assume that the mechanism in both cases is the same. . . .

Let us accept this hypothesis and assume that there are mechanisms in the human brain which inhibit muscular movements. . . .

Let us now see how the child's ability to inhibit movements, or, strictly speaking, to eliminate the last member of a reflex, is acquired by learning.

Childhood is generally characterized by extremely extensive reflex movements arising in response to relatively weak . . . external sensory stimulations. For example, reflexes from ear and eye spread to almost all the muscles of the body. The time comes, however, when the movements, so to speak, become grouped. One or two entire groups of muscles separate from the mass of other muscles which have functioned in a disorderly manner; having become more limited, the movements acquire a definite character. It is in this limiting process that the inhibitory mechanisms take part. For the sake of simplicity, let us examine the transition from the simultaneous flexion of all the fingers of the hand to the separate flexion of one finger. Assuming that the simultaneous flexion of all fingers is due to certain inborn properties of the child's make-up (which is really so), it is obvious that one finger can be moved separately only if the movement of the other fingers is inhibited. There is no other explanation. . . .

Thus, man not only learns to group his movements through the frequent repetition of associated reflexes, he, at the same time, acquires (also by means of reflexes) capacity to inhibit them. That is why psychic activity in the multitude of phenomena remains, so to speak, without external manifestation, i.e., in the form of thoughts, intentions, wishes, etc.

I shall now show the reader the first and most important result of man's capacity to inhibit the last member of a reflex. This can be summarized as *the ability to think, meditate, and reason.* What, actually, is the process of thinking? It is the series of interconnected notions and concepts which exists in man's consciousness at a given time and which is not expressed in external manifestations resulting from these psychical acts. But a psychical act, as the reader knows, cannot appear in consciousness without an external sensory stimulation. Consequently, thought is also subordinated to this law. It manifests, therefore, the beginning of a reflex and its continuation; only the end of the reflex, i.e. movement, is apparently absent.

A thought is the first two-thirds of a psychical reflex.

9.12

Rudolf Heidenhain

(1834–1897)

Sechenov's concept of intracortical inhibition was only a bold speculation. A firm basis for it was provided by Heidenhain, in an experiment published together with Nicholas Bubnoff, a Russian student whose death soon after interrupted a promising career. Heidenhain's interest in the physiological basis of hypnotic phenomena led to these experiments, which involved stimulation of the motor cortex in dogs under narcosis. The method thus rests on the prior demonstration of the motor area (10.7).

[II] . . . It is well known that we are able not only voluntarily to innervate muscles but also voluntarily to put muscles out of action. The question, however, whether the voluntary interruption of muscular activity is due simply to the cessation of impulses from the motor centers or to positive antagonistic effects which inhibit the action of these motor centers, has hardly ever been seriously considered and much less subjected to experiments. The observations reported . . . show that it is indeed possible to evoke from the periphery antagonistic effects, putting motor centers out of action. These peripheral stimuli were surprisingly small; in fact, much smaller than those which elicited activity of the centers from the same receptor apparatus. The foregoing observations necessarily lead to the question whether slight direct stimulation of the motor centers might not act in a way similar to slight peripheral stimuli and terminate an excitatory state.

Experimentation gave a positive answer. If either reflexly, or by a strong electrical stimulation of the cortex, a continuous muscular contraction was induced, it could be released by a much smaller stimulation of the self-same cortical point. This occurred either completely after a single stimulus or in steps after repeated stimuli. . . .

[III] . . . We do not wish to enter into a discussion of the nature of the

Bubnoff, N., and Heidenhain, R. Ueber Erregungs– und Hemmungsvorgänge innerhalb der motorischen Hirncentren. *Pflüger's Archiv für die gesammte Physiologie* 26 (1881): 137–200. Translated by G. von Bonin and W. S. McCullough, as "On excitatory and inhibitory processes within the motor centers of the brain." *Illinois Monographs in the Medical Sciences*, 4 (1944): 173–210. [Pp. 202–203, 206–210.]

impulses issuing from the cortex—a discussion which at present could not be brought to a conclusive end. Nonetheless, we would like to mention a conception advanced by several authors in order to emphasize its questionable value. Following Meynert and Wernicke, H. Munk maintains that movements are induced from the cortex only by "motor images" which originate in the cortex and that "with the origin of a motor image of a certain intensity that particular movement is immediately executed if it is not inhibited from somewhere." Drawing the full consequence of this conception, Wernicke . . . has pronounced the opinion that the electric stimulation of the cortex in its motor regions at first "evokes memory images of movements, motor images which evoke complex muscular effects by centrifugal fibers issuing from the ganglion cells which are involved." Quite apart from any other consequences, this conception seems to run afoul of the results of our experiments. For we have reported that electric stimulation of the same cortical point either induces movement or inhibits a movement induced in some other way—depending entirely on its intensity. Should the electric current evoke in the first case the image of a movement and in the second case the image of quiescence? It would be hard to find anybody who would dare to answer this question affirmatively.

In any event, investigations of the physiological processes in the brain should ignore as much as possible the contents of consciousness correlated with these processes if their goal is to interpret physical events. Whether it is an image or whether it is the will which induces a movement, in either case the psychic process will go hand in hand with a physical process in the cortex. It is this physical process which is the immediate cause of the motor excitation, and which is obviously the immediate object of the physiological investigations. The less physiology employs psychological conceptions, the surer will be the basis which it will one day be able to lay for a physiological psychology in the wider sense of the word.

When, in that spirit, we try to analyze the processes in the motor centers, it has to be emphasized that the motor nerve fibers which supply the various muscles and muscle-groups of the body do not find their first connections for the purpose of coordinating movements in the cortex but at lower levels. However, as we observed, cortex and subcortical centers have certain general properties in common.

Thus under normal conditions a transient stimulus which, directly or indirectly, acts on the motor centers, evokes only a transient state of excitation. Under certain conditions, however, every excitation of the motor centers assumes permanence.

If one clings to the conceptions of excitability deduced from experiments on nerve fibers, one will be prone to think that the tonic character of central excitations is due merely to the increased excitability of the center. However, the expression "increased excitability" does not explain very much. Moreover, "increased excitability" presupposes that weak stimuli are unusually strongly exciting. But we have seen just the opposite, namely that very weak peripheral or central stimuli may terminate a pre-existing excitation. This phenomenon does not fit into the conception that we simply have to do with "increased excitability." Rather, it proves that a weak stimulus must induce processes different in their nature from those which correspond to excitation.

Both phenomena—the tonic character assumed under certain circumstances by all excitations, as well as their disappearance after weak stimuli—indicate an unexpected complexity of the process of central innervation.

It appears that under normal conditions every central excitation finds or creates within the excited centers conditions which, as soon as the stimulus has disappeared, make this excitation vanish or decrease below threshold. If such a precise delimitation of central motor or sensory excitation did not exist, we would neither be able to execute intentionally movements of measurable duration nor would our sensations correspond to the temporal sequence of the extraneous stimuli producing them.

This very obvious train of thought leads to the conception that in central processes excitation must be coupled with another event which exerts a dampening influence on the induced excitation. The exact nature of these inhibitory influences, however, we are unable to define in detail, and we hope all the more to be excused since the exact nature of the excitatory process is also undefined. . . .

The assumption of inhibitory processes accompanying excitatory processes in the motor centers of the brain appears also to make intelligible the differences in the effect which a stimulation of the cortex and a stimulation of the subjacent white matter induce. . . . Other conditions being equal, the reaction time is longer, the contraction of the musculature generally smaller, and the muscular curve drawn out longer in the latter than in the former case. These differences can be understood by the assumption that direct cortical stimulation induces not only processes of excitation but simultaneously processes of inhibition. These processes distribute the development of the kinetic energies in the excited elements over a longer duration by increasing them at a later moment above threshold (prolongation of reaction time), and on the other hand keep them above that value for a longer time (drawing out of contraction curve), while simultaneously the absolute intensity of the excitation becomes smaller (decrease of muscular contraction). In these experiments, too, sensory stimuli of a certain intensity are effective. They lead to an increase of inhibition; hence the muscular contractions decrease and the reaction times and durations of the contractions increase simultaneously. The assumption of inhibitions as part and parcel of the mechanisms of central innervation affecting by their relative value—i.e. by the ratio of their intensity to that of the excitations—the quantitative aspects of the process of excitation both in its intensity and its temporal sequence, enables us to understand many other things which heretofore were enigmatic. If we assume, as we are almost driven to do, that inhibitions delimit not only the temporal but also the spatial spread of excitation, then it becomes clear that in deep morphine narcosis excitations spread unusually easily from the primarily excited centers to other ones. Quite correctly Munk pointed out that the tendency to respond to local stimulation of the cortex with general epileptic seizures is particularly noticeable in dogs subjected to large doses of morphine. A state of increased excitability which can be observed in many individuals as a consequence of morphine also indicates an easy spread of the state of excitation from the sensory to the motor centers. . . .

. . . These considerations do not, of course, furnish a theory of central innervation, but only some material for such a theory. Whatever shape that theory takes, it will have to reckon with the facts which we have reported. The further development of a theory will largely depend on our progress in the understanding and evaluation of inhibitory processes.

9.13

Charles Scott Sherrington

(1857–1952)

Sherrington's analysis of postural and locomotor reflexes of the decerebrate dog provides a dynamic picture of the native reflex mechanisms as the basis on which the superstructure of intentional behavior can be erected. He does not deal with "reflex arcs," but with behaviors built of interacting reflex components. His hypothesis regarding the synaptic seat of the inhibitory process was finally validated in the work of Eccles, who had studied with Sherrington's own student, Adrian.

Sherrington and Adrian shared a Nobel prize in 1932; Eccles received one in 1963.

Orderly sequence of movement characterizes the outward behaviour of animals. Not least so where, as in the earthworm crawling, or the insect in flight, or the fish swimming, every observer admits the coadjustment is essentially reflex. One act succeeds another without confusion. Yet, tracing this sequence to its external causes, we recognize that the usual thing in nature is not for one exciting stimulus to begin immediately

The integrative action of the nervous system. New Haven: Yale University Press, 1906. [Pp. 182, 190–192, 199, 233, 234.]

after another ceases, but for an array of environmental agents acting concurrently on the animal at any moment to exhibit correlative changes in regard to it, so that one or another group of them becomes—generally by increase in intensity—temporarily prepotent. . . . Thus each reflex in the mutilated animal breaks in upon a condition of relative equilibrium; and this latter is itself reflex. . . .

If it is advantageous for the transition from one reflex to another of like type to occur without a period of confusion, it is still more advantageous that it should be so in the case of transitions from one reflex to another of converse type. . . . In the transition from one reflex to another of antagonistic kind the avoidance of confusion of the two reflexes emphasizes at the same time the impossibility of co-ordinating them in a simultaneous combination. . . .

The process in virtue of which this transition from one antagonistic reflex to another occurs is obviously one of active intervention. In many cases the form which the intervention takes is inhibition. . . .

We do not yet understand the intimate nature of inhibition. In the cases before us now, its seat is certainly central, and in all probability is, as argued above, situated at points of synapsis. I have urged that a prominent physiological feature of the synapse is a synaptic membrane. It seems therefore to me that inhibition in such cases as those before us is probably referrable to a change in the condition of the synaptic membrane causing a block of conduction. . . .

Whatever the intimate nature of the inhibition, it is, however, only one part of the processes involved in transition from one antagonistic reflex to another. In the transition from the crossed extension-reflex to the flexion-reflex the inhibition of previous excitation in the extensor neurone is accompanied by excitation of the previously inhibited flexor neurone. And conversely in the transition from flexion-reflex to extension-reflex. . . . The process of transition, therefore, in many cases is one half of it inhibitory, one half excitatory. . . .

. . . The central organ is a vast network whose lines of conduction follow a certain scheme of pattern, but within that pattern the details of connection are, at the entrance to each common path, mutable. The gray matter may be compared with a telephone exchange, where, from moment to moment, though the end-points of the system are fixed, the connections between starting points and terminal points are changed to suit passing requirements, as the functional points are shifted at a great railway junction. In order to realize the exchange at work, one must add to its purely spatial plan the temporal datum that within certain limits the connections of the lines shift to and fro from minute to minute. An example is the "reciprocal innervation" of antagonistic muscles—when one muscle of the antagonistic couple is thrown into action the other is thrown out of action. This is only a widely spread case of the general rule that antagonistic reflexes interfere where they embouch upon the same final common paths. . . .

In the case of simple antagonistic muscles, and in the instances of simple spinal reflexes, the shifts of conductive pattern due to interaction at the mouths of common paths are of but small extent. The co-ordination covers, for instance, one limb or a pair of limbs. But the same principle extended to the reaction of the great arcs arising in the projicient receptor organs of the head, *e.g.* the eye, which deal with wide tracts of muscula- . ture *as a whole,* operates with more multiplex shift of the conductive pattern. Releasing forces acting on the brain from moment to moment shut out from activity whole regions of the nervous system, as they conversely call vast other regions into play. *The resultant singleness of action from moment to moment is a key-stone in the construction of the individual unity it is the specific office of the nervous system to perfect.* The interference of unlike reflexes and the alliance of like reflexes in their action upon their common paths seem to lie at the very root of the great psychical process of "attention."

Chapter 10

LOCALIZATION OF FUNCTION IN THE BRAIN

Theories of specialization of function within the brain were at first purely speculative, though basing themselves ostensibly on clinical data. Subsequently experimental evidence, derived at first from crude lesions, then from ablation studies, then from effects produced by electrical stimulation, and most recently from study of differential effects of drugs and chemicals and from recordings of electrical activity, have brought steadily increasing knowledge, stubbornly resisted at all times by those who held conceptions of mind as essentially unitary. Indeed, quite recently W. Riese wrote (A history of neurology, 1959) that the contemporary advance of "holistic" views has "marked the antagonism and final victory of the 'universalists' over the 'localists.'" The struggle is understandably bitter, for the opposite outcome would compel abandonment of Riese's view that "structures are only instruments, and it is not up to them to decide whether they may be used, and, if used, to what extent and for what purpose." To the degree that function is localized, mind becomes mechanism.

10.1

Gregor Reisch

(†1525)

The scheme of localization presented in this chapter was taken by Avicenna (980–1037) from late Hellenistic writers. Introduced into Europe through the school of Salerno, it was soon adopted universally, for Avicenna's authority rivaled that of Galen. This crude statement of it, with its woodcut illustration, has special interest because of a statement by Vesalius (8.4) that when he was a student of philosophy at Louvain (not when he was a student of medicine at Paris!) he was taught that this figure contained everything needful to know about the brain. An Italian translation at the end of the century (Margarita filosofica, Venice, 1599) not only omitted the illustration, but substituted one error for another by ending this short chapter with the words: "However, you should know that these divisions of the brain are not accepted by the anatomists, who in fact have demonstrated that the ventricles do not exist in it."

On the Nature, Number, and Organs
of the Internal Senses in General

Student: Your health, honored teacher!

Master: And yours, my son. What is the meaning of the happiness which shines in your face?

S: Listen. Everything that we discussed yesterday about the nature of the senses, I saw again in my sleep and understood very clearly, and I can scarcely wonder enough at this, that in sleep one can remember what happened when one was awake.

M: After you know something of the nature of the internal senses, as well as the external, this wonder of yours will cease.

S: Is it possible to explain all this in one day?

M: Indeed, for I will explain all this to you in brief. There is—not to hold you long in suspense—a faculty of the interior sense which perceives sensible things even in their absence. As we have indicated, sensible things are detected by means of their species and images. These are received by the external senses, and they pass through the nerves from the organ to the brain; there, with the help of the internal senses, they

Margarita philosophica, cum additionibus novi ab auctore suo studiossima revisione quarto super additis [The pearl of philosophy, with new additions, carefully revised by the author]. Basle, 1517. [Book X, Tract 2, Chapter 21.]

give rise to sensations even of remote sensible things. And now let me tell you in brief what you want to know: the number of the internal senses and their separate organs.

S: Very good.

M: There are five internal senses, to wit: the common sense, imagination, estimation, fantasy (which sometimes also is called imagination) and memory. Their organs in the substance of the brain are separated by very fine membranes; these separate the brain first into three ventricles,

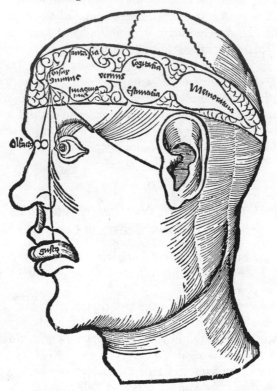

and of these the anterior and the middle ventricles, which are the largest, are again divided into two. The first part of the anterior ventricle is the organ of common sense, and the second part, of imagination. The first part of the middle ventricle is for estimation, and the second part for fantasy. The posterior ventricle is given over entirely to memory. This is enough to say about the organs. Let us now deal with their operations in the same order.

10.2

Juan Huarte

(1530?–1591?)

Huarte has been called the first modern psychologist because of his interest in individual differences. He not only rejects Galen's teaching on where the animal spirits are concocted, but he also rejects the accepted doctrine of localization of the faculties in separate ventricles, and prefers that the brain shall work as a unit. However, he finds that this brain may excel in judgment, imagination, or memory according as it excels in dryness, warmth, or moisture. This provides him with the basis for a theory of aptitudes which stirred so much interest that the book had 70 editions in half a dozen languages before 1700.

For Huarte's position on instinct, see 15.4.

[Ch. V] *It is proved that from the three qualities, hot, moist, and drie, proceed all the differences of mens wits.*

The reasonable soule making abode in the body, it is impossible that the same can performe contrary and different operations, if for each of them it use not a particular instrument. . . .

. . . With this selfe power of the soule, we understand, imagine, and remember. But if it be true, that every worke requires a particular instrument, it behooveth of necessitie, that within the braine there be one instrument for the understanding, one for the imagination, and another different from them for the memorie: for if all the braine were instrumentalized after one selfe manner, either the whole should be memorie, or the whole understanding, or the whole imagination. But we see that these are very different operations, and therefore it is of force that there be also a varietie in the instruments. But if we open by skill, and make an anatomie of the braine, we shall find the whole compounded after one manner, of one kind of substance, and alike, without parts of other kinds, or a different sort; onely there appeare foure little hollownesses, who (if we well marke them) have all one selfe composition and figure, without anything coming betweene which may breed a difference.

What the use and profit of these may be, and whereto they serve in the head, is not easily decideable: for *Galen* and the Anatomists, as well new as ancient, have laboured to find out the truth, but none of them hath precisely nor in particular, expressed whereto the right ventricle serveth,

Examen de ingenios para las sciencias [Baeza, 1575]. Translated by Richard Carew (from an Italian version by C. Camilli) as, *The examination of mens wits*. London, 1594. [Pp. 51–56, 58, 61, 63–64.]

nor the left, nor that which is placed in the middest of these two, nor the fourth, whose seat in the braine keepes the hinder part of the head. . . .

The truth of this matter is, that the fourth ventricle hath the office of digesting and altering the vitall spirits, and to convert them into animal, for that end which we have before remembred. And therefore nature hath severed the same so great a distance from the other three, and made that braine sundred apart, and so far off (as appeareth) to the end, that by his operation, he hinder not the contemplation of the rest. The three ventricles placed in the forepart, I doubt not, but that nature made them to none other end than to discourse and philosophise. Which is apparently prooved, for that in great studyings and contemplations, alwaies that part of the head finds it self agreed, which answereth these three concavities. The force of this argument is to be knowne, by consideration, that when the other powers are wearie of performing their workes, the instruments are alwaies agreeed, whose service they used; as in our much looking, the eyes are pained; and with much going, the soules of the feet wax sore.

Now the difficultie consists, to know in which of these ventricles the understanding is placed, in which the memorie, and in which the imagination, for they are so united and nere neighboured, that neither by the last argument, nor by any other notice, they can be distinguished or discerned. Then considering that the understanding cannot worke without the memorie be present, representing unto the same the figures and fantasies agreeable thereunto, it behooveth that the understanding part busie it selfe in beholding the fantasmes, and that the memorie cannot do it, if the imagination do not accompany the same (as we have already heretofore declared) we shall easily understand, that all the powers are united in every severall ventricle, and that the understanding is not solely in the one, nor the memory solely in the other, nor the imagination in the third, as the vulgar Philosophers have imagined, but that this union of powers is accustomably made in mans body, in as much as the one cannot worke without the aid of the other. . . .

In an infirmitie which the Phisitions tearme Resolution, or Palsie of the middle side, the operation is ordinarily lost of that ventricle which is strooken on that side, & if the other two remained not sound, & without endammageance, a man should thereby become witles, and void of reason. And yet for all this, by wanting that onely ventricle, there is a great abatement discerned in his operations, as well in those of the understanding, as of the imaginative, and memorie, as they shal also find in the losse of one sight, who were woont to behold with two; whereby we cleerely comprize, that in every ventricle are all the three powers, sithens by the annoiance of any one, all the three are weakened. Seeing then al the three ventricles are of one selfe composition, and that there rests not amongst them any varietie of parts, we may not leave to take the first qualities for an instrument, and to make so many generall differences of wits, as they are in number. For to thinke that the reasonable soule being in the body, can worke without some bodily instrument to assist her, is against all naturall Philosophie. But of the foure qualities, heat, cold, moisture, and drouth: all Phisitions leaave out cold, as unprofitable to any operation of the reasonable soule, wherethrough it is seene by experience in the other habilities, that if the same mount above heat, all the powers of man do badly performe their operations, neither can the stomacke digest his meat, nor the cods yeeld fruitfull seed, nor the muscles move the body, nor the brain discourse. . . .

. . . So there remaine drouth, moisture, and heat for the service of the reasonable facultie. But no Philosopher as yet wist to give to every difference of wit determinatly that which was his. . . .

. . . Memorie (verely) laies up and preserveth in it selfe, the things knowne by the sence, and by the mind, & is therin as it were their storehouse and receiving place, and not their inventer. And if this be the use thereof, it fals out apparent, that the same dependeth on moisture; for this makes the braine pliant, and the figure is imprinted by way of strayning. . . .

By this doctrine is perfectly seene that the understanding and memorie, are powers opposit and contrary, in sort, that the man who hath a great memorie, shall find a defect in his understanding, and he who hath a great understanding cannot enioy a good memorie: for it is impossible that the braine should of his owne nature, be at one selfe time drie and moist. . . .

From heat, which is the third qualitie, groweth the imaginative, for there is no other reasonable power in the braine, nor any other qualitie to which it may be assigned besides that, the sciences which appertaine to the imaginative, are those, which such utter as dote in their sicknesse, and not of those which appertaine to the understanding, or to the memorie. And frenzie, peevishness, and melancholy, being hot passions of the braine, it yeelds a great argument, to proove that imagination consists in heat. One thing breeds me a difficultie herein, and that is, that the imagination carrieth a contrarietie to the understanding, as also to the memorie, and the reason hereof is not to be gotten by experience, for in the braine may very wel be united much heat and much drinesse; and so likewise, much heat and much moisture, to a large quantitie: and for this cause, a man may have great understanding and a great imagination, & much memorie with much imagination: and verely, it is a miracle to find a man of great imagination, who hath a good understanding, and a sound memorie.

10.3

Pierre Jean Georges Cabanis

(1757–1808)

Fritsch and Hitzig are said to have discovered the motor area in 1870, but here is a statement by Cabanis, which is really only a digression in the discussion of another problem, which speaks of experimental verification that stimulating specific points on the brain results in contraction of specific muscles. There is no evidence that Cabanis himself performed this experiment, but he is too factual a writer to describe it on the basis of his own imagination or mere hearsay. One of his contemporaries must have demonstrated this experiment, but failed to publish it.

But it is not only with respect to sensations, but also with respect to movements, that the spontaneous action of the nervous system is often limited to certain isolated portions.

Every movement of a living part presupposes an analogous movement of which it is in some sort a representation, which takes place inside the cerebral center, or in the special center of the nerves which innervate that part. When we see a muscle move we may be sure that there is a corresponding movement of related points or divisions, either in the brain or in its offshoots. Visible movements that are not completed depend on other, hidden movements, which are likewise incomplete, just as, in clonic spasms, in which all parts of the musculature act at once, the nervous and cerebral divisions which govern these various parts must certainly be involved in a general convulsion, whether by direct excitation or by sympathy. Anatomy has taught us that certain lesions of the brain, of the spinal column, or of the ganglia, which have the effect of causing irregular movements in external organs, tend to do this to some organs rather than to others, and that these movements are circumscribed within rather narrow limits. Experiments performed on living animals confirm the same fact. If we prick different parts of the cerebral organ, or irritate them in any way at all, we see that the resulting convulsions which are usually produced by this method take place in different muscles by turns, and often they do not extend beyond those which are related to the irritated points.

Rapports du physique et du moral de l'homme [1802]. In *Oeuvres complètes de Cabanis*, vol. III. Paris, 1824. [Pp. 176–177.]

10.4

Franz Josef Gall

(1758–1828)

AND

Johann Kaspar Spurzheim

(1776–1832)

In 1802, Gall was forbidden to continue lecturing on "craniology" in Vienna because of his materialist tendency. Joined by his student Spurzheim, he started a lecture tour through German and French cities. Notoriety preceded them to Paris, which they reached in 1807. In March 1808, they delivered a report to the Institute, cautiously limiting it to matters of anatomy, a field in which Gall had many original contributions to offer. Pinel and Cuvier were among the members of a committee appointed to evaluate it. Their report was negative, doubtless swayed by the transparent wish of the emperor Napoleon. Gall and Spurzheim thereupon published their report [A] expanded by an extensive rebuttal of the unfavorable critique which it had received. The committee had carefully stated that its judgment on the originality of the anatomical theses had no bearing on the validity of the authors' well-known position regarding the functions of parts of the brain. Our first selection comes from a section in which Gall and Spurzheim insist that the brain's structure and its function are intimately related.

In the next year, the four-volume Anatomie et physiologie du système nerveux (1810–1819) began to appear. Spurzheim's collaboration with Gall ended about midway through the second volume. Our second selection [B] is taken from an advance publication of the first part of that second volume.

The point has often been made that quite apart from the weaknesses of phrenology and aside also from the genuine strength of Gall's contributions as an anatomist, he performed an important service by focusing attention on the problem of localization of brain functions. Spurzheim was the more active propagandist of the underlying philosophical position and its social implications.

[A] *Recherches sur le système nerveux en général, et sur celui du cerveau en particulier* [Investigations on the nervous system in general, and on that of the brain in particular]. Paris, 1809. [Pp. 228–232, 236, 253–254.]
[B] *Des dispositions innées* [On innate dispositions]. Paris, 1811. [Pp. 4–7.]

[A]

We believe, in effect, that the ensemble of the nerves is made up of several separate systems: that these systems differ from one another in their intimate structure as well as in their respective functions; that the functions or faculties depend directly on the development of the organs to which they belong; that among these various organs there exists more or less connection, and hence more or less reciprocal influence. We are careful to distinguish the common properties of all the systems from the specific functions of each, knowing well, for example, that feeling is an attribute of all the nerves, and sensation is an attribute of all the senses, although the sensation of sound can take place only in the organ of hearing, etc. . . . Where would the naturalist be, if he always had to limit himself to investigating the general properties of the physical world, such as weight, crystallization, etc., without ever attempting to grasp the relationships and the differences which characterize each species of objects?

It is only by submitting the different systems of nerves to a more scrupulous and more detailed examination than has ever been done before that we flatter ourselves to have made one of the most important steps of progress in anatomy and physiology. We do not limit ourselves to distinguishing the nervous systems of the viscera in the chest and abdomen, the spinal medulla, the medulla oblongata, and the brain as a whole, but we also find that the brain is made up of as many separate systems as there are distinct functions which it exercises; just as, in examining the senses, one will find them divided into as many kinds of apparatus, or complete systems, as there are essentially different sensations.

Now, the chief support for these ideas comes from the anatomical facts by which we have established that the nerves arise in different regions and from different masses of gray substance, and that the various separate systems in the brain are represented in the many fascicules, layers and convolutions.

If we were to accept all the crude ideas which have been advanced about the brain; if we were to admit that it is the source of all the nerves and that it is a composite of all their endings; how could we then ascribe to it any other function than those which belong to the nerves of sensation, movement, and the organs of nutrition, since it could no longer be anything but a joining of the cerebral endings of these nerves?

Is it not by mistakenly applying some general anatomical and physiological schema that differences among the nerves in regard to their internal structure have been denied? Because the bits of a polyp form other polyps, M. Cuvier compares the nerves with a magnet, which can be broken into pieces without each part losing the properties of the whole. That is why, by taking the nerves of a polyp as similar to those of more perfect animals, he does not look for differences of function except in the differences in external apparatus. . . .

Such accumulations of error, and the impressive reputation which until now has turned them into some sort of sacred object, are due in part to the custom which physiologists and even anatomists have had, of substituting metaphysical ideas which they have acquired in the schools for the facts of nature. The soul is simple, they say; therefore its seat also must be simple, and consequently there must be a single place where all the nerves take their start and where they all end: there is but *one* consciousness; therefore there can be but one seat of the soul. . . .

Unfortunately for all these reveries, we have proved that the author of nature followed quite a different plan in the creation. In general, nothing seems to us more ridiculous than that the naturalist, who has all of nature open to his discovery, should guide his research and his inductions by such vain and frivolous speculations. . . .

Indeed, when we compare the parts which constitute the brains of different animals with their diverse faculties, and compare the greater or lesser development of the former with the relative energy in the latter, we easily arrive at results which mere mechanical dissection would not even have led us to suspect. But one cannot do this without entering into the domain of the physiologist and the psychologist, who have besides several other sources of information at their disposal, which are no less certain and no less sure, from which they can derive positive information about the functions of certain cerebral parts. Therefore there need be nothing hypothetical or doubtful in this regard, as we shall show in our physiology of the brain. . . .

But if it is an eternal truth that animals which are deprived of any sort of intellect are also deprived of a brain, and provided only with interior nervous systems; that these systems are multiplied when the vegetative and organic life is more complicated; that any faculty of animal life, any instinct, talent or aptitude whatever, can never be seen except along with a brain; that the parts constituting the brain, from the worm to the man, increase and diversify in relation to and in the same proportion as the faculties; that all the facts join in proving that exceptional energy in any faculty always corresponds to the excitation and above all the extraordinary development of some part of the brain; that the derangement of a faculty is linked with the lesion or illness of a cerebral part; in the same way that the suffering or the loss of a sense is linked with the lesion or sickness of its physical apparatus; if, finally, it is an eternal truth that the brain is composed of a nervous system which is different from all the others, and which is divided into a number of other systems which are so distinct from one another that one can demonstrate to the eye the diversity of their origins, their fascicles, their directions, their points of joining—then it is altogether beyond doubt that the anatomy of the brain is in direct liaison and complete agreement with our doctrine of its functions; and the metaphysician can no longer say, in order to win the right to lose himself in the vagueness of speculations, that the operations of the soul are too obscure for it ever to be possible to discover their origins or their material conditions.

[B]

When we speak of innate penchants and faculties, of innate dispositions, or of innate moral and intellectual faculties, we do not intend to say thereby that there are *innate ideas* or *innate principles*. Our sensations and our ideas are due just as much to the external world, through the intermediate action of the senses, as to our interior organs, and since the impressions of the external world are accidental, and must precede perceptions, the sensations and ideas which particular objects of the external world give rise to (for example, a fish or a bird) are also accidental and cannot be innate. Nor can one regard as innate the sensations, ideas, or specific notions which include external things and accidents as integral parts; and although the faculties and the penchants are innate, the specific ideas relating to objects of the external world, which result from the action of these faculties and penchants on objects, are not innate. The faculty of loving, the sentiment of justice and injustice, ambition, the faculty of learning languages, that of comparing different sensations and ideas, of making judgments about them, and of drawing conclusions— this is what is innate. But the specific actions of our faculties, such and such judgments and comparisons, such and such perceptions—all these are not innate. So let us not be accused of renewing ancient errors about innate ideas and principles!

On the other hand, when we say that the exercise of the properties of the soul and the mind depend on material conditions, we do not mean that these faculties are a product of bodily structures. That would be to confuse the conditions and the effective cause. We confine ourselves strictly to observation. We consider the faculties of the soul only insofar as they become phenomena for us through the medium of organic substances; and, without going beyond the material conditions, we neither deny nor affirm anything except what can be judged from experience. We do not extend our research to living bodies, nor to the soul taken alone, but to the living man, a result of the union of body and soul. Consequently, we do not consider what faculties are by themselves; whether they should be regarded uniquely as the properties of a spiritual substance, the soul, or as properties of organized matter. In a word, we do not seek to explain the union of body and soul, nor their reciprocal influence, nor how this influence takes place, whether by the immediate action of God or by an ethereal fluid or a divine emanation. Whether souls are united to bodies early or late, whether they are endowed with different properties in each individual or whether they are quite similar in all, so that the phenomenal modifications are due solely to differences in bodily organization—whatever the decisions of theologians and metaphysicians on this question, our principle—to wit, that the qualities of the soul and the mind are innate and that their manifestations depend on organic materials—cannot suffer the least alteration.

We look with reason upon this principle as the basis for a physiology of the brain. If, instead of being able to demonstrate that our qualities are innate, and that their manifestation depends on the organization, one could prove that these properties are only the accidental product of external things and the external senses, or that they have no immediate relationship to organic materials, and that the soul could exercise its faculties in this life independently of organs, then we would search in vain for the instruments of the moral and intellectual qualities of the organism. It would be impossible to establish a doctrine of the functions of the brain and of its parts. Man, considered as a moral and intellectual being, would be placed outside the sphere of the observer of nature. If, on the contrary, we can demonstrate that an essential relationship exists between the exercise of the soul's properties and the organization, it will follow that investigations to discover the organs of man's moral and intellectual faculties are the most essential and most important study. And if we are also able to demonstrate that this relationship between the exercise of the soul's properties and the organization exists in the brain, it will no longer be possible to doubt that it is possible to establish a doctrine which will enable us to know the functions of this noblest part of the organism.

10.5

Pierre Flourens

(1794–1867)

Flourens' terse style makes him a favorite with anthologizers, but the following selections have not previously appeared in English translation to my knowledge. The modern reader cannot fail to be impressed by the remarkable agreement between his method and conclusions and those of

[A] *Recherches expérimentales sur les propriétés et les fonctions du système nerveux, dans les animaux vertébrés* [Experimental studies on the properties and functions of the nervous system in vertebrates]. Paris, 1824. [Pp. 155–163.]
[B] *Examen de la phrénologie* [Examination of phrenology. 1842]. Paris, 1845. [Pp. 117–118.]
[C] *De la vie et de l'intelligence* [On life and intelligence]. Paris, 1858. [Pp. 57–60.]

Lashley (10.9), showing that it is possible for a genial investigator to anticipate the errors as well as the "truths" of later generations.

The Examen de phrénologie did not appear until 14 years after Gall's death. Perhaps it was provoked less by the popularity of phrenology ("I have seen the progress of phrenology, and I have written this book") than by the statement of a certain Abbé Forichon (Materialism and phrenology, 1840) that since materialists had found it difficult to persuade people that one organ could perform all the wonders of mind, they were now offering a different organ for each faculty. Our brief selection is intended only to underline the depth of Flourens' feeling regarding the unity of the soul.

In the third selection, Flourens at 64 looks back proudly on his achievement, and turns it into an historical movement.

[A]

I removed the upper half of the cerebellum in one hen, the two cerebral lobes in another, both corpora quadrigemina in a third.

I put these three hens into the same living quarters. When I wanted to feed them, I sometimes counterfeited the call which had been used to summon them for feeding before the operation, and I threw the grain to them while continuing this call.

The hen without cerebral lobes heard nothing, suspected nothing, and did not move. The one without corpora quadrigemina heard very well, came toward the call and the sound which the grain made in falling, and when she arrived there, she was quite well able to find it without vision, and ate a good deal of it. The one without a cerebellum saw the grain, wanted to seize it, made a thousand efforts to do so without success (at least usually) and almost always went to one side when the grain came to it from the other, very much like drunken men who, when they want to go to the right, almost never fail to turn to the left.

I removed, as above, the two cerebral lobes from one hen, the two corpora quadrigemina from another, and the upper half of the cerebellum from a third.

Then I put them into the same living quarters which they had occupied before the operation, to which they were therefore accustomed. These quarters were kept well provisioned.

The hen without lobes died of hunger; the two others were able to seek their food, find it, choose it, and survived.

I have repeated this extraordinary opposition between the effects of the cerebral lobes, the corpora quadrigemina, and the cerebellum many times, on roosters, hens, pigeons, rabbits.

The opposition is complete in all respects:

10.5   Pierre Flourens

(1) The animal without lobes remains in a stupor; nothing can be more alert than the animal without a cerebellum; the one without tubercles is neither more nor less alert than ordinary.

(2) The first has no real sensations, no intellectual faculty; the second has all its sensations and all its faculties; the third has lost nothing except vision.

(3) The first and the third retain all their regular locomotor faculties; the second has lost them all.

(4) In summary, the first exhibits no spontaneous determination, shows no positive sensation, gives no sign of intelligence; it has therefore lost all its intelligence and all its intellectual faculties.

The third is impressionable to all the sorts of sensations, excepting only the sensations of vision; it gives all the signs of perfect intelligence; all its instincts manifest themselves and are developed energetically; it has therefore lost nothing except vision.

The second has lost neither sensations nor intellectual faculties; it has lost the faculty of moving in a coordinated manner.

Therefore the cerebral lobes are the unique recipient of sensation; the corpora quadrigemina are the principal primordial seat for the action of the retina, the iris and the optic nerve; the cerebellum is the seat for coordination of locomotor and prehensive movements. . . .

I split a hen's right cerebral lobe lengthwise; sight was immediately lost in the left eye.

However, the animal saw very well with the right eye; it heard, oriented itself, and found its food in the usual way.

The swelling of the split lobe was at first enormous. Seven or eight days later it had disappeared, and the animal recovered the sight of its left eye.

I then removed the left cerebral lobe; the animal continued to hear, to orient itself, and to feed itself, to all appearances, just as before; with the sole difference that it could no longer see except with the eye which it had first lost. . . .

I made a drake blind by extirpating the entire surface of both corpora quadrigemina.

Twenty days later, the animal had entirely recovered the sight of both eyes.

I removed the entire upper portion of a crow's cerebellum. Scarcely 12 days had passed when it had recovered all its equilibrium, all the regularity of its movements.

It would be superfluous to add further facts of this sort. I think that those which I have given are enough to establish in an incontestable manner:

(1) That lesions of the cerebral lobes, the corpora quadrigemina, and the cerebellum (when they do not exceed certain limits) are followed by recovery of the organ with complete reintegration of its functions;

(2) That a portion of these organs, rather small but definite, suffices for the full and complete exercise of their functions;

(3) That the physical conditions which influence the activity of these organs can be directly observed, and consequently can be rigorously established;

(4) Finally, that the functions of the cerebellum, the cerebral lobes, and the corpora quadrigemina are essentially distinct and separate, since each [function] can be separately conserved, destroyed, or recovered, according to whether the organ of each is conserved, destroyed, or recovered.

[B]

Inner sense tells me that I am *one;* Gall would have me *multiplex.* Inner sense tells me that I am *free;* Gall will have nothing of *moral freedom.* Inner sense assures me of the *continuity of my intelligence;* Cabanis and Broussais will have my intelligence no more than an *act.*

[C]

In my experiments on the brain, I set myself two problems, one physiological, the other philosophic.

(1) The Physiological Problem

The physiological problem was to localize the functions of the encephalon, that is to say, to see if each part of this organ has its own function, and what that function is.

For this, I had to find a method of experimentation, because previously there was none. People would merely make a hole in the skull, by means of a trephine, and thrust a probe through it into the brain. In that way they would injure sometimes one part, sometimes another, sometimes several parts together, and from this blind method they would draw confused results.

My method consisted in first uncovering the entire brain, and second, looking in this way at the limits of each part, guiding the hand always by the eye, and never making lesions which would cross over the proper limits of each distinct part. In a word, in examining, testing, interrogating one part after another, and always apart from the others.

This was my procedure; by this procedure the parts were separated;

the separation of the parts gave me separation of the functions. Each function which has a seat, a distinct organ, is a proper function and distinct from one which has another seat or another organ.

Proceeding in this manner, I obtained definite results.

By injuring only the *brain*, I had only the proper function of the brain, which is *intelligence*.

By injuring only the *cerebellum*, I had the proper function of the cerebellum, which is the *coordination* or equilibration of locomotor movements; by injuring only the *medulla oblongata*, and, within it, only the precise point which I have called the *vital center*, I obtained the sudden extinction of life, and I obtained this only at this point.

(2) The Philosophic Problem

The *philosophic* problem concerned me no less than the *physiological*. Throughout all ages, men have searched for the relationships:

(1) between *movement* and *will;*
(2) between *sensibility* and *intelligence;*
(3) between *sensation* and *perception;*
(4) between *intelligence* and *life.*

Now that is all resolved.

(1) *Movement* is completely independent of the *will;* because when the brain is removed, all volition is extinguished, and all the movements persist;

(2) *Sensibility* is not *intelligence,* because when the brain is removed, all intelligence is lost, and all sensibility (which resides elsewhere, that is to say, in the spinal medulla and the nerves) persists;

(3) *Sensation* is not *perception,* although it has been said that it is, because the *sensations* of *vision,* for example, are lost with one organ, the *corpora quadrigemina,* and the *perception* of *vision* with another, the brain;

(4) Finally, *intelligence* is completely distinct from *life,* and life is completely independent of intelligence, because, when the brain is removed, all intelligence is lost, absolutely lost, and nevertheless all life persists.

Therefore the philosophic problem is no less resolved, and no less certainly resolved, than the physiological problem.

10.6

Marc Dax

(*c.* 1775–*c.* 1840)

This painstaking research, completely overlooked in its time and all but forgotten since, not only provided a clue to localization of speech control, but showed the fallacy in Flourens' sweeping conclusions, which dominated the thinking of a generation. Notice the emphasis in the last paragraph that an injury to a cerebral hemisphere can interfere with one intellectual function while leaving others intact.

Identification of a speech area in the third frontal convolution of the left hemisphere was finally made by Broca in 1861. That paper is given complete by Herrnstein and Boring; excerpts from it appear in Clarke and O'Malley; Sahakian gives parts of a later paper by Broca.

In the month of September, 1800, I made the acquaintance of a former cavalry captain who had been wounded in battle by a sabre blow on the head, and who later suffered a great loss in his memory for words, although his memory for things remained undiminished.

I wanted very much to learn the reason for such a sharp distinction between the two memories.

After two or three months of fruitless search, I hoped that I had finally found the key to the enigma in the system of Dr. Gall, which was then beginning to spread in France. In fact, this writer assigns these two memories to different parts of the brain, and according to him one of these corresponds to a position just inside the orbits, and the other to a position at the base of the forehead.

I then inquired of the officer's family (for he had died a short while before) in what part of the skull he had been wounded. They told me that it was in the middle of the left parietal. This answer did not agree at all with the German physiologist's theory, and at the time it was of no use to the solution of my problem.

In 1806 the famous naturalist Broussonnet lost his memory for words, following an apoplectic attack which he survived for almost a year; but the fact that he lived in a city far from my own home deprived me for a long while of the ideas which the history of his illness, and the details of his autopsy, might have given me.

Lésions de la moitié gauche de l'encéphale coincidant avec l'oubli des signes de la pensée. [Lesions of the left half of the brain coinciding with loss of memory for words. Paper read at a medical congress in Montpellier, 1836.] In G. Dax, *L'Aphasie*. Paris, 1878. Pp. 9–13.

10.6 Marc Dax

In 1809 I collected a third observation on loss of memory for words, in a man who had cancer of the face, from which he died a few months after I saw him.

I could not connect these three cases, and they taught me nothing until, in 1811, I had occasion to read Cuvier's eloge for Broussonnet. I noticed among other things that a large ulcer had been found on the surface of the brain, on the left side. My thoughts immediately went back to the subject of my first observation, who had been wounded on the left side, and as to the third, I recalled very well that the cancerous tumor was on the left half of his face.

I was struck by this identity of location in the only three observations which I had been able to collect during eleven years; but on the other hand, they seemed to me too few to convince me that this would be a general law, even without considering the unlikelihood that the functions of one half of the brain could be so different from those of the other half. Nevertheless, a fourth case late in 1812, and a fifth early in 1813, gave me the hope that I might be able to convert my first appraisal into a general rule. . . .

Since then I have continued to collect similar observations, which now come to more than 40, without having found a single exception in all that time. Even if some exceptions should appear later they would not destroy the rule, so long as they are few in number. . . . I would not even consider an illness of the left hemisphere without any alteration of speech to constitute an exception, particularly if this illness were slight or if it had developed slowly. A true exception, such as I have not yet seen, would be an alteration in memory for words consequent to an ailment which occupied exclusively the right hemisphere. . . .

I believe I can conclude from all this, not that all ailments of the left hemisphere must alter verbal memory, but that when this memory has been altered by an ailment of the brain, the cause should be sought in a disorder of the left hemisphere, and it should be sought there even if both hemispheres are affected together.

Various interpretations have been given to the loss of memory for words. Gall and his school ascribe it to lesion of the anterior lobe of the brain; but a number of cases are known in which the anterior lobes have been destroyed without alteration of this memory.

M. Bouillaud seems to ascribe it to paralysis of the tongue, in a dissertation entitled, "Pathological and clinical investigations on the influence of the brain on muscular movements, and especially on those of the speech organs [1825]." But most of the patients with whom we are here concerned continue to speak, although they use one word in place of another; thus, their tongues are not paralyzed. I have made note of one, among others, who was completely deprived of speech, but when I asked him to move his tongue he did so with the greatest volubility; if he was given some disagreeable concoction to taste, he showed by his grimace that he could discriminate tastes very well. So in this case there was neither sensory nor motor paralysis of the tongue.

This absence of speech without paralysis of its principal organ was noted as early as the sixteenth century. In the collection of Schenkius one finds the following passage, written [in 1585] by a German physician named Oethius: "I have observed a number of cases in which, following apoplexy or other major head ailments, the patient cannot speak although the tongue is not paralysed, because the faculty of memory is extinct and words do not present themselves."

I prefer to adopt the explanation of Professor Lordat [1831], who attributes this phenomenon, not to paralysis of the tongue, but to an aberration in the synergy of the muscles involved in the exercise of speech, a synergy which is formed by the practice of simultaneous muscular movements which become mutually linked to one another, so that finally one evokes the other without intervention of the will. . . .

I hope that the new point of view which I have presented here will not only be useful in the therapy of the ailments which we are discussing, but that it will also throw a useful light on legal medicine. A patient of this type can write a will and direct his affairs, for his intelligence is ordinarily well conserved, and it would be unjust and cruel to declare him incompetent and to regard him as suffering from mental alienation. I hope also that it will give rise to investigations which will not be without use to the progress of science.

10.7

GustavTheodor Fritsch AND Eduard Hitzig
(1838–1927)   (1838–1907)

We have seen that the possibility of evoking specific motor response to stimulation of specific points on the brain was already known to Cabanis. But it did not fit into the scheme of either Gall or Flourens and seems to have been utterly suppressed, since it is not even mentioned by Fritsch and Hitzig in their thorough historical review. Rediscovery of this fact, along with Broca's designation of the speech area, compelled reassessment of the entire problem of brain function.

Portions of this paper dealing with method and results are given by both Clarke and O'Malley and Herrnstein and Boring. The following passages, of a theoretical nature, do not overlap with their selections.

Ueber die elektrische Erregbarkeit des Grosshirns [On the electrical excitability of the cerebrum]. *Archiv für Anatomie, Physiologie, und wissenschaftliche Medicin,* 1870: 300–332. [Pp. 322–325, 327–328, 332.]

10.7 Gustav Theodor Fritsch and Eduard Hitzig

The question must finally be raised, how it happened that so many earlier investigators, including the most illustrious names, reached contrary results. To this we have only one answer: "The method created the results." It is not possible that our predecessors could have laid bare the entire convex surface, for otherwise they *must* have obtained twitching movements.

In the dog, the hinder side wall of the skull, which does not lie over any motor parts, recommends itself by its formation for beginning the first trephine hole. Probably they started the operation here, and neglected to proceed frontally, because they started out from the mistaken view that the different areas on the surface were equivalent. They based themselves on the earlier developed and today still widespread assumption about the omnipresence of all mental functions in all parts of the cerebral cortex. If they had only considered a localization of mental functions, then the apparent non-excitability of some parts of the substratum would have been something to be taken for granted, and no part would have been left uninvestigated. . . .

If we now look back at the results of our investigation to this point and ask ourselves what has been gained thereby in knowledge of the characteristics of the central organ, then we have the responsibility to differentiate between what may rightly be regarded as established with certainty, and what has been made out as merely probable.

We can designate as a certain finding the fact, which has been demonstrated beyond a doubt and which can be reproduced at any moment, that there are central nervous structures which will respond immediately to one of our stimuli with a visible reaction. This in itself has a considerable theoretical importance for physiology. . . .

Equally certain is the fact that a substantial part of the nerve mass which makes up the cerebral hemispheres, one can say almost half, is directly related to muscular movement, while another portion apparently has at least nothing directly to do with it. Though this seems so simple and so obvious *now*, there was no clarity about it before now. . . . When such centers in the brain were discussed, even in the most recent period, mention was made only of basal parts, the pons, the thalamus, etc., and the explanation of findings regarding those portions was carefully confined to forms of expression that were as general as possible. Only a few brain anatomists, among whom Meynert must be named especially, have hitherto defended a strict localization of separate psychic functions, though in quite a different way from Gall's. . . .

[Among probable results] . . . We saw . . . that muscular contractions occurred in response to currents of minimal strength only when the electrodes were placed on certain specific points, and that they stopped, or would appear in other muscles, when the electrodes were removed from those positions even very slightly. This behavior permits only two possibilities. Either the stimulus is received by the ganglion cells lying in the immediate vicinity of the electrodes, and is converted into muscular movement by them, or the stimulable medullary fibers come especially close to the surface at these points, so that they are situated especially favorably for excitation. But since we can see no other reason why the fibers in question should come closest to the ganglion cells at just this point, except that they are destined to meet and enter the latter, we can in any case assume that precisely *these* ganglionic masses are intended for the production of organic stimuli for just *these* nerve fibers. . . .

From the sum of all our experiments it is clear that, contrary to what Flourens and most others after him have thought, the mind is by no means a kind of total function of the totality of the cerebral hemispheres, the expression of which can be mechanically disturbed as a whole but not in its separate parts, but far more certainly, separate mental functions, and probably all, when they enter into or when they arise out of material phenomena, are related to circumscribed centers of the cerebral cortex.

10.8

David Ferrier

(1843–1928)

Ferrier made detailed topographic analysis of motor and sensory areas in the dog and the monkey. His book was influential in establishing the view that the prefrontal area, where neither motor nor sensory functions are demonstrable, is important for intellectual work. But his ascription of inhibitory function to this area (see 16.8) was abandoned in the second edition of his book (1886), as physiologists generally rejected the concept of neural inhibition.

§ 78. Electrical irritation of the regions in advance and below [the middle frontal gyrus] in the brain of the monkey, was in general attended by negative results. This negative region also includes the island of Reil, which may be considered the starting point of the frontal convolutions. So likewise in the cat and dog, the regions in advance of the anterior limb of the sigmoid gyrus may be regarded as yielding no outward results, such phenomena as occur being irregular in character, and without doubt due to conduction of currents to the neighbouring parts.

. . . Removal or destruction by the cautery of the antero-frontal lobes

The functions of the brain. London, 1876. [Pp. 230–232.]

is not followed by any definite physiological results. The animals retain their appetites and instincts, and are capable of exhibiting emotional feeling. The sensory faculties . . . remain unimpaired. The powers of voluntary motion are retained in their integrity, and there is little to indicate the presence of such an extensive lesion, or removal of so large a part of the brain. I have removed the frontal lobes . . . almost completely in three monkeys, with the same negative results, and what is more remarkable, I found that the removal of these lobes in an animal which had recovered from ablation of the occipital lobes, caused no symptoms indicative of affection or impairment of the special sensory or motor faculties.

And yet, notwithstanding this apparent absence of physiological symptoms, I could perceive a very decided alteration in the animal's character and behaviour, though it is difficult to state in precise terms the nature of the change. The animals operated on were selected on account of their intelligent character. After the operation, though they might seem to one who had not compared their present with their past, fairly up to the average of monkey intelligence, they had undergone a considerable psychological alteration. Instead of, as before, being actively interested in their surroundings, and curiously prying into all that came within the field of their observation, they remained apathetic, or dull, or dozed off to sleep, responding only to the sensations or impressions of the moment, or varying their listlessness with restless and purposeless wanderings to and fro. While not actually deprived of intelligence, they had lost, to all appearance, the faculty of attentive and intelligent observation. . . .

What the physiological function of the frontal lobes may be is, therefore, not clearly indicated, either by the method of excitation or by the method of destruction. That the removal of the frontal part of the hemispheres in dogs caused no positive symptoms, in the domain of sensation or voluntary motion, is also proved by the experiments of Hitzig. And that extensive disease may occur in the frontal lobes in man, without any manifest symptoms during life, is likewise illustrated by numerous pathological cases, among which may be reckoned the celebrated 'American crow-bar case' [reported in 1850 by Bigelow]. . . .

245

10.9

Karl Spencer Lashley

(1890–1958)

Few men have pursued a problem so persistently, and at the same time with so much flexibility, as Lashley displayed in searching for the neural basis of learning. The conclusions reached in this book led him to study the implications of Gestalt theory and to perform studies on the transfer of learned responses to geometric patterns to other, remotely analogous patterns. He also studied the finer structure of the primate cortex, recognizing that the observed differences from one area to another must have functional significance. Despite this repeated questioning of his own results (cf. 13.12), he is too often remembered only for the principles of "mass action" and "vicarious functioning" as stated here. These conclusions were universally accepted by a generation of American psychologists and encouraged extreme scepticism about localization of function generally. His work with the rat reads like an extension of Flourens' work with the pigeon, but Lashley, unlike Flourens, recognized that this complicated the problem, but did not solve it.

[Ch. xi.] The doctrine of isolated reflex conduction has been widely influential in shaping current psychological theories. Its assumptions that reactions are determined by local conditions in limited groups of neurons, that learning consists of the modification of resistance in isolated synapses, that retention is the persistence of such modified conditions, all make for a conception of behavior as rigidly compartmentalized. Efficiency in any activity must depend upon the specific efficiency of the systems involved; and, since the condition of one synapse cannot influence that of others, there must be as many diverse capacities as there are independent reflex systems. . . .

There is no evidence to support this belief in identity of nervous elements. On the contrary, it is very doubtful if the same neurons or synapses are involved even in two similar reactions to the same stimulus. Our data seem to prove that the structural elements are relatively unimportant for integration and that the common elements must be some sort of dynamic patterns, determined by the relations or ratios among the parts of the system and not by the specific neurons activated. If this be true, we cannot, on the basis of our present knowledge of the nervous

Brain mechanisms in intelligence. A quantitative study of injuries to the brain. Chicago: University of Chicago Press, 1929. [Pp. 172–173, 175–176.]

system, set any limit to the kinds or amount of transfer possible or to the sort of relations which may be directly recognized. . . .

[Summary] The influence of the extent of cerebral destruction in the rat was tested for a variety of functions, including retention of maze habits formed before cerebral insult, and learning and retention of several habits after the insult. The results may be summarized as follows:

1. The capacity to form maze habits is reduced by destruction of cerebral tissue.

2. The reduction is roughly proportional to the amount of destruction.

3. The same retardation in learning is produced by equal amounts of destruction in any of the cyto-architectural fields. Hence the capacity to learn the maze is dependent upon the amount of functional cortical tissue and not upon its anatomical specialization. . . .

11. No difference in behavior in maze situations could be detected after lesions in different cerebral areas, and the retardation in learning is not referable to any sensory defects.

12. A review of the literature on cerebral function in other mammals, including man, indicates that, in spite of the greater specialization of cerebral areas in the higher forms, the problems of cerebral function are not greatly different from those raised by experiments with the rat.

From these facts the following inferences are drawn:

1. The learning process and the retention of habits are not dependent upon any finely localized structural changes within the cerebral cortex. The results are incompatible with theories of learning by changes in synaptic structure, or with any theories which assume that particular neural integrations are dependent upon definite anatomical paths specialized for them. Integration cannot be expressed in terms of connections between specific neurons.

2. The contribution of the different parts of a specialized area or of the whole cortex, in the case of non-localized functions, is qualitatively the same. There is not a summation of diverse functions, but a non-specialized dynamic function of the tissue as a whole.

3. Analysis of the maze habit indicates that its formation involves processes which are characteristic of intelligent behavior. Hence the results for the rat are generalized for cerebral functions in intelligence. Data on dementia in man are suggestive of conditions similar to those found after cerebral injury in the rat.

4. The mechanisms of integration are to be sought in the dynamic relations among the parts of the nervous system rather than in details of structural differentiation.

Walter Rudolf Hess

(1881–1973)

If the "new phrenology" was initiated by Fritsch and Hitzig's electrical stimulation of the motor cortex, what we may call the "third wave" of phrenology has its basis in Hess's technique of observing the behavior of freely moving animals while stimulating precise points in the brain stem through permanently implanted electrodes. This summary of the results of many years of research appeared in the year when the award of the Nobel prize attracted world attention to its author.

A separate category consists of those effects in which the application of the stimulus sets into motion very complex mechanisms that are accompanied under physiologic conditions by strong emotions. Perhaps the most striking example is one type of behavior of the cat, in which it looks as though it were being threatened by a dog. The animal *spits, snorts, or growls* at the same time; *the hair of its back stands on end,* and *its tail becomes bushy; its pupils widen,* sometimes to their maximum; and its *ears lie back,* or move back and forth (to frighten the non-existent enemy). The only thing missing from the total picture is the arched back. . . .

The points of stimulation at which the above described response pattern is elicited are grouped relatively close together in the *anterior hypothalamus.* . . .

Posterior to the focus of the defense reaction and partially overlapped by it lies a relatively small and narrow region that is associated with a different kind of instinctive behavior. Stimulation here produces *bulimia.* If the animal has previously taken neither milk nor meat, it now devours or drinks greedily. . . . In all cases, the latency is strikingly long, as compared with that of the defense reaction. . . . We must assume from the behavior of eager sniffing around for food not only that stimulation in the hypothalamus brings into action a subcortically directed mechanism (sniffing automatism), but also that the (electrically) induced state reaches consciousness, and that the higher sensory apparatus is also drawn into the coordinated total behavior. . . .

Sleep can also be obtained as a *direct stimulation effect.* This is the case if the points of the electrodes lie lateral to the ventral half of the massa intermedia. Often a reduced readiness of the animal to react appears within several minutes after insertion of the electrodes, or when

Das Zwischenhirn. Basle, 1949. Translated as *The functional organization of the diencephalon.* New York: Grune & Stratton, 1957. [Pp. 23–25, 27, 30, 77, 100–102, 125.] Reprinted by permission of the publisher and author.

stimuli of the *lowest potential stage* are used. During the same period spontaneous movements diminish more and more in striking fashion. At the very start, the cat shuts its eyes from time to time; the nictating membrane comes forward, and the pupils become narrow. Meanwhile, the animal sits down, lets its head sink forward, and falls asleep sitting. In other cases, the animal lies down with curled-up paws, sometimes on its side. . . . These different kinds of sleep are observed unequivocally in different animals and are thus worth mentioning. It is important that upon stimulation the cat does not appear to "pass out" suddenly, but seeks a comfortable position, which may not be found until after a few postural adjustments. . . .

. . . If the cat is left alone at rest, the effect can last for hours under certain conditions before the animal awakens spontaneously. On the other hand, the sleeplike state changes promptly as soon as a stimulus is applied in a motor region or a region of effective attack or defense. . . .

Long experience has shown that stimulation by a pulsating direct current of 8 cycles per second can provide an important means of interpreting experimental findings, since it makes possible a differentiation between two types of movement. Responses either follow the rhythm of the stimulus in the form of jerky movements or they show a more or less pronounced summation from slightly discontinuous to completely smooth, flowing movements. . . . Regardless of whether the animal is at rest or is locomoting, the electrical stimulation can be applied and can produce its effect, uninfluenced by mechanical hindrance and possible secondary reflexes of a limb in restraint. . . .

If we review the data obtained in the manner described, we perceive definite relationships between motor function and structure. These relations are no less precise than those found in the cortex! . . .

1. *Lowering of the head* is induced from the *posterior commisure* and from a region situated somewhat *lateral to and below* this. . . .

2. The opposite of sinking of the head, i. e., an intermittent *upward movement,* is attributed to a region that *lies medial to the tract of Vicq d'Azyr.* . . .

3. [For] ipsilateral turning . . . the corresponding region lies between the areas of pure rotation and pure head-sinking, with some as yet undefined spread laterally. . . .

4. With regard to *contralateral turning,* we find the corresponding region . . . *lateral to the field of rotation.* . . .

5. Motor effects in the *anterior extremities* and in the *face* are elicited from a region that lies *lateral* to that of *rotation* and *anterior* to that of *ipsilateral turning.* . . .

. . . The diencephalically elicited responses are conceptualized as compensatory postural mechanisms associated with the extrapyramidal motor system.

Chapter 11

MEMORY

In times past, when books were rare or nonexistent and authority the only unanswerable (verbal) argument, a quick and retentive memory was the greatest virtue of a student and a valuable asset for men in every form of public life. Therefore the improvement of memory rivaled physiognomy as the most important form of what we would now call "applied psychology." This early interest in memory fostered the development of association psychology, and therefore some important representatives of that movement are included in this chapter. Interest in memory also led to some of the earliest forms of psychological experiment. Most recently, investigation of the physiological processes involved in memory reveals that they are fundamentally similar to the basic phenomena of life.

11.1

Aristotle

(384–322 B.C.)

All things begin with Aristotle, but nothing more appropriately than memory, for surely no one in history has been so studiously committed to memory by so many generations of scholars. And after more than two

On memory and recollection. Translated by W. S. Hett. In *Aristotle: On the soul; Parva naturalia; On breath.* Cambridge, Mass.: Harvard University Press (Loeb Classical Library), 1957. Pp. 287–313. [449b, 451a–452a, 453a.] Reprinted by permission of the publisher and the Loeb Classical Library.

millennia, are we not still arguing the relative merits of similarity and contiguity as memory clues?

I. Our task is now to discuss memory and remembering: what it is, why it occurs and to what part of the soul this affection and that of recollection belongs. Men who have good memories are not the same as those who are good at recollecting, in fact generally speaking the slow-witted have better memories, but the quick-witted and those who learn easily are better at recollecting.

. . . Hence memory is found not only in man and beings which are capable of opinion and thought, but also in some other animals. If it formed part of the intellectual faculty, it would not belong, as it does, to many other animals; probably not to any mortal being, since even as it is it does not belong to all, because they have not all a consciousness of time; for as we said before, whenever a man actively remembers that he has seen, heard or learned something, he always has the additional consciousness that he did so *before;* now "before" and "after" relate to time.

It is obvious, then, that memory belongs to that part of the soul to which imagination belongs; all things which are imaginable are essentially objects of memory, and those which necessarily involve imagination are objects of memory only incidentally. . . .

II. It remains to speak about recollecting. . . .

Acts of recollection occur when one impluse naturally succeeds another; now if the sequence is necessary, it is plain that whoever experiences one impulse will also experience the next; but if the sequence is not necessary, but customary, the second experience will normally follow. But it happens that some impulses become habitual to us more readily from a single experience than others do from many; and so we remember some things that we have seen once better than others that we have seen many times. When we recollect, then, we re-experience one of our former impulses, until at last we experience that which customarily precedes the one which we require. This is why we follow the trail in order, starting in thought from the present, or some other concept, and from something similar or contrary to, or closely connected with, what we seek. This is how recollection takes place; for the impulses from these experiences are sometimes identical and sometimes simultaneous with those of what we seek, and sometimes form a part of them; so that the remaining portion which we experienced after that is relatively small.

This is the way in which men try to recollect, and the way in which they recollect, even if they do not try to: *viz.*, when one impulse follows upon another. Generally speaking, it is when other impulses, such as we have mentioned, have first been aroused that the particular impulse follows. We need not inquire how we remember when the extremes of the series are far apart, but only when they are near together; for it is clear that the method is the same in both cases, I mean by following a chain of succession, without previous search or recollection. For custom makes the impulses follow one another in a certain order. Thus when a man wishes to recall anything this will be his method; he will try to find a starting-point for an impulse which will lead to the one he seeks. This is why acts of recollection are achieved soonest and most successfully when they start from the beginning of a series; for just as the objects are related to each other in an order of succession, so are the impulses. Those subjects which possess an orderly arrangement, like mathematical problems, are the easiest to recollect; ill-arranged subjects are recovered with difficulty. It is in this that the difference between recollecting and learning afresh lies, that in the former one will be able in some way to move on by his own effort to the term next after the starting-point. When he cannot do this himself, but only through another agency, he no longer remembers.

It often happens that one cannot recollect at the moment, but can do so by searching, and finds what he wants. This occurs by his initiating many impulses, until at last he initiates one such that it will lead to the object of his search. For remembering consists in the potential existence in the mind of the effective stimulus; and this, as has been said, in such a way that the subject is stimulated from himself, and from the stimuli which he contains within him. But one must secure a starting-point. This is why some people seem, in recollecting, to proceed from *loci*. The reason for this is that they pass rapidly from one step to the next; for instance from milk to white, from white to air, from air to damp; from which one remembers autumn, if this is the season that he is trying to recall. . . .

We have said before that those who have good memories are not the same as those who recollect quickly. Recollecting differs from remembering not merely in the matter of time, but also because, while many other animals share in memory, one may say that none of the known animals can recollect except man. This is because recollecting is, as it were, a kind of inference; for when a man is recollecting he infers that he has seen or heard or experienced something of the sort before, and the process is a kind of search. This power can only belong by nature to such animals as have the faculty of deliberation; for deliberation too is a kind of inference.

11.2

Augustine

(354–430)

For Augustine, memory becomes another proof that there is a divine spark in human nature. But his dithyramb, besides being fine literature, brings into focus many problems which call for explanation through research.

[Book X.] 12. I will soar, then, beyond this power of my nature also {sensation}, ascending by degrees unto Him who made me. And I enter the fields and roomy chambers of memory, where are the treasures of countless images, imported into it from all manner of things by the senses. . . . When I am in this storehouse, I demand that what I wish should be brought forth, and some things immediately appear; others require to be longer sought after, and are dragged, as it were, out of some hidden receptacle; others, again, hurry forth in crowds, and while another thing is sought and inquired for, they leap into view, as if to say, "Is it not we, perchance?" These I drive away with the hand of my heart from before the face of my remembrance, until what I wish be discovered making its appearance out of its secret cell. Other things suggest themselves without effort, and in continuous order, just as they are called for,—those in front giving place to those that follow, and in giving place are treasured up again to be forthcoming when I wish it. All of which takes place when I repeat a thing from memory.

13. . . . And who can tell how these images are formed, notwithstanding that it is evident by which of the senses each has been fetched in and treasured up? For even while I live in darkness and silence, I can bring out colours in memory if I wish, and discern between black and white, and what others I wish; nor yet do sounds break in and disturb what is drawn in my eyes, and which I am considering, seeing that they also are there, and are concealed,—laid up, as it were, apart. . . . And though my tongue be at rest, and my throat silent, yet can I sing as much as I will; and those images of colours, which notwithstanding are there, do not interpose themselves and interrupt when another treasure is under consideration which flowed in through the ears. So the remaining things carried in and heaped up by the other senses, I recall at my pleasure. And I discern the scent of lilies from that of violets while smelling nothing; and I prefer honey to grape-syrup, a smooth thing to a rough, though then I neither taste nor handle, but only remember. . . .

The confessions of Saint Augustine. Translated by J. G. Pilkington [1876]. New York: Boni & Liveright, 1927. [Pp. 226–229, 233, 239–240.]

15. Great is this power of memory, exceeding great, O my God,—an inner chamber large and boundless! Who has plumbed the depths thereof? Yet it is a power of mine, and appertains unto my nature; nor do I myself grasp all that I am. Therefore is the mind too narrow to contain itself. And where should that be which it doth not contain of itself? Is it outside and not in itself: How is it then, that it doth not grasp itself? A great admiration rises upon me; astonishment seizes me. And men go forth to wonder at the heights of mountains, the huge waves of the sea, the broad flow of the rivers, the extent of the ocean, and the courses of the stars, and omit to wonder at themselves; nor do they marvel that when I spoke of all these things, I was not looking on them with my eyes, and yet could not speak of them unless those mountains, and waves, and rivers, and stars which I saw, and that ocean which I believe in, I saw inwardly in my memory, and with the same vast spaces between as when I saw them abroad. . . .

21. . . . . Without being joyous, I remember myself to have had joy; and without being sad, I call to mind my past sadness; and that of which I was once afraid, I remember without fear; and without desire recall a former desire. . . .

27. For the woman who lost her drachma, and searched for it with a lamp, unless she had remembered it, would never have found it. For when it was found, whence could she know whether it were the same, had she not remembered it? . . .

28. But how is it when the memory itself loses anything, as it happens when we forget anything and try to recall it? Where finally do we search, but in the memory itself? And there, if perchance one thing be offered for another, we refuse it, until we meet with what we seek; and when we do, we exclaim, "This is it!" which we should not do unless we remembered it. Assuredly, therefore, we had forgotten it. . . . And whence, save from the memory itself, does that present itself? For even when we recognize it as put in mind of it by another, it is thence it comes. For we do not believe it as something new, but, as we recall it, admit what was said to be correct. But if it were entirely blotted out of the mind, we should not, even when put in mind of it, recollect it. For we have not as yet entirely forgotten what we remember that we have forgotten. A lost notion, then, which we have entirely forgotten, we cannot even search for.

11.3

Henry Cornelius Agrippa

(1486–1535)

The use of special mnemonic devices is of very ancient origin. Agrippa tells a little of its history, while making the same sort of criticism which many a psychologist today will direct against memory systems.

Simonides is said to have invented his system of "local memory" (which will be described in detail below, by D'Assigny (11.6)) after a miraculous escape, when he was summoned from a feast a moment before the collapse of the building crushed all other participants beyond recognition. He was able to reconstruct the entire seating order, thus enabling each bereaved family to bury its own dead. This impressed him with how much memory can be aided by association with place.

[Ch. X. *Of the Art of Memory.*] Among these Arts, is to be reckon'd the Art of Memory; which, as Cicero saith, is nothing else but a certain method of Teaching, and Precept; like a thin Membrane, consisting of Characters, Places, and Representations; first invented by *Simonides Melito*, and perfected by *Metrodorus Sceptius*. But let it be what it will, more certain it is, that it can never come to good, where there is not a very good Natural Memory before; which sometimes it perplexes with such monstrous Apparitions, that instead of a new Memory, it is the cause of Madness and Phrenzies; and over-burdening the Natural memory with the Characters and Images of innumerable things and words, it occasions those that are not contented with the bounds of Nature, to run Mad with Art. This Art, when *Simonides* or some body else did offer to *Themistocles,* he refus'd it, saying, *He had more need of Forgetfulness than Memory;* said he, *I remember what I would not, but I cannot forget what I would.* As for *Metrodorus, Quintillian* thus writes concerning him: It was a great piece of vain Ostentation, saith he, to glory rather in his Memory by Art, than in that by Nature. Of this Art *Cicero* makes mention in his Book of Rhetoricks; *Quintillian,* in his Institutions; and *Seneca.* Among modern authors, *Francis Petrarch* hath writ something concerning it; together with *Mareol. Veronensis, Petrus Ravennas, Hermannus Buschius,* and others; though unworthy of a Catalogue, as being obscure Persons. Many there be, that at this day Profess the same, though they get more Infamy and dis-repute, than gain thereby; being a sort of rascally Fellows, that do many times impose upon silly Youth, only to

De incertitudine et vanitate scientiarum [Antwerp, 1531]. Translated as *The vanity of arts and sciences.* London, 1694. [Pp. 48–49.]

draw some small piece of Money from them for present Subsistance. Lastly, 'tis a childish Triumph to boast of a great Memory; besides that it is a thing of shame and disgrace to make a shew of great Reading, exposing a great Fair of words without doors, when the House within is altogether unfurnish'd.

11.4

Luis Vives

(1492–1540)

The account of memory in the De anima of this great humanist scholar is notable for including the important insight that association by contiguity does not apply indifferently to either member of a pair. (Cf. Dilly, 13.6). Again there is allusion to the widely used system of "local" memory. Vives' mention of the importance of emotion for memory is consistent with the attention he gives to emotion generally (see 20.3).

On Memory and Recollection

If something is first presented to the memory mixed with some exciting emotion, the subsequent recollection will be easier, prompter, and more lasting; so that our memory is very long for anything which entered the mind with great pleasure or pain. . . .

Memory acquires strength with exercise and frequent meditation, becoming more prompt in acquisition, greater in capacity, and more tenacious in retention. There is no other function of the soul which requires cultivation in this manner. The gifts of understanding do not deteriorate with rest and idleness, but rather become restored and acquire greater vigor. If memory is not exercised, it grows dull, becoming slower each day, more sluggish and inert.

Forgetting is explained in three ways: either because the very picture in memory is erased or destroyed directly; or it is smeared and broken up; or because it escapes our searching, whether because it is covered over and, as it were, concealed by a veil, as in sickness, or due to the excitement of emotion. The first is true forgetting, properly so called; the second is a disguise or blotting out; the third and fourth are concealment. . . .

The first kind of forgetting requires completely new learning; the

De anima et vita [On the soul and life]. Brussels, 1538. [Pp. 57–60.]

fourth calls for investigating the health of the body or the soul; the other two, a restoration and tracking down of what we are seeking, step by step. Thus, from a ring to the jeweler, thence to the queen's necklace, then to the war her husband is waging, from the war to the commanders, from the commanders to their ancestors or their children, then to the subjects which the children are studying—a process without limit. These steps spread out by every line of argument: from cause to effect, from effect to instrument, from part to whole, from thing to place, from place to person, from person to ancestors or offspring, to things alike and things opposite. To which foraging, there is no end. . . .

This reminiscence is either natural, the thought passing unconstrainedly from one thing to another, or it is voluntary, as under orders, when the soul persists in desiring to recall some certain thing. It is easier to recall things that have been written down in order; mathematical propositions especially are of this sort. Verses also lend themselves to faithful memorization, because of their orderly composition. . . . For this reason, whoever wishes to remember anything should give careful attention to the order in which he commits it to memory, and the teachers of this art give their pupils a certain place [schema] for memorizing things. For if two things have been apprehended together in fantasy, when one of them recurs, the other also will usually present itself. Therefore they use those locations in the art of memorizing, because at the sight of a place there will come to mind what we know happened in that place, or exists there.

When something pleasant happens to us at the same time that we hear some voice or a sound, we will afterward hear that sound with pleasure; if something sad, with sorrow. This is also to be observed in animals: if they are called by a certain sound to receive something desirable, they will return to that same sound readily and willingly; if they are whipped, the same sound afterwards is a terrifying thing, because of the memory of the punishment.

When two things occur together in memory, the more important one is often brought to mind by the lesser, not the contrary. By the more important, I mean the one that is better, more excellent, rarer and more precious, more highly esteemed; in fine, the one that means more to us. Thus, whenever I see a certain house in Brussels, within sight of the royal palace, I am reminded of Idiaquez, whose house that was, where often, whenever our affairs permitted, we had long delightful conversations about many things. But howsoever often I think of Idiaquez, I do not therefore think of that building, because in my soul the memory of Idiaquez is more notable than that of his house. It is the same with sounds, with tastes, with smells. When I was a boy in Valencia I suffered a fever, and I ate some cherries with a distorted sense of taste; many years later, whenever I ate the same fruit, I would not only remember the fever, but I seemed even to feel it. Therefore the places assigned for [prompting] memory should be bare, for if they have any distinctive marks or outstanding features, which are notable to us, these will cover up what they are to remind us of; the memory will then be carried away by this distinctive mark, and be so coupled with it that it will forget the rest, just as our stomachs prefer those foods best suited to their nature, neglecting others.

11.5

Cosmo Rosselli

(† 1578)

How serious a business mnemonic technique was may be judged from this work by a Dominican monk, which includes many varied devices to assist the memory. Our selection is one of many woodblocks depicting options for the exercise of the system of local memory.

This book also contains a finger alphabet to be used for the instruction of deaf mutes and a figure showing the localization of the faculties which agrees with that in Reisch (10.1), except that it shows four ventricles instead of three, the common sense being assigned to the anterior ventricle.

Thesaurus artificiosae memoriae [Treasury of memory devices]. Venice, 1579.

11.6

Marius D'Assigny

(1643–1717)

The greater part of this slender book is taken up with a discussion of the presumed physiology of memory and with suggestions about the diet and regimen to assist it. Then there are rules to be observed for the acts of memorizing, and these take into account such principles as order, interest, highlighting of first words, use of similarity and contrast, frequency, and the construction of mnemonic words. The final chapter gives instruction in the system of local memory, which we have seen ridiculed by Agrippa, alluded to by Vives, and elaborately illustrated by Rosselli.

Chap. IX   *Of Artificial or Fantastical Memory or Remembrance*

Artificial Memory, saith the Philosopher . . . is an imaginary Disposition in our mind of sensible things, upon which when our Memory reflects, by them it is admonish'd and assisted to remember more easily and distinctly things that are to be minded. . . . Now some prescribe the Imagination of a fair and regular Building, divided into many Rooms and Galleries, with differing Colors and distinct Pillars, which the Party must fancy to stand before him as so many Repositories where he is to place the Things or Ideas which he designs to remember, ordering them according to their several Circumstances and Qualifications, for the better assistance of Memory. Others, instead of a House, Palace or Building, have chosen such Beasts as answer to all the Alphabetical Letters in the Latin Tongue, and instead of Rooms have assigned their several Members for our Fancy to fix our Ideas there, and place them for our better remembrance: These are the Names of the Beasts, *Asinus, Basiliscus, Canis, Draco, Elephas, Faunus, Gryfus, Hircus, Juvencus, Leo, Mulus, Nectua, Ovis, Panthera, Qualea, Rhinoceros, Simia, Taurus, Ursus, Xystus, Hyena, Zacheus.* Every one of these they divide into five Parts or Places, into Head, Fore-feet, Belly, Hinder-feet, and Tail; for this is the Order that Nature it self directs, neither can our Imagination be disorder'd in reckoning or telling them over. So that by this means the Fancy may have one hundred and fifteen Places to imprint the Images of memorable things. Likewise in the Person speaking, we may fix the Ideas of things

The art of memory. A treatise useful for all, especially such as are to speak in public [1697]. Second edition. London, 1699. [Pp. 71–75, 77–78.]

to be remembered on his Head, Forehead, Eys, Mouth, Chin, and so downwards on all his Members. But if this way of Remembrance be beneficial, 'tis best when the Places where we design to leave and commit our Ideas are more known and familiar to us: As for example, the Town where we live, or the City that we are best acquainted with; our Mind must as it were enter by the Gate, and proceed to the several Streets and Quarters of the City, marking the public Places, Churches, Friends Houses, &c. by this means we may have an infinite number of Places to commit our Ideas. And because all Directions are best understood by Examples, I shall recommend these, that this method of remembering may better be comprehended. Suppose therefore a large and empty House, unto which we must not go often but seldom; suppose at the entrance there is one Room about three foot from the Door, the second about 12 or 15 foot, being in a Corner, the third likewise being distant about the same number of feet; and so likewise the fourth, fifth, sixth, seventh, and as many as you please, fancying upon them the number that denotes and distinguishes the Rooms and Corners the one from the other, that there may be no Mistake nor Confusion in our remembrance; or, if you please, distinguish the several Rooms by other Characters than Numbers. Now when we have well settled and divided the several Rooms and Corners in our Imagination, where we are to place the Ideas for our remembrance, we must contrive such a remarkable Fancy of that thing that we intend to put there as may not easily be forgotten, and such a Fancy as may be remarkable for Folly, Simplicity, Wisdom or Wonder, &c. For example, if I will remember any thing acted by another, I must fancy him in one of these Rooms acting in a ridiculous manner that which I design not to forget. Now the Figures that we must place there, ought to provoke to Pity, Wonder, Laughter or Scorn, that it may make a deeper Impression in our Fancy. Again, we may represent things by their Likeness or Contraries; for example, if we design to remember *Galen*, we will write the name of some famous Physician well known to us, or of some contemptible Mountebank. If we will remember *Ovidius Naso*, we shall represent a Man with a great nose; if *Plato*, we shall think upon a Person with large Shoulders; if *Crispus*, we shall fancy another with curl'd Hair, and so of other things. But this Method of remembering things is cumbersome and fantastical, and perhaps may not be sutable to every Temper and Person; neither is it proper, or of any use for the Delivery of a Discourse by Memory, but rather for the assisting our Remembrance not to forget some certain Passages of our Life, and of others, and we may make some use of it for the remembering of Sentences and Names.

I shall conclude with just setting down some other Rules which are prescribed by such as recommend this kind of Artificial Remembrance, for the better imprinting the Ideas in our Mind, and the avoiding Confusion. . . .

8. Such images are to be often recall'd to our mind in the same order as they were placed, with their several Circumstances and Properties, and such as are most remarkable and notable: for if by chance the Idea be blotted out, those Circumstances will quickly renew them in our memorative Faculty; and a frequent Repetition will make a deeper Impression in our Minds of the things that we desire not to forget; chiefly if this Repetition be made when we are going to lay down our Heads upon our Pillows: for it is observable, that what we think upon when we are going to sleep, we shall have fresh in our Fancy when we awake the next Morning. And in those Intervals that we lie quiet at Midnight without sleeping, we may easily imprime in our Imagination things that will not quickly be forgotten. The Mind will then be more susceptible, more retentive and tenacious of any Idea that we recommend to it with Deliberation, and free from the Incumbrance of Business: for he that will make use of his Memory, must know himself what time and season is most proper to imploy it, when it is most at liberty, and freest to receive the Impressions or Ideas of things. 'Tis with Memory as with the other Faculties and Abilities belonging to Man, there is a time for Action and a time when they are not fit, and a Temper that renders them unable to produce the natural Operations. Such Times therfore, Seasons and Tempers are to be chosen for the exercise of Memory when it is altogether disingaged from Troubles, Impediments, and all Incumbrances, and freest for Action. Our youthful Days are the most proper to begin to imploy this Faculty, for we then may speedily learn, and easily improve this Ability to our great Comfort and Advantage in the following course of our Lives. And as it has already bin observ'd, Exercise will render us by degrees more perfect: So that we shall never have cause to repent of the Labors and Pains that we take in this case at the beginning of our days.

11.7

Francis Galton

(1822–1911)

The experimental study of memory was initiated independently by Galton and by Ebbinghaus, using very different methods, at about the same time. We give two selections from this book, in the first of which Galton shows that local or "topical" memory schemata often arise spontaneously, par-

Inquiries into human faculty and its development. London, 1883. [Pp. 114–116, 119, 123, 126; 185–192, 195–197, 202–203.]

ticularly *in the handling of numbers. In the second he carries out an experimental study of his own associations and draws some important conclusions. It is not far from this to the use of word association lists for clinical diagnosis, as introduced first by Jung and developed further by Kent and Rosanoff. Both investigations are rich in suggestions relating to visual imagery, sex differences, childhood influences on thinking, and the like. Perhaps most important is his recognition that he has opened a way to quantitative study of the higher thought processes.*

Number Forms

Persons who are imaginative almost invariably think of *numerals* in some form of visual imagery. . . . The clearness of the images of numerals, and the number of them that can be mentally viewed at the same time, differs greatly in different persons. . . .

Now the strange psychological fact to which I desire to draw attention, is that among persons who visualize figures there are many who notice that the image of the same figure invariably makes its first appearance in the same direction, and at the same distance. . . . Consequently, when he thinks of the series of numerals 1, 2, 3, 4, etc., they show themselves in a definite pattern that always occupies an identical position in his field of view with respect to the direction in which he is looking. . . .

The pattern or "Form" in which the numerals are seen is by no means the same in different persons, but assumes the most grotesque variety of shapes, which run in all sorts of angles, bends, curves, and zigzags as reproduced in the various illustrations to this chapter. [There are 3 figures in the text, and 63 more on 3 plates, all distinctive.] The drawings, however, fail in giving the idea of their apparent size to those who see them; they usually occupy a wider range than the mental eye can take in at a single glance, and compel it to wander. Sometimes they are nearly panoramic. . . .

The peculiarity in question is found, speaking very roughly, in about 1 out of every 30 adult males or 15 females. It consists in the sudden and automatic appearance of a vivid and invariable "Form" in the mental field of view, whenever a numeral is thought of, and in which each numeral has its own definite place. This form may consist of a mere line of any shape, of a peculiarly arranged row or rows of figures, or of a shaded space. . . .

Nearly all of my correspondents speak with confidence of their Forms having been in existence as far back as they recollect. One states that he knows he possessed it at the age of four; another, that he learnt his multiplication table by the aid of the elaborate mental diagram he still uses. Not one in ten is able to suggest any clue as to their origin. . . .

These Forms are the most remarkable existing instances of what is called "topical" memory, the essence of which appears to lie in the establishment of a more exact system of division of labour in the different parts of the brain, than is usually carried on. Topical aids to memory are of the greatest service to many persons, and teachers of mnemonics make large use of them, as by advising a speaker to mentally associate the corners, etc., of a room with the chief divisions of the speech he is about to deliver. Those who feel the advantage of these aids most strongly are the most likely to cultivate the use of numerical forms. I have read many books on mnemonics, and cannot doubt their utility to some persons; to myself the system is of no avail whatever, but simply a stumbling-block, nevertheless I am well aware that many of my early associations are fanciful and silly.

Psychometric Experiments

When we attempt to trace the first steps in each operation of our minds, we are usually baulked by the difficulty of keeping watch, without embarrassing the freedom of its action. The difficulty is much more than the common and well-known one of attending to two things at once. It is especially due to the fact that the elementary operations of the mind are exceedingly faint and evanescent, and that it requires the utmost painstaking to watch them properly. It would seem impossible to give the required attention to the processes of thought, and yet to think as freely as if the mind had been in no way preoccupied. The peculiarity of the experiments I am about to describe is that I have succeeded in evading this difficulty. My method consists in allowing the mind to play freely for a very brief period, until a couple or so of ideas have passed through it, and then, while the traces or echoes of those ideas are still lingering in the brain, to turn the attention upon them with a sudden and complete awakening; to arrest, to scrutinize them, and to record their exact appearance. . . .

. . . My first experiments were these. On several occasions, but notably on one when I felt myself unusually capable of the kind of efforts required, I walked leisurely along Pall Mall, a distance of 450 yards, during which time I scrutinized with attention every successive object that caught my eyes, and I allowed my attention to rest on it until one or two thoughts had arisen through direct association with that object; then I took very brief mental note of them, and passed on to the next object. I never allowed my mind to ramble. The number of objects viewed was, I think, about 300, for I had subsequently repeated the same walk under similar conditions and endeavoured to estimate their number, with that result. It was impossible for me to recall in other than the vaguest way the numerous ideas that had passed through my mind; but of this, at least, I am sure, that samples of my whole life had passed before me, that many bygone incidents, which I had never suspected to have formed part of my stock of thoughts, had been glanced at as objects too familiar to awaken the attention. I saw at once that the brain was vastly more active than I had previously believed it to be, and I was perfectly amazed at the unexpected width of the field of its everyday operations. After an interval of some days, during which I kept my mind from dwelling on my first experiences, in order that it might retain as much freshness as possible for a second experiment, I repeated the walk, and was struck just as much as before by the variety of the ideas that presented themselves, and the number of events to which they referred, about which I had never consciously occupied myself of late years. But my admiration at the activity of the mind was seriously diminished by another observation which I then made, namely, that there had been a very great deal of repetition of thought. . . . I accordingly cast about for means of laying hold of these fleeting thoughts, and, submitting them to statistical analysis, to find out more about their tendency to repetition and other matters. . . . I selected a list of suitable words, and wrote them on different small sheets of paper. Taking care to dismiss them from my thoughts when not engaged upon them, and allowing some days to elapse before I began to use them, I laid one of these sheets with all due precautions under a book, but not wholly covered by it, so that when I leaned forward I could see one of the words, being previously quite ignorant of what the word would be. Also I held a small chronograph, which I started by pressing a spring the moment the word caught my eye, and which stopped of itself the instant I released the spring; and this I did so soon as about a couple of ideas in direct association with the word had arisen in my mind. . . . The list of words that I finally secured was 75 in number, though I began with more. I went through them on four separate occasions, under very different circumstances, in England and abroad, and at intervals of about a month. . . .

. . . I found that my list of 75 words gone over 4 times, had given rise to 505 ideas and 13 cases of puzzle, in which nothing sufficiently definite to note occurred within the brief maximum period of about 4 seconds, that I allowed myself to any single trial. Of those 505 only 289 were different. . . .

I was fully prepared to find much iteration in my ideas, but had little expected that out of every hundred words twenty-three would give rise to exactly the same association in every one of the four trials; twenty-three to the same association in three out of the four, and so on, the experiments having been purposely conducted under very different conditions of time and local circumstances. This shows much less variety in the mental stock of ideas than I had expected, and makes us feel that the roadways of our minds are worn into very deep ruts. I conclude from the proved number of faint and barely conscious thoughts, and from the proved iteration of them, that the mind is perpetually travelling over familiar ways without our memory retaining any impression of its excursions. . . .

I took pains to determine as far as feasible the dates of my life at which each of the associated ideas was first attached to the word. There were 124 cases in which identification was satisfactory. . . .

. . . Of the 48 earliest associations no less than 12, or one quarter of them occurred in each of the four trials; of the 57 associations first formed in manhood, 10, or about one-sixth of them, had a similar recurrence, but as to the 19 other associations first formed in quite recent times, not one of them occurred in the whole of the four trials. . . .

. . . If [these] figures . . . may be accepted as fairly correct for the world generally, it shows, still in a measurable degree, the large effect of early education in fixing our associations. It will of course be understood that I make no absurd profession of being able by these very few experiments to lay down statistical constants of universal application, but that my principal object is to show that a very large class of mental phenomena, that have hitherto been too vague to lay hold of, admit of being caught by the firm grip of genuine statistical inquiry. . . .

It would be very instructive to print the actual records at length, made by many experimenters, if the records could be clubbed together and thrown into a statistical form; but it would be too absurd to print one's own singly. They lay bare the foundations of a man's thoughts with curious distinctness, and exhibit his mental anatomy with more vividness and truth than he would probably care to publish to the world.

. . . I have desired to show how whole strata of mental operations that have lapsed out of ordinary consciousness, admit of being dragged into light, recorded and treated statistically, and how the obscurity that attends the initial steps of our thoughts can thus be pierced and dissipated. I then showed measurably the rate at which associations sprung up, their character, the date of their first formation, their tendency to recurrence, and their relative precedence. . . . Perhaps the strongest of the impressions left by these experiments regards the multifariousness of the work done by the mind in a state of half-consciousness, and the valid reason they afford for believing in the existence of still deeper strata of mental operations, sunk wholly below the level of consciousness, which may account for such mental phenomena as cannot otherwise be explained.

11.8

Hermann Ebbinghaus

(1850–1909)

Ebbinghaus brings the more ponderous German style and a more rigorous mathematical treatment to bear on the same problem. He deliberately restricted the scope of his work but built a solid foundation for future research. His detailed study of only so much as he could effectively control is in sharp contrast to Galton's broad perspectives.

[6] He who considers the complicated processes of the higher mental life or who is occupied with the still more complicated phenomena of the state and of society will in general be inclined to deny the possibility of keeping constant the conditions for psychological experimentation. . . .

However, care must be taken not to apply too much weight to these views . . . when dealing with fields other than those of the processes by the observation of which these views were obtained. All such unruly factors are of the greatest importance for higher mental processes. . . . The more lowly, commonplace, and constantly occurring processes are not in the least withdrawn from their influence, but we have it for the most part in our power, when it is a matter of consequence, to make this influence only slightly disturbing. Sensorial perception, for example, certainly occurs with greater or less accuracy according to the degree of interest. . . . But, in spite of that, we are on the whole sufficiently able to see a house just when we want to see it and to receive practically the same picture of it ten times in succession in case no objective change has occurred.

There is nothing *a priori* absurd in the assumption that ordinary retention and reproduction, which, according to general agreement, is ranked next to sensorial perception, should also behave like it in this respect. Whether this is actually the case or not . . . cannot be decided in advance. . . . We must try in experimental fashion to keep as constant as possible those circumstances whose influences on retention and reproduction is known or suspected, and then ascertain whether that is sufficient. . . .

. . . When are the circumstances, which will certainly offer differences enough to keen observation, sufficiently constant? The answer may be made:—When upon repetition of the experiment the results remain constant. . . .

Ueber das Gedächtniss [1885]. Translated by H. A. Ruger and Clara E. Bussenius, as *Memory: A contribution to experimental psychology*. New York: Teachers College, Columbia University, 1913. [Pp. 11–12, 22–24, 65, 75–78.]

{In sections 7 to 10, Ebbinghaus explains how the "law of error" may be used as a criterion in this judgment. This is an early application of statistical theory to psychological experiment, following the pioneering lead of Fechner.}

[11] In order to test practically, although only for a limited field, a way of penetrating more deeply into memory processes—and it is to these that the preceding considerations have been directed—I have hit upon the following method.

Out of the simple consonants of the alphabet and our eleven vowels and diphthongs all possible syllables of a certain sort were constructed, a vowel sound being placed between two consonants.

These syllables, about 2,300 in number, were mixed together and then drawn out by chance and used to construct series of different lengths, several of which each time formed the material for a test.

At the beginning a few rules were observed to prevent, in the construction of the syllables, too immediate repetition of similar sounds, but these were not strictly adhered to. Later they were abandoned and the matter left to chance. The syllables used each time were carefully laid aside till the whole number had been used, then they were mixed together and used again.

The aim of the tests carried on with these syllable series was, by means of repeated audible perusal of the separate series, to so impress them that immediately afterwards they could voluntarily just be reproduced. This aim was considered attained when, the initial syllable being given, a series could be recited at the first attempt, without hesitation, at a certain rate, and with the consciousness of being correct.

[12] The nonsense material, just described, offers many advantages, in part because of this very lack of meaning. . . .

However, the simplicity and homogeneity of the material must not be overestimated. It is still far from ideal. . . .

More indubitable are the advantages of our material in two other respects. In the first place it permits an inexhaustible amount of new combinations of quite homogeneous character, while different poems, different prose pieces always have something incomparable. It also makes possible a quantitative variation which is adequate and certain; whereas to break off before the end or to begin in the middle of the verse or the sentence leads to new complications because of various and unavoidable disturbances of the meanings.

Series of numbers, which I also tried, appeared impracticable for the more thorough tests. Their fundamental elements were too small in number and therefore too easily exhausted.

{Of the many types of experiments which Ebbinghaus carried out, we select that on "retention and oblivescence as a function of the time," using the "method of savings."}

[27] By the help of our method we have a possibility of indirectly ap-

proaching the problem {of retention and forgetting} in a small and definitely limited sphere, and, by means of keeping aloof for a while from any theory, perhaps of constructing one.

After a definite time, the hidden but yet existent dispositions laid down by the learning of a syllable-series may be strengthened by a further memorisation of the series, and thereby the remaining fragments may be united again to a whole. The work necessary for this compared with that necessary when such dispositions and fragments are absent gives a measure for what has been lost as well as for what remains. . . .

. . . If syllable series of a definite kind are learned by heart and then left to themselves, how will the process of forgetting go on when left merely to the influence of time or the daily events of life which fill it? The determination of the losses suffered was made in the way described: after certain intervals of time, the series memorised were relearned and the times necessary in both cases were compared.

The investigations in question fell in the year 1879–80 and comprised 163 double tests. Each double test consisted in learning eight series of 13 syllables each (with the exception of 38 double tests taken from 11–12 A.M. which contained only six series each) and then in relearning them after a definite time. The learning was continued until two errorless recitations of the series in question were possible. . . .

In spite of all irregularities in detail, {the results} group themselves as a whole with satisfactory certainty into an harmonious picture. As a proof of this the absolute amount of the saving in work is of less value {than the relative saving}. Accordingly I here tabulate the latter.

No.	After X hours	So much of the series learned was retained that in relearning a saving of $Q\%$ of the time of original learning was made	$P.E._m$	The amount forgotten was thus equivalent to $v\%$ of the original in terms of time of learning
	$X =$	$Q =$		$v =$
1	0.33	58.2	1	41.8
2	1.	44.2	1	55.8
3	8.8	35.8	1	64.2
4	24.	33.7	1.2	66.3
5	48.	27.8	1.4	72.2
6	6×24	25.4	1.3	74.6
7	31×24	21.1	0.8	78.9

[29] 1. It will probably be claimed that the fact that forgetting would be very rapid at the beginning of the process and very slow at the end should have been foreseen. However, it would be just as reasonable to be surprised at this initial rapidity and later slowness. . . . One hour after the end of the learning, the forgetting had already progressed so far that one

half the amount of the original work had to be expended before the series could be reproduced again; after 8 hours the work to be made up amounted to two-thirds of the first effort. . . . The decrease of this after-effect in the latter intervals of time is evidently so slow that it is easy to predict that a complete vanishing of the effect of the first memorisation of these series would, if they had been left to themselves, have occurred only after an indefinitely long period of time. . . .

3. Considering the special, individual, and uncertain character of our numerical results no one will desire at once to know what "law" is revealed in them. However, it is noteworthy that all the seven values which cover intervals of one-third of an hour in length to 31 days in length (thus from singlefold to 2,000-fold) may with tolerable approximation be put into a rather simple mathematical formula. I call: t the time in minutes counting from one minute before the end of the learning; b the saving of work evident in relearning, the equivalent of the amount remembered {behalten = retained} from the first learned expressed in percentage of the time necessary for this first learning; c and k two constants to be defined presently.

Then the following formula may be written:

$$b = \frac{100\,k}{(\log t)^c + k}$$

By using common logarithms and with merely approximate estimates, not involving exact calculation by the method of least squares,

$$k = 1.84$$
$$c = 1.25$$

Then the results are as follows:

t	b Observed	b Calculated	$\triangle$
20	58.2	57.0	+1.2
64	44.2	46.7	−2.5
526	35.8	34.5	+1.3
1440	33.7	30.4	+3.3
2 × 1440	27.8	28.1	−0.3
6 × 1440	25.4	24.9	+0.5
31 × 1440	21.1	21.2	−0.1

. . . Solving the formula for k we have

$$k = \frac{b\,(\log t)^c}{100 - b}$$

This expression, $100 - b$, the complement of the work saved, is nothing other than the work required for relearning, the equivalent of the amount forgotten from the first learning. Calling this, v {vergessen = forgotten; verloren = lost}, the following simple relation results:

$$\frac{b}{v} = \frac{k}{(\log t)^c}$$

To express it in words: when nonsense series of 13 syllables each were memorised and relearned after different intervals, the quotients of the work saved and the work required were about inversely proportional to a small power of the logarithm of those intervals of time. To express it more briefly and less accurately: the quotients of the amounts retained and the amounts forgotten were inversely as the logarithms of the times.

11.9

Georg Elias Müller

(1850–1934)

Müller's investigations of memory were monumental; the reports run to over 2,000 pages, and their mass discourages the close reading which they deserve. This research with Alfons Pilzecker, his assistant for many years, was the first to use the method of paired syllables (in which, during the recall, the first syllable of each pair is provided, the other to be supplied by the subject). It also called attention to two important phenomena: perseveration and retroactive inhibition. This analysis of perseveration may be said to be the first experimental breach in the theory that the "train of thoughts" is determined solely by association, and it also points to the existence of a separate short-term memory process. On perseveration, compare Spearman (17.12).

. . . After the appearance of any idea in consciousness, it has a tendency to perseverate, that is, a tendency, which ordinarily quickly fades away, to arise spontaneously in consciousness. This tendency is proportionately stronger as the attention was more intensively directed to the idea in question, and it increases if the idea or the series of ideas is very soon repeated. With frequent repetition it can easily happen that the idea or series of ideas appears in consciousness, at moments when other facts tending to consciousness are not especially strong or persistent, solely as a consequence of its tendency to perseverate. . . .

G. E. Müller and A. Pilzecker. Experimentelle Beiträge zur Lehre vom Gedächtniss [Experimental contributions to the theory of memory]. *Zeitschrift für Psychologie und Physiologie der Sinnesorgane,* Ergänzungsband 1 (1900). [Pp. 58, 62, 69–70, 72–75, 77, 179, 196–197.]

Just as in other similar investigations, the perseverative tendency of ideas showed itself in our experiments in the fact that with many subjects single syllables or pairs of syllables, in a series which had been read, would force themselves into consciousness even against the wish, during the time following the reading. . . .

It is quite impossible to explain the individual differences which exist in respect to the flow of ideas if, along with the associations, we do not also assume the perseverative tendencies, which just like the former vary in strength in different individuals under the same circumstances. . . .

Among our subjects, M. is the one who showed the strongest perseveration, while Frau M. was one of those with the weakest perseveration, although she surpassed all other subjects with respect to the durability of associations. How can one explain the difference which exists between these two persons in regard to the manner in which ideas follow one another, without the assumption of perseverative tendencies? . . .

. . . Strong perseverative tendencies exclude the capacity to shift the attention quickly and completely from one area of thought or activity to another. . . . However, along with this disadvantage of strong perseveration there are also certain advantages. It is certainly not always advantageous that after a lecture in which he has been excitedly engaged, M. is compelled to inwardly rehearse it for a long time afterward. But it is hardly a disadvantage that it is quite a natural thing for him to continuously carry with him, so to say, a problem on which he is engaged, and also again and again to think through fresh ideas which come to him from outside. . . .

. . . It would be an error to suppose that there is a relation between the strength of associations and that of perseverative tendencies, in the sense that a relatively high strength in the former entails a reduced intensity of the latter, and conversely. For although M. stands far behind his wife in regard to the strength of associations, he is still according to our results much superior in this respect to other subjects who, like her, show only weak perseverative tendencies. . . .

Perseverative tendencies are not an accidental or even useless addition to associations. . . . The flow of our ideas according to the laws of association is often interrupted by internal or external distractions. If after such distractions those ideas which had been prevented from exerting their reproductive effect did not have a tendency to reappear in consciousness of themselves, in too many cases a train of thought which had been begun, and was important to us, would be terminated. . . .

It is easy to see that individuals with strong perseveration would not be rightly placed in a profession which requires quick and frequent changes in the direction of attention, quick handling of numerous matters of very different kinds. . . .

[It was noticed that when two series are studied one after the other, and the paired associations are tested after, for example, 24 hours, retention was always better for the second series than for the first.] These results aroused in us the suspicion that in fact the strength of associations which had been fostered by reading a series of syllables underwent some impairment when the subject's mind was intensively engaged immediately or soon after. . . . Thus the supposition was forced upon us that the processes which serve to establish the associations for a series of syllables persist for a certain length of time after the reading, but that during this period they can be weakened by other simultaneous intense mental activity, so that the intense mental activity which results from reading a [second] series gives rise to an impairment or inhibition (more exactly: inhibition of development) of the associations for the [first] list. For lack of any shorter expression we shall designate this type of inhibition as *retroactive inhibition,* because it relates to the effectiveness of a process which superficially seems to have been completed, to the previously completed reading of a series of syllables. . . .

[A number of hypotheses for the explanation of retroactive inhibition are dismissed as inadequate.]

After all this, nothing remains but to assume that after the reading of a series of syllables, certain physiological processes which serve to strengthen the associations fostered by the reading of that series continue for a certain length of time, with gradually diminishing strength. These processes, and their beneficial effects on those associations, are more or less weakened if the subject experiences further mental effort in the interval immediately following the reading. . . .

The supposition seems justified that these physiological processes are the same as those on which the previously mentioned perseverative tendencies of ideas are based. The mental effort of a subject right after the reading of a list of syllables has first of all the direct effect previously mentioned, to weaken the perseverative tendencies of those syllables, and second, because these perseverative tendencies help to bring about a consolidation of those associations, it also has the effect of impairing those associations.

11.10

Holger Hydén

(born 1917)

In the year of this report, J. V. McConnell provided another type of evidence that chemical, rather than physical, change in the nervous system is basic to learning by his demonstration of "Memory transfer through cannibalism in planarians" (Journal of Neuropsychiatry, 3, Suppl. 1: 42–48). But Hydén's careful work, combining an ingeniously devised behavioral experiment with refined analytic techniques, opened hitherto unexpected vistas for research into the nature of memory. An article in the next volume of the Proceedings demonstrated similar change in the glial cells.

Hydén, a Swede, was awarded a Nobel prize in physiology in 1966.

As the nerve cells are rich in ribonucleic acid (RNA), the suggestion has been made that the RNA of the neurons may be linked with the capacity of the central nervous system to store information. . . .

Results are presented on the altered base ratio composition of nuclear RNA and cytoplasmic RNA from neurons of rats, subjected to a "trial-and-error" type of learning experiment during which a pattern of sensory and motor abilities was established in the rats. Concomitantly, the adenine/uracil ratio of the nuclear RNA increased significantly, and an increase of the total amount of the nerve cell RNA occurred. Requisite control experiments were carried out which excluded the possibility that the chemical changes observed were due to demands on the neural function *per se*.

The present paper . . . presents the results obtained from vestibular Deiters' nerve cells. These cells were chosen because they were directly involved in this learning performance, and because we wanted to use neurons from phylogenetically old parts of the brain in these first experiments and to avoid complicated cortical areas.

. . . A wooden cage (95 × 85 × 45 cm) with one side wall of glass was used for the experiments. At a height of 75 cm on one of the end walls, a small platform was arranged with a feeding cup. A 90-cm long steel wire, 1.5 mm in diameter, was strung between the floor and the platform. The experimental rats, kept on a minimal amount of food but with free access to water, were individually placed in the cage for 45 minutes

H. Hydén and E. Egyházi. Nuclear RNA changes of nerve cells during a learning experiment in rats. *Proceedings of the National Academy of Sciences* 48 (1962): 1366–1373.

daily. The only way for the animals to satisfy their food hunger was to learn how to balance up to the platform, an exceedingly difficult task of the trial-and-error type. These young rats took an average of four days to learn how to balance on the wire the full distance to the platform. On gaining the platform, a rat takes a small piece of food in his mouth and then walks down the wire in order to eat the food on the floor of the cage. On the first day, when they have learnt the performance, the rats usually balanced the whole way to the platform 3 to 5 times during the 45 minutes allotted, on the second day around 10 times, and on the third and fourth day around 20 times. The results presented in this paper are based on rats of the fourth day. . . .

As *functional controls,* rats of the same litter, stimulated in the following way, were used. The same part of the nervous system as in the learning experiments was stimulated with the difference that *the animal was passive* during the stimulation. The vestibular nerve was stimulated by rotating the animal through 120° horizontally and 30° vertically with 30 turns per minute and for 25 minutes twice daily for four days. . . .

. . . The amount of RNA per nerve cell increased significantly during the course of the trial-and-error experiment from 683 $\mu\mu$g to 751 $\mu\mu$g of RNA per isolated nerve cell. . . .

. . . A *significant change* occurred in the base ratios of the nuclear RNA in the learning experiment, with the adenine increasing, and the uracil decreasing. The ratio of nuclear adenine-uracil changed from 1.06 $\pm$ 0.08 in the controls to 1.35 $\pm$ 0.10 in the learning animals with a P value of 0.01. The nuclear RNA $(A + G)/(C + U)$ ratio changed from 0.91 in the controls to 1.03 in learning. The nuclear $(A + U)/(G + C)$ ratio remained at 0.72.

. . . The neuronal amount of RNA increased significantly, from 683 to 722 $\mu\mu$g per nerve cell, as a result of the rotatory vestibular stimulation.

The amount of RNA per nerve cell had thus increased as a result of stimulation. . . .

The base ratios of the nuclear RNA were next studied in these Dieters' nerve cells. The analysis of these functional controls showed no significant changes in the nuclear RNA base ratios as a result of vestibular stimulation during which the rats were passive.

Discussion.—The data presented thus links significant changes in the base ratio composition and production of nuclear RNA by neurons to the establishment of a sensory and motor pattern in rats during a learning experiment. The functional control experiment excludes, according to our view, the possibility that the qualitative chemical changes were caused by the demands of increased but "passive" activity.

The fact that the learning experiment is a more physiological stimulation than the vestibular experiment which is also stronger as stimulus on the vestibular apparatus than the learning experiment, supports the conclusion that the observed nuclear RNA changes are specific. . . .

In general terms the nuclear RNA changes presented in this study show that the neurons from an experienced animal are not the same biochemically as the neurons from an inexperienced one. . . .

A storage mechanism of information in the neurons, based on the data presented in this study, must be anchored in the genetic mechanism of cells. The learning capacity would therefore depend on the potentialities of the species, with different chromosomes having a capacity to produce their own type of RNA—within the potentialities of the DNA of the species.

The specific regions of the chromosomes in the neurons involved during the learning and establishment of a performance may be momentarily more active. We would like to suggest that the observed changes in the base ratios in the nuclei of neurons during learning is caused by specific regions of the chromosomes producing their specific RNA.

# Chapter 12

ASSOCIATIVE THINKING

Prior to the seventeenth century, human memory was regarded as only a servant of reason. Starting then, the effort was often made to reduce much or all of thinking to an irregular play of memories, a "train of imaginations" which later came to be called the association of ideas. This theory appealed strongly to empiricists, and its partisans, when it had been well developed as a school, were prone to overlook the important early contributions of writers not wholly within the empiricist tradition. I have tried to give them their due in the space gained by reducing to a minimum the selections from men who are already well anthologized!

The reader who seeks a connected view of the development should not fail to follow especially the cross-references to John Gay and David Hartley in other chapters.

René Descartes

(1596–1650)

Descartes would be the last to reduce human thinking generally to a sum of associations, but in this charming anecdote, he recognizes the part which minimal cues may play as unsuspected determinants of our behavior. This typically French tale makes an interesting contrast to Locke's dour English comment that "hatreds are often begotten" from the "accidental connexion of two ideas." Before Locke wrote on association, he must have been acquainted with this story as retold by Sylvain Régis (Système de la philosophie, 1691, vol. VI, p. 413), and very likely he heard it from Regis' own lips fifteen years earlier, in the year when he studied Cartesianism under his guidance at Montpellier.

. . . I now turn to your question about why we love one person more than another, before we know their merit. . . . I will speak only about the physical reason. It consists in a disposition of parts of our brain, which was placed there either by sensory objects, or by some other cause. Because objects touching our senses move certain parts of the brain, through interposition of the nerves, and make as it were certain folds, which unfold again when the object ceases to act; but the part where they have been remains disposed thereafter to take a similar fold from another object which resembles the previous one in some respect, even though not in all. For example, when I was a child, I loved a girl of my own age, who was somewhat crosseyed; as a result of which, the impression which sight made on my brain when I looked at her divergent eyes was so joined to that which also stirred in me the passion of love, that long afterwards, whenever I looked at crosseyed persons, I felt more inclined to love them than to love others, simply because they had this defect; and nevertheless I did not know that this was the reason. On the contrary, since I have reflected on the matter, and recognized that it is a defect, I am no longer moved by it. Thus, when we are led to love someone without knowing the reason, we may suppose that this is because they have some point of resemblance with someone whom we loved previously, even though we do not know what that is. . . .

Letter to Canut; June 6, 1647. In Ch. Adam and G. Milhaud, Eds., *Correspondance de Descartes.* Paris: Presses Universitaires de France, 1936–. Vol. VII, pp. 345–351. [Pp. 349–350.]

12.2

Thomas Hobbes

(1588–1679)

Hobbes was the first thorough reductionist since the ancient atomists. Not only did he say that all thinking is the recombination of elements previously experienced, in trains which rehearse earlier instances of contiguous experience, but he also made the useful distinction between what we now call free and controlled association. He is therefore the real founder of the association psychology, but because the suspicion of atheism was attached to his name, his contribution was not acknowledged by later associationists. Instead, they regarded Locke as their prophet, with what little justification we shall soon see.

Of the Consequence or Trayne of Imaginations

By *Consequence* or TRAYNE of Thoughts, I understand that succession of one Thought to another, which is called (to distinguish it from Discourse in words) *Mentall Discourse.*

When a man thinketh on anything whatsoever, His next Thought after, is not altogether so casuall as it seems to be. Not every Thought to every Thought succeeds indifferently. But as wee have no Imagination, whereof we have not formerly had Sense, in whole, or in parts; so we have no Transition from one Imagination to another, whereof we never had the like before in our Senses. The reason whereof is this. All Fancies are Motions within us, reliques of those made in the Sense: And those motions that immediately succeeded one another in the sense, continue also together after Sense: In so much as the former comming again to take place, and be praedominant, the later followeth, by coherence of the matter moved, in such manner, as water upon a plain Table is drawn which way any one part of it is guided by the finger. But because in sense, to one and the same thing perceived, sometimes one thing, sometimes another succeedeth, it comes to passe in time, that in the imagining of any thing, there is no certainty what we shall Imagine next; Onely this is certain, it shall be something that succeeded the same before, at one time or another.

This Trayne of Thoughts, or Mentall Discourse, is of two sorts. The first is *Unguided, without Design,* and inconstant; Wherein there is no

Leviathan, or the matter, forme, and power of a common-wealth ecclesiasticall and civill. London, 1651. [Part I, ch. 3; pp. 8–9, 11.]

Passionate Thought, to govern and direct those that follow, to it self, as the end and scope of some desire, or other passion: In which case the thoughts are said to wander, and seem impertinent one to another, as in a Dream. Such are Commonly the thoughts of men, that are not onely without company, but also without care of any thing; though even then their Thoughts are as busie as at other times, but without harmony; as the sound which a Lute out of tune would yeeld to any man; or in tune, to one that could not play. And yet in this wild ranging of the mind, a man may oft-times perceive the way of it, and the dependance of one thought upon another. . . .

The second is more constant; as being *regulated* by some desire, and designe. For the impression made by such things as wee desire, or feare, is strong, and permanent, or, (if it cease for a time,) of quick return: so strong it is sometimes, as to hinder and break our sleep. From Desire, ariseth the Thought of some means we have seen produce the like of that which we ayme at; and from the thought of that, the thought of means to that mean; and so continually, till we come to some beginning within our own power. . . .

The Trayne of regulated Thoughts is of two kinds; One, when of an effect imagined wee seek the causes, or means that produce it: and this is common to Man and Beast. The other is, when imagining anything whatsoever, wee seek all the possible effects, that can by it be produced; that is to say, we imagine what we can do with it, when wee have it. Of which I have not at any time seen any signe, but in man onely; for this is a curiosity hardly incident to the nature of any living creature that has no other Passion but sensuall, such as are hunger, thirst, lust, and anger. . . .

There is no other act of man's mind, that I can remember, naturally planted in him, so as to need no other thing, to the exercise of it, but to be born a man, and live with the use of his five Senses. Those other Faculties, of which I shall speak by and by, and which seem proper to man onely, are acquired, and encreased by study and industry; and of most men learned by instruction, and discipline; and proceed all from the invention of Words, and Speech. For besides Sense, and Thoughts, and the Trayne of thoughts, the mind of man has no other motion; though by the help of Speech, and Method, the same Facultyes may be improved to such a height, as to distinguish men from all other living Creatures.

12.3

John Locke

(1632–1704)

Locke, who was too reasonable a man to be even a thoroughgoing empiricist (in this selection, for example, he acknowledges the existence of
native antipathies), was not at all an associationist. Association had no part
in the original Essay, but in the fourth edition he added a chapter pointing
to the chance "connexion of ideas" (probably his rendering of "liaison des
idées," which he would have met in Malebranche) as a major source of
error in thinking. The more fortunate phrase, association of ideas, occurs
only in the chapter title and is perhaps derived from the word consocia-
tione which Molyneux used in the Latin edition which was being prepared
simultaneously and for which the chapter was indeed written. In time,
however, this phrase became so "rivetted" to Locke's name that the later
associationists came to look upon him as their founder. This error is so
persistent that the amused historian must concur with the dismayed Locke:
"When two things in themselves disjoin'd appear to the sight constantly
united . . . where will you begin to rectify the mistakes that follow?"

Of the Association of Ideas

§5. Some of our *Ideas* have a natural Correspondence and Connexion
one with another. It is the Office and Excellency of our Reason to trace
these, and hold them together in that Union and Correspondence which
is founded in their peculiar Beings. Besides this, there is another Connexion of *Ideas* wholly owing to *Chance* or *Custom*. *Ideas* that in themselves are not at all of kin, come to be so united in some Mens Minds,
that 'tis very hard to separate them, they always keep in company, and
the one no sooner at one time comes into the Understanding but its
Associate appears with it; and if they are more than two which are thus
united, the whole gang always inseparable shew themselves together.

§6. This strong Combination of *Ideas*, not ally'd by Nature, the Mind
makes in it self either voluntarily or by chance. . . . *Custom* settles habits
of Thinking in the Understanding, as well as of Determining in the
Will, and of Motions in the Body; all which seems to be but Trains of
Motion in the Animal Spirits, which once set a going continue on in the
same steps they have been used to, which by often treading are worn

An essay concerning humane understanding. Fourth edition. London, 1700. [Bk II,
Ch. 33; pp. 222–225.]

into a smooth path, and the Motion in it becomes easy and as if it were Natural. . . .

§7. . . . To this, perhaps, might be justly attributed most of the Sympathies and Antipathies observable in Men, which work as strongly, and produce as regular Effects as if they were Natural. . . . I say, most of the Antipathies, I do not say all, for some of them are truly Natural, depend upon our original Constitution, and are born with us. . . .

§9. This wrong Connexion in our Minds of *Ideas* in themselves, loose and independent one of another has such an influence, and is of so great force to set us awry in our Actions . . . that, perhaps, there is not any one thing that deserves more to be looked after.

§10. The *Ideas* of *Goblines* and *Sprights* have really no more to do with Darkness than Light, yet let but a foolish Maid inculcate these often on the Mind of a Child . . . possibly he shall never be able to separate them again so long as he lives. . . .

§11. . . . Thus Hatreds are often begotten from slight and almost innocent occasions. . . .

§18. . . . When two things in themselves disjoin'd appear to the sight constantly united; if the Eye sees these things rivetted which are loose, where will you begin to rectify the mistakes that follow in two *Ideas*, that they have been accustom'd so to join in their Minds, as to substitute one for the other, and, as I am apt to think, often without perceiving it themselves?

12.4

Francis Hutcheson

(1694–1746)

With such an introduction as Locke gave it, the principle of association was handicapped rather than assisted toward becoming the leading explanatory principle in British psychology. Berkeley (6.6) made a limited use of the concept, but without giving it a name. Now Francis Hutcheson uses it, name and all, to explain the origin of diversity in esthetic judgments. Like Hobbes, Hutcheson also will receive no credit for his contribution from later associationists, because of his predominantly nativist

An inquiry into the original of our ideas of beauty and virtue; in two treatises. In which the principles of the late Earl of Shaftesbury are explain'd and defended, against the author of the FABLE OF THE BEES: and the ideas OF MORAL GOOD and evil are establish'd, according to the sentiments of the Antient MORALISTS. With an attempt to introduce a MATHEMATICAL CALCULATION in subjects of MORALITY. London, 1725. [Pp. 68, 73–74, 76–78.]

*position. Indeed, he fails to take the obvious step of applying the principle
in his second treatise, to the development of moral attitudes. For that, see
John Gay (22.6), who in time exercised strong influence on David Hartley
(22.7, 13.8).*

*The long subtitle states Hutcheson's relations to Shaftesbury (22.4) and
Mandeville (22.5), and asserts his claim to priority in another area (25.1).*

3. We shall see afterwards, "That *Associations of Ideas* make Objects
pleasant, and delightful, which are not naturally apt to give any such
Pleasures; and the same way, the *casual Conjunctions of Ideas* may give
a Disgust, where there is nothing disagreeable in the Form it self." And
this is the occasion of many fantastick Aversions to Figures of some Animals, and to some other Forms: Thus *Swine, Serpents* of all Kinds, and
some *Insects* really beautiful enough, are beheld with Aversion by many
People, who have got *some accidental Ideas associated* to them. And for
Distastes of this Kind, no other Account can be given. . . .

8. . . . Nothing is more ordinary among those, who after Mr. Locke
have shaken off the groundless Opinions about *innate Ideas,* than to
alledge, "That all our Relish for *Beauty,* and *Order,* is either from *Advantage,* or *Custom,* or *Education,*" for no other Reason but the *Variety*
of *Fancys* in the World: and from this they conclude, "That our *Fancys*
do not arise from any *natural Power of Perception, or Sense.*" . . .

11. The *Association* of Ideas above hinted at, is one great Cause of the
apparent Diversity of Fancys in the *Sense of Beauty,* as well as in the
external Senses; and often makes Men have an aversion to Objects of
Beauty, and a liking to others void of it, but under different Conceptions
than those of *Beauty* or *Deformity.* And here it may not be improper to
give some instances of some of these *Associations.* The *Beauty* of *Trees,*
their *cool Shades,* and their *Aptness* to conceal from Observation, have
made *Groves* and *Woods* the usual Retreat to those who love *Solitude,*
especially to the *Religious,* the *Pensive,* the *Melancholy,* and the
Amorous. And do not we find that we have so join'd the Ideas of these
Dispositions of Mind with those external Objects, that they always
recur to us along with them? The Cunning of the *Heathen Priests* might
make such obscure Places the Scene of the fictitious Appearances of
their *Deitys;* and hence we join Ideas of something *Divine* to them. We
know the like Effect in the Ideas of our *Churches,* from the perpetual use
of them only in *religious Exercises.* The faint Light in *Gothick Buildings*
has had the same Association of a very foreign Idea, which our *Poet*
shews in his *Epithet.*

———*A Dim religious Light.* [Milton, *Il Penseroso.*]

In like manner it is known, "That often all the Circumstances of
Actions or *Places,* or *Dresses* of *Persons,* or *Voice,* or *Song,* which have
occurr'd at any time together, when we were strongly affected by any
Passion, will be so connected that any one of these will make all the rest

recur." And this is often the occasion both of great Pleasure and Pain, Delight and Aversion to many Objects, which of themselves might have been perfectly indifferent to us: but these *Approbations*, or *Distastes* are remote from the Ideas of *Beauty*, being plainly different Ideas.

12. There is also another Charm in *Musick* to various Persons, which is distinct from the *Harmony*, and is occasion'd by its raising agreeable Passions. The *human Voice* is obviously vary'd by all the stronger Passions; now when our *Ear* discerns any resemblance between the *Air* of a *Tune*, whether sung or play'd upon an Instrument, either in its *Time* or *Key*, or any other Circumstance, to the sound of the *human Voice* in any Passion, we shall be touch'd by it in a very sensible manner, and have *Melancholy, Joy, Gravity, Thoughtfulness* excited in us by a sort of *Sympathy* or *Contagion*. The same Connection is observable between the very *Air* of a *Tune*, and the *Words* expressing any Passion which we have heard it fitted to, so that they shall both recur to us together, tho but one of them affects our *Senses*. Now in such a diversity of pleasing or displeasing Ideas which may be conjoin'd with Forms of *Bodys*, or *Tunes*, when Men are of such different Dispositions, and prone to such a variety of Passions, it is no wonder "that they should often disagree in their Fancys of Objects, even altho their *Sense of Beauty* and *Harmony* were *perfectly uniform;*" because many other Ideas may either please or displease, according to Persons, Tempers, and past Circumstances. We know how agreeable a very *wild Country* may be to any Person who has spent the chearful Days of his Youth in it, and how disagreeable very *beautiful Places* may be if they were the Scenes of his Misery. And this may help us in many Cases to account for the Diversities of Fancy, without denying the *Uniformity* of our *internal Sense of Beauty*.

12.5

David Hume

(1711–1776)

Hume read Hutcheson, but it was with very different intent that he introduced the principle of association. Nevertheless, his reference to it as "a gentle force, which commonly prevails" shows how little he was prepared to found a system upon it. That step was reserved for Hartley, ten years later, whose contribution is presented in the next chapter (13.8) because

A treatise of human nature, being an attempt to introduce the experimental method of reasoning into moral subjects. 3 volumes. London, 1739–1740. [Vol. I, p. 26–27, 30.]

he breaks associationism out of the intellectual mold and applies it to behavior generally. Hume's definition of three "qualities" giving rise to associations provides an important reference point for all future discussions.

[Book I, Part I, Sect. IV.] . . . Were ideas entirely loose and unconnected, chance alone wou'd join them; and 'tis impossible the same simple ideas should fall regularly into complex ones (as they commonly do) without some bond of union among them, some associating quality, by which one idea naturally introduces another. This uniting principle among ideas is not to be consider'd as an inseparable connexion; for that has been already excluded from the imagination: Nor yet are we to conclude, that without it the mind cannot join two ideas; for nothing is more free than that faculty: but we are only to regard it as a gentle force, which commonly prevails, and is the cause why, among other things, languages so nearly correspond to each other; nature in a manner pointing out to every one those simple ideas, which are most proper to be united into a complex one. The qualities, from which this association arises, and by which the mind is after this manner convey'd from one idea to another, are three, viz. RESEMBLANCE, CONTIGUITY in time or place, and CAUSE and EFFECT. . . .

These are therefore the principles of union or cohesion among our simple ideas, and in the imagination supply the place of that inseparable connexion, by which they are united in our memory. Here is a kind of ATTRACTION, which in the mental world will be found to have as extraordinary effects as in the natural, and to shew itself in as many and as various forms. Its effects are every where conspicuous; but as to its causes, they are mostly unknown, and must be resolv'd into *original qualities of human nature, which I pretend not to explain.*

12.6

Henry Home, Lord Kames

(1696–1782)

In A history of the association psychology *(1921), H. C. Warren mentioned as post-Hartleyan eighteenth-century associationists Abraham Tucker (see 21.7), Joseph Priestley (see 20.9), Erasmus Darwin (see 15.10), and Archibald Alison, author of* Essays on the nature and principles of taste *(1790). But Dugald Stewart (in* Elements of the philosophy of the human mind, *1792) credited Kames and Gerard with showing that the*

Elements of criticism. 3 volumes. Edinburgh, 1762. [Vol. 1, pp. 21–28, 32–33, 40–41.]

"principles of association among our ideas" are far more numerous than
the three which had been enumerated by Hume. In selections from their
writings, we see how they rely on this variety of principles to differentiate
the styles of men. (See also Burke's comments on association (20.8),
which antedate all those named above.)

A man while awake is sensible of a continued train of perceptions and
ideas passing in his mind. It requires no activity on his part to carry on
the train: nor has he power to vary it by calling up an object at will. At
the same time we learn from daily experience, that a train of thought is
not merely casual. And if it depend not upon will, nor upon chance, we
must try to evolve by what law it is governed. The subject is of importance in the science of human nature; and I promise beforehand, that it
will be found of great importance in the fine arts.

It appears that the relations by which things are linked together, have
a great influence in directing the train of thought; and we find by experience, that objects are connected in the mind precisely as they are
externally. Beginning then with things external, we find that they are
not more remarkable by their inherent properties than by their various
relations. We cannot anywhere extend our view without perceiving
things connected together by certain relations. One thing perceived to
be a cause, is connected with its several effects; some things are connected by contiguity in time, others by contiguity in place; some are connected by resemblance, some by contrast; some go before, some follow.
Not a single thing appears solitary, and altogether devoid of connection.
The only difference is, that some are intimately connected, some more
slightly; some near, some at a distance.

Experience as well as reason may satisfy us, that the train of mental
perceptions is in a great measure regulated by the foregoing relations.
Where a number of things are linked together, the idea of any one suggests the rest; and in this manner is a train of thoughts composed. Such
is the law of succession; whether an original law, or whether directed
by some latent principle, is doubtful; and probably will forever remain
so. This law, however, is not inviolable. It sometimes happens, though
rarely, that an idea presents itself to the mind without any connection, so
far at least as can be discovered.

But though we have not the absolute command of ideas, yet the Will
hath a considerable influence in directing the order of connected ideas.
There are few things but what are connected with many others. By this
means, when any thing becomes an object, whether in a direct survey,
or ideally only, it generally suggests many of its connections. Among
these a choice is afforded. We can insist upon one, rejecting others; and
we can even insist upon what has the slightest connection. Where ideas
are left to their natural course, they are generally continued through the
strongest connections. The mind extends its view to a son more readily

than to a servant, and more readily to a neighbour than to one living at a distance. This order may be varied at will, but still within the limits of connected objects. In short, every train of ideas must be a chain, in which the particular ideas are linked to each other. We may vary the order of a natural train; but not so as to dissolve it altogether, by carrying on our thoughts in a loose manner without any connection. So far doth our power extend; and that power is sufficient for all useful purposes. To give us more power, would probably be detrimental, instead of being salutary.

Will is not the only cause that prevents a train of thought from being continued through the strongest connections. Much depends on the present tone of mind; for a subject that accords with this tone is always welcome. Thus, in good spirits, a chearful subject will be introduced by the slightest connection; and one that is melancholy, not less readily in low spirits. Again, an interesting subject is recalled, from time to time, by any connection indifferently, strong or weak. . . .

Another cause clearly distinguishable from that now mentioned, hath also a considerable influence over the train of ideas. In some minds of a singular frame, thoughts and circumstances crowd upon each other by the slightest connection. I ascribe this to a defect in the faculty of discernment. A person who cannot accurately distinguish betwixt a slight connection and one that is more solid, is equally affected with both. Such a person must necessarily have a great command of ideas, because they are introduced by any relation indifferently; and the slighter relations, being without number, must furnish ideas without end. . . .

On the other hand, a man of accurate judgement cannot have a great flow of ideas. The slighter relations making no figure in his mind, have no power to introduce ideas. And hence it is, that accurate judgement is not friendly to declamation or copious eloquence. This reasoning is confirmed by experience; for it is a noted observation, That a great or comprehensive memory is seldom connected with a good judgement. . . .

It appears then that we are framed by nature to relish order and connection. When an object is introduced by a proper connection, we are conscious of a certain pleasure arising from that circumstance. Among objects of equal rank, the pleasure is proportioned to the degree of connection: but among unequal objects, where we require a certain order, the pleasure arises chiefly from an orderly arrangement. Of this one may be made sensible, in tracing objects contrary to the course of nature, or contrary to our sense of order. The mind proceeds with alacrity from a whole to its parts, and from a principle to its accessories; but in the contrary direction, it is sensible of a sort of retrograde motion, which is unpleasant. And here may be remarked the great influence of order upon the mind of man. Grandeur, which makes a deep impression, inclines us, in running over any series, to proceed from small to great, rather than from great to small. But order prevails over this tendency; and in passing from the whole to its parts, and from a subject to its ornaments, affords pleasure as well as facility, which are not felt in the opposite course. . . .

There is perhaps not another instance of a building so great erected upon a foundation so slight in appearance, as that which is erected upon the relations of objects and their arrangement. Relations make no capital figure in the mind: the bulk of them are transitory, and some extremely trivial. They are however the links that, uniting our perceptions into one connected chain, produce connection of action, because perceptions and actions have an intimate correspondence. But it is not sufficient for the conduct of life that our actions be linked together, however intimately: it is beside necessary that they proceed in a certain order; and this also is provided for by an original propensity. Thus order and connection, while they admit sufficient variety, introduce a method in the management of affairs. Without them our conduct would be fluctuating and desultory; and we would be hurried from thought to thought, and from action to action, entirely at the mercy of chance.

12.7

Alexander Gerard

(1728–1795)

Gerard names as associating principles Vicinity (in time or place), Resemblance, Contrariety, Coexistence, Cause and Effect, and Order (in time, place, nature, and custom). Each is discussed at length before entering on his argument that an important source of difference among men is in the relative strength of these principles.

[Part II, Sec. IV] From the account which has been already given of the principles of association, it is easy to collect, That there is a broad foundation laid in the nature of the human imagination, for great extent and variety of genius. There are many relations of ideas, which fit them for being associated; almost every perception bears some of these relations to many different ideas; habit and the passions multiply and vary the instruments of association: by these means there are innumerable handles by which the imagination may seize such ideas as it has occasion for. Genius has, in some men, great force and compass: but a vigorous construction of the associating principles is sufficient to account for it, however great it be; for if they be vigorous, any one perception may introduce a great multitude of others, and that by means of many

An essay on genius. London, 1774. [Pp. 184–185, 215–216, 218–222.]

different relations. The principles of association likewise being so various, cannot but admit many distinct combinations and modifications, by which genius will be moulded into a great diversity of forms. In order therefore to prepare the way for a discovery of the varieties of genius, it will be proper to make some reflections on the principles of association, which have been separately illustrated. . . .

[Sec. VII] All the associating principles have some degree of force in every man. There is perhaps no person on whom any one of them has no influence at all. But in almost every man, some one of them is predominant: on every subject, a man is apt to follow one relation rather than any other, and to conceive chiefly such ideas as are, by that relation, connected with the present perception. Whence this proceeds, is perhaps inexplicable; it must, in a great measure, be resolved into original differences in the constitution of the mind; but the thing itself is evident in the most simple and common instances. If different persons set themselves to recollect a company, one naturally recollects it by running over the places occupied by those who composed it; another enumerates them according to their several professions, conditions, ages, or sexes; another according to their respective families and connexions: in the first person, vicinity or order; in the second, resemblance; in the third, the relation of cause and effect, is the predominant principle of association. . . .

Here is a direct foundation for a permanent variety of genius. In some man of genius or another, each of the associating principles is predominant; and whichever of them is, it forms a turn of genius suitable to it, and different from what the prevalence of any other would have produced. Invention in different arts and sciences, is dependent on very different relations of perceptions: genius for a particular art or science, will therefore be formed by the prevalence of that principle of association which chiefly leads to invention in it. . . .

Most commonly, the great divisions of genius arise from the prevalence of one *principle* of association or another; and the more minute variation from the prevalence of different *modifications* of the same principle. Yet these modifications are sometimes so dissimilar, that the predominance of one or another of them produces a difference of genius as great as could be produced by the predominance of principles totally distinct. . . . The same actions which the historian relates, may be also considered by the philosopher, their motives attended to, and conclusions deduced from them, concerning the constitution of human nature: in this he is influenced by the same relation of cause and effect, but by a different species of it; and accordingly he shows a kind of genius totally distinct from that of the historian. I shall give an example which is still more striking. In reducing bodies to regular divisions and subdivisions, the natural historian is conducted altogether by the principle of resemblance; yet no two sorts of genius are perhaps more different than that for natural history, and that for poetry. In accounting for the phenomena of bodies, the philosopher follows a quite different relation, that of cause and effect; but the genius of a natural historian, is much more akin to philosophical, than to poetical genius.

12.8

Thomas Brown

(1778–1820)

Although the future of associationism was to lie in its use as a simplifying and reductionistic principle, we have seen that most of the Scottish authors using it (including Hutcheson, Kames, Gerard, and Alison) looked upon it as a source of complication and enrichment of experience. Thomas Reid preferred the term "suggestion" as leaving scope for the "active powers" still to determine the course of mental events. Brown follows this usage, but his detailed specification of secondary laws lays the foundation for an argument which would point to "the inaccuracy or imperfection of the analyses which have led philosophers to rank, under distinct intellectual powers, phenomena that appear, on minuter analysis, not to differ in any respect from the common phenomena of simple suggestion [Lect. 45]."

The influence of Kames and Gerard appears in a lengthy discussion of the influence of constitution on genius, under the sixth law, occupying as much space as all the illustrations provided for the other eight laws.

. . . When Mr. Hume reduced, to the three orders of *resemblance, contiguity,* and *causation,* the relations on which he believed association to depend, he considered himself as stating only facts which were before familiar to every one, and *did* state only facts that were perfectly familiar. In like manner, when I reduce under a few heads those modifying circumstances, which seem to me as *secondary* laws, to guide, in every particular case, the momentary direction of the primary, my object is not to discover facts that are new, or little observed, but to arrange facts that, separately, are well known.

The *first* circumstance, which presents itself, as modifying the influence of the primary laws, in inducing one associate conception rather than another, is the length of time during which the original feelings from which they flowed, continued, when they coexisted, or succeeded each other. . . .

Lectures on the philosophy of the human mind. 4 volumes. Edinburgh, 1820. [Lecture 37. Vol. II; pp. 270–273, 278–279, 281–283, 285–286.]

12.8 Thomas Brown

In the *second* place, the parts of a train appear to be more closely and firmly associated, as the original feelings have been *more lively*. We remember brilliant objects, more than those which are faint and obscure. We remember for our whole lifetime, the occasions of great joy or sorrow. . . .

In the *third* place, the parts of any train are more readily suggested, in proportion as they have been more *frequently renewed*. . . .

In the *fourth* place, the feelings are connected more strongly, in proportion as they are *more or less recent*. . . .

In the *fifth* place, our successive feelings are associated more closely, as *each has existed less with other feelings*. The song, which we have never heard but from one person, can scarcely be heard again by us, without recalling that person to our memory; but there is obviously much less chance of this particular suggestion, if we have heard the same air and words frequently sung by others.

In the *sixth* place, the influence of the primary laws of suggestion is greatly modified by *original constitutional differences*, whether these are to be referred to the mind itself, or to varieties of bodily temperament. Such constitutional differences affect the primary laws in two ways,—first, by augmenting and extending the influence of all of them, as in the varieties of *the general power of remembering*, so observable in different individuals. Secondly, they modify the influence of the primary laws, by giving *greater proportional vigour* to *one set* of tendencies of suggestion than to another. . . .

The primary laws of association . . . are not less modified by constitutional diversities of another kind. These are the diversities of what is called temper, or disposition. It is thus we speak of one person of a *gloomy*, and of another of a *cheerful* disposition; and we avoid the one, and seek the company of the other, as if with perfect confidence, that the trains of thought which rise by spontaneous suggestion to the minds of each will be *different*, and will be in accordance with that variety of character which we have supposed. . . .

. . . The primary laws are modified, not by constitutional and permanent differences only, but by differences which occur in the same individual, according to the varying emotion of the hour. . . .

The temporary diversities of state, that give rise to varieties of suggestion are not *mental* only, but *corporeal;* and this *difference of bodily state* furnishes another *secondary law*, in modification of the *primary*. . . . How different are the trains of thought in *health* and in *sickness*, after a *temperate meal* and after a *luxurious excess!* It is not to the *animal powers* only, that the burthen of digestion may become oppressive, but to the *intellectual* also; and often to the *intellectual* powers even more than to the *animal*. . . .

There is yet another principle which modifies the primary laws of suggestion with very powerful influence. This is the principle of habit. . . .

When men of different professions observe the same circumstances, listen to the same story, or peruse the same work, their subsequent suggestions are far from being the same; and, could the future differences of the associate feelings that are to rise, be foreseen by us at the time, we should probably be able to trace many of them to former *professional peculiarities*, which are thus always unfortunately apt to be more and more aggravated by the very suggestions to which they have themselves given rise. . . .

In addition, then, to the primary laws of suggestion, which are founded on the mere relations of the objects or feelings to each other, it appears that there is another set of laws, the operation of which is in-dispensible to account for the variety in the effects of the former. To these I have given the name of *secondary laws of suggestion.* . . .

Even *one* of these secondary laws, alone, may be sufficient to change completely the suggestion which would *otherwise* have arisen from the operation of the primary laws; and it is not wonderful, therefore, that when many of them, as they usually do, *concur* in one joint effect, the result in different individuals should be so various. . . .

By the consideration of these *secondary laws of suggestion,* then, the difficulty, which the consideration of the *primary laws* left unexplained, is at once removed. We see now how *one* suggestion takes place rather than *another,* when, by the operation of the *mere primary laws,* many suggestions might arise equally; the influence of the *secondary laws* modifying this general tendency, and modifying it, of course, variously, as themselves are various.

12.9

James Mill

(1773–1836)

James Mill (Scot by birth, if not by philosophic affiliation) enforces parsimony. Nothing is left of Brown's secondary laws but vividness and frequency, and our selection closes with what seems almost a deliberate reductio ad absurdum of the associationist position.

The chapter from which this selection is taken is wholly reprinted in Rand; Herrnstein and Boring give about 90 percent of it.

Our ideas spring up, or exist, in the order in which the sensations ex-isted, of which they are the copies.

Analysis of the phenomena of the human mind. 2 volumes. London, 1829. [Vol. 1, pp. 56, 61, 68–71, 79–82.]

This is the general law of the "Association of Ideas"; by which term, let it be remembered, nothing is here meant to be expressed, but the order of occurrence. . . .

7. The causes of strength in association seem all to be resolvable into two; the vividness of the associated feelings; and the frequency of the association. . . .

8. Where two or more ideas have been often repeated together, and the association has become very strong, they sometimes spring up in such close combination as not to be distinguishable. . . .

The idea expressed by the term weight, appears so perfectly simple, that he is a good metaphysician, who can trace its composition. Yet it involves, of course, the idea of resistance, which we have shewn above to be compounded, and to involve the feeling attendant upon the contraction of muscles; and the feeling, or feelings, denominated Will; it involves the idea, not of resistance simply, but of resistance in a particular direction; the idea of direction, therefore, is included in it, and in that are involved the ideas of extension, and of place and motion, some of the most complicated phenomena of the human mind. . . .

The idea of extension is derived from the muscular feelings in what we call the motion of parts of our own bodies; as for example, the hands. I move my hand along a line; I have certain sensations; on account of these sensations, I call the line long, or extended. . . . In the idea of extension, there are included three of the most complex of our ideas; motion; time, which is included in motion; and space, which is included in direction. . . .

It is to this great law of association, that we trace the formation of our ideas of what we call external objects; that is, the ideas of a certain number of sensations, received together so frequently that they coalesce as it were, and are spoken of under the idea of unity. Hence, what we call the idea of a tree, the idea of a stone, the idea of a horse, the idea of a man. . . .

11. Mr. Hume, and after him other philosophers, have said that our ideas are associated according to three principles; Contiguity in time and place, Causation, and Resemblance. The Contiguity in time and place, must mean, that of the sensations; and so far it is affirmed, that the order of the ideas follows that of the sensations. Contiguity of two sensations in time, means the successive order. Contiguity of two sensations in place, means the synchronous order. We have explained the mode in which ideas are associated, in the synchronous, as well as the successive order, and have traced the principle of contiguity to its proper source.

Causation, the second of Mr. Hume's principles, is the same with contiguity in time, or the order of succession. Causation is only a name for the order established between an antecedent and a consequent; that is, the established or constant antecedence of the one, and consequence of the other. Resemblance only remains, as an alleged principle of association, and it is necessary to inquire whether it is included in the laws which have been above expounded. I believe it will be found that we are accustomed to see like things together. When we see a tree, we generally see more trees than one; when we see an ox, we generally see more oxen than one; a sheep, more sheep than one; a man, more men than one. From this observation, I think, we may refer resemblance to the law of frequency, of which it seems to form only a particular case. . . .

12. Not only do simple ideas, by strong association, run together, and form complex ideas: but a complex idea, when the simple ideas which compose it have become so consolidated that it always appears as one, is capable of entering into combinations with other ideas, both simple and complex. . . .

Some of the most familiar objects with which we are acquainted furnish instances of these unions of complex and duplex ideas.

Brick is one complex idea, mortar is another complex idea; these ideas, with ideas of position and quantity, compose my idea of a wall. My idea of a plank is a complex idea, my idea of a rafter is a complex idea, my idea of a nail is a complex idea. These, united with the same ideas of position and quantity, compose my duplex idea of a floor. In the same manner my complex idea of glass, and wood, and others, compose my duplex idea of a window; and these duplex ideas, united together, compose my idea of a house, which is made up of various duplex ideas. How many complex, or duplex ideas, are all united in the idea of furniture? How many more in the idea of merchandize? How many more in the idea called Every Thing?

12.10

John Stuart Mill

(1806–1873)

John Stuart Mill relaxed a great deal the rigidity of the system which his father had constructed on a strict contiguity principle. He restored the principle of similarity, and his statement that the idea of Extension cannot be resolved into more elementary ideas which constitute it contradicted the underlying principle of the Analysis.

This selection introduces the concept of mental chemistry, which would

A system of logic, ratiocinative and inductive, being a connected view of the principles of evidence and the methods of scientific investigation. 2 volumes. London, 1843. [Vol. II, pp. 500–503.]

later be used by Wundt. John Mill credited both his father and Thomas Brown with an appreciation of this principle, but only from an excess of generosity prompted by filial respect. It is true that Brown used the word, but not with the meaning which John Mill attached to it. To emphasize the value of introspective analysis, Brown held up as a model "the analytic art of chymistry, which does for us only what the microscope does" and "tells us, what, with livelier perceptive organs, we might have known, without a single experiment" (Lectures, Ch. X). His "spontaneous chymistry of the mind" contained no hint of interactive effects, but only required "the most attentive reflection to separate . . . the assemblages [emphasis added] which even a few years may have produced." James Mill emphasized this feature of analysis in his very title and did not go beyond it. Chemistry had advanced in the intervening years, and now John Mill uses the phrase "mental chemistry" in a totally new sense.

[Book VI, Ch. 4.] §3. The subject, then, of Psychology, is the uniformities of succession, the laws, whether ultimate or derivative, according to which one mental state succeeds another; is caused by, or at the least, is caused to follow, another. Of these laws, some are general, others more special. The following are examples of the most general laws.

First: Whenever any state of consciousness has once been excited in us, no matter by what cause; an inferior degree of the same state of consciousness, a state of consciousness resembling the former but inferior in intensity, is capable of being reproduced in us, without the presence of any such cause as excited it at first. Thus, if we have once seen or touched an object, we can afterwards think of the object though it be absent from our sight or from our touch. . . . This law is expressed by saying, in the language of Hume, that every mental *impression* has its *idea*.

Secondly: These Ideas, or secondary mental states, are excited by our impressions, or by other ideas, according to certain laws which are called Laws of Association. Of these laws the first is, that similar ideas tend to excite one another. The second is, that when two impressions have been frequently experienced (or even thought of) either simultaneously or in immediate succession, then whenever one of these impressions or the idea of it recurs, it tends to excite the idea of the other. The third law is, that greater intensity in either or both of the impressions, is equivalent, in rendering them excitable by one another, to a greater frequency of conjunction. . . .

. . . It is obvious that complex laws of thought and feeling not only may, but must, be generated from these simple laws. And it is to be remarked, that the case is not always one of Composition of Causes: the effect of concurring causes is not always precisely the sum of the effects of those causes when separate, nor even always an effect of the same kind with them. Reverting to the distinction which occupies so prominent a place in the history of induction; the laws of the phenomena of mind are sometimes analogous to mechanical, but sometimes also to chemical laws. When many impressions or ideas are operating in the mind together, there sometimes takes place a process, of a similar kind to chemical combination. When impressions have been so often experienced in conjunction, that each of them calls up readily and instantaneously the ideas of the whole group, those ideas sometimes melt and coalesce into one another, and appear not several ideas, but one; in the same manner as when the seven prismatic colours are presented to the eye in rapid succession, the sensation produced is that of white. But as in this last case it is correct to say that the seven colours when they rapidly follow one another *generate* white, but not that they actually *are* white; so it appears to me that the Complex Idea, formed by the blending together of several simpler ones, should, when it really appears simple, (that is, when the separate elements are not consciously distinguishable in it,) be said to *result from*, or be *generated by*, the simple ideas, not to *consist* of them. Our idea of an orange really *consists* of the simple ideas of a certain colour, a certain form, a certain taste and smell, &c., because we can by interrogating our consciousness, perceive all these elements in the idea. But we cannot perceive, in so apparently simple a feeling as our perception of the shape of an object by the eye, all that multitude of ideas derived from other senses, without which it is well ascertained that no such visual perception would ever have had existence; nor, in our idea of Extension, can we discover those elementary ideas of resistance, derived from our muscular frame, in which Dr. Brown has rendered it highly probable that the idea originates. These therefore are cases of mental chemistry: in which it is proper to say that the simple ideas generate, rather than that they compose, the complex ones.

With respect to all the other constituents of the mind, its beliefs, its abstruser conceptions, its sentiments, emotions, and volitions; there are some (among whom are Hartley, and the author of the *Analysis*) who think that the whole of these are generated from simple ideas of sensation, by a chemistry similar to that which we have just exemplified. I am unable to satisfy myself that this conclusion is, in the present state of our knowledge, fully made out.

12.11

Alexander Bain

(1818–1903)

After exhaustive discussion of the applications of the laws of contiguity and similarity, and of compound associations, Bain closes his book on Intellect with the chapter "Of constructive association." The emphasis on trial and error, and on the importance of a rich reserve of associative bonds for it to operate on, will reappear in Thorndike's "connectionism."

1. Throughout the whole of the preceding exposition we have had in view the literal resuscitation, revival, or reinstatement of former sensations, images, emotions, and trains of thought. No special reference has been made to the operation known by such names as Imagination, Creation, Constructiveness, Origination; through which we are supposed to put together new forms, or to construct images, conceptions, pictures, and modes of working such as we have never before had any experience of. Yet the genius of the painter, poet, musician, and inventor in the arts and sciences, evidently implies such a process as this.

Under the head of similarity we have had to recognise a power tending to originality and invention, as when in virtue of the identifying of two things formerly considered remote from each other, whatever is known of the one is instantly transferred to the other, thereby constituting a new and instructive combination of ideas. Such was the case when Franklin's identification of electricity and thunder led to the extension of all the properties of the Leyden jar to explain a thunder-storm. The power of recalling like by like in spite of remoteness, disguise, and false lures enters, as we have seen, into a very large number of inventive efforts, particularly in science. But we have now to consider constructions of a much higher order of complexity. There are discoveries that seem nothing short of absolute creations, as for example, the whole science of Mathematics; while in the Fine Arts, a Gothic cathedral, a frieze of the Parthenon, a Paradise Lost, are very far from repetitions of experienced objects, even with all the power of extension that the highest reach of the identifying faculty can impart.

Nevertheless, I mean to affirm that the intellectual forces operating in those creations are no other than the associating forces already discussed. . . .

3. The facility the mind has in passing from mere repetition into new

The senses and the intellect. London, 1855. [Pp. 571–575.]

combinations is perhaps most obvious in the use of language. Scarcely any succession of words uttered in everyday intercourse is precisely the same as any other succession formerly said or heard by the speaker. It seems particularly easy for us to adapt and modify this acquisition in an endless variety of ways. . . .

. . . Two utterances are present to the mind; the articulate activity is awakened and repeats these utterances perhaps in two or three ways; one is hit upon such as to satisfy the purpose of the moment, and being hit upon is retained and repeated. The effort of substitution once or twice put in practice becomes easy; the mind knows as it were to carry on the current of words so far, then stop, and fall into a different current, so as thereby to produce a third different from either. It is a part of the voluntary command that we acquire over our actions, that we can stop a train at any stage, and commence another train from that point, and this is all that is required in such a case of verbal substitution as we have now supposed. . . . The constructiveness, therefore, lies not in any purely intellectual operation, but in the command that the volition has obtained over the movements, by virtue of which command these are suspended and commenced at pleasure in the service of a particular end. The intellectual forces bring to mind the former acquisitions bearing on the situation, and if no one previous form is strictly applicable, it is a property of the volition to take part of one and part of another, and to make successive trials if necessary, until the want is satisfied.

Throughout the whole wide-ranging operation of adapting old forms of words to new meanings, this is essentially the process pursued. When all the elements requisite for a new combination are at hand, a volition alone is needed to make the selection and adaptation suited to the end in view. When there is not a sufficiency of forms within reach of the present recollection, the process of intellectual recovery must be plied to bring up others, until the desired combination is attained. A voluntary effort is quite equal to the task of cutting down and making up, choosing and rejecting, sorting and re-sorting; the feeling that possesses the mind of the end to be served, is the criterion to judge by, and when this is satisfied the volition ceases, the stimulus being no longer present. In all difficult operations, for purposes or ends, the rule of trial and error is the grand and final resort.

It would thus appear that the first condition of good verbal combinations for the expression of meaning is a sufficient abundance of already formed combinations to choose from, in other words, the effect depends on the previous acquisitions, and on the associating forces whereby old forms are revived for the new occasions. If a complex meaning has to be expressed, every part of this meaning will revive by contiguity and similarity some former idea of an identical or like nature, and the language therewith associated; and out of the mixed assemblage of foregone phrases, the volition must combine a whole into the requisite unity, by trial and error. The more abundant and choice the material supplied from the past by the forces of intellectual recovery, the better will be the combination that it is possible for the mind to form by the selecting effort.

# Chapter 13

THE LEARNED ACT

Because learning has been so much the focus of psychological theory in our century, it surprises us to see how small a part it played in earlier psychology. Such discussion of learning as did occur was almost entirely in intellectual terms, and it was regarded as a joint function of memory and reason. Not until the eighteenth century, with its emphasis on the perfectibility of man, do psychologists begin to deal with learning as a central rather than a peripheral problem. On the other hand, there had always been a need to explain behavioral change in animals in nonintellectual terms, and therefore it is not surprising that the real roots of learning theory should appear first in discussions of animal rather than of human behavior.

13.1

Erasistratus

(flourished 260 B.C.)

Erasistratus must be considered the greatest physiologist before Galen, who in effect developed his system farther. When Galen refers to Erasistratus, it is usually to emphasize a difference in views, but that is not the

As cited in Galen, "On habits." In *Greek medicine: Being extracts illustrative of medical writers from Hippocrates to Galen.* Translated and annotated by Arthur J. Brock. London: J. M. Dent & Sons, 1929. [P. 185.]

case in this selection. (However, Galen does in a later passage state that he does not consider the "habitual evacuations" as true habits.) This follows a passage in which Hippocrates has been cited at length on the importance of habits of eating and drinking. The entire context is quite medical, dealing primarily with the effects of habituation on the vital functions, but it goes on to apply the same point of view to intellectual functions.

Next Erasistratus, in the second book of his treatise "On Paralysis," writes as follows:—"Whoever is to exercise medicine properly must pay a great deal of attention to what is habitual and what not. The following are examples of what I mean. People carry out numerous familiar tasks without fatigue, whereas a few unwonted tasks tire them. Some persons digest familiar food more easily—although it be naturally difficult of digestion—than easily digested food to which they are not accustomed. Again, the body calls for its customary evacuations, even although these be useless, if they have developed into a habit; and when deprived of them it falls into disease. This is the case, for instance, with the haemorrhoidal flux and the evacuations which some people habitually administer to themselves; and even where sores open from time to time with ichorous discharge, and sometimes in the purgings (*choleras*) which take place at certain epochs. For the body demands all these various discharges, although they are useless, and when they do not occur at the ordinary times, people who are used to having them fall seriously ill. The following sort of thing may also be observed. Suppose we are asked to quote two or three lines out of the middle of an epic or iambic poem which we know; being unused to this, we do not readily manage it, but when we come to these same lines in their natural order, we say them easily; further, with practice, we can do even the previous task as well.

"The following also may occur. People who are unused to learning, learn little, and that slowly, while those more accustomed do much more and do it more easily. The same thing also happens in connection with research. Those who are altogether unfamiliar with this become blinded and bewildered as soon as their minds begin to work; they readily withdraw from the inquiry, in a state of mental fatigue and exhaustion, much like people who attempt to race without having been trained. He, on the other hand, who is accustomed to research, seeks and penetrates everywhere mentally, passing constantly from one topic to another; nor does he ever give up his investigation; he pursues it not merely for a matter of days, but throughout his whole life. Also by transferring his mind to other ideas which are yet not foreign to the question at issue, he persists till he reaches the solution."

13.2

Leo Africanus

(*c.* 1494–1552)

The skills of animal trainers were at a high level long before the days of Pavlov and Skinner. Medieval falconers trained their birds with highly sophisticated techniques. (See P. T. Mountjoy et al., in the Journal of the History of the Behavioral Sciences, 1969, 5, 59–67.) In a thirteenth-century sermon by Jacques de Vitry, there is a tale about a knight who contrived to obtain for himself a fine horse belonging to a priest by borrowing it for several days. During that time, he repeatedly spurred it violently just after saying the words "Make haste, O Lord, to deliver me," a phrase which the priest often spoke as he recited his Hours while riding. Returned to its master, the horse seemed to have become strangely unmanageable, and the priest sadly parted with it. (C. Beeson, A primer of medieval Latin, ch. XIV.) In the sixteenth century, Bishop Rorarius introduced a discussion of animal reason with an anecdote about a dog which performed amazingly to musical cues. The following account of street entertainment in six-teenth-century Cairo provides clear evidence of a sophisticated approach to animal training.

At my being in Cairo I saw a camell dance; which arte of dancing howe he learned of his master I will heere in fewe words report. They take a yoong camell, and put him for halfe an hower togither into a place like a bathstove prepared for the same purpose, the floore whereof is het with fire; then play they without upon a drum, whereat the camell, not so much in regard of the noise, as of the hot pavement which offendeth his feete, lifteth up one legge after another in maner of a dance, and having beene accustomed unto this exercise for the space of a yeere or ten moneths, they then present him unto the publike view of the people, when as hearing the noise of a drum, and remembering the time when he trode upon the hot floore, he presently falleth a dancing and leaping: and so, use being turned into a kind of nature, he perpetually observeth the same custome.

The history and description of Africa, and of the notable things therein contained {1556}. Written by Al-Hassan Ibn-Mohammed Al-Wezaz Al-Fasi, a Moor, baptised as Giovanni Leone, but better known as Leo Africanus. Done into English in the year 1600, by John Pory. Reprinted by the Hakluyt Society, 1896. [P. 942.]

13.3

Luis Vives

(1492–1540)

Vives conformed to the thought of his times by devoting much more space to memory (see 11.4) than to nonverbal learning, but he does include a chapter on habit. In it we see, as clearly as anywhere, that practical interest in behavior which has made him a nominee for that widely distributed title, "the first modern psychologist." Note the use of assuefactio, which will reappear in the two following selections.

Habit

The faculties give birth to actions. In this, as in everything which the soul does, the faculties accept the gifts of nature. For some acts follow directly from the natural powers, as soon as they have had the opportunity to ripen and gain control. These acts, like seeing and hearing, are no less natural than the faculties themselves: for these senses are definitely natural, being present in the child at birth, and in puppies after nine days. These actions are not the product of any thought or exercise whatever; to be well done, they need only ripe strength and good disposition. But there are other acts which require exercise and practice in order that they shall be done swiftly and correctly. From exercise comes habituation [*assuefactio*], which includes both facility in the act and a disposition to it. In Greek this is called ἕξις which we translate as *habit;* this is a readiness to perform acts similar to those which gave rise to it. Habituation pertains not only to actions, but also to passions, which are indeed a kind of action of the animal faculties, although their force is exerted passively; therefore we call both of them actions.

It sometimes happens that an act is natural as to kind but in its forms, attributes or details it depends on exercise. Thus we receive our senses directly from nature, for seeing, hearing, tasting, smelling, touching. But it is habit which gives them the power to tolerate sights which are disagreeable, hideous and terrifying, horrifying noises, bitter and acid tastes, and other things of this sort. It is habituation which gives rise to the skill and readiness of the master, as well as the aptness of his instruments; for just as the carver and the painter become more skilled and more expert, their instruments, such as the hand, also become more apt; and this is sometimes true even of the external instruments, provided they do not

De anima et vita [On the soul and life]. Brussels, 1538. [Pp. 116–118.]

deteriorate due to the resistance of the material, as happens to the brush, the axe, the saw and the plane. The same may be said of the effect of habit on the soul, which it renders more docile, while giving the spirits a greater disposition for the same employments; although sometimes they can be harmed by immoderate use, and are thus destroyed. The soul is drawn along by custom in established ways, which are called propensities; thus anything which has been confirmed by long habit acquires almost the strength of nature, and then we do it not only without difficulty, but with pleasure, and things that are familiar become enjoyable. Not only in what we do, but also in what we suffer, in anything which is hurtful to our nature, custome lessens the annoyance and the suffering of the senses; thus illness and pain are reduced by familiarity. Therefore they are wise who advise us to choose the best conduct for our lives, which by habit will become agreeable in the future; and Plato says that it matters not a little how we were shaped and what habits we formed in childhood. This rooting of habit is given to our soul, like everything else, for its own good. For if we are to do what is good and proper, use and exertise are required; for if time and repetition did not strengthen our faculties, so that afterwards we can do our tasks more easily and expeditiously, learn more aptly, and pursue them with more pleasure, all the work we undertake would be in vain, and our mind would always come to its noble tasks unprepared; nor would we do anything well, if we could not improve with time. So much as to the things we do of our own will, but as to those which we suffer unwillingly, how miserable would the condition of our life be if, being exposed to so many things that are bitter and harsh, habituation did not bring us consolation. Just as habit grows and is strengthened with time, so also time and disuse diminish it, as well as any very violent assault, whether internal, as from poison or illness, or external, as from a wound or a blow. In this way some persons lose the knowledge of how to read as a result of sickness, and others from being struck by a stone or a staff; this seems to me to depend more on the condition of the instruments than on that of the master, because those to whom this happens, when later they recover from their illness, also recover their prior skill, which would not happen if the master had lost the traces which had been imprinted by habituation.

13.4

Kenelm Digby

(1603–1665)

Although Digby is probably most often remembered for the absurdity of his venture into medicine in defense of "the powder of sympathy" which may cure a wound when applied to the weapon that had inflicted it, in his account of animal behavior he is at great pains to give a purely physical account of actions which most of his contemporaries attributed to sympathies and antipathies of occult origin. From a discussion of that subject (see 15.5) he goes on to describe how antipathies may be overcome by "assuefaction" (a word we have already met in Vives). He rejects the idea that intelligence can be involved in such behavioral change in animals. There seems little reason to say, as has been done, that Digby's discussion of assuefaction anticipates the conditioned reflex. Here, as with Vives before him and Charleton soon after, it is clearly habituation.

Digby's book appeared in Paris because he spent many years in exile from England to escape persecution as a Catholic.

[First treatise, Ch. XXXVII. 5.] Unto some of these causes all antipathies may be reduced: and the like reason may be given for the sympathies we see betweene some creatures. The litle corporeities which issue from the one, have such a conformity with the temper of the other, that it is thereby moved to ioyne itself unto the body from whence they flow, and affecteth union with it in that way, as it receiveth the impression. If the smell do please it, the beast will alwayes be smelling at it: if the tast, nothing shall hinder it from feeding upon it when it can reach it. The fishermen upon the banke over against newfound land, do report that there flocketh about them a kind of bird, so greedy of the fishes livers which they take there, as that to come at them and feede upon them, they will suffer the men to take them in their handes; and will not fly away, as long as any of their desired meate is in theyr eye: whence the French men that fish there, do call them *Happe foyes* [liver snatchers]. The like power, a certaine worme hath with nightingales.

And thus you see, how they are strong impressions upon sense, and not any discourse of reason, that do governe beastes in their actions: for if their avoyding men, did proceed from any sagacity in their nature, surely they would exercise it, when they see that for a bitte of meate they incurre their destruction: and yet neyther the examples of their

Two treatises. In the one of which, the nature of bodies; in the other, the nature of mans soule; is looked into. . . . Paris, 1644. [Pp. 333–334.]

fellowes killed before their eyes in the same pursuite, nor the blowes which themselves do feele; can serve them for warning, where the sense is so strongly affected: but as soon as the blowe that removed them is passed, (if it miste killing or laming them) and they be gotten on wing againe, they will returne to their prey as eagerly and confidently as if nothing were there to hinder them.

[6.] This then being the true reason of all sympathy and antipathy, we can not admitt that any beastes should love or hate one an other, for any other cause, then some of those we have touched. All which are reduced to locall motion, and to materiall application of bodies of one nature, to bodies of an other; and are as well transmitted to their yong ones, as begotten in themselves: and as the satisfying of their sense is more prevalent in the *Happe foyes* than the feare which from other groundes is begotten in their fantasy; and so maketh them approach to what the other would drive them from.

In like manner, any aversion of the fantasy may be mastered not only by a more powerfull agent upon the present sense, but also by assuefaction, and by bringing into the fantasy with pleasing circumstances that obiect which before was displeasing and affrightfull to it: as we see that all sortes of beastes or birdes, if they be taken yong may be tamed and will live quietly together. Dogges that are used to hunt and kill deere, will live friendly with one that is bred with them; and that fawne which otherwise would have beene affraide of them, by such education groweth confident and playeth boldely with them. Of which we can no longer remaine in doubt, if we will beleeve the story of a tygar (accounted the cruellest beaste of all others) who being shutt up with a deere, that had been bred with him from a kidde, and from his being a whelpe; and no meate given him, used meanes to breake prison, when was halfe starved, rather than he would hurt his familiar friend. You will not suspect that it was a morall consideration, which made him so kinde: but the deere had never come into his fantasy accompanied with other circumstances, then of play or of warmth: and therefore hunger (which calleth only the species of meate out of the memory into the fantasy) would never bring the deere thither, for remedy of that passion. . . .

And thus the deere was beholding to the tygar's fantasy, not to his discourse of morall honesty, for his life.

13.5

Walter Charleton

(1619–1707)

Walter Charleton is likewise determined to explain animal behavior in terms of the actions of bodies on one another. Here habit is clearly no more than habituation. The selection is from Book III, Ch. XI: "Of the Motive, Vertue, Habit, Gravity, and Levity of Concretions."

Of the Motive Vertue, Habit, Etc.

[Sec. I, 10.] As for that Appendix of a Faculty, which not only Philosophers, but the people also name a HABIT; Experience daily teacheth, that there are some Faculties, (in Animals especially) which by only frequency of acting grow more prompt and fit to act: and upon consequence, that that Hability or promptness for action, is nothing but a Facility of doing, or repeating that action, which the same Faculty, by the same instruments, hath frequently done before.

[11.] And, as to the *Reason* of this Facility; though it arise in some measure from the Power or Faculty it self, or the Spirits, as being accustomed to one certain motion: yet doth it chiefly depend upon the Disposition of the *Organs,* or instruments which the Faculty makes use of in the performance of its proper action. For, because the Organ is alwayes a Dissimilar or Compound body, consisting of some parts that are crass and rigid; we are to conceive it to be at first somewhat stubborn, and not easily flexible to such various motions, as the Faculty requires to its several operations: and therefore, as when we would have a Wand to be every way easily flexible, we are gently and frequently to bend it, that so the tenour of its fibres running longwise through it, may be here and there and everywhere made more lax, without any sensible divulsion; so if we desire to have our hands expedite for the performance of all those difficult motions that are necessary to the playing of a Lesson on the Lute, we must by degrees master that rigidity or clumsiness in the Nerves, Tendons, Muscles and joints of our fingers, yea in the very skin and all other parts of our hands. Thus also Infants, while they stammer, and strive again and again to pronounce a word clearly and distinctly, do no more than by degrees master the stiffness and sluggish-

Physiologia Epicuro-Gassendo-Charltoniana: or a fabric of science natural, upon the hypothesis of atoms, founded by Epicurus, repaired by Petrus Gassendi, augmented by Walter Charleton. The first part [all published]. London, 1654. [Pp. 273–274.]

ness of their tongues and other vocal organs, and so make them more flexible and voluble: and when by assuefaction they have made them easily flexible to all the motions required to the formation of that idiome, then at length come they to speak it plainly and perfectly. The same is also true, concerning the Brain, and those Organical parts therein, that are inservient to the act of Imagination, and by the imagination to the act of Discourse. For, though the Mind, when divorced from the body, can operate most readily, and knows no difficulty or impediment in the act of Intellection; as being Immaterial, and so wanting no organs for the exercise of the reasoning Faculty: yet nevertheless, while it is adliged to the body and its material instruments, doth it remain subject to some impediment in the execution of its functions; and because that impediment consisteth only in the less aptitude or inconformity of its proper organs, therefore the way to remove that impediment, is only by Assuefaction of it to study and ratiocination. And from this Assuefaction may the Mind be affirmed to acquire a certain Habit or Promptitude to perform its proper Actions; insomuch as by reason of that Habit, it operates more freely and expeditely: but, yet, in stricter Logick, that Habit ariseth chiefly to its Organs; as may be inferred only from hence, that the Organs are capable of increment and decrement, and to increase and decrease, is competent only to a thing that consisteth of parts; such is the Organ, not the Mind.

[12.] Nor is the acquisition of a Habit by assuefaction proper only to Man, but is common also to *all Living Creatures,* such especially as are used to the hand and government of Man, as Horses, Doggs, Hawks, and all prating and singing Birds. And where we affirmed, that some Faculties are capable of advancement to perfection by Habit; we intended, that there are other faculties which are *incapable* thereof, as chiefly the *Natural Faculties* in Animals, and such as are not subject to the regiment of the Will: though still we acknowledge that some of these there are, which upon change of temperament in their respective Organs, may acquire such a certain Habit, as may oppose the original inclination; and of this sort the principal is the Nutrient Faculty, which may be accustomed even to Poison. Lastly, when we, said *Chiefly in Animals;* we were unwilling totally to exclude *Plants;* because they also seem (at least Analogically) to acquire a kind of Habit: as is evident from their constant retaining of any posture or incurvation, which the hand of the gardiner hath imposed upon them, while they were tender and flexible; as also that they may by degrees be accustomed to foreign soils, and (what is more admirable) if in their transplantation those parts of them, which at first respected the South or East, be converted to the North or West, they seldome thrive, never attain their due procerity. Nay, if the Experiments of some Physitians be true, *Minerals* also may be admitted to attain a Habit by assuefaction: for *Baptista van Helmont* . . . reports that He hath found a Saphire become so much the more efficacious an

Attractive of the pestilential Venome from the Vitals, by how much the more frequently it hath been circumduced about Carbuncles or Plague Sores; as if Custome multiplied its Amuletary Virtue and taught it a more speedy way of conquest.

13.6

Antoine Dilly

(?–1676)

This book is the only published work of an obscure Jesuit priest who died in the year of its publication. The theory presented herein, which is essentially the drainage theory of learning as developed in the late nineteenth century by James and McDougall, is a direct development of the Cartesian automaton theory. It is especially notable because Dilly did not merely link simultaneous events, as Descartes had done and as most associationists continued to do, but described a process whereby the weaker stimulus comes to evoke the response formerly attached to the stronger stimulus— a true conditioning paradigm. (Compare Vives, 11.4, and our comment thereon.)

It is known that Locke read this book and brought it back to England with him.

We should also take careful note, and we will come back to this later, that because the brain is of a soft substance it is capable of receiving and retaining the impressions which external objects make upon it, which perhaps consist in nothing more than the facility which is conserved by pores in the brain, which have been opened by means of them, to reopen in the same manner either by themselves or as a result of the fortuitous flow of the animal spirits, like a book which has been opened several times at the same place. Now these impressions are nothing more than the traces the animal spirits leave by depressing the hairs which bristle on the fibers of the brain, just as a man who walks through a field covered with grass makes a sort of path which lasts for some time, and he can even wear this out so strongly that it will never disappear; also, one can traverse it more easily the second time than the first, the third time than the second, and so forth. . . .

De l'ame des be'tes, ou après avoir démontré la spiritualité de l'ame de l'homme, l'on explique par la seule machine, les actions les plus surprenantes des animaux [The animal soul; in which, after demonstrating the spirituality of the human soul, the most surprising actions of animals are explained as merely mechanical]. Lyon, 1676. [Pp. 221–222, 224–225, 227–231.]

We should also take note that when two objects act together their traces usually unite, that is to say the animal spirits which, due to the impression of these two objects, flowed into different fibers of the brain, in order then to inflate different muscles, happening to cross in their paths, mix together and become a single stream, which will go to only one of the two places to which these spirits would have flowed if they had not joined. From this it follows, first, that the only movements which result will be those excited by the object which made the stronger impression; secondly, the movements which would have been produced by the weaker object will not take place, but thereafter, even if it appears alone, it cannot act on the brain without exciting the movements which accompany the action of the object whose traces have been fused with its own. This joining of species (as we shall henceforth refer to such fused traces) happens very frequently, not only when the paths of the animal spirits cross, but even when they run near one another; for when one of the two streams disturbs the parts lying close to its own course, it no doubt causes the other to move towards that side, because it meets less resistance in that way . . . due to the agitation of the parts which lie between the two [currents]. . . .

If we accept what has been said in the previous chapter, I see nothing easier than to explain the discipline of animals: because if I want to train a dog to stand on its two hind legs, I merely hold him in that position for some time, in order to obtain a free and easy passage for the animal spirits into those parts, and so that the pores which let the spirits escape acquire greater facility at opening in this way. Further, when the animal wants to change its posture, I will threaten it with a stick, and since his brain is naturally disposed so that at this sight it opens at those points required to make him stop, and check him from approaching the stick, there is no reason to be surprised that he will stay fixed in this position. And thus after I have repeated the same thing several times, this habit will become so strong that afterwards he will keep it by himself.

If then we want to make him dance to the sound of a violin, we need only walk in front of him, while he is in this posture, offering him some bread, because he will be disposed to approach this food and follow it; so that if a violin is played at the same time, the species of the sound of this instrument will be so well joined with that of the bread that after this has been repeated several times, the sound of the violin by itself will be able to make the dog dance. . . .

If furthermore I want this dog to jump when I pronounce the name of the king of France, and to bark when he hears that of the king of Spain, then I will hold a stick horizontally a little above the ground, and when he is quite hungry I will offer him some bread on the other side of the stick while at the same time speaking the words at the sound of which I want him to jump. It is plain that since he is obliged to get over the stick to come and eat the bread, he will jump on this occasion, and the two species being joined in this manner, after this has been done several times, the dog afterwards will jump as well for the words alone as he does when the bread is there. If on the contrary I strike him when I pronounce the name of the king of Spain, it is certain that he will bark, and that afterwards he will do this whenever these same words are spoken.

13.7

Thomas Willis

(1621–1675)

This selection is from Chapter VI "Of the science or knowledge of brutes," in which the description of learning is joined with unrestrained neurological speculation.

Therefore, that we may seek out as it were the several footsteps, by which all brute Animals are imbued with the Knowledg of things; we ought first to distinguish here, that some of their Knowledg is born with them . . . being infused by the most high Creator, and impressed like a Character, from their first formation, on the beginnings, or on their very Natures themselves, which is wont commonly to be called *Natural Instinct;* But others acquired, to wit, which by degrees is learned, by the incursion of sensible things, Imitation, humane Institution, and other ways, and is carryed to a greater degree of Perfection in some than in others; yet in some, this acquired Knowledg, as also Cunning, depend wholly on the natural Instinct, and being polished by frequent use and habit, and Carried a little further, seem to be certain additions only. . . .

For secondly, besides the natural Instincts, living Brutes are wont to be taught by sensible species, to wit, to profit in the Knowledge of several things, and to acquire certain habits of practice: But this happens not equally to all nor at all times. For in many Animals newly brought forth, natural Instinct is of some force, but then the Impressions of sensible things little or nothing affect the sensitive soul: Because, altho the flamy part of the Soul is enough inkindled in the Brain, yet because the Brain and its Appendix, abounds with much humidity, therefore the Spirituous Effluvias, or the lucid part of the Soul which ought to irradiate these Bodies, is very much obscured, as the beam of the Sun passing thorow a

[*De anima brutorum* . . . , 1672.] *Two discourses concerning the soul of brutes, which is that of the vital and sensitive of man.* Englished by S. Pordage. London, 1683. [Pp. 34–38.]

thick Cloud: Wherefore at this time, the strokes of sensible things, being not deeply fixed, are presently obliterated, and in them local motions hardly follow: yea in some Beasts, in whom the blood being continually and habitually thick, and who have a less Clear Brain, tho through their whole Life some acts of the Exterior Senses and Motions are performed, yet few Characters are left, of any interiour Knowledg. Wherefore, we shall here inquire only concerning Brutes, that are more docil, to wit, in whom are besides local motions, and the five Exterior Senses, Memory, and Imagination; and in these we may conceive this kind of Introduction, or Method of Institution, concerning the Exquisite Knowledge, by the sense with which they are wont to be imbued.

Therefore, as soon as the Brain in the more perfect Brutes grows Clear, and the Constitution of the Animal Spirits becomes sufficiently lucid and defecated, the exterior Objects being brought to the Organs of the Senses, make Impressions, which being from thence transmitted, for the continuing the Series or Order of the Animal Spirits inwards, towards the streaked Bodies, affect the Common Sensory; and when as a sensible Impulse of the same, like a waving of Waters, is carried further into the Callous Body, and thence into the *Cortex* or shelly substance of the Brain, a Perception is brought in, concerning the Species of the thing admitted, by the Sense, to which presently succeeds the Imagination, and marks or prints of its Type being left, constitutes the Memory; But in the mean time, whilst the sensible Impression being brought to the common Sensory, effects there the Perception of the thing felt; as some direct Species of it, tending further creates the Imagination and Memory; so other reflected Species of the same Object, as they appear either Congruous or Incongruous, produce the Appetite, and local motions its Executors; that is, the Animal Spirits looking inwards, for the Act of Sension, being struck back, leap towards the streaked Bodies; and when as these Spirits presently possessing the Beginnings of the Nerves, irritate others, they make a desire of flying from the thing felt, and a motion of this or that member or part, to be stirred up: Then, because this Kind, or that Kind of Motion succeeds once or twice, to this or to that Sension, afterwards, for the most part, this Motion follows that Sension as the Effect follows the Cause: and according to this manner, by the admitting the Idea's of sensible things, both the Knowledg of several things, and the habits of things to be done, or of local Motions, are by little and little produced: For indeed, from the beginning, almost every Motion of the animated Body is stirred up by the Contact of the outward Object; to wit, the Animal Spirits residing within the Organ, are driven inward, being strucken by the Object, and so (as we have said) constitute Sension or Feeling; then, like as a Flood sliding along the Banks of the shore, is at last beaten back, so, because this waving or inward turning down of the Animal spirits, being partly reflected from the Common Sensory, is at last directed outwards, and is partly stretched forth even into the inmost part of the Brain, presently local Motion succeeds the Sension; and at the same time, a Character being affixed on the Brain, by the sense of the thing perceived, it impresses there, Marks or *Vestigia* of the same, for the Phantasie and the Memory then affected, and afterwards to be affected; but afterwards, when as the Prints or Marks of very many Acts of this Kind of Sensation and Imagination, as so many Tracts or Ways, are ingraven in the Brain, the Animal Spirits, oftentimes of their own accord, without any other forewarning, and without the presence of an Exterior Object, being stirred up into Motion, for as much, as the[y] Fall into the footsteps before made, represent the Image of the former thing; with which, when the Appetite is affected, it desiring the thing objected to the Imagination, causes spontaneous Actions, and as it were drawn forth from an inward Principle. As for Examples sake, The Stomach of a Horse, feeding in a barren Ground or fallow Land, being incited by hunger, stirs up and variously agitates the Animal Spirits flowing within the Brain; the Spirits being thus moved by accident, because they run into the footsteps formerly made, they call to mind the former more plentiful Pasture fed on by the Horse, and the Meadows at a great distance, then the Imagination of the desirable thing, (which then is cast before it, by no outward Sense, but only from the Memory,) stops at the Appetite: that is, the Spirits implanted in the streaked Bodies, are affected by that Motion of the spirits flowing within the middle part or Marrow of the Brain; who from thence presently after their former accustomed manner, enter the origines of the Nerves, and actuating the Nervous System after their wonted manner by the same Series, produce local Motions, by which the hungry Horse is carried from place to place, till he has found out the Imagined Pasture, and indeed enjoyes that good the Image of which was painted in his Brain.

After this manner, the sensible Species being intromitted, by the benefit of the Exterior Organs, in the more perfect Brutes, for that they affix their Characters on the Brain, and there leave them, they constitute the Faculties of Phantasie and Memory, as it were Store-houses full of Notions; further, stirring up the Appetite into local Motions, agreeable to the Sensions frequently, they produce an habit of Acting; so that some Beasts being Taught or Instructed for a long time, by the assiduous Incursion of the Objects, are able to know and remember many things, and further learn manifold works; to wit, to perform them by a Complicated and Continued series and succession of very many Actions. Moreover, this Kind of acquired Knowledge of the Brutes, and the Practical habits introduced through the Acts of the Senses, are wont to be promoted by some other means, to a greater degree of perfection.

For in the third place, it happens to these by often Experience that the Beasts are not only made more certain of simple things, but it teaches them to form certain Propositions, and from thence to draw certain Conclusions. Because, draught Beasts, having sometimes found water to be

Cooling, they seek it far as a remedy of too much heat; wherefore, when their Precordia grow hot, running to the River they drink of it, and if they are hot in their whole Body they fearlessly lye down in the same. In truth, many Actions which appear admirable in Brutes came to them at first by some accident, which being often repeated by Experience, pass into Habits, which seem to shew very much of Cunning and Sagacity; because, the sensitive soul is easily accustomed to every Institution or Performance, and its actions begun by Chance, and often repeated, pass into a Manner and Custom. . . .

Living Brutes are taught by Example, by the Imitation and Institution of others of the same or of a diverse Kind, to perform certain more excellent Actions. Hence it is that the Ape so plainly imitates Man, that by some, it is thought a more imperfect Species of him. For this Animal being extreamly mimical, as it is indued with a most Capacious and hot Brain, it imitates to an hair, almost all the Gestures that it happens to see, presently with a ready and expeditious Composing of its Members, and is furnished with a notable Memory, and retains all its tricks which it has once acted very firmly afterwards, and is wont to repeat them at its pleasure. They are very admirable habits, which Horses, Doggs, and Birds get, being carefully instructed by the Discipline of Man; and not only from Men but being taught first by their Companions, they imbibe altogether new and more Excellent Customs: so one Dog ordinarily teaches another to hunt, and one Bird another to compose harmonious notes and various tunes. It were an Easy matter to bring very many Instances of this Kind. But we shall hasten to other things.

Having thus enumerated the Chief Helps from Nature and Art, by which living Brutes do profit in the Knowledge of things, and are instructed by the Habits of Acting, we shall now inquire, to what hight most of them or all of them put together, can arrive.

. . . According to this sort of *Analyzing*, the most Intricate Actions of Brutes, which seem to contain Ratiocination, may be explained, and reduced into Competent notions of the sensitive Soul.

13.8

David Hartley

(1705–1757)

David Hartley, a physician with strong convictions on theological matters, combined science and piety to create a man-machine which can associate on equal terms with like fabrications of twentieth-century behaviorism.

Observations on man, his frame, his duty, and his expectations. 2 vols. London, 1749. [Pp. 58, 65, 102–107, 109, 256–259.]

13.8　David Hartley

He tells us that he took the doctrine of vibrations from Newton (8.9) and the theory of association from Gay (22.6). Blending these, he established what has been called the first physiological psychology, and is certainly the first thorough-going application of association theory, thus founding the association school. The device of vibratiuncles, or diminutive vibrations, permitted him to establish associations indifferently among sensations (i.e., immediate effects of stimulation), ideas (their lingering traces), and motions (their somatic effects).

Three short paragraphs which contain an outline of the hypothetical foundation of his system are followed by some examples of its application, particularly in the acquisition of speech and its use in control of behavior. Infant babbling is described very much in the terms of Floyd Allport's "circular reflex" (27.6).

See 22.7 for Hartley's position on free will and morality, a problem of the highest concern to him.

[Prop. 9] *Sensory Vibrations, by being often repeated, beget, in the medullary Substance of the Brain, a Disposition to diminutive Vibrations, which may also be called Vibratiuncles and Miniatures, corresponding to themselves respectively.* . . .

[Prop. 10]) *Any Sensations A, B, C, &c. by being associated with one another a sufficient Number of Times, get such a Power over the corresponding Ideas a, ab, c, &c. that any one of the Sensations, A, when impressed alone, shall be able to excite in the Mind b, c, &c. the Ideas of the rest.* . . .

[Prop. 20, Corollary 7] . . . *If any Sensation A, Idea B, or muscular Motion C, be associated for a sufficient Number of times with any other Sensation D, Idea E, or muscular Motion F, it will, at last, excite d, the simple Idea belonging to the Sensation D, the very Idea E, or the very muscular Motion F.*

[Prop. 21] *The voluntary and semivoluntary Motions are deducible from Association, in the manner laid down in the last Proposition.* . . .

After the Actions, which are most perfectly voluntary, have been rendered so by one Set of Associations, they may, by another, be made to depend upon the most diminutive Sensations, Ideas, and Motions, such as the Mind scarce regards, or is conscious of; and which therefore it can scarce recollect the Moment after the Action is over. Hence it follows, that Association not only converts automatic Actions into voluntary, but voluntary ones into automatic. . . . I shall call them automatic Motions of the secondary Kind, to distinguish them both from those which are originally automatic, and from the voluntary ones. . . .

The Fingers of young Children bend upon almost every Impression which is made upon the Palm of the Hand, thus performing the Action of Grasping, in the original automatic Manner. After a sufficient Repetition of the motory Vibrations which concur in this Action, their Vibratiuncles are generated, and associated strongly with other Vibrations or Vibratiuncles, the most common of which, I suppose, are those excited by the Sight of a favourite Play-thing which the Child uses to grasp, and hold in his Hand. He ought, therefore, according to the Doctrine of Association, to perform and repeat the Action of Grasping, upon having such a Play-thing presented to his Sight. But it is a known Fact, that Children do this. By pursuing the same Method of Reasoning, we may see how, after a sufficient Repetition of the proper Associations, the Sound of the Words *grasp, take hold, &c.* The Sight of the Nurse's Hand in a State of Contraction, the Idea of a Hand, and particularly of the Child's own Hand, in that State, and innumerable other associated Circumstances, *i.e.* Sensations, Ideas, and Motions, will put the Child upon Grasping, till, at last, that Idea, or State of Mind which we may call the Will to grasp, is generated, and sufficiently associated with the Action to produce it instantaneously. It is therefore perfectly voluntary in this Case; and, by the innumerable Repetitions of it in this perfectly voluntary State, it comes, at last, to obtain a sufficient Connexion with so many diminutive Sensations, Ideas, and Motions, as to follow them in the same Manner as originally automatic Actions do the corresponding Sensations, and consequently to be automatic secondarily. . . .

. . . The newborn Child is not able to produce a Sound at all, unless the Muscles of the Trunk and Larynx be stimulated thereto by the Impression of Pain on some Part of the Body. As the Child advances in Age, the frequent Returns of this Action facilitate it; so that it recurs from less and less Pains, from Pleasures, from mere Sensations, and, lastly, from slight associated Circumstances. . . . It is evident, that an articulate Sound, or one approaching thereto, will sometimes be produced by this conjoint Action of the Muscles of the Trunk, Larynx, Tongue, and Lips; and that both these articulate Sounds, and inarticulate ones, will often recur, from the Recurrence of the same accidental Causes. After they have recurred a sufficient Number of times, the Impression which these Sounds, articulate and inarticulate, make upon the Ear, will become an associated Circumstance (for the Child always hears himself speak, at the same time that he exerts the Action) sufficient to produce a Repetition of them. And thus it is, that Children repeat the same Sounds over and over again, for many Successions, the Impression of the last Sound upon the Ear exciting a fresh one, and so on, till the Organs be tired. It follows therefore, that if any of the Attendants make any of the Sounds familiar to the Child, he will be excited from this Impression, considered as an associated Circumstance, to return it. But the Attendants make articulate Sounds chiefly; there will therefore be a considerable Balance in favour of such, and that of a growing Nature: So that the Child's articulate Sounds will be more and more frequent every Day—his inarticulate ones grow into Disuse. Suppose now, that he compounds these simple articulate Sounds, making complex ones, which approach to familiar Words at some times, at others such as are quite foreign to the Words of his native Language, and that the first get an ever-growing Balance in their Favour, from the Cause just now taken notice of; also, that they are associated with Visible Objects, Actions, &c. and it will be easily seen, that the young Child ought, from the Nature of Association, to learn to speak much in the same Manner as he is found in Fact to do. Speech will also become a perfectly voluntary Action, *i.e.* the Child will be able to utter any Word or Sentence proposed to him by others, or by himself, from a mere Exertion of the Will, as much as to grasp: Only here the introductory Circumstance, *viz.* the Impression of the Sound on the Ear, the Idea of this Sound, or the preceding Motion in pronouncing the preceding Word, is evident; and therefore makes it probable, that the same thing takes place in other Cases. In like manner, Speech, after it has been voluntary for a due Time, will become secondarily automatic, *i.e.* will follow associated Circumstances, without any express Exertion of the Will. . . .

And thus . . . we are enabled to account for all the Motions of the human Body, upon Principles which, tho' they may be fictitious, are, at least, clear and intelligible. The Doctrine of Vibrations explains all the original automatic Motions, that of Association the voluntary and secondarily automatic ones. . . .

[Prop. 77] *To examine how far the Motions that are most perfectly voluntary, such as those of Walking, Handling, and Speaking . . . are agreeable to the foregoing Theory.* . . .

The new-born Child is unable to walk on account of the want of Strength to support his Body, as well as of complex and decomplex motory Vibratiuncles, generated by Association, and depending upon Sensations and Ideas by Association also. As he gets Strength, he advances likewise in the Number and Variety of compound Motions of the Limbs, their Species being determined by the Nature of the Articulations, the Position of the Muscles, the automatic Motions excited by Friction, accidental Flexures and Extensions made by the Nurse, &c. When he is tolerably perfect in the Rudiments of walking, the View of a favourite Plaything will excite various Motions in the Limbs; and thus if he be set upon his Legs, and his Body carried forward by the Nurse, an imperfect Atttempt to walk follows of course. It is made more perfect gradually by his Improvement in the Rudiments, by the Nurse's moving his Legs alternately in the proper Manner, by his Desire of going up to Persons, Playthings, &c. and thence repeating the Process which has succeeded (for he makes innumerable Trials, both successful and unsuccessful); and by his seeing others walk, and endeavouring to imitate them. . . .

When the Child can walk up to an Object that he desires to walk up to, the Action may be termed voluntary; *i.e.* the Use of Language will then justify this Appelation. But it appears from the Reasoning here used, that this Kind and Degree of voluntary Power over his Motions is generated by proper Combinations and Associations of the automatic Motions. . . . voluntary Powers may therefore result from Association, as is asserted in these papers.

When he is arrived at such a Perfection in Walking, as to walk readily upon being desired by another Person, the Action is deemed still more voluntary. One Reason of which is, that the Child, in some Cases, does not walk when desired, whilst yet the Circumstances are apparently the same as when he does. For here the unapparent Cause of Walking, or not walking, is *Will*. However, it follows from this Theory, that all this is still owing to Association, or to something equally suitable to the foregoing Theory; *e.g.* to the then present Strength or Weakness of the Association of the Words of the Command with the Action of Walking, to its proceeding from this or that Person, in this or that manner, to the Child's being in an active or inactive State, attentive or inattentive, disposed by other Circumstances to move as directed, or to move in a different Way, &c. A careful Observation of the Fact will always shew, as far as is reasonable to expect in so nice a Matter, that when Children do different Things, the real Circumstances, natural or associated, are proportionably different, and that the State of the Mind called *Will* depends upon this Difference. This Degree of voluntary Power is therefore, in like manner, of an acquired Nature. . . .

Walking passes into the secondarily automatic State more perfectly perhaps, than any other Action; for Adults seldom exert any Degree of Volition here, sufficient to affect the Power of Consciousness or Memory for the least perceptible Moment of Time. Now this Transition of Walking, from its voluntary to its secondarily automatic State, must be acknowledged by all to proceed merely from Association. And it seems to follow by Parity of Reason, that the Transition of primarily automatic Actions into voluntary ones may be merely from Association also, since it is evident, that Association has at least a very great and extensive Influence there.

13.9

Alexander Bain

(1818–1903)

Aside from Hartley, British association psychology was purely intellectualistic. Even Thomas Brown's "secondary laws" (12.8) did not include any recognition that the outcome of an action would influence associative

[A] *The senses and the intellect*. London, 1855. [Pp. 291–296.]
[B] Ibid. 2nd ed. London, 1864. [Pp. 306–309.]
[C] *The emotions and the will*. London, 1859. [P. 343.]

strength. The importance of pleasure as motivation was universally acknowledged, but the problem of how it did its work was not faced. The major point of dispute was whether the principles of associationism could be reduced to contiguity (as by James Mill) or must include other factors such as cause-and-effect and similarity. Bain changes this, and can be said to open an era in modern psychology not only because of the newly realistic physiological orientation (in place of Hartley's purely hypothetical physiology) but also because of his statement of what later became, with Thorndike, the Law of Effect. We give it both in its initial form, in which pain was the motivating force, and in the revised statement of 1864. Finally, we give a short passage in which Bain again uses the phrase "trial and error," which was to become so popular with the behaviorists (cf. 12.11).

[A]

27. We must now therefore specifically consider what there is in volition over and beyond the spontaneous discharge of active impulses upon our various moving organs,—limbs, body, voice, tongue, eyes, &c. If we look at this kind of impulse closely, we shall see wherein its defect or insufficiency lies, namely, in the random nature of it. . . .

There is a power in certain feelings or emotions to originate movements of the various active organs. A connexion is formed either by instinct or by acquisition, or by both together, between our emotional states and our active states, sufficient to constitute a link of cause and effect between the one and the other. And the question arises whether this link is original or acquired.

Dr. Reid has no hesitation in classing the voluntary command of our organs, that is, the sequence of feeling and action implied in all acts of will among instincts. . . .

This assertion of Dr. Reid's may be simply met by appealing to the facts. It is not true that human beings possess at birth any voluntary command of their limbs whatsoever. A babe of two months old cannot use its hands in obedience to its desires. The infant can grasp nothing, can scarcely fix its eyes on anything. Dr. Reid might just as easily assert that the movements of a ballet-dancer are instinctive, or that we are born with an already established link of causation in our minds between the wish to paint a landscape and the movements of a painter's arm. If the more perfect command of our voluntary movements implied in every art be an acquisition, so is the less perfect command of these movements that grows upon a child during the first year of life. At the very moment of birth, voluntary action is all but a nonentity.

28. According to this view, therefore, there is a process of acquirement in the establishing of those links of feeling and action which volition

implies. . . . The acquisition must needs repose upon some fundamental property of our nature that may properly be styled an Instinct. . . .

29. I will endeavour to indicate what seems to me to be the circumstance that leads to this remarkable union between the two great isolated facts of our nature, namely, on the one hand, feelings inciting to movement in general, but to no action in particular, and, on the other hand, the spontaneous movements already spoken of.

If, at the moment of some acute pain, there should accidentally occur a spontaneous movement, and if that movement sensibly alleviates the pain, then it is that the volitional impulse belonging to the feeling will show itself. The movement accidentally begun through some other influence, will be sustained through this influence of the painful emotion. In the original situation of things, the acute feeling is unable of itself to bring on the precise movement that would modify the suffering; there is no primordial link between a state of suffering and a train of alleviating movements. But should the proper movement be once actually begun, and cause a felt diminution of the acute agony, the spur that belongs to states of pain would suffice to sustain this movement. Once assume that the two waves occur together in the same cerebral seat—a wave of painful emotion, and a wave of spontaneous action tending to subdue the pain,—there would arise an influence out of the former to sustain and prolong the activity of the latter. The emotion cannot invite, suggest, or waken up the appropriate action; nevertheless, the appropriate action once there and sensibly telling upon the irritation, is thereupon kept going by the active influence, the volitional spur of the irritated consciousness. In short, if the state of pain cannot awaken a dormant action, a present feeling can at least maintain a present action. This, as far as I can make out, is the original position of things in the matter of volition. . . .

[B]

[Par. 27 remains substantially as in the first edition.]

28. According to this view, then, there must be a process of *acquirement*, in the establishing of those links uniting feeling with action, which volition implies. But the acquisition must itself repose upon some primordial fact, or instinct, of our nature. The point is to ascertain what connexion there is, at the outset of life, between our feelings and our movements, which the course of our experience and education converts into mature volitions.

I will endeavour to indicate what seems to me the precise situation wherein a feeling prompts an action in the beginning.

Although in the completely-formed will, a state of pleasure can induce the actions necessary for prolonging it,—as when a crowd follows a military band,—in the infancy of the being, pleasure can induce action of some kind, but not necessarily of the right kind. There is no relevance in the heightened movements of the child under pleasure, no proper direction given to them for sustaining or increasing that pleasure, as would happen at a later period. Still, there is an effect of quickened energy when an agreeable feeling suddenly takes possession of the mind. We have seen that an increase of vital power is a concomitant of pleasure; . . . which increase passes sometimes to the organic functions alone, and sometimes to the active functions or the muscles, and not infrequently to all parts, especially in the freshness of early life. Now the important result as regards the will, is the *muscular* accession. If the system is previously quiescent, there will be a burst of energy; if already acting, the action will be increased. Still there will be no determination in one course rather than in another; there will be no preference, and therefore no proper volition.

But suppose now that the movements arising out of mere physical exuberance, should be accidentally such as to increase the pleasurable feeling of the moment; the very fact of such increased pleasure would imply the other fact of increased energy of the system, and of those very movements then at work. The pleasure would in this way feed itself, and we should have something amounting substantially to a volition. Spontaneity, or accident, has brought certain movements into play; the effect of those movements is to induce a burst of new pleasure: but we cannot induce pleasure without inducing new energy to the physical system, and therefore to the members acting at the moment. So long as these movements add to the pleasure, so long they add to their own stimulation. Let them cease to yield new accessions of delight, and there will be an end to their farther acceleration as the result of increased vital energy.

29. Before producing actual instances, let us complete the general statement by supposing the opposite condition, that of pain. Let movements be commenced as before, through the spontaneous energy of the healthy system, but let these movements occasion a sudden feeling of pain. In doing so, they occasion also, in virtue of the connexion above contended for, an abatement of the vital energies, which abatement, extending to the movements, brings them more or less to a stand-still. . . . Thus, then, we see that when movement concurs with pain, the pain arrests the movement through its general depressing agency; while, on the other hand, a movement bringing pleasure is sustained and promoted through the connection between pleasure and exalted energy.

30. . . . A third case, of equal, if not greater, frequency in animal life, is the following:—A creature is in pain, or under a depressing condition of mind; the direct consequence, or natural accompaniment, is a lowered state of the vital energies. Nevertheless random movements are still performed; the spontaneity may not always be exhausted; and perhaps the pain has produced that other effect of spasmodic irritation of the nerves.

At all events movements occur; the limbs are thrown about, the head is tossed from side to side, and so forth. Now, let the pain instantly cease. Mentally, the result is a great reaction, in fact a burst of pleasure; physically, there concurs the usual elation of the system, moving members among the rest. The movements that were going on when the pain ceased, receive a sudden accession of power out of the general fund, and are made all the more energetic. . . .

[C]

13. . . . It is an original property of our feelings to prompt the active system one way or another; but there is no original connexion between the several feelings and the actions that are relevant in each particular case. To arrive at this goal, we need all the resources of spontaneity, trial and error, and the adhesive growth of the proper couples when they can once be got together. The first steps of our volitional education are a jumble of spluttering, stumbling, and all but despairing hopelessness. Instead of a clear and distinct curriculum, we have to wait upon the accidents, and improve them when they come.

13.10

Edward Lee Thorndike

(1874–1949)

Bain's theory and Morgan's urging (14.10) bore their fruit in Thorndike's experimental procedures, and his development of the so-called Law of Effect. It seems hardly comprehensible that years later Thorndike could write that James and Galton had influenced him most, and list Bain in a group of those who "seemed to me to give wrong answers." But Thorndike is prophetic in his statement that learning must become the central focus of psychological research, and that perhaps only a quantitative difference exists between men and animals.

[A] Animal intelligence. *Psychological Review Monograph Supplement* No. 8, 1898. Reprinted as Chapter 2 of *Animal intelligence.* New York, 1911. [Pp. 22, 26–28, 36–38, 54, 153–155.]
[B] The mental life of monkeys. *Psychological Review Monograph Supplement* No. 15, 1901. Reprinted as Chapter 5 of *Animal intelligence.* New York, 1911. [Pp. 239–240.]
[C] *Animal intelligence.* New York, 1911. [Pp. 243–245, 247–248.]

[A]

. . . The main purpose of the study of the animal mind is to learn the development of mental life down through the phylum, to trace in particular the origin of human faculty. In relation to this chief purpose of comparative psychology the associative processes assume a role predominant over that of sense-powers or instinct, for in a study of the associative processes lies the solution of the problem. . . . For the origin and development of human faculty we must look to these processes of association in lower animals. . . .

. . . I chose for my general method one which, simple as it is, possesses several other marked advantages besides those which accompany experiment of any sort. It was merely to put animals when hungry in inclosures from which they could escape by some simple act, such as pulling at a loop of cord, pressing a lever, or stepping on a platform. . . . The animal was put in the inclosure, food was left outside in sight, and his actions observed. Besides recording his general behavior, special notice was taken of how he succeeded in doing the necessary act (in case he did succeed), and a record was kept of the time that he was in the box before performing the successful pull, or clawing, or bite. This was repeated until the animal had formed a perfect association between the sense-impression of the interior of that box and the impulse leading to the successful movement. . . .

If, on the other hand, after a certain time the animal did not succeed, he was taken out, but *not fed*. If, after a sufficient number of trials, he failed to get out, the case was recorded as one of complete failure. . . .

. . . No personal factor is present save in the observation and interpretation. . . . The curves showing the progress of the formation of associations, which are obtained from the records of the times taken by the animals in successive trials, are facts which may be obtained by any observer who can tell time. . . .

The starting point for the formation of any association in these cases, then, is the set of instinctive activities which are aroused when a cat feels discomfort in the box either because of confinement or a desire for food. This discomfort, plus the sense-impression of a surrounding, confining wall, expresses itself, prior to any experience, in squeezings, clawings, bitings, etc. From among these movements one is selected by success. But this is the starting point only in the case of the first box experienced. After that the cat has associated with the feeling of confinement certain impulses which have led to success more than others and are thereby strengthened. A cat that has learned to escape from A by clawing has, when put into C or G, a greater tendency to claw at things than it instinctively had at the start, and a less tendency to squeeze through holes. A very pleasant form of this decrease in instinctive impulses was noticed in the gradual cessation of howling and mewing. However, the useless instinctive impulses die out slowly, and often play an important part even after the cat has had experience with six or eight boxes. And what is important in our previous statement, namely, that the activity of an animal when first put into a new box is not directed by an appreciation of *that* box's character, but by certain general impulses to act, is not affected by this modification. Most of this activity is determined by heredity; some of it, by previous experience. . . .

Starting, then, with its store of instinctive impulses, the cat hits upon the successful movement, and gradually associates it with the sense-impressions of the interior of the box until the connection is perfect, so that it performs the act as soon as confronted with the sense-impression. The formation of each association may be represented graphically by a time-curve. . . .

We have in these time-curves a fairly adequate measure of what the ordinary cat can do, and how it does it. . . . If other investigators . . . will take other cats and dogs, especially those supposed by owners to be extraordinarily intelligent, and experiment with them in this way, we shall soon get a notion of how much variation there is among animals in the direction of more or superior intelligence. . . . No phenomena are more capable of exact and thorough investigation by experiment than the associations of animal consciousness. Never will you get a better psychological subject than a hungry cat. . . .

. . . Our work has described a method, crude but promising, and has made the beginning of an exact estimate of just what associations, simple and compound, an animal can form, how quickly he forms them, and how long he retains them. It has described the method of formation, and, on the condition that our subjects were representative, has rejected reason, comparison or inference, perception of similarity, and imitation. It has denied the existence in animals of any important stock of free ideas or impulses, and so has denied that animal association is homologous with the association of human psychology. It has homologized it with a certain limited form of human association. It has proposed, as necessary steps in the evolution of human faculty, a vast increase in the number of associations, signs of which appear in the primates, and a freeing of the elements thereof into independent existence. It has given us an increased insight into various mental processes. It has convinced the writer, if not the reader, that the old speculations about what an animal could do, what it thought, and how what it thought grew into what human beings think, were a long way from the truth, and *not on the road to it.*

. . . I believe that our best service has been to show that animal intellection is made up of a lot of specific connections, whose elements are restricted to them, and which subserve practical ends *directly,* and to homologize it with the intellection involved in such human associations as regulate the conduct of a man playing tennis. The fundamental phenomenon which I find presented in animal consciousness is one which can harden into inherited connections and reflexes, on the one hand, and thus connect naturally with a host of the phenomena of animal life; on the other hand, it emphasizes the fact that our mental life has grown up as a mediation between stimulus and reaction. . . . If, as seems probable, the primates display a vast increase of associations, and a stock of free-swimming ideas, our view gives to the line of descent a meaning which it never could have so long as the question was the vague one of more or less 'intelligence.' . . . It turns out apparently that a modest study of the facts of association in animals has given us a working hypothesis for a comparative psychology.

[B]

4. In their method of learning, the monkeys do not advance far beyond the generalized mammalian type, but in their proficiency in that method they do. They seem at least to form associations very much faster, and they form many more. They also seem superior in the delicacy and in the complexity of the associations formed and the connections seem to be more permanent.

This progress may seem, and doubtless will to the thinker who looks upon the human intellect as a collection of functions of which ideation, judgment and reasoning are chief, to be slight. To my mind it is not so in reality. For it seems to me highly probable that the so-called 'higher' intellectual processes of human beings are but secondary results of the general function of having free ideas and that this general function is the result of the formation after the fashion of the animals of a very great number of associations. I should therefore say, "Let us not wonder at the comparative absence of free ideas in the monkeys, much less at the absence of inferences or concepts. Let us not wonder that the only demonstrable intellectual advance of the monkeys over the mammals in general is the change from a few, narrowly confined, practical associations to a multitude of all sorts, for that may turn out to be at the bottom the only *demonstrable advance of man,* an advance which in connection with a brain acting with increased delicacy and irritability, brings in its train the functions which mark off human mental faculty from that of all other animals.

. . . I have already hinted that we ought to turn our views of human psychology upside down and study what is now casually referred to in a chapter on habit or on the development of the will, as the general psychological law, of which the commonly named processes are derivatives. When this is done, we shall not only relieve human mentality from its isolation and see its real relationships with other forms; we may also come to know more about it, may even elevate our psychologies to the explanatory level and connect mental processes with nervous activities without arousing a sneer from the logician or a grin from the neurologist.

[C]

. . . The law of original behavior, or the law of instinct, is then that *to any situation an animal will, apart from learning, respond by virtue of the inherited nature of its reception-, connection-, and action-systems.* . . . .

The Law of Effect is that: *Of several responses made to the same situation, those which are accompanied or closely followed by satisfaction to the animal will, other things being equal, be more firmly connected with the situation, so that, when it recurs, they will be more likely to recur; those which are accompanied or closely followed by discomfort to the animal will, other things being equal, have their connections with that situation weakened, so that, when it recurs, they will be less likely to occur. The greater the satisfaction or discomfort, the greater the strengthening or weakening of the bond.*

The Law of Exercise is that: *Any response to a situation will, other things being equal, be more strongly connected with the situation in proportion to the number of times it has been connected with that situation and to the average vigor and duration of the connections.* . . .

By a satisfying state of affairs is meant one which the animal does nothing to avoid, often doing such things as attain and preserve it. By a discomforting or annoying state of affairs is meant one which the animal commonly avoids and abandons. . . .

As a provisional hypothesis for what satisfies and what annoys an animal, I suggest the following:—

A neurone modifies the intimacy of its synapses so as to keep intimate those by whose intimacy its other life processes are favored and to weaken the intimacy of those whereby its other life processes are hindered. The animal's action-system as a whole consequently does nothing to avoid that response whereby the life processes of the neurones other than connection-changing are maintained, but does cease those responses whereby such life processes of the neurones are hindered. . . .

. . . The learning of an animal is an instinct of its neurones.

13.11

Knight Dunlap

(1875–1949)

Here Dunlap presents for the first time his technique of negative practice for the elimination of undesirable habits. He extended its use to the treatment of masturbation and homosexuality and even recommended purposeful forgetting as a means of imprinting facts on the memory! A fuller treatment is given in his book, Habits: their making and unmaking (1932). *This technique makes Dunlap a pioneer in the history of behavior modification. The principles of learning, or habit formation, as they are taught by contemporary psychologists, include as fundamental the principles of recency and frequency. . . .*

Behind these principles, however, there is a more fundamental assumption, which was sharply indicated by William James, but which has seemed too obvious to need statement by those of us who have nevertheless continued in the Jamesian philosophy. This assumption is as follows: *A* response (that is, even a single response) *to a given stimulus pattern definitely increases the probability that on the reoccurrence of the same, or substantially the same, stimulus pattern, the same, or approximately the same, response will occur.* This principle I shall call the *alpha-postulate* of learning. . . .

For nearly twenty-five years the present writer has been teaching, explicitly and implicitly, this orthodox doctrine, and attempting to fit the facts somehow to the theory. . . .

The cumulative effect of the difficulty of fitting facts to the theory, however, has, although no longer ago than last summer, suggested that it would be much simpler to fit the theory to the facts. It has seemed well, therefore, to question the fundamental assumption on which we have proceeded.

If we no longer take the assumption of the positive effect of response as a divinely revealed truth, but as a mere postulate, it is at once seen that there are two other postulates possible. One of these, the *beta-postulate*, as I shall call it, is that response, in itself, has *no* effect on the future probability of the same stimulus pattern producing the same response; the other, the *gamma-postulate*, is that the response *decreases* the probability. . . .

If "repetition" has in itself no effect, but is important merely in that through it certain positive factors have their chance to operate, then it

A revision of the fundamental law of habit formation. *Science* 67 (1928): 360–362.

at once becomes a live possibility that negative factors also may be allowed to operate through repetition. Thus would be explained the apparent "neutralizing" of the effects of repetition, not as actual neutralizing in this sense, but as either the operation of negative factors in the absence of positive, or the prevalence of the negative factors over the positive.

The deductions from our postulate are still more interesting. If the negative factors, those which decrease the probability of the recurrence of the response, can be discovered, repetition may be used practically for the abolition of a habit already formed. This is, I think, a new idea, and worth trying, even aside from the possible light the results may throw on our postulate. Can we, for example, cure stammering, through causing the patient to stammer voluntarily in as nearly as possible the same way in which he ordinarily stammers? Can we abolish tics through causing the tic to occur? If so, we should have a method of "catharsis" of enormous value, and the method should be applicable to a host of minor defects of response and conduct, as well as to such major troubles. . . .

The first opportunity which occurred for the testing of this method lay in an idiosyncrasy of my own in typewriting. For some years I have been annoyed, when typing rapidly, by an occasional transposition of the letters of a word, the word "the" being especially troublesome, so that in reading over a manuscript of my own typing I would sometimes find two, three or more of these transpositions into "hte." Several times I have attempted, by careful practice, to train myself out of the habit. The fact that in the majority of cases I actually wrote "the," exchanging it for "hte" only in a minority of cases and when typing rapidly, in itself indicates the futility of increased repetition of the "right" spelling.

On the basis of the neutral postulate, I now proceeded to try the typing of "hte" voluntarily, as a means of destroying it. I set to work deliberately and wrote about a half page, single spaced, of the "hte" combination, with the futuric thought that this was a "word" that I would *not* write in the future (unless deliberately and voluntarily). Somewhat over a week later, I followed this with a second "practice period," writing less than a third of a page. This was over three months ago. Since that time I have typed many pages, some rapidly, but have not found on reading them over a single case of "hte"! This may sound too easy to be true, but as a matter of fact a long-standing and troublesome habit has disappeared. . . .

The application of the method to speech defects offers an interesting field. . . .

. . . It is hard to set the limits of practical applications, and from present indications a vast number of hitherto insoluble problems may be solved in this way.

13.12

Karl Spencer Lashley

(1890–1958)

Testing with an open mind what everyone had long taken for granted, Lashley exposed fatal weaknesses in the hypothesis that changes at the synapses, or other local changes in the nervous system, account for learning.

[I] . . . In experiments extending over the past 30 years I have been trying to trace conditioned reflex paths through the brain or to find the locus of specific memory traces. . . .

[II] I first became skeptical of the supposed path of the conditioned reflex when I found that rats, trained in a differential reaction to light, showed no reduction in accuracy of performance when almost the entire motor cortex, along with the frontal poles of the brain, was removed. . . .

Incisions were made through the cortex and underlying fibres of the rat's brain such as to sever the visual areas more or less completely from the motor regions of the brain. The rats were then trained . . . to jump to a white triangle and to avoid a white *x* when both figures are on a black background, but to choose the *x* and avoid the triangle if the background is striped. . . . This is the most difficult visual generalization that we have been able to teach the rat. Animals with incisions . . . which practically separate the motor regions from the visual, were able to learn this reaction as quickly as did normal controls.

[III.] . . . Rats were trained on the maze, then knife cuts were made through the cortex and underlying fibres, separating different functional areas or cutting through functional areas. The incisions were long, averaging half of the entire length of the cerebral hemispheres. After recovery the animals were tested in retention of the maze habit. In other experiments the incisions were made before training and their effect upon the rate of initial learning was tested. In neither initial learning nor in retention could any certain effect of separating the various parts of the cortex be demonstrated. . . .

Such results are certainly puzzling. They leave us with almost no understanding of the function of the associative fibres which extend across from one part of the cortex to another. . . .

[IV.] . . . A number of experiments with the rat have shown that habits of visual discrimination survive the destruction of any part of the cerebral

In search of the engram. *Symposia of the Society for Experimental Biology*, No. IV: *Physiological mechanisms in animal behavior*. Cambridge: University Press, 1950. Pp. 454–482. [Pp. 455–457, 459–460, 463–464, 477–480.]

cortex except the primary visual projection area. . . . There is no indication of specialized memory areas outside the primary sensory fields. . . .

. . . Is there a greater cortical differentiation in anthropoid apes and man? . . . Bilateral removal of the entire prefrontal granular cortex in five chimpanzees in our laboratory has not resulted in any memory defect. . . . Adult chimpanzees, trained in such complicated habits as choosing an object, like a model shown, retain the habits after removal of the entire prefrontal cortex. . . .

[X.] This series of experiments has yielded a good bit of information about what and where the memory trace is not. It has discovered nothing directly of the real nature of the engram. I sometimes feel, in reviewing the evidence on the localization of the memory trace, that the necessary conclusion is that learning just is not possible. It is difficult to conceive of a mechanism which can satisfy the conditions set for it. Nevertheless, in spite of such evidence against it, learning does sometimes occur. . . . Some general conclusions are, I believe, justified by the evidence.

(1) It seems certain that the theory of well-defined conditioned reflex paths from sense organ via association areas to the motor cortex is false. . . .

(2) It is not possible to demonstrate the isolated localization of a memory trace anywhere within the nervous system. . . .

(3) The so-called associative areas are not storehouses for specific memories. They seem to be concerned with modes of organization and with general facilitation or maintenance of the level of vigilance. The defects which occur after their destruction are not amnesias but difficulties in the performance of tasks which involve abstraction and generalization, or conflict of purposes. . . .

(4) The trace of any activity is not an isolated connexion between sensory and motor elements. It is tied in with the whole complex of spatial and temporal axes of nervous activity which forms a constant substratum of behaviour. . . .

(5) . . . Somehow, equivalent traces are established throughout the functional area. . . .

(6) Consideration of the numerical relations of sensory and other cells in the brain makes it certain, I believe, that all of the cells of the brain must be in almost constant activity, either firing or actively inhibited. There is no great excess of cells which can be reserved as the seat of special memories. The complexity of the functions involved in reproductive memory implies that every instance of recall requires the activity of literally millions of neurons. The same neurons which retain the memory traces of one experience must also participate in countless other activities.

. . . From the numerical relations involved, I believe that even the reservation of individual synapses for special associative reactions is impossible.

13.13

Burrhus Frederick Skinner

(born 1904)

In closing this chapter with Skinner, we despairingly omit two giant figures. Pavlov's classical conditioning procedure has been the basis for a vast experimental literature, and his insistence on the necessity for cortical inhibitory processes to explain such phenomena as extinction and discriminative learning has earned him a place in the pantheon of science. Clark Hull's insistence that learning does not take place without reinforcement and that reinforcement must always involve an element of tension-reduction, along with his development of an elaborate body of theory stated in mathematico-deductive terms, provided the foundation and impetus for another vast body of experimentation by countless followers. We commend them (needlessly) to the reader's attention.

Skinner turns away from theoretical speculation and advocates instead a "descriptive behaviorism" which seeks only to discover empirically the means by which behavior can be (in the phrase of John B. Watson) "predicted and controlled." His success in "shaping" the behavior of animals encouraged a vigorous growth of techniques for "behavior modification"—a learning technology which seeks to supplant psychotherapy.

Operant conditioning shapes behavior as a sculptor shapes a lump of clay. Although at some point the sculptor seems to have produced an entirely novel object, we can always follow the process back to the original undifferentiated lump, and we can make the successive stages by which we return to this condition as small as we wish. At no point does anything emerge which is very different from what preceded it. The final product seems to have a special unity or integrity of design, but we cannot find a point at which this suddenly appears. In this same sense, an operant is not something which appears full grown in the behavior of the organism. It is the result of a continuous shaping process.

The pigeon experiment demonstrates this clearly. "Raising the head" is not a discrete unit of behavior. It does not come, so to speak, in a separate package. We reinforce only slightly exceptional values of the behavior observed while the pigeon is standing or moving about. We succeed in shifting the whole range of heights at which the head is held, but there is nothing which can accurately be described as a new "re-

Science and human behavior. New York: Macmillan, 1953. [Pp. 91–93.] Reprinted by permission of The Macmillan Company. Copyright 1953 by The Macmillan Company.

sponse." A response such as turning the latch in a problem box appears to be a more discrete unit, but only because the continuity with other behavior is more difficult to observe. In the pigeon, the response of pecking at a spot on the wall of the experimental box seems to differ from stretching the neck because no other behavior of the pigeon resembles it. If in reinforcing such a response we simply wait for it to occur—and we may have to wait many hours or days or weeks—the whole unit appears to emerge in its final form and to be strengthened as such. There may be no appreciable behavior which we could describe as "almost pecking the spot."

The continuous connection between such an operant and the general behavior of the bird can nevertheless easily be demonstrated. It is the basis of a practical procedure for setting up a complex response. To get the pigeon to peck the spot as quickly as possible we proceed as follows: We first give the bird food when it turns slightly in the direction of the spot from any part of the cage. This increases the frequency of such behavior. We then withhold reinforcement until a slight movement is made toward the spot. This again alters the general distribution of behavior without producing a new unit. We continue by reinforcing positions successively closer to the spot, then by reinforcing only when the head is moved slightly forward, and finally only when the beak actually makes contact with the spot. We may reach this final response in a remarkably short time. A hungry bird, well adapted to the situation and to the food tray, can usually be brought to respond in this way in two or three minutes.

The original probability of the response in its final form is very low; in some cases it may even be zero. In this way we can build complicated operants which would never appear in the repertoire of the organism otherwise. By reinforcing a series of successive approximations, we bring a rare response to a very high probability in a short time. This is an effective procedure because it recognizes and utilizes the continuous nature of a complex act. The total act of turning toward the spot from any point [in] the box, walking toward it, raising the head, and striking the spot may seem to be a functionally coherent unit of behavior; but it is constructed by a continual process of differential reinforcement from undifferentiated behavior, just as the sculptor shapes his figure from a lump of clay. When we wait for a single complete instance, we reinforce a similar sequence but far less effectively because the earlier steps are not optimally strengthened. . . .

Through the reinforcement of slightly exceptional instances of his behavior, a child learns to raise himself, to stand, to walk, to grasp objects, and to move them about. Later on, through the same process, he learns to talk, to sing, to dance, to play games—in short, to exhibit the enormous repertoire characteristic of the normal adult.

Chapter 14

ANIMAL SPEECH AND REASON

"Discourse" originally denoted the course or movement of thinking; it later was applied to speech. The change in meaning reflected the general belief that thought is not possible except in words, and some psychologists hold to this view even today. Descartes particularly emphasized speech as a criterion by which to distinguish a thinking animal (man) from mere machines, and the lively eighteenth-century discussion on the speech of animals was only an offshoot of the debate continuing from the seventeenth century as to whether animals are capable of reason.

Although this chapter is mainly concerned with the "speech" of animals, it includes a few selections which deal with the relation between language and thought in humans. On this, see also Hartley on the development of speech in children (13.8) and Preyer on thought without speech in the infant (18.2).

14.1

Aristotle

(384–322 B.C.)

*As usual, Aristotle writes as a naturalist. He finds a varying degree of
kinship between men and animals, in both intellectual and emotional
spheres.*

In the great majority of animals there are traces of psychical qualities or
attitudes, which qualities are more markedly differentiated in the case of
human beings. For just as we pointed out resemblances in the physical
organs, so in a number of animals we observe gentleness or fierceness,
mildness or cross temper, courage or timidity, fear or confidence, high
spirit or low cunning, and, with regard to intelligence, something equivalent to sagacity. Some of these qualities in man, as compared with the
corresponding qualities in animals, differ only quantitatively: that is to
say, a man has more or less of this quality, and an animal has more or less
of some other; other qualities in man are represented by analogous and
not identical qualities: for instance, just as in man we find knowledge,
wisdom, and sagacity, so in certain animals there exists some other
natural potentiality akin to these. The truth of this statement will be the
more clearly apprehended if we have regard to the phenomena of childhood: for in children may be observed the traces and seeds of what will
one day be settled psychological habits, though psychologically a child
hardly differs for the time being from an animal; so that one is quite justified in saying that, as regards man and animals, certain psychical qualities are identical with one another, whilst others resemble, and others are
analogous to, each other. . . .

In regard to sensibility, some animals give no indication whatsoever of
it, whilst others indicate it but indistinctly. Further, the substance of
some of these intermediate creatures is fleshlike, as is the case with the
so-called tethya (or ascidians) and the acalephae (or sea-anemones);
but the sponge is in every respect like a vegetable. And so throughout the
entire animal scale there is a graduated differentiation in amount of
vitality and in capacity for motion.

A similar statement holds good with regard to habits of life. Thus of
plants that spring from seed the one function seems to be the reproduction of their own particular species, and the sphere of action with certain

The history of animals. Translated by D'Arcy Wentworth Thompson. In J. A. Smith
and W. D. Ross (Eds.), *The works of Aristotle.* Vol. IV. Oxford University Press,
1910. [Book VIII, Ch. 1.]

animals is similarly limited. The faculty of reproduction, then, is common to all alike. If sensibility be superadded, then their lives will differ from one another in respect to sexual intercourse through the varying amount of pleasure derived therefrom, and also in regard to modes of parturition and ways of rearing their young. Some animals, like plants, simply procreate their own species at definite seasons; other animals busy themselves also in procuring food for their young, and after they are reared quit them and have no further dealings with them; other animals are more intelligent and endowed with memory, and they live with their offspring for a longer period and on a more social footing.

The life of animals, then, may be divided into two acts—procreation and feeding; for on these two acts all their interests and life concentrate. Their food depends chiefly on the substance of which they are severally constituted; for the source of their growth in all cases will be this substance. And whatsoever is in conformity with nature is pleasant, and all animals pursue pleasure in keeping with their nature.

14.2

Albertus Magnus

(1193–1280)

The twenty-first book in this massive work by the teacher of Thomas Aquinas has the title, "On perfect and imperfect animals, and the cause of perfection and imperfection." It is in effect a treatise on comparative psychology, since the gauge of "perfection" is the possession of the various external and internal senses. In this selection, the anthropocentrism of Christian psychology very nearly reduces learning to the taking of instruction from man, the ordained lord over all the animals.

Some animals remember what was in the senses, some do not. And that some do not remember what was in the senses we know from the fact that memory is the recall of what was first apprehended through the senses, in the absence of the sensible object. For example, we see satiated vultures leave the site of a body, and later recall again from memory the site and the body; and in the same way flocks return to the sheepfold, birds to their nests, and the like. However, because other animals do not pursue a sensible object which is not present, and do not return to the previously apprehended sensible object, we know that they do not have

De animalibus [On animals]. Edited by Hermann Stadler. *Beiträge zur Geschichte der Philosophie des Mittelalters*. Vols. 15 and 16, 1921. [Vol. 16, pp. 1326–1328.]

a memory of what was previously apprehended; such as the flies who, when we chase them off, fly back heedless of the blow which they have previously received. We also see that certain animals have no home, and that they do not pursue absent sensible objects.

Furthermore, we see that some animals have a certain wisdom about things relating to themselves, and nevertheless cannot be taught, as is evident in bees, who have great wisdom in gathering although they are not taught, and likewise the ants. Their wisdom leads them to provide stores for themselves. But the fact that they do not come to a man's call, nor fear his hostile swings, nor take flight from fearful sounds, shows that they cannot be taught by man's instruction. Some say that this is because they cannot hear sounds, however this hypothesis is unacceptable, for they are seen to hear sounds. But however it may be regarding their hearing, this without doubt is true, that they do not hear sounds for instruction, so as to be called by name and taught as many animals are taught, like dogs, monkeys, and certain others.

For animals can hear in two ways: for some it is merely a sense, while for others it is not only a sense but also a teachable sense. And this can happen [in the second sense] in two ways, for a sense is teachable according to whether sounds and words are apprehended as giving knowledge of the intents of the sounds or the speaker, for this is the way that sounds and words are used for instruction. . . . They provide either a confused or a clear indication of the intent. They cause a confused indication in brutes, a clear indication in men. And thus, to the extent that animals possess hearing as a teachable sense, as well as a memory which retains the indications of discipline either confusedly or clearly, they are teachable and they apprehend instruction confusedly or clearly. Hence many animals do many things [in obedience] to man's voice: the elephant bends its knee in the presence of the king at a spoken signal, and dogs do many similar things. But bees and other small animals in no wise perceive sounds and words for [purposes of] instruction, no matter how vigorous their memory. This therefore is the basis of discipline in some animals. And this kind of discipline is totally absent in very small animals like bees, wasps, spiders, fleas, and other vermin of this sort.

Nevertheless, animals are seen to profit somewhat from experience. Experience indeed gives rise in memory to things which have there the power and faculty of [direct] experience, and we see that through experience many animals besides men have knowledge of individual things. For example, a weasel that is wounded in a fight with a serpent uses, against the venom, a leaf of chicory (which some call hog's-snout); and we see many other similar things which we introduced previously. But they do not profit from experience to arrive at universals, at arts and reasons, but they only profit from it in the way we have just said.

However, some animals are so advanced in this ability that they can imitate some arts, although they cannot attain arts. And we see animals do this in two ways: for those in whom both vision and hearing are teachable do what they see, and retain what they hear, like monkeys. Those whose hearing is teachable, to the extent that it is vigorously so, may even be able to make their intentions known to each other, as for example the pygmies, who can talk although they are irrational animals; and therefore with respect to animal faculties the pygmy is the most perfect animal after man, and it can be seen that among all the animals he has the best memory and the best apprehension of auditory signs, so that he seems to have something like an imitation of reason, although he lacks reason. For reason is the faculty of the soul which discourses on what has been apprehended by experience and in memory, according to their special natures or syllogistically, so as to elicit from them universals, principles of the arts and sciences, by comparisons of similar things. The pygmies cannot do this, for they do not separate what they hear from the sensible intentions, and thus the sensible intentions are committed to memory, and are gathered up and collected through speech. And therefore although the pygmies speak, they do not reason nor do they speak of universals, but rather they direct their words to the particular things of which they speak. Their speech is like a shadow resulting from the collapse of reason. For there are two kinds of reason, one of which is a reflection of the senses and of memory, and this is the perception of experience. The other is possessed in the degree to which one attains the simplicity of intellect, and from this comes the deduction of universals, which is the basis of the arts and sciences. Pygmies however have only the first kind, and therefore they have only a shadow of reason, for all the light of reason is in the second kind. I call shadow that which results from the darkness of sensible matter and the things which cling to matter. And therefore pygmies have no perception of subjects of discussion, nor do they perceive anything of the rules of argumentation. Their speech is like the speech of fools who are by nature stupid and therefore cannot perceive reason. But there is this difference, that pygmies are deprived of reason by [their] nature, while fools are not deprived of reason but of the use of reason, through some accident of melancholy or some other accident.

14.3

Francis Bacon, Lord Verulam

(1561–1626)

This "forest of groves" consists of 1,000 numbered paragraphs, 100 in each of ten chapters, presenting as many empirical observations intended to give impetus to the development of inductive science. Here, Bacon's observations concerning the speech of birds and animals interest us especially. See 20.4 for another selection, reflecting Bacon's reliance on animal spirits to explain physiological aspects of the passions.

Rawley was Bacon's secretary.

[236] It is a Thing strange in Nature, when it is attentively considered; How *Children*, and some *Birds*, learne to *imitate Speech*. They take no *Marke* (at all) of the *Motion* of the *Mouth* of Him that speaketh; For *Birds* are as well taught in the *Darke*, as by *Light*. The *Sounds* of *Speech* are very Curious and Exquisite: So one would thinke it were a Lesson hard to learne. It is true, that it is done with time, and by little and little, and with many Essayes and Proffers: But all this dischargeth not the Wonder. It would make a Man thinke (though this which we shall say may seeme exceeding strange) that there is some *Transmission* of Spirits; and that the *Spirits* of the *Teacher* put in Motion, should worke with the *Spirits* of the *Learner*, a Pre-disposition to offer to *Imitate*; And so to perfect the *Imitation* by degrees. But touching *Operations* by *Transmissions* of *Spirits*, (which is one of the highest Secrets in Nature,) we shall speake in due place; Chiefly when we come to enquire of *Imagination*. But as for *Imitation*, it is certaine, that there is in Men, and other Creatures, a predisposition to *Imitate*. We see how ready Apes and Monkies are, to *imitate* all Motions of Man: And in the Catching of Dottrels, we see, how the Foolish Bird playeth the Ape in Gestures: And no Man (in effect) doth accompany with others, but he learneth, (ere he is aware,) some Gesture, or Voice, or Fashion of the other.

[237] In *Imitation* of *Sounds*, that *Man* should be the *Teacher*, is no Part of the Matter; For *Birds* will learne one of another; And there is no Reward, by feeding, or the like, given them for the *Imitation*; And besides, you shall have Parrots, that will not only *imitate* Voices, but Laughing, Knocking, Squeaking of a Doore upon the Hinges, or of a Cart-wheele; And (in effect) any other *Noise* they heare.

[238] No *Beast* can *imitate* the *Speech* of *Man*, but *Birds* onely; For the Ape it selfe, that is so ready to *imitate* otherwise, attaineth not any

Sylva sylvarum: or a naturall historie. In ten centuries. Published after the author's death by William Rawley. London, 1627. [Pp. 64–65.]

degree of *Imitation* of Speech. It is true, that I have knowne a Dog, that if one howled in his *Eare*, he would fall a howling a great while. What should be the Aptnesse of *Birds*, in comparison of *Beasts*, to *imitate* the *Speech* of *Man*, may be further enquired. We see that *Beasts* have those Parts, which they count the *Instruments* of *Speech*, (as *Lips, Teeth, &c.*) liker unto *Man*, than *Birds*. As for the *Necke*, by which the *Throat* passeth; we see many *Beasts* have it, for the Length, as much as *Birds*. What better *Gorge*, or Artire [artery?], *Birds* have, may be further enquired. The *Birds* that are knowne to be Speakers, are *Parrots, Pyes, Iayes, Dawes*, and *Ravens*. Of which Parrots have an adunque Bill, but the rest not.

[239] But I conceive, that the *Aptnesse* of *Birds*, is not so much in the *Conformitie* of the *Organs* of *Speech*, as in their *Attention*. For *Speech* must come by *Hearing*, and *Learning;* And *Birds* give more heed, and marke *Sounds*, more than *Beasts;* Because naturally they are more delighted with them, and practise them more; As appeareth in their *Singing*. We see also, that those that teach *Birds* to sing, doe keepe them Waking, to increase their *Attention*. We see also, that *Cock-Birds*, amongst *Singing-Birds*, are ever the better *Singers;* which may be, because they are more lively, and listen more.

14.4

René Descartes

(1496–1650)

Descartes' position on speech as the mark of humanity has stood up well with time, as witness E. H. Lenneberg's Biological foundations of language *(1967).*

. . . if there were such Machines which had organs, and the exteriour figure of an Ape, or of any other unreasonable creature, we should finde no means of knowing them not to be altogether of the same nature as those Animals: whereas, if there were any which resembled our bodies, and imitated our actions as much as morally it were possible, we should always have two most certain ways to know, that for all that they were not reall men: The first of which is, that they could never have the use of speech, nor of other signes in framing it, as we have, to declare our thoughts to others: for we may well conceive, that a Machine may be so made, that it may utter words, and even some proper to the corporal

A discourse of a method for the well guiding of reason, and the discovery of truth in the sciences *[1637]. Anonymous translation. London, 1649. [Pp. 91–94.]*

actions, which may cause some change in its organs; as if we touch it in some part, and it should ask what we would say; or so as it might cry out that one hurts it, and the like: but not that they can diversifie them to answer sensibly to all what shall be spoken in its presence, as the dullest men may do. . . . For 'tis a very remarkable thing, that there are no men so dull and so stupid, without excepting those who are out of their wits, but are capable to rank severall words together, and of them to compose a Discourse, by which they make known their thoughts: and that on the contrary, there is no other creature, how perfect or happily soever brought forth, which can do the like. The which happens, not because they want organs; for we know, that Pyes and Parrots can utter words even as we can, and yet cannot speak like us; that is to say, with evidence that they think what they say. Whereas Men, being born deaf and dumb, and deprived of those organs which seem to make others speak, as much or more than beasts, usually invent of themselves to be understood by those, who commonly being with them, have the leisure to learn their expressions. And this not onely witnesseth, that Beasts have lesse reason than men, but that they have none at all. For we see there needs not much to learn to speak: and forasmuch as we observe inequality among Beasts of the same kind, aswell as amongst men, and that some are more easily managed then others; 'tis not to be believed, but that an Ape or a Parrot which were the most perfect of its kinde, should therein equall the most stupid child, or at least a child of a distracted brain, if their souls were not of a nature wholly different from ours. And we ought not to confound words with naturall motions, which witness passions, and may be imitated by Machines aswell as by Animals; nor think (as some of the Ancients) that beasts speak, although we do not understand their language: for if it were true, since they have divers organs which relate to ours, they could as well make themselves understood by us, as by their like.

14.5

Guillaume-Hyacinthe Bougeant

(1690–1743)

For this tongue-in-cheek solution to the problem of animal mind, its Jesuit author ended his days in confinement at La Flêche, which was not relaxed despite a contrite abnegation. The English translation drew a

Amusement philosophique sur le langage des bestes [Paris, 1739]. Translated anonymously, as *A philosophical amusement upon the language of beasts and birds.* Second edition, corrected. London, 1740. [Pp. 3–4, 9–13, 15–18, 26.]

quite serious rebuttal from John Hildrop, a clergyman (Free thoughts upon the brute creation, 1742).

The setting of this discussion is typical for a French book of the period: a long letter to a lady friend, written from the country, continuing an interrupted conversation. Only by a strong effort do I exclude many passages of great literary charm not absolutely essential to the argument. It is a product of that elegant Parisian salon society out of which such other works as those of La Mettrie (1.8, 14.6), Condillac (15.7, 16.6), and Helvetius (4.4, 17.4, 21.6) will soon develop.

Have Brutes any Understanding? I am convinced you will not so much as hesitate upon an Answer to this Question. *Descartes* shall in vain tell you that Beasts are Machines: that all their Actions may be accounted for by the Laws of Mechanism: that before him, and even from the time of St. *Austin*, some Philosophers have had something like the same Notion. You have a Bitch which you love, and which you think yourself reciprocally loved by. Now I defy all the *Cartesians* in the World to persuade you that your Bitch is a meer Machine. Pray consider what a ridiculous Cast this Opinion would give all of us who love Horses, Dogs, and Birds. Imagine to yourself a Man who should love his Watch as we love a Dog, and caress it because he should think himself dearly beloved by it, so as to think that when it points out Twelve or One o'Clock, it does it knowingly and out of Tenderness to him. Were *Descartes's* Opinion true, such would indeed be the Folly of all who believe that their Dogs have an Affection for them, and love them with Knowledge and what we call Sentiment. . . .

Let me pray you to do one Thing. Go to the *Indies*, to *China* or *Japan*, and there you will find Philosophers of the Heathen, Deist, or Atheist Kind, who will argue if not with greater Capacity, at least with greater Freedom. One will tell you that God has created several Species of Spirits, some more perfect, such as the good and bad *Genii* are; some less perfect, which are Men, and others much more imperfect still, which are the Beasts. Another will tell you, that the Distinction of the Spirit and Matter is chimerical and impossible to be demonstrated; that he sees no Manner of Inconveniency in thinking that there is but one Substance which you may call by what Name you please; that this Substance has in Beasts as well as in Men an Organization, a Modification, a Motion, something in short which makes it think more or less perfectly: And these Gentlemen acknowledging neither the Principles of the Christian Religion nor the Authority of the Church; you will be under the Necessity (in order to attack them in their Retrenchments) either to begin by making them Christians, or to go back to metaphysical Principles very difficult to be unravelled. But I hope you will spare yourself the Trouble of the Voyage, and chuse, as I myself do, to stick close to this greatest of Principles, *viz.* All these Systems are contrary to the Christian Religion; of course they are absolutely false.

Be comforted, Madam, here is another Hypothesis, which has nothing common with any of those I just laid before you. It is a System intirely new, which will divert you at least by its Singularity, and which I shall here repeat to you in the very words of the Author himself, whom I heard producing it a while since in Company, and with an Air of Gravity mixed with Buffoonery, which made it doubtful whether he was himself perfectly persuaded of it. . . .

Reason, said he, naturally inclines us to believe that Beasts have a spiritual Soul; and the only Thing which opposes this Sentiment is, the Consequences that might be inferred from it; and this, among others; that Men would differ from Beasts only by the Degree of *Plus* and *Minus;* which would demolish the very Foundations of all Religion. Therefore, added he, if I can elude all these Consequences, if I can assign to Beasts a spiritual Soul without striking at the Doctrines of Religion; it is evident that my System being moreover the most agreeable to Reason, is the only warrantable Hypothesis. . . .

Religion teaches us that the Devils, from the very Moment they had sinned, were reprobate, and that they are doomed to burn forever in Hell. But the Church has not as yet determined whether they do actually indure the Torments to which they are condemned. It may then be thought that they do not as yet suffer them, and that the Execution of the Verdict brought against them, is reserved for the Day of the final Judgment. . . .

. . . It is an Article of our Faith that the Devil tempts us in order to provoke us to Sin: that he lays Snares to make us fall: That he is for ever roving about us, as St. *Peter* has it, watching an Occasion to devour us. He fills our Minds with wicked Suggestions: He seizes upon Bodies, and when he has once made himself Master of them, he does not always betray his Presence by Fits of Madness. He sometimes Laughs, he Sings, and delights in puzzling the Ministers of the Church who attempt to conjure him forth. He argues with the utmost Coolness, as when he tempted *Jesus Christ* in the Desart, and seduced *Eve* in the earthly Paradise. Now imagine to yourself some Body in Hell, such as Scripture represents it, penetrated through his whole Substance, devoured and consumed by a Fire, whose Violence is beyond every thing; and then consider if a Man or a Spirit in that Condition can possibly be taken up with any other Thought than that of the horrid Torture he endures. If you tell me that he is transported with Fury, and that all his Moments are constantly filled by new Fits of Rage and Despair, I shall necessarily conceive it. But that he should have leisure enough to think of tempting and shifting with us, is altogether incomprehensible. . . . Let us then conclude, that the Devils do not as yet undergo their Torments. . . .

. . . What I pretend to infer, said he, is, that till Doom's-Day comes,

God, in order not to suffer so many Legions of reprobate Spirits to be of no use, has distributed them thro' the several Spaces of the World, to serve the Designs of his Providence, and make his Omnipotence to appear. Some continuing in their natural State, busy themselves in tempting Men, about seducing and tormenting them, either immediately as *Job's Devil,* and those that lay hold of human Bodies, or by the Ministry of Sorcerers, and of Phantoms. These wicked Spirits are those whom the Scripture calls the *Powers of Darkness,* and the *Powers of the Air.* God, with the others, makes Millions of Beasts of all Kinds, which serve for the several Uses of Man, which fill the Universe, and cause the Wisdom and Omnipotence of the Creator to be admired. By that Means, added he, I easily conceive how on the one Hand the Devils can tempt us, and on the other how Beasts can think, know, have Sentiments and a Spiritual Soul, without any way striking at the Doctrines of Religion. I am no longer surprised to see them have Dexterity, Fore-cast, Memory, and Judgment. I should rather have occasion to wonder at their having no more of those Qualities, since their Soul very likely is more perfect than ours. But I discover the Reason of this. It is because in Beasts as well as in ourselves, the Operations of the Mind are dependent on the material Organs of the Machine to which it is united, and these Organs being grosser and less perfect in Beasts than in us, it follows that the Knowledge, the Thoughts, and the other Spiritual Operations of Beasts must of course be less perfect than ours; and if these proud Spirits know their own dismal State, what an Humiliation must it be to them, thus to see themselves reduced to the Condition of Beasts! But, whether they know it or no, so shameful a Degradation is still with regard to them that primary Effect of the Divine Vengeance I just mentioned. It is an anticipated Hell.

Here a very beautiful Lady, whom this Discourse put out of Humour, could not help interrupting the Author of the new System. Sir, said she with a good deal of Fire, it is of little Consequence to me whether the Devils be humbled or no, and actually suffer the Tortures of Hell; but I will never allow Beasts to be Devils. How! shall my *little* Bitch be a Devil that lies with me all Night and caresses me all Day? I never will grant you that. And I say the same of my *Parrot,* added a young Lady; it is a charming Creature; but if I was persuaded it was a little Devil, I am sure that I should no longer indure it. I conceive, said the Author, how great your Aversion for this System must be, and I excuse it: But give yourself the trouble to reflect upon it, and you shall see that it is only the Result of a Prejudice which must be conquered by Reason. Do we love Beasts for their own sakes? No. As they are altogether Strangers to human Society, they can have no other Appointment but that of being useful and amusing. And what care we whether it be a Devil or some other Being that serves and amuses us? The Thought of it, far from shocking pleases me mightily. I with Gratitude admire the Goodness of the Creator, who gave me so many little Devils to serve and amuse me. If I am told that these poor Devils are doomed to suffer eternal Tortures, I admire God's Decrees; but I have no manner of Share in this dreadful Sentence. I leave the Execution of it to the Sovereign Judge, and notwithstanding this I live with my little Devils as I do with a Multitude of People of whom Religion informs me that a great number shall be damned....

I know not, Madam, what You will think of a System so new and so very singular. But I must tell you that its very great Singularity was mighty agreeable to the whole Company; some took it merely for a Piece of Wit and an ingenious Pleasantry; others look'd upon it as a System that deserved to be seriously believed. For my part, as you know I am a perfect Pyrrhonian in Point of Systems; I was contented with giving the Author the Praises, which good Breeding requires in a Case like this, without explaining myself farther. The Truth is that I knew and still know not what to think of it.

14.6

Julien Offray de La Mettrie

(1709–1751)

Since La Mettrie argued that matter can think, he could not accept the sharp division which Descartes established in asserting that no animal can speak. He proposed what many subsequently have tried, but always without success: to test the limits of education for an ape by patiently trying to teach it speech.

Let us pause to contemplate the varying capacity of animals to learn....

Among animals, some learn to speak and sing; they remember tunes, and strike the notes as easily as a musician. Others, for instance the ape, show more intelligence, and yet can not learn music. What is the reason for this, except some defect in the organs of speech? But is this defect so essential to the structure that it could never be remedied? In a word, would it be absolutely impossible to teach the ape a language? I do not think so.

I should choose a large ape in preference to any other, until by some good fortune another kind should be discovered, more like us, for nothing

L'Homme machine [1748]. Translated by Gertrude C. Bussey as *Man a machine*. La Salle, Ill.: Open Court Publishing Co., 1912. (Includes the complete French text.) [Pp. 100–103.]

prevents there being such an one in regions unknown to us. The ape resembles us so strongly that naturalists have called it "wild man" or "man of the woods." I should take it in the condition of the pupils of Amman, that is to say, I should not want it to be too young or too old; for apes that are brought to Europe are usually too old. I would choose the one with the most intelligent face, and the one which, in a thousand little ways, best lived up to its look of intelligence. Finally not considering myself worthy to be his master, I should put him in the school of that excellent teacher whom I have just named, or with another teacher equally skilled, if there is one.

You know by Amman's work, and by all those who have interpreted his method, all the wonders he has been able to accomplish for those born deaf. In their eyes he has discovered ears, as he himself explains, and in how short a time! In short he taught them to hear, speak, read, and write. I grant that a deaf person's eyes see more clearly and are keener than if he were not deaf, for the loss of one member or sense can increase the strength or acuteness of another, but apes see and hear, they understand what they hear and see, and grasp so perfectly the signs that are made to them, that I doubt not that they would surpass the pupils of Amman in any other game or exercise. Why then should the education of monkeys be impossible? Why might not the monkey, by dint of great pains, at last imitate after the manner of deaf mutes, the motions necessary for pronunciation? I do not dare decide whether the monkey's organs of speech, however trained, would be capable of articulation. But because of the great analogy between ape and man and because there is no known animal whose external and internal organs so strikingly resemble man's, it would surprise me if speech were absolutely impossible to the ape. . . .

Could not the device which opens the Eustachian canal of the deaf, open that of the apes? Might not a happy desire to imitate the master's pronunciation, liberate the organs of speech in animals that imitate so many other signs with such skill and intelligence? Not only do I defy any one to name any really conclusive experiment which proves my view impossible and absurd; but such is the likeness of the structure and functions of the ape to ours that I have very little doubt that if this animal were properly trained he might at last be taught to pronounce, and consequently to know, a language. Then he would no longer be a wild man, nor a defective man, but he would be a perfect man, a little gentleman, with as much matter of muscle as we have, for thinking and profiting by his education.

14.7

Herbert Spencer

(1820–1903)

Four years before the appearance of Darwin's Origin of species, Spencer emphasized the importance of an evolutionary point of view for psychology. Of course his view of evolution at that time was Lamarckian, but Darwin also was a Lamarckian in part, never supposing that his principle of natural selection provided the whole answer. Spencer's influence was especially strong on such American psychologists as Mark Baldwin (18.3) and Stanley Hall (22.10).

§122. Looking at life in its lowest developments, we find that only the most prevalent coexistences and sequences in the environment, have any simultaneous and successive changes corresponding to them in the organism. . . . Every step upwards must consist in adding to the previously-adjusted relations which the organism exhibits, some further relation parallel to a further relation in the environment. . . .

§126. . . . Those more complex forms of internal change which constitute the subject matter of Psychology, cannot be adequately comprehended without a previous comprehension of those simple forms of it which constitute life in its unintelligent phases. . . .

§180. As, in the environment, there exist relations of all orders of persistency, from the absolute to the fortuitous; it follows that in an intelligence displaying any high degree of correspondence, there must exist all grades of strength in the connections between states of consciousness. As a high intelligence is only thus possible, it is manifestly a condition of intelligence in general, that the antecedents and consequents of psychical changes shall admit of all degrees of cohesion. And the fundamental question to be determined, is:—How are these various degrees of cohesion adjusted?

Concerning their adjustment, there appear to be but two possible hypotheses, of which all other hypotheses can be but variations. It may on the one hand be asserted, that the strength of the tendency which each particular state of consciousness has to follow any other, is fixed beforehand by a Creator—that there is a pre-established harmony between the inner and outer relations. On the other hand it may be asserted, that the strength of the tendency which each particular state of consciousness has to follow any other, depends upon the frequency

Principles of psychology. London, 1855. [Pp. 376–378, 383–384, 523–526, 572–573, 577–579, 583.]

with which the two have been connected in experience—that the harmony between the inner and outer relations, arises from the fact, that the outer relations produce the inner relations. . . .

While, for the first hypothesis, there is no evidence, for the second the evidence is overwhelming. . . .

The only orders of psychical sequence which do not obviously come within this general law, are those which we class as reflex and instinctive —those which are as well performed on the first occasion as ever afterwards—those which are apparently established antecedent to experience. But there are not wanting facts which indicate that, rightly interpreted, the law covers all these cases too. Though it is manifest that reflex and instinctive sequences are not determined by the experiences of the *individual* organism manifesting them; yet there still remains the hypothesis that they are determined by the experiences of the *race* of organisms forming its ancestry, which by infinite repetition in countless successive generations have established these sequences as organic relations: and all the facts that are accessible to us, go to support this hypothesis. . . .

§196. But will the experience hypothesis also suffice to explain the evolution of the higher forms of rationality out of the lower? It will. From the reasoning from particulars to particulars—familiarly exhibited by children, by domestic animals, and by the superior mammals at large —the progress to inductive and deductive reasoning is similarly unbroken, and similarly determined by the accumulation of experiences. . . .

Were it not for the prevalent anxiety to establish some positive distinction between animal intelligence and human intelligence, it would scarcely be needful to assign any proof of this. . . . Every one is bound to admit, that as the rationality of an infant is no higher than that of a domestic animal, if so high; and as, from the rationality of the infant to that of the man, the progress is through insensible steps; there is also a series of insensible steps through which brute rationality may pass into human rationality. And further, it must be admitted that as the assimilation of experiences of successively increasing complexity, alone suffices for the unfolding of reason in the individual human being; so must it alone suffice for the evolution of reason in general.

Equally conclusive is the argument from the history of civilization, or from the comparison of different existing human races. . . .

§197. And here seems to be the fittest place for pointing out how the general doctrine that has been developed, supplies a reconciliation between the experience-hypothesis as commonly interpreted, and the antagonist hypothesis of the transcendentalists. . . .

As most who have read thus far will have perceived, both the general argument unfolded in the synthetical divisions of this work, and many of the special arguments by which it has been supported, imply a tacit adhesion to the development hypothesis—the hypothesis that Life in its multitudinous and infinitely-varied embodiments, has arisen out of the lowest and simplest beginnings, by steps as gradual as those which evolve a homogeneous microscopic germ into a complex organism. This tacit admission, which the progress of the argument has rendered much more obvious than I anticipated it would become, I do not hesitate to acknowledge. . . .

For, joined with this hypothesis, the simple universal law that the cohesion of psychical states is proportionate to the frequency with which they have followed one another in experience, requires but to be supplemented by the law that habitual psychical successions entail some hereditary tendency to such successions, which, under persistent conditions, will become cumulative in generation after generation, to supply an explanation of all psychological phenomena; and, among others, of the so-called "forms of thought." Just as we saw that the establishment of those compound reflex actions which we call instincts, is comprehensible on the principle that inner relations are, by perpetual repetition, organized into correspondence with outer relations; so, the establishment of those consolidated, those indissoluble, those instinctive mental relations constituting our ideas of Space and Time, is comprehensible on the same principle. . . .

In the sense, then, that there exist in the nervous system certain pre-established relations answering to relations in the environment, there is truth in the doctrine of "forms of thought"—not the truth for which its advocates contend, but a parallel truth. Corresponding to absolute external relations, there are developed in the nervous system absolute internal relations—relations that are developed before birth; that are antecedent to, and independent of, individual experiences; and that are automatically established along with the very first cognitions. And, as here understood, it is not only these fundamental relations which are thus pre-determined; but also hosts of other relations of a more or less constant kind, which are congenitally represented by more or less complete nervous connections. On the other hand, I hold that these pre-established internal relations, though independent of the experience of the individual, are not independent of experience in general; but that they have been established by the accumulated experience of preceding organisms. The corollary from the general argument that has been elaborated, is, that the brain represents an infinitude of experiences received during the evolution of life in general: the most uniform and frequent of which, have been successively bequeathed, principal and interest; and have thus slowly amounted to that high intelligence which lies latent in the brain of the infant—which the infant in the course of its after life exercises and usually strengthens or further complicates—and which, with minute additions, it again bequeaths to future generations. And thus it happens that the European comes to have from twenty to thirty cubic inches more brain than the Papuan. Thus it happens that faculties, as that of music, which scarcely exist in the inferior human races, become congenital in the superior ones. Thus it happens that out of savages unable to count even up to the number of their fingers, and speaking a language containing only nouns and verbs, come at length our Newtons and Shakespeares.

14.8

George John Romanes

(1848–1894)

This was the first "comparative" psychology, and in it Romanes made an effort to demonstrate the continuity of mind throughout the animal kingdom, including man. The material he used was largely anecdotal, and because lesser men who used the same sort of material far less critically than he have vanished in the mists of history, he has been left as the one most often named as the exponent of this method. It is true that his accounts were often anthropomorphic, but one should not forget that he was also an experimenter to whom we owe our first knowledge of the operation of the nerve-net in the jellyfish. The criterion of intelligence which he states here is essentially the same which tough-minded Jacques Loeb advanced at the end of the century when he said that "consciousness is a metaphysical term for phenomena which are determined by associative memory" (Comparative physiology of the brain, 1899, p. 12). However, he applies it in a way which seems to endorse Pflüger's (9.10) conclusion about consciousness in the spinal frog.

Before we begin to consider the phenomena of mind throughout the animal kingdom it is desirable that we should understand, as far as possible, what it is that we exactly mean by mind. . . . It is evident that in our study of animal intelligence we are wholly restricted to the objective method. Starting from what I know subjectively of the operations of my own individual mind, and the activities which in my own organism they prompt, I proceed by analogy to infer from the observable activities of other organisms what are the mental operations that underlie them.
. . . Two conditions require to be satisfied before we even begin to imagine that observable activities are indicative of mind; first, the activities must be displayed by a living organism; and secondly, they must be of a kind to suggest the presence of two elements which we recognise as the distinctive characteristics of mind as such—consciousness and choice.

Animal intelligence. London, 1882. [Pp. 1–5.]

So far, then, the case seems simple enough. Wherever we see a living organism apparently exerting intentional choice, we might infer that it is conscious choice, and therefore that the organism has a mind. But further reflection shows us that this is just what we cannot do; for although it is true that there is no mind without the power of conscious choice, it is not true that all apparent choice is due to mind. In our own organisms, for instance, we find a great many adaptive movements performed without much choice or even consciousness coming into play at all—such, for instance, as in the beating of our hearts. And not only so, but physiological experiments and pathological lesions prove that in our own and in other organisms the mechanism of the nervous system is sufficient, without the intervention of consciousness, to produce muscular movements of a highly co-ordinate and apparently intentional character. . . .

. . . It thus becomes evident that before we can predicate the bare existence of mind in the lower animals, we need some yet more definite criterion of mind than that which is supplied by the adaptive actions of a living organism, howsoever apparently intentional such actions may be. Such a criterion I have now to lay down, and I think it is one that is as practically adequate as it is theoretically legitimate.

Objectively considered, the only distinction between adaptive movements due to reflex action and adaptive movements due to mental perception, consists in the former depending on inherited mechanisms within the nervous system being so constructed as to effect *particular* adaptive movements in response to *particular* stimulations, while the latter are independent of any such inherited adjustment of special mechanisms to the exigencies of special circumstances. . . . Without at present going into the question concerning the relation of body and mind, or waiting to ask whether cases of mental adjustment are not really quite as *mechanical* in the sense of being the necessary result or correlative to a chain of physical sequences due to a physical stimulation, it is enough to point to the variable and incalculable character of mental adjustments as distinguished from the constant and forseeable character of reflex adjustments. All, in fact, that in an objective sense we can mean by a mental adjustment is an adjustment of a kind that has not been definitely fixed by heredity as the only adjustment possible in the given circumstances of stimulation. . . .

It is, then, adaptive action by a living organism in cases where the inherited machinery of the nervous system does not furnish data for our prevision of what the adaptive action must necessarily be—it is only here that we recognise the objective evidence of mind. The criterion of mind, therefore, which I propose . . . is as follows:—Does the organism learn to make new adjustments, or to modify old ones, in accordance with the results of its own individual experience? If it does so, the fact cannot be due merely to reflex action in the sense above described, for it is impossible that heredity can have provided in advance for innovations upon, or alterations of, its machinery during the lifetime of a particular individual.

. . . In my use of this criterion I shall always regard it as fixing only the upper limit of non-mental action; I shall never regard it as fixing the lower limit of mental action. For it is clear that long before mind has advanced sufficiently far in the scale of development to become amenable to the test in question, it has probably begun to dawn as nascent subjectivity. In other words, because a lowly organised animal does *not* learn by its own individual experience, we may not therefore conclude that in performing its natural or ancestral adaptations to appropriate stimuli consciousness, or the mind-element, is wholly absent; we can only say that this element, if present, reveals no evidence of the fact. But, on the other hand, if a lowly organised animal *does* learn by its own individual experience, we are in possession of the best available evidence of conscious memory leading to intentional adaptation. Therefore our criterion applies to the upper limit of non-mental action, not to the lower limit of mental.

14.9

Richard Lynch Garner

(1848–1920)

Eighteenth-century authors loved to discuss the language of animals, and many then and since have debated whether apes could learn human speech, but Garner took hold of the problem in a different way: to learn the speech of monkeys. By escaping the limits of anthropocentrism, he is able to demonstrate conclusively that they do possess language and to learn something of its range and limitations. Subsequently, during a quarter-century of research in African jungles, Garner traded roles by placing himself and his recording equipment in a steel mesh cage, and succeeded in demonstrating the similarity of chimpanzee language in different regions.

From childhood, I have believed that all kinds of animals have some mode of speech by which they can talk among their own kind; and I have often wondered why man has never tried to learn it. . . .

I regarded the task of learning the speech of monkeys as very much the same as learning that of some strange race of mankind—more difficult in the degree of its inferiority, but less in volume.

Year by year, as new ideas were revealed to me, new barriers arose,

The speech of monkeys. New York, 1892. [Pp. 3, 5–7, 86–87, 91–93, 108–109.]

and I began to realize how great a task was mine. One difficulty was to utter the sounds I heard, another was to recall them, and yet another to translate them. But impelled by an inordinate hope and not discouraged by poor success, I continued my studies as best I could in the gardens of New York, Philadelphia, Cincinnati, and Chicago, and with such specimens as I could find from time to time with travelling shows, hand-organs, aboard some ship, or kept as a family pet. I must acknowledge my debt of gratitude to all these little creatures who have aided me in the study of their native tongue.

Having contended for some years with the difficulties mentioned, a new idea dawned upon me. . . . [I] proposed the novel experiment of acting as interpreter between two monkeys. . . . I separated two monkeys which had occupied the same cage together for some time, and placed them in separate rooms of the building, where they could not see or hear each other. I then arranged the phonograph near the cage of the female, and by various means induced her to utter a few sounds. . . . The machine was then placed near the cage containing the male and the record repeated to him, and his conduct closely studied. He gave evident signs of recognizing the sounds, and at once began a search for the mysterious monkey doing the talking. His perplexity at this strange affair cannot well be described. The familiar voice of his mate would induce him to approach, but that squeaking, chattering horn was a feature he could not comprehend. He traced the sounds, however, to the source from which they came, and failing to find his mate, thrust his arm into the horn quite up to his shoulder, then withdrew it, and peeped into it again and again. . . . In this experiment for the first time in the history of language was the simian speech reduced to record, and while the results were not fully up to my hopes, they served to inspire me to further efforts to find the fountain-head from which flows out the great river of human speech. . . .

Up to this time I have been able to determine, with a fair degree of certainty, nine words or sounds belonging to Capuchins, some of which sounds are so inflected as to have two or three different meanings, I think. The sound which I have translated food, and found to have a much wider meaning, long perplexed me, because I found it used under so many conditions, and had not been able to detect any difference of modulation. I find one form of this sound used for food in general, but when modulated in a certain way seems to specify the kind of food. I observed that this sound seemed to be a salutation or peace-making term with them, which I attributed to the fact that food was the central thought of every monkey's life, and that consequently that word would naturally be the most important of his whole speech. During the past winter I found that another modulation of this word expressed a wish to obtain a thing, and appeared to me to be almost equivalent to the word "give," when used in the imperative mood; something like this: "Give me that." I have succeeded a great many times, by the use of this word, in inducing McGinty to give me a part of his food, and on many occasions to hand me from his cage a ball, a club, or some such thing that I had given him to play with. . . .

From a number of sounds uttered by the Rhesus monkeys, I finally selected a word which, for many reasons, I believed meant food, and was the equivalent in meaning to that word in the Capuchin tongue. The phonetic character of the word differs very widely. . . .

One of the most unique of my experiments I made in Central Park in the autumn of 1891. I secured a very fine phonograph record of the food-sound of the Rhesus monkeys belonging to the park. During the following night there arrived at the park a shipment of Rhesus monkeys just from their home in the east of Asia. There were seven of these new monkeys, three adult females and four babies. . . . At my request the superintendant had these monkeys stored in the vacant room in the upper story of the old armory building. . . . About sunrise I repaired to this room, where I had my phonograph placed in order. . . . I delivered to them the sounds contained on my cylinder which I had recorded on the day preceding. Up to this time not a sound had been uttered by any inmate of the shipping-cage. The instant my phonograph began to reproduce the record, the seven new monkeys began to answer vociferously. After having delivered this record to them, I gave them time to become quiet again. I showed them some carrots and apples, on seeing which they began to utter the same sounds which they had uttered before, and this time I secured a good record of their sounds to compare with the others. . . .

More than a year ago, I made some splendid records of the sounds of the two chimpanzees in the Cincinnati collection. . . . I was able to discern as many as seven different phones, all of which come within the scope of the human vocal organs. I learned one of these sounds, and on a subsequent visit to Cincinnati I succeeded in attracting the attention of the female and eliciting from her a response. She would come to the lattice door of the inner cage by which I was standing, and when I would give utterance to the sound she would press her face against the door and answer it with a like sound. The male, however, did not appear to notice it with any degree of concern. I have no idea what the sound meant, and my opportunities have not been such that I could translate it with the remotest degree of certainty.

14.10

Conway Lloyd Morgan

(1852–1936)

Bain (12.11) used the phrase "trial and error" and explained (13.9) how accidental success influences habit formation. Subsequently, the debate over Darwinism encouraged much "anecdotal" reporting of animal feats, particularly to support the view that animals reason. Morgan now stresses the need for careful observation, but he himself does not take the step to planned experiment. But compare Tony's escape from the garden, in this selection, with Thorndike's problem-box experiments (13.10).

The first part of this selection includes the statement of the famous "canon" for which Morgan is most often remembered.

Unfortunately many able men who are eminently fitted to make and record exact observations on the habits and activities of animals have not undergone the training necessary to enable them to deal with the psychological aspect of the question. The skilled naturalist or biologist is seldom also skilled in psychological analysis. Notwithstanding therefore the admirable and invaluable observations of our great naturalists, we cannot help feeling that their psychological conclusions are hardly on the same level as that reached by their conclusions in the purely biological field. . . .

. . . There is one basal principle . . . (which) may be thus stated:— *In no case may we interpret an action as the outcome of the exercise of a higher psychical faculty, if it can be interpreted as the outcome of the exercise of one which stands lower in the psychological scale. . . .*

. . . If we apply the term "reasoning" to the process by which an animal, profiting by experience, adapts his actions to somewhat varying circumstances, there can be no hesitation whatever in giving an affirmative answer to the question ["Do animals reason?"]. But if by reasoning we mean the process of drawing a logical inference; if we define reason in such a way that it is necessary for the reasoning being as such, to think the *therefore,* then we cannot answer the question so readily. . . .

Tony, the fox-terrier, already introduced to my readers, when he wants to go out into the road, puts his head under the latch of the gate, lifts it, and waits for the gate to swing open. Now an observer of the dog's intelligent action might well suppose that he clearly perceived how the end in view was to be gained, and the most appropriate means for ef-

Introduction to comparative psychology. London, 1894. [Pp. 52–53, 287–291.]

fecting his purpose. The following chain of ideas might be supposed to pass through the dog's mind, not, indeed, in a clear-cut logical form, but at any rate in a rough and practically serviceable way: "Why does the gate remain shut? The latch holds it. I'll lift the latch. Now it is no longer held, therefore it swings open." But is it necessary to assume that there were ideas involving, even in the most rudimentary way, the why and the wherefore? May not the action be quite well explained on the hypothesis that the dog acted under the sole guidance of sense-experience? I think it not unlikely that two chance observers, both witnesses of the action, might long discuss it from different standpoints: the one contending that it was probably based on practical experience, and therefore intelligent as I use this word; the other asking, in reply, what practical experience the dog could have had of gates swinging open of themselves when the latch was raised, insisting on the purposive nature of the action, and asserting that it unquestionably involved a clear perception of the relationship of the *how* of the gates opening, and, as it swung back when the latch was raised, of the *therefore* involved. Eventually the two observers might agree to differ, and each go on his way, more convinced than ever of the correctness of his own view, and of the fact that preconceived ideas may blind a man to the most obvious conclusions.

But if, now, one had an opportunity of seeing how such a clever trick originated, if one had watched all the stages of its genesis, then one would presumably be in a better position to offer an opinion in the matter than either of the chance observers who saw it only in its final and perfected form. With regard to this particular trick of Tony's I am in that position. I watched from the first the development of the habit. The facts are as follows: I may premise that the gate is of iron, and has iron bars running vertically with interspaces of five or six inches between. On either side is a wall or low parapet, on which are similar vertical rails. The latch of the gate is at a level of about a foot above that of the top of the low wall. When it is lifted the gate swings open by its own weight. The gate separates a small garden of only a few square yards area, from the road. When the dog is put out of the front door he naturally wants to get out into the road, where there is often much to interest him; cats to be worried, other dogs with whom to establish a sniffing acquaintance, and so forth. I said just now that I watched the development of the habit from the beginning. This perhaps is a slight exaggeration. I was sitting at a window above the garden, and heard the dog put out of the door. I therefore watched him. He ran up and down the low wall, and put his head out between the iron bars, now here, now there, now elsewhere, anxiously gazing into the road. This he did for quite three or four minutes. At length it so happened that he put out his head beneath the latch, which, as I have said, is at a convenient height for his doing so, being about a foot above the level of the wall.

The latch was thus lifted. He withdrew his head, and began to look out elsewhere, when he found that the gate was swinging open, and out be bolted. After that, whenever I took him out, I shut the gate in his face, and waited till he opened it for himself and joined me. I did not give him any assistance in any way, but just waited and watched, sometimes putting him back and making him open it again. Gradually he went, after fewer pokings of his head out in the wrong place, to the one opening at which the latch was lifted. But it was nearly three weeks from my first noticing his actions from the window before he went at once and with precision to the right place and put his head without any ineffectual fumbling beneath the latch. Even now he always lifts it with the back of his head and not with his muzzle which would be easier for him.

With regard to this particular trick, then, I venture to affirm that, *when we know the whole history of it,* Tony's action is quite similar in kind to that of my little chick, Blackie, which, profiting by a chance experience, pulled down the corner of the newspaper and escaped from my experimental poultry-yard. As it stands, it is quite within the range of sense-experience; nay more, it affords a pretty example of the application of sense-experience to new circumstances. It is typically intelligent. . . .

Now what I am particularly anxious to enforce is, not the adoption of the usage of the word "reason" in its narrower sense, though I think that this is desirable; or the hypothesis that animals do not reason in this sense, though I think that this is probable; but rather than what we need is careful investigation in place of anecdotal reporting. Unfortunately the opportunities for investigation are not numerous. One may keep dogs and other animals for years, and find few opportunities of investigating what has even a semblance of reasoning. And if a friend tells one of the clever performance of his dog, the time for investigation may have passed. No one, by observing Tony opening the gate *now*, could ascertain the stages of the development of this intelligent action. Still opportunities do present themselves; and if those who take a scientific interest in zoological psychology will endeavour to utilize to the full these opportunities, and will record the results of experimental investigation, we shall acquire a better acquaintance with the psychological processes in animals than we could gain by a thousand anecdotes. In zoological psychology we have got beyond the anecdotal stage, we have reached the stage of experimental investigation.

14.11

Karl von Frisch

(born 1886)

One of the most romantic chapters in the history of science has been the long story of Frisch's patient deciphering of the manner in which foraging bees communicate. Almost a half-century of work is summarized in his book, The dance language and orientation of bees *(Harvard University Press, 1967). We translate parts of his first publication on this problem, in which he recognizes that the bees dance in several styles but has as yet no intimation of what different meanings they convey. At first he set up his experimental tables at a short distance from the hive, and for many years this kept him from recognizing that a bee could also "instruct" others as to the approximate distance and direction to the find!*

In 1973, von Frisch shared a Nobel prize with Lorenz (see 15.15) and N. Tinbergen.

During past years, when I wanted to train bees to colors in order to test their color sense, I would first place a bit of honeycomb on the experimental table. After a little while it would be discovered by a bee hunting for food, which would at once begin gathering, and would quickly bring a large number of its fellows from the hive. . . . The honey was then removed, and I would start the training by placing a dish of sugar water on a piece of colored paper. When the bees emptied the dish, I usually allowed an interval of perhaps half an hour before I refilled it. For with uninterrupted feeding the number of bees coming to the place of training grew so out of hand as to interfere with the experiment.

Under these circumstances on innumerable occasions I made the following observation: At the end of each feeding period 50 or 100 bees would be swarming around the place and trying to reach the empty dish. But after only a few minutes their number decreased markedly, gradually more and more of them flew away, and finally the place was almost totally abandoned, with now and then a single bee flying up as if to see whether there might not again be something to take. If it found nothing, it would return to the hive after a short search. But as soon as sugar water was poured in, and the first bees returned to the hive with full honey-bags, the others also came flying and within a few minutes almost the whole swarm that had been visiting the training place was mobile again.

Ueber die "Sprache" der Bienen [On the "language" of the bees]. *Münchener medizinische Wochenschrift*, 67 (1920): 566–569. [Pp. 567, 569.]

Had the first bees that found the dish filled told the others that there was food again? . . .

Not much could be learned from further observations at the feeding place. We must see what is happening inside the hive. For this purpose I had a bee-case prepared in which the cells were not arranged in the usual manner, over and behind one another, but all side by side, so that through the glass panes of the two broad sides one could see all the cells and all the bees inside the hive. . . . All the bees to be used in the experiment were numbered by a simple system, so that each could easily be recognized both at the feeding place and inside the hive, and not confused with any of its comrades.

Usually only about 20 bees were permitted to approach the feeding place and were numbered. All new (unnumbered) animals which came later were immediately killed. . . . This limitation was necessary in order not to lose track of them. How clear the phenomenon is can be shown by an example: On the morning of July 25, 1919, I drew a new swarm of 24 bees to my feeding place and numbered them. At 12:15 I removed the feeding dish and did not replace it until 2:34. After this interval of more than 2 hours the animals seemed to have given up the hunt for sugar water, and it took a whole half hour until the first bee, which was No. 24, finally flew up to the dish at 3:05. It drank its fill, and at 3:09 returned to the hive. After 2 minutes, at 3:11, No. 5 and No. 16 came to the feeding dish, at 3:12 No. 17, about half a minute later No. 6, and at 3:13 No. 24 returned from the hive to the dish, followed after 1 minute by No. 2, so that now, 5 minutes after the first visit by No. 24, five other bees sat beside it at the dish, having apparently come at her instigation. And although not a single bee had made an appearance at the feeding place for half an hour before, within a half hour after three-fourths of the morning swarm were busily engaged in gathering sugar water. . . .

During an interval in feeding the numbered bees sit around idly on the cells, generally not too far from the flight-hole. Now and then one comes to life. It becomes restless, begins to creep about, slowly starts moving downwards, leaves the hive and flies to the feeding place. If it finds no sugar water there it turns home again, creeps slowly along the cells and comes to rest in one spot or another without making itself conspicuous in any way. Quite otherwise, if the dish has meanwhile been filled. Then it pumps its honey-stomach full, flies to the hive and runs up the comb of cells as if seized by a feverish excitement, stopping now and then to give some of its sugar water to other bees which seem to be waiting for it, and then plays out a scene which is so full of charm and fascination that one may despair of being able to describe it in dry words. It begins with a dance which I may call a "round dance," which obviously brings excitement to its immediate environment. The dance consists in tripping about in circles very swiftly, but often turning by

180 degrees, so that the direction is always changing. These circles are tight, usually enclosing only one cell, the bee running about on the 6 neighboring cells, making one or two circles in one direction, sometimes only a half or three-fourths of a circumference, then suddenly turning about and going in the opposite sense. It does this at the same spot for 3, 5, 10 seconds, often even for half a minute. Then it runs a little distance to repeat the same thing at another spot, or it may suddenly break off dancing, run in great haste to the flight-hole and return to the feeding place. Just as characteristic as this behavior is the reaction which it elicits in the others. As soon as the bee begins the dance, those sitting nearby turn so as to come into direct contact with it, head on, trying with their outstretched feelers to hold her body and thus tripping after her to join in the swift round dance with all its turnings. If the bees whose attention is aroused in this manner are *unnumbered,* that is, those who have no relation to our feeding place, then most of them let go of the whirling bee without any further consequence. But if in its dance it accidentally comes into contact with one of the *numbered* bees, that knows the feeding place and has been sitting idle on the comb during the interval, then it also reacts in the same manner, but then, without worrying any further about its whirling colleague, it hurries directly to the flight-hole and to the feeding-place. . . .

We have made a step of progress concerning a question about which only vague suppositions were hitherto possible. We now know for sure: Bees have an active means of communication regarding the presence of food, and this by a kind of sign-language which, however, is based on touch rather than vision, in keeping with the darkness of the hive. How rich the "vocabulary" of this sign language is, and whether in addition to this there is also some primitive communication by sound, remains to be investigated. The difficulties which stand in the way of the solution of these questions are great, and therefore many years will pass before we have half an understanding of the language of the bees.

Chapter 15

INSTINCT CONTROVERSY

It is commonly supposed that rejection of instinct is a recent, even a twentieth-century development, and that mystical notions about animal instinct have a very long heritage. Ancient authors wrote of animals as "instructed by nature," but they had no word for instinct, though that word has often been put into their mouths by translators. The Latin *instinctus*, meaning incitement (and derived from the same root as stimulus) was never applied to animals. The phrase natural instinct originated late in the thirteenth century, but it should be translated natural (i.e., bodily) impulse, and it was definitely not a mystical concept. The unqualified word instinct was first applied to animals at about the start of the seventeenth century by writers who did indeed conceive of instinct as an inexplicable and supernatural force directing behavior, but they provoked a vigorous counterreaction. The eighteenth century showed its commitment to the limitless power of education in nothing else so clearly as in its scorn for instinct. Darwinism gave a new aspect to pro-instinct arguments, but the twentieth-century anti-instinct movement has introduced nothing essentially new.

15.1

Lucius Annaeus Seneca

(*c.* 3 B.C.–A.D. 65)

Seneca's Letter No. 121 of the Letters to Lucilius, also called the Moral Epistles, deals with the problem of the unlearned adequacy of animal behavior. It has been called the first explicit statement of an instinct theory, but a careful reading will show that this would require a definition of instinct as "innate understanding" rather than as "blind impulse" or "chained reflex acts." In Grummere's translation, this letter carries the title "On instinct in animals," but the word instinct does not appear in the text of the letter, although in less careful translations it may appear several times. Even at this time, it is clear, the subject is already controversial, for Seneca argues against a more mechanistic view according to which these actions are forced rather than guided by some measure of understanding.

. . . We were once debating whether all animals had any feelings about their "constitution." That this is the case is proved particularly by their making motions of such fitness and nimbleness that they seem to be trained for the purpose. Every being is clever in its own line. The skilled workman handles his tools with an ease born of experience; the pilot knows how to steer his ship skilfully; the artist can quickly lay on the colours which he has prepared in great variety for the purpose of rendering the likeness, and passes with ready eye and hand from palette to canvas. In the same way an animal is agile in all that pertains to the use of its body. We are apt to wonder at skilled dancers because their gestures are perfectly adapted to the meaning of the piece and its accompanying emotions, and their movements match the speed of the dialogue. But that which art gives to the craftsman, is given to the animal by nature. No animal handles its limbs with difficulty, no animal is at a loss how to use its body. This function they exercise immediately at birth. They come into this world with this knowledge; they are born full-trained.

But people reply: "The reason why animals are so dexterous in the use of their limbs is that if they move them unnaturally, they will feel pain. They are *compelled* to do thus, according to your school, and it is fear rather than will-power which moves them in the right direction."

Ad Lucilium epistolae morales [Letters to Lucilius on moral questions]. With an English translation by R. M. Grummere. 3 volumes. Cambridge, Mass.: Harvard University Press, Loeb Classical Library, 1953. [Vol. III, pp. 399–401, 407–411.] Reprinted by permission of the publisher and the Loeb Classical Library.

This idea is wrong. Bodies driven by a compelling force move slowly; but those which move of their own accord possess alertness. The proof that it is not fear of pain which prompts them thus, is, that even when pain checks them they struggle to carry out their natural motions. Thus the child who is trying to stand and is becoming used to carry his own weight, on beginning to test his strength, falls and rises again and again with tears until through painful effort he has trained himself to the demands of nature. And certain animals with hard shells, when turned on their backs, twist and grope with their feet and make motions side-ways until they are restored to their proper position. The tortoise on his back feels no suffering; but he is restless because he misses his natural condition, and does not cease to shake himself about until he stands once more upon his feet.

So all these animals have a consciousness of their physical constitution, and for that reason can manage their limbs as readily as they do; nor have we any better proof that they come into being equipped with this knowledge than the fact that no animal is unskilled in the use of its body. . . .

Nature brings up her own offspring and does not cast them away; and because the most assured security is that which is nearest, every man has been entrusted to his own self. Therefore . . . even young animals, on issuing from the mother's womb or from the egg, know at once of their own accord what is harmful for them, and avoid death-dealing things. They even shrink when they notice the shadow of birds of prey which flit overhead.

No animal, when it enters upon life, is free from the fear of death. People may ask: "How can an animal at birth have an understanding of things wholesome or destructive?" The first question, however, is *whether* it can have such understanding, and not *how* it can understand. And it is clear that they have such understanding from the fact that, even if you add understanding, they will act no more adequately than they did in the first place. Why should the hen show no fear of the peacock or the goose, and yet run from the hawk, which is a so much smaller animal not even familiar to the hen? Why should young chickens fear a cat and not a dog? These fowls clearly have a presentiment of harm—one not based on actual experiments; for they avoid a thing before they can possibly have experience of it. Furthermore, in order that you may not suppose this to be the result of chance, they do not shrink form certain other things which you would expect them to fear, nor do they ever forget vigilance and care in this regard; they all possess equally the faculty of avoiding what is destructive. Besides, their fear does not grow as their lives lengthen.

Hence indeed it is evident that these animals have not reached such a condition through experience; it is because of an inborn desire for self-preservation. The teachings of experience are slow and irregular; but whatever Nature communicates belongs equally to everyone, and comes immediately. If, however, you require an explanation, shall I tell you how it is that every living thing tries to understand that which is harmful? It feels that it is constructed of flesh; and so it perceives to what an extent flesh may be cut or burned or crushed, and what animals are equipped with the power of doing this damage; it is of animals of this sort that it derives an unfavourable and hostile idea. These tendencies are closely connected; for each animal at the same time consults its own safety, seeking that which helps it, and shrinks from that which will harm it. Impulses towards useful objects, and revulsion from the opposite, are according to nature; without any reflection to prompt the idea, and without any advice, whatever Nature has prescribed, is done.

Do you see how skillful bees are in building their cells? How completely harmonious in sharing and enduring toil? Do you not see how the spider weaves a web so subtle that man's hand cannot imitate it; and what a task it is to arrange the threads, some directed straight towards the center, for the sake of making the web solid, and others running in circles and lessening in thickness—for the purpose of tangling and catching in a sort of net the smaller insects for whose ruin the spider spreads the web? This art is born, not taught, and for this reason no animal is more skilled than any other. You will notice that all spider-webs are equally fine, and that the openings in all honeycomb cells are identical in shape. Whatever art communicates is uncertain and uneven; but Nature's assignments are always uniform. Nature has communicated nothing except the duty of taking care of themselves and the skill to do so; that is why living and learning begin at the same time. No wonder that living things are born with a gift whose absence would make birth useless. This is the first equipment that Nature granted them for the maintenance of their existence—the quality of adaptability and self-love. They could not survive except by desiring to do so. Nor would this desire alone have made them prosper, but without it nothing could have prospered. In no animal can you observe any low esteem, or even any carelessness, of self. Dumb beasts, sluggish in other respects, are clever at living. So you will see that creatures which are useless to others are alert for their own preservation.

15.2

Galen

(131–200)

Galen's discussions of unlearned animal behavior make him a pioneer comparative psychologist, but they invariably occur as digressions from other topics. From De usu partium, we give first a passage which is actually the elision from an earlier selection (4.2) on the human hand, and second, a discussion of sucking behavior which is incidental to the treatment of the process of birth. The final selection in this group reports what is probably the earliest truly psychological experiment of which a clear record survives, and it occurs in the course of a discussion of diseases affecting male sexual response.

Galen, like Seneca, sees animal behavior as guided by an "untaught perception" rather than as "blind." The phrase attributed to Hippocrates was used by him in relation to involuntary digestive processes, not to behavior in the usual sense.

Translation of the last selection has been based also on the Greek and Latin texts of the Opera omnia edited by C. G. Kühn (Leipzig, 1821–1833).

[A]

In observing newborn animals striving to exert themselves before their parts are perfected, we can see clearly that it is not the bodily parts that lead the soul to be timid or brave or wise. Now I have often seen a young calf butting before its horns have sprouted, a colt kicking with hoofs still soft, a shote, quite small, trying to defend itself with jaws innocent of tusks, and a newborn puppy attempting to bite with its teeth still tender. For every animal has, untaught, a perception of the faculties of its own soul and the virtues resident in its parts. Or why else, when it is possible for the small boar to bite with its little teeth, does he not use them for battle instead of longing to use those {weapons} which he does not yet

[A] *De usu partium.* Translated by Margaret Tallmadge May, as *On the usefulness of the parts of the body.* 2 vols. Ithaca: Cornell University Press, 1968. [Bk. I, Ch. 3 (pp. 70–71).] Copyright © 1968 by Cornell University. Used by permission of Cornell University Press.
[B] Ibid. [Bk. XV, Ch. 7 (p. 673).]
[C] De locis affectis [On the seats of ailments]. In *Oeuvres anatomiques, physiologiques et médicales de Galien.* Translated (into French) by Ch. Daremberg. 2 vols. Paris, 1854–1856. Vol. II, pp. 468–705. [Bk. VI, Ch. 6 (pp. 700–702).]

have? How, then, is it possible to say that animals learn the usefulness of their parts from the parts themselves, when they obviously know their usefulness even before they have them. Now if you like, take three eggs, an eagle's, a duck's, and a serpent's; warm them, and in due season hatch them out; and you will see two of the animals that have been formed making trial of their wings even before they are able to fly, and the other, though still soft and weak, wiggling and struggling to crawl. And if you raise them to maturity under one and the same roof and then take them out in the open and let them go, the eagle will fly up high in the air, the duck will fly down onto some marshy lake, and the serpent will creep away into the earth. Afterwards, without having learned, the eagle, I think will hunt its prey, the duck will swim, and the serpent lurk in its den. "For," says Hippocrates, "the instincts {natures} of animals are untaught." So it seems to me that the other animals acquire their skills by instinct {nature} rather than by reason, bees, for example, molding [their wax], ants working at their treasuries and labyrinths, and spiders spinning and weaving. I judge from the fact that they are untaught.

[B]

Then is it right to praise Nature only for these things [i.e., the process of birth], or has the greatest wonder of them all—the instruction of the animal being born in the actions of all the parts—not yet been told? For not only did she prepare a mouth, esophagus, and stomach as instruments of nutrition; she also produced an animal that understands right from the beginning how these are to be used, and she instilled into it a certain instinctive {natural} faculty of wisdom by which each animal arrives at the nutriment suitable for it. I shall explain all the other animals at another time. For man she prepared milk as nutriment, producing two things at one appointed time, nutriment in the breasts of the mother, and in the infants to be nourished an eager desire for such a juice. Now if the nipple of a breast is put into the mouth of a newborn child, he immediately compresses it with his lips, immediately draws in the juice by opening his jaws, and then by curving his tongue pushes it down into his throat, as if he had practised this for a long time.

[C]

Nature, which has shaped and completed the parts of the body, made them so that they are able to perform their proper functions without instruction. I did a very important experiment on this capability by raising a kid which had never seen its mother. I dissected some pregnant she-goats, taking account of what anatomists have learned concerning the economy of the fetus. When I found one that was vigorous, I detached it from its mother in the usual manner. I removed it before it had seen its mother, and carrying it indoors, I put it down in the midst of a number of vessels which were filled, one with wine and another with oil, this one with honey and that one with milk, and others with various liquids; there were even a few which were filled with cereals and with fruits. First we watched this little kid walk as if it had been taught that it had feet for walking. Then we saw him shake off the moisture he had received from his mother, then scratch his side with one foot; sniff at each of the vessels placed in the room, and after having sniffed at all of them, drink the milk. Seeing which we all exclaimed, what Hippocrates had said: "the natures of animals are without instruction." In raising this kid we subsequently established that he did not nourish himself with milk only, but with other substances placed on the ground. Since the time when the kid had been lifted from its mother was near the spring equinox, at the end of two months I brought him the tender shoots of branches and of plants, and having sniffed at all of them, he immediately turned away from some and proceeded to taste others, and after having tasted them he ate those which are the usual food of adult goats. This fact may mean little, but here is something which means much. After having browsed on the leaves and young shoots he drank, and a little later he started to ruminate. The sight of this caused all who were present to exclaim with astonishment at the natural faculties of animals. Assuredly, it was a great thing for a hungry animal to take food with its mouth and its teeth, but for it to bring back into its mouth the food which had descended into the stomach, in order to chew it for a long time and grind it fine, and then to carry it not into the stomach itself but into another cavity—this seemed to us a most wondrous spectacle. Common folk disdain such works of nature, and are surprised only by strange spectacles. Nevertheless, is it not surprising that physicians who are most skilled in anatomy inquire as to which muscle is stretched by a given joint, for example by the ischium, and by what muscles it is flexed, which muscles move it obliquely in two directions, and which move it circularly to either side, whereas the kid immediately performs the movements that it wishes in every joint, just as men do, though neither men nor goats know by which muscle each movement is performed? And, if we take the movements of the tongue as an example, how can we not be surprised if, although we find anatomists disagreeing among themselves not only as to the number of its muscles but also regarding their functions, meanwhile we see that nature teaches children how they shall imitate this speech or that, how they shall move their tongues and what muscles will produce the very sound itself? The same is true for vocalization and respiration of all other animals, and, to be brief, of voluntary functions. Who is not amazed to see these organs knowing freely of themselves what to do, while such serious differences of opinion exist among anatomists regarding these functions, and they argue about how they are accomplished and by which organs, and how all animals breathe and utter sounds immediately after birth?

15.3

Saint Thomas Aquinas

(1225–1274)

Aquinas is often said to be the originator of the Church's doctrine on instinct, but his use of the term still has little relationship to either scientific or unscientific concepts of instinct in modern times. It is true that he (or some contemporary) was the first to apply the word instinctus to animals, but a conservative translation of this would be "impulse" not "instinct." When applied by Aquinas to men, this word may refer either to divine incitement to prophecy (usually translated "instinct") or to satanic incitement to evil (usually translated "instigation"). Aquinas never applies it to animals without the qualifying word "natural," thus consistently distinguishing between natural (i.e. bodily) and spiritual (i.e. noncorporeal) impulses to action. In [A] I have translated instinctus as "impulse." This would also be a more conservative translation in each of the excerpts from the Summa. These may be compared with Aquinas on innate moral judgments of men (22.1).

[A]

13. . . . . [Among the criteria of complete sensory knowledge:] it is necessary [to perceive] some intentions which the senses do not apprehend, such as harmfulness and usefulness and others of this sort. Men attain such knowledge by means of inquiry and comparison, but other animals by a certain natural impulse, as the sheep naturally flees from the wolf as something harmful. From this we see that in other animals this is arranged by the faculty of estimation; but in man by the cognitive faculty, which collates the particular intentions. Therefore it is called the particular reason, and the passive intellect.

[A] Disputatio de anima. Pp. 281–362 in *Quaestiones disputatae*, Vol. II. Edited by P. Bazzi. Rome, 1949. [P. 330a.]
[B] *The Summa Theologica of Saint Thomas Aquinas*. Literally translated by Fathers of the Dominican Province. 20 volumes. New York: Benziger Brothers, 1912–1925. [Vol. IV, p. 148; vol. VI, pp. 181, 189, 469.]

[*B*]

[I, *Q*, 83 (1)] For the sheep, seeing the wolf, judges it to be shunned, from a natural and not a free judgment; because it judges not from deliberation, but from natural instinct. And the same thing is to be said of any judgment in brute animals. But man acts from judgment, because by his apprehensive power he judges that something should be avoided or sought.

[I-II, *Q*. 15 (2)] But irrational animals have not the command of the appetitive movement; for this is in them through natural instinct.

[I-II, *Q*. 16 (2)] Animals by means of their members do something from natural instinct; not through knowing the relations of their members to these operations.

[I-II. *Q*. 41 (1)] The senses do not apprehend the future: but from apprehending the present, an animal is moved by natural instinct to hope for a future good, or to fear a future evil.

15.4

Juan Huarte

(1530?–1591?)

By the sixteenth century, a mystical concept of instinct had replaced the naturalistic concept of Aquinas, and against this Huarte protests vigorously. He emphasizes somatic determinants of behavior (which does not stop him from believing in sudden accessions of knowledge independent of experience, due to changes of "temperature"), and he evidently regards the instinct concept of his contemporaries as nonsomatic.

References to instinct become more frequent after this date. Shakespeare was perhaps the first to apply the word to animals without the qualifier "natural" (Henry IV, Part I). The first really extended defense of animal instinct is in a refutation of Huarte's immensely popular book by Guibelet (Examen de l'examen des esprits, 1631), and there the doctrine does have a mystical quality, being linked to occult heavenly forces, rather than to the forces of the terrestrial elements which are accessible to human understanding.

The temperature of the four first qualities (which we heretofore termed Nature) hath so great force, to cause that (of plants, brute beasts, and

Examen de ingenios para las sciencias [1575]. Translated (from the Italian version of Camillo Camilli) by Richard Carew, as *The examination of mens wits*. London, 1594. [Pp. 33, 36–38, 40.]

man) each one set himselfe to performe those workes which are proper
to his kind, that they arrive to that utmost bound of perfection which
may be attained, sodainly & without any others teaching them; the plants
know how to forme roots under ground, and by way of them to draw
nourishment to retaine it, to digest it, and to drive foorth the excrements:
and the brute beasts likewise so soone as they are borne, know that
which is agreeable to their nature, and flie the things which are naughtie
and noisome. And that which makes them most to marvell who are not
seene {i.e., versed} in naturall Philosophie, is, that a man having his
braine well tempered, and of that disposition which is requisit for this
or that science, sodainly and without having ever learned it of any, he
speaketh and uttereth such exquisit matters, as could hardly win credit.
Vulgar Philosophers, seeing the marvellous works which brute beasts performe, affirme it holds no cause of marvell, because they do it by naturall
instinct, in as much as nature sheweth and teacheth each in his kind
what he is to do. And in this they say very well, for we have alreadie
alleaged and prooved, that nature is nothing else than this temperature
of the foure first qualities, and that this is the schoolemaister who
teacheth the soules in what sort they are to worke: but they tearme instinct of nature a certaine masse of things, which rise from the noddocke
upward, neyther could they ever expound or give us to understand,
what it is. . . .

. . . The manner which *Galen* held to behold and discerne by eyesight
the wisedome of the sensitive soule, was to take a yoong kid, but newly
kidded, which set on the ground, begins to go (as if it had bene told and
taught that his legs were made to that purpose) and after that, he shakes
from his backe the superfluous moisture which he brought with him from
his mothers belly, and lifting up the one foot, scrapes behind his eare;
and setting before him sundrie platters with wine, water, vinegre, oile,
and milke, after he hath smelt them all, he fed onely on that of milke.
Which being beheld by divers Philosophers there present, they all with
one voice cried out, That *Hippocrates* had great reason to say, that soules
were skilful without the instruction of any teacher. But *Galen* held not
himselfe contented with this one proofe, for two months after he caused
the same kid, being very hungrie, to be brought into the field, where
smelling at many hearbs, he did eat only those, whereon goats accustomably feed.

But if *Galen*, as he set himselfe to contemplat the demeanure of this
kid, had done the like with three or foure together, he should have
seene some gone better than other some, shrug themselves better, scratch
better, and performe better al the other actions which we have recounted.
And if *Galen* had reared two colts, bred of one horse and mare, he
should have seene the one to pace with more grace than the other, and
to gallop and stop better, and shew more fidelitie. And if he had taken
an ayrie of Faulcons, and manned them, he should have found the

first good of wing, the second good of prey, and the third ravening and ill conditioned. The like shall we find in hounds, who being whelpes of the same litter, the one for perfection of hunting, will seeme to want but speech, and the other have no more inclination thereunto, than if he had bene engendered by a heardmans bandog.

All this cannot be reduced to those vaine instincts of nature; which the Philosophers faine. For if you aske for what cause one dog hath more instinct than another, both coming of one kind, and whelpes of one sire, I cannot coniecture what they may answer, save to flie backe to their old leaning post, saying, That God hath taught the one better than the other, and given him a more naturall instinct. And if we demaund the reason, why this good hound, being yet but a whelpe, is a perfect hunter, and growing in age, hath no such sufficiencie: and contrariewise, another being yoong cannot hunt at all, and waxing old, is wylie and readie; I know not what they can yeeld in replie. My selfe at least would say, that the towardly hunting of one dog more than an other, growes from the better temperature of his brain: and againe, that his well hunting whilest he is yoong, and his decay in age, is occasioned by means that in one age he partakes the temperature which is requisit to the qualities of hunting, and in the other not. Whence we infer, that sithens the temperature of the foure first qualities is the reason and cause, for which one brute beast better performs the works of his kind than another, that this temperature is the schoolemaister which teacheth the sensitive soule what it is to do. . . .

. . . The child so soone as it is borne, knowes to sucke, and fashion his lips to draw foorth the milke, and this so redily, as not the wisest man can do the like. And herewithall, it assures the qualities which are incident to the preservation of his nature, shuns that which is noisome and dammageable thereunto, knowes to weepe and laugh, without being taught by any. And if this be not so, let the vulgar Philosophers tell me awhile, who hath taught the children to do these things, or by what sence they have learned it. Well I know they will answer, That God hath given them this naturall instinct as to the brute beasts, wherein they say not ill, if the naturall instinct be the selfe same with the temperature.

15.5

Kenelm Digby

(1603–1665)

Digby constructs a chain of hypotheses to demonstrate that the breeding and nesting behavior of birds, taken as an example of instinctive behavior generally, can be explained as a series of mechanically forced responses. His emphasis on the bird's discomfort as a motivating force essentially repeats an argument which Seneca had already rejected in the first century.

[First Treatise. Ch XXXVII, 4.] But it is time that we come to the third sort of actions performed by beastes, which we promised to discourse of. These seeme to be more admirable, then any we have yet touched: and are chiefly concerning the breeding of their yong ones. Above all others, the orderly course of birds in this affaire is most remarkable. After they have coupled they make their nest, they line it with mosse, straw, and feathers; they lay their egges, they sett upon them, they hatch them, they feede their yong ones, and they teach them to flye: all which they do with so continuate and regular a methode, as no man can direct or imagine a better.

But as for the regularity, orderlinesse, and continuance of these actions, the matter is easy enough to be conceived: for seeing that the operation of the male, maketh a change in the female; and that this change beginning from the very first, groweth by time into divers proportions; it is no wonder that it breedeth divers dispositions in the female, which cause her to do different actions, correspondent to those divers dispositions. Now, those actions must of necessity be constant and orderly, because the causes whence they proceed, are such.

But to determine in particular, how it cometh to passe, that every change in the female, disposeth her to such and such actions, there is the difficulty; and it is no small one: as well, for that there are no carefull and due observations, made of the effects and circumstances, which should guide us to judge of their causes; as because these actions, are the most refined ones of sensitive creatures; and do flow from the toppe and perfection of their nature; and are the last straine of their utmost vigour, unto which all others are subordinate. . . .

So I conceive, it will be sufficient for us in this, to shew how these actions may be done by the senses, and by the motion of corporeall spirits, and by materiall impressions upon them; without being con-

Two treatises. In the one of which, the nature of bodies; in the other, the nature of mans soule; is looked into. Paris, 1664. [Pp. 322–324, 326–327.]

371

strained to resort unto an immateriall principle, which must furnish birdes with reason and discourse: in which, it is not necessary for my purpose, to determine precisely every steppe, by which these actions are performed, and to settle the rigorous truth of them: but leaving that unto those, who shall take paines to deliver the history of their nature, I will content my selfe with the possibility and probability of my coniectures. The first of which qualities, I am obliged to make plaine, but the later concerneth this treatise no more, then it would do a man to enquire anxiously into the particulars of what it is that a beast is doing, whiles looking upon it, at a great distance, he perceiveth plainely that it moveth it selfe: and his arrant is, but to be assured whether it be alive or dead: which the moving of it selfe in common, doth sufficiently demonstrate, without descending into a particular search, of what his motions are.

But lett us come to the matter: first, I conceive no man will make any difficulty in allowing, that it is the temper of the bloud and spirits in birdes (brought thereunto by the quality of their foode, and by the season of the yeare) which maketh them accouple with one an other; and not any ayme or desire of having yong ones, that occasioneth this action in them. Then it followeth that the hennes egges will encrease in her belly; and when they grow bigge, they can not choose but be troublesome unto her; and therefore, must of necessity breede in her an inclination to rest in some soft place, and to be ridde of them. And as we see a dogg or a catt pressed by nature, searcheth about to find a convenient place to disburthen themselves in, not only of their yong ones, but even of their excrements; so do birdes, whose egges within them, making them heavy and unfitt to flye, they beginn to sitt much, and are pleased in a soft and warme place: and thereupon, they are delighted with strawes and mosse, and other gentle substances; and so carry them to their sitting place: which that they do not by designe, is evident by the manner of it; for when they have mette with a straw or other fitt materiall, they fly not with it directly to their nest, but first to a bough of some tree, or to the toppe of a house; and there they hoppe and dance a while with it in their beakes; and from thence skippe to an other place, where they entertaine themselves in like manner: and at the last, they gett to their nest: where if the strawes should lye confusedly, their endes would pricke and hurt them: and therefore they turne and alter their positions till they lye smooth: which we that looke upon the effect, and compare them with our performing of like actions (if we had occasion) may call a iuditious ordering of them, whereas in them, it is nothing but removing such thinges as presse upon their sense, untill they cause them no more paine or unquietnesse.

Their plastering of their nestes, may be attributed to the great heat raigning in them at that time; which maketh them still be dabbling in moist clay, and in water, and in gravell, (without which, all birdes will soone grow sicke, blind, and at length dye) which for the coolnesse of it, they bring home to their nestes in their beakes and upon their feete; and when it groweth dry, and consequently troublesome to them, they wipe it off, and rubbe their durty parts upon the place where they use to sitt; and then flye for more to refresh themselves withall.

Out of all which actions (sett on foote by the wise orderer of nature, to compasse a remote end, quite different from the immediate end that every one of them is done for) there resulteth a fitt and convenient place for these litle builders (that know not why they do, whiles they build themselves houses) to lye in, and to lay their egges in. Which the next yeare, when the like occasion occureth, they build againe, peradventure then, as much through memory of the former, as upon their temper and other circumstances, moving their fantasy in such sort as we have sett downe. . . .

And thus you see how this long *series* of actions, may have orderly causes, made and chained together, by him that knew what was fitting for the worke he went about. Of which, though it is likely I have missed of the right ones (as it can not choose but happen in all disquisitions, where one is the first to break the yce, and is so slenderly informed of the particular circumstances of the matter in question, as I professe to be in this) yet I conceive this discourse doth plainely shew, that he who hath done more than we are able to comprehend and understand, may have sett causes sufficient for all these effects, in a better order, and in compleater rankes, then those which we have here expressed: and yet in them so coursely hewed out, appeareth a possibility of having the work done by corporeall agents. Surely it were very well worth the while, for some curious and iuditious person, to observe carefully and often, the severall steppes of nature in this progresse: for I am strongly persuaded, that by such industry, we might in time arrive to very particular knowledge of the immediate and precise causes, that worke all these effects. And I conceive, that such observation needeth not be very troublesome; as not requiring any great variety of creatures to institute it upon; for by marking carefully all that passeth among our homebred hennes, I beleeve it were easy to guesse very neerely at all the rest.

15.6

Walter Charleton

(1619–1707)

Charleton was a physician of some note, one of the founding members of the Royal Society of London and a president of the Royal College of Surgeons. He was one of the first to accept Harvey's theory of the circulation of the blood, and he was the principal advocate in England of the Epicurean revival initiated by Gassendi in France. In advocating this atomistic philosophy, he took pains to emphasize that his religious views remained orthodox, and in fact he did not extend it, as Hobbes did, to the explanation of all human reason. Like Digby, he tried to explain all animal behavior on purely physical grounds (compare the selection on animal learning, 13.5), and for his analysis of instinct he uses the old stock example of the sheep's "antipathy" to the wolf. (The behavior itself is no myth, and Weyer (cf. 24.4) tells a story about a trickster who made a good income by ridding barns of evil spirits until his secret had been discovered, which was to secrete a fresh wolf pelt under the barn, which he would then as secretly remove to earn his fee.)

[Book III. Ch IV, I.] In the THIRD and last Division of *Special* Occult Qualities, or such as are vulgarly imputed to *Sensible* Creatures; the Pens of Schollars have been so profuse, that should we but recount, and with all possible succinctness, enquire into the Verity and Causes of but the one Half of them; our Discourses would take up more sheets of Paper, than are allowed to the Longest Chancery Bill: wherefore, as in the former, so in this, we shall select and examine only a Few of them, but such as are most in vogue, and whose Reasons, if judiciously accomodated, suffice to the Solution of the Rest.

[2] (1) The *Antipathy of a Sheep to a Woolf*, is the common argument of wonder; and nothing is more frequent, than to hear men ascribe it to a provident Instinct, or haereditary and invincible Hatred, that a Lamb, which never saw a Woolf before, and so could not retain the impression of any harme done or attempted by him, should be invaded with horror and trembling at first interview, and run from him: nay, some have magnified the secret so far, as to affirme the Antipathy to be Equall on both sides. Concerning this, therefore, we observe; that the Enmity is not Reciprocal: For, He that can be persuaded, that the Woolf hates the Sheep, only because he worries and preys upon him, and not

Physiologia Epicuro-Gassendo-Charletoniana: or a fabric of natural science erected upon the most ancient hypothesis of atoms. London, 1654. [Pp. 362–363.]

rather, that the Woolf loves the sheep, because it is a weak and helpless Animal, and its flesh is both pleasant and convenient food for him: we shall not despair to persuade Him, that Himself also hates a sheep, because he finds his pallate and stomach delighted and relieved with Mutton. Nor is the Enmity on the sheeps side Invincible; for, ourselves have seen a Lamb brought, by Custom, to so great familiarity with a Woolf, that He would play with him, and bleat, as after the Dam when the Woolf hath removed out of the room: and the like kindness have we very lately observed betwixt a Lamb and Lyon of the Lord Generall *Cromwells*, kept at *Sion* house, and afterward publikely shewed in *London*. Again, the Fear, which surpriseth the Lamb at first sight of a Woolf, seems not to arise from any Hereditary Impression derived from the Dam, or Sire, or Both; as well because all Inbredd or traduced Antipathies are invincible, as that none of the Progenitors of the Lamb, for many Ages, ever saw or received any impression of injury from a Woolf, here with us in *England*. Besides, in case they had, and though it be indisputable, that some Beasts are afraid of men, and other Beasts, meerly from the memory of some Harme received from some man, or Beast of the same species; the Idea of him, that did the Harme, remaining impressed upon the table of the Memory, and being freshly brought again to the Phansy, whenever the sense brings in the like species: yet is it not likely, that the same Idea should be propagated by Generation to the issue, after so many hundred removes, and traduced from one Individual to the whole species, throughout the world.

The Cause, therefore, why All Sheep generally are startled and offended at sight of a Woolf, seems to be only this; that when the Woolf converts his eyes upon a sheep, as a pleasing and inviting object, and that whereupon Appetite hath wholly engaged his Imagination, he instantly darts forth from his brain certain streams of subtle Effluvia's, which being part of thos Spirits, whereof his newly formed Idea of dilaniating and devouring the sheep, is composed, serve as Forerunners or Messengers of destruction to the sheep; and being transmitted to his Common Sensory, through his optick nerves, most highly misaffect the same, and so cause the sheep to fear, and endeavour the praeservation of his life, by flight.

[3.] This receives sufficient Confirmation from hence; that not only such Aversions, as arise from the Contrariety of Constitutions in several Animals, are commonly observed to produce those Effects of Fear, Trembling and flight from the objects, from which offensive impressions are derived, by the mediation of disagreeing Spirits or Emanations: but even the seeing them in a passion of Anger, or Fury, doth suddainly cause the like. For, violent Passions ever alter the Spirits, and Characterize them with the idea at that time most praevalent in the Imagination of the Passionate; so that those spirits issuing from the body of the Animal, in that height of Passion, and insinuating themselves into the brain of the other Animal contrarily disposed, must of necessity highly disgust and offend it. Which is the most likely Reason that hath hitherto been given, Why *Bees* seldom sting men of a mild and peaceful disposition: but will by no means endure, nor be reconciled to others of a froward, cholerick, and waspish nature. The same also may serve to answer that common Quaere, Why some *Bold and Confident* persons, having tuned their spirits to the highest key of Anger and Indignation, have *daunted* not only fierce *Mastiffs,* but even *Lyons, Panthers,* and other Wild and ravenous Beasts, meerly by their threatening looks, and put them to flight by the Artillery of their scornful Eyes. And this Key, wherewith we have unlockt the secret betwixt the Lamb and Woolf, will also open those like Antipathies supposed to be betwixt the *Dove* and *Falcon,* the *Chicken* and *Kite,* and all other weak Animals, and such as use to make them their prey.

15.7

Étienne Bonnot de Condillac

(1715–1780)

Condillac was an extreme reductionist who went beyond Locke by reducing all knowledge and all mental processes to effects of sensation (see 15.6). If correct, his theory had to apply to animals as well as men, and in this book he seeks to demonstrate that it does. Condillac, who frequented the fashionable intellectual salons of Paris, describes animals which are no more real than his famous statue was a man. Nevertheless, the major thesis of this discussion was accepted and argued forcibly by Georges Le Roy (see 21.8), a man who did have firsthand acquaintance with animals. Condillac had enormous influence on French thinking during the last half of the eighteenth century, and it soon became the fashion to sneer at instinct and to dismiss it as a meaningless word.

We commonly say that animals are limited to instinct, and that reason is man's lot. These two words, *instinct* and *reason,* which are not at all explained, satisfy everyone, and they take the place of a reasoned system.

Instinct is either nothing, or it is the beginning of knowledge; for the actions of animals can depend on only three principles: pure mechanism; blind feeling which neither compares nor judges; or feeling which compares, judges, knows. Now, I have shown that the two first principles are absolutely inadequate.

Traité des animaux [Treatise on animals]. Paris, 1755. [Pp. 105–112.]

15.7 Étienne Bonnot de Condillac

But what degree of knowledge is it that constitutes instinct? This is something which must vary according to the organization of different animals. Those that have a greater number of senses and of needs more often have occasion to make comparisons and to perform judgments. Their instinct therefore comprises a greater degree of knowledge. It is not possible to determine this [with precision]: it is greater or less even from one individual to another of the same species. Therefore we must not be satisfied to look upon instinct as a principle which directs the animal in an altogether mysterious manner. We must not be satisfied with comparing all the actions of beasts with those movements which we make, as we say, mechanically, as if this word *mechanically* explained everything. But let us investigate how these movements are made, and we will form a precise idea of what is called *instinct*.

If we want to look and to walk merely in order to go from one place to another, it is not always necessary to think about it; we often look and walk merely by habit. But if we wish to discern more things in objects, or if we wish to walk more gracefully, then reflection must guide us; it must govern our faculties, until we have made a habit of this new way of looking or walking. Then it will have nothing more to do, until we want to do something we have not done before, until we have new needs, or seek to use new means to satisfy those we already have.

Thus there are in a way two *selves* in each man: the self of habit and the self of reflection. The first looks, touches, directs all the animal faculties. Its purpose is to guide the body, to protect it from all accident, continuously to keep watch for its preservation.

The second, abandoning all the details to the first, turns to other things. It occupies itself with the concern of adding to our pleasures. Its successes increase its desires, its failures renew them with greater strength. Obstacles are so many spurs, curiosity stirs it ceaselessly, industry shapes its character. The former is activated by objects whose impressions produce in the soul ideas, needs, and desires which determine appropriate bodily movements that are necessary for the conservation of the animal. The latter is excited by all those things which, by arousing our curiosity, lead us to increase our needs. . . .

Now if we subtract the reflecting self from a complete man, one can see that, having only the self of habit, he would no longer know how to conduct himself when he experiences one of those needs which call for new views and new combinations. But he would still conduct himself perfectly well whenever he had to do nothing but repeat what he was used to doing. The self of habit suffices, then, for the needs which are absolutely necessary for the conservation of the animal. Now instinct is nothing but this habit deprived of reflection.

In truth, it is by reflection that animals acquire instinct, but since they have few needs, the time soon comes when they have done everything that reflection can teach them. Nothing remains for them except to repeat the same things day by day. Therefore they do not need anything but habits, and they should be limited to instinct. . . .

These principles once established, it is easy to see why the instinct of beasts is sometimes surer than our reason, and even than our habits.

Having few needs they form few habits; always doing the same things, they do them better. . . .

Instinct is therefore better proportioned to the needs of beasts, than reason is to our own, and that is why it ordinarily seems so sure. . . .

. . . Our judgments would be just as sure, if we used judgment as little as they. We fall into more errors, only because we acquire more knowledge. Of all creatures, the one that is least likely to be deceived is the one that has the smallest share of intelligence.

15.8

Hermann Samuel Reimarus

(1694–1768)

In the period following Condillac, most writers dismissed instinct as a metaphysical-religious notion. (An important exception is Bonnet. In De la contemplation de la nature (1764), he wrote à la Digby: "I will not say that the spider spreads its net to capture flies, but that it captures flies because it spreads its net . . . and it spreads its net because it has a need to spin.") Reimarus, a Deist, presented a theory of instinct from the standpoint of "natural theology," or the argument that nature's evident design is proof of divine creation. The book was soon translated into French and exercised great influence. It is not without reason that German writers especially regard this book as the beginning of modern instinct theory.

56. An orderly skill in the performance of voluntary actions, which serves a certain purpose even though it may undergo numerous variations, is called an *art*. Animals by nature possess such orderly skills in their voluntary actions, and, although numerous deviations are inherently possible, these actions serve for the preservation and welfare of themselves and of their species; therefore animals by nature possess certain *innate arts*. And since each animal has a natural urge, that is, an instinct, to exercise its innate arts for the satisfaction of its needs, therefore each

Allgemeine Betrachtungen über die Triebe der Thiere, hauptsächlich über ihre Kunsttriebe [General observations on the instincts of animals, particularly regarding their instinctual arts. 1760.] Zweite Ausgabe. Hamburg, 1762. [Pp. 94–97, 304–305, 317–320.]

378

according to its kind does possess certain natural *instinctual arts,* which give them the aptitude to regularly apply special means for the preservation and welfare of themselves and their species.

Because we humans for the most part possess only acquired arts and skills, we commonly merge the essential concept of a skill or ability with the idea that it is acquired by diligent practice. But the cause of a thing, and the way it is brought about, really have nothing to do with its essential concept. Plants and animal bodies are just as much machines as clocks are, even if they are not made by human hands, but by nature. The movement of natural bodies is just as much movement as that which men bring about in their own limbs and in other bodies. So even if humans themselves had no performance skills which were not acquired, would it follow that none can be innate in animals? I think this would no more follow than that animals cannot be born with hair, wool, feathers and shells because men are born naked, and must prepare all their coverings by their own effort. However, I will show below that men also possess some innate performance skills, though fewer than animals, and I shall try to develop a concept of their *a priori* possibility; therefore human skills also must be divided into the innate and the acquired. . . .

57. Accordingly, the concept of instinctual arts contains nothing that is merely an arbitrary intellectual construction, which might be deceptive. Whether we call them instincts, impulses, arts, artlike, or instinctual arts, or do without all of these words, experience still clearly shows us that animals are moved to perform certain similar actions, which constitute the most serviceable means for preservation and welfare of themselves and their species, and that they display an orderly skill in these actions the very first time that they perform them, which sometimes is immediately after birth. Now, when a word is used to denote something which evident experience shows to be real, one cannot truthfully say that it is a meaningless word, a mere empty sound. [In a long footnote, Reimarus points out that such words as *lightning* and *gravity* would also be without meaning, if we were required to have an adequate explanation for every phenomenon we named.] . . .

130(6). It is possible that certain animals have sensations of a kind which men do not know about and of which we can form no conception. Material things have many powers, and they can act on one another in thousands of ways. It is only a matter of having the organs that are capable of receiving the impression. Without such organs, the material characteristics cannot be recognized. If we did not have a nose, or if its nerve surface were not equipped to receive the special impressions of sulphurous effluvia, we would not know what a smell is, and we would not understand how animals can track down and discover this or that remote object, which they can neither see nor hear. But it is evident that many species of animals have some organs which men do not possess, and that these do not serve the animals for locomotion, although they may move these organs as if they were trying thereby to discover the characteristics of material objects. We also notice in the behavior of animals that they must have sensations from many things, and many attributes or changes in things, which we cannot detect with any of our senses or sense organs; in particular, as regards changes to come in the weather, some animals are like living forecasting barometers, thermometers and hygrometers. Therefore it is possible that many animal species have one or more senses which are not included among the five known senses. . . .

132. We thus recognize that all animals are equipped with the necessary senses, some with senses sharper and finer than those of men, and perhaps also with quite different ones; that they therefore sense many things of which we do not feel a trace, or that in their perceptions they are capable of more acute discrimination than we. Also, that the internal structure of their sense organs, and the pleasure or displeasure which they experience thereby from external things, is entirely in agreement with the manner of their living and provides them, in the absence of reason, with an almost infallible stimulus; so that they recognize everything which is genuinely either good or bad for them, and then either approach or flee as indicated. . . . Just the animals' sharp sense of smell, for example, gives us much insight into how they are able to find suitable food and prey; how they can so precisely recognize and discriminate their own kind and other species; how they avoid and flee many harmful objects and other animals; remove excrement and the dead from their nests; discover and trace a desired path. . . . These external senses must then provide the soul with impressions and perceptions such that, due to a natural connection with their bodies, they are blindly determined to perform harmonious movements of certain muscles and organs which are suited thereto, and almost fully prepared. I say that voluntary movements are blindly determined because the soul is not conscious of the source of its inclinations, nor does it knowingly decide to excite a movement in this or that part of the body. This natural connection between sensations and blindly willed movements of certain parts is indeed a mystery, the operation of which we shall never be able to understand; but it is based on the experience of men as well as animals, and I have given clear examples of it, which show the secret understanding between the soul and the mechanical excitations of bodily parts, or the influence of our sensitive being over the preformed mechanism. I include among these, yawning at the sight of someone who yawns, the eyes tearing at the sight of eyes with ugly sores, the mouth watering in the presence of food, vomiting because of a nauseating idea, weeping from sorrow, laughing from joy, blushing from shame, and tumescence of the genital organs because of lascivious thoughts. But if we want examples more definitely useful, then we think about the onset and continuance of respiration in infants, their crying because of pain, sucking and swallowing milk, facial expressions with which they communicate their feelings, and other actions

which are excited either by pleasure or displeasure. In all of these there is a predetermined mechanism which is brought into action by a sense stimulus and blind will, and which may be called a *sensory mechanism*. Many animal acts seem to be so formed, where everything in the body is arranged and ready for the movement in advance, needing only a first push from the sensory impression and from blind appetite—just as a fireworks display is all arranged on the stage, so that with a single spark and a push it goes into action and gives the whole desired performance.

15.9

William Smellie

(1740–1795)

Beyond its immediate relevance to the topic of instinct, this is a good statement of the view that excessive concern with the dignity of man keeps us from studying the mechanism of behavior in an objective manner. Although Smellie maintains that man has a rich instinctual endowment, he does not carry this so far as to question that distance perception must be learned. This work was continued in a second volume published posthumously (see 19.8). As a young man he edited the first edition of the Encyclopedia Brittanica (3 volumes, 1771).

The author is not to be identified with the famous obstetrician of the same name who died in 1763.

[Ch. V.] Many theories have been invented with a view to explain the instinctive actions of animals; but none of them have received the general approbation of Philosophers. This want of success in the investigation of a subject so curious and so interesting must be owing to the operation of some powerful causes. Two of these causes appear to be a want of attention to the general oeconomy and manners of animals, and mistaken notions concerning the dignity of human nature. From perusing the compositions of most authors who have written upon animal instinct, it is evident, that they have chiefly derived their ideas, not from the various mental qualities discoverable in different species of animals, but from the feelings and propensities of their own minds. Some of them, at the same time, are so averse to allow brutes a participation of that intellect which man possesses in such an eminent degree, that they consider every animal action to be the result of pure mechanism. But the

The philosophy of natural history. Edinburgh, 1790. [Pp. 144–146, 150–153, 155–156, 158–159.]

great source of error on this subject is the uniform attempt to distinguish instinctive from rational motives. I shall, however, endeavour to show that no such distinction exists, and that the reasoning faculty itself is a necessary result of instinct. . . .

I.   *Of Pure Instincts*

By *pure* instincts, I mean those, which, independent of all instruction or experience, instantaneously produce certain actions when particular objects are presented to animals, or when they are influenced by peculiar feelings. Of this class the following are examples.

In the human species, the instinct of sucking is exerted immediately after birth. This instinct is not excited by any smell peculiar to the mother, to milk or to any other substance; for infants suck indiscriminately every thing brought into contact with their mouths. The desire for sucking, therefore, is innate, and coeval with the appetite for air.

The voiding of urine and excrement, sneezing, retraction of the muscles upon the application of any painful stimulus, the moving of the eye-lids, and other parts of the body, are likewise effects of original instincts, and essential to the existence of young animals.

The love of light is exhibited by infants at a very early period. I have remarked evident symptoms of this attachment on the third day after birth. When children are farther advanced, marks of the various passions gradually appear. The passion of fear is discoverable at the age of two months. It is called forth by approaching the hand to the child's eye, and by any sudden motion or unusual noise. I once instituted a course of experiments to ascertain the periods when the various passions, principles, or propensities, of the human mind are unfolded, and to mark the causes which first produced them. But, in less than five months after the birth of the child, the business became too complicated and extensive for the time I had to bestow on subjects of this nature.

The brute creation affords innumerable examples of pure instincts. . . .

II.   *Of instincts which can accommodate themselves to peculiar circumstances and situations*

To this class many human instincts may be referred. But, as these instinctive propensities are likewise highly improveable by experience and observation, examples of them will fall more naturally to be given under the third class. . . .

The ostrich has been accused of unnaturalness, because she leaves her eggs to be hatched by the heat of the sun. In Senegal, where the heat is great, she neglects her eggs during the day, but sits upon them in the night. At the Cape of Good Hope, however, where the degree of heat is less, the ostrich, like other birds, sits upon her eggs both day and night. . . .

In countries infested with monkeys, many birds, which, in other climates, build in bushes and the clefts of trees, suspend their nests upon slender twigs, and, by this ingenious device, elude the rapacity of their enemies. . . .

III. *The third class comprehends all those instincts which are improveable by experience and observation*

The superiority of man over the other animals seems to depend chiefly on the great number of instincts with which his mind is endowed. Traces of every instinct he possesses are discoverable in the brute creation. But no particular species enjoys the whole. On the contrary, most animals are limited to a small number. This appears to be the reason why the instincts of brutes are stronger, and more steady in their operation, than those of man. A being actuated by a great variety of motives must necessarily reason, or, in other words, hesitate in his choice. Its conduct, therefore, must often waver; and he will have the appearance of being inferior to another creature who is stimulated by a smaller number of motives. Man, accordingly, has been considered as the most vacillant and inconsistent of all animals. The remark is just; but, instead of a censure, it is an encomium on the species. The actions of a dog, or a monkey, for the same reason, are more various, whimsical, and uncertain, than those of a sheep or a cow.

Most human instincts receive improvement from experience and observation, and are capable of a thousand modifications. This is another source of man's superiority over the brutes. When we are stimulated by a particular instinct, instead of instantly obeying the impulse, another instinct arises in opposition, creates hesitation, and often totally extinguishes the original motive to action. The instinct of fear is daily counteracted by ambition or resentment; and, in some minds, fear is too powerful for resentment, or any other instinct we possess. The instinct of anger is often restrained by the apprehension of danger, by the sense of propriety, by contempt, and even by compassion. Sympathy, which is one of our most amiable instincts, frequently yields to anger, ambition, and other motives. The instinct or sense of morality is too often thwarted by ambition, resentment, love, fear, and several of what I call modified or compound instincts, such as avarice, envy, &c. . . .

From the examples I have given, it appears that instinct is an original quality of mind, which, in many animals, may be improved, modified, and extended, by experience; that some instincts are coeval with birth; and that others, as fear, anger, the principle of imitation, and the power of reasoning, or balancing motives, are gradually unfolded, according to the exigencies of the animal. One of the strongest instincts appears not till near the age of puberty; but, by bad example, and improper situations, this instinctive desire is often prematurely excited. . . . Instincts exist before they act. . . . Instinct should be limited to such actions as every individual of a species exerts without the aid either of experience or imitation. Hence instinct may be defined, 'Every original quality of mind which produces particular feelings or actions, when the proper objects are presented to it.' . . . Insects have fewer instincts than men or quadrupeds, but the exertions of insects are so uniform and steady, that they excite the admiration of every beholder. . . .

This view of instinct is simple, removes every objection to the existence of mind in brutes, and unfolds all their actions, by referring them to motives perfectly similar to those by which man is actuated. There is, perhaps, a greater difference between the mental powers of some animals than between those of man and the most sagacious brutes. Instincts may be considered as so many internal senses, of which some animals have a greater, and others a smaller number. These senses, in different species, are likewise more or less ductile; and the animals possessing them are, of course, more or less susceptible of improving, and of acquiring knowledge. . . .

Brutes, like men, learn to see objects in their proper position, to judge of distances and heights, and of hurtful, pleasureable, or indifferent bodies. Without some portion of reason, therefore, they could never acquire the faculty of making a proper use of their senses. . . .

From the above facts and reasoning, it seems to be apparent, that instincts are original qualities of mind; that every animal is possessed of some of these qualities; that the intelligence and resources of animals are proportioned to the number of instincts with which their minds are endowed; that all animals are, in some measure, rational beings; and that the dignity and superiority of the human intellect are necessary results, not of the conformation of our bodies, but of the great variety of instincts which nature has been pleased to confer on the species.

15.10

Erasmus Darwin

(1731–1802)

The grandfather of Charles Darwin earned respect throughout Europe for theoretical works which have never been surpassed as examples of uncompromising reductionism. On the other hand, his boldness in this book, his most important work, led him to anticipate, as his grandson later remarked, "the views and erroneous grounds of opinions of Lamarck." In the treatment of instinct, we take in stride the explanation of postnatal responses as developed by intrauterine practice, because this has become a familiar idea in the twentieth century, but we are startled when the expressive features of fear are explained on the basis of a single association with the accidental events of birth, in preference to admitting that they may be due to a native organization.

This book provided the young Thomas Brown with an opportunity to establish his reputation by a merciless detailed critique (Observations on the Zoonomia of Erasmus Darwin, 1798). Regarding instinct, Brown wrote:

> Those who defend instinct as a "divine something, a kind of inspiration," are, indeed, worthy of ridicule. But, if by the term instinct be meant *a predisposition to certain actions, when certain sensations exist*, the admission of it is so far from being ridiculous, that, without it, the phenomena of animation cannot possibly be explained. Instinctive actions, therefore, are . . . to be considered, as the result of principles, original in the frame; so that, when the mind is affected, in a certain manner, a certain action, independently of experience, necessarily ensues.

II. We experience some sensations, and perform some actions before our nativity; the sensations of cold and warmth, agitation and rest, fulness and inanition, are instances of the former; and the repeated struggles of the limbs of the foetus, which begin about the middle of gestation, and those motions by which it frequently wraps the umbilical cord around its neck or body, and even sometimes ties it on a knot; are instances of the latter.

By a due attention to these circumstances many of the actions of young animals, which at first sight seemed only referable to an inexplicable instinct, will appear to have been acquired like all other animal actions, that are attended with consciousness, *by the repeated efforts of our muscles under the conduct of our sensations or desires.*

Zoonomia, or the laws of organic life. 2 vols. London, 1794–1796. [Vol. 1, pp. 137–141, 146–148.]

The chick in the shell begins to move its feet and legs on the sixth day of incubation (Mattreican); or on the seventh day (Langley); afterwards they are seen to move themselves gently in the liquid that surrounds them, and to open and shut their mouths (Harvey). Puppies before the membranes are broken, that involve them, are seen to move themselves, to put out their tongues, and to open and shut their mouths, (Harvey, Gipson, Riolan, Haller). And calves lick themselves and swallow many of their hairs before their nativity: which however puppies do not, (Swammerdam, Flemyng). And towards the end of gestation, the foetus of all animals are proved to drink part of the liquid in which they swim, (Haller). . . .

III. It has been deemed a surprising instance of instinct, that calves and chickens should be able to walk by a few efforts almost immediately after their nativity: whilst the human infant in those countries where he is not incumbered with clothes, as in India, is five or six months, and in our climate almost a twelvemonth, before he can safely stand upon his feet.

The struggles of all animals in the womb must resemble their mode of swimming, as by this kind of motion they can best change their attitude in the water. But the swimming of the calf and chicken resemble their manner of walking, which they thus have in part acquired before their nativity, and hence accomplish it afterwards with very few efforts, whilst the swimming of the human creature resembles that of the frog, and totally differs from his mode of walking. . . .

IV. From the facts mentioned in No. 2 of this Section, it is evinced that the foetus learns to swallow before its nativity; for it is seen to open its mouth, and its stomach is found filled with the liquid that surrounds it. It opens its mouth, either instigated by hunger, or by the irksomeness of a continued attitude of the muscles of its face; the liquor amnii, in which it swims, is agreeable to its palate, as it consists of a nourishing material, (Haller). It is tempted to experience its taste further in the mouth, and by a few efforts learns to swallow, in the same manner as we learn all other animal actions, which are attended with consciousness, *by the repeated efforts of our muscles under the conduct of our sensations or volitions.*

The inspiration of air into the lungs is so totally different from that of swallowing a fluid in which we are immersed, that it cannot be acquired before our nativity. But at this time, when the circulation of the blood is no longer continued through the placenta, that suffocating sensation, which we feel about the precordia, when we are in want of fresh air, disagreeably affects the infant; and all the muscles of the body are excited into action to relieve this oppression; those of the breast, ribs, and diaphragm are found to answer this purpose, and thus respiration is discovered, and is continued throughout our lives, as often as the oppression begins to recur. . . .

At length, by the direction of its sense of smell, or by the officious care of its mother, the young animal approaches the odoriferous rill of its future nourishment, already experienced to swallow. But in the act of swallowing, it is necessary nearly to close the mouth, whether the creature be immersed in the fluid it is about to drink, or not: hence, when the child first attempts to suck, it does not slightly compress the nipple between its lips, and suck as an adult person would do, by absorbing the milk; but it takes the whole nipple into its mouth for this purpose, compresses it between its gums, and thus repeatedly chewing (as it were) the nipple, presses out the milk; exactly in the same manner as it is drawn from the teats of cows by the hands of the milkmaid. The celebrated Harvey observes, that the foetus in the womb must have sucked in a part of its nourishment, because it knows how to suck the minute it is born, as any one may experience by putting a finger between its lips, and because in a few days it forgets this art of sucking, and cannot without some difficulty again acquire it (Excit. de gener. anim. 48). The same observation is made by Hippocrates.

A little further experience teaches the young animal to suck by absorption, as well as by compression; that is, to open the chest as in the beginning of respiration, and thus to rarefy the air in the mouth, that the pressure of the denser external atmosphere may contribute to force out the milk.

The chick yet in the shell has learnt to drink by swallowing a part of the white of the egg for its food; but not having experienced how to take up and swallow solid feeds, or grains, is either taught by the solicitous industry of its mother; or by many repeated attempts is enabled at length to distinguish and to swallow this kind of nourishment. . . .

VII. There are two ways by which we become acquainted with the passions of others: first, by having observed the effects of them, as of fear or anger, on our own bodies, we know at sight when others are under the influence of these affections. So when two cocks are preparing to fight, each feels the feathers rise round his own neck, and knows from the same sign the disposition of his adversary: and children long before they can speak, or understand the language of their parents, may be frightened by an angry countenance, or soothed by smiles and blandishments.

Secondly, when we put ourselves into the attitude that any passion naturally occasions, we soon in some degree acquire that passion. . . .

These then are the natural signs by which we understand each other, and on this slender basis is built all human language. For without some natural signs, no artificial ones could have been invented or understood, as is very ingeniously observed by Dr. Reid.

VIII. The origin of this universal language is a subject of the highest curiosity, the knowledge of which has always been thought utterly inaccessible. A part of which we shall however here attempt. . . .

1.   *Of Fear*

As soon as the young animal is born, the first important sensations, that occur to him, are occasioned by the oppression about his precordia for want of respiration, and by his sudden transition from ninety-eight degrees of heat into so cold a climate. —He trembles, that is, he exerts alternately all the muscles of his body, to enfranchise himself from the oppression about his bosom, and begins to breathe with frequent and short respirations; at the same time the cold contracts his red skin, gradually turning it pale; the contents of the bladder and of the bowels are evacuated: and from the experience of these first disagreeable sensations the passion of fear is excited, which is no other than the expectation of disagreeable sensations. This early association of motions and sensations persists throughout life; the passion of fear produces a cold and pale skin, with tremblings, quick respiration, and an evacuation of the bladder and bowels, and thus constitutes the natural or universal language of this passion.

15.11

Pierre Jean Georges Cabanis

(1757–1808)

Cabanis placed great stress on the distinction between the external senses, which before his time were almost the only senses considered as determinants of behavior, and the internal bodily senses—quite a different matter from the "internal senses" of the older psychology, such as imagination and memory. He believed that instinctive behavior consists largely of responses to internal sensation. He also stresses the importance of prenatal experience in establishing these responses, thus (like Erasmus Darwin) anticipating the theory presented in the twentieth century by Zing Yang Kuo.

. . . We have already recognized . . . that the action of the nervous system . . . consists in receiving impressions from its sensitive endings and bringing them together at a central point, from which, by a true reaction, there depart all the analogous and subsequent determinations which put into play all the parts [of the body] which fall within the

Rapports du physique et du moral de l'homme [Relations between the body and the mind of man. Paris, 1802]. Vols. III and IV of *Oeuvres complètes de Cabanis.* 5 vols. Paris, 1823–1825. [Vol. IV, pp. 317–319, 321, 323–325.]

sphere of activity of this same central point. We have established, further, that a greater or lesser number of these nervous centers may exist in an animal system, either primitively or through being formed by later habits of living, and although these are subordinated to the common center, they have their own way of feeling, exercise their own kind of influence, and often remain isolated in their respective domains, with respect to the impressions they receive or the movements they execute. We have also seen that the reaction in the common center assumes a volitional character, so that is where the *self* resides. All the centers act upon it in some measure, in proportion to their importance, and therefore the determinations formed within it embrace all of them, and relate to all their various functions and their special states. . . .

However, . . . there is an important difference of which we must take note. Since the *self* resides in the common center, all those operations which do not go outside the domains of the partial centers can produce no perceived judgment nor sensed volition. Because the impressions which come from the internal nerve endings are far from being so distinct, or susceptible to such methodical arrangement and classification, as those which are transmitted by the sense organs properly so called, there is always something confused and indeterminate about them and about their effects, as we easily recognize must be the case.

Thus the earliest tendencies and the first instinctive modes of action are a consequence of the laws of the formation and development of organs; they relate especially to the internal impressions and to the determinations which the latter produce in the entire animal system. Those that are formed in later periods of life depend more on the influence of the medley of impressions coming from the external world, which are gathered by the senses, but they always owe their birth to the state of the nervous ramifications which are spread through the viscera and the principal organs, and sometimes to the intimate disposition of the cerebral system itself. They always preserve some imprint of this vague character which shows that they have little dependence on the judgment and its will.

. . . In effect, all these instinctive tendencies are bound up with the intimate nature of the organization. Their first lines are no doubt engraved in the cerebral system at the very moment when the fetus is formed, and if they do not develop all their energy until the animal is nearly adult this is because, in order to be exercised, they need considerable strength in the organs. However this may be, we put into the second class of instinctive habits and determinations—that is, those which show themselves in later periods, more or less distant from the time of birth— penchants which are produced by the development of certain special organs: for example, those brought on by the maturity of the generative organs; appetite or distaste for certain foods, or certain remedies, which we notice in many ailments; instincts and even emotions which are foreign to the species but which are characteristic of certain strange affections of the nervous system.

... [In any case] the instinctive tendencies which appear in the course of life, like those which the animal manifests at birth, result from internal impressions which are in their origin absolutely independent of those received by the sense organs properly so called; although they soon are blended into all the sensations and they may be modified to a certain point by judgment and will.

The observations stated in this memoir, and those previously brought together in the physiological description of the sensations, leave not the slightest doubt about either the existence of a system of penchants and determinations which are formed by impressions that are almost foreign to those of the external world, or about the characteristics which distinguish these determinations and these penchants from the volitions based on judgments more or less clearly felt, but genuinely carried by the *self;* nor even about the circumstances which almost always intermingle and combine, and sometimes confuse, these two sorts of determinations. I dare to believe that these juxtaposed observations throw a new light on the study of man.

15.12

Johann Kaspar Spurzheim

(1776–1832)

As a theoretical structure, phrenology rested on three supports: the variety of innate behavioral dispositions, the dependence of these on neural structures, and the possibility of diagnosing individual differences from physiognomical characteristics, particularly from the shape of the skull. The weakness of this last leg caused it to topple, but it is a mistake to suppose that nothing can be salvaged from the remains. In this selection some shrewd observations on animal behavior provide a basis for questionable generalizations about human talents and interests.

On the Influence of Circumstances

It is a very common manner of speaking to say that suffering and deprivation cause animals and men to act; that necessity leads to invention;

Essai philosophique sur la nature morale et intellectuelle de l'homme [A philosophical essay on the moral and intellectual nature of man]. Paris, 1820. [Pp. 60–63.]

that it is the cause for the birth of talent; that revolutions produce great men; that society is the source of the needs and passions which are the great motives of human action; that food and climate determine our behavior; etc. In brief, that external circumstances create the faculties. . . .

On Suffering

Situations of suffering or pain are an important cause of activity in men and animals, for sensitive creatures love and seek pleasure, and have an aversion toward anything painful. Nightingales, quails, starlings, woodcocks, swallows, wild geese, and many other birds emigrate at certain seasons, because they lack food, or because the temperature is unfavorable to them. But neither cold nor lack of food suffices to make birds migrate, for sparrows and blackbirds remain throughout the winter, although they often perish from hunger and cold. On the other hand, nightingales leave us before the lack of food becomes apparent, and sometimes they return before they are able to obtain the insects which are their favorite food. The dog and the monkey, which astonish us by their intelligence, often have need to seek shelter from inclement weather. A dog can dig a burrow as well as a mole, and the monkey could construct a cabin by the use of his hands. But expose these animals to cold and rain, put the dog in a place where he could easily dig, give the monkey material for building, and see if they know how to protect themselves from inclement weather. Meanwhile, the beaver will use his talent as soon as you furnish him with tree branches, even if you keep him in a closed room. . . .

. . . A certain degree of suffering or unhappiness causes men and animals to act in accordance with the talents with which they have been endowed, but it does not produce their faculties. Introduce a dog into an enclosure where there are rabbits, squirrels and hares: the rabbits will burrow in their tunnels, the squirrels will climb the trees, and the hares will leap the wall. In the same way, different people who are reduced to the same state of suffering will draw on their special faculties: one escapes suffering through his talent for music, another by his mechanical skill, a third by his gift for language or mathematics, while still others have no resource except manual labor, or charity.

On the other hand, some people prefer poverty, when it is inseparable from the satisfaction of their talents, to an excellent position which would oblige them to renounce their favorite occupations. Thus, suffering serves only as a means of stimulation, but it does not give birth to any faculties.

15.13

William James

(1842–1910)

Like most of James's often-quoted chapters, that on "Instinct" appeared first in magazines of general circulation. (This chapter appeared in Scribner's Magazine and Popular Science Monthly during 1887.) But the ideas are seriously and clearly stated, and they exercised great influence on the next generation of American psychologists, Thorndike among them. As in every author who has written observantly on this question, there is a stress on the importance of the particular releasing stimulus. Like Smellie, James believes that humans have more instincts, not fewer, but he has a different explanation for why we fail to regard them as such. In fact, more than 40 pages of this chapter are given to a listing and description of instinctive behaviors in man, ranging from sucking and biting, constructiveness and play, cleanliness (why not, when it is so obvious in cats?), through modesty, and parental love.

This selection shows James's inimitable combination of subjective sensitivity, literary imagination, and physiological orientation.

INSTINCT is usually defined as the faculty of acting in such a way as to produce certain ends, without foresight of the ends, and without previous education in the performance. That instincts, as thus defined, exist on an enormous scale in the animal kingdom needs no proof. They are the functional correlatives of structure. With the presence of a certain organ goes, one may say, almost always a native aptitude for its use. . . .

. . . Although the naturalist may, for his own convenience, class these reactions under general heads, he must not forget that in the animal it is a particular sensation or perception or image which calls them forth.

At first this view astounds us by the enormous number of special adjustments it supposes animals to possess readymade in anticipation of the outer things among which they are to dwell. *Can* mutual dependence be so intricate and go so far? Is each thing born fitted to particular things, and to them exclusively, as locks are fitted to their keys? Undoubtedly this must be believed to be so. Each nook and cranny of creation, down to our very skin and entrails, has its living inhabitants, with organs suited to the place, to devour and digest the food it harbors and to meet the

Principles of psychology. 2 vols. New York, 1890. [Vol. II, pp. 383–388, 390–391, 394–395, 398, 400–402.]

dangers it conceals; and the minuteness of adaptation thus shown in the way of *structure* knows no bounds. Even so there are no bounds to the minuteness of adaptation in the way of *conduct* which the several inhabitants display.

The older writings on instinct are ineffectual wastes of words, because their authors never came down to this definite and simple point of view, but smothered everything in vague wonder at the clairvoyant and prophetic power of the animals—so superior to anything in man—and at the beneficence of God in endowing them with such a gift. But God's beneficence endows them, first of all, with a nervous system; and, turning our attention to this, makes instinct immediately appear neither more nor less wonderful than all the other facts of life. . . .

Now, why do the various animals do what seem to us such strange things, in the presence of such outlandish stimuli? Why does the hen, for example, submit herself to the tedium of incubating such a fearfully uninteresting set of objects as a nestful of eggs, unless she have some sort of a prophetic inkling of the result? The only answer is *ad hominem.* We can only interpret the instincts of brutes by what we know of instincts in ourselves. Why do men always lie down, when they can, on soft beds rather than on hard floors? Why do they sit round the stove on a cold day? Why, in a room, do they place themselves, ninetynine times out of a hundred, with their faces towards its middle rather than to the wall? Why do they prefer saddle of mutton and champagne to hard-tack and ditch-water? Why does the maiden interest the youth so that everything about her seems more important and significant than anything else in the world? Nothing more can be said than that these are human ways, and that every creature *likes* its own ways, and takes to the following of them as a matter of course. Science may come and consider these ways, and find that most of them are useful. But it is not for the sake of their utility that they are followed, but because at the moment of following them we feel that that is the only appropriate and natural thing to do. Not one man in a billion, when taking his dinner, ever thinks of utility. He eats because the food tastes good and makes him want more. If you ask him *why* he should want to eat more of what tastes like that, instead of revering you for a philosopher he will probably laugh at you for a fool. The connection between savory sensation and the act it awakens is for him absolute and *selbstverständlich,* an '*a priori* synthesis' of the most perfect sort, needing no proof but its own evidence. It takes, in short, what Berkeley calls a mind debauched by learning to carry the process of making the natural seem strange, so far as to ask for the *why* of any instinctive human act. To the metaphysician alone can such questions occur as: Why do we smile, when pleased, and not scowl? Why are we unable to talk to a crowd as we talk to a single friend? Why does a particular maiden turn our wits so upside-down? The common man can only say, *"Of course* we smile, *of course* our heart palpitates at the sight of the crowd, *of course* we love the maiden, that beautiful soul clad in that perfect form, so palpably and flagrantly made from all eternity to be loved!"

And so, probably, does each animal feel about the particular things it tends to do in presence of particular objects. They, too, are *a priori* syntheses. To the lion it is the lioness which is made to be loved; to the bear, the she-bear. To the broody hen the notion would probably seem monstrous that there should be a creature in the world to whom a nestful of eggs was not the utterly fascinating and precious and never-to-be-too-much-sat-upon object which it is to her.

Thus we may be sure that, however mysterious some animals' instincts may appear to us, our instincts will appear no less mysterious to them. And we may conclude that, to the animal which obeys it, every impulse and every step of every instinct shines with its own sufficient light, and seems at the moment the only eternally right and proper thing to do. It is done for its own sake exclusively. What voluptuous thrill may not shake a fly, when she at last discovers the one particular leaf, or carrion, or bit of dung, that out of all the world can stimulate her ovipositor to its discharge? Does not the discharge then seem to her the only fitting thing? And need she care or know anything about the future maggot and its food? . . .

. . . Man has a far greater variety of *impulses* than any other animal; and any one of these impulses, taken by itself, is as 'blind' as the lowest instinct can be; but, owing to man's memory, power of reflection, and power of inference, they come each one to be felt by him, after he has once yielded to them and experienced their results, in connection with a *foresight* of those results. . . . It is obvious that *every instinctive act, in an animal with memory, must cease to be 'blind' after being once repeated,* and must be accompanied with foresight of its 'end' just so far as that end may have fallen under the animal's cognizance. An insect that lays her eggs in a place where she never sees them hatched must always do so 'blindly;' but a hen who has already hatched a brood can hardly be assumed to sit with perfect 'blindness' on her second nest. . . .

It is plain, then, that, *no matter how well endowed an animal may originally be in the way of instincts, his resultant actions will be much modified if the instincts combine with experience,* if in addition to impulses he have memories, associations, inferences, and expectations, on any considerable scale. . . .

Here we immediately reap the good fruits of our simple physiological conception of what an instinct is. If it be a mere excito-motor impulse, due to the pre-existence of a certain 'reflex arc' in the nerve-centres of the creature, of course it must follow the law of all such reflex arcs. One liability of such arcs is to have their activity 'inhibited,' by other processes going on at the same time. It makes no difference whether the arc be organized at birth, or ripen spontaneously later, or be due to acquired habit, it must take its chances with all the other arcs, and sometimes succeed, and sometimes fail, in drafting off the currents through itself. The mystical view of an instinct would make it invariable. The physiological view would require it to show occasional irregularities in any animal in whom the number of separate instincts, and the possible entrance of the same stimulus into several of them, were great. And such irregularities are what every superior animal's instincts do show in abundance. . . .

1. The law of inhibition of instincts by habits is this: *When objects of a certain class elicit from an animal a certain sort of reaction, it often happens that the animal becomes partial to the first specimen of the class on which it has reacted, and will not afterward react on any other specimen.*

The selection of a particular hole to live in, of a particular mate, of a particular feeding-ground, a particular variety of diet, a particular anything, in short, out of a possible multitude, is a very wide-spread tendency among animals, even those low down in the scale. The limpet will return to the same sticking-place in its rock, and the lobster to its favorite nook on the sea-bottom. The rabbit will deposit its dung in the same corner; the bird makes its nest on the same bough. But each of these preferences carries with it an insensibility to *other* opportunities and occasions—an insensibility which can only be described physiologically as an inhibition of new impulses by the habit of old ones already formed. . . .

2. This leads us to the *law of transitoriness,* which is this: *Many instincts ripen at a certain age and then fade away.* A consequence of this law is that if, during the time of such an instinct's vivacity, objects adequate to arouse it are met with, a *habit* of acting on them is formed, which remains when the original instinct has passed away; but that if no such objects are met with, then no habit will be formed; and, later on in life, when the animal meets the objects, he will altogether fail to react, as at the earlier epoch he would instinctively have done. . . .

Leaving lower animals aside, and turning to human instincts, we see the law of transiency corroborated on the widest scale by the alternation of different interests and passions as human life goes on. With the child, life is all play and fairy-tales and learning the external properties of 'things;' with the youth, it is bodily exercises of a more systematic sort, novels of the real world, boon-fellowship and song, friendship and love, nature, travel and adventure, science and philosophy; with the man, ambition and policy, acquisitiveness, responsibility to others, and the selfish zest of the battle of life. . . . In all pedagogy the great thing is to strike the iron while hot, and to seize the wave of the pupil's interest in each successive subject before its ebb has come, so that knowledge may be got and a habit of skill acquired—a headway of interest, in short, secured, on which afterward the individual may float. . . .

The natural conclusion to draw from this transiency of instincts is that *most instincts are implanted for the sake of giving rise to habits, and that, this purpose once accomplished, the instincts themselves, as such, have no raison d'être in the psychical economy, and consequently fade away.* That occasionally an instinct should fade before circumstances permit of a habit being formed, or that, if the habit be formed, other factors than the pure instinct should modify its course, need not surprise us. Life is full of the imperfect adjustment to individual cases, of arrangements which, taking the species as a whole, are quite orderly and regular. Instincts cannot be expected to escape this general risk.

15.14

Zing Yang Kuo

(1898–1970)

The rise of behaviorism was accompanied by a vigorous anti-instinct movement, in which there was no more ardent crusader than Kuo. Neither his experimental shaping of the behavior of kittens toward rats, nor his patient observation of the appearance in embryo of components of later response patterns of the chick, can be considered as particularly important experimental evidence. But his impassioned theoretical discussions were extraordinarily convincing at the time, and they formulated the problem in the way many American investigators have viewed it ever since. This is the pure voice of behaviorism in its heyday, rejecting the possibility of any hereditary patterning of the nervous system as only a disguise for a psychic implant.

[A]

In reviewing the results of this study, one is impressed with the fact that the behavior of the cat toward the rat is much more complex and much more variable than most psychologists would have thought. Shall we explain such complexity and variability of the cat's behavior in terms of instinct or in terms of learning? I do not think that these concepts are adequate to describe the responses of the cat to the rat. Nor do we need

[A] The genesis of the cat's responses to the rat. *Journal of Comparative Psychology* 11 (1931): 1–35. [Pp. 32–35.]
[B] Ontogeny of embryonic behavior in aves. IV. The influence of embryonic movements upon the behavior after hatching. *Journal of Comparative Psychology* 14 (1932): 109–122. [Pp. 120–121.]

any such concepts. We have presented the actual behavior picture of the cat towards the rat in terms of stimulus and response together with the life history of the cat. Do we need to add that such responses are instinctive, such and such are learned by trial and error, and such and such are due to insight or ideation? Do we need to add that in our findings the cat shows instincts of rat-killing and rat-eating as well [as] the instinct to love the rat? Do we need to resort to such concepts as modification of instinct, periodicity of instinct, waning of instinct and the like in order to explain the results of our study?

The cat is a small-sized tiger. Its bodily make-up is especially fitted for capturing small animals; its body and legs are fitted for swift movements, its sharp paws and teeth are fitted for capturing and devouring; and its eyes and ears too, are very helpful in guiding its capturing responses. Here we have a machine so manufactured that under ordinary circumstances it will kill or even eat animals smaller than itself, such as rats, birds, etc. But its swift bodily make-up may also make it playful in response to small animals or small objects especially moving objects. Is it necessary to add that this machine has been endowed by heredity, through its nervous system with the instinct to kill rats and other small animals, and also another instinct to play with them? Should this machine become as large as a tiger, it may even ignore smaller animals such as rats, etc., but will seek to kill much larger ones including men. Shall we say then, that this larger machine possesses an instinct to kill man, and another instinct to pity and forgive rats and other smaller animals? To me, the organismic pattern (please note that I do not mean neural pattern!) or bodily make-up and the size should be sufficient to tell why the cat behaves like cat, the tiger like tiger or the monkey like monkey. The cat has a cat-body and hence the rat-killing behavior; the tiger has a tiger body, and hence man-killing behavior. The chimpanzee has a chimpanzee body, and so uses sticks and does many things almost human. Have the cat and the tiger any instincts? Does the chimpanzee possess any insight? Is the cat's behavior toward the rat hereditary or learned through trial and error, or by imitation? To me, all such questions are useless as well as meaningless. . . .

The point I am here making is that the mere proof or disproof of an instinct, i.e., action which can be performed without learning, the mere experiments on trial and error learning and the mere test to show the presence or absence of insight or intelligence and imitation will not lead us anywhere. We need to know the potential range or repertory of activities of a given species. We need to know the physiological and genetic or developmental aspects of each behavior. The behavior of an organism is a *passive* affair. How an animal or man will behave in a given moment depends on how it has been brought up and how it is stimulated. Without sufficient knowledge of the physiology of behavior and of the behavior history of the organism, prediction would be impossible. Our study has shown that kittens can be made to kill a rat, to love it, to fear it or to play with it: it depends on the life history of the kitten. . . . Prediction of behavior implies knowledge of behavior range, behavior physiology and behavior history. . . . Our behavior researches in the past have been in the wrong direction, because *instead of finding how we could build nature into the animal, we have tried to find nature in the animal.* Nothing is more natural than for the cat to "love" the rat. And if one insists that the cat has an instinct to kill the rat, I must add that it has an instinct to love the rat too. In behavior nature is what can be built in and not what is supposed to unfold from within. The science of behavior is the science of building nature into animals and men by the most economic methods available (of course, "nature" can be built in only within the potential limit of the organismic pattern). But so far our experimental researches have not been directed towards this goal.

[B]

. . . Recently I have maintained that the concepts of both instinct and habit must be abandoned. Behavior is neither prenatally nor postnatally acquired, nor is it hereditary. *The development of behavior is an absolutely gradual and continuous process.* In this continuous stream of behavioral development we can not pick up at a certain period one bit of response and assign to it the name of instinct and take another bit and call it a habit. The real nature of behavior can not be understood unless its underlying physiology and the entire developmental history are known. . . .

Unfortunately, modern animal psychology, not to say human psychology, has been built upon a wrong premise. Investigations on animal behavior have been centered upon the problems of sensory capacity, instincts, and trial and error learning. The workers in the field have so busied themselves with maze or puzzle box experiments, with counting the number of errors, with juggling with statistical figures to reveal the degree of the God-endowed intelligence in the albino rat, and with attempts to determine whether or not a given act can be performed without learning, that the developmental aspect of behavior is almost entirely neglected. If it is realized that behavior begins long before birth and that every previous movement has its effect upon subsequent ones either directly or indirectly, it must be admitted that the direction of our behavior researches must be radically changed. The present condition of animal psychology is just like the older morphology which was not worked out from the developmental standpoint. Indeed, if it is true that scientific morphology depends on embryology, it must be equally true that scientific knowledge of behavior can only come from embryological studies.

15.15

Konrad Lorenz

(born 1903)

Although Lorenz himself often points to earlier research by the Americans C. O. Whitman and W. Craig and by his own teachers O. Heinroth and J. von Uexküll as anticipating the basic viewpoints of ethology, this paper is usually regarded as the event which marked the beginning of ethology as a movement. In it, Lorenz states at least three important ideas which are outlined in the following summary passage: (a) the specificity of "releasers" for instinctive acts; (b) "imprinting" as a form of behavioral plasticity which cannot be considered as learning in the usual sense; and (c) the use of phyletic sequences of instinctive behaviors for taxonomic purposes.

In 1973, Lorenz shared a Nobel prize with von Frisch (see 14.11) and another outstanding ethologist, N. Tinbergen.

From the many stimuli which emanate from one animal and impinge upon the sense-organs of a conspecific, we have attempted to select those which elicit in the latter social responses in the widest sense of the term. We have discovered that the stimuli and stimulus combinations to which the animal *instinctively* responds with specific responses belong to a category quite different from those whose elicitatory effect depends upon *acquired* properties. . . .

The instinctive, *innate* releasing schemata play a particular role in the behaviour of birds. If the releasing schema of a response is innately determined, it always corresponds to a relatively *simple* combination of individual stimuli, which as a unitary whole represent a key to a specific instinctive response. . . .

The innate schema attains great importance in responses which have a conspecific as their object. With responses whose object is *some entity in the external environment*, the innate schema can only be adapted to stimuli which are an inherent property of this entity *from the outset*. . . . With responses directed toward *conspecifics*, on the other hand, both the development of the innate releasing schema and that of the relevant stimulus-key are within the evolutionary framework of one species. *Organs* and *instinctive behaviour patterns* which are exclusively con-

Der Kumpan in der Umwelt des Vogels. *Journal für Ornithologie* 83 (1935): 137–312, 389–413. Translated by R. Martin, as "Companions as factors in the bird's environment." Pp. 101–258 in K. Lorenz, *Studies in animal and human behaviour,* Vol. I. Cambridge, Mass.: Harvard University Press, and London: Methuen & Co., 1970. [Pp. 243–249.] Excerpted by permission of the publishers.

cerned in the transmission of key stimuli (sign stimuli) achieve a high degree of specialization, always progressing in parallel with the evolution of corresponding, matching releasing schemata. Such organs and instinctive behaviour patterns are briefly termed *releasers*. . . .

I should like to emphasize, as the most important result of this investigation of instinctive behaviour patterns oriented toward conspecifics, the fact that *not all acquired behaviour can be equated with experience and that not all processes of acquisition can be equated with learning*. We have seen that in many cases the object appropriate to innately-determined instinctive behaviour patterns is not instinctively recognized as such, but that recognition of the object is acquired through a quite specific process, *which has nothing to do with learning*. . . .

An instinctive behaviour pattern adapted towards a conspecific, yet initially incorporated without an object, is fixated upon an object in the environment at a quite specific time, at a quite specific developmental stage of the bird. This specification of the object can take place hand-in-hand with the emergence of the motor component of the instinctive behaviour pattern, but it can also precede the latter by a matter of months or even years. In the normal free-living existence of the species, the conditions are so organized that the choice of object of the instinctive behaviour patterns is reliably limited to a conspecific which represents the biologically-appropriate object. If the young bird is *not* surrounded by conspecifics at the psychological period for object-selection, the responses concerned are oriented towards some other environmental object, usually towards a living organism (as long as such is available) but otherwise towards some inanimate object.

The process of object-acquisition is separated from any genuine learning process by two factors, and rendered parallel to another process of acquisition which is known from the mechanics of embryogeny and is referred to in that context as inductive determination. In the first place, this process is *irreversible*, whereas the concept of learning necessarily incorporates the condition that the acquired element can be both forgotten and revised. Secondly, the process is bound to a sharply-demarcated developmental condition of the individual, which often exists only for a few hours.

The process of acquisition of the object of instinctive behaviour patterns oriented toward conspecifics, which are initially incorporated without the object, has been termed *imprinting*. . . .

The interplay between the innate companions schema and object-imprinting varies greatly from species to species. There is every transition from species like the Greylag goose, which possess extremely broad companion schemata incorporating few characters, to birds in which virtually all of the releasing schemata are innately determined, so that no room is left for variability due to imprinting. It can be reliably stated that within the Class Aves the latter form of behaviour is likely to be the more primitive.

The assumption of a fundamental dichotomy between instinctive behaviour patterns on one hand and feats of learning and intelligence on the other has not encountered difficulty at any stage. On the contrary, it has aided us in understanding a number of otherwise incomprehensible behaviour patterns. There has been no cause for regret that the mutability of instinctive patterns through experience was flatly discounted and that the instinct was treated *as an organ,* whose individual range of variation can be neglected in the general biological description of a species. . . .

The inseparable relationship between the development of an organ and the evolution of the instinct governing its use is virtually nowhere as conspicuous and undeniable as it is in the social ethology of birds. Whatever the factors which determine the biological adaptiveness in the development of an organ, they are doubtless the same as those which also govern the development of the relevant instincts. . . . We find with great frequency *'phylogenetic' series of releasers,* in which innate behaviour patterns without a corresponding underlining organ occur at one end, with highly-specialized organs developed for the emphasis of virtually-identical and doubtless homologous motor patterns at the other extreme. . . . In consequence, we are often able to determine genetic relationships with a degree of accuracy seldom available to the comparative morphologist.

Chapter 16

HUMAN UNDERSTANDING

From ancient times to the present, man has prided himself above all on his capacity to reason. When Godliness was most prized, this was the token of his Godliness. (Compare Gregory of Nyssa, 4.3; Augustine, 11.2; Maimonides, 1.4.) By modern man it has been viewed as the instrument of self-directed progress toward human betterment. But does it merely respond to pressures of his environment in quasi-mechanical ways, as the associationists would maintain, or does it achieve saltatory creative syntheses? The latest word seems to be that man as machine has a computer-brain, like many of his own most sophisticated devices.

16.1

Robert Burton

(1577–1640)

Robert Burton found it convenient to provide his readers with a summary statement of the then accepted view of human cognition and volition. It is convenient for us to take this as a starting point. It is an eclectic sum-

The anatomy of melancholy, what it is. With all the kinds, causes, symptomes, prognostickes, and severall cures of it. By Democritus Iunior. Oxford, 1621. [Pp. 39–41, 43–45.]

mary, which contains no hint of the revolution which will begin with Hobbes, only eleven years Burton's junior. A statement about the faculties of the sensitive soul, including imagination and memory, has preceded this exposition of understanding and the will.

The selection is from the First Partition, Section I, Member 2.

Of the Rationall Soule

In the precedent Subsections, I have anatomised those inferiour Faculties of the Soule; the *Rationall* remaineth, *a pleasant, but a doubtfull Subiect*, as one termes it, and with the like brevity to be discussed. . . . This *Reasonable Soule*, which *Austin* [Augustine] calles a Spirituall substance, moving it selfe, is defined by Philosophers to be *the first substantiall Act of a Naturall, Humane, Organicall Body, by which a man lives, perceives, and understands, freely doing all things, and with election.* Out of which Definition we may gather, that this *Rationall Soule* includes the powers, and performes the duties of the two other, which are contained in it, and all three Faculties make one *Soule*, which is inorganicall of it selfe, although it bc in all parts, & incorporcall, using their Organs, and working by them. It is divided into two chiefe parts, differing in office onely, not in Essence. The *Understanding*, which is the *Rationall* power *apprehending*: the *Will*, which is the *Rationall* power *moving*, to which two, all the other *Rationall* powers are subiect and reduced.

Of tho Understunding

Understanding, is a power of the Soule, by which we perceive, know, remember, and Iudge, aswell Singulars as Universals, having certain innate notices or beginnings of arts, a reflecting action, by which it iudgeth of his owne doings, and examines them. Out of this Definition besides his chiefe office, which is to apprehend, iudge all which he performes, without the helpe of any Instruments or Organs, three differences appeare betwixt a man and a beast. As first, the sence onely comprehends *Singularities*, the Understanding *universalities*. Secondly, the sence hath no innate notions, thirdly, Bruts can not reflect upon themselves. Bees indeed make neate and curious workes, and many other Creatures besides, but when they have done, they cannot iudge of them. His obiect is God, *Ens;* all nature, and whatever is to bee understood: which successively it apprehends. The obiect first moving the *Understanding*, is some sensible thing, after by discoursing the Minde findes out the corporeall substance, and from thence the spirituall. His actions, some say, are *Apprehension, Composition, Division, Discoursing, Reasoning, Memory,* which some include in *Invention,* and *Iudgment.* The common Divisions are of the Understanding, *Agent* and *Patient. Speculative,* and *Practicke.* In *Habite,* or in *Act. Simple,* or *Compound.* The *Agent* is that which is called the *Wit* of Man, *acumen* or subtilty, *sharpnesse* of invention, when he doth invent of himselfe without a Teacher, or learnes anew, which abstracts those intelligible Species from the Phantasie, and transferres them to the passive Understanding, *because there is nothing in the Understanding, which was not first in the sence:* that which the Imagination hath taken from the Sence, this *Agent* iudgeth of, whether it be true or false; and being so iudged, he committes it to the *Passible* to bee kept. The *Agent* is a Doctor or Teacher, the Passive a Scholler; and his office is to keepe, and farther iudge of such things as are committed to his charge: as a bare and rased table at first, capable of all formes & notions. Now these *Notions* are two-fold, *Actions or Habits:* Actions, by which we take Notions of, and perceive things; *Habits,* which are durable lights and notions, which wee may use when we will. . . .

Of the Will

Will, is the other power of the *Rationall Soule, which covets or avoides such things as have beene before iudged, and apprehended by the Understanding.* If good, it approves it, if evill, it abhorres it; so that his obiect is good, or evill. *Aristotle* cals this our *Rationall Appetite;* for as in the *Sensative,* we are carried to good or bad by our *Appetite,* ruled and directed by Sence: so in this we are carried by *Reason.* Besides, the *Sensative Appetite* hath a particular obiect, good or bad, this an universall immateriall, that respects onely things delectable and pleasant, this Honest. Againe, they differ in liberty. The *Sensuall appetite* seeing an obiect, if it bee a convenient good, cannot but desire it; if evill, avoide it: but this is free in his Essence, *much now depraved, obscured, and fallen from his first perfection; yet in some of his operations still free,* as to go, walke, moove at his pleasure, and to choose whether it will doe, or not doe, steale, or not steale. Otherwise in vaine were Lawes, Deliberations, Dehortations, Exhortations, Counsels, Praecepts, Rewards, Promises, Threates and punishments: and God should be the Author of sinne. . . .

The actions of the *will* are *Velle* and *Nolle,* will and nill: which two wordes comprehend all, and they are, Good or Bad, accordingly as they are directed: and some of them freely performed by himselfe, although the Stoicks absolutely deny it, and will have all things inevitably done by *Destiny,* imposing a fatal necessity upon us, which wee may not resist; yet wee say that our will is free in respect of us, and things contingent, howsoever in respect of God's determinate counsell, they are inevitable and necessary. Some other actions of the *Will* are performed by the inferiour powers, which obey him as the *Sensative and Moving Appetite,* as to open our eyes, to goe hether and thether, not to touch a Booke, to speak faire or foule, but this *Appetite* is many times rebellious in us. It was, as I said, once well agreeing with reason in us, and there was an excellent consent and harmony betwixt them, but that is now dissolved, they often jarre, *Reason* is over-borne by *Passion*. . . . as so many wilde horses runne away with a chariot, and will not be curbed. . . .

Those *Naturall* and *Vegetall* powers, are not commanded by *Will* at all; for *who can adde one cubit to his stature?* These other may, but are not, and thence come all those headstrong Passions, and violent perturbations of the Minde; And many times vitious Habits, customes, ferall Diseases, because we give so much sway to our Appetite, and follow our inclination, like so many beasts.

16.2

Ignace Gaston Pardies

(1636?–1673)

In his effort to clarify the differences between human and animal perception, Pardies establishes a distinction between two kinds of human thinking. Thus he anticipates that "steadily developing climate of thought regarding the unconscious mind" which, according to Lancelot Whyte (The Unconscious before Freud, 1960), began about 1680 and owed its impulse to English and German, but not to French authors! We shall discuss the significance of this further in connection with Leibnitz (16.5).

[78] Spiritual knowledge, or intellectual knowledge if you prefer, is an intimate perception by which we perceive an object in such a manner that we are aware of this very fact; that is to say, it is a perception of which an essential, indivisible part is a reflection made upon itself, so that we know very well that we know. But sensory knowledge is a simple perception of an object without this reflection. . . .

[80] But we sometimes also have perceptions which do not by any means include this sort of reflection, and in which we perceive without being aware that we are perceiving. . . .

[82] And to become fully convinced of this, we only need to reflect on what happens to us every day when we are reading a book with some application. We are attentive to the meaning of the words, and we have no attention for thinking about the letters which, by their various shapes

De la connaissance des bestes [1672]. [Concerning the knowledge of beasts.] Paris, 1678. [Arts. 78, 80, 82–85; pp. 171, 175, 181–190.]

and arrangement, make up the whole tenor of the discourse. We pay no attention to whether the characters are well formed or not, as long as the impression is clear enough not to impede us. There might be some italic mixed in with the roman, without our becoming aware of it; and sometimes our application may be so great that we do not even reflect on what language the book is written in. One must acknowledge that in this case we do not perceive the letters and the words with that perceptive reflection which would allow us to give an account to ourselves of what we are perceiving, and which would make us aware that we are perceiving. Yet it is clear that we have seen all these letters, that we have noticed their shapes, that we have distinguished them from one another, that we have considered the relations by which they form words; and that without this, we would never have been able to penetrate the meaning which, nevertheless, we have well understood. . . .

[84] It is true that there are sometimes perceptions so fine and delicate that, even though they are spiritual, they escape our knowledge, so that we are unaware of them, or at least we cannot remember having been aware of them, as often happens in dreams, where we have often had such reflective perceptions without being able to recall them. . . .

[85] But this very fact, that there are perceptions so fine and delicate that, however much we try, we cannot notice them or remember them— this is what I wish to show, and these are what I call sensory perceptions. Do not say that we have forgotten them, because in order to forget, one first had to know them. Now we never knew what we perceived in the cases which I have described, and if while we were reading some one were to interrupt us, and ask for a description of the letters and the type, we would find it as difficult as if we had not been reading at all, and we would have to cast our eyes again upon the book in order to notice the printing. It is true that we forget what we have seen effectively in dreams; but finally we can remember, at least generally, having seen something, and if someone mentions some detail of it, we remember that it was so. . . . But here there is nothing of that sort. In vain we torment ourselves trying to recall to the mind what we may have seen. It is in vain that we are questioned and examined, because the more we reflect upon it, the more we see that indeed we never knew how a certain letter was made; so that although we saw it clearly and distinguished it from all the others, we never perceived it with that sort of perception which makes us intimately aware of the very fact that we are perceiving. Therefore I do not think that anyone will any longer contest that we have certain perceptions of which we are unaware, and which we have called sensory knowledge, to differentiate it from the intellectual experience whose essential quality is that it makes us indivisibly aware that we are perceiving.

16.3

Nicholas Malebranche

(1638–1715)

Malebranche, as he opens his Search for truth, attempts to define both the passive nature of human understanding and the degree of voluntary control left to man, which is essential if he is to have moral responsibility. Reading what he says about perception, one should bear in mind that the primary meaning of this word in French was the receipt of rents and taxes, and this connotation colors what he has to say about the nature of perceiving (i.e., receiving) sensory information.

Malebranche's views were of course carefully studied by Locke, and they form the background against which one must consider not only Locke's own solution to the problem of the limits of human understanding, but also his relation to the later French sensationist psychologists, particularly Condillac, for whom thinking was decidedly more passive than for Locke.

The Mind of Man, being neither Material nor Extended, is undoubtedly a simple Substance, indivisible, and without any Composition of Parts; Notwithstanding it has been the Custom to distinguish in it two Faculties, namely, the *Understanding* and the *Will*. . . .

But because these Idea's are very Abstract, and fall not under the Imagination, it seems not amiss to express them by the Resemblance they bear to the Properties belonging to Matter, which being easie to be Imagin'd, will render the Notions which may conveniently be apply'd to those two Words *Understanding* and *Will*, more distinct, and also more familiar *to Us*; only this Caution must be observ'd, that these Resemblances betwixt the Mind and Matter, are not perfectly just; And that these two kinds of Beings are only compar'd in order to make the Mind more Attentive, and to make others, as it were, *sensible* of our meaning.

Matter, or Extension, contains in it two Properties or Faculties; the first Faculty is that of receiving different Figures, and the second is its capacity of being mov'd: In like manner the Mind of Man includes two Faculties; the first, which is the *Understanding*, is that of receiving many Idea's, that is, of perceiving many things; the second, which is the *Will*, is the Faculty of receiving many Inclinations, or of *Willing* different

De la recherche de la vérité, où l'on traite de la nature de l'esprit de l'homme, et de l'usage qu'il en doit faire pour eviter l'erreur dans les sciences [The search for truth, in which the nature of man's mind is considered, and the use which he should make of it to avoid error in the sciences]. Paris, 1674–1675. Translated by T. Taylor as *Father Malebranche* his Treatise concerning the search after truth [1694]. Second edition. London, 1700. [Pp. 1–3.]

things. We will begin with an explication of the Resemblances the first of the faculties belonging to *Matter*, has to the first of the two faculties appertaining to the *Mind*.

Extension is capable of admitting two kinds of Figures, The one is only External, as the Roundness of a piece of Wax, the other is Internal, and is peculiar to all the little parts the Wax is compos'd of; for it is most certain that all the little parts which go to the Composition of a piece of Wax, are of a Figure very different from those, which constitute a piece of Iron. Therefore I call that which is external, barely *Figure*, and I term the internal Figure, *Configuration;* which is peculiarly necessary to the Wax to make it what it is.

So likewise it may be said that the Idea's of the Soul are of two sorts, taking the name of *Idea* in general for whatever the Mind immediately perceives. The first give Us a Representation of something without Us, as of a *Square*, or an House, *&c.* The second represent to Us only what we find within Us, as our Sensations, *Pain, Pleasure*, or the like. For we shall make it plain hereafter, that these last Idea's are only a *manner* of the Mind's *existing*; and for that reason I call them the *Modifications* of the Mind.

Thus also the Inclinations of the Soul might be call'd *Modifications* of the same Soul: For it being manifest that the Inclination of the Will is a *manner* of *existing* of the Soul, it might be term'd a *Modification* of the Soul; just as Motion in Bodies, being a *manner* of *existing* of those Bodies, might be said to be a *Modification* of Matter: Notwithstanding I do not term the Inclinations of the Will, or the Motions of Matter, *Modifications*, for as much as both those Inclinations, and those Motions have commonly a reference to something that's external; for the *Inclinations* stand related unto *Good*, and the *Motions* have a reference to some separate Body. But the *Figures* and *Configurations* of Bodies, and the *Sensations* of the Soul have no necessary relation to any thing without. . . .

The first, and principal Agreement, *or Resemblance*, that is found betwixt the Faculty which matter has of receiving different Figures, and different Configurations; and that which the Soul has of receiving different Idea's, and different Modifications is this, That as the Faculty of receiving different Figures, and different Configurations in Bodies, is intirely *passive*, and contains nothing at all of Action, so the faculty of receiving different Idea's and different Modifications in the Mind, is altogether *passive* and includes no Action at all. I call that Faculty or Capacity, the Soul has of receiving all these things, the UNDERSTANDING.

Whence we ought to conclude, That 'tis the *Understanding* which *perceives;* since 'tis only its business to receive the Idea's of Objects: For, for the Soul to perceive an Object, and to receive the Idea which represents it, is one and the same thing: 'Tis also the *Understanding* which perceives the Modifications of the Soul, since I mean by this word *Under-*

standing, that passive Faculty of the Soul, by means of which it receives all the different *Modifications* it is capable of. For it is the same thing for the Soul to receive a *mode* of *existence,* which we call *pain,* as to perceive Pain, since it has no other way of *receiving* Pain, than by the *Perception* of it; whence it may be inferr'd, that 'tis the *Understanding* that *imagines* the Objects that are absent, and is *sensible* of those that are present; and that the *Senses* and *Imagination,* are nothing but the *Understanding,* perceiving Objects by the Organs of the Body, as shall be explain'd hereafter.

But because in the Sensation of Pain, or any thing else, Men generally perceive it by the mediation of the Organs of *Sense;* they customarily say they are the Senses which perceive it, without knowing distinctly what it is they mean by the word *Sense:* They fancy there is some Faculty distinct from the Soul, which renders It, or the Body capable of Sensation, as believing the Organs of Sense do really participate of our Perceptions. They imagine the Body is so assistant to the Mind, in its Sensations, that if the Mind was separate from the Body, it could have no *Sensation* at all. But these thoughts are the effects of Prejudice; and because in the State we are in, we are *sensible* of nothing but through the use of the Instruments of Sense, as shall be shewn elsewhere more at large. . . .

The other Faculty of Matter is that of its being capable of receiving many *Motions,* and the other Faculty of the Soul is that power it has of receiving many *Inclinations.* . . .

So that by the word WILL, I would be conceiv'd to design, *That natural Motion or Impression which carries us towards Good universal, and undetermin'd.* And by that of LIBERTY, I mean nothing more than *The Power the Mind has of turning that Impression towards agreeable Objects; and terminating our natural Inclinations upon some particular Object, which before were loose and undetermin'd,* except towards general or universal Good; that is to say, towards God, who is alone universal Good, since 'tis he alone who comprehends in himself all Goods. . . .

But it must be observ'd, that the Mind consider'd under so strong a bent towards Good in general, cannot determine its Motion towards a particular Good, unless the same Mind, consider'd as susceptible of Idea's, has knowledge of that particular Good; I would say, to make use of the ordinary terms, that the Will is a *blind Power,* that can make no advances to things but what are represented to it by the *Understanding;* so that the Will can not diversly determine its Propensity to Good, or over-rule the *direct* Bent of his natural Inclinations, but by commanding the *Understanding* to represent it to some particular Object. The power then that the *Will* has of determining its Inclinations, necessarily contains an ability of applying the Understanding to the Objects which it likes.

16.4

John Locke

(1632–1704)

Since history is a chain, it is not possible to select one link as more impor-
tant than all the rest. But historiography is selective, and there is probably
no other book, Aristotle in this instance not excepted, which is so indis-
pensable as Locke's Essay to a series of readings in the history of psy-
chology. Nor is this without good reason, for Locke can be said to open
a new era in the thinking of men about the nature of their own minds.
Selections can therefore be found in every general source book. I have
chosen to string together capsule statements of what seems most essential
for the history of psychology.

The central thought of the Essay is to dispute Cartesian thinking about
innate ideas and hence about the superiority of rational over empirical
evidence. But Locke acknowledges two sources of empirical data, one being
reflection, which gives us ideas "which could not be had from things out-
side." This side of his thinking was neglected, almost suppressed, by most
of his followers. Meanwhile, the rejection of innateness leads to rejection
of nonconscious thinking, and the emphasis on sensation leads to atomism.

[Bk. I, Ch. I] §1. . . . The Understanding, like the Eye, whilst it makes
us see, and perceive all other Things, takes no notice of it self: And it
requires Art and Pains to set it at a distance, and make it its own
Object. . . .

§2. . . . I shall not at present meddle with the Physical Consideration of
the Mind; or trouble my self to examine, wherein its Essence consists,
or by what Motions of our Spirits, or Alterations of our Bodies, we come
to have any Sensation by our Organs, or any *Idea's* in our Understandings;
and whether those *Idea's* do in their Formation, any, or all of them, depend on Matter, or no. . . . It shall suffice to my present Purpose, to consider the discerning Faculties of a Man, as they are employ'd about the
Objects, which they have to do with. . . .

§3. . . . I shall enquire into the Original of those *Idea's*, Notions, or
whatever else you please to call them, which a Man observes, and is
conscious to himself he has in his Mind; and the ways whereby the
Understanding comes to be furnished with them.

Secondly, I shall endeavour to shew, what *Knowledge* the Understanding hath by those *Idea's;* and the Certainty, Evidence, and Extent
of it. . . .

An essay concerning humane understanding. London, 1690. [Pp. 1–4, 8, 11, 27, 34,
36–39, 44–46.]

§5. . . . The Candle, that is set up in us, shines bright enough for all our Purposes. . . . And we shall then use our Understandings right, when we entertain all Objects in that Way and Proportion, that they are suited to our Faculties . . . and not . . . demand Certainty, where Probability only is to be had. . . .

§8. . . . The word *Idea* . . . I have used . . . to express whatever is meant by *Phantasm, Notion, Species,* or whatever it is, which the Mind can be employ'd about in thinking. . . .

[Ch. II] §1. It is an Established Opinion amongst some Men, That there are in the Understanding certain *innate Principles;* some Primary Notions . . . which the Soul receives in its very first Being; and brings into the World with it. . . .

. . . I shall set down the Reasons, that made me doubt of the Truth of that Opinion. . . .

§15. The Senses at first let in particular *Idea's,* and furnish the yet empty Cabinet: And the Mind by degrees growing familiar with some of them, they are lodged in the Memory, and Names got to them. Afterwards the Mind proceeding further, abstracts them, and by Degrees learns the use of general Names. . . . But though the having of general *Idea's,* and the use of general Words and Reason usually grow together: yet, I see not, how this any way proves them innate. The Knowledge of some Truths, I confess, is very early in the Mind; but in a way that shews them not to be Innate. For, if we will observe, we shall find it still to be about *Idea's,* not innate, but acquired: It being about those first, which are imprinted by external Things, with which Infants have earliest to do, and which make the most frequent Impressions on their Senses. . . .

§23. . . . So, that in all Propositions that are assented to, at first hearing the Terms of the Proposition, their standing for such *Idea's,* and the *Idea's* themselves that they stand for, being neither of them innate, I would fain know what there is remaining in such Propositions that is innate. . . .

[Ch. IV] §2. If we will attently consider new born *Children,* we shall have little Reason, to think, that they bring many *Idea's* into the World with them. For, bating, perhaps, some faint *Idea's,* of Hunger, and Thirst, and Warmth, and some Pains which they may *have* felt in the Womb, there is *not* the least appearance of any setled *Idea's* at all in them; especially of *Ideas, answering the Terms, which make up those universal Propositions,* that are esteemed innate Principles. One may perceive how, by degrees, afterwards *Idea's* come into their Minds; and that they get no more, nor no other, than what Experience, and the Observation of Things, that come in their way, furnish them with; which might be enough to satisfie us, that they are not Original Characters, stamped on the Mind. . . .

§21. To conclude, some *Ideas* forwardly offer themselves to all mens Understandings; and some sorts of Truths result from any *Ideas,* as soon as the Mind puts them into Propositions: Other Truths require a train of *Ideas* placed in order, a due comparing of them, and deductions made with attention, before they can be discovered, and assented to. Some of the first sort, because of their general and easie reception, have been mistaken for innate: But the truth is, *Ideas* and Notions are no more born with us, than Arts and Sciences; though some of them, indeed, offer themselves to our Faculties, more readily than others; and therefore are more generally received. . . .

§23. When Men have found some general Propositions that could not be doubted of, as soon as understood, it was, I know, *a short and easy way to conclude them innate.* . . . Whereas had they examined the ways, whereby men came to the knowledge of many universal *Truths,* they would have found . . . that they were discovered by the application of those Faculties, that were fitted by Nature to receive and judge of them, when duely employ'd about them. . . .

[Bk. II, Ch. I] §1. Every Man being conscious to himself, That he thinks, and that which his Mind is employ'd about whilst thinking, being the *Ideas,* that are there, 'tis past doubt, that Men have in their Minds several *Ideas,* such as are those expressed by the words, *Whiteness, Hardness, Sweetness, Thinking, Motion, Man, Elephant, Army, Drunkenness,* and others: It is in the first place then to be enquired, How comes he by them? . . .

§2. Let us then suppose the Mind to be, as we say, white Paper, void of all Characters, without any *Ideas;* How comes it to be furnished? . . . To this I answer, in one word, From *Experience.* . . . Our Observation employ'd either about *external sensible Objects; or about the internal Operations of our Minds, perceived and reflected on by our selves, is that, which supplies our Understanding with all the materials of thinking.* These Two are the Fountains of Knowledge. . . .

§3. First, *Our Senses . . . convey into the Mind,* several distinct *Perceptions* of things. . . .

§4. Secondly, the other Fountain, from which Experience furnisheth the Understanding with *Ideas,* is the *Perception of the Operations of our own Minds* within us, as it is employ'd about the *Idea's* it has got; which Operations, when the Soul comes to reflect on, and consider, do furnish the Understanding with another Sett of *Ideas,* which could not be had from things without; and such are, *Perception, Thinking, Doubting, Believing, Reasoning, Knowing, Willing,* and all the different actings of our own Minds. . . . This Source of *Ideas,* every Man has wholly in himself: And though it be not Sense, as having nothing to do with external Objects; yet it is very like it, and might properly enough be call'd internal Sense. But as I call the other *Sensation,* so I call this *REFLECTION.* . . .

§5. . . . We have nothing in our Minds, which did not come in, one of these two ways. . . .

§10. . . . I confess my self to have one of those dull Souls, that doth not perceive it self always to contemplate its *Ideas,* nor can conceive it any more necessary for the *Soul always to think,* than for the Body always to move; the perception of *Idea's* being (as I conceive) to the Soul, what motion is to the Body, not its Essence, but Operation. . . .

[Added in 1694: I do not say, there is no Soul in a Man, because he is not sensible of it in his sleep: But I do say, he cannot think at any time waking or sleeping, without being sensible of it. Our being sensible of it is not necessary to any thing, but to our thoughts; and to them it is; and to them it will always be necessary, till we can think without being conscious of it. . . .]

§20. I see no Reason, therefore to believe, that the *Soul thinks before the Senses have furnish'd it with Ideas* to think on. . . .

§21. He that will suffer himself, to be informed by Observation and Experience . . . will find few Signs of a Soul accustomed to much thinking in a new born Child, and much fewer of any Reasoning at all. . . .

§22. Follow a *Child* from its Birth, and observe the alterations that time makes; and you shall find, as the mind by the Senses comes more and more to be furnished with *Ideas,* it comes to be more and more awake; thinks more, the more it has matter to think on. . . .

§23. If it shall be demanded then, *When a man begins to have any Ideas?* I think, the true Answer is, When he first has any *Sensation.* . . .

§25. . . . These *simple Ideas,* when offered to the Mind, *the Understanding can* no more refuse to have, nor alter, when they are imprinted, nor blot them out, and make new ones in it self, than a mirror can refuse, alter, or obliterate the Images or *Ideas,* which the Objects set before it do therein produce. As the Bodies that surround us, do diversly affect our Organs, the mind is forced to receive the Impressions; and cannot avoid the Perception of those *Ideas* that are annexed to them. . . .

[Ch. II] §2. . . . When the Understanding is once stored with these simple *Ideas,* it has the Power to repeat, compare, and unite them even to an almost infinite Variety, and so can make at Pleasure new complex *Ideas.* But it is not in the Power of the most exalted Wit, or enlarged Understanding, by any quickness or variety of Thought, to *invent or frame one new simple* Idea in the Mind, not taken in by the ways before mentioned: nor can any Force of the Understanding, *destroy* those that are there.

16.5

Gottfried Wilhelm Leibnitz

(1646–1716)

After the appearance of a French translation of Locke's Essay, Leibnitz wrote an extensive critique which he did not publish due to Locke's death in 1704. Our selection, taken from the preface, states the theory of "petites perceptions," and also introduces a word coined by Leibnitz, apperception. Comparison of this passage with the selection from Pardies (16.2) will show that Leibnitz was not altogether original in either the concept of subconscious perceptions or in the notion of apperception. By his own admission, Leibnitz enjoyed an "uncommon friendship" with Pardies in the years 1672 and 1673, and the two young men must have engaged in discussions about these topics, as they appear in the book by Pardies. These ideas exercised strong influence on the future development of German psychology, giving rise to concepts of threshold, unconscious dynamics, and a variety of theories in which active apperception is offered as an alternative to association to explain creativity in human thinking.

I do not know whether it will be so easy to harmonize him [Locke] with us and with the Cartesians, when he maintains that the mind does not always think, and particularly that it is without perception when we sleep without dreaming; and he objects that since bodies can exist without motion, souls can also exist without thought. . . .

. . . There are a thousand indications which make us think that there are at every moment an infinite number of *perceptions* in us, but without apperception and reflection, *i.e.* changes in the soul itself of which we are not conscious, because the impressions are either too slight and too great in number, or too even, so that they have nothing sufficiently distinguishing them from each other; but joined to others, they do not fail to produce their effect and to make themselves felt at least confusedly in the mass. Thus it is that habit makes us take no notice of the motion of a mill or a waterfall when we have lived quite near it for some time. It is not that the motion does not always strike our organs, and that something no longer enters into the soul corresponding thereto, in virtue of the harmony of the soul and the body, but these impressions which are in the soul and the body, being destitute of the attractions of novelty, are not strong enough to attract our attention and our memory, attached to

Nouveaux essais sur l'entendement humain [Written c. 1704, published 1765]. Translated by A. G. Langley, as *New essays concerning human understanding*. New York: Macmillan, 1896. [Pp. 47–48, 50–51.]

objects more engrossing. For all attention requires memory, and often when we are not admonished, so to speak, and warned to take note of some of our own present perceptions, we allow them to pass without reflection, and even without being noticed; but if any one directs our attention to them immediately after, and makes us notice, for example, some noise which was just heard, we remember it, and are conscious of having had at the time some feeling of it. Thus there were perceptions of which we were not conscious at once, consciousness arising in this case only from the warning after some interval, however small it may be. And to judge still better of the minute perceptions which we cannot distinguish in the crowd, I am wont to make use of the example of the roar or noise of the sea which strikes one when on its shore. To understand this noise as it is made, it would be necessary to hear the parts which compose this whole, *i.e.* the noise of each wave, although each of these little noises makes itself known only in the confused collection of all the others, *i.e.* in the roar itself, and would not be noticed if the wave which makes it were alone. For it must be that we are affected a little by the motion of this wave, and that we have some perception of each one of these noises, small as they are; otherwise we would not have that of a hundred thousand waves, since a hundred thousand nothings cannot make something. One never sleeps so soundly as not to have some feeble and confused sensation, and one would never be awakened by the greatest noise in the world if he did not have some perception of its small beginning. . . .

These minute perceptions are, then, of greater efficacy in their results than one supposes. They form I know not what, these tastes, these images of the sense-qualities, clear in the mass, but confused in the parts, these impressions which surrounding bodies make upon us, which involve the infinite, this connection which each being has with all the rest of the universe. . . .

In a word, *the insensible perceptions* are as eminently useful in Pneumatology as are the insensible corpuscles in Physics, and it is equally unreasonable to reject the one or the other under the pretext that they are out of reach of our senses. Nothing is accomplished all at once, and it is one of my great maxims, and one of the most verified, that *nature makes no leaps:* a maxim which I called the *Law of Continuity*. . . . And all this makes one indeed think that the *noticeable perceptions* also arise by degrees from those which are too minute to be observed. To think otherwise, is to have little knowledge of the immense subtilty of things which always and everywhere surrounds an actual infinite.

16.6

Étienne Bonnot de Condillac

(1714–1780)

*In his earlier works, Condillac had been an interpreter of Locke to the
French. But in the Treatise on sensations, which appeared in 1754, he
outdid Locke by far and wrote a reductionist psychology which limited all
mental processes to sensory terms. The form of this work, in which a
"statue" endowed initially only with sensibility gradually developed higher
mental processes and motivation, was apparently influenced by Diderot's
fancied gathering of men "out of their senses" (see 7.9). The next year,
1755, Condillac published the Traité des Animaux (see 15.7), which included a defense against the accusation that he had plagiarized Buffon.
The first edition also included Condillac's own synopsis of the earlier work,
which is here abridged.*

*Condillac's followers for half a century thought that he had written the
definitive psychology, sweeping away all metaphysical illusions.*

For Locke's theory of "uneasiness" see 21.5.

The principal purpose of this work is to show how all our knowledge
and all our faculties come from the senses, or, to speak more exactly,
from sensations. . . .

The *Treatise on Sensations* is the only work which strips man of all his
habits. . . . Whoever attains a thorough understanding of the system of
our sensations will agree that it is no longer necessary to have recourse to
the vague words instinct, mechanical movement, and the like.

If a man had no reason to concern himself with his sensations, the impressions that objects make on him would pass like shadows, and leave
no trace. . . . But the nature of our sensations does not permit him to
remain wrapped in this lethargy. Because they are necessarily either
agreeable or disagreeable, he has an interest in seeking some and ridding
himself of others. The livelier this contrast of pleasures and pains, the
more will it give rise to action in the soul.

The privation of an object which we judge to be necessary for our happiness gives us malaise or uneasiness which we call *need*, and from which
desires are born. . . . Locke was the first to notice that uneasiness caused
by privation of some object is the source of our decisions. But he made
restlessness arise from desire, and precisely the contrary is the fact. . . .

Extrait raisonée du traité des sensations [Synopsis of the treatise on sensations].
Oeuvres philosophiques de Condillac. Ed. by G. Le Roy. 3 vols. Paris, 1947–1951.
[Vol. I, pp. 321–335.]

16.6 Étienne Bonnot de Condillac

It remained to show that this uneasiness is the prime source of our habits of touching, seeing, hearing, feeling, tasting, comparing, judging, reflecting, desiring, loving, hating, fearing, hoping, wishing; that out of it, in a word, all the habits of the soul and the body are born. . . .

But it was not enough to go back to sensation. To discover the progress of all our knowledge and all our faculties, it was important to separate out what we owe to each sense, an investigation which had never before been attempted. This gave rise to the four parts of the *Treatise on Sensations*.

Part One deals with the senses which do not, by themselves, make judgments concerning external objects.

Part Two deals with touch, the only sense which does make judgments concerning external objects by itself.

Part Three, with how touch teaches the other senses to judge external objects.

Part Four, with the needs, ideas, and industry of an isolated man who enjoys all his senses.

Synopsis of Part One

The *Treatise on Sensations* has this defect: when one reads at the outset that *judgment, reflection, emotion, in a word, all the soul's operations, are nothing but sensation itself which has undergone different transformations,* it strikes one as a paradox devoid of all proof; but one has scarcely finished reading the book when one is tempted to say, *That is a very simple truth, of which no one is ignorant.* . . .

If a multitude of sensations are presented simultaneously and with the same or almost the same intensity, a man is still no more than a sensory animal: experience alone is enough to convince us that the multitude of sensations deprives the mind of all its actions.

But let us allow only one sensation to remain, or, even without removing the others entirely, let us reduce their strength; the mind is at once occupied more especially with the sensation which has kept its intensity; this sensation becomes attention, without any need for supposing anything else in the soul.

. . . Thus a sensation is attention, either because it is by itself, or because it is more intense than all the others.

If a new sensation acquires more intensity than the first, then it becomes attention in its turn. . . .

Our capacity for sensing is now divided between the sensation which we had [formerly] and the one we have [presently]. We perceive them both at once, but we perceive them differently: one seems past, the other seems present.

. . . Now, this feeling is called *sensation* when the impression is being presently made on the senses, and it is called *memory* when it is completed and no longer in process. Memory is therefore nothing but transformed sensation.

In this way we are capable of two attentions: one is exercised by memory, the other by the senses.

As soon as there is double attention, there is comparison. . . . The acts of comparison and judgment are nothing but attention itself. In this way sensation successively becomes attention, comparison, judgment. . . .

There are no sensations which are indifferent except comparatively; each in itself is either agreeable or disagreeable. To feel, and not to feel either good or bad, are contradictory expressions. . . .

Consequently, we cannot feel badly, or less well than previously, without comparing our present state with the past. The more we make this comparison, the more we feel that restlessness which causes us to judge that it is important for us to change the situation; we feel the need of something better. Memory soon recalls the object which we believe could contribute to our happiness, and instantly the action of all our faculties is turned to this object. This action of the faculties is what we call *desire.* . . .

In the Treatise, these matters are given in detail. It is shown there how, in passing from need to need, from desire to desire, imagination is formed, the emotions are born, the soul acquires increased activity from moment to moment, and advances from knowledge to knowledge.

. . . We never lose sight of this principle during the whole work, and we never assume any operations in the soul of the statue, any movement in its body, without indicating the motive that determines it.

This first part also had the purpose of considering, separately and together, smell, hearing, taste, and vision; and a truth which immediately presents itself is that these senses by themselves give us no knowledge of external objects. . . .

A living creature limited to smell would feel nothing but himself in the sensations which he experienced. Present him with odoriferous objects, and he will have the feeling of his existence; if you do not present them, he will not feel it. He does not exist for himself except by smells. He believes himself to be those very smells, and cannot think otherwise. . . .

The final purpose of Part One is to show the extent and the limits of discernment by the senses with which it deals. We see how the statue limited to smell forms particular ideas, abstract ideas, ideas of number; what sort of particular and general truths it knows; what notions it forms of possibility and impossibility; and how it judges duration from the succession of its sensations. . . .

16.6 Étienne Bonnot de Condillac

Synopsis of Part Two

. . . Consider a man at the start of his existence. As long as he does not move, he will experience only those sensations which the surrounding air can give him. He will be hot and cold, he will have pleasure and pain. But these will still be only modifications which remain, so to speak, concentrated in his soul. He will not even learn from them that there is an atmosphere which surrounds him, nor even that he has a body. . . .

His hand moves, and touches various objects: immediately sensations of solidity and resistance are joined to the sensations of hot and cold.

As soon as these sensations are joined together, he can no longer feel himself without at the same time feeling something other than himself; heat and cold continue to be modifications of his soul, but become at the same time modifications of something solid. Henceforth they relate both to the soul and to the objects external to it; they extend themselves to the objects, and carry the soul with them.

Thus the sensation of solidity is the only one which can force this man to go outside himself. . . .

. . . Refuse him this single sensation, allow him all the others, and he will take no cognizance of anything but himself. . . .

Synopsis of Part Three

. . . It is touch which instructs [the other] senses, which by themselves have only the property of modifying the soul. As soon as objects take certain forms, certain sizes, beneath the hand, smell, hearing, vision and taste compete in spreading their sensations over them, and the modifications of the soul become qualities of all that exists outside it.

Once these habits are formed, one has difficulty in separating out what belongs to each sense. . . .

At the first instant when our eye admits light, our soul is modified: these modifications consist only in it, and they can as yet have neither shape nor extension.

Some circumstance causes us to place our hands on our eyes, and immediately the feelings which we have been experiencing are weakened or disappear completely. We take the hand away, and the feeling is reproduced. Astonished, we repeat the experiment, and we conclude that these sensations relate to the organ which our hand touched. . . .

From curiosity or restlessness, we put our hand in front of our eyes, we remove it, we bring it near, and the surface we see seems to change. . . .

Then we touch an object on which our sight is fixed; I will suppose, for example, that it is one color, blue. On this assumption, the blue which appeared at first to be at an indeterminate distance must now seem at the same distance as the surface which the hand is touching. . . . The hand says in some sense to vision: *the blue is on each part that I traverse;* and vision, through repetition of this judgment, makes so great a habit of it that it comes to feel the blue where it has judged it to be. . . .

Synopsis of Part Four

When all the senses have been instructed, it only remains to examine the needs which must be satisfied for our conservation. . . . We see how man, who was at first only a sensitive animal, becomes a reflective animal, capable of watching over his conservation. . . .

16.7

Charles Bonnet

(1720–1793)

Locke had made the sensory process passive, but he permitted the mind some activity in its operations on the sensory elements. Condillac, by reducing all mental processes to sensation, made the mind completely passive. To this Bonnet replies, and in doing so he formulates the drainage theory of attention, which would be popular for 150 years.

126. There is a certain way of talking about the Soul which does not seem right to me: that is, when one says that the Soul is *passive* when it *feels* or *perceives. Passivity,* if I may use this word, is directly opposed to *Activity.* An absolutely passive Being is one that cannot exercise any kind of *Action.* To *act* is to produce a certain *effect,* a certain *modification.* How can a passive Being be susceptible of modification? How could the *modifying* Force exert itself upon a Subject that was incapable of *resistance* or *reaction?* . . .

133. Now I must remind my Reader of the Situation in which I left my Statue.

It had experienced two different Sensations at the same time: one was excited by the presence of a *Violet;* the other was recalled by this, and this recalled Sensation was the odor of a *Rose.*

I made the supposition that the odor of the *Violet* was more pleasing to the Statue than the Odor of the *Rose,* and I showed how this could

Essai analytique sur les facultés de l'âme [Analytical essay on the faculties of the soul]. Copenhagen, 1760.

happen. Thereupon, I set myself this Question: *what will happen in the Soul of our Statue when two different sensations cause it to experience greater or lesser pleasure?* This Question led me to examine [the nature of] Activity, and this examination leads me back to the same Question.

134. The Statue therefore *distinguishes* between the two Sensations which now affect it. It feels that one affects it more *agreeably* than the other. Therefore it is more pleased with one than with the other. Therefore it *prefers* one to the other.

But: what is this preference? What results from it? . . .

135. This preference which the Statue gives to the Sensation which pleases it *more* is an *action* which the Statue exerts on that Sensation. To *prefer* is not to *feel*, it is to *determine, to act.* The preference cannot be a *modification* in the *Faculty of feeling;* the modifications of this Faculty are only *Sensations,* and *degrees* of Sensations. A Being that experienced Sensations, but was not *active,* would simply be *affected,* and no more would result inwardly, from this diversity of Impressions which it experienced, than the *pleasure* or *pain* attached to these impressions, and the *recall* of these impressions by each in consequence of their *physical linkage* which is independent of the *Soul.*

But the Soul of our Statue is endowed with Activity: . . . therefore the Statue can *determine* in favor of the Sensation which *pleases it more:* the *effect* of this determination is the *Attention* which the Statue gives to that Sensation.

136. Therefore ATTENTION is a *modification* in the *Activity* of the Soul; or, to express myself in other words, it is a *certain exertion* of the *motive Force* of the Soul upon the fibers of the brain.

If my reader doubts this fact; if he suspects that I make Attention more a *physical* thing than it really is, I remind him of what he himself experiences when he turns his attention to some Object.

He turns his eye away from the surrounding Objects; thus he *weakens* the *impression* that those Objects make. He *fixes* his view on the Object of his Attention; he concentrates it on that Object; he *tenses* the organ for that Object, if I may so express myself.

Does not all this prove the *intervention* of the Body in the act of *Attention?* But if my reader wants another proof of this Fact, I recall to him further that he becomes *fatigued* when he fixes his gaze too long on an Object. This fatigue may even go to the point of *pain,* whether he was considering that Object with the eyes of the Spirit, or with the eyes of the Body. Now, is not the Seat of this fatigue, of this pain, in the Organs?

Finally, how does one cure this fatigue, this pain? By *rest,* or by *changing* the Object. Why by rest? because it is a *cessation of Action.* When the Soul ceases to act on the *Fibers* on which it had been acting, the *tension* which it has imposed on them *diminishes, weakens, disappears,* Why *by changing the Object?* because then the Soul is *no longer* acting on the *same* fibers. Each perception has fibers which belong to it.

137. Thus EXPERIENCE proves that *Attention* involves a certain exertion of the Soul's *motive Force* on the Fibers of the Brain. . . .

138. What effect does the Soul produce on these Fibers? . . .

When some motive leads me to turn my attention to one [of several] Objects, I fix my eyes upon it. Immediately the *Perception* of this Object becomes *more lively;* the Perception of neighboring Objects *becomes weakened.* Soon I discover peculiarities in this Object which had at first escaped me. To the extent that my attention increases, the impressions of the Object are *strengthened* and *multiplied.* Finally, all this grows to a point where I am almost not affected at all except by this Object.

139. Those are the Facts; what do they teach us? That Attention increases the *intensity* of movements imprinted by Objects. One cannot reject this conclusion. The *vivacity* of Sensations is necessarily proportional to the intensity of the movements which excite them. A Sensation *grows weaker* to the extent that the action of the Object *diminishes,* and this action is a *movement* imprinted on the Organ. . . .

142. To the extent that the Perception of an Object is made *more lively* by Attention, the Perception of *neighboring* Objects *becomes weaker.* This is another *effect* of Attention which I must explain by the Principles which I have stated.

The *sensory* and *motor* Fibers have need of Spirits in order to perform their functions.

Anything that tends to increase or diminish the *quantity* of the *Nervous* Fluid, increases or diminishes the *Activity* of the Fibers.

The Nervous Fluid is therefore distributed to the Fibers in a certain relation to the *sum* of the actions which they must exercise.

The *quantity* of the Nervous Fluid is *fixed.* Therefore it cannot flow in greater abundance into certain Fibers, except by taking away from what the neighboring Fibers are able to receive at the same time.

Attention augments the movement of the Fibers on which it acts. The stronger the Attention, or the more sustained it is, the greater is this augmentation.

The *Spirits* are therefore drawn from the neighboring Fibers, toward those on which the Attention is exercised.

This *drainage* [dérivation], in proportion to the amount of movement imposed by the Attention, may reach the point that the neighboring Fibers are too depleted of Spirits to be able to make any sensible impression on the soul. This impression on the Soul may become nil, or almost nil.

16.8

David Ferrier

(1843–1928)

John B. Watson is frequently credited with introducing the theory that thought is implicit speech. Actually, Bain had said that "in speech we have a series of actions fixed in trains by association, and which we can perform either actually or mentally at pleasure, the mental action being nothing else than a sort of whisper, or approach to a whisper, instead of the full-spoken utterance." With his usual good sense, Bain did not assert that thinking always involves this "sort of whisper." David Ferrier gave the theory a fuller statement and combined it with the concept of cortical inhibition. As a neurologist, he was of course acquainted with Sechenov's work on inhibitory centers in the frog, but probably he was not aware of the Reflexes of the brain (see 9.11).

Like most of his contemporaries, Ferrier subsequently abandoned the notion of neural inhibition.

§103. Both the voluntary excitation of ideas and the concentration of consciousness by which the current of ideation is controlled, seem to be essentially dependent on the motor centres. . . .

In calling up an idea, or when engaged in the attentive consideration of some idea or ideas, we are in reality throwing into action, but in an inhibited or suppressed manner, the movements with which the sensory factors of ideation are associated in organic cohesion.

We think of form by initiating and then inhibiting the movements of the eyes or hands through which and by which ideas of form have been gained and persist. . . . In the case of ideas, the motor element of which is not apparent, the method of excitation can be referred to the articulatory movements with which as symbols ideas are associated. This is, in fact, the most usual method of recalling ideas in general. We recall an object in idea by pronouncing the name in a suppressed manner. We think, therefore, and direct the current of thought in a great measure by means of internal speech.

This is essentially the case with respect to the recalling of abstract ideas as contradistinguished from concrete and particular.

The abstract qualities and relations of objects exist only by reason of words, and we think of the concrete or particular instances out of which the general or abstract have been formed, by making the symbolic movements of articulation with which these ideas cohere.

The functions of the brain. London, 1876. [Pp. 284–288.]

An aphasic individual is incapable of abstract ideation or trains of thought. He thinks only in particulars, and his thoughts are conditioned mainly by present impressions on his organs of sense, arousing ideas according to the usual laws of association.

The recall of an idea being thus apparently dependent on excitation of the motor element of its composition, the power of fixing the attention and concentrating consciousness depends, further, on inhibition of the movement.

During the time we are engaged in attentive ideation we suppress actual movements, but keep up in a state of greater or less tension the centres of the movement or movements with which the various sensory factors of ideation cohere.

By checking the tendency to outward diffusion in actual motion, we thereby increase the internal diffusion, and concentrate consciousness. For the degree of consciousness is inversely proportional to the amount of external diffusion in action. In the deepest attention, every movement which would diminish internal diffusion is likewise inhibited. Hence, in deep thought, even automatic actions are inhibited, and a man who becomes deep in thought while he walks, may be observed to stand still. . . .

In proportion to the development and degree of education of the centres of inhibition do acts of volition lose their impulsive character, and acquire the aspect of deliberation. Present impulses or feelings, instead of at once exciting action, as in the infant, stimulate the centres of inhibition simultaneously, and suspend action until, under the influence of attention, the associations engendered by past experience between actions and their pleasurable or painful consequences, near and remote, have arisen in consciousness. If the centres of inhibition, and therefore the faculty of attention, are weak, or present impulses unusually strong, volition is impulsive rather than deliberate.

The centres of inhibition being thus the essential factor of attention, constitute the organic base of all the higher intellectual faculties. And in proportion to their development we should expect a corresponding intellectual power. . . .

§104. In proportion to the development of the faculty of attention are the intellectual and reflective powers manifested. This is in accordance with the anatomical development of the frontal lobes of the brain, and we have various experimental and pathological data for localising in these the centres of inhibition, the physiological substrata of this psychological faculty.

It has already been shown that electrical irritation of the antero-frontal lobes causes no motor manifestation, a fact which, though a negative one, is consistent with the view that, though not actually motor, they are inhibitory-motor, and expend their energy in inducing internal changes in the centres of actual motor execution. . . .

The removal of the frontal lobes causes no motor paralysis, or other evident physiological effects, but causes a form of mental degradation, which may be reduced in ultimate analysis to loss of the faculty of attention. . . .

The development of the frontal lobes is greatest in man with the highest intellectual powers, and taking one man with another, the greatest intellectual power is characteristic of the one with the greatest frontal development.

The phrenologists have, I think, good grounds for localising the reflective faculties in the frontal regions of the brain, and there is nothing inherently improbable in the view that frontal development in special regions may be indicative of the power of concentration of thought and intellectual capacity in special directions.

16.9

Oswald Külpe

(1862–1915)

The "Würzburg school" of psychologists, who worked under Külpe's direction on the experimental analysis of the thought process, included Mayer, Orth, Marbe, Watt, Ach, and Karl Bühler. Instead of reporting any of their research directly, we take this selection from Külpe's invited address before the Fifth Congress of the German Society for Experimental Psychology in 1912.

Earlier psychology generally did not give sufficient attention to the problem of thinking. And the experimental movement at first had so much to do to establish order in the enormous house of sensations, images, and feelings, that it was only relatively late that it could take on the airy thoughts. The robust sensory content of pricks and pressures, of tastes and smells, of sounds and colors, first made themselves evident in consciousness, were most easily perceived, and after them their images, and pleasures and pains. That there might be something other than these, something without their perceptual consistency, escaped the eye of the investigator, which was not trained to perceive this. Scientific experience had prepared them to notice stimuli and sensations, afterimages, contrast phenomena and imaginative alterations of reality. Whatever did not have this character, simply did not seem to exist. And thus it was that the first experimental psychologists who performed experiments on

Ueber die Bedeutung der modernen Denkpsychologie. [On the significance of the modern psychology of thinking. 1912.] Pp. 297–331 in O. Külpe, *Vorlesungen über Psychologie*, Stuttgart: Hirzel Verlag, 1922. [Pp. 301–306, 315–317.]

word meanings had nothing to report unless some imaginal representations or accompanying phenomena appeared. In many other cases, especially when the word signified something abstract or general, they found "nothing." The fact that a word could be understood without releasing an image, that a sentence could be grasped and a judgment could be made although it could not be proved that anything more than its sound had entered into consciousness, did not lead these psychologists to assume and to ascertain the existence of imageless content alongside of the image content. . . .

What finally led psychologists to a different theory was *the systematic application of introspection.* Previously it had been the custom not to require a report after each trial, on all the experiences during it, but to collect occasional protocols from the experimental subjects about exceptional or abnormal phenomena, and only after a whole series had been completed to ask for a summary report about the main points which could still be remembered. In that way, only the most obvious material came to light. Also, preoccupation with the concepts of sensations, feelings and images served to hinder noticing and describing anything which was neither sensation nor feeling nor image. But as soon as introspectively trained observers were asked to give full and unrestricted reports about the experience during each trial, immediately after it was completed, the necessity for broadening the earlier concepts and definitions became obvious. They discovered within themselves processes, states, tendencies, acts, which did not fit into the schema of the older psychology. The experimental subjects began to talk in the speech of life, and to assign only a subordinate significance, for their inner worlds, to images. They knew and thought, judged and understood, grasped meanings and interpreted relationships, without receiving any real support from occasionally appearing sensory material. Let us take a pair of examples. The subject is asked: Do you understand the saying, *The gold, as soon as it had recognized the jewel, worshipped its brighter gleam and became its vassal?* In the protocol he says: "First I was surprised by the conspicuous appearance of the word *gold;* understanding was immediate, though the word *recognized* caused a little difficulty. Then the thought came to me of a general translation to human circumstances, and in this the recognition of a ranking by worth was included. Finally I had something of a vista of infinite possibilities for application of this metaphor." —Here a process of understanding is described, taking place without images, and also without more than fragmentary speech. Nor would it be possible to understand how sensory contents of consciousness, or mere words, could give rise to the recognition of a ranking by worth, or a vista of infinite possibilities. Or another example: Do you understand the saying, *Thinking is so extraordinarily difficult that many people prefer to make judgments?* The protocol reads: "Right after the end of the sentence, I knew what it was about. But the thought was still quite unclear. In order to reach clarity, I repeated the sentence slowly, and as I finished it the thought was clear, which I can now repeat thus: Here the *judgment* is a kind of thoughtless statement and way of disposing of the matter in contrast to the self-searching of *thinking*. Aside from the words of the saying which I heard and repeated, nothing imagelike appeared in consciousness." —Here again is a not altogether simple process of imageless thinking. And it is significant that both subjects have said that understanding of more difficult sayings takes place in just the same way. It is therefore no artifact of the laboratory, but the blossoming life of reality, which is made evident in these experiments. We can bring in a great many examples from daily experience which contain thinking of this sort. We read or hear: *Man should be noble, good, and helpful, for only this distinguishes him from the other creatures.* Or: *My memory and my pride fight with each other. My memory says: you did it; my pride says: you cannot have done it. Finally my memory gives in.* . . . In such cases, who experiences images, and for whom are such images the basis, the necessary conditions for understanding? And who can assert that such words alone would be enough to represent the meaning? No, such cases give proof of the existence of imageless content of consciousness, particularly of thoughts.

But if there are thoughts which are different from images of colors and tones, of forests and gardens, of people and animals, then this difference must also carry over to how these thoughts behave, their forms, their course or progress. We know how images are governed by laws. Everyone talks about association and reproduction, about the emergence of an image, about its excitation by others, its combination with others. We memorize a poem or a series of syllables. It is not enough to know their content, their meaning; we must learn it word for word in order to be able to reproduce it faithfully later. We foster firm associations between the successive or paired elements of the poem or the series of syllables, and for this we need a fairly long time and a great many repetitions. If thoughts were nothing but images, the same sort of tedious effort would be needed to memorize them. But a consideration of the way in which we assimilate the meaning of a poem shows us at once that this is quite another matter. One careful reading often suffices so that we can reproduce the thought content. And by such purely mental assimilation we go on to achievements of such broad scope as to reproduce the thoughts that were contained in a sermon, a lecture, a dramatic performance, a novel or a scientific book, and a long conversation. How independent this is of the sound of words we often learn to our regret. So often we would like to be able to repeat some apt expression, a pithy sentence or a beautiful metaphor. But although the meaning of what was said remains with us, we can no longer recollect the form in which it was stated. . . .

The independent significance of the task [*Aufgabe*], and of the determining tendency which emerges from it, were also disastrous for association psychology. An *Aufgabe* is not a motive for reproduction in the usual sense. It must be accepted, the subject must set himself accordingly; it gives a certain direction to his activity. . . . A change in *Aufgabe* is therefore an experimental intervention which is at least as important as a change in the external conditions of the experiment.

This importance of the *Aufgabe* and its effects on the structure and the course of mental processes cannot be explained by associative psychology. To the contrary, Ach [in 1905] was able to show that even associations of considerable strength could be overcome by an opposed *Aufgabe*. The power which a determining tendency itself asserts is not only greater than the known tendencies to reproduction, but it also comes from deeper sources and it is not tied to associative conditions in its effects.

We have studied the influence of the *Aufgabe* in simple cases. For example, the subject is to find a part of the whole, or to state a classification for a certain specific character. In these experiments it has been consistently shown that the *Aufgabe* is much more significant for the outcome than the particular stimuli which are given. In the flight of phenomena, it is the fixed point of reference. The words change from trial to trial; the task remains the same at least for a series, for an experimental hour. It is the *Aufgabe* which gives a certain direction to activity. The word "chemistry" may receive many different answers: one can think of it as a science, or emphasize its usefulness or think of the elements and their compounds, which are its subject matter, and so forth. Whether it is seen as a part or subordinated to a whole depends solely on the compulsion of the determining tendency. . . . Of course errors sometimes occur; one may perhaps name another part, or give a classification, instead of naming the whole. But the number of errors is relatively small, and it therefore proves how greatly the determining tendency influences the flow of ideas.

16.10

Max Wertheimer

(1880–1943)

Gestalt psychology traces its birth as a self-conscious school from the publication in 1912 of Wertheimer's study of illusory visual movement, the phi-phenomenon. That publication was "pregnant" with Gestalt theory,

Untersuchungen zur Lehre von der Gestalt, I. Prinzipielle Bemerkungen [Investigations of Gestalt theory, I. Statements of principle.] *Psychologische Forschung* 1 (1921): 47–58. [Pp. 47–50, 52–56.] Used by permission of Springer-Verlag, West Berlin.

but it gave no explicit formulation, and the events of World War I delayed further publication. This selection is taken from the first issue of the journal which was established as the house organ of the Gestalt movement. It is a sharpened expression of a point of view characteristic of many German psychologists, and already expressed by Herbart (see 25.4) and Johannes Müller (see 7.11)—the rejection of association as mechanical, and insistence on the creative aspects of thinking. Gestalt theory found a way to restore spontaneity to thinking, which had been reduced to a passive mechanism by the triumph of associationism. (Herbart had done this by inhibitory interactions, and Wundt by "apperception.")

This article was condensed in a paraphrase by W. D. Ellis in his Source Book of Gestalt Psychology (1938).

In its concrete work on specific problems—despite all differences of opinion on general theoretical questions—scientific psychology almost universally applies one basic and highly significant point of view regarding mental phenomena: a point of view which must always strike any ingenuous person as strange, wooden, and monstrous (although it is inwardly closely bound up with very characteristic features of the modern world-view). Again and again this point of view is postulated as a matter of course in dealing with concrete scientific problems, because, compared with vaguer points of view, it does have undoubted advantages in respect to scientific exactness, and this is particularly so because we are disposed to regard some of its essential characteristics as requisites for any sort of proper scientific procedure.

For example, we readily accept as a matter of course that in order to attain a scientific understanding of mental phenomena generally, we must first of all plainly postulate "elements" which are basic to the complex multiplicity of coexisting psychological events, and that we can arrive at a correct description and explanation of the complex processes by applying general laws which apply to these elements, through combination of the elements, through *and*-connections. . . .

This fundamental point of view is characterized by two basic theses which we may formulate quite simply:

I. The mosaic or bundle hypothesis:

Every "complex" is based first of all on a sum of elementary contents or pieces (sensations, etc.), existing side-by-side. Basically what we are dealing with is an additive multiplicity made up of different kinds of pieces (a "bundle"); anything over and above this and-summation of elements is somehow erected on top of it. For example, "residues" of earlier perceptions are added to the sensations, as well as feelings and all sorts of factors, such as "attentive processes," interpretive processes, volitional processes, etc.

Memory also tacks itself on to this sum of contents.

II. The association thesis:

If Content A has frequently occurred together with Content B ("in spatial contiguity"), a tendency arises for the appearance of A to be followed, as a consequence, by appearance of B.

(If pum-lap has occurred frequently, and if pum should now enter awareness, then lap also will happen. In this way my friend is associatively "connected" with his telephone number.) . . .

The detailed formulation of these theses is of no importance here. One can substitute any other formulation to fit a particular theoretical orientation, without changing the essential point. . . .

What the two theses have in common, as a matter of principle, is the use of *and-summations*. Complexes are built up out of pieces which exist before anything else—a first and a second and a third . . . [*sic*]—and these provide the foundation for everything else. Each, with respect to the others, "also" exists. They are in principle independent of one another as to content, lacking any "inherence" as such, unless we mean one that arises "from below," and again out of pieces. If on top of these there arise higher structures, connections, complexes, then they are erected secondarily, from the bottom up, on top of this *and-summation* (although in this process various newly appearing functions, acts, attentional behaviors, etc., do play a role).

It is in principle a matter of indifference what elements are thus joined together, simultaneously, adjacently, sequentially. The "content" or the relatedness of contents is really irrelevant to their coexistence. There are no inherent factors which are conditions for this togetherness, but content-alien, extraneous factors, such as, for example, simultaneous viewing, or the fact that they had frequently been together before, etc.

It is like a blind manipulation of all different kinds of building stones. Which ones come together, what it all leads to, what happens, is a matter of "*contingencies*."

The picture is that of a manifold which is put together out of pieces that fit together mechanically, and which takes its essential character primarily from this sum. Technically, the first thesis might be put this way: the total output of a series of machines, standing in a row, side by side, is equal to the sum of their separate outputs. And the second thesis —stated without polish:—It doesn't matter what we add on, everything is "sticky," and it will all stick together if we push the pieces together often enough, and the more often the better.

In short: a fundamental *and*-summation, progress from the bottom up, with everything mechanical, indifferently thrown together by chance. . . .

In contrast:

Only rarely, only under definite characteristic conditions, only within narrow limits, and perhaps never except approximately, do we really have and-summations; *it is not appropriate to regard this limiting case as a typical basis for events.*

Only rarely: for example when suffering from a bad cold, in cases of utter stupidity, at characteristic points when the process of thinking is not proceeding smoothly; when things which are grossly "disparate" and truly irrelevant to each other are presented together, compelling piece-meal apprehension of them (as in analysis and dissolution of arbitrary configurations without meaning); under experimental conditions which give a "set" that favors "determination of the parts," "dissolution of the configuration," and leveling of impressions.

Within very narrow limits: the "range of consciousness" is extraordinar-ily small for piecemeal objects; it is functionally tied to the degree of configuration (a fact which has considerable biological value). The same for readiness to notice something, to be impressed by it, to remember it.

Perhaps never except approximately: Even when we at first seem to have piecemeal summative apprehension, a more penetrating description often shows that the case is otherwise (and functional regularities con-firm this). Even in the examples given above—the very impression of a "chaos" is far from being a simple apprehension of an and-summation, and often it is only a typical habit of scientific thinking which leads to assuming it. The genuine occurrence of piecemeal and-phenomena can only be attained to a slight degree, and it is always accompanied by the danger of an artificial condition, by the danger that the phenomena themselves will be changed, will be flattened and drained of what is most essential to them. . . .

Phenomena are in themselves "structured" in varying degrees: they are more or less definitely structured, more or less definite wholes and whole-processes, which as wholes possess very concrete characteristics, including inner regularities, characteristic whole-tendencies, and influ-ences which the whole exercises on its parts.

"Pieces" for the most part are to be regarded in a concrete manner "as parts" of whole-processes. . . .

It is in principle not at all accidental which things are joined together, which seem to be "apprehended together," which are "filled in" (nor in principle are these events determined by blind, irrelevant, "external" factors, as for example by fragmentary habits). [These outcomes are] rather largely determined by *concrete laws of configuration.* We see tendencies to definite "superior configurations," movements of the whole, laws which determine how the parts are "conditioned by inner necessity" and "demanded" by the essential conditions of the whole.

Therefore it is not the "pieces" which are to be set up as the starting point, as a foundation which gives rise [to the whole] by and-connections and as a result of conditions which are in principle foreign to the matter. They exist largely as parts which are conditioned by the whole, and which are to be understood "as parts" of the whole. . . .

Gestalten therefore are not "[mental] contents added to the sum [of elements]," not "arbitrary" structures "subjectively erected" upon parts that are first given, which are contingent and "only subjectively determined;" they are not simple, blind, additional "qualities," which are basically as fragmentary and unmanageable as the "elements"; not something "added to the material" or "merely formal." Rather they are wholes and whole-processes with numerous quite definite inner, essential laws; they are structures with concrete structural principles. . . .

It is readily apparent that these theses also open definite approaches to problems quite different from those of perception and memory—to problems of *psychic* and *intellectual* values; and also, that this general statement of the problem implies important philosophical consequences. . . .

Attentional processes themselves include essential Gestalt processes; memory attaches itself first of all to whole-characteristics and structural connections; the most essential aspect of the memory process (and likewise of "experience") is not reducible to the retention of sums [of elements] and their order, nor of the whole insofar as that is a merely summative, fragmentary whole. Association and habit, in the sense of connections between things existing together, regardless of content (mechanical memory in general) is only a limiting case.

Processes of thinking, processes involved *in the original solution of a problem,* processes involved *in grasping and comprehending* (in the full meaning of these words, that is, in the fundamental transition from something that is not understood to something that is understood), processes involved *in the perception of a problem*—are quite distinct from mere memory phenomena, with which they seemed to be holpelessly amalgamated "as a train of ideas;" quite distinct from processes of piecemeal generalization, piecemeal subtractive abstractions, combinations, etc. They show themselves in their essential nature to be *Gestalt processes with concrete characteristics of a very definite sort* (which have their analogies on one hand in perception, and on the other in processes of *feeling* and *volition*).

16.11

Kenneth J. W. Craik

(1914–1945)

Kenneth Craik was among the first to foresee the possibilities of developing computers as servo-mechanisms which could perform complex tasks, and he perceived the analogy between these "thinking machines" and our

On the nature of explanation. London and New York: Cambridge University Press, 1943. [Pp. 50–61.]

*own brains. Unfortunately, he did not live to participate in the develop-
ments which followed. The line of thought presented here is related to the
thesis of Köhler's book on "physical configurations" (Die physischen Gestalten in Ruhe und im stationären Zustand, 1920), as well as to the important paper by Köhler and Wallach on figural aftereffects (1944). These
may be regarded as special cases of the sort of symbolization which Craik
has in mind, although he certainly contemplates an isomorphism which
is not so spatially restricted as those of the Gestalt theorists. Considerations
which make the Köhler-Wallach hypothesis of electrical fields in the brain
untenable, do not apply to Craik's hypothesis.*

[Ch. V.] One of the most fundamental properties of thought is its power
of predicting events. This gives it immense adaptive and constructive
significance as noted by Dewey and other pragmatists. It enables us, for
instance, to design bridges with a sufficient factor of safety instead of
building them haphazard and waiting to see whether they collapse, and
to predict consequences of recondite physical or chemical processes whose
value may often be more theoretical than practical. . . .

Surely, however, this process of prediction is not unique to minds,
though no doubt it is hard to imitate the flexibility and versatility of
mental prediction. A calculating machine, an anti-aircraft 'predictor',
and Kelvin's tidal predictor all show the same ability. In all these latter
cases, the physical process which it is desired to predict is *imitated*
by some mechanical device or model which is cheaper, or quicker, or
more convenient in operation. . . .

. . . I have not committed myself to a definite picture of the mechanisms
of synaptic resistance, facilitation, etc.; but I have tried, in the succeeding pages, to indicate what I suspect to be the fundamental feature of
neural machinery—its power to parallel or model external events—and
have emphasized the fundamental role of this process of paralleling in
calculating machines. Thus, it is perhaps better to start with a definite
idea as to the kind of tasks mechanism can accomplish in calculations,
and the tasks it would have to accomplish in order to play a part in
thought, rather than to draw analogies between the nervous system and
some specific mechanism such as a telephone exchange and leave the
matter there. A telephone exchange may resemble the nervous system
in just the sense I think important; but the essential point is the principle
underlying the similarity. . . .

Any kind of working model of a process is, in a sense, an analogy. Being
different it is bound somewhere to break down by showing properties not
found in the process it imitates or by not possessing properties possessed
by the process it imitates. . . .

We have now to inquire how the neural mechanism, in producing
numerical measurement and calculation, has managed to function in a
way so much more universal and flexible than any other. Our question,

to emphasize it once again, is not to ask what kind of thing a number is, but to think what kind of machine could represent so many physically possible or impossible, and yet self-consistent processes as number does. . . .

This greatly extended power is not unique to a mind; it could be illustrated by calculating machines. A machine working on a graphical principle might try to represent squaring and cubing by pointers moving along the x, y, and z axes; it would inevitably come to a standstill or repeat itself when the volume of the cube equalled its own volume. On the other hand, a machine working on the principle of picking up gear-teeth by a repeated-multiplication process could go on raising any number to any power however large if it had sufficient dials on it.

It is likely then that the nervous system is in a fortunate position, as far as modelling physical processes is concerned, in that it has only to produce combinations of excited arcs, not physical objects; its 'answer' need only be a combination of consistent patterns of excitation—not a new object that is physically and chemically stable. . . .

My hypothesis then is that thought, models, or parallels, reality—that its essential feature is not 'the mind', 'the self', 'sense-data', nor propositions but symbolism, and that this symbolism is largely of the same kind as that which is familiar to us in mechanical devices which aid thought and calculation. . . .

It is generally agreed that thought employs symbols such as written or spoken words or tokens; but it is not generally considered whether the whole of thought may not consist of a process of symbolism, nor is the nature of symbolism and its presence or absence in the inorganic world discussed. Further, it has been usual to restrict the word 'symbol' to words or tokens, which still leaves the processes of the relating of words to form sentences and the processes of inference and implication mysterious and unique. . . .

There are plenty of instances in nature of processes which parallel each other—the emptying of pools and the discharge of a cat's fur which has become electrified, the transmission of sound and electromagnetic and ocean waves, and so forth. As mentioned above, human thought has a definite function; it provides a convenient small-scale model of a process so that we can, for instance, design a bridge in our minds and know that it will bear a train passing over it instead of having to conduct a number of full-scale experiments; and the thinking of animals represents on a more restricted scale the ability to represent, say, danger before it comes and leads to avoidance instead of repeated bitter experience. . . .

Thus there are instances of symbolisation in nature; we use such instances as an aid in thinking; there is evidence of similar mechanisms at work in our own sensory and central nervous systems; and the function of such symbolisation is plain. If the organism carries a 'small-scale model' of external reality and of its own possible reactions within its head, it is able to try out various alternatives, conclude which is the best of them, react to future situations before they arise, utilise the knowledge of past events in dealing with the present and future, and in every way to react in a much fuller, safer, and more competent, manner to the emergencies which face it. . . . Is it not possible, therefore, that our brains themselves utilise [mechanisms which] can parallel phenomena in the external world as a calculating machine can parellel the development of strains in a bridge?

 # Chapter 17

LEVELS OF
INTELLIGENCE

Awareness of individual differences in capacity for verbal learning and problem-solving has no doubt existed as long as men consciously studied behavior. Because reason, or intelligence, was long regarded as an attribute of the incorporeal soul, a link of man to God, there was reluctance to think of these differences otherwise than as indirect effects of damage to the bodily instruments through which the mind must express itself. (Cf. 8.3.) One of the earliest references to mental retardation is in the selection from Albertus Magnus (14.2), where he stated that Pygmies (whom he regarded as irrational animals) are "deprived of reason by nature, while the moron . . . is not deprived of reason but of the power to use reason." Intellectual deficiency has a prominent place in this chapter because advances in understanding the nature of intelligence have often grown out of efforts to deal with those who were deficient in it because of some developmental anomaly.

17.1

Juan Huarte

(1530?–1591?)

The subtitle of this work appears as follows on the title page of the translation:

In whicch, by discovering the varietie of natures, is shewed for what profession each one is apt, and how far he shall profit therein

It is a promise he never fulfills, but his insistence that physical factors determine the strength of the various faculties was revolutionary, and by many thought irreligious. Which aspect of temperament relates to each faculty has already been stated in an earlier selection (10.2); Huarte's views on instinct are given in 15.4.

[Chap. II.]   *That Nature Is That Which Makes a Man of Habilities to Learne.*

It is an opinion very common and ordinarie amongst the antient Philosophers, to say, That Nature is she who makes a man of habilitie to learne, and that art with her precepts and rules gives a facilitie thereunto, but then use and experience, which he reapes of particular things, maker him mightie in working. Yet none of them over chewed in par ticular, what thing this nature was, nor in what ranke of causes it ought to be placed: only they affirmed, that this, wanting in him who learned, art, experience, teachers, bookes, and travaile are of none availe. . . .

The token whereon I ground my judgement, when I would discover whether a man have a wit appropriat to Naturall Philosophie, is, to see whether he be addicted to reduce all matters to miracle, without distinction; and contrariwise, such as hold not themselves contented, untill they know the particular cause of everie effect, leave no occasion to mistrust the goodnesse of their wit. . . .

To returne then to that sentence so often used by naturall Philosophers, that *Nature makes able;* we must understand that there are wits, and there are Abilities, which God bestoweth upon men besides naturall order, as was the wisedome of the Apostles, who being simple and of base account, were miraculously enlightened and replenished with

Examen de ingenios para las sciencias [Baeza, 1575]. Translated by Richard Carew (from the Italian version of Camillo Camilli) as *The examination of mens wits*. London, 1594. [Pp. 13, 17, 19–25.]

knowledge and learning. Of this sort of abilitie & wisdome, it cannot be verefied, that nature makes able; for this is a worke, which is to be imputed immediately unto God, & not unto nature: The like is to be understood of the wisedome of the prophets, and of all those to whome God graunted some grace infused. Another sort of abilitie is found in men, which springs of their being begotten, with that order and consent of causes which are established by God to this end: and of this sort it may be sayd with truth; *Nature makes able....*

This varietie of wits, it is a matter certaine that it springs not from the reasonable soule, for that is one selfe in all ages, without having received in his forces and substaunce any alteration: but man hath in every age a divers temperature, and a contrarie disposition, by means whereof, the soule doth other workes in childhood, other in youth, and other in old age. Whence we draw an evident argument, that one selfe soule, doing contrarie workes in one selfe bodie, for that it partakes in every age a contrarie temperature, when of young men, the one is able, and the other unapt, this growes for that the one of them enioies a divers temperature from the other. And this for that it is the beginning of all the workes of the reasonable soule, was by the Phisitions and the Philosophers, termed Nature; of which signification, this sentence is properly verefied, that *Nature makes able.*

For confirmation of this doctrine, *Galen* writ a booke, wherein he prooveth, That the maners of the soule, follow the temperature of the body, in which it keepes residence, and that by reason of the heat, the coldness, the moisture, and the drouth, of the territorie where men inhabit, of the meats which they feed on, of the waters which they drinke, and of the aire which they breath: some are blockish, and some wise: some of woorth, and some base: some cruel, and some merciful: many straight brested, and many large: part lyers, and part true speakers: sundrie traitors, and sundrie faythfull: somewhere unquiet, and somewhere stayed: there double, here single: one pinching, another liberall: this man shamefast, and that shamelesse: such hard, and such light of beleefe. . . . Finally, all that which *Galen* writeth in this his booke, is the groundplot of this my Treatise, albeit he declares not in particular, the differences of the habilities which are in men, neither as touching the sciences which everie one requires in particular. Notwithstanding, he understood that it was necessarie to depart the sciences amongst yoong men, and to give ech one that which to his naturall habilitie was requisit, in as much as he sayd, That well ordered common wealths, ought to have men of great wisedome and knowledge, who might in their tender age, discover ech ones wit and naturall sharpnesse, to the end they might be set to learne that art which was agreeable, and not leave it to their owne election.

438

[Chap. III.] *What Part of the Body Ought to Be Well Tempered, That a Young Man May Have Habilitie.*

Mans body hath so many varieties of parts and powers (applied ech to his end) that it shal not stray from our purpose, but rather growes a matter of necessitie, to know first, what member was ordained by nature for the principall instrument, to the end man might become wise and advised. For it is a thing apparant, that we discourse not with our foot, nor walke on our head, nor see with our nostrils, nor heare with our eies, but that every of these parts hath his use and particular disposition, for the worke which it is to accomplish. . . .

Foure conditions the braine ought to enioy, to the end the reasonable soule may therewith commodiously performe the workes which appertaine to understanding and wisdome. The first, good composition; the second, that his parts be well united; the third, that the heat exceed not the cold, nor the moist the drie; the fourth, that his substance be made of parts suitable and verie delicate.

In the good composition, are contained other foure things: the first is, good figure: the second, quantitie sufficient: the third, that in the braine the foure ventricles be distinct and severed, each duly bestowed in his seat and place: the fourth, that the capablenesse of these be neither greater nor less than is convenient for their workings.

17.2

Thomas Hobbes

(1588–1679)

Because Hobbes was a partisan of absolute royal power, we may be surprised to find him arguing also for the essential equality of all men, but this equality provides a basis for the social contract which he regards as the foundation of a stable society. Studying Hobbes, it is hard to believe that his politics determined his psychology. He is realistic enough to take man as he finds him.

Hobbes not only accepts Descartes' argument about the essential equality of men as reasoning creatures, but he seems to argue this with more sincerity than Descartes. Both men agree that the differences arise because men turn their thoughts to different things. Descartes conforms to tradition by viewing the passions as interfering with correct thinking (see 20.6);

Leviathan, or the matter, forme, and power of a common-wealth ecclesiasticall and civill. London, 1651. [Part I, chs. 8 and 13; pp. 32–35, 60–61.]

Hobbes sees them as directing our thoughts, and he thus initiates a fruitful line of theory.

Of the Vertues Commonly Called Intellectuall; and their Contrary Defects.

Vertue generally, in all sorts of subjects, is somewhat that is valued for eminence; and consisteth in comparison. For if all things were equally in all men, nothing would be prized. And by *Vertues* INTELLECTUAL are alwayes understood such abilityes of the mind as men praise, value, and desire should be in themselves; and go commonly under the name of a *good witte*; though the same word *Witte*, he used also, to distinguish one certain ability from the rest.

These *Vertues* are of two sorts; *Naturall* and *Acquired*. By Naturall, I mean not, that which a man hath from his Birth: for that is nothing else but Sense, wherein men differ so little one from another, and from brute Beasts, as it is not to be reckoned amongst Vertues. But I mean that *Witte*, which is gotten by Use onely, and Experience; without Method, Culture, or Instruction. This NATURALL WITTE, consisteth principally in two things; *Celerity of Imagining* (that is, swift succession of one thought to another;) and *steddy direction* to some approved end. On the Contary a slow Imagination, maketh that Defect, or fault of the mind, which is commonly called DULNESSE, *Stupidity*, and sometimes by other names that signifie slownesse of motion, or difficulty to be moved.

And this difference of quicknesse, is caused by the difference of mens passions; that love and dislike, some one thing, some another; and therefore some mens thoughts run one way, some another; and are held to, and observe differently the things that passe through their imagination. And whereas in this succession of mens thoughts, there is nothing to observe in the things they think on, but either in what they be *like one another*, or in what they be *unlike*, or *what they serve for*, or *how they serve to such a purpose;* Those that observe their similitudes, in case they be such as are but rarely observed by others, are sayd to have a *Good Wit;* by which, in this occasion, is meant a *Good Fancy*. But they that observe their differences, and dissimilitudes, which is called *Distinguishing*, and *Discerning*, and *Judging* between thing and thing; in case, such discerning be not easie, are said to have a *good Judgement:* and particularly in matter of conversation and businesse; wherein, times, places, and persons are to be discerned, this Vertue is called DISCRETION. The former, that is, Fancy, without the help of Judgement, is not commended as a Vertue: but the later which is Judgement, and Discretion, is commended for it selfe, without the help of Fancy. Besides the Discretion of times, places, and persons, necessary to a good Fancy, there is required also an often application of his thoughts to their End; that is to say, to some use to be made of them. This done; he that hath this Vertue, will be easily fitted with similitudes, that will please, not only by illustration of his discourse, and adorning it with new and apt metaphors; but also, by the rarity of their invention. But without Stedinesse, and Direction to some End, a great Fancy is one kind of Madnesse; such as they have, that entring into any discourse, are snatched from their purpose, by every thing that comes in their thought, into so many, and so long digressions, and Parentheses, that they utterly lose themselves; Which kind of folly, I know no particular name for: but the cause of it is, sometimes want of experience; whereby that seemeth to a man new and rare, which doth not so to others: sometimes Pusillanimity; by which that seems great to him, which other men think a trifle: and whatsoever is new, or great, and therefore thought fit to be told, withdrawes a man by degrees from the intended way of his discourse. . . .

When the thoughts of a man, that has a designe in hand, running over a multitude of things, observes how they conduce to that designe; or what designe they may conduce unto; if his observations be such as are not easie, or usuall, This wit of his is called PRUDENCE; and dependeth on much Experience, and Memory of the like things, and their consequences heretofore. In which there is not so much difference of Men, as there is in their Fancies and Judgements; Because the Experience of men equall in age, is not much unequall, as to the quantity; but lyes in different occasions; every one having his private designs. To govern well a family, and a kingdome, are not different degrees of Prudence; but different forms of businesse; no more then to draw a picture in little, or as great, or greater then the life, are different degrees of Art. A plain husband-man is more Prudent in affaires of his own house, than a Privy Counseller in the affaires of another man. . . .

As for *acquired Wit* (I mean acquired by method and instruction;) there is none but Reason; which is grounded on the right use of Speech; and produceth the Sciences. . . .

The causes of this difference of Witts are in the Passions: and the difference of Passions, proceedeth partly from the different Constitution of the body, and partly from different Education. For if the difference proceeded from the temper of the brain, and the organs of Sense, either exterior or interior, there would be no lesse difference of men in their Sight, Hearing, or other Senses, than in their Fancies, and Discretions. It proceeds therefore from the Passions; which are different, not onely from the difference of mens complexions; but also from their difference of customes and education.

The Passions that most of all cause the differences of Wit, are principally, the more or less Desire of Power, of Riches, of Knowledge, and of Honour. All which may be reduced to the first, that is Desire of Power. For Riches, Knowledge and Honour are but severall sorts of Power.

And therefore, a man who has no great Passion for any of these things; but is as men terme it indifferent; though he may be so farre a good man, as to be free from giving offence; yet he cannot possibly have either a great Fancy, or much Judgement. For the Thoughts, are to the Desires, as Scouts, and Spies, to range abroad, and find the way to the things Desired: All Steddinesse of the minds motion, and all quicknesse of the same, proceeding from thence. For as to have no Desire, is to be Dead: so to have weak Passions, is Dulnesse; and to have Passions indifferently for every thing, GIDDINESSE and *Distraction;* and to have stronger, and more vehement Passions for any thing, than is ordinarily seen in others, is that which men call MADNESSE.

Whereof there be almost as many kinds, as of the Passions themselves. Sometimes the extraordinary and extravagant Passion, proceedeth from the evil constitution of the organs of the Body, or harme done them; and sometimes the hurt, and indisposition of the Organs, is caused by the vehemence, or long continuance of the Passion. But in both cases the Madnesse is of one and the same nature.

Of the Naturall Condition of Mankind, as Concerning their Felicity, and Misery.

Nature hath made men so equall, in the faculties of body, and mind; as that though there bee found one man sometimes manifestly stronger in body, or of quicker mind then another; yet when all is reckoned together, the difference between man, and man, is not so considerable, as that one man can thereupon claim to himselfe any benefit, to which another may not pretend, as well as he. For as to the strength of body, the weakest has strength enough to kill the strongest either by secret machination, or by confederacy with others, that are in the same danger with himselfe.

And as to the faculties of the mind, (setting aside the arts grounded upon words . . .) I find yet a greater equality amongst men, than that of strength. For Prudence, is but Experience: which equall time, equally bestowes on all men, in those things they equally apply themselves unto. That which may perhaps make such equality incredible, is but a vain conceipt of ones owne wisdome, which almost all men think they have in a greater degree, than the Vulgar; that is, than all men but themselves, and a few others, whom by Fame, or for concurring with themselves, they approve. For such is the nature of men, that howsoever they may acknowledge many others to be more witty, or more eloquent, or more learned; Yet they will hardly believe there be many so wise as themselves: For they see their own wit at hand, and other mens at a distance. But this proveth rather that men are in that point equall, than unequall. For there is not ordinarily a greater signe of the equall distribution of any thing, than that every man is contented with his share.

17.3

Jan Amos Comenius (Komensky)

(1592–1671)

The appearance of printed books opened the way to education outside the monasteries and to the rise of interest in pedagogic method (the first peda-gogs being, for the most part, tutors to the sons of noblemen), the development of textbooks, and discussion about the part education plays in shaping character. Comenius, a Czech, took a prominent part in this movement. Although his enthusiasm was initially fired by nationalism, the resulting political exile helped to make him an international figure. He was invited to Sweden to organize its public educational system and to England for the same purpose, but that mission was terminated by the same political unrest which drove Hobbes into exile. He is best known for his Orbis pictus, the world in pictures, which appeared in many multilingual editions. It contained more than 150 woodblock illustrations, each accompanied by word-lists (in the original edition) in Latin, Bohemian, Hungarian, and German. He also wrote on the theory of education, and we give his statement on the right of every child to all the education from which it can profit.

[Ch. 5.] 5. The philosophers call man a microcosm, a world in miniature, which envelops everything that is spread broad and wide, visibly, in the macrocosm. . . . And so the intelligence of people as they enter the world may appropriately be compared to a grain of corn, or a seed. Although the form of the plant or the tree is not yet present in the latter, nevertheless the plant or the tree does truly live therein, as it will reveal itself, when the seed that has been planted in the earth spreads little roots beneath itself and branchings above, which are then transformed by natural powers into branches and twigs, soon to be covered with leaves, bedecked by flowers and by fruit. Therefore it is not necessary to bring anything into men from without, but it is only a matter of unfolding or unpeeling what is already wrapped within him, and demonstrating the meaning of each part. . . .

7. Further there is implanted in man a desire for knowledge, and not only a capacity to sustain work, but an impulse to work. This shows itself early in childhood, and it remains with us all through life. Who does not wish continuously to hear, and see, and do new things? Who

Opera didactica omnia [The complete pedagogy]. Amsterdam, 1657. Selections re-translated from the German edition, *Grosse Didaktik*, Berlin, 1957. [Pp. 72–73, 81–83, 85, 93, 111–112.]

443

does not take daily pleasure in going someplace, talking to someone, asking about something, repeating something? For this is the situation: eyes, ears, touch, reason itself are forever seeking nourishment, going outside themselves; and there is nothing so unsupportable to a living creature as quiet and monotony. . . .

[Ch. 7.] 1. Nature, as we have seen, gives the need for science, morality, and religion; she does not give science, virtue, and religion themselves. Therefore someone has well defined man as an educable animal, because he cannot indeed become a man unless he is educated to it. . . .

4. Man is fitted for work by his body, but we see that only the mere capacity is innate: he must learn bit by bit how to sit, to stand, to walk, to move his hands constructively. . . .

6. There have been men who were kidnapped by wild animals in their infancy, and brought up among them; they knew no more than animals, indeed, they could do no more than wild animals with their tongue, their hands and feet, unless afterward they lived for a while among men. . . .

10. Thus we see that all those who are born as men need education in order to become truly men, and not wild animals. . . .

[Ch. 9.] 1. Not only the children of the eminent, but all alike, noble and commoners, rich and poor, boys and girls, in every town and city, every house and village, must be given schooling. . . .

[Ch. 12.] 16. You will say: but just the same there are great dumbheads, who cannot be taught anything. The answer: there is no mirror so dirty that it cannot give at least some sort of picture, no slate so rough that we cannot at least write something, somehow, on it. Furthermore, if someone hands you a dirty or spattered mirror, you must first smooth it, then you will be able to use it. If young people are thus sharpened and polished, no doubt they will all be so well smoothed and sharpened that, finally, they will all grasp everything. (I stand firmly on my assertion, for my reasons are unshaken.) No doubt the difference will appear, that the duller ones will notice that they have only a rather shallow knowledge of things, but they notice that anyhow; the capable ones, on the other hand, as their effort extends from one thing to another, will plunge deeper and deeper into things, and collect new and very useful observations about them, in many ways. Finally, even if there are some who are thoroughly unteachable, just as knotty wood is unsuitable for cabinet work, still our assertion remains true for average minds, of whom, by God's grace, there always are the most. We see utterly stupid people as rarely as we see people who are missing an arm or a leg from birth. For blindness, deafness, crippling, and disease are surely only rarely innate: we bring these on far more often by our own fault. It is the same with extraordinary feeblemindedness.

17.4

Claude Helvetius

(1715–1771)

Helvetius, born with a silver spoon which he quickly turned to gold and jewels, wealthy, gifted, and universally loved, retired from a lucrative post to make himself, as he hoped, a literary benefactor to all mankind. The book he wrote was sentenced to the flames, which came near to singeing his own handsome head. The opinions he expressed on the dependence of intelligence on motivation and the basic equality of all "well organized" men, joined with his disdainful criticism of the priesthood, made him a direct if unacknowledged forebear of Watsonian behaviorism. More immediately, he helped to shape Bentham's ideas on morals and legislation.

Helvetius stated his views again, even more bluntly, in a book designedly posthumous: Man, his education and his needs (1773).

(For this selection, I have not used the 1759 English translation because of its awkwardness and inaccuracies.)

[III.] *Whether Genius Should be Considered to be a Gift of Nature or an Effect of Education*

[Ch. 1.] In this discourse I shall consider the influence which nature and education exercise on the mind. In order to do this, I must first state what I mean by *nature*.

This word may rouse in us a confused idea of a being or a force which has endowed us with all our senses. Now the senses are the source of all our ideas: if we are deprived of any sense, we are deprived of all the ideas relating to it, and for this reason one who is born blind has no idea of colors. In this meaning, it is clear, intelligence must be considered as wholly a gift of nature.

But if we take the word in a different meaning, and if we suppose that among men who are well formed, endowed with all their senses, and with no evident defect in their organization, nature has nevertheless placed such great differences and such unequal dispositions to intelligence, that some are organized to be stupid and others to be clever, then the question becomes more delicate.

I grant that when one considers the great inequalities of intelligence among men, we cannot at first fail to recognize the same differences as among their bodies, some of which are weak and delicate, while others

De l'esprit [On the mind]. Paris, 1758.

are strong and robust. What, we ask, can be the cause of such differences, since nature [ordinarily] operates in a uniform manner?

. . . To what shall we attribute the great inequality of intelligence which we notice among men who seem to have had the same education?

In order to answer this objection we must first of all consider whether different men can, strictly speaking, receive the same education; and to do this we must define the idea we attach to the word *education*.

If by *education* we understand simply something that has been received from the same teachers in the same towns, then in this sense education is the same for an infinite number of men.

But if we give this word a truer and wider meaning, and if by it we understand in general everything which serves to instruct us, then I say that no one receives the same education, because each of us has as his teachers, if I may be allowed to so express myself, the form of government under which he lives, his friends, his mistresses, the people by whom he is surrounded, the books he reads, and finally chance, that is to say, an infinity of events whose causes and connections we cannot perceive, because of our ignorance. Now, this chance has a greater share in our education than is generally supposed. . . .

. . . If we include under education everything which serves for our instruction, then chance must necessarily have the greatest share in it, and since no one is ever placed in exactly the same combination of circumstances, no one ever receives exactly the same education.

This fact admitted, who can say that it is not a difference in education which produces the difference we see among minds? and that men are not like those trees of the same species whose seeds, which are indestructible and absolutely the same, but never fall upon exactly the same soil, nor are exposed to the same winds, the same sun, the same rains, must in their development necessarily assume an infinite number of different forms. I may therefore conclude that the inequality in the minds of men can be indifferently regarded as an effect of nature or of education. But, however true this conclusion may be, it is still quite vague, and comes down, so to say, to a *perhaps;* therefore I think that I should consider this question from a fresh point of view, based on principles which are more certain and exact. To do that it must be reduced to simple points, going back to the origin of our ideas and the development of our mind. We must remember that a man can do nothing but sense, and remember, and observe similarities and differences, that is, the relationships existing either among the objects he observes or those which he remembers. Therefore nature cannot endow men with more or less disposition to intellect except by giving some, as compared to others, greater refinement of the senses, greater extent of memory, or greater capacity of attention. . . .

[In Chapters 2 and 3, Helvetius demonstrates that neither sharper senses nor better memory can be the basis for higher intelligence.]

17.4 Claude Helvetius

[Ch. 4.] I have shown that the great inequality in minds does not depend either on the degree of perfection of the sense organs or on that of memory. Therefore we can search for its cause only in an unequal capacity for attention.

Since it is more or less attention which engraves objects more or less deeply into memory, and makes us more or less perceptive of the relationships which form the greater part of our true and false judgments; and since we owe almost all our ideas to attention, it is plain (some will say) that the unequal strength of men's minds depends on their unequal capacity for attention. . . .

All the men whom I call well organized are capable of attention, because they all learn to read, they learn their language, and they can understand the first propositions of Euclid. Now any man capable of understanding these first propositions has the physical capacity to understand them all. Indeed, in geometry as in any other science, the degree of ease with which a truth is grasped depends on the greater or lesser number of antecedent propositions which one must have present in memory, in order to understand it. . . .

But, some will say, if all men are endowed with the attention needed to excel in one field, when habit has not rendered them incapable of it, it still remains true that this attention is more difficult for some than for others. To what other cause can we attribute this difference in ease of attention if not to differences in the perfection of the organization?

Before answering this question directly, I shall observe that attention is not foreign to man's nature. When we find it difficult to maintain attention, it is generally because we mistake the fatigue of boredom and impatience for the fatigue of application. Indeed, if there is no man without desires then there is none without attention. When it has become habitual, attention even becomes a need. What makes it fatiguing is the motive which brings us to it. If it is from necessity, poverty, or fear, attention is painful. If it is from the hope of pleasure, attention itself becomes a pleasure. Give the same man two scribbled pages to decipher, one dealing with a question of law, and the other a letter from his mistress. Who will doubt that attention will be as painful in the first case as it is pleasurable in the second? From this observation we may easily explain why attention is more difficult for some men than for others. To do this it is not necessary to postulate any difference in organization between them: it is enough to say that the degree of effort in attention is always proportional to the degree of pleasure which each man sees as the recompense for this effort. . . .

[Helvetius now argues at length that differences in "passion" are the real basis for differences in intellectual achievement, and that passion is influenced more by social environment than by native endowment.]

[Ch. 15.] . . . The general conclusion of what I have said about the origin of the passions is that it is sensory pain and pleasure which cause

447

men to act and to think, and it is only these balanced forces which give movement to the moral world.

Our passions are therefore the immediate effects of physical sensibility. Now, all men are sensitive, and susceptible to passion; all, therefore, carry in themselves the productive seed of genius. . . .

[Ch. 30.] . . . The general conclusion of this discourse is that genius is common, but the circumstances proper to its development are very rare. If we may compare the profane with the sacred, we may say that in this respect, many are called but few are chosen.

Thus the inequality of intelligence which we notice among men depends on the government under which they live, on the more or less fortunate age in which they are born, on the good or less good education which they receive, on the more or less lively desire which they have to distinguish themselves, and finally on the degree of greatness or fecundity in the ideas which are the object of their meditation.

Thus the man of genius is nothing but the product of the circumstances in which men find themselves. Hence too, the whole art of education consists in putting young people into that combination of circumstances which is proper to develop in them the seed of genius and of virtue. It is not the love of paradox which has led me to this conclusion, but only a desire for the happiness of men. I have felt both that good education would spread enlightenment and virtue, and consequently happiness, in society; and also that the current opinion that genius and virtue are pure gifts of nature is much opposed to progress in the science of education, and favors laziness and neglect in this regard. By examining, from this point of view, what influence nature and education have upon us, I have perceived that it is education which makes us what we are. Consequently, I have thought that it is the duty of a citizen to state a fact which will draw attention to the means for improving that education.

17.5

Jean-Marc-Gaspard Itard

(1775–1838)

We have heard Digby (7.4) and Comenius (17.3) on the subject of "wild men." One of the most famous was the "wild boy of Aveyron," captured in 1799 and brought to Paris as a curiosity, where he disappointed expectations based on Rousseau's theories of the "noble savage." After Pinel diagnosed him as an idiot, most persons assumed he had simply been abandoned by disgusted parents. Itard rejected this conclusion, and courageously undertook the boy's education. He devoted a superhuman effort to the task, and nine months later he wrote the optimistic report from which this selection is taken. A second report, in 1806 (which is also translated in the volume from which this selection is taken), revealed the probable limits of education for this unfortunate young man, who was still unable to master the first rudiments of speech. Itard regarded his patient as the victim of a prolonged experience of social isolation, starting at the age of four or five and continuing for about seven years. He correctly assumed that more than a few months of education would be needed to overcome this experience, but he discovered that some of its effects were irreversible.

. . . The conclusion may be drawn from the greater part of my observations . . . that the child known under the name of the *Savage of Aveyron* is endowed with the free use of all his senses; that he can compare, discern, and judge, and finally apply all the faculties of his understanding to the objects related to his instruction. It is essential to note that these happy changes have occurred during the short space of nine months in a subject believed to be incapable of attention; and the conclusion will follow that his education is possible, if it is not even already guaranteed, by this early success, quite apart from any results which time may bring—time which in its unalterable course seems to give the child, in powers and development, all that it takes away from man in the decline of his life.

And meanwhile what important consequences for the philosophic and natural history of the human race already follow from this first series of

De l'éducation d'un homme sauvage, or des premiers développemens physiques et moraux du Jeune Sauvage de l'Aveyron. [On the education of a Savage, or the early physical and mental development of the young savage of Aveyron.] Paris, 1801. Translated by George and Muriel Humphrey, as *The wild boy of Aveyron.* New York: Appleton-Century-Crofts, 1932, 1962. [Pp. 48–50.]

observations. . . . It has appeared to me that at least the following conclusions may be drawn.

(1) That man is inferior to a large number of animals in the pure state of nature, a state of nullity and barbarism that has been falsely painted in the most seductive colors. . . .

(2) That the moral superiority said to be *natural* to man is only the result of civilization, which raises him above other animals by a great and powerful force. This force is the preeminent sensibility of his kind, an essential peculiarity from which proceed the imitative faculties and that continual urge which drives him to seek new sensations in new needs.

(3) That this imitative force . . . rapidly wanes with age, with isolation, and with all the causes which tend to blunt the nervous sensibility; from which it results that the articulation of sounds, of all the effects of imitation unquestionably the most incomprehensible and the most useful, must encounter innumerable obstacles at any age later than that of early childhood.

(4) That in the most isolated savage as in the most highly civilized man, there exists a constant relation between ideas and needs. . . .

(5) That in the present state of our knowledge of physiology the progress of education can and ought to be illumined by the light of modern medicine which, of all the natural sciences, can help most powerfully towards the perfection of the human species by detecting the organic and intellectual peculiarities of each individual and determining therefrom what education ought to do for him and what society can expect from him.

17.6

Franz Joseph Gall

(1758–1828)

AND

Johann Kaspar Spurzheim

(1776–1832)

Gall and his younger coworker Spurzheim not only emphasized the dependence of mental functions on the brain at a time when this was still not generally acknowledged, but they insisted also on the dependence of particular functions on particular portions of the brain (see 10.4). Not surprisingly, this led them to recognize distinctions in the general picture of mental defect.

This book, with its wide-ranging title, represents the advance publication of the first three chapters of the second volume of the four-volume Anatomy and physiology of the nervous system (1810–1811). The collaboration of the two authors ceased at about this time.

In the various degrees of imbecility, to the extent that the organization of the brain approaches perfection, and the particular organs are more or less developed and perfected, the respective faculties of these organs manifest themselves proportionately. Individuals who are in this stage of development show some particular dispositions and penchants; their gestures become more meaningful; they even reach the point of speaking short phrases, which are fairly logical. Thus their functions progress along with the organization, until weakness of the mind no longer shows itself except in a few points, or in a single point. Thus we see that all individuals who are called imbeciles are not completely such. Parents and physicians have difficulty in understanding how a child who acquits himself well in everything there is to do around the house, and who exhibits exact sensations, sensibility and even cleverness, can nevertheless be called an imbecile. That is nevertheless the case with a number of children who can hear, but do not learn to speak. We have drawn attention to this in dealing with the functions of the sense of hearing,

Des dispositions innées de l'âme et de l'esprit, du materialisme, du fatalisme, et de la liberté morale, avec des réflexions sur l'éducation et sur la législation criminelle [On the innate dispositions of the soul and the mind, on materialism, fatalism, and moral liberty, with thoughts on education and criminal legislation]. Paris, 1811. [Pp. 28–30.]

and when we deal with the articulated language which is specific to man we will show that the cause of this accident is a defective organization, the result of which is incapacity to concentrate the attention, to compare and to coordinate the ideas.

At Hamburg we saw a young man, 16 years of age, in whom the lower anterior parts of the head were well developed; but his forehead was scarcely an inch high, because the upper anterior parts of the brain had been impeded in their development. In consequence, he enjoyed only the exercise of the functions influenced by the lower anterior portions. He learned names, numbers, dates, history, and he repeated everything mechanically. But he completely lacked combination, comparison of ideas, and judgment. He was rightly regarded as an imbecile, and he could not have been employed at anything. In the course of this work we shall have several opportunities to confirm this proposition: that the defective development of the organs always results in the weakness of their functions.

17.7

Johann Kaspar Spurzheim

(1776–1832)

Spurzheim was much more successful than his master as an advocate of the cause of phrenology (a designation which he accepted, but which Gall refused to condone because of its mentalistic connotations). Here we have a statement of the position that the old "faculties" must be discarded. It is often said that phrenology simply took over the existing faculty psychology, but actually it contributed largely to the multiplication of the faculties in the later Scottish psychology. What they worked toward, however confusedly, was what we now call the factoring of intelligence.

Spurzheim calls his essay "philosophic" to indicate that it is a scientific treatment of what had previously been regarded as a metaphysical problem.

In physical respects, zoologists divide and subdivide animals; they examine and denote all the peculiarities of their structure; but they are content to view the mental aspect in a general way. Everything the animal does with consciousness, they express with the word *instinct*. They eat and drink by instinct. Why does the nightingale sing? By instinct. Why do birds build nests? By instinct. . . . It is really a very con-

Essai philosophique sur la nature morale et intellectuelle de l'homme [A philosophical essay on the moral and intellectual nature of man]. Paris, 1820. [Pp. 3–4, 8–9, 18, 22, 24–25, 28.]

venient explanation. Instinct is the true talisman which presents all shapes and produces all animal functions. . . .

. . . [However,] instinct is not a single principle; an animal can be endowed with one instinct and not another. Therefore we must specify the kinds of instinct which we observe in animals. . . .

With respect to intelligence, we must repeat what we said about the instinct of animals. First, there are several different kinds of intelligence, and one can have one kind and be deprived of another. Great painters cannot always become great musicians, and *vice versa*. Profound mathematicians will sometimes make bad poets, and excellent generals miserable legislators. Thus daily experience proves that there are different kinds of intelligence, which therefore ought to be specified.

Secondly, the causes of different kinds of intellectual manifestations have not yet been determined, and need special research. Indeed, it is false [to say] that men always act with intelligence. . . . All the gestures, movements and attitudes which accompany the various emotions of the soul take place involuntarily. . . . Modern philosophers are therefore mistaken to believe that intelligence is the sole source of our actions, and that everything which we call will, feeling and desire, results from it; that bad actions depend solely on errors of judgment; and that, to make men better, it would suffice to cultivate their understanding. . . .

Let us begin by examining one of the supposed fundamental faculties of the mind, *attention*, which, according to the opinion of the philosophers, is applied to all sorts of functions. But . . . how shall we understand the variations of attention in different species of animals and in different individuals of the same species, or how can we have one kind of attention which is strong, another which is weak, and be deprived of a third kind? Hens are attracted by grain, the eagle is on the watch for pigeons, the fox directs its attention to a passing hare, while the cow browses tranquilly in the grass. . . . Children are not equally attentive to different subjects. . . . Therefore attention cannot be a single faculty; for the one possessing it should be able to apply it to all sorts of objects. . . .

Memory is another mode of the mind's activity which is ordinarily regarded as a primitive faculty; but this is an abstract term which signifies any repetition of intellectual operations. This explains why memory varies in type and energy in different persons, and why no one has a memory which is equally good for all kinds of knowledge. . . .

. . . Nor is judgment a special faculty, for the same person who is endowed with one kind of judgment sometimes has very little of another kind, or entirely lacks a third kind. The great mathematician who is a perfect judge of numbers and dimensions can be deceived with respect to musical harmony or the colors of a painting. . . .

Imagination, or the faculty of invention, is also regarded as a fundamental power of the understanding. But if there is a primitive faculty which is the basis of all inventions in the arts and sciences, how can we conceive of its acting differently in different persons? Why is a great composer of music unable to compose ingenious machines? . . . It must [therefore] be admitted that men make improvements or inventions in the area of action of the dispositions which they possess, and that there is no faculty of invention. Each faculty has its laws, and the individual who is endowed with it in the highest degree may often discover unknown effects. That is what is called invention. . . .

It follows from all these remarks . . . that all the ideologists have hitherto only envisaged certain modes of action of the faculties, and certain laws according to which the mind acts, but that the special or fundamental faculties of the understanding are still unknown.

17.8

Edouard Séguin

(1812–1880)

Séguin was the student of Itard. He greatly advanced the differential diagnosis of mental retardation as well as the education of children so handicapped.

A physiologist should not concern himself with intelligence except as a function. It has been said, more from the point of view of physiology than from that of a psychologist, that *man is an intelligence served by organs.* If just a word would suffice to give an understanding of an idea which is full of implications, I would say in turn: *the idiot is an intelligence poorly served by imperfect organs:* but I would not be understood, and I hasten to resume a strict analysis of my subject.

Whatever notion one may have of mind, intelligence, human understanding, whatever one wishes to call it, and no matter what opinions are current in psychology, I look upon psychology as a science which is just as positive as botany, and I follow Dr. Collineau in saying that it is *a science of observation, where things are to be observed and put in their places, and nothing is to be created or imagined.* . . .

What does it matter to me what names psychologists give to intellec-

Traitement moral, hygiène et éducation des idiots, et des autres enfants arriérés ou retardés dans leur développement, agités de mouvements involontaires, débiles, muets non-sourds, bègues, etc. [The moral treatment, hygiene and education of idiots and other children backward or retarded in their development, agitated by involuntary movements, debilitated, mute without deafness, stammerers, etc.]. Paris, 1846. [Pp. 163, 165, 169–170, 331–333, 340, 343–344.]

tual functions? I am not here concerned with those names. What we must do is to set up groups of functions, that can be observed.

In order to study intellectual functions by groups, we must first take note that psychological functions are of three kinds: perceptive, discriminative, and elective or spontaneous; and that they have different names depending on whether they are concerned with three orders of phenomena—matter, mind, and feeling—taken in three times—past, present, and future. In effect, any intellectual operation starts with a perception, a discrimination, or an election; in the past, the present, or the future; relative to a moral, intellectual, or material fact.

Starting from this generalization, although at first one may not recognize the traces of psychological functions in the majority of idiots, more persistent observation makes their exercise of these same functions so evident that one will almost refuse to believe that they are organized differently from everyone else. At this stage in the study of idiocy one is tempted to believe that one is suffering from an hallucination, and that we are looking at a creature who seems to lack only the words which Jesus spoke to the paralytic: Stand up and walk. . . .

He does not lack any intellectual faculty; but he does not have the necessary freedom to apply his so-called intellectual faculties to moral and abstract phenomena; he lacks the synergy, the spontaneity, out of which moral volitions arise.

The idiot enjoys the exercise of all his intellectual faculties, but he will not apply them except to concrete phenomena; and only to those concrete phenomena which by their texture, form, taste, smell, sound, or some other particular property (which often he alone appreciates) rouses in him a desire, a manifestation of intelligence, of life. But there is more: not only does the idiot not willingly respond to any but concrete phenomena—not only does he limit those concrete phenomena to which he will respond to a very small number, sometimes to a single one; but you must not imagine that he has a clear idea of even this unique phenomenon, or this small number. By no means.

With idiots, the problem of education is not [as with the deaf] to substitute one unusual mode of perception for another which does not exist; it consists quite simply in the possibility of regulating the use of the senses, multiplying notions, making more fertile the ideas, desires, and passions of creatures who, left to themselves, would stay without ties, without relationships to the outside world, who would remain *idiots*. It is a question of vital dynamics. For example, the method of instruction which I propose does not teach a deaf idiot to hear, nor even to substitute vision for hearing; but it teaches him to listen to what he already hears without being conscious of the phenomena of audition, and consequently without listening and without entering into communication with his fellows by means of the sense of hearing. I recognize that even after this result has been attained, with the help of the methods which I propose, much still remains to be done. Sensations may become precise without being varied, swift, and numerous; they may be varied, swift, and numerous, and still not furnish material for fertile cerebral activity in intellectual operations; and the senses of an idiot may acquire great perfection while the intellectual faculties do not undergo the desired development. (No doubt that is what will happen in most cases of profound idiocy, since the brain itself is the seat of a serious condition which disturbs the psychological functions.) But that is also the moment at which I propose to replace the sensorial exercises, which form the first part of my treatise on the education of idiots, with intellectual exercises which, along with an appropriate regime, can alter the condition of the brain, by pulling it out of its asthenic state through the use of mechanical, intellectual, and emotional excitants. Indeed, all [these] methods . . . may fail, due to the seriousness of the brain condition which they are intended to combat, and the idiot may never become capable of entering society as a man; but at least he will return to his family, with his bad habits corrected, more obedient, more active, in better health, more affectionate toward the persons who have given him their affection and support, and always improved.

No doubt this is not the result one has in mind when one expends rather considerable sums on the education of a child; but neither is that the most usual outcome of the method we have described. Most frequently, a child to whom my method is applied from an early age . . . emerges from my instruction equipped with a sufficient stock of notions, aptitudes, ideas, so that he can be useful to himself and to others, and sometimes so that he can live freely under the governance of his own will, which has been enlightened by intelligence and morality. . . .

. . . I would blush to take as the basis for my instruction the mnemotechnical artifices which are used in ordinary education. . . .

Education should embrace: (1) activity; (2) intelligence; (3) the will. These correspond to the three aspects of the human being: emotion, intellect, and morality. Activity is emotion translated into action; intelligence is a function of the intellect; the will is spontaneity transformed by morality. Placed in this order, these three functions . . . are in an order which is the inverse of that of their importance in human destiny; but they are in the order in which education must take them, in order to develop them. In other words, the education of activity must come before that of intelligence, and the education of intelligence must come before that of the will, because men move and feel before they have knowledge, and they have knowledge long before they are conscious of the morality of their actions and of their ideas.

17.9

J. Langdon H. Down

(1828–1896)

The differential diagnosis of a developmental anomaly must precede the discovery of etiology, which then makes treatment or prevention possible. The cause of "Down's syndrome" has now been traced to "non-disjunction during meiosis of one pair of small telocentrics" (Lejeune, Gauthier and Turpin, Comtes rendus de l'Acad. des Sciences 248(1959): 1721–1722) since identified as the 21st chromosome pair. The condition can be diagnosed early enough for preventive abortion. Down perceptively describes behavioral characteristics of these lovable though unfortunate children. Although today we raise our eyebrows at the naiveté which led him to call them "Mongolian," his reasoning was in keeping with the thought of his time—the age of imperialist expansion by European powers.

I have for some time had my attention directed to the possibility of making a classification of the feeble-minded, by arranging them around various ethnic standards,—in other words, framing a natural system to supplement the information to be derived by an inquiry into the history of the case.

I have been able to find among the large number of idiots and imbeciles which come under my observation . . . that a considerable portion can be fairly referred to one of the great divisions of the human family other than the class from which they have sprung. Of course, there are numerous representatives of the great Caucasian family. Several well-marked examples of the Ethiopian variety have come under my notice, presenting the characteristic malar bones, the prominent eyes, the puffy lips, and retreating chin. The wooly hair has also been present, although not always black, nor has the skin acquired pigmentary deposit. They have been specimens of white negroes, although of European descent.

Some arrange themselves around the Malay variety, and present in their soft, black, curly hair, their prominent upper jaws and capacious mouths, types of the family which people the South Sea Islands.

Nor have there been wanting the analogues of the people who with shortened foreheads, prominent cheeks, deep-set eyes, and slightly apish nose, originally inhabited the American Continent.

The great Mongolian family has numerous representatives, and it is to this division, I wish, in this paper, to call special attention. A very large

Observations on an ethnic classification of idiots. London Hospital Clinical Lectures and Reports 3 (1866): 259–262. [Pp. 260–262.]

number of congenital idiots are typical Mongols. So marked is this, that when placed side by side, it is difficult to believe that the specimens compared are not children of the same parents. The number of idiots who arrange themselves around the Mongolian type is so great, and they present such a close resemblance to one another in mental power, that I shall describe an idiot member of this racial division, selected from the large number that have fallen under my observation.

The hair is not black, as in the real Mongol, but of a brownish colour, straight and scanty. The face is flat and broad, and destitute of prominence. The cheeks are roundish, and extended laterally. The eyes are obliquely placed, and the internal canthi more than normally distant from one another. The palpebral fissure is very narrow. The forehead is wrinkled transversely from the constant assistance which the levatores palpebrarum derive from the occipito-frontalis muscle in the opening of the eyes. The lips are large and thick with transverse fissures. The tongue is long, thick, and is much roughened. The nose is small. The skin has a slight dirty yellowish tinge, and is deficient in elasticity, giving the appearance of being too large for the body.

The boy's aspect is such that it is difficult to realize that he is the child of Europeans, but so frequently are these characters presented, that there can be no doubt that these ethnic features are the result of degeneration.

The Mongolian type of idiocy occurs in more than ten percent of the cases which are presented to me. They are always congenital idiots, and never result from accidents after uterine life. They are, for the most part, instances of degeneracy arising from tuberculosis in the parents. They are cases which very much repay judicious treatment. They require highly azotised food with a considerable amount of oleaginous material. They have considerable power of imitation, even bordering on being mimics. They are humorous, and a lively sense of the ridiculous often colours their mimicry. This faculty of imitation may be cultivated to a very great extent, and a practical direction given to the results obtained. They are usually able to speak; the speech is thick and indistinct, but may be improved very greatly by a well-directed scheme of tongue gymnastics. The co-ordinating faculty is abnormal, but not so defective that it cannot be greatly strengthened. By systematic training, considerable manipulative power may be obtained.

The circulation is feeble, and whatever advance is made intellectually in the summer, some amount of retrogression may be expected in the winter. Their mental and physical capabilities are, in fact, *directly* as the temperature.

The improvement which training effects in them is greatly in excess of what would be predicated if one did not know the characteristics of the type. The life expectancy, however, is far below the average, and the tendency is to the tuberculosis, which I believe to be the hereditary origin of the degeneracy. . . .

These examples of the result of degeneracy among mankind, appear to me to furnish some arguments in favour of the unity of the human species.

17.10

Francis Galton

(1822–1911)

Building in part on Quetelet's generalization (25.6) about the normal distribution of human traits, Galton established a scheme of classification under which idiots and geniuses are included as extremes of the same distribution.

I propose to show in this book that a man's natural abilities are derived by inheritance, under exactly the same limitations as are the form and physical features of the whole organic world. Consequently, as it is easy, notwithstanding those limitations, to obtain by careful selection a permanent breed of dogs or horses gifted with peculiar powers of running, or of doing anything else, so it would be quite practicable to produce a highly-gifted race of men by judicious marriages during several consecutive generations. I shall show that social agencies of an ordinary character, whose influences are little suspected, are at this moment working towards the degradation of human nature, and that others are working towards its improvement. I conclude that each generation has enormous power over the natural gifts of those that follow, and maintain that it is a duty we owe to humanity to investigate the range of that power, and to exercise it in a way that, without being unwise towards ourselves, shall be most advantageous to future inhabitants of the earth.

[Ch. 3.]   *Classification of Men According to Their Natural Gifts*

. . . The range of mental powers between—I will not say the highest Caucasian and the lowest savage—but between the greatest and least of English intellects, is enormous. There is a continuity of natural ability reaching from one knows not what height, and descending to one can hardly say what depth. I propose in this chapter to range men according

Hereditary genius: an inquiry into its laws and consequences. London, 1869. [Pp. 1, 26, 33–36.]

to their natural abilities, putting them into classes separated by equal degrees of merit, and to show the relative number of individuals included in the several classes. Perhaps some persons might be inclined to make an offhand guess that the number of men included in the several classes would be pretty equal. If he thinks so, I can assure him that he is most egregiously mistaken.

The method I shall employ for discovering all this, is an application of the very curious theoretical law of "deviation from an average." . . .

The number of grades into which we may divide ability is purely a matter of option. We may consult our convenience by sorting Englishmen into a few large classes, or into many small ones. I will select a system of classification that shall be easily comparable with the numbers of eminent men, as determined in the previous chapter. We have seen that 250 men per million become eminent; accordingly, I have so contrived the classes in the following table that the two highest, F and G, together with X (which includes all classes beyond G, and which are unclassed), shall amount to about that number—namely, to 248 per million:—

Classification of Men According to Their natural gifts[1]

Grades of natural ability, separated by equal intervals		Number of men comprised in the several grades of natural ability, whether in respect to their general powers, or to special aptitudes	
Below average	Above average	Proportionate, viz. one in	In each million of the same age
a	A	4	256,791
b	B	6	162,279
c	C	16	63,563
d	D	64	15,696
e	E	413	2,423
f	F	4,300	233
g	G	79,000	14
x (all grades below g)	X (all grades above G)	1,000,000	1
On either side of average			500,000
Total, both sides			1,000,000

[1] The original table includes six additional columns, giving representation in each age-decade of the adult male population.

. . . It will be seen that more than half of each million is contained in the two mediocre classes *a* and *A;* the four mediocre classes *a, b, A, B,* contain more than four-fifths, and the six mediocre classes more than nineteen-twentieths of the entire population. Thus, the rarity of commanding ability, and the vast abundance of mediocrity, is no accident, but follows of necessity, from the very nature of these things. . . .

Hence we arrive at the undeniable, but unexpected conclusion, that eminently gifted men are raised as much above mediocrity as idiots are depressed below it; a fact that is calculated to considerably enlarge our ideas of the enormous differences of intellectual gifts between man and man.

17.11

Alfred Binet   AND   Théodore Simon

(1857–1911)   (1873–1961)

Starting about 1905, the very versatile Alfred Binet, assisted in this phase of his activities by Théodore Simon, developed a series of tests designed to assist in the identification of children who would be unable to benefit from the usual school instruction. The new technique was quickly adapted for use in English-speaking countries, and one of the centers for its diffusion in the United States was the Vineland Training School, in New Jersey, which published two volumes of translations of the articles appearing in L'Année psychologique between 1905 and 1911.

[A]

In October, 1904, the Minister of Public Instruction named a commission which was charged with the study of measures to be taken for insuring the benefits of instruction to defective children. . . . This commission . . . decided that no child suspected of retardation should be eliminated from the ordinary school and admitted into a special class, without first being subjected to a pedagogical and medical examination from which it could be certified that because of the state of his intelligence, he was unable to profit, in an average measure, from the instruction given in the ordinary schools.

[A] Upon the necessity of establishing a scientific diagnosis of inferior states of intelligence [1905]. Pp. 9–36, in *The development of intelligence in children*. Translated by Eliz. S. Kite. Vineland, N.J., 1916. [P. 9.] Reprinted by permission of the Training School Unit of the American Institute for Mental Studies.
[B] New methods for the diagnosis of the intellectual level of subnormals [1905]. *Idem*, pp. 37–90. [Pp. 40–44.]
[C] The development of intelligence in the child [1908]. *Idem*, pp. 182–273. [Pp. 261–265, 272–273.]

[B]

The fundamental idea of [the psychological] method is the establishment of what we shall call a measuring scale of intelligence. This scale is composed of a series of tests of increasing difficulty, starting from the lowest intellectual level that can be observed, and ending with that of average normal intelligence. Each group in the series corresponds to a different mental level.

This scale properly speaking does not permit the measure of the intelligence, because intellectual qualities are not superposable, and therefore cannot be measured as linear surfaces are measured, but are on the contrary, a classification, a hierarchy among diverse intelligences; and for the necessities of practice this classification is equivalent to a measure. We shall therefore be able to know, after studying two individuals, if one rises above the other and to how many degrees, if one rises above the average level of other individuals considered as normal, or if he remains below. Understanding the normal progress of intellectual development among normals, we shall be able to determine how many years such an individual is advanced or retarded. In a word we shall be able to determine to what degrees of the scale idiocy, imbecility, and moronity correspond. . . .

It seems to us that in intelligence there is a fundamental faculty, the alteration or the lack of which, is of the utmost importance for practical life. This faculty is judgment, otherwise called good sense, practical sense initiative, the faculty of adapting one's self to circumstances. To judge well, to comprehend well, to reason well, these are the essential activities of intelligence. A person may be a moron or an imbecile if he is lacking in judgment; but with good judgment he can never be either. . . . We may measure the acuteness of the sensibility of subjects; nothing could be easier. But we should do this, not so much to find out the state of their sensibility as to learn the exactitude of their judgment.

The same remark holds good for the study of the memory. . . .

As a result of all this investigation, in the scale which we present we accord the first place to judgment; that which is of importance to us is not certain errors which the subject commits, but absurd errors, which prove that he lacks judgment. We have even made special provision to encourage people to make absurd replies. In spite of the accuracy of this directing idea, it will be easily understood that it has been impossible to permit of its regulating exclusively our examinations. For example, one can not make tests of judgment on children of less than two years when one begins to watch their first gleams of intelligence. Much is gained when one can discern in them traces of coordination, the first delineation of attention and memory. We shall therefore bring out in our lists some tests of memory; but so far as we are able, we shall give these tests such a turn as to invite the subject to make absurd replies, and thus under cover of a test of memory, we shall have an appreciation of their judgment. . . .

[C]

Our principal conclusion is that we actually possess an instrument which will allow us to measure the intellectual development of young children whose age is included between three and twelve years. This method appears to us practical, convenient and rapid. . . .

One question remains to be examined. To what purpose are these studies? In reading the reflections which we have interspersed in the course of our treatise, it will be seen that a profound knowledge of the normal intellectual development of the child would not only be of great interest but useful in formulating a course of instruction really adapted to their aptitudes. . . . The instruction should always be according to the natural evolution of the child, and not precede it by a year or two. In other words the child should be taught only what he is sufficiently mature to understand; all precocious instruction is lost time, for it is not assimilated. . . .

It now remains to explain the use of our measuring scale which we consider a standard of the child's intelligence. Of what use is a measure of intelligence? Without doubt one could conceive many possible applications of the process, in dreaming of a future where the social sphere would be better organized than ours; where every one would work according to his known aptitudes in such a way that no particle of psychic force should be lost for society. That would be the ideal city. It is indeed far from us. But we have to remain among the sterner and the matter-of-fact realities of life, since we here deal with practical experiments which are the most commonplace realities.

We shall not speak of parents; although a father and mother who raise a child themselves, who watch over him and study him fondly, would have great satisfaction in knowing that the intelligence of a child can be measured, and would willingly make the necessary effort to find out if their own child is intelligent. We think especially of teachers who love their profession, who interest themselves in their pupils, and who understand that the first condition of instructing them well, is to know them. . . .

But we are of the opinion that the most valuable use of our scale will not be its application to the normal pupils, but rather to those of inferior grades of intelligence. . . .

. . . The most serious criticisms that one can make of the actual medical practice is that if by chance, a child of normal intelligence were presented at a clinic, the alienist would not be able to know that he is dealing with a normal child. He will be unable for a very simple reason; he does not know what is necessary in order for a child to be normal; let us add that everyone is equally ignorant of how an individual intelligence can be studied and measured. . . .

During the past year one of us examined 25 children who for various reasons had been admitted to Sainte-Anne and later confined at the Bicêtre, at Salpêtrière, or at other places. We applied the procedure of our measuring scale to all these children, and thus proved that *three of them were at age in intelligence, and two others were a year advanced beyond the average.*

. . . To two of these children who showed normal intelligence, we regret to say that the term *mental debility* had been applied without consideration. The third had received the term, truly extraordinary of its kind, of *"enfant idiot."* . . . A doctor had written concerning him, "Idiotic, with attacks of furious anger. Wishes to bite. Does not know how to read or write." This last is a little too naive. Since the normal child does not know how to read or write at seven years, to be astonished that T— who is just seven is still illiterate, is like reproaching a three year old baby for not knowing how to play the piano. Finally, one of these children who was a year in advance was classed as a moron; and as to the other nothing was said concerning his mentality. Nothing could show more clearly, that with the means which it has at its disposal, the mental clinic is not in a position to diagnose correctly a child's intelligence. . . .

These examples to which we could add many others show that the methods of measuring the individual intelligence have not a speculative interest alone; by the direction, by the organization of all the investigations, psychology has furnished the proof (we do not say for the first time but in a more positive manner than ever before), that it is in a fair way to become a science of great social utility.

17.12

Charles E. Spearman

(1863–1945)

In 1904, while Binet was constructing his test on the assumption that "judgment" is the single important ability to be tested, Spearman argued that "all branches of intellectual activity have in common one fundamental function . . . whereas the remaining or specific elements seem in every case to be wholly different from that in all the others." (" 'General intelligence,'

The abilities of man; their nature and measurement. New York: The Macmillan Company, 1927. [Pp. 73–75, 411–413.]

objectively determined and measured," American Journal of Psychology 15: 201–293.)

With continued research, Spearman and his collaborators found other general factors, one of which corresponded to the perseveration reported by Müller and Pilzecker (11.9). They also confirmed Gall's old contention that there is no general memory factor.

Spearman's work provided the basis from which Thurstone, using far more powerful techniques of multivariate analysis, started his search for "primary mental factors." And this, in turn, provided the impetus for early factor analytic studies of personality structure, such as those by J. P. Guilford and R. B. Cattell.

The start of the whole inquiry was a curious observation made in the correlations calculated between the measurements of different abilities. . . . These correlations were noticed to tend towards a peculiar arrangement, which could be expressed in a definite mathematical formula. . . .
. . . In it, as usual, the letter r stands for any correlation, whilst its two subscripts indicate the two abilities . . . that are correlated.

$$r_{ap} \times r_{bq} - r_{aq} \times r_{bp} = 0$$

This formula has been termed the *tetrad equation* and the value constituting the left side of it is the *tetrad difference*. . . .
. . . Whenever the tetrad equation holds throughout any table of correlations, and *only* when it does so, then every individual measurement of every ability (or of any other variable that enters into the table) can be divided into two independent parts which possess the following momentous properties. The one part has been called the "general factor" and denoted by the letter g; it is so named because, although varying freely from individual to individual, it remains the same for any one individual in respect of all the correlated abilities. The second part has been called the "specific factor" and denoted by the letter s. It not only varies from individual to individual, but even for any one individual from each ability to another. The proof of this all-important mathematical theorem has gradually evolved through successive stages of completeness, and may now be regarded as complete.

Although, however, both of these factors occur in every ability, they need not be equally influential in all. On the contrary, the very earliest application of this mathematical theorem to psychological correlations showed that there the g has a much greater relative influence or "weight" in some of the abilities tested than in others.

First and foremost among the results of all these investigations has been a Copernican revolution in point of view. We have not—as all others —set out from an ill-defined mental entity the "intelligence," and then sought to obtain a quantitative value characterising this. Instead, we have started from a perfectly defined quantitative value "g," and then have demonstrated what mental entity or entities this really characterises. The g proved to be a factor which enters into the measurements of ability of all kinds, and which is throughout constant for any individual, although varying greatly for different individuals. It showed itself to be involved invariably and exclusively in all operations of eductive nature, whatever might be the class of relation or the sort of fundaments at issue. It was found to be equally concerned with each of the two general dimensions of ability, Clearness and Speed. It also applied in similar manner to both the dimensions of span, which are Intensity and Extensity. But it revealed a surprisingly complete independence of all manifestations of Retentivity. Whether there is any advantage in attaching to this g, the old mishandled label of "intelligence," seems at least dubious.

Only second in importance to the establishment of g has been that of another factor as also possessing functional unity of acting as a behaviour unit. This consists in the first kind of retentivity (see above), and may be called general mental inertia or lag; another convenient name for it, especially when present to excess, is perseveration. Comparative freedom from it, which with Garnet we may call c, has proved to be the main ground on which persons become reputed for "quickness" or for "originality." It would seem to have an extraordinary importance —hitherto almost wholly overlooked—for education, medicine, and industry.

Yet a third cognitive functional unity has been discovered; it appertains to the oscillations of mental efficiency. . . .

As for the second kind of Retentivity, or the tendency to retain dispositions, this has shown itself *not* to possess any such functional unity (though commonly assumed to do so). Normally, the individual whose dispositions are quickly formed and lastingly retained for one kind of mental operation has little or no general superiority for other kinds.

Still another great functional unity [W] has revealed its existence; this, although not in itself of cognitive nature, yet has a dominating influence upon all exercise or even estimation of cognitive ability. On trying to express it by any current name, perhaps the least unsatisfactory— though still seriously misleading—would be "self-control." It has shown itself to be chiefly responsible for the fact of one person's ability seeming to be more "profound" or more inclined to "common sense" than that of persons otherwise equally capable.

Altogether, then, there are four factors with claims to the character of universality. But only one of them, g, is of such a nature as to manifest appreciable individual differences in the ordinary tests of "intelligence."

17.13

Lewis Madison Terman

(1877–1956)

These volumes present early reports on a still-continuing longitudinal study of "geniuses" selected in California schools in 1921. (Volume II, by Catherine M. Cox, deals with The early mental traits of three hundred geniuses, and is concerned with historical figures.) Although the conclusions are almost a triumphal affirmation of the hopes envisaged by Galton in his pioneering studies of genius, Terman is not blind to the social realities which make the total picture less than idyllic: Harriet, a Negro girl tested as having an IQ of 147 at age 12, is working as a children's maid at 18; and after a newspaper report about the genius of a family of children of mixed Japanese and American parentage, the president of Stanford University received a letter from a former United States senator "protesting violently against the peddling of such nonsense by a university professor and suggesting that the President should do something to put an end to it [p. 297]." The main conclusions stated here continue to stand the test of time, as for example in Terman's article on "Scientists and nonscientists in a group of 800 gifted men" (Psychological Monographs, 1954).

A large part of both Volume I and Volume III has been devoted to a delineation of the characteristic traits of gifted children considered as a group. This seemed necessary because of the large amount of erroneous opinion that has been disseminated in connection with this aspect of the problem. . . . It seems to have been satisfactorily demonstrated that:

1. Gifted children come predominantly from family stocks of decidedly superior intellectual endowment and of slightly superior physical endowment;

2. These family stocks have greatly decreased in fecundity during the last two generations and have already reached the point where they are not maintaining themselves;

3. The mean IQ of siblings of children who are in the IQ range above 140 is about 123, or almost exactly what would be expected if the correlation between siblings in the general population were in the neighborhood of .45 or .50;

4. Intellectually gifted children, either because of better endowment or better physical care, or both, are as a group slightly superior to the generality of children in health and physique and tend to remain so;

Genetic studies of genius. Volumes I and III. Stanford: Stanford University Press, 1925 and 1930. [Vol. III: *The promise of youth,* with Barbara Stoddard Burks and Dortha Williams Jensen, pp. 472–477.] Excerpted with permission of the publisher.

5. Children above 140 IQ are not as a group characterized by intellectual one-sidedness, emotional instability, lack of sociality or of social adaptability, or other types of maladjusted personality;

6. Indeed in practically every personality and character trait such children average much better than the general school population. . . .

It is to be hoped that the superstitions so commonly accepted relative to intellectually superior children have been permanently swept away by the factual data these studies have presented. It is simply not true that such children are especially prone to be puny, over-specialized in their abilities and interests, emotionally unstable, socially unadaptable, psychotic, and morally undependable; nor is it true that they usually deteriorate to the level of mediocrity as adult life is approached. Educational reforms in the direction of special classes, special curricula, and special classroom procedures can now be confidently formulated upon this foundation of established truth. . . . One would like to believe that the stage is set for one of the most important educational reforms of the century; a reform that would have for its end the discovery, conservation, and intensive cultivation of every form of exceptional talent. . . .

The composite portraiture method is useful, just as concepts and generalizations are useful in the shorthand of thinking. Nevertheless, the composite portrait, like any other kind of average, has its limitations. . . .

For example, it is true that the gifted children as a group have held their own intellectually, but it is no less true that some of them have changed significantly in their intelligence ratings. . . .

Making due allowances for complicating factors in measuring IQ constancy, one can hardly avoid the conclusion that there are individual children in our gifted group who have shown very marked changes in IQ. Some of these changes have been in the direction of IQ increase, others of them in the direction of decrease. The important fact which seems to have been definitely established is that there sometimes occur genuine changes in the rate of intellectual growth which cannot be accounted for on the basis of general health, educational opportunity, or other environmental influences. The opinion has often been advanced that something like this is true, but convincing evidence has hitherto been lacking, previous data having been limited entirely to retests by a single fallible intelligence [test] without supporting evidence.

 # Chapter 18

CHILD DEVELOPMENT

Before Darwin, child psychology was limited to occasional bits and snatches such as Aristotle's mention that children do not dream before the age of four [!] or Locke's reminder that supposedly innate truths are not known to children in advance of experience. In the eighteenth century Smellie recognized the need for the systematic study of infant behavior (see 15.9), but he could not spare the time. Augustine aside, history provides scarcely any example of truly understanding observation of children's behavior before the nineteenth century, when Fröbel, founder of the kindergarten, recognized the need for growth which must precede formal learning. Child psychology as a special field came into being because men mistakenly thought that through the study of early child development they might learn something about the development of the human mind from its "primitive" to its "civilized" form. Even today, children are studied less from an interest in the child per se than from an interest in the roots of his adult pathologies!

18.1

Saint Augustine

(354–430)

If Augustine had not stated his "cogito" (3.1), nor given his remarkable appraisal of memory (11.2), or made any of a number of other contributions to psychology (e.g., 21.3), he would deserve a place in the history of psychology as the first to observe infants with open eyes. In his Confessions we read accounts based not on his own memories but on the observation of children, doubtless including his own well-loved son. The dogma of original sin helps to focus his attention on the temper tantrum and sibling rivalry, but this does not detract from the authenticity of his account.

8. Afterwards I began to laugh,—at first in sleep, then when waking. For this I have heard mentioned of myself, and I believe it (though I cannot remember it), for we see the same in other infants. And now little by little I realized where I was, and wished to tell my wishes to those who might satisfy them, but I could not: for my wants were within me, while they were without, and could not by any faculty of theirs enter into my soul. So I cast about limbs and voice, making the few and feeble signs I could, like, though indeed not much like, unto what I wished; and when I was not satisfied—either not being understood, or because it would have been injurious to me—I grew indignant that my elders were not subject unto me, and that those on whom I had no claim did not wait on me, and avenged myself on them by tears. That infants are such I have been able to learn by watching them; and they, though unknowing, have better shown me that I was such an one than my nurses who knew it. . . .

11. . . . Or was it good, even for a time, to strive to get by crying that which, if given, would be hurtful—to be bitterly indignant that those who were free and its elders, and those to whom it owed its being, besides many others wiser than it, who would not give way to the nod of its good pleasure, were not subject unto it—to endeavour to harm, by struggling as much as it could, because those commands were not obeyed which only could have been obeyed to its hurt? Then, in the weakness of the infant's limbs, and not in its will, lies its innocency. I myself have seen and known an infant to be jealous though it could not speak. It became pale, and cast bitter looks on its foster-brother. Who is ignorant of this? Mothers and nurses tell us that they appease these things by I know

The confessions of Saint Augustine. Translated by J. G. Pilkington [1876]. New York: Boni & Liveright, 1927. [Pp. 6–7, 9–10.]

not what remedies; and may this be taken for innocence, that when the fountain of milk is flowing fresh and abundant, one who has need should not be allowed to share it, though needing that nourishment to sustain life? Yet we look leniently on these things, not because they are not faults, nor because the faults are small, but because they will vanish as age increases. For although you may allow these things now, you could not bear them with equanimity if found in an older person. ·

18.2

William Preyer

(1842–1897)

Modern interest in the "child mind" arose as a direct result of Darwinism. Darwin himself published a "Biographical sketch of an infant mind," based on observations of his own son (Mind 2(1877): 285–294). Preyer's work must have been initiated at just about this time, and it was followed by similar studies by Miss Shinn, the Scupins, and others. Preyer was a physiologist interested in many aspects of psychology, and the value of his painstaking observations is enhanced by his conviction that a child should be allowed to develop freely, without undue training, through his early years. With regard to the choice of our selection, it may be noted that he himself wrote: "Of all the facts which I have established . . . the one which is most contrary to traditional doctrines is the formation of concepts without language, and it is on this that I place the greatest emphasis (P. 393)."

There exists a somewhat awkward translation based on the second (1884) edition, by H. W. Brown (New York: Appleton, 1888–1889).

. . . At this time—on the 319th day—there took place a remarkable experiment in acoustics which testifies to great intellectual progress. The child struck a dish several times with a spoon. Then by accident he touched the dish with his free hand; the sound was dampened, and this difference astonished him. He took the spoon in his other hand, struck the dish with it, again dampened it, etc. In the evening the experiment was repeated with the same success. Obviously, the causality-function had emerged strongly, for this is what provoked the experiment. Was the cause of the dampening . . . in the hand or in the dish? The other hand had the same dampening effect, so the cause did not pertain to one hand. The child must have interpreted his sound-experience somewhat in this

Die Seele des Kindes [The mind of the child, 1882]. Fourth edition. Leipzig, 1895. [Pp. 58, 212–213, 229–231, 234–235, 237–238, 241.]

manner, at a time when he did not yet know how to speak a single word. . . .

It is noteworthy that one day (in the 14th month) my child opened and closed the lid of a tankard that stood beside me no fewer than 79 times, without pausing for a moment. Meanwhile his strained attention bespoke the participation of his intellect: "What makes the noise?" he would have thought, if he had been able to speak. For later he asked often enough, whenever he heard a strange sound, "What makes like that?" But even the child who still knows no speech can think this way, like an intelligent animal. But the animal would not have lifted the lid so often on his own initiative, because in it the causality-function is much less developed. . . .

There is a widespread prejudice that "without speech there is no understanding." Subtle distinctions between understanding and reasoning have limited the application of this rule to the latter. But even the rule that "without verbal speech there is no reasoning" is unproven.

The question is: *Can thinking exist without words?*

It is difficult or impossible for the thinker himself to answer this question, for he has long forgotten the time when he learned to speak. Even if he catches himself arriving at logical results without continuity in the thoughts that take place in unspoken words, he still cannot admit that he has been thinking without words. There was a gap in the series: but it was in a series of thoughts. Gaps alone cannot constitute thinking, for they arise only after words have been brought together into thoughts, and therefore they cannot serve as evidence for thinking without words. . . .

But the child who knows no speech, who has not been prematurely spoiled by the suppression of his own efforts to express himself, and who learns to think just as he learns to see and to hear—this child will clearly show an attentive observer that long before he has any acquaintance with words as a means of communication among adults, and long before his first successful efforts to express himself in articulated words, even before he has learned a single word, he connects images in a logical manner and forms concepts, which is to say, he *thinks*. Thinking is indeed an inner speech, but there is also a speech without words.

Factual proof of this has already been given [in the two examples above].

But it will not be superfluous to bring together several observations regarding the development of understanding in the child, without regard to the learning of speech, to serve as an introduction to investigation of the latter.

Memory, concept formation based on the connection of the earliest memory images due to their joint physiological stimulation, and purposeful movements which tend to reduce the child's exertions, all occur in the child independently of verbal speech. There is a sort of embryonic child-logic which has no need of words. In this regard, every child is self-taught. This will be demonstrated by a concise explanation of these three factors.

. . . In the second quarter of the first year, if an infant is brought into a room that he has never seen before, his facial expression changes, he shows surprise. The new light sensations, the changed distribution of lights and shadows, arouse his attention; when he is brought back to his previous environment, he no longer shows surprise. That room *has lost the stimulus of novelty:* the child retains a *memory* of it; it is *imprinted* on him.

Long before the 30th week healthy children distinguish human faces—first those of the mother and the nursemaid, then that of the father, who is less often seen, and all three from every stranger. Faces are probably the first things that are clearly perceived by the eye. . . . My child could localize his mother's voice and face even in the second month, but he could not point it out before the second year. . . .

Innate in all children is the ability to connect sensory impressions which are related to the feeding process either with each other or with their memory images, when afterward some of these appear alone. As a result of these associations, purposive movement-images and movements arise, which are directed toward getting more food. . . .

In the 16th month my boy saw a closed box, from which he had received a cookie some days before. He immediately made begging motions with his hands, but he could speak no word. In the 21st month I took a zwieback out of the pocket of a coat which was hanging in a wardrobe, along with many others, and gave it to him. When he had eaten it, he went by himself right to the wardrobe and looked for another zwieback in the correct coat. The child at this time could not have been thinking the unspoken words, "get zwieback, wardrobe, coat, pocket, look" because he did not know them. . . .

A child's logic naturally operates with concepts which are much broader than those of the adult, and therefore much poorer in content. They are concepts which the adult no longer forms. But this does not mean that the child proceeds illogically, even if clumsily. A few examples may clarify this. . . .

Before an adult uses a watering can to water flowers, he will look to see if there is any water in it. The child of one-and-a-half enjoys going from flower to flower with the empty watering can and spraying each of them just as if water were coming out. For him, the concept "watering can" is identical with the concept "filled watering can," because at first this was the only concept he had learned. The same thing happens with dipping a pencil into an empty ink bottle.

A great deal of what is ascribed to fantasy in early childhood is based on the formation of such vague concepts, on the inability to unite constant indicators into sharply defined concepts. . . .

In many of the instances which I have reported there is not the slightest sign of any influence of spoken words. Whether there has as yet been no effort at speech, or whether a small vocabulary has already been formed, the instances of childhood intelligence which I have observed prove that the logical activity of the child can reach a high level without any knowledge of verbal speech, and independently of it. Nor is there any reason to regard the intelligent actions of children, who do not as yet clothe any of their ideas in words, as specifically different from the intelligent (non-instinctual) actions of clever chimpanzees. The difference consists rather in that the latter are unable to form such clear and abstract concepts, and above all so many and such complicated combinations of ideas, as are formed by the gifted human child *before he has learned to speak.* Once he has learned to speak, the gap becomes so wide that what had seemed in many respects an equal becomes a repulsive caricature of the human.

To understand the true difference between man and animal, we must learn how ideas become purposively connected with words, and how the learning of speech takes place thereafter. That is why all parents should observe both processes more exactly than is the custom, because in this way pathological mental phenomena will be recognized early and more certainly, even in cases in which sleeping is not disturbed.

18.3

James Mark Baldwin

(1861–1934)

Baldwin, along with Stanley Hall, preached the gospel of evolution in American psychology, but they did so from the text of Herbert Spencer more than from that of Charles Darwin. Baldwin was far from being the first to draw a parallel between the thinking of children and that of so-called "primitive" man. In a paper on "The mental characteristics of primitive man" (Journal of the Anthropological Institute of Great Britain and Ireland 1(1872): 74–84), C. S. Wake asserted that "the aborigenes of Australia, as compared with the races who have made further progress in mental cultures, are yet in the condition of children," and that they must "show approximately the condition in which man generally must have existed in the primeval ages."

Mental development in the child and the race. New York: Macmillan, 1894. [Pp. 12–17, 27.]

18.3   James Mark Baldwin

If we adopt a distinction in terminology which the biologists use, and call the development of a single life or mind its *ontogenesis*, and, on the other hand, call the life history of the race, or of consciousness in all the forms of animal life, the *phylogenesis* of mind, it will be seen that what I have said about infant psychology falls under the former head. . . .

The phrase 'Race Psychology' is commonly used in a narrow sense, having reference to the characteristic mental peculiarities of various peoples, tribes, stages of civilization, cults, etc. That is, the word 'race' is applied to the human race. The points of comparison, on the other hand, between human and animal consciousness, fall under so-called Comparative Psychology. I take the liberty, however, of extending the meaning of the former phrase to include this history of consciousness, very much as the phrase 'race experience' is used to include the full wealth of inheritance derived, as it is held to be, from ancestral life of whatever kind. The problem of 'race psychology' then becomes the problem of the phylogenetic development of consciousness, just as 'individual psychology' deals with its ontogenetic development, both being legitimate branches of genetic as opposed to functional psychology.

The question of race psychology, as thus understood, is an extremely important and, until very lately, a greatly neglected question. The presumption in favour of mental phylogenesis, arising from the modern evolution theory in biology, cannot be duly weighed without the most careful detailed comparative work and the fairest interpretation of the concomitance existing between nervous and mental growth everywhere. As far as theoretical human psychology has to do with questions of the nature of mind, as opposed to questions of function, it is, I hold, largely independent of questions of origin; but in as far as data of origin must be included in the answer to questions of function, just so far do they come to throw light on the deeper problems of the nature of the mind as well.

Assuming, then, that there is a phylogenetic problem,—that is, assuming that mind has had a natural history in the animal series,—we are at liberty to use what we know of the correspondence between nerve process and conscious process, in man and the higher animals, to arrive at hypotheses for its solution: to expect general analogies to hold between nervous development and mental development, one of which is the deduction of race history epochs from individual history epochs through the repetition of phylogenesis in ontogenesis, called in biology 'Recapitulation'; to view the plan of development of the two series of facts taken together as a common one in race history, as we are convinced it is in individual history by an overwhelming weight of evidence; to accept the criteria established by biological research on one side of this correspondence,—the organic,—while we expect biology to accept the criteria established on the other side by psychology; and, finally, to admit with equal freedom the possibility of an absolute beginning of either series at points, if such be found, at which the best conceived criteria on either side fall of application. For example: if biology has the right to make it a legitimate problem whether the organic exhibits a kind of function over and above that supplied by the chemical affinities which are the necessary presuppositions of life, then the psychologist has the equal right, after the same candid rehearsal of the facts in support of his criteria, to submit for examination the claim, let us say, that 'judgments of worth' represent a kind of deliverance which vital functions as such do not give rise to. . . .

Students of biology consider the argument for organic evolution especially strong in view of the analogy between race and individual development. The individual in embryo passes through stages which represent morphologically, to a degree, the stages actually found in the ancestral animal series. A similar analogy, when inquired into on the side of consciousness, seems on the surface true, since we find more and more developed stages of conscious function in a series corresponding in the main with the stages of nervous growth in the animals; and then we find this growth paralleled in its great features in the mental development of the human infant.

The race series seems to require, both on organic grounds and from evidence regarding consciousness, a development whose major terms are somewhat in this order, *i.e.,* simple contractility with the organic analogue of pleasure and pain; nervous integration corresponding to special sense functions, including the congeries of muscular sensations, and some adaptive movements; nervous integration to a degree to which corresponds mental presentation of objects with higher motor organization and reflex attention; greater co-ordination, having on the conscious side memory, conscious imitation, impulse, instinct, instinctive emotion; finally, cerebral function with conscious thought, voluntary action, and ideal emotion. Without insisting on the details of this sketch—intended at this point for no more than a sketch—certain great epochs of functional differentiation may be clearly seen. First, the epoch of the rudimentary sense processes, the pleasure and pain process, and simple motor adaptation, called for convenience the 'affective epoch'; second, the epoch of presentation, memory, imitation, defensive action, instinct, which passes by gradations into, third, the epoch of complex presentation, complex motor co-ordination, of conquest, of offensive action, and rudimentary volition. These, the second and third together, I should characterize, on the side of consciousness, as the 'epoch of objective reference'; and, finally, the epoch of thought, reflection, self-assertion, social organization, union of forces, co-operation; the 'epoch of subjective reference,' which, in human history, merges into the 'social and ethical epoch.' . . .

The analogy of this series . . . with that of the infant's growth, is, in the main, very clear: the child begins in its prenatal and early post-natal experience with blank sensations and pleasure and pain with the motor adaptations to which they lead, passes into a stage of apprehension of objects with response to them by 'suggestion,' imitation, etc., gets to be more or less self-controlled, imaginative, and volitional, and ultimately becomes reflective, social, and ethical. . . .

These considerations also seem, from the psychological side, to support the general theory of 'race experience' as held by the evolutionists of both [Lamarckian and Darwinian] schools. The whole tendency of current psychology is toward a functional view of experience, *i.e.*, toward the view that memory is a form of mental reinstatement or habit, that character is disposition for action, that the brain develops by enlargement of function on the basis of earlier function, and that the mind proceeds upon its past, even when it does not know its indebtedness. The value of ancestral experience is seen in what it makes me to be for opinion and action now—by whatever process it may have come down from my father to myself.

Now this is what evolution claims for race-experience. It says what is present in the mind now, in the way of function, is due somehow to the past. Nervous inheritance provides for the apparatus, and mental inheritance sums up the experience. Hence if individual mental development does not epitomize race development and yet it be true that man has developed, then the 'race experience hypothesis' becomes absolutely essential to genetic psychology, just as animal physiology would be the main resource of human morphology, if the animal embryos did not show Recapitulation.

18.4

James Sully

(1842–1923)

Experimental psychology was slow to take root in Britain, but James Sully's perceptive contributions to the study of child behavior were a notable aspect of the awakening movement toward the "new psychology." The same evolutionary doctrine is present here as in Baldwin and in Hall, but it is softened by a sensitive appreciation for the child's way of thinking.

. . . We find in the drawings of untrained children from about the age of three to that of eight or ten a curious mode of dealing with the most familiar forms. At no stage of this child-art can we find what we should

Studies of childhood. London, 1895. [Pp. 382–383, 385, 394–396.]

regard as elements of artistic value: yet it has its quaint and its suggestive side.

The first thing that strikes us here is that this child-delineation, crude and bizarre as it is, illustrates a process of development. Thus we have (*a*) the stage of vague formless scribble, (*b*) that of primitive design, typified by what I have called the lunar scheme of the human face, and (*c*) that of a more sophisticated treatment of the human figure, as well as of animal forms.

This process of art-evolution has striking analogies with that of organic evolution. It is clearly a movement from the vague or indefinite to the definite, a process of gradual specialisation. Not only so, we may note that it begins with the representation of those rounded or ovoid contours which seem to constitute the basal forms of animal organisms, and proceeds like organic evolution by a gradual differentiation of the 'homogeneous' structure through the addition of detailed parts or organs. These organs in their turn gradually assume their characteristic forms. It is, perhaps, worth observing here that some of the early drawings of animals are strongly suggestive of embryo forms.

If now we examine this early drawing on its representative side we find that it is crude and defective enough. It proceeds by getting a bare outline of the object, with at most one or two details thrown in. The form neither of the whole nor of the parts is correctly rendered. Thus in drawing the foot it is enough for the child to indicate the angle: the direction of the foot-line is comparatively immaterial. In this respect a child's drawing differs from a truly artistic sketch or suggestive indication by a few characteristic lines, which is absolutely correct so far as it goes. The child is content with a schematic treatment, which involves an appreciable and even considerable departure from truthful representation. Thus the primitive lunar drawing of the human face is manifestly rather a diagrammatic scheme than an imitative representation of a concrete form. . . .

The art of children is a thing by itself, and must not straight away be classed with the rude art of the untrained adult. As adult, the latter has knowledge and technical resources above those of the little child; and these points of superiority show themselves, for example, in the fine delineation of animal forms by Africans and others. At the same time, after allowing for these differences, it is, I think, incontestable that a number of characteristic traits in children's drawings are reflected in those of untutored savages. . . .

We are apt to think that children when they look at things at all scrutinise them closely, and afterwards imagine clearly what they have observed. But this assumption is hardly justified. No doubt they often surprise us by their attention to small unimportant details of objects, especially when these are new and odd-looking. But it is a long way from this to a careful methodic investigation of objects. Children's observation is for the most part capriciously selective and one-sided. . . .

This being so it may be said that defects of observation are reflected in children's drawing through all its phases. Thus the primitive bare schematism of the human face answers to an incomplete observation and consequently incomplete mode of imagination, just as it answers to a want of artistic purpose and to technical incapacity. How far defective observation assists at this first stage I do not feel sure. Further experimental inquiries are needed on this point. I lean to the view already expressed, that at this stage manual reproduction is far behind visual imagination.

When, however, we come to the delineation of an object under its different aspects the defects of mental representation assume a much graver character. We must bear in mind that a child soon gets beyond the stage of recalling and imagining the particular look of an object, say the front view of his mother's face, or of his house. He begins as soon as he understands and imitates others' language to synthesise such pictorial images of particular visual presentations or appearances into the wholes which we call ideas of things. . . . A child of five or six, so far from being immersed in individual presentations and concrete objects, as is often supposed, has carried out a respectable measure of generalisation, and this largely by the help of language. Thus a 'man' reduced to visual terms has come to mean for him (according to his well-known verbal formula) something with a head, two eyes, etc., etc., which he does not need to represent in a mental picture because the verbal formula serves to connect the features in his memory. . . .

Since the process at this sophisticated stage is controlled by knowledge of things as wholes and not by representations of concrete appearances or views, we can understand why the visible result does not shock the draughtsman. The little descriptor does not need to compare the look of his drawing with that of the real object: it is right as a description anyhow. . . . We may say then that what a lively fancy did in the earlier play-stages childish logic does now, it blinds the artist to the actual look of what his pencil has created.

Use soon adds its magic force, and the impossible combination, the two eyes stuck on at the side of the profile nose, the two legs of the rider untroubled by the capacious trunk of the animal which he strides, the man wholly exposed to view inside the boat or carriage, gets stereotyped into the right mode of linear description.

All this shows that the child's eye at a surprisingly early period loses its primal 'innocence,' grows 'sophisticated' in the sense that instead of seeing what is really presented it sees, or pretends to see, what knowledge and logic tell it is there. In other words his sense-perceptions have for artistic purposes been corrupted by a too large admixture of intelligence. This corruption is closely analogous to what we all experience when we lose the primal simplicity of the eye for colour, and impart into our 'visual impressions,' as we call them, elements of memory and inference, saying, for example, that a distant mountain side is 'green' just because we can make out that it is grass-covered and know that grass when looked at nearer is of a green colour.

18.5

Karl Groos

(1861–1946)

Herbert Spencer had regarded play as only a means to consume surplus energy. Groos develops the theory that it has direct utility in aiding the development of essential behaviors. His volume on human play followed one on the play of animals (Die Spiele der Thiere, 1896).

In the attempt to form a biological estimate of play independently of the Lamarckian principle we must constantly bear in mind the value and origin of youthful play, and therefore we must begin with instinct in its more limited sense. We find in all creatures a number of innate capacities which are essential for the preservation of species. In many animals these capacities appear as finely developed reflexes and instincts, needing but little if any practice for the fulfilment of their function. With the higher animals, and above all with man, it is essentially otherwise. Although the number of his hereditary instincts is considerable—perhaps larger than with any other creature—yet he comes into the world an absolutely helpless and undeveloped being which must grow in every other sense, as well as physiologically, in order to be an individual of independent capabilities. The period of youth renders such growth possible. If it is asked why an arrangement apparently so awkward has arisen, we may reply that instinctive apparatus being inadequate for his life tasks, a period of parental protection is necessary to enable him to acquire imitatively and experimentally the capacities adapted to his individual needs. The more complicated the life tasks, the more necessary are these preparations; the longer this natural education continues, the more vivid do the inherited capacities become. Play is the agency employed to develop crude powers and prepare them for life's uses, and from our biological standpoint we can say: From the moment when the intellectual development of a

Die Spiele der Menschen. Jena, 1899. Translated by Eliz. A. Baldwin, as *The play of man.* New York: Appleton, 1901. [Pp. 374–376.]

species becomes more useful in the "struggle for life" than the most perfect instinct, will natural selection favour those individuals in whom the less elaborated faculties have more chance of being worked out by practice under the protection of parents—that is to say, those individuals that play. Play depends, then, first of all on the elaboration of immature capacities to full equality with perfected instinct, and secondly on the evolution of hereditary qualities to a degree far transcending this, to a state of adaptability and versatility surpassing the most perfect instinct. . . .

The imitative impulse is an inborn faculty resembling instinct whose first effect is to supplement instinct by means of individual acquirements; secondly, it preserves those race heritages which survive only through tradition. The first of these functions falls in the biological domain, while the second belongs to social play. The former may be advantageously observed in the world of birds, which learn the characteristic song of their kind by the help of playful experimentation to a great degree, but never get it so perfectly as when they hear the song of older birds as a model. Children, too, exemplify it clearly in the transition from their lall-monologue to speech; in their tussling, where many of the movements are instinctive, but are materially assisted by imitation of older boys; in the nursing of dolls by little girls, who would probably not make any use of the instinct during childhood but for imitation; and in many other cases. Imitation is clearly playful in such instances, so far as it is both unconscious and practical.

From the biological standpoint, too, imitative play is an important agent in supplementing instincts, usually tending to render them more plastic, and thus further the opening of new paths for the development of intelligence.

18.6

Sigmund Freud

(1856–1939)

Besides laying the basis for that great mass of psychoanalytic literature concerned with "the psychosexual development of the child," this work first compelled the attention of psychologists generally to an aspect of

Drei Abhandlungen zur Sexualtheorie. Leipzig and Vienna, 1905. Translated by J. Strachey, as *Three essays on the theory of sexuality.* New York: Basic Books, and London: The Hogarth Press, Ltd., 1962. [Pp. 39, 42, 45, 47–54, 88–89.] Reprinted by permission of Basic Books and the Hogarth Press, Ltd., Sigmund Freud Copyrights Ltd. and the Institute for Psycho-Analysis. This book is part of the Standard Edition of the Complete Psychological Works of Sigmund Freud.

child behavior which they had been ignoring. The selection is chiefly from the second essay, on "The transformations of puberty." The final paragraph (from the third essay) is prophetic of the large amount of experimental material which demonstrates that animals as well, such as cats and monkeys, are unable adequately to fulfill their sexual and parental roles if they have not enjoyed the timely caresses of a mother.

One feature of the popular view of the sexual instinct is that it is absent in childhood and only awakens in the period of life described as puberty. This, however, is not merely a simple error but one that has had grave consequences, for it is mainly to this idea that we owe our present ignorance of the fundamental conditions of sexual life. . . .

. . . Infantile amnesia, which turns everyone's childhood into something like a prehistoric epoch and conceals from him the beginnings of his own sexual life, is responsible for the fact that in general no importance is attached to childhood in the development of sexual life. . . .

There seems no doubt that germs of sexual impulses are already present in the new-born child and that these continue to develop for a time, but are then overtaken by a progressive process of suppression; this in turn is itself interrupted by periodical advances in sexual development or may be held up by individual peculiarities. . . .

For reasons which will appear later, I shall take thumb-sucking (or sensual sucking) as a sample of the sexual manifestations of childhood. . . .

. . . It is clear that the behaviour of a child who indulges in thumb-sucking is determined by a search for some pleasure which has already been experienced and is now remembered. . . . It is also easy to guess the occasions on which the child had his first experiences of the pleasure which he is now striving to renew. It was the child's first and most vital activity, his sucking at his mother's breast, or at substitutes for it, that must have familiarized him with this pleasure. The child's lips, in our view, behave like an erotogenic zone, and no doubt stimulation by the warm flow of milk is the cause of the pleasurable sensation. . . . No one who has seen a baby sinking back satiated from the breast and falling asleep with flushed cheeks and a blissful smile can escape the reflection that this picture persists as a prototype of the expression of sexual satisfaction in later life. The need for repeating the sexual satisfaction now becomes detached from the need for taking nourishment—a separation which becomes inevitable when the teeth appear and food is no longer taken in only by sucking, but is also chewed up. The child does not make use of an extraneous body for his sucking, but prefers a part of his own skin because it is more convenient, because it makes him independent of the external world, which he is not yet able to control, and because in that way he provides himself, as it were, with a second erotogenic zone, though one of an inferior kind. . . .

18.6 Sigmund Freud

The character of erotogenicity can be attached to some parts of the body in a particularly marked way. There are predestined erotogenic zones, as is shown in the example of sucking. . . .

Like the labial zone, the anal zone is well suited by its position to act as a medium through which sexuality may attach itself to other somatic functions. It is to be presumed that the erotogenic significance of this part of the body is very great from the first. . . .

Children who are making use of the susceptibility to erotogenic stimulation of the anal zone betray themselves by holding back their stool till its accumulation brings about violent muscular contractions and, as it passes through the anus, is able to produce powerful stimulation of the mucous membrane. . . .

Among the erotogenic zones that form part of the child's body there is one which certainly does not play the opening part, and which cannot be the vehicle of the oldest sexual impulses, but which is destined to great things in the future. In both male and female children it is brought into connection with micturition . . . so that there can be no lack of stimulation of it by secretions which may give an early start to sexual excitation. The sexual activities of this erotogenic zone, which forms part of the sexual organs proper, are the beginning of what is later to become "normal" sexual life. The anatomical situation of this region, the secretions in which it is bathed, the washing and rubbing to which it is subjected in the course of a child's toilet, . . . make it inevitable that the pleasurable feeling which this part of the body is capable of producing should be noticed by children even during their earliest infancy, and should give rise to a need for its repetition. If we consider this whole range of contrivances and bear in mind that both making a mess and measures for keeping clean are bound to operate in much the same way, it is scarcely possible to avoid the conclusion that the foundations for the future primacy over sexual activity exercised by this erotogenic zone are established by early infantile masturbation, which scarcely a single individual escapes. . . .

. . . All through the period of latency children learn to feel for other people who help them in their helplessness and satisfy their needs a love which is on the model of, and a continuation of, their relation as sucklings to their nursing mother. There may perhaps be an inclination to dispute the possibility of identifying a child's affection and esteem for those who look after him with sexual love. I think, however, that a closer psychological examination may make it possible to establish this identity beyond any doubt. A child's intercourse with anyone responsible for his care affords him an unending source of sexual excitation and satisfaction from his erotogenic zones. This is especially so since the person in charge of him, who, after all, is as a rule his mother, herself regards him with feelings that are derived from her own sexual life: she strokes him, kisses him, rocks him and quite clearly treats him as a substitute for a complete sexual object. A mother would probably be horrified if she were made aware that all her marks of affection were rousing her child's sexual instinct and preparing for its later intensity. She regards what she does as asexual, 'pure' love, since, after all, she carefully avoids applying more excitations to the child's genitals than are unavoidable in nursery care. As we know, however, the sexual instinct is not aroused only by direct excitation of the genital zone. What we call affection will unfailingly show its effects one day on the genital zones as well. Moreover, if the mother understood more of the high importance of the part played by instincts in mental life as a whole—in all its ethical and psychical achievements—she would spare herself any self-reproaches even after her enlightenment. She is only fulfilling her task in teaching the child to love.

18.7

Arnold Gesell

(1880–1961)

This is one of the many books in which Gesell and his collaborators present results of studies establishing developmental norms for preschool children by a series of play-like performance tests administered in a standard situation. To dramatize the developmental stages, children of different ages were observed together in pairs. In the youngest of eight pairs, the children were aged four and six months; in the oldest, four and five years. We give the beginning and end of one of these pair-comparisons.

Gesell emphasized the importance of maturation at a time when this was an unpopular concept with psychologists.

Two Years Versus *Three Years*

Initial reactions. Both children enter reception room dressed in cloak and bonnet. Mild timidity is evident in facial expression. When it is suggested that the children take off cloak and bonnet, TWO begins to cry and clings to skirt of mother. This fear subsides in a few minutes, as soon as she is shown a few toys. Both children remove their wraps without further assistance. TWO is talkative; THREE is silent during the

The mental growth of the pre-school child. New York: Macmillan, 1925. [Pp. 262–263, 265–266.] Reprinted by permission of the Gesell Institute of Child Development and Gerhard A. Gesell.

initial period of adjustment. Both children enter the examining room in confident manner; they show a real interest in their new surroundings; but there is a trace of anxiety.

When presented with saucer, plate, and cup, TWO at once utilizes them as play material, taking up each object in turn and bringing the spoon into relation with the plate and cup. She plays in a combining manner. THREE is more interested in watching TWO and also follows closely all the movements of the examiner. THREE has no inhibition in regard to the material, but makes no play responses. When asked, "What do you do with the cup," she points to saucer and then places the cup in the saucer and then the spoon into the saucer in a very purposive and sensible manner. TWO watches THREE, duplicates the actions, and then pretends to drink.

On the multiple choice and command test, THREE without any error places the cube in box and cup and plate in turn; TWO likewise. THREE is more sedate in all these situations, TWO is more playful.

Both children simultaneously and without an imitation model begin to build a tower *when nine blocks are placed before each one of them.* TWO builds a tower of four; THREE builds a tower of nine blocks. Following the tower THREE makes a horizontal row of nine blocks. THREE makes a good attempt at duplicating a *bridge from a model* but tries to put two blocks side by side on top of one, an impossible engineering feat. TWO does not imitate either a train or a bridge but persists in building towers only.

THREE promptly adjusts to *performance box* and *places square* in rectangular hole; TWO makes imitative effort at putting square in all three holes but does not turn it adaptively on edge. When *shown,* she holds the block properly but persists in an effort to place it in the opening cornerwise. After second demonstration she still tries to put it in each of the two small holes but finally succeeds in placing it in the rectangular hole. On third trial she adjusts promptly. It took TWO about three minutes to accomplish this reaction and it took THREE five seconds. . . .

When presented with one-ounce bottle and box of pellets, she [THREE] takes pleasure in filling the bottle with pellets, one by one, breaking apart those that are stuck together. She also turns the bottle upside down when asked to return the pellets. Her attention in this is well sustained and when she has difficulty in pouring out the pellets, she shakes the bottle vigorously in an adaptive manner.

When THREE sees moist pellets adhering to the side of the bottle, she makes an adaptive effort to get them out with a little wooden rod.

TWO shows the same initial interest in putting pellets into bottle and even attempts to put them in before requested to do so. Her attention, however, is more readily distracted by the other objects on the table. When she drops a pellet, which is oftener than with THREE, she recovers it before placing the others in. Her coordination is accurate but it takes her much longer to place in the pellets. This slowness makes her movements seem more cautious whereas they really indicate less skill.

In taking the pellets out of the bottle she is also more awkward and spills them about more than THREE. When asked to take out the two pellets which cling to the side of the bottle she tries to thrust in her finger and to shake vigorously, and later thrusts in the wooden rod which is given to her but uses it much less purposively than THREE. Her pellets and bottle behavior, however, is definitely superior to that of the eighteen-months level. Later she begins to play with the pellets by putting them into the box instead of into bottle. In putting them into box she uses her whole hand; in putting them into bottle she uses index finger and thumb.

Reactions of children to each other. When THREE and TWO are both *brought* to the *small test table* and are seated at either end there is no conflict or dispute, but THREE at once seizes the two pellets and eats them, after which her interest soon declines. Both soon leave the table, but spontaneously return to the test table; and THREE initiates a game in which she pretends to feed TWO.

This final little scene epitomizes in a manner the difference between these two levels. Not only is the psychologist throughout the examination conscious of the greater maturity of social attitude of THREE when compared with TWO; but THREE, herself, recognizes TWO as her junior. In a similar manner, TWO yesterday treated EIGHTEEN [months] as her junior and assumed a corresponding attitude of seniority.

18.8

Kurt Koffka

(1886–1941)

One of the original Gestalt triumvirate (with Max Wertheimer and Wolfgang Köhler), Koffka was, in Boring's words, "always the most vocal evangelist of these three men." His book on child psychology first demonstrated that Gestalt principles had application outside the relatively narrow field of perception. In 1924 (before political events drove Wertheimer and Köhler, along with many other scientists, out of Germany) he came to the United States; from 1927 until his death he was at Smith. Thus he did much to attract the attention of American psychologists to Gestalt theory.

Grundlagen der psychischen Entwicklung [1921]. Translated by R. M. Ogden, as *The growth of the mind: an introduction to child psychology.* Second edition, revised. New York: Humanities Press, Inc., and London: Routledge & Kegan Paul, Ltd., 1928. [Pp. 147–150.]

18.8 Kurt Koffka

If the theory of original chaos were correct, one would expect "simple" stimuli to be the first to arouse the reaction and interest of the child; because simple stimuli ought to be the ones first to be singled out from the chaos for association with one another. But all our experience runs counter to this assumption. It is not the stimuli the psychologist takes to be simple, because they correspond to his elementary sensations, that are most influential in the behaviour of a baby. The first differentiated reactions to sound are aroused by the human voice whose stimuli (and "sensations") are very complicated, indeed. For instance, at the end of the first month the infant begins to scream when it hears another baby scream. Between the first and second month the infant reacts to the human voice with a smile, at first without differentiating between a friendly, neutral, or scolding voice. This differentiation occurs in the fourth or fifth month, when a smile is the reaction to friendly and inviting speech, while angry words evoke crying and general symptoms of discomfort. Nor is the interest of a suckling aroused by a single colour, but by human faces, as Miss Shinn has expressly reported to be the case with her niece after the child's twenty-fifth day. During the second month the friendly gaze of an adult makes the infant smile. At the end of two months, the mere presence of an adult may have a quieting influence upon the child. This reaction is so specific that during the first half-year of his life the infant will smile only at another human being—not, for instance, at a toy, however much the toy may attract his attention. Think what sort of experience must parallel the process of distinguishing, among an infinite variety of chaotic images, the father's from the mother's face (and more than this, a friendly from an unfriendly countenance), the sensations of which are constantly undergoing change. . . .

As early as the middle of the first year of life an influence of the parents' facial expression upon the child may be noted. According to the chaos-theory, the phenomena corresponding to a human face can be nothing but a confused mass of the most varied light-, dark-, and colour-sensations, all in a constant state of alteration—changing with every movement of the person observed, or of the child himself, and likewise subject to every change of illumination. Yet the child recognizes its mother's face as early as the second month, and in the middle of the first year the reaction to a "friendly" face is quite different from the reaction to an "angry" face. Furthermore, this difference is of a kind which obliges us to conclude that "friendly" and "angry" faces are phenomenal facts to the infant, and not mere distributions of light and shade. It seems quite impossible to explain this behaviour by experience, upon the assumption that these phenomena arise from an original chaos of sensations in which single visual sensations combine with one another, together with pleasant or unpleasant consequences. One of Köhler's observations is here in point: "By suddenly showing signs of the greatest terror, while staring at a certain spot as though possessed, it is not difficult to make all the

487

chimpanzees in the station look at the same place at once. Immediately all the black company starts as if it had been struck by lightning, and proceeds to stare at the same spot, even though nothing is to be seen there. According to the usual view this involves an inference drawn by analogy from what is taking place in 'my consciousness.' " The animals understand this terror-stricken direction of the gaze *immediately*, and an inference by analogy from Köhler's consciousness of terror would be an altogether absurd explanation.

Is it not possible that phenomena, such as "friendliness" and "unfriendliness," are very primitive—even more so than the visual impression of a "blue spot"? However absurd this possibility may seem to a psychologist who regards all consciousness as being ultimately made up of elements, it ceases to be absurd if we bear in mind that all psychological phenomena stand in the closest relation to objective behaviour. "Friendliness" and "unfriendliness" certainly influence behaviour, whereas it is not easy to understand how the behaviour of so primitive an organism as the human infant could be motivated by a "blue spot." If phenomena are to be construed from behaviour, must we not attribute to them, first of all, such properties as might occasion activity? Certainly the fact that something is being done furnishes the basis for an inference that certain phenomena accompany the behaviour in question. But this means that we must assume that features like "threatening" or "tempting" are more primitive and elementary contents of perception than those we learn of as "elements" in the text-books of psychology.

18.9

Jean Piaget

(born 1896)

Piaget brought to psychology a point of view developed during early precocious research in biology. His distinctive method of clinical-experimental observation of the thought processes of children extends a tradition initiated by Alfred Binet and Édouard Claparède. The resulting theory defines a series of necessary stages in mental development which, although they are shaped largely by social factors, parallel analogous stages in biological evolution. This theory has defied all attempts at lucid summarization. (See J. H. Flavell, The developmental psychology of Jean Piaget, 1963, for what is perhaps the best effort.) Understood or not, Piaget has provided the

La représentation du monde chez l'enfant. Paris: Alcan, 1926. Translated by J. and A. Tomlinson, as *The child's conception of the world.* New York: Humanities Press, Inc., and London: Routledge & Kegan Paul, Ltd., 1929. [Pp. 123–124, 132, 152–153, 166–168.]

focus for a great deal of recent research in developmental psychology, and a challenge to anyone entering this field.

[Ch IV.] The aim of this chapter is to trace the consequences of the realism analysed in the preceding chapters. . . .

. . . The child is a realist, since he supposes thought to be inseparable from its object, names from the things named, and dreams to be external. His realism consists in a spontaneous and immediate tendency to confuse the sign and the thing signified, internal and external, and the psychical and the physical.

The results of this realism are twofold. Firstly, the limits the child draws between the self and the external world are much less rigid than our own; secondly, the realism is further extended by "participations" and spontaneous ideas of a magical nature. . . .

Following the definition of M. Lévy-Bruhl, we shall give the name "participation" to that relation which primitive thought believes to exist between two beings or two phenomena which it regards either as partially identical or as having a direct influence on one another, although there is no spatial contact nor intelligible causal connection between them. The application of this conception to the child's thought may be disputed, but it is merely a question of words. It may be that the child's idea of "participation" differs from that of the primitive, but they resemble one another, and this is sufficient to authorise us in choosing our vocabulary from among the expressions which have been found most adequate in describing primitive thought. There is no intention of suggesting the identity of the different forms of participation that may be distinguished. . . .

If we admit this assimilation of the world to the self and the self to the world, participation and magical causality become intelligible. On one hand, the movements of the body itself must be confused with any sort of external movement, and on the other, desires, pleasures and pains must be situated, not in the self, but in the absolute, in a world which, from the adult point of view, we should describe as common to all, but which from the infant's point of view is the only possible world. It follows when the infant sees his limbs move at his own will, he must feel that he is commanding the world. Thus on seeing a baby joyfully watching the movements of his feet, one has the impression of the joy felt by a god in directing from a distance the movements of the stars. Inversely, when the baby takes delight in movements situated in the outside world, such as the movement of the ribbons of its cradle, he must feel an immediate bond between these movements and his delight in them. In short, for a mind that cannot distinguish, or does so but dimly, the self from the external world, everything participates in the nature of and can influence everything else. To put it another way, participation results from a lack of differentiation between the consciousness of the action of the self on the self and the consciousness of the action of the self on things. . . .

In the first three chapters we tried to show that the distinction between thought and the external world is not innate in the child but is only gradually evolved and built up by a slow process. One result of this is of primary importance to the study of causality, namely that the child is a realist in its thought and that its progress consists in ridding itself of this initial realism. In fact, during the primitive stages, since the child is not yet conscious of his subjectivity, all reality appears to be of one unvaried type by reason of the confusion between the data of the external world and those of the internal. Reality is impregnated with self and thought is conceived as belonging to the category of physical matter. From the point of view of causality, all the universe is felt to be in communion with and obedient to the self. There is participation and magic. The desires and commands of the self are felt to be absolute, since the subject's own point of view is regarded as the only one possible. There is integral egocentricity through lack of consciousness of self.

We are thus drawn to a conclusion parallel to that to which we were led by our earlier studies of child logic. In his manner of reasoning, equally, the child is only concerned with himself, and ignores more or less completely the points of view of others. But, in logic also, if the child sees everything from his own point of view, it is because he believes all the world to think like himself. He has not yet discovered the multiplicity of possible perspectives and remains blind to all but his own as if that were the only one possible. Also he states his views without proof since he feels no need to convince. The results of this are seen in play, make-belief, the tendency to believe without proof, the absence of deductive reasoning; in syncretism also which connects all things in terms of primitive subjective associations; in the absence of all relativity among ideas; and finally in "transductive" reasoning which, through the agency of syncretism, leads from one particular to another, heedless both of logical necessity and of general laws, because lacking in feeling for the reciprocal nature of all relationship.

There are two forms of egocentricity, the first logical and the second ontological. Just as the child makes his own truth, so he makes his own reality; he feels the resistance of matter no more than he feels the difficulty of giving proofs. He states without proof and he commands without limit. Magic on the ontological plane, and conviction without proof on the logical; participation in the domain of being, and "transduction" in that of reasoning are thus the two converging products of the same phenomenon. At the root both of magic and of conviction without proof lie the same egocentric illusions, namely, confusion between one's own thought and that of others and confusion between the self and the external world.

Ontological egocentricity is a principle essential to the comprehension of the child's world. Just as logical egocentricity provided the key to the child's judgment and reasoning, so ontological egocentricity provides that to his conceptions of reality and causality. Precausality and finalism are, in fact, directly derived from this egocentricity, since, in their assumption that man is the centre of the universe, they consist in a confusion of relationships of a causal and physical nature with those of psychological origin. These primitive relationships come to be justified by animism and artificialism {topics to which the remainder of the book is devoted} and from their lingering traces are finally made up the integral dynamism which impregnates the child's ideas on meteorology and physics.

18.10

René Spitz

(born 1887)

Although Spitz's methodology has been severely criticized, his observations had undoubted importance. Along with comparable studies by William Goldfarb on older children, they demonstrated the need to provide foster homes rather than institutionalized care for orphan children. Harry Harlow's experimental analysis of the problem, using more expendable monkey-subjects, gave the coup de grace to the early-behaviorist myth about the harm done by mother-love. Perhaps all this indirectly helped nourish the rival myth that maternal rejection is the principal root of autism and schizophrenia.

Emotions are not present ready-made from birth. Like any other sector of the human personality they have to develop. . . .

Two distinct emotional responses are differentiated in the course of the first two months of life. They appear to correspond to pleasure and displeasure, and they seem to appear in reaction to physical stimulation.

A response to psychological stimulation seems to present itself for the first time in the third month, when the infant smiles in response to a human partner's face.

Somewhat later displeasure also is manifested in response not only to physical, but also to psychological stimulation. It can be observed in the

The role of ecological factors in emotional development in infancy. *Child Development* 20 (1949): 145–155. [Pp. 146–151.] Reprinted by permission of The Society for Research in Child Development, Inc. © The Society for Research in Child Development, Inc.

reaction of the infant to being left alone when its human partner goes away.

After the sixth month negative emotions take the lead. Anxiety is differentiated from the displeasure reaction. . . .

In the following two months possessive emotions toward toys are manifested. Jealousy appears in the ninth and tenth months; between the tenth and twelfth months disappointment, anger, love, sympathy, friendliness, enjoyment, and a positive sense of property become observable. The age levels mentioned should not be considered as definite limits. They designate approximate ages at which these emotions appear and may vary widely both according to individuals and circumstances.

The significant part of this emotional development is that during the whole of the first year emotional discrimination is manifested approximately two months earlier than any other form of perception. The three months smiling response, which is the infant's smiling recognition of the human partner's face, appears at an age at which no other object is recognized. Even food, the most familiar object in the baby's life, is recognized only more than two months later. The displeasure which the infant manifests at four months when left by its partner, appears two months earlier than the displeasure shown by the child when its toy is taken away. The eight months anxiety shown by the child when confronted with strangers is a sign that it has achieved the capacity to discriminate between friend and stranger. This appears two months earlier than the child's capacity to differentiate toys and other objects from each other. Thus emotional development acts as the trailbreaker for all other perceptual development during infancy.

These are the main stations of emotional development which we were able to locate in the course of the first year of life. For the purpose of our other investigations they served as points of orientation. These points of orientation we combined with the well-known findings on physical and mental development, investigated in such excellent detail by Gesell, Buehler, McGraw, Goodenough, Thompson, Pratt, Shirley and many others. We applied the combination of these two viewpoints for the purpose of comparing infants raised under different ecological circumstances.

A brief summary of the first such investigation made by us may serve as an illustration. . . .

The investigation in question was carried out in two institutions which we had the opportunity to observe simultaneously. Both institutions had certain similarities: the infants received adequate food, hygiene and asepsis were strictly enforced, the housing of the children was excellent, and medical care more than adequate. In both institutions the infants were admitted shortly after birth.

The institutions differed in one single factor. This factor was the amount of emotional interchange offered. In institution No. 1, which we have called "Nursery," the children were raised by their own mothers. In institution No. 2, which we have called "Foundlinghome," the children were raised from the third month by overworked nursing personnel: one nurse had to care for from eight to twelve children. Thus the available emotional interchange between child and mother formed the one independent variable in the comparison of the two groups.

The response to this variable showed itself in many different ways. Perhaps the most comprehensive index of this response is offered by the monthly averages of the developmental quotients of these children. . . . [See Figure.]

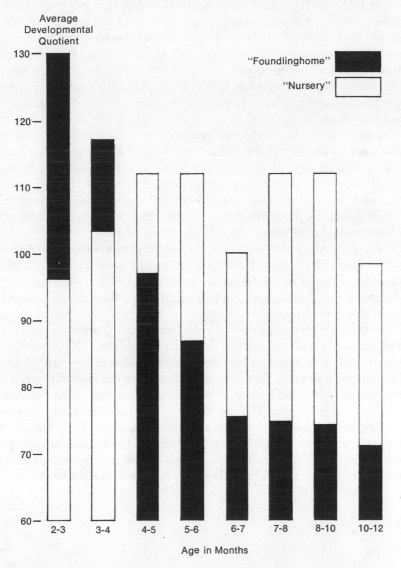

Comparison of Development in "Nursery" and "Foundlinghome"

The contrast in the development of the children in the two institutions is striking. But this twelve months chart does not tell the whole story. The children in "Foundlinghome" continued their downward slide and by the end of the second year reached a developmental quotient of 45. We have here an impressive example of how the absence of one psychosocial factor, that of emotional interchange with the mother, results in a complete reversal of a developmental trend. . . .

It should be realized that the factor which was present in the first case, but eliminated in the second, is the pivot of all development in the first year. It is the mother-child relation. By choosing this factor as our independent variable we were able to observe its vital importance. While the children in "Nursery" developed into normal healthy toddlers, a two-year observation of "Foundlinghome" showed that the emotionally starved children never learned to speak, to walk, to feed themselves. With one or two exceptions in a total of 91 children, those who survived were human wrecks who behaved either in the manner of agitated or of apathetic idiots.

The most impressive evidence probably is a comparison of the mortality rates of the two institutions. "Nursery" in this respect has an outstanding record, far better than the average of the country. In a five years' observation period during which we observed a total of 239 children, each for one year or more, "Nursery" did not lose a single child through death. In "Foundlinghome" on the other hand, 37 per cent of the children died during a two years' observation period.

The high mortality is but the most extreme consequence of the general decline, both physical and psychological, which is shown by children completely starved of emotional interchange.

We have called this condition marasmus, from the picture it shows; or hospitalism according to its etiology. . . .

The results of this study caused us to focus our attention on the mother-child relation in all our further research on infants. We strove to examine whether in less spectacular conditions also it was truly such an all-important influence. Closer investigation bore out this impression. We could establish, in the course of our further research, with the help of statistical methods, that the regularity in the emergence of emotional response, and subsequently of developmental progress both physical and mental, is predicated on adequate mother-child relations. Inappropriate mother-child relations resulted regularly either in the absence of developmental progress, emotional or otherwise, or in paradoxical responses.

Chapter 19

DREAMS

There is one common element in all theories of dreaming: an awareness that under conditions of sleep we lose rational control over our thought processes, and something other than reason directs them. But as to what that something else is, there are many opinions. Leaving aside mystical explanations of a quasi-religious nature, there remain mechanical influences of residual sensory processes, revival of recent experiences, effects of disturbed bodily processes, excessive response to stimuli which in the waking state would go unnoticed, impulses of our own irrational nature, and effects of habit. Although Plato had recognized the irrational element in dreams, this was not an important theme in psychology before Freud, although it was not uncommon to say that in one form or another the "true character" showed itself in dreams. Modern readers will probably be surprised that Smellie, in the eighteenth century, recommended keeping a regular record of dreams, to be written down immediately upon awakening.

19.1

Plato

(427–347 B.C.)

In a short digression, Plato appeals to the dream as proof that "lawless desires" exist in all men.

[Book IX.] I. . . . Of our unnecessary pleasures and appetites there are some lawless ones, I think, which probably are to be found in us all, but which, when controlled by the laws and the better desires in alliance with reason, can in some men be altogether got rid of, or so nearly so that only a few weak ones remain, while in others the remnant is stronger and more numerous. . . . {These desires} are awakened in sleep when the rest of the soul, the rational, gentle and dominant part, slumbers, but the beastly and savage part, replete with food and wine, gambols and, repelling sleep, endeavours to sally forth and satisfy its own instincts {ἤθη; literally, dispositions}. You are aware that in such case there is nothing it will not venture to undertake as being released from all sense of shame and all reason. It does not shrink from attempting to lie with a mother in fancy or with anyone else, man, god or brute. It is ready for any foul deed of blood; it abstains from no food, and, in a word, falls short of no extreme of folly and shamelessness. . . . But when, I suppose, a man's condition is healthy and sober, and he goes to sleep after arousing his rational part and entertaining it with fair words and thoughts, and attaining to clear self-consciousness, while he has neither starved nor indulged to repletion his appetitive part, so that it may be lulled to sleep and not disturb the better part by its pleasure or pain, but may suffer that in isolated purity to examine and reach out towards and apprehend some of the things unknown to it, past, present or future; and when he has in like manner tamed his passionate part, and does not after a quarrel fall asleep with anger still awake within him, but if he has thus quieted the two elements in his soul and quickened the third, in which reason resides, and so goes to his rest, you are aware that in such case he is most likely to apprehend truth, and the visions of his dreams are least likely to be lawless. . . . The point that we have to notice is this, that in fact there exists in every one of us, even in some reputed most respectable, a terrible, fierce and lawless brood of desires, which it seems are revealed in our sleep.

The Republic. With an English translation by Paul Shorey. 2 vols. Cambridge, Mass.: Harvard University Press, Loeb Classical Library, 1930–1935. [Vol. II, pp. 335–339; 571–572.] Reprinted by permission of the publisher and the Loeb Classical Library.

19.2

Aristotle

(384–322 B.C.)

For Aristotle the dream is an illusion in which we misinterpret faint residual sensory impressions in ways that are influenced by our emotional states.

II. What a dream is and how it originates, we can best study from the circumstances which attend sleep. For the sensible objects corresponding to each sense organ produce sensation in us, and the affection produced by them persists in the sense organs not only while the sensations are active, but also after they have gone. . . .

. . . This is clear in cases of continuous perception; for even when we change our sensation the affection goes on, for instance, when we turn from sunlight to darkness; the result is that we see nothing, because the movement produced in our eyes by the light still persists. Again if we look for a long time at one colour—say white or green—any object to which we shift our gaze appears to be that colour. And if, after looking at the sun or some other bright object, we shut our eyes, then, if we watch carefully, it appears in the same direct line as we saw it before, first of all in its own proper colour; then it changes to red, and then to purple, until it fades to black and disappears. The same persistence of vision occurs when we turn our gaze from moving objects—*e.g.*, rivers, especially when they flow very rapidly; for then objects really at rest appear to be moving. . . .

With regard to our original inquiry, one fact, which is clear from what we have said, may be laid down—that the sensation still remains perceptible even after the external object perceived has gone, and moreover that we are easily deceived about our perceptions when we are in emotional states, some in one state and others in another; *e.g.*, the coward in his fear, the lover in his love; so that even from a very faint resemblance the coward thinks that he sees his enemy, and the lover his loved one; and in proportion to his excitement, his imagination is stimulated by a more remote resemblance. Similarly in fits of anger and in all forms of desire all are easily deceived, and the more easily, the more they are under the influence of emotion. So men in fever sometimes think that they see animals on the walls from the slight resemblance of marks in a pattern. Sometimes the illusion corresponds to the degree of emotion, so

On dreams. In *Aristotle: On the soul; Parva naturalia; On breath.* With an English translation by W. S. Hett. Cambridge, Mass.: Harvard University Press, Loeb Classical Library, 1957. Pp. 347–371. [Pp. 353–355, 359–363; 459a–459b, 460b–461a.] Reprinted by permission of the publisher and the Loeb Classical Library.

that those who are not very ill are aware that the impression is false, but if the malady is more severe, they move themselves in accordance with what they think they see. The reason why this happens is that the controlling sense does not judge these things by the same faculty as that by which sense images occur. This is proved by the fact that the sun appears to measure a foot across, but something else often contradicts this impression. So again when the fingers are crossed one object [between them] appears to be two, but yet we deny that there are two; for sight has more authority than touch. . . .

III. It is evident from the foregoing that stimuli arising from sense-impressions, both those which are derived from without and those which have their origin within the body, occúr not only when we are awake, but also when the affection we call sleep supervenes, and even more at that time. In the daytime, when the senses and the mind are active, they are thrust aside or obscured just in the same way as a smaller fire is obscured by a greater, and small pains and pleasures by great, although when the latter have ceased even the small ones come to the surface; but at night, because the particular senses are at rest and cannot function, owing to the heat's reversing its flow and passing from the outside to the inside, these stimuli reach the starting-point of sensation and become noticeable, as the bustle subsides. One may suppose that, like the eddies often seen in rivers, each movement takes place continuously, often with unchanging pattern, but often again dividing into other shapes owing to some obstruction. For this reason no dreams occur after food or to the very young such as infants; for the movement is considerable owing to the heat arising from the food. Hence, just as in a liquid, if one disturbs it violently, sometimes no image appears, and sometimes it appears but is entirely distorted, so that it seems quite different from what it really is, although when the movement has ceased, the reflections are clear and plain; so also in sleep, the images or residuary movements that arise from the sense-impressions are altogether obscured owing to the aforesaid movement when it is too great, and sometimes the visions appear confused and monstrous, and the dreams are morbid, as occurs with the melancholic, the feverish and the intoxicated; for all these affections, being spirituous, produce much movement and confusion.

19.3

Lucretius (Titus Lucretius Carus)

(†55 B.C.)

Although the imaginal content of the dream is based on "idols" or sensory replicas of objects, entering through the senses, when the normal passages of the senses are closed by sleep the mind may still perceive such idols as it is especially tuned to, by reason of its customary and recent activities.

And generally to whatever pursuit a man is closely tied down and strongly attached, on whatever subject we have previously much dwelt, the mind having been put to a more than usual strain in it, during sleep we for the most part fancy that we are engaged in the same; lawyers think they plead causes and draw up covenants of sale, generals that they fight and engage in battle, sailors that they wage and carry on war with the winds, we think we pursue our task and investigate the nature of things constantly and consign it when discovered to writings in our native tongue. So all other pursuits and arts are seen for the most part during sleep to occupy and mock the minds of men. And whenever men have given during many days in succession undivided attention to games, we generally see that after they have ceased to perceive these with their senses, there yet remain passages open in the mind through which the same idols of things may enter. Thus for many days those same objects present themselves to the eyes, so that even when awake they see dancers as they think moving their pliant limbs, and receive into the ears the clear music of the harp and speaking strings, and behold the same spectators and at the same time the varied decorations of the stage in all their brilliancy. So great is the influence of zeal and inclination, so great is the influence of the things in which men have been habitually engaged, and not men only but all living creatures. Thus you will see stout horses, even when their bodies are lying down, yet in their sleep sweat and pant without ceasing and strain their powers to the utmost as if for the prize, or as if the barriers were thrown open. And often during soft repose the dogs of hunters do yet all at once throw about their legs and suddenly utter cries and repeatedly snuff the air with their nostrils, as though they had found and were on the tracks of wild beasts; and after they are awake often chase the shadowy idols of stags, as though they saw them in full flight, until they have shaken off their delusions and come to themselves again. And the fawning brood of dogs brought up tame in the house haste to shake their body and raise it up from the ground, as if

On the nature of things (De rerum natura). Translated by H. A. J. Munro. Fourth edition finally revised. Cambridge, 1886. [Book IV, lines 962–1036.]

they beheld unknown faces and features. And the fiercer the different breeds are, the greater rage they must display in sleep. But the various kinds of birds flee and suddenly in the night time trouble with their wings the groves of the gods, when in gentle sleep hawks and pursuing birds have appeared to shew fight and offer battle. Again the minds of men which pursue and carry on the same in like manner; kings take by storm, are taken, join battle, raise a loud cry as if stabbed on the spot. Many struggle hard and utter groans in pain, and as if gnawed by the bite of panther or cruel lion fill all the place with loud cries. Many during sleep speak of important affairs and have often disclosed their own guilt. Many meet death; many as if tumbling down from high precipices to the ground with their whole body, are scared with terror and after sleep as if out of their judgment scarce come to themselves again, quite disordered by their body's turmoil: Again a thirsty man sits down beside a river or a pleasant spring and gulps down wellnigh all the stream. Cleanly people often, when sound asleep, believing that they are lifting their dress beside a urinal or the public vessels, pour forth the filtered liquid of their whole body, and the Babylonian coverlets of surpassing brilliancy are drenched. Then too those, into the boiling currents of whose age seed is for the first time passing, when the ripe fulness of days has produced it in their limbs, idols encounter from without from what body soever, harbingers of a glorious face and a beautiful bloom, which stir and excite the frame.

19.4

Gregory of Nyssa

(335?–395?)

Gregory is evidently troubled because the mind continues to be some degree active even when "reason" is asleep. He explains this by assuming that "some appearances of the operations of the mind are accidentally moulded in the less rational part of the soul." A hint of prophecy is permitted into what is for the most part response to physiological events.

[XIII.] 5. Hence the mind of man clearly proves its claim to connection with his nature, itself also co-operating and moving with the nature in its sound and waking state, but remaining unmoved when it is abandoned

On the making of man. Translated by H. A. Wilson. In *A select library of Nicene and post-Nicene Fathers of the Christian Church*. Second series, vol. V: Gregory of Nyssa. London, 1893. Pp. 387–427. [Pp. 400–402.]

to sleep, unless any one supposes that the imagery of dreams is a motion of the mind exercised in sleep. We for our part say that it is only the conscious and sound action of the intellect which we ought to refer to mind; and as to the fantastic nonsense which occurs to us in sleep, we suppose that some appearances of the operations of the mind are accidentally moulded in the less rational part of the soul; for the soul, being by sleep dissociated from the senses, is also of necessity outside the range of the operations of the mind; for it is through the senses that the union of mind with man takes place; therefore when the senses are at rest, the intellect also must needs be inactive; and an evidence of this is the fact that the dreamer often seems to be in absurd and impossible situations, which would not happen if the soul were then guided by reason and intellect.

6. It seems to me, however, that when the soul is at rest so far as concerns its more excellent faculties (so far, I mean, as concerns the operations of mind and sense), the nutritive part of it alone is operative during sleep, and that some shadows and echoes of those things which happen in our waking moments—of the operations both of sense and of intellect—which are impressed upon it by that part of the soul which is capable of memory, that these, I say, are pictured as chance will have it, some echo of memory still lingering in this division of the soul.

7. With these, then, the man is beguiled, not led to acquaintance with the things that present themselves by any train of·thought, but wandering among confused and inconsequent delusions. But just as in his bodily operations, while each of the parts individually acts in some way according to the power which naturally resides in it, there arises also in the limb that is at rest a state sympathetic with that which is in motion, similarly in the case of the soul, even if one part is at rest and another in motion, the whole is affected in sympathy with the part; for it is not natural that the natural unity should be in any way severed, though one of the faculties included in it is in turn supreme in virtue of its active operation. But as, when men are awake and busy, the mind is supreme, and sense ministers to it, yet the faculty which regulates the body is not dissociated from them (for the mind furnishes the food for its wants, the sense receives what is furnished, and the nutritive faculty of the body appropriates to itself that which is given to it), so in sleep the supremacy of these faculties is in some way reversed in us, and while the less rational becomes supreme, the operation of the other ceases indeed, yet is not absolutely extinguished; but while the nutritive faculty is then busied with digestion during sleep, and keeps all our nature occupied with itself, the faculty of sense is neither entirely severed from it (for that cannot be separated which has once been naturally joined), nor yet can its activity revive, as it is hindered by the inaction during sleep of the organs of sense; and by the same reasoning (the mind also being united to the sensitive part of the soul) it would follow that we should

say that the mind moves with the latter when it is in motion, and rests with it when it is quiescent.

8. As naturally happens with fire when it is heaped over with chaff, and no breath fans the flames—it neither consumes what lies beside it, nor is entirely quenched, but instead of flame it rises through the air in the form of smoke; yet if it should obtain any breath of air, it turns the smoke to flame—in the same way the mind when hidden by the inaction of the senses in sleep is neither able to shine out through them, nor yet is quite extinguished, but has, so to say, a smouldering activity, operating to a certain extent, but unable to operate farther. . . .

10. For this cause memory is confused, and foreknowledge, though rendered doubtful by certain veils, is imaged in shadows of our waking pursuits, and often indicates to us something of what is going to happen: for by its subtlety of nature the mind has some advantage, in ability to behold things, over mere corporeal grossness; yet it cannot make its meaning clear by direct methods, so that the information of the matter in hand should be plain and evident, but its declaration of the future is ambiguous and doubtful,—what those who interpret such things call an "enigma." . . .

15. I also knew another cause of the fancies of sleep, when attending one of my relations attacked by frenzy; who being annoyed by food given him in too great quantity for his strength, kept crying out and finding fault with those who were about him for filling intestines with dung and putting them upon him: and when his body was rapidly tending to perspire he blamed those who were with him for having water ready to wet him with as he lay: and he did not cease calling out till the result showed the meaning of these complaints: for all at once a copious sweat broke out over his body, and a relaxation of the bowels explained the weight in the intestines. The same condition which, while his sober judgment was dulled by disease, his nature underwent, being sympathetically affected by the condition of the body—not being without perception of what was amiss, but being unable clearly to express its pain, by reason of the distraction resulting from the disease—this, probably, if the intelligent principle of the soul were lulled to rest, not from infirmity but from natural sleep, might appear as a dream to one similarly situated, the breaking out of perspiration being expressed by water, and the pain occasioned by the food, by the weight of intestines.

16. This view also is taken by those skilled in medicine, that according to the differences of complaints the visions of dreams appear differently to the patients: that the visions of those of weak stomachs are of one kind, those of persons suffering from injury to the cerebral membrane of another, those of persons in fevers of yet another; that those of patients suffering from bilious and from phlegmatic affections are diverse, and those again of plethoric patients in wasting disease, are different; whence we may see that the nutritive and vegetative faculty

of the soul has in it by commixture some seed of the intelligent element, which is in some sense brought into likeness to the particular state of the body, being adapted in its fancies according to the complaint which has seized upon it.

17. Moreover, most men's dreams are conformed to the state of their character: the brave man's fancies are of one kind, the coward's of another; the wanton man's dreams of one kind, the continent man's of another; the liberal man and the avaricious man are subject to different fancies; while these fancies are nowhere framed in the intellect, but by the less rational disposition of the soul, which forms even in dreams the semblance of those things to which each is accustomed by the practice of his waking hours.

19.5

Thomas Hobbes

(1588–1679)

The influence of Aristotle is clearly evident in Hobbes, but now the internal organs provide most of the substance for imagination to work upon, and the disordered sequence of dream thoughts is attributed to their uneven influence.

The bracketed words were added in the second (1651) edition, having perhaps been accidentally omitted from the first.

As standing water put into motion by the stroke of a *stone,* or blast of winde, doth *not presently* give over moving as soon as the winde ceaseth, or the stone setleth: so *neither* doth the *effect* cease which the *Object* hath wrought upon the *Brain.* So soon as ever, by turning aside of the Organs, the *Object ceaseth* to work; that is to say, Though the *Sense* be *past,* the *Image* or conception *remaineth;* but more *obscure* while we are *awake,* because some *object* or other continually *plieth* and solliciteth our Eyes, and Ears, *keeping* the Minde in a *stronger* motion, whereby the *weaker* doth *not* easily *appear.* And this obscure conception is that we call *Phantasie,* or *Imagination: Imagination* being (to define it) *conception remaining, and by little and little decaying from and after the act of Sense.*

Humane nature: or, the fundamental elements of policie. Being a discoverie of the faculties, acts, and passions of the soul of man, from their original causes; according to such philosophical principles as are not commonly known or asserted. London, 1650. [Pp. 19–23.]

2. But when *present* Sense is *not,* as in *Sleep,* there the *Images* remaining after Sense (when there be many) as in Dreams, are *not obscure,* but *strong* and *clear,* as in Sense it self. The reason is, That which obscured and made the conceptions weak, namely Sense, and present *operation* of the Object, is *removed:* for *Sleep* is the *privation of the act of Sense,* (the power remaining) and *Dreams* are the *Imagination* of them that *sleep.*

3. The *causes* of Dreams (if they be natural) are the *actions* or violence of the *inward* parts of a man upon his *Brain,* by which the *passages* of Sense by Sleep *benummed,* are *restored* to their motion. The signes by which this appeareth to be so, are the *differences* of Dreams (old men commonly dream oftner, and have their dreams more painfuller then young) proceeding from the *different* accidents of mans body; as Dreams of *Lust,* or Dreams of *Anger,* according as the Heart, or other parts within, work more or less upon the Brain, by more or less *heat;* so also the descents of different *sorts of Flegm* maketh us [a dream of different tasts of meates and drinks; and I] believe there is a *reciprocation* of motion from the Brain to the Vital parts, and back from the Vital parts to the Brain; whereby not onely *Imagination* begetteth *motion* in those parts; but also motion in those parts begetteth Imagination like to that by which it was gotten. If this be true, and that *sad* imaginations nourish the *Spleen,* then we see also a cause, why a strong *Spleen* reciprocally causeth *fearful dreams,* and why the effects of *Lasciviousness* may in a dream produce the image of some person that had *caused* them. Another signe that dreams are caused by the action of the inward parts, is the *disorder* and casual consequence of one conception or Image to another: for when we are *waking,* the *antecedent* thought or conception introduceth & is cause of the *consequent,* (as the water followeth a mans finger upon a dry and level table) but in *Dreams* there is commonly *no coherence,* (and when there is, it is by chance) which must needs proceed from this, That the *Brain* in dreams is *not restored* to its motion in every part alike; whereby it cometh to pass, that our Thoughts appear like the Stars between the flying Clouds, not in the order which a Man would chuse to observe them, but as the uncertain flight of broken Clouds permits.

19.6

Marin Cureau de la Chambre

(1594–1669)

La Chambre, the protégé and friend of chancellor Séguier, an important patron of literature and the sciences, was also physician to Richelieu, Mazarin, and Louis XIV—all fortunately for him long-lived men. He is said to have served the king as a consultant on his appointments, and it is clear that his medical practice was sometimes of the nature of psychotherapy. One wonders if he ever interpreted the dreams of these renowned patients. Here we meet a mechanism of wish-fulfilment!

[Violent anger makes sleep well nigh impossible, but] when it is a little appeased, it permits sleep to deaden the senses in order to repair the damage that has been caused by wakefulness and toil.

But in such rest as [this sleep] can give, it still preserves, in the soul and the humors, the remains of the storm which anger had excited there. For [this sleep] is usually crossed by a thousand kinds of dreams which are filled with fire and conflagration, threats, combats and victories. Sometimes the cause of these dreams is that the imagination is still full of images that were left there by the emotion, and still feeling as one might say the impulse which had been given it by the desire for revenge, it is insensibly carried away and thus continues its original plans. It always brings these to a successful conclusion, since in sleep it is no longer governed by sense or by reason, but takes counsel only from self-love and from the pride which anger brings with it. That is the source of the strength felt by a man who sleeps on his anger. It seems to him that he is always stronger and more skilful; he never sees his enemy otherwise than weak and conquered; he never undertakes any combat from which he does not emerge victorious and triumphant.

But it sometimes also happens that the soul is quite calm, and nothing is left in it of the agitation which the emotion had introduced, and that nevertheless all these illusions continue. Perhaps the movement of agitation lasts longer here than in the soul, or perhaps the bile which had been separated from the blood has not been able so soon to regain its original place; either of these reasons is capable of producing those same violent dreams about which we have been speaking. The difficulty is to know how this can happen, in view of the fact that these things do not

Les charactères des passions, II. Où il est traitté de la nature et des effets des passions courageuses [The signs of the emotions, II. The nature and the effects of the courageous emotions]. Paris, 1645. [Pp. 454–458.]

affect the senses, which are stupefied, nor, consequently, the imagination, which works only with images which it receives from the senses. And even if the senses were free to act, it does not seem that they could know anything about what is taking place inside the veins. What, then, can excite all these phantoms and chimeras in the soul, which are so closely related to the movements which the spirits undergo, and are disordered just like the humors?

We must certainly admit that, besides the external knowledge which the senses give it, the soul has another interior and secret knowledge provided by nature, by means of which it sees and knows everything that is taking place in the organs. With this information the soul, which is present everywhere in the body, readily notices everything which happens there, and then communicates it to the imagination, which is a kind of central point for all knowledge. But since this (internal) knowledge is obscure and confused, it does not instruct the imagination clearly, but only gives it a general view. It does not form correct images, which represent the objects as they are, but only such as have some relation and correspondence with them. So when the bile has been stirred up, even though the soul does not know what it is, it does know that it is a warm and ardent humor; and from the report which it then gives to the imagination, the latter imagines the brilliant colors, the flames and conflagrations which conform to this vague notion which it has received. And because it also knows that this humor serves in both anger and audacity, in order to destroy the enemies against whom these emotions are always directed . . . it immediately thinks of objects and plans for assault and combat, and of imaginary enemies.

19.7

Thomas Willis

(1621–1675)

As Hobbes follows Aristotle, so Willis seems to follow Lucretius, both in the emphasis on organic stimulation and in permitting the restless spirits to engage in habitual pursuits. This discussion of dreams falls within his first, "physiological" discourse, but it shows the almost-complete reliance on somatic causes of mental illness which characterizes his second "pathological" discourse, including the discussion there "of delirium and phrensie."

[*De anima brutorum,* . . . 1672.] *Two discourses concerning the soul of brutes, which is that of the vital and sensitive of man.* Englished by S. Pordage. London, 1683. [Pp. 93–94.]

The Nature, Causes and Effects of Sleep, being unfolded after this manner, before we wholly leave its Consideration, it will not be far from the Matter, to subjoyn something of Dreams, we shall here purposely pass over what manner of Signification they have, both Natural, as they indicate the intemperance of the Brain, and also fatidical, as if they were inspired by a *Daemon,* and are affirmed to Prophesie things to come: we shall only inquire by what Motion, and agitation of the Animal Spirits, Dreams are produced in the Brain. We say therefore, that the Animal Spirits, although they affect naturally alternate times of Motion and Rest, and whil'st they indulge Rest, instilling fresh Nervous Humor to the Brain, they suffer themselves to be bound together with Embraces, as it were with Chains, that they may not enter into Motion; yet it for the most part happens, that some Spirits easily cast off this Bond, and love to wander hither and thither, in the deep silence of the Rest. And indeed Dreams are only the Excursions of some Spirits in the Brain, from their bond or tye, which, whil'st the rest are strictly bound together, wander about, without any Guide or Ruler; and repeat the types or shaddows of Motions, as it were Dances before learnt; and are wont to represent the Cogitations of things, though after a very confused manner. The Spirits which being got loose, variously run about, whil'st the rest are bound together, gain the Liberty of Motion, by a twofold means. To wit, some Spirits, fly from the Captivity of Sleep, for the most part, by reason of the Heat and Agitation of the Brain, as by Drinking of Wine, the fume of Tobacco, immoderate Exercise, as also by the Passions, and more hard study, is wont to arise: for by these means, the Spirits are stirred up, by a certain Stimulation or Provokement, and are driven as it were into rage, that, though Sleep creep upon them, all of them will not be bound or restrained, but that some of them will walk about the Sepulchers of the rest, like Spectres in a Church-yard, and Cause stupendious Apparitions of things. Another Exsuscitation of some Spirits in the Brain, whereby Dreams are produced, is made by reason of some Spirits being disturbed in other Parts, as in the Praecordia, Stomach, Spleen, Genitals, &c. By which, whil'st the same Perturbation is Communicated by the Nerves to the Brain, perhaps one or two Handfuls or Bands of Spirits, there stirred up, causes various Phantasies to be represented. In the disease called the *Incubus* or Night-Mare, when the Praecordia are stop'd in their Motion, or otherwise hindred, by reason of the Nerves being bound together, we Dream some Animal or heavy weight lying upon the Breast, stops our Breathing. The Genital Humor growing turgid or swelling up in the Vessels, and irritating them, produces immodest Dreams. Undigested and gross Meats, eaten at Supper, because they aggravate or lye heavy in the Ventricle, and trouble it, render Sleep also troubled, and infested with terrible and affrightful Phantasies; in like manner we might easily shew, that it is the same with many other Parts.

Whil'st as it were private Troops of Spirits, being excited in the Brain, carrying themselves hither and thither, exercise the Phantasie, their Divergency or Excursions happen sometimes regularly, sometimes inordinately: and therefore Dreams, represent either the Series of things before acted, or only *Chimera's,* or Notions altogether incongruous and disagreeing. Further, whil'st the Animal Spirits, being agitated by this means, within the Brain, produce Dreams or the Images of Cogitations, do often leap back, into the Nervous Stock, and there stirring up other Spirits, produce divers sorts of local Motions: wherefore some Men also, when they sleep soundly, are wont to rise out of their Bed, to walk here and there, oftentimes to put on their Cloaths, to open the Doors, go up Stairs, and to pass over Rocky places, which they could scarce go over when Awake; in the mean time if they meet with any Obstacle in their Progress, they either advisedly pass by it, or remove it out of the way. . . . Yea, it is observed of most of these Night-walkers like Spirits, that being awakned, they scarce remember any thing of what they did, or acted in their Sleep; as if they suffer'd something that was different from other Dreamers; for these think that they perform local Motions, when indeed there is no such thing, but the others move from place to place, and yet know nothing of it. In Dreamers, the Spirits being stirred up, spread or are carried wholly inwards, towards the Callous Body, and affect only the Imagination and Memory: but in those walking in their Sleep, some handfuls or bands of them, being awakned, direct their tendency only outwards, towards the moving Parts, in the mean time, the Common Sense, Imagination, and Memory are not at all affected.

19.8

William Smellie

(1740–1795)

David Hume wrote in 1739 that "several moralists have recommended it as an excellent method of becoming acquainted with our own hearts, and knowing our progress in virtue, to recollect our dreams in a morning, and examine them with the same rigour that we would our most serious and most deliberate actions." What Smellie adds is the sound advice that recording our dreams instantly upon awakening will develop in us a capacity for remembering them in greater detail. As illustration he describes a series of four dreams "recorded thirty years ago." In one of these he suffers the

The philosophy of natural history. II. Edinburgh, 1799. [Pp. 375–377.]

embarrassment of having his breeches fall down in a festive ballroom scene. In another he is witness to "a furious dispute between Dr. Munro and Dr. Whytt concerning the use of the Deltoid Muscle!" He offers no interpretations.

Every Person may derive Advantage from Dreams

To know one's self is the most important of all knowledge, and, at the same time, the most difficult to attain. Mankind are so artful in disguising the real motives of their actions, so ingenious in deceiving themselves, so averse to the discovery of vice or imperfection in their sentiments or behaviour, so keenly engaged in the occupations of life, and so prone to contrast themselves with the most profligate of the species, that they generally rest satisfied with their condition, and seldom inquire with any degree of impartiality into the real character or temperament of their minds. A more simple method of acquiring a knowledge of ourselves must be acceptable to every person who thinks himself interested in the inquiry. This end, I presume, may be accomplished by a moderate attention to our dreams. *Dreaming* must here be understood in the most common acceptation of the word; for an inquiry into the natural tendency of imagination while awake, would engage us in a struggle with all the obstructions to self-knowledge formerly suggested. Let us, then, attend to those particular vices which we are most inclined to indulge in sleep. That vice which is most frequently and most luxuriously indulged in our dreams, may safely be esteemed our predominant passion. Though motives of interest, decency, and the opinions of our friends, may have restrained us from actual gratification, and created a delusive belief that we are no longer subject to its solicitations; yet, if the imaginary gratification constitutes an agreeable dream; if it is then indulged without check or remorse, we may freely conclude, that we still remain its humble votaries, and that those motives which deter from actual indulgence are not the genuine motives which virtue inspires.

This method of discovering our real characters, it may be said, is more uncertain, and attended with greater difficulty than deliberate self-examination. But, we should reflect, that, during sleep, the mind is more ingenuous, less inclined to palliate its real motives, less influenced by public opinion, and, in general, more open and candid, than when the senses are awake. It is true, that, by the return of external objects, business, and intercourse with the world, dreams are apt to escape from the memory, and that this circumstance, in some measure, deprives us of the advantages which might otherwise result from them. This is, indeed, the only difficulty we have to encounter; but it is not unsurmountable. It may be removed by a few minutes labour every morning. Let any person who wishes to know his real character, as soon as he gets up, revolve, as accurately as he can, those thoughts which made the deepest impression upon him while he was asleep, what scenes gave him pleasure or pain, what actions he approved or disapproved, and let him instantly write them in a book kept for the purpose. In opposition to a *Diary,* this book may be entitled *A Nocturnal.* The nocturnalist, however, must be careful to give a candid account of his sleeping transactions, marking with accuracy the various feelings which the particular incidents excited. At first, perhaps, his business will be soon executed. But the mere habit of writing, so ductile is the human mind, will soon make him both more attentive to his dreams, and increase his faculty of remembering them.

19.9

Sigmund Freud

(1859–1939)

Freud's Interpretation of Dreams appeared in 1900. The very title, with its mystic connotations, was like a chip on the shoulder. The book was at first poorly received and was a failure from the publishing standpoint. In later years Freud more than once referred to it as his most important work, the one which gave him most satisfaction. A briefer statement of the theory was published soon after in a medical journal, and from this we give one section (IX), containing the heart of the theory.

Now that we have established the concept of repression and have brought dream-distortion into relation with repressed psychical material, we can express in general terms the principal findings to which we have been led by the analysis of dreams. In the case of dreams which are intelligible and have a meaning, we have found that they are undisguised wish-fulfilments; that is, that in their case the dream-situation represents as fulfilled a wish which is known to consciousness, which is left over from daytime life, and which is deservedly of interest. Analysis has taught us something entirely analogous in the case of obscure and confused dreams: once again the dream-situation represents a wish as fulfilled—a wish which invariably arises from the dream-thoughts, but

Ueber den Traum. *Grenzfragen des Nerven- und Seelenlebens,* 1901, pp. 307–344. Translated by James Strachey, as "On dreams." *Standard Edition of the complete psychological works of Sigmund Freud,* Vol. V. New York: W. W. Norton & Company, Inc. and London: Hogarth Press, 1952. Pp. 631–686. [Pp. 674–675.] Copyright 1952 by W. W. Norton & Company, Inc. Reprinted by permission of the Hogarth Press, W. W. Norton & Company, Sigmund Freud Copyrights and The Institute of Psycho-Analysis.

one which is represented in an unrecognizable form and can only be explained when it has been traced back in analysis. The wish in such cases is either itself a repressed one and alien to consciousness, or it is intimately connected with repressed thoughts and is based upon them. Thus the formula for such dreams is as follows: *they are disguised fulfilments of repressed wishes.* It is interesting in this connection to observe that the popular belief that dreams always foretell the future is confirmed. Actually the future which the dream shows us is not the one which *will* occur but the one which we should *like* to occur. The popular mind is behaving here as it usually does: what it wishes, it believes.

Dreams fall into three classes according to their attitude to wishfulfilment. The first class consists of those which represent an unrepressed wish undisguisedly; these are the dreams of an infantile type which become ever rarer in adults. Secondly there are the dreams which express a repressed wish disguisedly; these no doubt form the overwhelming majority of all our dreams, and require analysis before they can be understood. In the third place there are the dreams which represent a repressed wish, but do so with insufficient or no disguise. These last dreams are invariably accompanied by anxiety, which interrupts them. In their case anxiety takes the place of dream-distortion; and in dreams of the second class anxiety is only avoided owing to the dream-work. There is no great difficulty in proving that the ideational content which produces anxiety in us in dreams was once a wish but has since undergone repression.

There are also clear dreams with a distressing content, which, however, is not felt as distressing in the dream itself. For this reason they cannot be counted as anxiety-dreams; but they have always been taken as evidence of the fact that dreams are without meaning and have no psychical value. An analysis of a dream of this kind will show that we are dealing with well-disguised fulfilments of repressed wishes, that is to say with a dream of the second class; it will also show how admirably the process of displacement is adapted for disguising wishes.

A girl had a dream of seeing her sister's only surviving child lying dead in the same surroundings in which a few years earlier she had in fact seen the dead body of her sister's *first* child. She felt no pain over this; but she naturally rejected the idea that this situation represented any wish of hers. Nor was there any need to suppose this. It had been beside the first child's coffin, however, that, years before, she had seen and spoken to the man she was in love with; if the second child died, she would no doubt meet the man again in her sister's house. She longed for such a meeting, but fought against the feeling. On the dream-day she had bought a ticket for a lecture which was to be given by this same man, to whom she was still devoted. Her dream was a simple dream of impatience of the kind that often occurs before journeys, visits to the theatre, and similar enjoyments that lie ahead. But in order to disguise this longing from her, the situation was displaced on to an event of a kind most unsuitable for producing a feeling of enjoyment, though it had in fact done so in the past. It is to be observed that the emotional behaviour in the dream was appropriate to the real content which lay in the background and not to what was pushed into the foreground. The dream-situation anticipated the meeting she had so long desired; it offered no basis for any painful feelings.

19.10

Nathaniel Kleitman AND Eugene Aserinsky

(born 1895)   (born 1921)

Kleitman's earlier research had established the periodicity of sleep, particularly as manifested in cyclic changes in EEG records. This study provided researchers with a method by which to determine when their subjects were dreaming and stimulated a great flood of experimental studies of dreaming. It made REM, if not a household, at least a classroom word.

. . . The purpose of the present work was to re-examine the condition of ocular motility during the whole course of undisturbed sleep and to clarify the relationship of the eye movements to other events recorded simultaneously.

[Method.] One 10-year-old boy and 26 adults including two women were subjects for the several sets of experiments. . . . Preparations were completed so that each subject could retire at his usual or preferred time. . . .

Eye movements were recorded as an electro-oculogram (EOG). The latter is a record of the changes of the resting potential of the eye (corneo-retinal potential) with respect to fixed electrodes near the eye. . . .

[Results.] Two types of eye movements were observed. First, there was a slow, lateral movement similar to that seen in sleeping infants and in adults during sleep and anesthesia. A single excursion of this type was usually completed in 3–4 seconds; the highest frequencies were in the order of the respiratory rate, i.e. 15/min., whereas the lower frequencies were less than 1/min. . . . The second type of ocular activity was characterized by rapid, jerky motions of relatively short arc and by completion of a single rotation in about 1 second. . . . Inasmuch as a

Two types of ocular motility during sleep. *Journal of Applied Physiology* 8 (1955): 1–10.

nomenclature describing these movements is lacking, the first type of movement will be referred to as *slow eye movement* and the second type as *rapid eye movement.* . . .

Slow eye movements were seen at the onset of sleep and together with and after every body movement throughout sleep. When the subjects were awake and when the alpha rhythm [EEG] was definite (subjects presumably relaxed) these lateral movements were especially prominent. However, these motions were not discernible despite the presence of alpha waves when the subjects were aware of the observer's presence. . . .

From 1 to 5 hours (average, 3 hr.) after the onset of sleep, the first group of rapid eye movements appeared simultaneously in both eyes. They persisted for a variable duration, disappearing and then reappearing, until about 20 minutes later the last cluster of movements could be discerned. After 2 hours of ocular quiescence (including slow eye movement) there usually occurred another period of rapid eye movement which did not differ significantly in duration from the first period. Again, about 1½ hours later, a third period of such movement sometimes appeared. With longer sleep, a fourth period of rapid eye movement appeared. The interval between successive eye movement periods was progressively shorter. . . .

The peculiar rapid eye movements suggested the possibility that they might be associated with dreaming. Consequently, 10 subjects in 14 experiments were interrogated after intervals with and without rapid eye movements, care being taken that the EEG's in both situations were at least superficially similar. . . . The subjects were awakened by voice and asked whether dreaming was recalled, and if so, to describe in a few words the dream content or any visual imagery which could be remembered. . . .

Twenty out of twenty-seven replies, from individuals who were awakened after rapid eye movements had been observed, yielded detailed dream descriptions in contrast to 19 out of 23 replies from persons awakened in the absence of eye movements, which revealed complete failure to recall dreaming. . . . Thus the recall of dreaming was associated with the prior occurrence of rapid eye movements at a probability level of less than 0.001. . . .

[Discussion.] Although no attempt was made to secure a thorough account of the recalled dream events during the extremely brief interrogation, there were reports revealing strikingly vivid visual imagery, especially after the subjects were awakened following the eye movements. It is indeed highly probable that the rapid eye movements are directly associated with visual imagery in dreaming.

The duration of the rapid eye movement *period* might suggest that a single dream lasts about 25 minutes. It is nevertheless possible that a period may encompass more than one dream. . . . Also, the data at hand do not support the contention that dreams last throughout sleep or that they 'regulate' the depth of sleep. The regularity of occurrence of eye movement periods, furthermore, makes it unwarranted to assert a causal relationship between emotion, mental conflict or external stimulation with the onset of dreaming although those factors conceivably may modify dream content. If anything, such prosaic events as the diurnal fall in body temperature or increase of proprioceptive impulses from the periphery may be the direct cause of CNS changes which manifest themselves as dreaming.

# Chapter 20

EMOTION

In the period following the death of Aristotle (that is, after the fall of Alexander and in the decline of Grecian political and military power) there was a strong upsurge of ethical interest among Greek philosophers. The persistent Hellenic theme of moderation expressed itself differently in two rival schools, those of Zeno the Stoic and of Epicurus, who in different ways derogated the emotions. Later, after the center of learning had moved to Alexandria, Neoplatonists followed the Stoic lead, and from them the Christians in their turn accepted the thesis that the body is to be regarded as a prison for the soul and the passions as pathologies induced by the coarseness of body. In ensuing centuries the study of emotion was neglected, all emotion being labeled evil, except an ideal love of God. Vives presents the first clear break in this tradition, anticipating the strong interest in the passions during the seventeenth century. That century also saw the revival of Epicurean atomism by Gassendi. The eighteenth century gave Epicureanism a new meaning, and it began to glorify the passions. From then on, emotion was increasingly recognized as an essential part of man, a key to his behavior: that man is as much a passionate as a rational animal.

Starting in the eighteenth century, this has been an area of sharp controversy between nativists and empiricists—a controversy perhaps foreshadowed by the Stoic doctrine that emotions are only opinions.

20.1

Zeno the Stoic

(*c.* 350?–258? B.C.)

Zeno presents a rational ethic which warns against permitting reason to be perverted or overcome by passion. Later critics often ridiculed the Stoic contention that a wise man is incapable of fear, as in a tale of a prominent Stoic who lost his philosophic mien during a storm at sea. But the theory evidently had its attraction, since Descartes (who displayed a wise caution by not publishing L'Homme during his lifetime) did not include fear among the primary emotions.

We know Zeno and Epicurus only at second hand, and we shall present their views through the accounts given in Stanley's History of Philosophy, constructed by an exhaustive compilation of everything reported by such ancient authors as Diogenes Laertes, Cicero, Stobeus, and Plutarch.

Of Eupathies

As soon as any object is presented to us, which seemeth good, Nature . . . drives us on to the acquisition thereof, which being done constantly and prudently, is call'd Will; imprudently and excessively, Desire.

Moreover, while we are so moved, that we are in some good, that happeneth also two ways, when the Soul is mov'd quietly and constantly according to reason, this is called Joy; when vainly and excessively, Pleasure.

In like manner, as we desire good things by nature, so by nature we decline the Ill: This declination, if done according to reason, is called *Caution,* if without reason, *Fear.* Caution is only in a wise man, of Fear he is not capable.

Hence it appeareth, that there are three kinds of good affections of the Mind, called *Eupathies,* or *Constancies: Joy, Caution, Will.*

1. *Joy* is contrary to Pleasure, as being a rational Evaluation of the Mind.
2. *Caution* is contrary to Fear, as being a rational declination of ill.
3. *Will* is contrary to desire, as being a rational Appetite.

These are primary Eupathies; and as under the primary Passions are comprehended many subordinate passions; so are there secondary eupathies subordinate to those. . . .

Notwithstanding that Eupathies and Passions are contrary; yet there

Thomas Stanley, *History of philosophy* [1655]. Third edition. London, 1701. [Pp. 321–323.]

are but three Eupathies, though there are four Passions; for there is no Eupathy contrary to Grief.

Of Passions

From falsities proceedeth a perversity of Intellect, hence spring up several passions, and causes of disorder.

Zeno defineth passion, a praeternatural motion of the Soul, (or as *Cicero* renders it, *a commotion of the Soul, averse from right Reason, against Nature.*) *Others more briefly, a mere vehement Appetite. More vehement they call that, which recedeth from the constancy of Nature,* and is contrary to nature, whereupon all passion is an excessive stupid desire.

The kinds of Passion arise from two opinionated goods, and two opinionated Evils, so they are four. From the good, *desire* and *pleasure;* pleasure from present good, desire from future; from the ill, *Fear* and *Grief;* fear from the future, grief from the present. . . . Thus *desire* and *fear* go foremost, that to apparent good, this to apparent ill; *pleasure* and *grief* follows; pleasure, when we attain what we desire, grief, when we incur what we fear.

All passions arise from *Judgment* and *Opinion*, whence they are more strictly defined, (that it may appear not only how vicious they are, but also that they are in our power) thus;

Grief is a fresh opinion of present ill, wherein it seemeth fit that the mind be contracted and dejected, or a contraction of the Soul caused by opinion of present ill.

Pleasure is a fresh opinion of present good, wherein it seemeth good that the Mind be exalted, or an irrational elevation of mind to something that seemeth eligible.

Fear is an opinion of eminent ill, which seemeth to be intolerable; or a contraction of the Soul disobedient to Reason, caused by expectation of ill.

Desire is an opinion of good to come, that if it were present, it were fit for our use, or an appetite disobedient to Reason, caused by the opinion of consequent good.

These four are, as *Hecato* saith, primary passions, under each of which there are subordinate passions, several species belonging to their proper genus. . . .

In all these Passions there is Opinion. Opinion is a weak assent. Hence passions (as *Chrysippus* in his Book of *Passions* affirms) are Judgments; for Avarice is an opinion, or false Judgment that Money is good; Drunkenness and Intemperance, are the like. Opinion is likewise sudden from the contractive motion of an unreasonable elation of the Mind, unreasonable and praeternatural, in as much as it is not obedient to reason. For every passion is violent: Wherefore oftentimes, though we see in those that are transported by passions, the inconvenience thereof; yet notwithstanding, the same Persons that condemn it, are carried away by it, as by a headstrong Horse, and therefore properly may use that saying:

Against my Judgment Nature forceth me, Meaning by Judgment, the knowledge of right things; for Man is carried beyond Nature by Passion, to transgress natural reason and right.

All those who are led by Passion, are diverted from Reason, but in another manner than those who are deceived. For the deceived, as for example, They who think Atomes to be the principles of all things, when they come to know that they are not, change their Judgment: But, those that are in passion, although that they are taught not to grieve, or fear, or give way to any passion in the Soul, yet they do not put them off, but are lead on by their passions, until they come to be subject to their tyranical sway.

20.2

Epicurus

(342?–270 B.C.)

In contrast to the rational ethic of Stoicism, Epicurus taught a scientific ethic based on atomism. His finding that pleasure cannot occur except as the counterpart to a prior pain led to the conclusion that an avoidance of all desire is not only the most rational, but in the long run the least unpleasurable plan for living. In keeping with this scientific basis, the Epicurean theory links men and animals more closely, and provides the basis for differentiating among men according to their propensity, not merely for passion, but for different kinds of passion.

Of the Affections or Passions of the Soul

There is besides Sense another part of the Irrational Soul, which may be called Affectuous, or Passionate, from the Affections or Passions raised in it. It is also termed the Appetite or Desire, from the chief Affection which it hath, called Appetite or Desire; some distinguish it into Concupiscible and Irascible.

Now whereas it was already said, that the affections which follow

Thomas Stanley, *History of philosophy* [1655]. Third edition. London, 1701. [Pp. 590–591.]

Sense, are produced in the organs of Sense, those which follow opinion in the Breast; hereupon there being two principal affections, Pleasure, and Pain; the first, familiar, and suitable to the Soul; the other, incommodious, and unsuitable to Nature. It is manifest, that both these are excited, not in the Breast only, where Pleasure, for the most part, comes under the name of Joy, Gladness, Exultation, Mirth; and Pain, under that of Grief, Sorrow, Anguish, &c. but also in the other parts, in which, when they are restored to that state, Pleasure.

If all the parts could continue in their natural state, either there would be no affection, or if there were any, it must be called Pleasure, from the quiet and calmness of that state. But because either by reason of the continual motion of principles in the Body of an Animal, some things depart from it, others come to it; some are taken asunder, others put together, &c. or by reason of the motion which is in the things round about, some things are brought which insinuate into them, change, invert, disjoin, &c. pain is caused, (from the first occasion, as by Hunger, Thirst, Sickness; from the second, as by burning, bruising, wresting, wounding,) therefore the affection of pain seems to be first produced: And withal, because it is of an opposite nature, that of aversation or avoidance of it, and of the thing that bringeth it, to which, for that reason, is attributed the name of Ill.

Hereupon followeth a desire of exemption from pain, or of that state which is void of pain, and consequently of the thing by which it may be expelled, and to which, for that reason, is given the name of Good; and then the pain being taken away, and the thing reduced into a better, that is, into its natural state, pleasure is excited, and goeth along with it; so as there would not be pleasure, if some kind of pain did not go before, as is easily observable even from hunger and thirst and the pleasure that is taken in eating and drinking.

For this pleasure is only made, because (most of the parts being dissipated by the action of the intrinsecal heat, by which means the body itself becomes rarify'd, all Nature destroy'd, and the stomach especially grip'd, or otherwise some little Bodies of heat rolling about it, make it glow, whereby is caused pain) because, I say, meat cometh, and supplieth the defects, supports the limbs, stoppeth the desire of eating, which gapeth throughout the members and the veins; Drink comes and extinguishes the heat, moistneth the parts which before were dry, and reduceth them to their first state. And besides, both are made with a smooth and pleasing sense of Nature, which, it is manifest, is then absent, when a Man eats, not being hungry; or drinks, not being athirst.

Thus the general affections of the soul seem to be these four, Pain and Pleasure, the Extreme; Aversion and Desire, the Intermediate. I say, General, because the rest are kinds of these, and made by opinion intervening, and may be reduced principally to Desire and Avoidance. . . .

Natural and Necessary are those, which take away, both the indigence, and the Pain proceeding from the Indigence; such is that of Meat, of Drink, of Cloathing, to expel the Cold. Natural, but not Necessary, are those which only vary the Pleasure but are not absolutely Necessary to the taking away of the Pain, as those which are of delicate Meats, even that which is of Venereal Delights, to which Nature gives a Beginning, but from which a Man may abstain without inconvenience. Lastly, neither Natural nor Necessary are those, which contribute nothing to the taking away of any Pain, caused by some indigence of Nature, but are begot only by Opinion; such are for Instance, those of Crowns, Statues, Ornaments, Rich Cloathing, Gold, Silver, Ivory, and the like.

Moreover, it is to be observed, That whereas Pleasure consists in the fruition of Good, Pain is suffering Ill; for this Reason, the first is produced with a kind of dilatation and depression thereof; and therefore it is not to be wondred at, if the Soul dilates herself as much as she can, to make way for the Good to come into her, and contracts herself to prevent Ill.

There is a Diffusion, or Dilatation; for as soon as ever the Form of a good and pleasing thing strikes the Sense, or moveth the Mind, the little Bodies, of which it consists, so insinuate into the organs of Sense, or into the Heart itself, as that being accommodated as well to the Soul, as to the Body, they, in a more particular manner, gently stroke and delight the Soul, and, like little Chains, allure and draw it towards that thing out of which they were sent: Whereupon the Soul being turned towards, and intent upon that thing, gives a great leap, as it were, towards it, with all the strength it hath, that it may enjoy it.

On the other side there is Cantraction, because as soon as ever the Form of a painful thing strikes the Sense, or the Mind, the little Bodies of which it consists, as so many little Darts or Needles, prick the very Soul together with the Organ, in such manner, that they loosen its Contexture, while she, to prevent them as much as she can, shuts herself up, and retires to her very Centre or Root, where the Heart or Intellect is placed.

It will not be necessary to repeat what we formerly said, that it depends upon the contexture of the Soul, why one Animal is more inclined to Anger, another to Fear, a third to calm smooth Motions; nor to add, that this difference is found in Men also, according as their Souls participate more of a fiery, or a flatuous, or of an aerial Principle. Or we may observe even in Men that are polished by Learning, these Seeds cannot be so rooted out, but that one is more propense to Anger, another more subject to Fear, a third more prone to Clemency than he ought. Moreover, the difference of manners, which is observed to be so great, not amongst Animals only, but in Men from one another, is plainly enough derived from the various commistion of these Seeds.

20.3

Luis Vives

(1492–1540)

The treatment of the emotions by Vives brings a startling departure from the Stoic-Christian condemnation of passion as irrational. He portrays emotion not as evil, but as an adaptive mechanism, and the importance he attributes to it appears in the fact that he devotes almost half of his entire work to this topic. The physiological description of fear in this selection is also new and certainly shows that Descartes, a century later, was not the first to attempt such a description.

The acts of those faculties which nature has given us to pursue what is good and to avoid what is evil are called passions or emotion. . . . Good and bad, as we speak of them now, do not mean what are really such, but what each one for himself judges to be such. . . .

There are certain movements of the soul, or truly natural impulses, which arise from bodily effects, such as to desire food when hungry and drink when thirsty, to grieve when we are ill or pressed by black bile, to rejoice when pure clear blood surrounds the heart, to be pained by injury. These movements precede judgment; all others, however swift, follow the determination of judgment. For the soul makes no movement without a prior judgment as to whether the object of its action is good or evil; this is the case even with animals, in whom imagination alone produces no effect without the assistance of the estimative faculty, which in them takes the place of judgment. . . . However, this judgment is not always based on an examination of reasons. It can result from the picture formed in imagination, and this is more often the case. Thus fantasy by itself, through its excitement, can give rise to a kind of opinion and judgment as to whether an object is good or bad, and from this we feel perturbations throughout the soul—we are fearful or happy, we weep, we are sad. The soul turns to those parts of the body which are especially dominated by the imagination. We therefore attribute to the emotions the same qualities which belong to the natural body: some are hot, some cold; some are moist, some dry; in some these qualities are mixed, for all these qualities are joined in the human body. Whatever the nature of a particular emotion may be, it is easily aroused and grows strong in a body of the same nature, but not in one of opposite nature. . . .

The first effect of fear is to constrict and weaken the heart. To give it assistance, nature sends the heat of the upper parts, and if that is not

De anima et vita [Of the soul and life]. Brussels, 1538. [Pp. 146–147, 243–246, 249.]

enough, it takes that of the lower parts as well. Hence paleness, and chills. The quaking of the heart causes the whole body to quake, following the heart's motion, and from this comes stammering and hesitation in speech. This is also to be seen in other emotions in which the heart beats quickly, as in anger or joy, and in physical exercise. But in fear the voice is weak, because the heat has gone from the heart and the upper parts, while in anger it is strong, because the heat rises. The hairs bristle, because the vessels are constricted by cold, which makes the hairs stiff. Those who have little blood around the heart are cowards. Those whose hearts are large in proportion to [the quantity of] the blood are timid, like the hare. The dove and the deer are also timid, because they lack the bile by which the blood can be inflamed. But in those in whom the yellow bile swells freely, the blood also boils about the praecordia, and they are bold and vigorous. Those in whom the blood is thick and hot and plentiful around the heart, are secure in their souls and courageous, for they have an abundance of heat, which is very potent for confidence, and this is conserved for a long time by the firm, dense matter. But if the heat is scanty, and is drawn back into the breast, the heart becomes weak and trembles greatly. Therefore when the face becomes flushed in fear this is proof that the soul is ignoble; braver is the one who grows pale, for [in him] nature strengthens the heart by sending it reserves of heat and blood from other parts. Furthermore when the heat descends, fear grows, being abandoned by the heart, and the bowels may be loosened. And for a natural reason Homer said of a coward that his heart fell into his heels. It is to be noted that all constriction of the heart, that which takes place in grief and in terror as well as in disgust and in the restraint and inhibition of desire, is called anxiety. This often takes place without emotion, when some thick humor burdens the heart. These are the effects of fear on the body. The effect which it has on the soul is to disturb it and to confuse the thoughts. He was quite right who said: "How can anyone examine the heavens and the elements, when he is perpetually burdened with all the fear of poverty, servitude, and sickness?" And likewise he who said, "Fear throws all wisdom out of my soul." . . .

The consequences of fear are dejection, self-degradation, flattery, suspicion, and caution, which stimulates strong souls to seek remedies for their ills, but in weak souls causes consternation, terror, dispiritedness, as well as sluggishness, hopelessness, and prostration, as if that which impends and threatens were actually overwhelming the victim with force. Therefore the soul has no greater misery than fear, no baser servitude. This is why hatred against one who is feared is sharpened, as on a whetstone, just as against a tyrant. The soul desires to assert its freedom, and, recovering strength, the cold blood is reheated, and by a vigorous contraction it enkindles vengeance in the brain. This often makes brave men of those who have been afraid of despotic masters, and causes them to turn upon those who previously had oppressed them. . . .

Fear has been given to man, so that he can guard himself against injurious things, before they reach him.

20.4

Francis Bacon, Lord Verulam

(1561–1626)

Bacon died two years before the publication of Harvey's discovery of the circulation of the blood. Here we see every conceivable somatic expression of the emotions referred to the movement of animal spirits. Soon it will be possible to refer much of this to the movements of the blood.

[713] The *Passions* of the *Minde*, worke upon the *Body* the *Impressions* following. *Feare* causeth *Palenesse; Trembling;* The *Standing* of the *Haire upright; Starting;* and *Skritching.* The *Palenesse* is caused, for that the *Bloud* runneth inward, to succour the *Heart.* The *Trembling* is caused, for that through the *Flight* of the *Spirits* inward, the *Outward Parts* are destituted, and not sustained. *Standing Upright* of the *Haire* is caused, for that by the *Shutting* of the *Pores* of the *Skin,* the *Haire* that lyeth asloape, must needs Rise. *Starting* is both an *Apprehension* of the *Thing feared;* (And, in that kinde, it is a *Motion* of *Shrincking;*) And likewise an *Inquisition,* in the beginning, what the *Matter* should be, (And in that kinde it is a *Motion* of *Erection;*) And therefore, when a *Man* would listen suddenly to any Thing, he *Starteth;* For the *Starting* is an *Erection* of the *Spirits* to attend. *Skritching* is an *Appetite* of *Expelling* that which suddenly striketh the *Spirits:* For it must be noted, that many *Motions,* though they bee unprofitable to expell that which hurteth, yet they are *Offers* of *Nature,* and cause *Motions* by *Consent;* As in *Groaning,* or *Crying* upon *Paine.*

[714] *Griefe* and *Paine* cause *Sighing; Sobbing; Groaning; Screaming;* and *Roaring; Teares; Distorting* of the *Face; Grinding* of the *Teeth; Sweating. Sighing* is caused by the *Drawing* in of a greater *Quantity* of *Breath* to refresh the *Heart* that laboureth: like a great *Draught* when one is thirsty. *Sobbing* is the same Thing stronger. *Groaning,* and *Screaming,* and *Roaring,* are caused by an *Appetite* of *Expulsion,* as hath beene

Sylva sylvarum: or a naturall historie. In ten centuries. Published after the author's death by William Rawley. London, 1627. [Pp. 184–187.]

said: For when the *Spirits* cannot expell the Thing that hurteth, in their
Strife to do it, by *Motion* of *Consent,* they expell the *Voice.* And this is,
when the *Spirits* yeeld, and give over to resist; For if one doe constantly
resist *Paine,* he will not groane. *Teares* are caused by a *Contraction* of
the *Spirits* of the *Braine;* Which *Contraction* by consequence astringeth
the *Moisture* of the *Braine,* and thereby sendeth *Teares* into the *Eyes.*
And this *Contraction,* or *Compression* causeth also *Wringing* of the
Hands; For *Wringing* is a *Gesture* of *Expression* of *Moisture.* The *Distorting* of the *Face* is caused by a *Contention,* first to beare and resist,
and then to expell; Which maketh the Parts knit first, and afterwards
open. *Grinding* of the *Teeth* is caused (likewise) by a *Gathering* and
Serring of the *Spirits* together to resist; Which maketh the *Teeth* also
to set hard one against another. *Sweating* is also a *Compound Motion*
by the *Labour* of the *Spirits,* first to resist, and then to expell.

[715] *Ioy* causeth a *Chearefulnesse,* and *Vigour* in the *Eyes; Singing;
Leaping; Dancing;* And sometimes *Teares.* All these are the effects of
the *Dilatation* and *Comming* forth of the *Spirits* into the *Outward Parts;*
Which maketh them more *Lively,* and *Stirring.* We know it hath beene
seen, that *Excessive Sudden Ioy* hath caused *Present Death,* while the
Spirits did spread so much, as they could not retire againe. As for
Teares, they are the Effects of *Compression* of the *Moisture* of the *Braine,*
upon *Dilatation* of the *Spirits.* For *Compression* of the *Spirits* worketh
an *Expression* of the *Moisture* of the *Braine,* by *Consent,* as hath beene
said in *Griefe.* But then in *Ioy,* it worketh it diversly; *viz.* By *Propulsion*
of the *Moisture,* when the *Spirits* dilate, and occupy more Roome.

[716] *Anger* causeth *Palenesse* in some, and the *Going* and *Comming
of the Colour* in Others: also *Trembling* in some; *Swelling; Foaming* at
the *Mouth; Stamping; Bending* of the *Fist. Palenesse,* and *Going,* and
Comming of the *Colour,* are caused by the *Burning* of the *Spirits* about
the *Heart;* Which to refresh themselves, call in more *Spirits* from the
Outward Parts. And if the Palenesse be alone, without *Sending forth*
the *Colour* againe, it is commonly ioyned with some Feare; but in many
there is no *Palenesse* at all, but contrariwise *Rednesse* about the *Cheekes,*
and *Gills;* Which is by the *Sending forth* of the *Spirits* in an *Appetite* to
Revenge. Trembling in *Anger* is likewise by a *Calling* in of the *Spirits;*
And is commonly, when *Anger* is ioyned with *Fear. Swelling* is caused,
both by a *Dilatation* of the *Spirits* by *Over-Heating,* and by a *Liquefaction*
or *Boyling* of the *Humours* thereupon. *Foaming* at the *Mouth* is from
the same *Cause,* being an *Ebullition. Stamping,* and *Bending* of the
Fist, are caused by an *Imagination* of the *Act* of *Revenge. . . .*

[720] *Wonder* causeth *Astonishment,* or an *Immoveable Posture* of the
Body; Casting up of the *Eyes* to *Heaven;* And *Lifting* up of the *Hands.*
For *Astonishment,* it is caused by the *Fixing* of the *Minde* upon one
Object of *Cogitation,* whereby it doth not spatiate and transcurre, as it
useth: For in *Wonder* the *Spirits* fly not, as in *Feare;* But onely settle,

and are made lesse apt to move. As for the *Casting* up of the *Eyes*, and *Lifting* up of the *Hands*, it is a *Kinde* of *Appeale* to the *Deity;* Which is the *Authour*, by *Power*, and *Providence*, of *Strange Wonders*.

[721] *Laughing* causeth a *Dilatation* of the *Mouth*, and *Lips;* A *Continued Expulsion* of the *Breath*, with the loud *Noise*, which makes the *Interiection* of *Laughing; Shaking* of the *Breast*, and *Sides; Running* of the *Eyes* with *Water*, if it be Violent, and Continued. Wherein first it is to be understood, that *Laughing* is scarce (properly) a *Passion*, but hath his *Source* from the *Intellect;* For in *Laughing* there ever precedeth a *Conceit* of somewhat *Ridiculous*. And therefore it is Proper to *Man*. Secondly, that the *Cause* of *Laughing* is but a *Light Touch* of the *Spirits*, and not so deepe an *Impression* as in other *Passions*. And therefore, (that which hath no *Affinity* with the *Passions* of the *Minde*,) it is moved, and that in great vehemency, onely by *Tickling* some *Parts* of the *Body:* And we see that *Men* even in a *Grieved* State of *Minde*, yet cannot sometimes forbeare *Laughing*. Thirdly, it is ever ioyned with some *Degree* of *Delight:* And therefore *Exhilaration* hath some *Affinity* with *Ioy*, though it be a much *Lighter Motion*. . . . Fourthly, that the *Obiect* of it is *Deformity*, *Absurdity*, *Shrew'd Turnes*, and the like. Now to speake of the *Causes* of the *Effects* before mentioned, whereunto these *Generall Notes* give some *Light*. For the *Dilatation* of the *Mouth* and *Lips*, *Continued Expulsion* of the *Breath* and *Voice*, and *Shaking* of the *Breast* and *Sides*, they proceed (all) from the *Dilatation* of the *Spirits;* Especially being *Sudden*. So likewise, the *Running* of the *Eyes* with *Water*, (as hath beene formerly touched, where we spake of the *Teares* of *Ioy* and *Griefe*) is an *Effect* of *Dilatation* of the *Spirits*. And for *Suddennesse*, it is a great *Part* of the *Matter:* For we see, that any *Shrew'd Turne* that lighteth upon Another; Or any *Deformity*, &c. moveth *Laughter* in the Instant; Which after a little time it doth not. So we cannot *Laugh* at any Thing after it is *Stale*, but whilest it is *New:* And even in *Tickling*, if you *Tickle* the *Sides*, and give warning; Or give a *Hard* or *Continued Touch*, it doth not move *Laughter* so much.

[722] *Lust* causeth a *Flagrancy* in the *Eyes;* and *Priapisme*. The *Cause* of both these is, for that in *Lust* the *Sight*, and the *Touch*, are the Things desired: And therefore the *Spirits* resort to those parts which are most affected. And note well in generall, (For that great Use may be made of the *Observation*,) that (evermore) the *Spirits*, in all *Passions*, resort most to the *Parts*, that labour most, or are most affected. As in the last, which hath been mentioned, they resort to the *Eyes*, and *Venereous Parts:* In *Feare*, and *Anger*, to the *Heart:* In *Shame* to the *Face:* And in *Light Dislikes* to the *Head*.

20.5

Marin Cureau de La Chambre

(1594–1669)

For some facts about the author, see 19.6. La Chambre wrote many psychological books, the most important being Les charactères des passions, *in five volumes, 1640–1662. In stating his plan for this work, he said: "Because among the simple passions there are some which tend toward the good, others which attack the evil, and others which flee from it, I have thought that instead of arranging them as is ordinarily done with their opposites, it would be more suitable to examine them in that order." Thus he abandoned the traditional rationalistic categorization, and adopted a naturalistic one, and specifically stated for the first time a theory of a tripartite division of the emotions, so common in modern use. (Compare, for example, Karen Horney's classification of neurotic responses as "toward people, away from people, or against people.")*

In these selections, emphasis is placed for the first time on the social nature of emotion, and the "signs of the emotions" are recognized as social stimuli, anticipating an important feature of ethological theory.

[A]

Why do we rest our hands on our hips, when facing someone in anger or in threat? No doubt to make these parts more firm, in order that the muscles of respiration, which they support, may act more powerfully. By this means the voice is given greater strength and endurance. Therefore we do not merely place our hands on our hips, but also push the arms and elbows forward, so that by this spreading of the shoulders they become more firm, all to the same purpose. . . .

Let us say only that although anger often causes great disturbance in the soul and the body, it is not always the enemy of health and reason. It is absolutely necessary for timid and sluggish spirits, and for cold and coarse constitutions. In all others one can compare it to the winds which, impetuous as they are, chase away mists and vapors, clearing the air, and rendering it purer and healthier. Indeed, if one tries to check its course, and hold it back, without permitting it at least verbal expression,

[A] *Les charactères des passions, Vol. II. Des passions courageuses* [The signs of the emotions: Of the courageous emotions] Paris, 1645. [Pp. 444, 467.]
[B] Ibid., Vol. V. *Des larmes, de la crainte, du désespoir* [Of weeping, fear, and despair]. [Paris, 1662.] Amsterdam, 1663. [Pp. 25–27.]

it is stored up for a long time in the soul and finally changes the state of the humors, giving rise to severe and pernicious sicknesses. Deaf to the counsels of reason, it thinks of revenge as the goal to be attained, and it will not stop its movement until it is avenged in some fashion. So although the will may check the acts over which it has control, such as words, blows, and the like, those over which it has no control, such as the movement of the heart and the agitation of the humors, necessarily continue, and they become even more violent because of the restraint imposed on them, and they last still longer because the vengeance which ought to terminate them has been prevented.

[B]

To establish our [view] on a more solid basis, we admit indeed that the same object which causes pain also excites tears, and that tears never appear unless one feels an evil which changes the constitution of the soul or of the body. But to tell the truth this is only the distant object: the proximate one, and that which is the immediate cause of tears, is the pain itself, or rather the vexatious state of the soul in this passion. But even this does not suffice, because this condition occurs in all kinds of pain. It must be, then, that the soul intends to make its unhappy state known. For however great the pain may be, if the soul did not propose to make it known, it would shed no tears; as we see in extreme afflictions which astonish us and deprive us of the freedom to form any intent.

Now in order to make something known, one must not be alone, one must be in company. That is why tears soon dry up in solitude; the approach of friends renews them; and the recital of our misfortunes, although then they are much lighter, makes tears flow much more than the pain alone could do at its greatest violence. Why do you think compassion makes us cry, if not to show that we are touched by the misfortunes that we see others suffer? And why are women, children, and all weak persons so quick to tears, if not because they want to make known their weakness and the need they have for the help of others. Thus the soul seeks to disclose its unhappy state by its tears; if it did not have this intent, its pain might be very great, it might even be insupportable, but tears would not appear.

All this fits very well with what we said [Vol. I] about laughter, which is to joy what tears are to sorrow. For it does not suffice that the object which excites laughter be novel and amusing, nor that the soul feels the surprising joy which that gives. The soul must have the intent to show the state in which it is, that is to say, the amused surprise which it feels. That is why laughter does not occur when alone any more than tears, and we can say that both of these actions do not belong to man simply as an animal, but as a sociable animal, that they are instruments of the society for which he is destined, ingenious words which without a sound express the sentiments of his heart far more clearly than those which are spoken by the voice.

I know very well that they often escape us in solitude, and that there are those who laugh and cry when they are alone. But are there not also those who talk to themselves, although speech is altogether reserved for society? Laughter and tears are no doubt a mute speech which nature uses to make our condition known, and consequently, like other speech, they require communication and company. And if we do these things when alone, it is a disorder of the soul which causes this irregularity, either from the violence of the passion or from sickness of the mind; for there are fools who laugh, and melancholics who weep, at any time and for any cause.

20.6

René Descartes

(1596–1650)

Two intellectual women figure in Descartes' life: the exiled Princess Elizabeth, who asked him to write about the passions, and the powerful Queen Christina of Sweden, to whom the resulting book was dedicated. We have seen (in Vives, Bacon, La Chambre) how needless it is to credit Descartes with being the first to give a physiological account of emotion, as is sometimes done. But Descartes has an amazing ability to anticipate later discovery. We allude in this case to his purely cerebral "admiration," or wonder, which is in effect cortical arousal as we now know it, joined with the overt behavior of what Pavlov would call the "orientation reflex."

[70] Admiration is a sudden surprise of the Soul, which causeth in her an inclination to consider with attention the objects which seem rare, and extraordinary to her; it is caused first by an impression in the brain, that represents the object, as rare and consequently, worthy to be seriously considered: after that, by the motion of the spirits, which are disposed by this impression to tend with might and main, towards that place of the brain where it is, to fortifie, and conserve it there; as also they are thereby disposed to passe from thence into the muscles, which serve to hold the organs of the senses in the same scituation they are, that it may be fomented by them, if it bee by them that it was formed.

Les passions de l'âme. Amsterdam, 1649. Translated anonymously, as *The passions of the soule.* London, 1650. [Pp. 55–58, 77, 82–83.]

[71] And this Passion hath this peculiar quality; it is observed not to be attended by any alteration in the heart, and the blood, as the other Passions are; the reason whereof is, that having neither good nor evill for its object, but only the knowledge of the thing admired, it hath no relation to the heart, and blood, on which depend all the good of the body, but only with the brain, where dwell the organs of the senses subservient to this knowledge.

[72] This doth not hinder it from being exceeding powerfull, notwithstanding the surprise, that is, the sudden, and unexpected arrivall of the impression that alters the motion of the spirits: which surprize is proper, and peculiar to this Passion: so that if at any time it doe happen to any of the rest, as it usually does to all, and encreaseth them, it is because Admiration is joyned with them; and the power of it consists in two things, to wit, the novelty, and for that the motion which it causeth, from the very beginning hath its full strength; for it is certain, such a motive is more operative, then those which being weak at first, and growing but by little, and little, may easily be diverted; also, it is certain that those objects of the senses which are new, touch the brain in certain parts, where it used not to be touched, and that these parts being more tender, or less firme then those that frequent agitation hath hardned, augments the operation of the motion which they excite there; which will not be deemed incredible, if it bee considered, that is the like reason which causeth the soles of our feet, accustomed to a pretty stubborn touch by the weight of the body they bear, but very little to feel this touch when we goe: whereas another far lighter and softer (when they are tickled) is almost insupportable to us, onely because it is not usuall.

[73] And the surprize hath so much power, to cause the spirits in the cavities of the brain, to bend their course from thence to the place where the impression of the object admired is, that it sometimes drives them all thither, and finds them such work to conserve this impression, that there are none which passe from thence into the muscles, nor yet so much as deviate any way from the first tracts they followed into the brain: this causes all the body to be unmoveable like a statue, and that one can onely perceive the first represented face of the object, and consequently not acquire any further knowledge of it; it is thus when a man is said to be astonished: for astonishment is an excesse of admiration, which can never be but evill. . . .

[96] The five Passions {love, hatred, desire, joy and sadness, which with admiration comprise the six primary passions} which I have here begun to explain are so joyned, or opposed to one another, that it is easier to consider them all together, then to treat distinctly of each, as I handled Admiration: and their cause is not like that, in the brain onely, but also in the Heart, Spleen, Liver, and all other parts of the body, in as much as they serve to the production of the blood, and afterwards of the spirits. For although all the veins convey the blood they contain, into the

heart, yet it sometimes falls out, that the blood of some of them is driven with a stronger force than the rest, and it happens also that the overtures through which it enters into the heart, or those through which it goes out, are more dilated or contracted one time than another. . . .

[104] In Joy, not onely the nerves of the spleen, Liver, stomach or intestines act, but those in the rest of the body; and particularly that about the Orifices of the heart, which opening and dilating these Orifices, enable the blood which the rest of the nerves have driven from the veins to the heart, to get in there, and issue forth in greater quantity then ordinary: and because the blood which then gets into the heart hath often passed and repassed through it, coming from the arteries into the veines; it easily dilates, and produces spirits, whose parts being very equall, and subtle, are fit to form, and fortifie the impressions of the brain, which deal lively, and quiet thoughts to the Soul.

[105] Contrariwise, in Sadness the Orifices of the heart are hugely straitened by the small nerve that environs them, and the blood of the veins is no whit agitated: which causeth but very little to go to the heart, and in the mean while the passages through which the juyce of meats glides from the stomack, and entrails to the Liver, are open, wherefore the appetite diminisheth not, unlesse Hatred, which is an ordinary companion of Sadness, close them.

20.7

Nicholas Malebranche

(1638–1715)

The details of Descartes' broad sketch were filled in by Malebranche, combining careful introspection with due attention to the most recent physiological research.

[Bk V, Ch. III] Seven things may be distinguished in each of our Passions, save Admiration only, which is indeed but an Imperfect Passion.

The first is the Judgment the Mind makes of an Object, or rather the confused or distinct View of the Relation that Object has to us.

The Second is a New Determination of the Motion of the Will towards that Object, provided it *be* or *seem* to be a *Good*. . . .

But if that particular Object be considered as Evil, or able to deprive us of some Good, there happens no New Determination in the Motion

De la recherche de la vérité [Paris, 1674]. Translated by T. Taylor, as *Treatise concerning the search after truth*. 2 vols. Second edition. London, 1700. [Vol. 2, pp. 6–9.]

of the Will; but only the Motion towards the *Good,* oppos'd to that seemingly *evil* Object, is augmented.... For indeed we *hate* only because we *love,* and the Evil that is without us is judg'd no farther Evil, than with reference to the Good of which it deprives us....

The third thing to be observ'd in every Passion is the Sensation that attends them; the Sensation of Love, Hatred, Desire, Joy, Sorrow, which are all different in the different Passions.

The fourth thing is a new Determination of the course of the Animal Spirits and Blood to the outward and inward parts of the Body. Before the View of the Object of the Passion, the vital Spirits were dispers'd throughout the whole Body, for the preservation of all its parts in general; but at the appearance of that new Object, all this Order and Oeconomy is disturb'd, and most part of the Spirits are thrown into the Muscles of the Arms, Legs, Face, and other exteriour parts of the Body, to put them in a disposition suitable to the ruling Passion, and to give it such a gesture and motion, as are necessary for the obtaining or avoiding the imminent Good or Evil: But if its own Forces are insufficient for its occasions, these same Spirits are distributed in such a manner as make it machinally utter certain words and cries; and which diffuse over the Face and the rest of the Body, such an air and comportment, as is capable of actuating others with the same Passion it self is possess'd with. For Men and Beasts having a mutual cohesion by the Eyes and Ears, when any one of them is in a violent Commotion, it necessarily affects the Spectators and Hearers, and naturally makes upon their Imagination such an Impression as troubles them, and moves them to preserve it.

As to the rest of the Animal Spirits, they violently descend into the Heart, Lungs, Liver, Spleen, and other *Viscera,* thence to draw contributions, and to hasten those parts to send forth a sufficient and timely supply of Spirits, necessary to preserve the Body in that extraordinary Contention.

The fifth thing is a sensible Commotion of the Soul, who feels her self agitated by an unexpected overflow of Spirits....

The sixth thing are several Sensations of Love, Hatred, Joy, Desire, Sorrow, that are produced, not by the Intellectual view of Good or Evil, as those that have been already mention'd, but by the various concussions that are caus'd in the Brain by the Animal Spirits.

The seventh thing is a certain Sensation of Joy, or rather internal Satisfaction, which detains the Soul in her Passion, and assures her that she is in the fittest State she can be, in reference to the Object she considers. This internal satisfaction attends all the Passions whatsoever, whether they proceed from the sight of an Evil, or from the sight of a Good, Sorrow as well as Joy. This satisfaction makes all the Passions pleasant, and induces us to yield our consent, and give up ourselves to them; and 'tis that satisfaction which must be overcome by the Delights of Grace, and the Comforts of Faith and Reason....

But if those Humours always flowed in the same manner into the Heart; if they received an equal Fermentation in different times, and the Spirits, that are made of them, regularly ascended into the Brain, we should not see such hasty Changes in the Motions of the Passions. For instance, the sight of a Magistrate would not stop, of a sudden, the extravagant Transports of an enraged Person, persuing his Revenge; and his Face, all fiery with Blood and Spirits, would not in an instant turn pale and wan for fear of Punishment.

So, to hinder those Humours that are mixed with the Blood from entering the Heart constantly in the same manner, there are Nerves that surround all the Avenues thereof, which being compressed or dilated . . . shut up or open the way to those Humours. And lest the said Humours should undergo the same Agitation and Fermentation in the Heart in divers times; there are other Nerves that cause the Beatings of it, which being not equally agitated in the different Motions of the Spirits, drive not the Blood with the same force into the Arteries. . . .

Last of all, to regulate with the greatest Accuracy and Readiness the Course of the Spirits, there are Nerves surrounding the Arteries, as well those that end in the Brain, as those that carry the Blood into the other parts of the Body; so that the Concussion of the Brain, which accompanies the unexpected Sight of some Circumstance, for which 'tis convenient that the Motions of the Passion should be alter'd, suddenly determine the Course of the Spirits to the Nerves thus surrounding the Arteries; that by their Contraction they may shut up the Passage to the Blood that ascends into the Brain, and by their Dilatation lay it open to that which runs into all the other Parts of the Body.

When those Arteries that carry the Blood to the Brain are free and open; and on the contrary, those that disperse it through the rest of the Body are strongly bound up by these Nerves, the Head must all be full of Blood, and the Face appear all fiery; but some circumstance altering the Commotion of the Brain, that caused that Disposition in the Nerves, the Arteries that were strait bound are loosened, and on the contrary, the Arteries of the Brain strongly contracted. Then is the Head emptied of Bloud, the Face covered with Paleness, and the small quantity of Blood, which issues from the Heart, and which the Nerves before mentioned admit into it, as the Fewel to keep in Life, descends most or all into the lower parts of the Body; the Brain wants Animal Spirits, and all the rest of the body is seized with Weakness and Trembling.

20.8

Edmund Burke

(1729–1797)

*In the latter half of the eighteenth century, the doctrine of association had
taken such firm hold that Burke is apologetic in arguing for the importance
of native dispositions. But the young man who, in time, would show his
courage in affairs of state, displays it here by challenging the authority of
Locke. This book influenced Moses Mendelssohn in his speculations that
there must be "feelings" which are independent of volition as well as Kant
who wrote a short book with a very similar title.*

[Part IV, Sect. II. Association.] It is no small bar in the way of our en-
quiries into the causes of the passions, that the occasion of many of
them are given, and that their governing motions are impressed at a
time when we have not capacity to reflect on them; at a time of which all
sorts of memory is worn out of our minds. For besides such things as
affect us in various manners according to their natural powers, there are
associations made at that early season, which we find it very hard afterwards to distinguish from natural effects. Not to mention the unaccountable antipathies which we find in many persons, we all find it impossible
to remember when a steep became more terrible than a plain; or fire or
water more dreadful than a clod of earth; though all these are very
probably either conclusions from experience, or arising from the premo-
nitions of others; and some of them impressed, in all likelihood, pretty
late. But as it must be allowed that many things affect us after a certain
manner, not by any natural powers they have for that purpose, but by
association; so it would be absurd on the other hand, to say that nothing
affects us otherwise; since some things must have been originally and
naturally agreeable or disagreeable, from which the others derive their
associated powers; and it would be, I fancy, to little purpose to look for
the causes of our passions in association, until we fail of them in the
natural properties of things. . . .

[Sect. XIV. Locke's opinion concerning darkness, considered.] It is Mr.
Locke's opinion, that darkness is not naturally an idea of terror; and that,
though an excessive light is painful to the sense, that the greatest excess
of darkness is no ways troublesome. He observes indeed in another place,
that a nurse or an old woman having once associated the idea of ghosts
and goblins with that of darkness; night ever after becomes painful and
horrible to the imagination. The authority of this great man is doubtless

A philosophical enquiry into the origin of our ideas of the sublime and beautiful.
London, 1757. [Pp. 120–121, 140–142.]

as great, as that of any man can be, and it seems to stand in the way of our general principle. We have considered darkness as a cause of the sublime; and we have all along considered the sublime as depending on some modification of pain or terror; so that, if darkness be no way painful or terrible to any, who have not had their minds early tainted with superstitions, it can be no source of the sublime to them. But with all deference to such an authority; it seems to me, that an association of a more general nature; an association which takes in all mankind may make darkness terrible; for in utter darkness, it is impossible to know in what degree of safety we stand; we are ignorant of the objects that surround us; we may every moment strike against some dangerous obstruction; we may fall down a precipice the first step we take; and if any enemy approach, we know not in what quarter to defend ourselves; in such a case strength is no sure protection; wisdom can only act by guess; the boldest are staggered, and he who would pray for nothing else towards his defence, is forced to pray for light. . . .

As to the association of ghosts and goblins; surely it is more natural to think, that darkness being originally an idea of terror, was chosen as a scene for such terrible representations, than that such representations have made darkness terrible. The mind of man very easily slides into an error of the former sort; but it is very hard to imagine, that the effect of an idea so universally terrible in all times, and in all countries, as darkness has been, could possibly have been owing to a set of idle stories, or to any cause of a nature so trivial, and of an operation so precarious.

20.9

Joseph Priestley

(1773–1804)

Chemist and nonconformist minister, Priestley was an enthusiastic supporter of Hartley's association theories. However, as a sober scientist he recognized that the system was only weakened by the hypothesis of vibratiuncles, and he edited an abridgement excluding this irrelevancy. Priestley concerned himself alike with electricity, chemistry (he first isolated oxygen), and theology. His critique of Reid's Inquiry is wholly directed against the doctrine of instinct. Priestley emigrated to America to find what he hoped would be a more congenial environment, and certainly the views he expresses here are shared by most American psychologists.

An examination of Dr. Reid's Inquiry into the human mind on the principles of common sense. London, 1774. [Pp. 89–92.]

Unfortunately for the American mystique, they do not survive the test of experiment.

Of the Natural Signs of the Passions

One would think that a man must never have heard of the general principle of the *association of ideas,* who could possibly take it into his head that certain features, modulations of the voice, and attitudes of the body, require any other principle, in order to suggest the idea and belief of certain thoughts, purposes, and dispositions of mind. Dr. Reid indeed asserts, in proof of this, that 'an infant may be put into a fright by an angry countenance, and soothed again by smiles and blandishments,' p. 89. Now I have had children of my own, and have made many observations and experiments of this kind upon them, and upon this authority I do not hesitate absolutely to deny the fact with respect to them; and I have no doubt but that the same is the case with respect to all other infants; unless those of Dr. Reid should be as different from mine as are our notions of human nature. But nature, I believe, is pretty uniform in her operations and productions, how differently soever we may conceive of them.

Dr. Reid talks of an *infant,* being put into a fright. On the contrary, I assert that an infant (unless by an infant he should mean a child who has had a good deal of experience, and of course has made many observations on the connections of things) is absolutely incapable of terror. I am positive that no child ever showed the least symptom of fear or apprehension, till he had actually received hurts, and had felt pain; and that children have no fear of any particular persons or things, but in consequence of some connection between that person or thing and the pain they have felt. . . .

I, moreover, do not hesitate to say, that if it were possible always to beat and terrify a child with a placid countenance, so as never to assume that appearance but in those circumstances, and always to soothe him with what we call an angry countenance, this natural and necessary connection of ideas that Dr. Reid talks of would be reversed, and we should see the child frighted with a smile, and delighted with a frown.

In fact, there is no more reason to believe that a child is naturally afraid of a frown, than he is afraid of being in the dark; and of this children certainly discover no sign, till they have either found something disagreeable to them in the dark, or have been told that there is something dreadful in it.

20.10

Xavier Bichat

(1771–1802)

Bichat drew a sharp distinction between what he called "two lives," the organic and the animal, and he had great influence on early nineteenth-century thought regarding the nature of involuntary behavior. In this selection, however, he recognizes that the division is not so absolute that emotions, a part of the organic life as he conceives it, do not powerfully influence striped muscle responses. He looks to an influence of blood upon the brain to explain an interaction for which he can find no anatomical basis, but of course he does not suspect that special endocrine secretions may be responsible.

The Passions Regulate the Actions of Animal Life though They Have Their Seat in Organic Life

Though the passions are the particular attribute of organic life, they have however, an influence on the motions of animal life which it is necessary to inquire into. The voluntary muscles are frequently put in play by them; sometimes they have a stimulating action, and sometimes they appear to act in a sedative manner.

Observe the man agitated by anger and fury; you will find his muscular powers are doubled, are exercised with an energy which he himself cannot moderate; where shall we look for the source of this increase? It is manifestly in the heart.

This organ is the natural *exciter* of the brain by means of the blood which it sends to it, as I shall prove in the course of this work, so that according as the excitement is more or less powerful, the cerebral energy will be greater or less, and we have seen that the effect of anger is to give an extreme vivacity to the circulation, and consequently to send towards the brain a large quantity of blood in a given time. A similar effect results in the paroxysms of ardent fevers, in the use of wine to a certain degree, &c.

The brain when strongly excited, communicates force to the muscles which are subject to its influence; their motions become, to use the expression, involuntary: thus is the will a stranger to those muscular spasms produced by a cause which irritates the medullary organs, as the splinter

Recherches physiologiques sur la vie et la mort [Paris, 1800]. Translated from the second (1802) edition by Tobias Watkins, as *Physiological researches upon life and death.* Philadelphia, 1809. [Pp. 52–56.]

of a bone, blood, pus in wounds of the head, or the handle of any instrument in our use.

The analogy is exact; the blood arriving at the brain in larger quantities than usual, produces upon it the effect of those different exciters just mentioned. It is, however, passive in these different motions. It is, to be sure, from it that the necessary irradiations proceed as usual, but these irradiations are produced there in spite of it, and we have not the power to suspend them.

Observe further, that in anger, a constant connexion exists between the contractions of the heart and those of the locomotive organs: where the former are augmented, the latter increase also; if an equilibrium is established on the one side, we soon observe it on the other. In no other case, on the contrary, does any appearance of this connexion manifest itself; the action of the heart remains the same notwithstanding numerous variations in the locomotive muscular system. In convulsions or paralysis, of which this system is the seat, the circulation is never either retarded or accelerated.

In anger we see the kind of influence which organic life exercises over animal life. In fear where, on the one hand, the enfeebled powers of the heart push on to the brain less blood, and consequently direct thither a slighter cause of excitement; and where on the other hand a feebleness of action is remarked in the external muscles, we observe plainly the connexion between the cause and effect. This passion offers in the first degree, the phenomenon which is presented in the last, by those powerful emotions, which suspending all at once the effort of the heart, produce a sudden cessation of animal life, and consequently syncope.

But how shall we apply the thousand varied modifications which the other passions at every instant, give to the motions which belong to this life? How explain the cause of those infinite shades which succeed each other so often with an inconceivable rapidity in the changeable picture of the face? or why independent of the will, the forehead frowns or expresses cheerfulness, the eyes look fierce or languishing, bright or obscure, &c.

All the muscles which are the agents of these motions receive their nerves from the brain, and are ordinarily voluntary. Why do they cease to be so in the passions? Why do they enter into that class of motions of organic life, which are exercised without our direction, or without even our consciousness? The following is, I think, the most probable explanation of this phenomenon.

Numerous sympathetic relations unite all the internal viscera with the brain or its different parts. Every day's practice affords us examples of affections of this organ, arising sympathetically from those of the stomach, liver, intestines, spleen, &c. This being premised, as the effect of every kind of passion is to produce an affection, a change of force in some one of these viscera, it will also excite sympathetically either the brain wholly, or only some of its parts whose reaction on the muscles which receive it from the nerves, will produce in them those motions which are observed. In the production of these motions, the cerebral organ is, if we may say so, passive, while it is active when the will presides over its efforts.

What happens in the passions is similar to what we observe in diseases of the internal organs, which produce sympathetically spasms, weakness or even paralysis of the locomotive muscles.

Perhaps the internal organs do not act upon the voluntary muscles by the intermediate excitement of the brain, but by direct nervous communications; how they act is of no consequence. The question here is not as to their mode of action, but as to the existence of these sympathetic communications.

What is most essential, is the fact itself; what is evidently in support of it is: on the one part, the affection of an internal organ by the passions; on the other part, the determinate motion to this affection in muscles over which this organ has no influence, in the ordinary series of the phenomena of the two lives. This is certainly sympathy; for between it and what is presented to us by convulsions and spasms of the face, occasioned by an injury in the *phrenic* centre, by a wound in the stomach, &c. the only difference is in the cause which affects the internal organ. . . .

This then, generally is the way in which the passions snatch from the empire of the will, motions which are naturally voluntary, and in which they appropriate to themselves, if I may thus express myself, the phenomena of animal life, though they hold their seat essentially in organic life.

When they are violent, the powerful affection of the internal organs produces such impetuosity in the sympathetic motions of the muscles that the ordinary action of the brain is absolutely null. But the first impression being past, the usual mode of locomotion returns. . . .

There is in almost all the passions, a mixture or a succession of the motions of animal to those of organic life; so that, in almost all, the muscular action is directed partly by the brain in the natural order, and partly has its seat in the organic viscera, the heart, liver, stomach, &c. These two foci (foyers) alternately predominating over each other, or remaining in equilibrium, constitute by their mode of influence, all the numerous varieties which our moral affections present to us.

20.11

Alexander Bain

(1818–1903)

The "botanizing" tendency for which Bain was often criticized is nowhere stronger than in his description of the emotions. In other words, he is thorough and systematic, and overlooks no scintilla of available knowledge pertaining to their physiological or subjective character.

In this selection, the pages from his first chapter give what is very nearly an anticipation of the James-Lange theory, but one should hold in mind that the Jamesian view is not consistent with modern research, while Bain's more moderate approach, in which the somatic expression of the emotion is an essential component but far from the whole, is. There follow pages from his chapter on "terror," and these also include anticipations of modern views. As "loss of support" and "loud noise" anticipates Watson, so "breach of expectation" anticipates Hebb.

[Ch. I.]   *Of Emotion in General*

2. The fundamental proposition, respecting Emotion generally, may be expressed in these words: The state of Feeling, or the subjective consciousness which is known to each person by his own experience, is associated with a *diffusive action* over the system, through the medium of the cerebral hemispheres. In other words, the physical fact that accompanies and supports the mental fact, without making or constituting that fact, is an agitation of all those bodily members more immediately allied with the brain by nervous communication.

The organs first affected, by a wave of nervous influence emanating from the brain, are the moving members. Some of these are more readily agitated than others—for example, the features of the face; which therefore constitute the principal medium of the expression of feeling. But observation shows that all parts of the moving system are liable to be affected by an emotional wave: while a very important series of effects is produced upon the secreting and excreting apparatus of the body. . . .

6. . . . It is the common impression even with those who give full credit to the concurrence of the brain in every mental experience, that the brain is alone concerned, or that the agitation, whatever it may be, is confined to the encephalic mass. To this view I oppose the doctrine of the participation of the muscles and secreting organs in the circle of effects. I be-

The emotions and the will. London, 1859. [Pp. 5, 9–10, 13–14, 27, 73–77, 81–82.]

lieve that there must be not merely a free opening inwards to the hemispheres, but also a free vent outwards by the outgoing nerves that supply the muscles and other parts that are found to be in sympathy with the mind.

The emotion of Fear, for example, would not have its characteristic mental development if the currents from the brain to the moving organs and viscera were arrested. What we take merely as signs of the emotion are a part of its own essential workings, in whose absence it would be something entirely different. . . .

10. . . . The various emotions of the human mind exhibit differences in regard to the organs and parts more especially affected by them. Although the course of diffusion through the cerebral hemispheres would appear to lie open in every direction, yet some emotional stimuli choose directions peculiar to themselves, or occupy by preference some one set of organs. One remarkable example of this distinctness of outlet is furnished by the contrasted expressions of pleasure and pain in the features of the face. In pleasure, the muscles affected are those that elevate the eyebrows and distend the mouth; in pain, the opposing muscles are made to contract. No account can be given of the cerebral process that determines this preference. The stimulants of pleasure and pain flow into the brain through the same channel of sense, the course of diffusion through the multiplied connexions of the cerebral mass is equally open to both, yet there is something that determines the flow in either case towards certain specific quarters, and not to all parts indiscriminately.

With respect to the glandular or secreting organs affected by an emotional wave, there are notable preferences observed. Thus the lachrymal secretion is in close connexion with the cerebral hemispheres, and lies open to the spreading influence excited under strong feeling; but while some kinds of emotion affect at once the flow of this secretion, others, equally strong, never seem to reach it. In like manner, all the other secretions affected by states of mind are more immediately acted on, each by a separate class of emotions. The distinctness in the physical outgoings of different feelings corresponds with that variety of tone and character that they possess in the consciousness of the individual, and is a basis for the classification of the mental emotions. . . .

17. The tendency to diffusive agitation throughout the ramifications of the nervous system having been laid down as a constant fact in regard to consciousness, or feeling, generally, one prominent point in the definition of any feeling must needs be the mode of diffusion accompanying, or embodying, that particular state. . . . To whatever extent we may be able to ascertain or divine the manner of diffusion, and the localities more especially affected in each case, these facts are proper to be specified in the description of the feeling. They are the natural language of emotion, being read and understood by all observers as furnishing the clue to the

character of the accompanying consciousness; and any delineation that omits them must be defective. . . .

[Ch. X.]   *Emotion of Terror*

1. This passion may be described as a tremulous excitement originating in pain, apprehension, uncertainty, or strangeness; causing a feeling of intense misery, while wasting the energies, and subduing the spirit, and finally impressing the intellect to an undue degree with the things that arouse it. . . .

The apprehension of evil is a more specific agent of terror than present suffering. . . .

The element of Uncertainty is next to be noticed as indicating a principal source of various forms of the passion. Nothing more readily dissolves the composure of the frame than the sense of the unstable, or insecure. The strongest illustration of this is afforded by the giving way of the bodily support. . . .

Any breach of expectation is eminently discomposing. The whole frame being thrown into a certain attitude for meeting a given effect, there is a violent unhingement caused by the occurrence of something totally different. . . .

2. Next as to the diffusion and physical embodiments of the passion. . . .

The known aspect of terror is made up of a relaxation of parts commonly tense, and the tension of other parts beyond the ordinary degree, showing a transference of power, or a loss on one side, and gain on the other. The tension is seen in the stare of the eyes, elevation of the eyebrows, and inflation of the nostril—in the hair standing on end under the increased action of the muscle of the scalp, and in the contraction or creeping of the skin. A convulsive clench of the hand, and the violent seizure of some near object of protection, indicate the same tumultuous pouring out of force into new directions. The vocalizing muscles are strongly affected. The relaxation is seen in the dropping of the jaw, in the enfeebled expiration, in the loosening of the sphincters, and in the action upon the alimentary canal. . . .

The derangement of the secretions is a consequence of the same withdrawal of nervous power, whichever way acting. The odours suddenly developed by fright in animals and human beings are owing to this derangement. The inky fluid emitted by the cuttle-fish when pursued, is known to be an incontinent discharge of the animal's fluid excretion. The loss of appetite is a symptom of enfeebled digestion from the withdrawal of power. The flow of saliva is checked. The general convulsive tremor, the opposite of nervous and muscular tone, is a proof of the same deprivation. So the cold sweat and the pallor of the skin enter into the same train of consequences. . . .

7. . . . The infant brain is an easy prey to fear. Actual pain which leads to the outburst of grief has also the tendency to induce the peculiar disturbance characteristic of this passion. But in their case, as most usually, it is not actual bodily suffering, so much as outward appearances of a strange and menacing character, that cause the effect. The remote and intangible are pre-eminently the unnerving influences. Children are frightened by any unusual intensity of sensation, as by a violent squeeze, a sharp taste or odour, a loud sound, a strong glare of light, or a sudden and quick movement. By growth and familiarity, the nervous system becomes hardened to such agencies, and not only resists their discomposing effect, but also comes to relish their pungency. To these succeed as causes of fear, the apprehension of known evil, as the threat of punishment, the dread of a fall, a scald, or anything that has already given severe pain. Darkness is not necessarily a source of terror to children, but very easily becomes so by the slightest suggestion of possible danger. Should any cause of fear ever enter the mind, the being left alone in the dark makes it flame up to an incontrollable pitch. Darkness is like an atmosphere of oxygen to a spark of apprehension.

20.12

Alfred Lehmann

(1858–1921)

Mosso in Italy and Féré in France pioneered the use of measures of physiological response during intellectual work. In 1885 the Dane, Carl Lange, argued that physiological events, not psychic feelings, are primary in emotion, and in the United States William James independently stated this theory, using the memorable phrase "We are afraid because we run." But the pioneer in developing the "method of expression" for experimental study of the somatic aspects of emotion was another Dane, Alfred Lehmann, a student of Wundt. He used a pneumograph (a pneumatic tube around the chest) to record breathing and a plethysmograph (another such tube around the arm) to measure changes in blood circulation. Each instrument activated a Marey tambour which recorded on the smoked paper of a rotating cylinder—the kymograph which Helmholtz, Ludwig,

Die Hauptgesetze des menschlichen Gefühlslebens [The principal laws of human emotional life]. Translated into German by W. Bendixen from the Danish original. Leipzig, 1892. [Pp. 109–113.]

and others had used in studying muscular reactions. Thus, the descriptions based on visual observation gave way to recorded response, and the road was opened toward GSR, EEG, and other sophisticated devices of the present.

We give the account of one experiment, and the conclusions based on a series of experiments.

137. I succeeded in evoking an intense outbreak of anger in M, who was a somewhat reactive subject, while he sat in the apparatus. After completing a series of experiments, some of which were fairly unpleasant, I told him finally that for recreation he would be allowed a fine cigarette, the effect of which we wished to observe. Previously I had arranged with an assistant that on a signal from me he would strike the cigarette out of M's mouth. I hoped in this way to produce a really bitter mood, and I was prepared to urge M, with strong argument, to sit quietly, in the event that in his bitterness he threatened to spoil the experiment by movements that were too energetic. This succeeded far beyond my expectations. . . . As soon as the form of the volume curve started to show that M was feeling good under the influence of the tobacco, I gave the signal, and a strong and well-aimed flick of the hand dashed the cigarette to the floor, sparks spraying as it fell. M, as he himself said, was furious, for it only occurred to him long after the experiment that the whole thing was a staged affair; in other respects, he remained as still as possible. Involuntary movements of course could not be avoided, and probably for that reason there is the sudden strong increase in volume, which was followed by a significant but temporary decrease right at the start of the experiment. After a few slight irregularities, which probably also derive from muscular movements, the curve shows a slow increase in volume above the normal level and a very slight pulse.

138. The breathing curve also is very interesting. An increased but irregular (uncoordinated) innervation of the voluntary muscles can be clearly recognized in the jagged, quite abnormal respiratory movements, which are relatively deep. Since the cylinder was now almost all used up, I had to stop the kymograph for two minutes, in order to be able to record the end of the emotion. During these two minutes the volume curve rose significantly, and the pulse strokes meanwhile almost completely returned to their normal height. The volume remained maximal for some time and then fell off relatively quickly as the pulse strokes rose above their normal height.

139. . . . The interpretation of changes in the volume curve is not easy. . . . It does appear clearly that the [initial] constriction of the vessels is resolved by a marked relaxation and increase in volume. It seems beyond question that there is a constriction followed by congestion as a reaction thereto.

140. Naturally the few experiments which we have described above do

543

not begin to exhaust the wide range of emotional responses, with their many transitional forms. . . . In the nature of the case it is extremely difficult to evoke most of these states in a mere experiment, and for most of them the experimenter must rely on a happy accident playing into his hands. . . . Despite the great amount of research which still remains to be done, there are three points which in my estimation have been well illuminated by these investigations. . . .

142. *All kinds of pleasurably toned states are accompanied by dilatation of the vessels at the surface of the body, elevated innervation of the voluntary muscles (especially the respiratory muscles) and probably an increase in the extent of the heart movements. Unpleasantly toned states are accompanied by constriction of the vessels at the surface of the body, disturbances of various kinds in the innervation of the voluntary and organic muscles, and probably usually by relaxation of the interior vessels, in association with a reduction in the extent of heart movements.*

143. *. . . There is a relationship of dependency between the feeling tone of the conscious state at a given moment and the state of innervation of the various muscles of the organism at that time. . . .*

145. *There is at present no particular basis for the assumption that vasomotor changes are the cause of the other changes in innervation which accompany the different emotions. With respect to most emotions, the relationship between these must still be regarded as an open question.*

20.13

Walter B. Cannon

(1871–1945)

Between 1909 and 1914, Cannon and his students published an important series of research papers dealing with the mobilization of the body's resources in emergency, which were soon afterward summarized in the book, Bodily changes in pain, hunger, fear and rage (1915). In this paper, Cannon addresses himself to psychologists, drawing their attention to the implication that the subjective qualities of different emotional states must depend on central, not peripheral factors.

From the evidence just given it appears that any high degree of excitement in the central nervous system, whether felt as anger, terror, pain, anxiety, joy, grief or deep disgust, is likely to break over the threshold

The interrelations of emotions as suggested by recent physiological researches. *American Journal of Psychology* 25 (1914): 256–282. [Pp. 279–282.]

of the sympathetic division and disturb the quiet of all the organs which that division innervates. . . .

If various strong emotions can thus be expressed in the diffused activities of a single division of the autonomic—the division which accelerates the heart, inhibits the movements of the stomach and intestines, contracts the blood vessels, erects the hairs, liberates sugar, and discharges adrenalin—it would appear that the bodily conditions which have been assumed, by some psychologists, to distinguish emotions from one another must be sought for elsewhere than in the viscera. We do not "feel sorry because we cry," as James contended, but we cry because, when we are sorry or overjoyed or violently angry or full of tender affection—when any one of these diverse emotional states is present—there are nervous discharges by sympathetic channels to various viscera, including the lachrymal glands. And in terror and rage and intense elation, for example, the responses in the viscera seem too uniform to offer a satisfactory means of distinguishing states which, in man at least, are subjectively very different. For this reason I am inclined to urge that the visceral changes merely contribute to an emotional complex more or less indefinite, but still pertinent feelings of disturbance, in organs of which we are not usually conscious. . . .

If these differences are due to central changes, why is it not always possible by voluntary innervations to produce emotions? We can laugh and cry and tremble. But forced laughter does not bring happiness nor forced sobbing sorrow, and the trembling from cold rouses neither anger nor fear. The muscle positions and tensions are there, but the experiencing of such bodily changes does not seem even approximately to rouse an emotion in us. The *voluntary* assumption of an attitude seems to leave out the "feeling." It is probable, however, that no attitude which we can assume has all the elements in it which appear in the complete response to a stirring situation. But is not this because the natural response is a pattern reaction, like inborn reflexes of a low order, such as sneezing, in which impulses flash through peculiarly cooperating neurone groups of the central system, suddenly, unexpectedly, and in a manner not exactly reproducible by volition, and thus they throw the skeletal muscles into peculiar attitudes and, if sufficiently intense, rush out in diffuse discharges that cause tremors and vascular perturbations? The typical facial and bodily expressions, automatically assumed in different emotions and so well known as to constitute the common language between man and beast, indicate the discharge of peculiar groupings of neurones in the several affective states. That these responses occur instantly and spontaneously when the appropriate "situation," actual or vividly imagined, is present, shows that they are ingrained in the nervous organization. At least one such pattern, that of anger, persists after removal of the hemispheres,—the decorticated dog, by growling and biting when handled, has the appearance of being enraged; the decerebrate cat when vigorously stimulated retracts its lips and tongue, stares with dilated pupils, snarls, and snaps its jaws. On the other hand, stroking the hair, whistling, gently calling, or yelling to produce fright have not the slightest effect in evoking from the decorticated dog, signs of joy, affection or fear, nor does the animal manifest any sexual feeling. The absence of bodily indications of these emotions is quite as significant as the presence of the signs of anger. For, since expressions of anger can persist without the cortex, there is little reason why the complexes of other emotional expressions, if their "machinery" exists below the cortex, should not also be elicitable. That they are not elicitable suggests that they require a more elaborately organized grouping of neurones than does anger—possibly what the cortex, or the cortex in combination with basal ganglia, would provide.

The contrast between the brevity of the "pseudoaffective reactions" in the decerebrate cat, though the viscera are still connected with the central nervous system, and the normal duration of emotional expression in the dog with body separated from the head region, has been used by Sherrington to weigh the importance of the visceral and cerebral factors. And for reasons given above, as well as for the reasons he has offered, I agree with Sherrington's conclusion "that the reverberation from the trunk, limbs and viscera counts for relatively little, even in the primitive emotions of the dog, as compared with the cerebral reverberation to which is adjunct the psychical component of emotional reaction."

20.14

Philip Bard

(born 1898)

Bard's research on the cortical inhibition of a hypothalamic rage pattern, which points also to the higher cortical disinhibition of rage in intact animals, is one of the important evidences favoring the Cannon-Bard central theory of emotion as against the James-Lange peripheral theory. This discussion is based largely on experiments performed with V. B. Mountcastle, reported in 1947.

It has been established that after removal of all cerebral cortex a cat or dog is capable of displaying a type of behavior which in intensity and pattern closely resembles the activity which constitutes the expression of anger shown by normal members of the same species. The rage reactions

Central nervous mechanisms for the expression of anger in animals. *In* Martin L. Reymert, ed., *Feelings and emotions. The Mooseheart symposium.* New York: McGraw-Hill, 1950. Pp. 211–237. [Pp. 211–212, 223–224, 235–236.]

of decorticate animals differ from those of their normal fellows chiefly in being poorly directed in respect to the provoking stimulus. Further, all available evidence suggests that removal of cortex leads to the development of a hyperexcitability in the sense that stimuli which preoperatively had proved quite indifferent or even productive of signs of pleasure suffice to provoke a marked display of anger. Such, in brief, are the experimental facts which have led to the development of two closely related ideas: (a) that subcortical structures are responsible for the basic pattern of rage reactions, and (b) that the cerebral cortex normally exerts an inhibitory influence on these subcortical mechanisms. . . .

Evidence that the hypothalamus is concerned in the production of angry behavior was first obtained in a study devoted to the delimitation of the subcortical region responsible for the so-called "sham-rage" of decorticate cats. It was found in acute experiments that removal of all cerebral tissue rostral, dorsal, and lateral to the hypothalamus, *i.e.*, neocortex, rhinencephalic portions of the forebrain, striatum, pallidum, and dorsal diencephalon, is followed by "sham rage," whereas this vigorous patterned activity fails to develop after truncation of the brain stem at any level below the caudal hypothalamus. Acute ablation experiments thus indicate that the hypothalamus contains neural machinery that is prepotent among the brain-stem mechanisms which confer on the decorticate animal the capacity to exhibit at low threshold a full expression of anger. . . .

In our experience the only restricted bilateral forebrain removals that produce a state of ferocity in cats are ones that include the amygdala. This structure is a complex gray mass composed of several distinct cell groups. It lies just dorsal to the anterior portion of the pyriform lobe and lateral to the first portion of the optic tract. . . . Its chief efferent projections appear to be distributed to the hypothalamus and preoptic area. . . .

The results obtained in this investigation indicate that in cats there originates from or passes through the region of the amygdala an influence which powerfully inhibits the brain-stem mechanisms concerned in the execution of angry behavior. There is also evidence that a similar but weaker influence emanates from the limbic cortex; it may be channeled through or near the amygdaloid complex. . . .

The production of placidity by removal of neocortex alone and the conversion of this specific refractory state to one of savageness by removal of certain forebrain structures show that the telencephalic mechanisms which influence angry behavior are organized as a series of checks and balances. The inhibitory influences become dominant when neocortex is removed. Therefore normally the neocortex must exert an effect that is predominantly opposite in sign, *i.e.*, one that tends to lower the threshold of rage reactions. Further, it is obvious that in the management of expression of anger the neocortex does more than this. In the cats that became ferocious as a result of bilateral ablations of the amygdala and pyriform cortex, rage reactions could be evoked by stimuli, *e.g.*, visual, that are ineffective in wholly decorticate animals. The effectiveness of such stimulation depends on neocortex. Another obvious operation of neocortical influence in these same animals was the accuracy and the calculated timing of their attacks upon the source of the stimulation. In the absence of neocortex such attacks are stereotyped and undirected or very poorly directed.

Finally, mention must be made of what appears to be an extraordinary discrepancy between certain of the results obtained in cats and observations that have been made on monkeys [by Klüver and Bucy, 1939]. . . . We are inclined to think that this fascinating problem will be solved in specific anatomical terms.

Chapter 21

MOTIVATION AND CONFLICT

The beginnings of motivational theory are found, in part, in the rival Stoic and Epicurean theories of emotion. The early Christians were influenced mostly by the Stoic tradition, but they added an infusion of unphilosophic passion, which is not surprising since they did not accept the underlying Stoic thesis of the supremacy of reason. Paul and Augustine give eloquent expression to the ambivalence of human motives. Pleasure and pain, which were asserted to be the guides of behavior in the ancient Epicureanism, were again acknowledged as supreme by the new epicureanism of the eighteenth century. Locke opened a new vein with his emphasis on "uneasiness," which the French sensationists carried forward in their discussion of needs as motivating forces, foreshadowing the modern behaviorist position that tensions arising from the primary needs of the organism are the source of all motivation. British associationism continued to cling, for the most part, to calculating credits and debits of pleasure and pain, thus providing a basis for later reinforcement theory, and for contemporary research into the neural basis of these aspects of experience.

The special problem of the innateness of dispositions to "good" and "bad" behavior is reserved for the following chapter.

21.1

Epictetus

(1st Century A.D.)

The thoughts of Epictetus, a Stoic Greek philosopher, were collected by one of his auditors, Flavius Arrianus, into eight volumes of discourses or dissertations, of which four survive. Later Flavius condensed these into an Encheiridion or "handbook." Augustine spoke of Epictetus as the best of the Stoics, and with this recommendation the Encheiridion was endorsed by the Church and studied as a text by Christian monks.

The selection below illustrates the Stoic emphasis on self-control and the exaltation of reason as the supreme virtue. (In this selection, the third paragraph is not from the Encheiridion proper, but is interpolated by the translator from the Dissertations.)

[Bk. II. Ch. III.] 1. Each thing that allures the mind, or offers an advantage, or is loved by you, remember to speak of it as it is, from the smallest thing upward. If you love an earthen jar, then, think, *I love an earthen jar,* for so shall you not be troubled when it breaks. And when you kiss your little child, or wife, think, *I kiss a mortal;* and so shall you not be troubled when they die.

2. When you are about to take in hand some action, bethink you what it is that you are about to do. If you go to the bath, represent to yourself all that takes place there—the squirting of water, the slapping, the scolding, the pilfering; and then shall you take the matter in hand more safely, saying straightway: *I desire to be bathed, and maintain my purpose according to Nature.* And even so with each and every action. For thus, if aught should occur to cross you in your bathing, this thought shall be straightway at hand: *But not this alone did I desire; but also to maintain my purpose according to Nature. And I shall not maintain it if I have indignation at what happens here.*

3. The first difference between the vulgar man and the philosopher: The one saith, *Woe is me for my child, my brother, woe for my father;* but the other, if ever he shall be compelled to say, *Woe is me,* checks himself and saith, *for myself.* For nothing that the Will willeth not can hinder or hurt the Will, but itself only can hurt itself. If then, indeed, we too incline to this, that when we are afflicted we accuse ourselves, and recollect that nothing else than Opinion can cause us any trouble or unsettlement, I swear by all the Gods we have advanced! But as it is, we

The teaching of Epictetus: being the "Encheiridion of Epictetus," with selections from the "Dissertations" and "Fragments." Translated by T. W. Rolleston. Third edition, revised. London, n.d. (First published 1881.) [Pp. 50–51.]

have from the beginning travelled a different road. While we are still children, if haply we stumbled as we were gaping about, the nurse did not chide us, but beat the stone. For what had the stone done? Ought it to have moved out of the way, for your child's folly? Again, if we find nothing to eat after coming from the bath, never doth the tutor check our desire, but he beats the cook. Man, we did not set thee to be a tutor of the cook, but of our child—him shall you train, him improve. And thus, even when full-grown, we appear as children. For a child in music is he who hath not learned music, and in letters, one who hath not learned letters, and in life, one undisciplined in philosophy.

4. It is not things, but the opinions about the things, that trouble mankind. Thus Death is nothing terrible, if it were so, it would have appeared so to Socrates. But the opinion we have about Death, that it is terrible, *that* it is wherein the terror lieth. When, therefore, we are hindered or troubled or grieved, never let us blame any other than ourselves; that is to say, our opinions. A man undisciplined in philosophy blames others in matters in which he fares ill; one who begins to be disciplined blames himself; one who is disciplined, neither others nor himself.

21.2

Paul of Tarsus

(c. A.D. 15–67?)

This letter, written in A.D. 56, deals with the relation of legalism to righteousness. The conflict of sin is stated in terms that fit the general framework of the Stoic antithesis of mind and body, but the philosophic detachment is gone. This passage also calls to mind the words which the poet Ovid had put not long before into the mouth of Medea (and which we shall meet more than once in the next chapter): I know and approve the good, but I do evil.

For we know that the law is spiritual: but I am carnal, sold under sin. For that which I do, I allow not: for what I would, that I do not; but what I hate, that do I. If then I do that which I would not, I consent unto the law that *it is* good. Now then it is no more I that do it, but sin that dwelleth in me. For I know that in me (that is, in my flesh,) dwelleth no good thing: for to will is present with me; but to perform that which is good I find not. For the good that I would, I do not: but the evil which

Epistle to the Romans. (Authorized Version.) [7:14–24.]

I would not, that I do. Now if I do that I would not, it is no more I that do it, but sin that dwelleth in me. I find then a law, that, when I would do good, evil is present with me. For I delight in the law of God after the inward man: But I see another law in my members, warring against the law of my mind, and bringing me into captivity to the law of sin which is in my members. O wretched man that I am! who shall deliver me from the body of this death?

21.3

Saint Augustine

(354–430)

Augustine's treatment of conflict and ambivalence is of a very personal nature. He has experienced them. His conversion was long delayed by his reluctance to give up the delights of the flesh. His sense of guilt was stirred especially when he heard from a visiting countryman, Pontitianus, the story of his own conversion. The awareness of inner conflict, that "willing" does not always issue directly into "doing," is vividly stated. While relating this incident, Augustine recalls the conflicts of his adolescent years, and I have seized the chance to introduce the selection with a few eloquent sentences from the account of that earlier period.

For Paul, as for Plato and the Stoics, conflict was between mind and body. For Augustine, it is within the mind, that is, he experiences true intrapsychic conflict.

[Book III] 1. To Carthage I came, where a cauldron of unholy loves bubbled up all around me. I loved not as yet, yet I loved to love; and, with a hidden want, I abhorred myself that I wanted not. I searched about for something to love, in love with loving, and hating security, and a way not beset with snares.

[Book VIII] 16. Such was the story of Pontitianus. But Thou, O Lord, whilst he was speaking, didst turn me towards myself, taking me from behind my back, where I had placed myself while unwilling to exercise self-scrutiny; and Thou didst set me face to face with myself, that I might behold how foul I was, and how crooked and sordid, bespotted and ulcerous. And I beheld and loathed myself; and whither to fly from myself I discovered not. . . .

The confessions of Saint Augustine. Translated by J. G. Pilkington, 1876. New York: Boni & Liveright, 1927. [Pp. 41, 175–177, 179–180.]

17. . . . For many of my years (perhaps twelve) had passed since my nineteenth, when, on the reading of Cicero's *Hortensius,* I was roused to a desire for wisdom; and still I was delaying to reject mere worldly happiness. . . . I, miserable young man, supremely miserable even in the very outset of my youth, had entreated chastity of Thee, and said, "Grant me chastity and continency, but not yet." For I was afraid that Thou shouldest hear me soon, and soon deliver me from the disease of con- cupiscence, which I desired to have satisfied rather than extinguished. . . .

18. . . . And now had the day arrived in which I was to be laid bare to myself, and my conscience was to chide me. . . . With what scourge of rebuke lashed I not my soul to make it follow me, struggle to go after Thee! Yet it drew back; it refused, and exercised not itself. . . .

21. Whence is this monstrous thing? and why is it? The mind com- mands the body, and it obeys forthwith; the mind commands itself, and is resisted. The mind commands the hand to be moved, and such readi- ness is there that the command is scarce to be distinguished from the obedience. Yet the mind is mind, and the hand is body. The mind com- mands the mind to will, and yet, though it be itself, it obeyeth not. Whence this monstrous thing? and why is it? I repeat, it commands itself to will, and would not give the command unless it willed; yet is not that done which it commandeth. But it willeth not entirely; therefore it com- mandeth not entirely. For so far forth it commandeth, as it willeth; and so far forth is the thing commanded not done, as it willeth not. For the will commandeth that there be a will;—not another, but itself. But it doth not command entirely, therefore that is not which it commandeth. For were it entire, it would not even command it to be, because it would already be. It is, therefore, no monstrous thing partly to will, partly to be unwilling, but an infirmity of the mind, that it does not wholly rise, sustained by truth, {because} pressed down by custom. And so there are two wills, because one of them is not entire; and the one is supplied with what the other needs.

21.4

Kenelm Digby

(1603–1665)

In his second treatise, dealing with "the nature of mans soule," Digby gives reason all its due, but to explain its limited effectiveness in the con- trol of behavior he gives a mechano-physiological account of how the

Two treatises, in the one of which, the nature of bodies; in the other, the nature of mans soule; is looked into. Paris, 1644. [Pp. 386–392.]

conflict of reason and passion plays itself out in a battle of spirits for possession first of the imagination and then of the very muscles. (Although but an amateur physician, Digby was a professional military commander, which accounts for his metaphor.)

[Ch. IV.] *How a man proceedeth to Action*

[1.] . . . If only sense were the fountaine from whence [man's] actions spring, we should observe no other straine in any of them, then meerely that according to which beasts performe theirs: they would proceede ever more in a constant unvaryable tenour, according to the law of materiall things, one body working upon an other, in such sort as we have declared in the former Treatise.

On the other side, if a man were all understanding, and had not this bright lampe enclosed in a pitcher of clay, the beames of it would shine without any allay of dimmenesse, through all he did. . . .

[2.] We may then safely conclude, that in humane nature there are two different centers, from whence crosse actions do flow: the one he hath common with beasts, and whose principles and lawes we delivered in the former Treatise, where we discoursed of life, and the motions of life and of passions: the other is the subject of our present enquiry; which in this place, expecteth at our handes, that we should consider how it demeaneth itselfe, and what it doth in us, when by its guidance we proceede to any action. Experience must be our informer in generall: after which, our discourse shall anatomise what that presenteth us in bulke. She giveth us notice of three especial effects of our understanding: first, that it ordereth a right those conceptions which are brought unto it: secondly, that when they appeare to be not sufficient for the intended worke, it casteth about and seeketh out others: and thirdly, that it strengtheneth those actions which spring from it; and keepeth them regular and firme and constant to their beginnings and principles. Unto which last seemeth to belong, that it sometimes checketh its own thoughts, and bringeth backe those it would have, and appeareth to keepe as it were a watch over its owne wayes. . . .

[5.] But the third operation, is that which giveth clearest evidence of the peculiar and distinct working of the understanding: for if we marke the contestation and strife within us, betweene our sensual part and his antagonist which mainteneth the resolution sett by reason, and observe how exceedingly their courses and proceedings differ from one an other; we shall more plainely discerne the nature, and power, and efficacy of both of them. We may perceive that the motions against *Reason,* rise up turbulently, as it were in billowes, and like a hill of boyling water (as truly *Passion* is a conglobation of spirits) do putt us into an unquiet and distempered heate and confusion: on the other side, *Reason* endeavoureth to keepe us in our due temper, by sometimes commanding downe this growing sea; otherwhiles, by contending in some measure the desires of it, and so diverting an other way its unruly force: sometimes she terrifyeth it, by the proposall of offensive things ioyned unto those it is so earnest to enioy: againe, sometimes she preventeth it, by cutting of all the causes and helpes that promote on its impotent desires, and by engaging before hand the power of it in other things, and the like.

All which do evidently convince, that as *Reason* hath a great strength and power in opposition of sense, so it must be a quite different thing, and of a contrary nature unto it; we may adde, that the worke of *Reason* can never be well performed, but in a great quiet and tranquillity; whereas the motions of *Passion*, are alwayes accompanied with disorder and perturbation: so as it appeareth manifestly, that the force of *Reason*, is not purely the force of its instruments, but the force of its instruments as they are guided, and as the quantities of them are proportioned by it: and this force of *Reason*, is different from the force of its instruments in themselves, in such sort as the force of a song, is different from the force of the same soundes, whereof it is composed, taken without that order which the musitian putteth in them: for otherwise the more spirits that are raysed by any thought (which spirits are the instruments whereby *Reason* performeth all her operations in us) the more strongly *Reason* should worke; the contrary of which is evident, for we see that too great aboundance of spirits confoundeth *Reason*. . . .

[7.] . . . [We] end this Chapter, with collecting out of what is said, how it fareth with us, when we do any thing against *Reason*, or against our owne knowledge. If this happen by surprise, it is plaine that the watch of *Reason* was not so strong as it should have beene, to prevent the admittance or continuance of those thoughts, which worke that transgression. Againe, if it be occasioned by *Passion*, it is evident that in this case, the multitude and violence of those spirits which *Passion* sendeth boyling up to the fantasie, is so great, as the other spirits, which are in the iurisdiction and government of *Reason*, are not able for the present to ballance them and stay their impetuosity, whiles she maketh truth appeare. Sometimes we may observe, that *Reason* hath warning enough, to muster together all her forces, to encounter, as it were in sett battaile, the assault of some concupiscence, that sendeth his unruly bands to take possession of the fansie, and constraine it to serve their desires, and by it to bring *Reason* to their bente. Now if in this pitched field she loose the bridle, and be carried away against her owne resolutions, and be forced like a captive to obey the others lawes, it is cleare that her strength was not so great as the contrary factions.

The cause of which is evident; for we know that she can do nothing but by the assistance of the spirits which inhabite the braine: now then it followeth, that if she have not the command of those spirits which flocke thither, she must of necessity be carried along by the streame of the greater and stronger multitude; which in our case, is the throng of those which are sent up into the braine by the desired object; and they come thither so thicke and so forcibly, that they displace the others which fought under *Reasons* standard; which if they do totally, and excluding reasons party, do entirely possesse the fansie with their troupes, (as in maddenesse and in extremity of suddaine passion it happeneth) then must *Reason* wholy follow their sway, without any struggling at all against it; for whatsoever beateth on the fansie, occasioneth her to worke; and therefore when nothing beateth there but the messengers of some sensuall object, she can make no resistance to what they impose: but if it happen that these tumultuary ones, be not the only spirits which beate there, but that *Reason* hath likewise some under her iurisdiction, which keepe possession for her, though they be too weake to turne the others out of dores; then it is true, she can still direct fairely, how in that case a man should governe himselfe; but when he cometh to execute, he findeth his sinews already possessed, and swelled with the contrary spirits; and they keeping out the smaller and weaker number, which reason hath ranked in order, and would furnish those partes withall, he is drawn even against his iudgment and *Reason*, to obey their appetites, and to move himselfe in prosecution of what they propose. . . . And in this case, a man forseeth his misery all the way he rouleth towardes it, and leapeth into the precipice with his eyes open; which showeth that the army of thoughts on *Reasons* side, should be encreased in number, to have her strong enough to wage battaile with the rebellious adversary: or else, that her adversary should be so much weakened, that she, though not growne stronger in her selfe, yet might, through the others enfeebling, be able to make her party good; (and hence is the use of corporeall mortifications, to subiect our *Passions* to the beheast of *Reason*).

21.5

John Locke

(1632–1704)

In the first edition of the Essay, Locke had written that "Pleasure and pain and that which causes them—good and evil, are the hinges on which our passions turn." He also accepted the conventional view that behavior is guided by judgments regarding expected good and evil outcomes, and

Essay concerning humane understanding. Second edition. London, 1694. [Pp. 134–136.]

explained differences in conduct by the fact that "the same thing is not good to every man." The psychological weakness of this position had already been exposed by Bayle (22.3). Locke abandoned it in the second edition and found a new guiding principle closer to modern views and even suggestive of the future concept of homeostasis: that behavior is guided by discomforts rather than by anticipated outcomes.

[Book II, Ch. XXI.] § 31. To return then to the Enquiry, *what is it that determines the Will in regard to our Actions?* And that upon second thoughts, I am apt to imagine is not, as is generally supposed, the greater good in view: But some (and for the most part the most pressing) uneasiness a Man is at present under: This is that which successively determines the *Will*, and sets us upon those Actions, we perform. This, *Uneasiness* we may call, as it is Desire; which is an uneasiness of the mind for want of some absent good. All pain of the body of what sort soever, and disquiet of the mind is uneasiness: And with this is always join'd Desire, equal to the pain or uneasiness felt; and is scarce distinguishable from it. For desire being nothing but an uneasiness in the want of an absent good, in reference to any pain felt, ease is that absent good; and till that ease be attained, we may call it desire, no body feeling pain, that he wishes not to be eased of, with a desire equal to that pain, and inseparable from it. Besides this desire of ease from pain, there is another of absent positive good, and here also the desire and uneasiness is equal: As much as we desire any absent good, so much are we in pain for it: But here all absent good does not, according to the greatness it has, or is acknowledg'd, and confess'd to have, cause pain equal to that greatness; as all pain causes desire equal to it self: Because the absence of good is not always a pain, as the presence of pain is. And therefore absent good may be looked on, and considered without desire. But so much as there is any where of desire, so much there is of uneasiness. . . .

§ 33. Good & evil, present and absent, 'tis true, work upon the mind: But that which immediately determines the *Will* from time to time to every voluntary action is the uneasiness of *desire,* fixed on some absent good, either negative, as indolency to one in pain; or positive, as enjoyment of pleasure. That it is this uneasiness, that determines the *Will* to the successive voluntary actions, whereof the greatest part of our lives is made up, and by which we are conducted through different courses to different ends, I shall endeavour to shew both from Experience, and the reason of the thing.

§ 34. When a Man is perfectly content with the State he is in, which is when he is perfectly without any uneasiness, what industry, what action, what *Will* is there left, but to continue in it? of this every Man's observation will satisfie him. And thus we see our All-wise Maker, suitable to our constitution and frame, and knowing what it is that determines the *Will,* has put into man the uneasiness of hunger and thirst, and other natural desires, that return at their Seasons, to move and determine their *Wills*, for the preservation of themselves, and the continuation of their Species. For I think we may conclude, that, if the bare contemplation of these good ends, to which we are carried by these several uneasinesses, had been sufficient to determine the will, and set us on work, we should have had none of these natural pains, and perhaps in this World, little or no pain at all. It is better to marry than to burn, says St. Paul, whereby we may see what it is that chiefly drives men into the enjoyment of conjugal life. A little burning felt pushes us more powerfully, than greater pleasures in prospect draw or allure.

§ 35. It seems so establish'd and settled a maxim by the general consent of all Mankind, That good, the greater good, determines the will, that I do not at all wonder, that when I first publish'd my thoughts on this Subject, I took it for granted; and I imagine, that by a great many I shall be thought more excusable for having then done so, than that now I have ventur'd to recede from so received an Opinion. But yet upon a stricter enquiry, I am forced to conclude, that *good, the greater good,* though apprehended and acknowledged to be so, does not determine the *will*, until our desire, raised proportionably to it, makes us uneasie in the want of it. Convince a Man never so much, that plenty has its advantages over poverty; make him see and own, that the handsome conveniences of life are better than nasty penury; yet as long as he is content with the latter, and finds no uneasiness in it, he moves not; his *will* never is determin'd to any action, that shall bring him out of it. Let a Man be never so well perswaded of the advantages of virtue, that it is as necessary to a Man, who has any great aims in this World, or hopes in the next, as food to life; yet till he *hungers and thirsts after righteousness;* till he feels an uneasiness in the want of it, his *will* will not be determin'd to any action in pursuit of this confessed greater good; but any other uneasiness he feels in himself, shall take place, and carry his *will* to other actions. On the other side, let a Drunkard see, that his Health decays, his Estate wastes; Discredit and Diseases, and the want of all things, even of his beloved Drink, attends him in the course he follows; yet the returns of uneasiness to miss his Companions, the habitual thirst after his Cups at the usual time drives him to the Tavern, though he have in his view the loss of health and plenty, and perhaps of the joys of another life; the least of which is no inconsiderable good, but such as, he confesses, is far greater, than the tickling of his palatt with a glass of Wine, or the idle chat of a soaking Club. 'Tis not for want of viewing the greater good; for he sees, and acknowledges it, and in the intervals of his drinking hours, will take resolutions to pursue the greater good; but when the uneasiness to miss his accustomed delight returns, the greater acknowledged good loses its hold, and the present uneasiness determines the *will* to the accustomed action, which thereby gets stronger footing to prevail again the next occasion; though he at the same time make secret promises to himself, that he will do so no more; this is the last time he will act against the attainment of those greater goods. And, thus he is from time to time in the State of that unhappy complainer, *Video meliora proboque Deteriora sequor;* which sentence, allowed for true, and made good by constant Experience, may this, and possibly no other way be easily made intelligible.

21.6

Claude Helvetius

(1715–1771)

Helvetius, who relinquished his lucrative post as tax collector to pursue a literary career, was well qualified to recognize ennui (translated below as lassitude) as a major motivator of civilized man. The theme will be developed further by his friend Le Roy, in the following selection.

Gifted himself in so many ways, Helvetius also argued that the secret of genius lies not in native endowment but in the motivating force of the passions (see 17.4). This leads him naturally enough into an anticipation of modern research on interests as a tool of vocational counseling.

The first part of the selection is from Essay 3, Chapter 5, "Of the powers that act upon the soul." The second is from Essay 4, Chapter 16, "The method of discovering that kind of study for which we are best qualified."

[Essay 3, Ch 5] Lassitude, or wearisomeness of inaction, is a more general and powerful spring than is imagined. Of all pains, this is doubtless the least; but nevertheless it is one. The desire of happiness makes us always consider the absence of pleasure as an evil. We would have the necessary intervals that separate the lively pleasures always connected with the gratification of our natural wants, filled up with some of those sensations that are always agreeable when they are not painful: we therefore constantly desire new impressions, in order to put us in mind every instant of our existence; because every one of these informations affords us pleasure. Thus the savage, as soon as he has satisfied his wants, runs to the banks of a river, where the rapid succession of the waves that drive each other forward makes every moment new impressions upon him: for this reason, we prefer the sight of objects in motion to those at rest: and we proverbially say, that fire makes company; that is, it helps us to deliver us from lassitude.

De l'esprit [Paris, 1758]. Translated anonymously as *De l'esprit, or essays on the mind, and its several faculties.* London, 1759. [Pp. 146–147, 319–321, 323–324.]

It is this necessity of being put in motion, and the kind of inquietude produced in the mind by the absence of any impression, that contains in part the principle of the inconstancy and improvement of the human mind, and which forcing it to actuate all our senses must, after a revolution of an infinite number of ages, invent and carry to perfection the arts and sciences, and at length lead to the decay of taste.

In fact, if the impressions made upon us are the more agreeable in proportion as they are more lively, and if the duration of the same impression blunts its vivacity, we must be desirous of those new impressions that produce in our minds the pleasure of surprise: artists ambitious of pleasing us, and exciting in us these kinds of impressions, ought therefore, after having in part exhausted the combinations of beauty, to substitute in its room the singular, because it makes a newer, and consequently a more lively impression upon us. This, in polite {i.e. civilized} nations occasions the decay of taste.

To know still better the effect of lassitude upon us, and what the activity of this principle is capable of producing, let us observe mankind with an attentive eye; and we shall perceive, that the fear of lassitude prompts most of them to thought and action. In order to save themselves from it, at the hazard of too strong, and consequently disagreeable impressions, men search with the greatest eagerness for every thing capable of putting them in motion: it is this desire that makes the common people run to see an execution, and the people of fashion a play; and it is the same motive in a gloomy devotion, and even in the austere exercises of pennance, that frequently affords old women a remedy against the tiresomeness of inaction; for God, who by all possible means endeavours to bring sinners to himself, commonly uses with respect to them that of lassitude.

But especially at the age when the strong passions are enchained, either by morals, or the form of government, the wearisomeness of inaction plays its greatest part: it then becomes the universal mover.

[Essay 4, Ch. 16] In order to know our abilities, we must examine with what kind of object chance and education have principally charged the memory, and what degree of love we have for glory. Upon this combination we may determine the kind of study to which we ought to apply ourselves.

There is no man intirely destitute of knowledge. According as we have in the memory more physical or historical facts, more images or sentiments, we shall have a greater or less aptitude to natural philosophy, politics, or poetry. . . .

The objects which chance and education place in our memory, are indeed the primary matter of the mind; but it remains there dead and inactive, till it is put into a ferment by the passions. It then produces a new assemblage of ideas, images, or sentiments, to which we give the name of genius, wit, or talents.

After having discovered what is the number, and what the species of objects deposited in the magazine of the memory, before we can determine on any kind of study, we must calculate to what a degree we are sensible of glory. We are liable to mistake in this particular, and to give the name of passion to mere inclination; nothing, however . . . is more easily distinguished. We have a strong passion when we are animated with a single desire, and all our thoughts and actions are subordinate to it. We have only inclinations, when the mind is divided by an infinite number of nearly equal desires. The more numerous these desires are, the more moderate are our inclinations; on the contrary, the less our desires are multiplied, the more nearly do they approach to unity, and the more do these inclinations become lively, and the readier to be changed into passions. It is then the unity, or at least the pre-eminence of one desire over all the others, that constitutes passion.

The passions being once determined, we must know their strength, and, for this purpose, examine the degree of enthusiasm we feel for great men. This is in early youth a pretty exact standard of our love of glory. I say, in early youth; because, being then more susceptible of the passions, we deliver our selves the more freely up to our enthusiasm. Besides, we have then no motives to degrade merit and abilities, and we may still hope to see esteemed in ourselves what we esteem in others; this is not the case with those who are grown to manhood. Whoever has attained to a certain age without having any merit, always indulges the contempt of abilities, to comfort himself for the want of them. . . . As we esteem in others only such ideas as are analogous to our own, our respect for wit is always proportioned to the wit we have ourselves; we celebrate great men only when we are made to be great. Why did Caesar weep on his stopping before the bust of Alexander? It was because he was Caesar. Why do we not weep at the sight of the same bust? It is because we are not Caesar.

We may then from the degree of esteem conceived for great men, measure the degree of our love of glory, and, consequently, come to a resolution in the choice of our studies. The choice is always good, wherever the strength of the passions is proportioned to the difficulty of the success. Now it is more difficult to succeed in any one art or science in proportion to the number of men employed in it, and to their having carried it nearer to perfection. . . . He who is not intoxicated with the love of glory, ought to seek for it in winding paths, and particularly to avoid the roads beaten by the men of the greatest understandings. . . .

I have said enough on this subject; and shall conclude, from the principles established in this chapter, that all the mental abilities are produced by the objects placed in our memory, and by those objects being put into a fermentation by the love of glory. . . . Upon which I shall observe, that if there is an art of exciting in us strong passions, if there are easy means of filling the memory of a young man with a certain species of ideas and objects, there are, consequently, certain methods of forming men of genius. . . .

Moreover, this knowledge of the mind may not only be of use to individuals, but also to the public: it may enlighten ministers with respect to the knowledge of making a proper choice, and enable them to distinguish men of superior abilities.

21.7

Abraham Tucker

(1705–1774)

A country gentleman of ample means, Tucker wrote in an unhurried style, and for the four volumes which appeared in his own lifetime he used the pseudonym "Edward Search." Bishop Paley credited him with "more original thinking and observation upon the several subjects that he has taken in hand, than in any other [writer], not to say, than in all others put together. His talent also for illustration is unrivalled [Works, 1849, p. 408]." In a long chapter on "Satisfaction," Tucker fills in the bare schema that Locke left, excusing the thoroughness of his critique by stating that though he might "not pretend to a clearer, perhaps [he might] to a more microscopic eye." The reader will note, beyond his "talent for illustration," how his "original thinking" shows in a brilliant anticipation of the need for special neural structures to provide experiences of satisfaction and discomfort. Tucker made a not inconsiderable contribution to the advance of associationist thinking, not only in England but also in Germany, where his work appeared in translation in 1771. An abridgement by William Hazlitt (1807) received wider circulation than the original.

[Ch. 6.] 8. . . . Mr. Locke ascribes the change of action solely to uneasiness, and the continuance of it to satisfaction: it behooves me then to give my reasons for departing from so great an authority. . . .

. . . I think one may produce instances wherein we depart from our design and change our measures without being driven by the lash of uneasiness. Suppose a man sitting down to his harpsichord intending to

The light of nature pursued [1768–1778]. Second edition, revised. 7 volumes. London, 1805. [Vol. I, pp. 112–115, 190–192.]

play through an opera of Corelli: in the midst of his diversion enters a messenger to tell him, that, if he will come away directly to the minister, he may be instated in a considerable preferment he had long wished and ardently sought for. Is it uneasiness or joy that makes him leave his music and run to catch up his hat? Suppose a company of young folks agreeably entertained in dancing; somebody tells them of a fine fire-work just going to be played off in a neighbouring garden: I will not ensure that they shall not run instantly to the window. When their curiosity a little abates and before the sight begins to cloy, some one puts them in mind of their dancing, perhaps the rest take the admonition and they run back to their sport as hastily as they quitted it. Surely this is a change of action and a departure from the plan laid down for the employment of the night: Yet I appeal to any gentleman or lady, who may have experienced such an incident, whether they feel the least spice of uneasiness either in breaking off their diversion or returning to it again. On the other hand, suppose a man travelling through a lonely forest infested with a gang of desperate villains, who murder all they meet, he sees them coming towards him and has but just time to jump into a stinking bog where he can hide his head behind a little bush: the rogues halt at a small distance from him, where they sit chattering perhaps an hour or two, all which time I suppose he will hardly quit his lurking hole. Now what holds him to this continuance of action? is it satisfaction? He sees none and expects none by sticking up to the shoulders in dirt and nastiness. Is it any other than the uneasy dread of falling into their hands, where he can expect nothing but misery and destruction? . . .

37. The ninth and last remark I have to make upon satisfaction and uneasiness is this, That they are perceptions of a kind peculiar to themselves, analogous to none others we have, yet capable of joining company with any others. We neither hear, nor see, nor taste, nor imagine them, yet find some degree or other of them in almost every thing we hear, or see, or taste, or reflect upon. But though they often change their companions, they never change their nature: the same thing may become uneasy that before was satisfactory, but satisfaction never cloys, and uneasiness never loses its sting. Sometimes nature assigns them their places on her original constitution of the subjects, and sometimes custom, practice or accident, introduce them. To some sensations and reflections they adhere strongly, not to be removed at all or not without much labour, time, and difficulty; and upon others they sit so lightly that the least breath of air can blow them away. They have their seasons of absence and residence, lasting longer or shorter as it happens, and often trip nimbly from object to object without tarrying a moment upon any: and when separated make no other difference in the idea they leave, than that of their being gone. For in a picture that you looked upon at first with delight and afterwards with indifference, you shall perceive no alteration of form or colour or other circumstance than that it once gave you

pleasure, but now affords you none. Sometimes they propagate their own likeness upon different subjects, at others, they come into one another's places successively in the same. One while they come and go unaccountably, at another one may discern the causes of their migration: for an idea, whereto satisfaction was annexed, entering into a compound which is afterwards divided again, the satisfaction shall rest upon a different part from that whereto it was at first united: and a satisfactory end shall render the means conducive thereto satisfactory after the end is removed out of view. Some things please by their novelty, and others displease from their strangeness: custom brings the latter to be pleasant, but repetition makes the former nauseous.

All which seems to indicate that there is some particular spring or nerve appropriated to affect us with satisfaction or uneasiness, which never moves unless touched by some of the nerves bringing us our other ideas: and that the body, being a very complicated machine, as well in the grosser as the finer of its organs, they delight or disturb us in various degrees according as in the variety of their play they approach nearer or remove further from the springs of satisfaction or uneasiness. For as the difference of our ideas depends probably upon the form, or magnitude, or motion, or force of the organs exhibiting them, one cannot suppose the same organ by the variations of its play affecting us either with pleasure or pain without producing an alteration in our ideas.

21.8

Georges Le Roy

(1723–1789)

The anonymously published Letters on animals, offered as the work of "a doctor of Nuremberg," attacked the instinct doctrine, not in Condillac's bookish manner (see 15.7), but with the firsthand knowledge of animal behavior which one should expect from an author who is the king's master of the hunt. It included a "Letter on man," which points to the importance of boredom (in effect, the need for novel stimulation) as a source of human progress. Le Roy develops the insight of Helvetius into an appreciation of what Maslow called the "hierarchy of motives." Included is an awareness of the very different role of sex as a motivating force in men as compared with animals.

It was Le Roy who got Helvetius into no end of trouble by persuading

Lettres sur les animaux [1764]. New, enlarged edition. Nuremberg [falsely], 1781. [Pp. 210–221.]

him to publish De l'esprit *in France, under his own name, despite its strong anticlerical tone. Le Roy cleverly managed the censorship hurdle, but after the inevitable furor the book was nevertheless officially condemned. Le Roy was more discreet with his own harmless book.*

There are in man's constitution many more natural needs than in those of all other animals. Even if his intelligence were not essentially superior to theirs, he would necessarily acquire a great superiority over all other species, because of his needs and the means he possesses. It is not that the need for food, which can become one of the most pressing, would naturally force him to be very industrious. His taste and his constitution have led him to accommodate himself to different kinds of food, and therefore he is less in danger of lacking food than other species are. Hunting, fishing, dairy herds, the fruits of the soil—all satisfy his appetite equally. It is not the hungry man who is difficult to satiate, but the squeamish one, whose desires are troublesome when aroused; perhaps the soil furnished natural man coarse food enough, without much labor, to maintain his vigor. . . . If man had no need but to be fed, society would be much less necessary to him. It would have been established without difficulty, and perhaps we would not have cause to admire all the progress which industry has achieved, due to his other needs.

In most climates, man is condemned, under pain of suffering or even death, to clothe himself. Therefore this is a need which we must rank among those of highest necessity, and it may have pushed man to more thought and invention than the need to feed himself. Not that men could not, at first, cover themselves with the skins of the animals they had killed, without preparing them in any way, but they could not do this for long without being forced, because of the inconvenience, to think of some means for making this simple garment better suited to its purpose. These reflections gave birth to the arts of treating skins to make them more supple and more durable, and stitching them together so that one would be more completely and more comfortably covered. . . . Need, that universal teacher of all sensitive creatures, gives learned lessons in this respect to those who otherwise are the most stupid and uncouth. But no matter how well clothed a man may be, he is still so much at the mercy of intemperate weather that a shelter is just as necessary to him as a garment. Though he may begin by taking refuge in a tree trunk . . . his need will lead him to gathering leaves and branches . . . [and finally] to constructing a cabin. . . .

Love too, no doubt, is one of man's most pressing needs. It makes itself felt with overwhelming force above all when the other needs are satisfied. This terrible passion, which torments and perpetuates all living creatures, has no special season for man. It is almost always active during his vigorous years, even when moral ideas, whether real or illusory, add nothing to its natural vivacity, and its enjoyment only slackens the desire for an instant, but does not extinguish it. Hope for the moment to come is confused with intoxication in the present, and gives this passion a character of permanence which can scarcely fail to establish a durable association between male and female. . . . In addition to the advantages and the mutual assistance which result from this association, this bond soon acquires new force from the birth of children, whose needs increase the relationships which the father and mother already have with each other. . . . But the needs which we have mentioned are not the only ones which man receives from nature. There are other dispositions which render society at least very interesting to him, and which, perhaps more than the primary needs, influence his efforts, his progress, and his crimes. Man not only has the need to be fed, clothed, sheltered from harsh weather, and even to experience, for a portion of his life, the lively emotions of love. All this together may suffice for an isolated man, because the necessity of providing for them will occupy his time, and scarcely leave any for sleep. This indeed is what happens to those unfortunates who are doomed by poverty to unending fatigue in order to sustain themselves. But excessive toil, concern and fear leave them with only a painful sense of their existence. They do not enjoy it; they suffer it, and are made aware of it only by their suffering. When men have the means to satisfy all the needs of which we have been speaking; when nature's boons leave them, in this regard, without immediate concern for the future; in short, when they seem to have nothing to do but to enjoy a happy leisure—then a new need torments them, to have a lively feeling of their own existence. We are aware of ourselves only through our immediate sensations, or our ideas. If they are to make us happy they must interest us, and unfortunately, even the sensations which interest us most become weakened when they are continuous. When we look at something for a long time, it becomes like a receding object, which we perceive only as an image that is confused and ill-defined. The need for animated existence, coupled with the continual debilitation of our sensations, produce in us a mechanical unease, vague desires which are aroused by the insistent recollection of an earlier condition. We are therefore forced, if we would be happy, either to continually change the objects [of our attention] or to push our sensations to extremes of the same kind. Hence arises an inconstancy which resolution cannot check, and an infinite progression of desires which are stimulated by memory, but are always destroyed by enjoyment. This disposition, which makes the unrest of boredom follow even the most interesting emotions, is the torment of idle and civilized man, as we shall see by examining its effects on society. But we shall also see that this torment is the source of a portion of his efforts and his progress. The need for a lively sense of existence is balanced in man by another disposition which he has in common with all other sensitive creatures, laziness or the love of rest. This inertial force does not act powerfully except on society's idle class. Under all other conditions it is subjugated by more stimulating needs. But, although it is at first difficult to believe, this is the greatest motive to activity in man. The perspective of rest, which made Pyrrho run, still fatigues every ambitious man who wants to get ahead, every miser who accumulates more than he needs, every man who has a passion for glory and a fear of rivals. Love of rest and desire for animated existence are two contradictory needs which influence and modify one another. Man fears labor; every kind of effort troubles and fatigues him, at least when he is not stirred by passion. Above all, the labor of thinking is insupportable for anyone to whom habit has not made it easy. But boredom becomes just as much a burden as work itself. To the idle man, it seems as if a portion of his existence is escaping him. He moves about mechanically; he is forced to seek external objects which will stir him by their action and excite in him the feeling of being alive. Since he has no activity of his own, he needs to be passive. He needs extraordinary spectacles, the novelty of which will rouse his numbed organs. This malaise is less known to savage men. . . . But if the savage has once enjoyed a lively sense of existence—if, for example, strong liquor has excited this feeling in him —he becomes very greedy for it, and he will sacrifice everything to satisfy this new need.

21.9

Jeremy Bentham

(1748–1832)

Bentham learned from Helvetius (as Henry Sedgwick noted in his Outlines of the history of ethics) that just as individuals are guided by considerations of self-interest, so society's moral judgments are its expressions of common interest, and therefore a sound ethic should be based on a principle of greatest general advantage, or, in the phrase he borrowed from Hutcheson (25.1), "the greatest happiness for the greatest numbers." Therefore Bentham based his system on a demonstration, or an assumption, that pleasure and pain are the only determiners of human conduct. This principle was accepted totally by his friend James Mill, thereafter by John Stuart Mill (who as a boy was taught to revere the aged Bentham, and as a man wrote Utilitarianism) and subsequently by

An introduction to the principles of morals and legislation [1789]. In *The Works of Jeremy Bentham*, Vol. I. Edinburgh, 1838. [Pp 1.]

Mill's friend Alexander Bain, who translated it into a basis for all learning, independent of reason (see 13.9).

1. Nature has placed mankind under the governance of two sovereign masters, *pain* and *pleasure*. It is for them alone to point out what we ought to do, as well as to determine what we shall do. On the one hand the standard of right and wrong, on the other the chain of causes and effects, are fastened to their throne. They govern us in all we do, in all we say, in all we think: every effort we can make to throw off our subjection, will serve but to demonstrate and confirm it. In words a man may pretend to abjure their empire; but in reality he will remain subject to it all the while. The *principle of utility* recognises this subjection, and assumes it for the foundation of that system, the object of which is to rear the fabric of felicity by the hands of reason and of law. Systems which attempt to question it, deal in sounds instead of sense, in caprice instead of reason, in darkness instead of light. . . .

. . . By the principle of utility is meant that principle which approves or disapproves of every action whatsoever, according to the tendency which it appears to have to augment or diminish the happiness of the party whose interest is in question: or, what is the same thing in other words, to promote or to oppose that happiness. I say of every action whatsoever; and therefore not only of every action of a private individual, but of every measure of government.

21.10

Alexander Bain

(1818–1903)

All great thinkers have experienced, and many have expressed, the force of intellectual motivation. At first it is the "need to know," but later the need to establish understanding of relationships. Bain's statement of this important source of motivation is especially notable, partly because it is related to his insistence that construction of analogies is the essential feature of intellectual creativity and partly because it anticipates Festinger's principle of cognitive dissonance. The selection comes from a chapter on "Emotions of intellect."

1. The operations of the Intellect give occasion to a certain select class of feelings, which concern both our pleasures and our actions. . . .

The emotions and the will. London, 1859. [Pp. 199–201, 205.]

The trains of contiguous association, as exemplified in memory and routine, present no special stimulant of the emotions. They constitute a case of mere exercise, and gratify or pain the individual according to the condition of mental vigour and freshness at the time. It is under similarity that the great fund of emotion-giving situations is placed. Those identifications of likeness in remote objects, and under deep disguises strike the mind with an effect of surprise, brilliancy, exhilaration, or charm. . . . On the other hand, Inconsistency, want of unity, or positive discord, are forms of pain that influence us to a considerable degree, and derive importance from inspiring the virtues of Truth, Integrity, and Justice; being, in fact, a constituent element of the Moral Sense.

2. The emotion of similarity, or the feeling excited by a flash of identification between things never regarded as like before, is generically of the nature of agreeable Surprise; this, in fact, is one of the ordinary occasions of that outburst. When we suddenly discover, or have pointed out to us for the first time, a likeness between two objects lying far apart and never considered as of the same class, we are arrested, startled, and excited into a pleasing wonderment. . . .

3. The peculiar mode of the pleasurable surprise varies with the subject. . . . In the identities struck by science,—the generalizations, abstractions, classification, inductions, and deductions that constitute scientific discovery,—the sudden shock of wonder is accompanied with a marked degree of the pleasure of *rebound,* the lightening of an intellectual burden, or the solving of a difficulty that formerly weighed on the mind. . . . The labor of intellectual comprehension is reduced by every new discovery of likeness; and the first feeling of this gives a rush of delight, the delight we feel when we are relieved of some long-standing burden, or discharged from a laborious obligation. If the effect is to resolve an apparent contradiction, there is the same gladdening reaction from the depression of embarrassment. . . .

6. . . . Contrary statements, opinions, or appearances, operate on the mind as a painful jar, and stimulate a corresponding desire for a reconciliation. When we hear the same event described by two persons who contradict each other, we are said to be distracted, or pulled two ways at once; a certain suffering is caused by the attempt to entertain contrary accounts of one thing. This susceptibility is most felt in minds where the intelligence is highly developed; indeed, with the great mass of men it counts for very little except with reference to further consequences. Any strong emotion is sufficient to make the untutored mind swallow a contradiction with ease; but they that have been accustomed to sift opinions, and reject the untenable and contradictory, feel an intellectual revulsion when conflicting doctrines are propounded. This intellectual sensitiveness usually leads to the abandonment of one of the contraries, or else to a total suspension of judgment, that is to say,

a repudiation for the time of both the one and the other. As a spur to the volition, therefore, no motive is stronger in the mind of the intellectual man than the pain of inconsistency.

21.11

Edward J. Kempf

(born 1885)

Kempf's emphasis on the role of the autonomic functions in governing behavior (as well as, phylogenetically, in shaping the very process of evolution) reflects the influence of behaviorism in its emphasis on the importance of peripheral organs rather than of the brain in the process of thinking. It is perhaps the first attempt to use the principle of homeostasis as the central principle in psychological theory. It is a twentieth-century restatement of the eighteenth-century thought that passions, not reason, rule our conduct.

In the higher animals and man an autonomic or affect-producing sensori-motor system exists which uses a projicient sensori-motor system as a means to project and keep itself in contact with the environment. The affective sensori-motor system has specialized physiological functions and a definite anatomical structure, consisting of the entire autonomic apparatus and the sympathetic or unstriped part of the striped muscle cells. The latter make a reënforcing affective contribution to the personality through the postural tonus of the striped muscles, particularly the facial muscles and extensor and flexor muscles of the skeleton. (The nervous division of this cellular system has often been referred to as an involuntary, or vegetative, or sympathetic nervous system.)

The projicient sensori-motor apparatus has also specialized functions and a distinct anatomical structure in the entire cerebro-spinal apparatus (so-called voluntary) which does not include those autonomic centers and their nerve fibers which are embedded in it. (The projicient sensori-motor apparatus, it appears from the nature of postural tonus and kinesthetic imagery, is, in a sense, the thinking apparatus of the organism.)

The theory advanced is that *whenever the autonomic or affective sensori-motor apparatus is disturbed or forced into a state of unrest, either through the necessities of growth, metabolism, or endogenous or exog-*

The autonomic functions and the personality. *Nervous and Mental Disease Monograph Series*, No. 28. 1921. [Pp. 1–2, 141.] Reprinted by permission of the Smith Ely Jelliffe Trust.

*enous stimuli, it compels the projicient sensori-motor apparatus to so
adjust the receptors in the environment as to acquire stimuli which have
the capacity to produce adequate postural readjustments in the autonomic apparatus. In this manner, only, the disturbance of function may
be neutralized. The constant tendency of the autonomic apparatus is to
so organize the projicient apparatus into a means as to acquire a maximum of affective gratification with a minimum expenditure of energy
or effort.*

This continuous dynamic pressure determines the tendency towards
perfection through practice, eliminates the useless and stabilizes the useful. It determines the evolution of organic structure, of personality, behavior and achievement. The healthy individual is a dynamic entity that
has an elastic though limited quotient of energy, hence the tendency
to attain a maximum influence upon the environment with a minimum
expenditure of his resources conserves the unused resources for further
extension of power and influence. In commerce men are constantly striving to find methods of reducing the waste of power and of extending the
control of power. Each invention that improves a method in either direction causes the old method to be discarded. This principle is also
to be seen in the individual's refinement of his personality, as speech
and movements, until he attains a comfortable maximum of skill.

In discussing the above conception of the dynamic nature of the personality the entire organism is conceived as a unity and the *central
nervous system is reduced to a means, or instrument, for, first the integration of the various physiological divisions into a functional unity, and,
second, the reënforcement of their powers.*

[Shepherd Ivory] Franz has concluded from his experiments on the
variations in distribution of motor centers that "the same forms of behavior are not always due to the activities of the same cerebral cells."
When such data and conclusions are associated with the recent work
on the influence of the proprioceptive arc and postural tonus, the old,
unfounded notions about the supremacy of the cerebral cortex and localized origin in the cortex of the controlling forces of behavior must be
considered to have been thoroughly undermined by the more recent
contribution to the knowledge of the nervous system. . . .

The affective stream should be seen as a continuous but complex
stream of afferent impulses arising, peripherally, from the receptors in
the autonomic apparatus. The thought content of consciousness is largely
determined by the nature of the affective stream as it affects the postural tonus of the striped muscles. Because of the relations of postural
muscle tonus and kinesthetic imagery, the projicient apparatus may be
regarded, in a sense, as the thinking apparatus of the body, trying to
acquire means to please the affect.

Therefore, in the psychoanalytic study of any personality, or of an
act or fantasy, such as an hallucination, a work of art, a poem, play,

novel, or Darwin's contributions to knowledge of evolution, the formula to be followed is:

Affective Craving x Environmental Resistance = Behavior.

Given the Behavior and the Resistance, the nature of the Wishes may be quite accurately inferred; or

Given the Wishes and the Resistance, the Behavior may be quite accurately predicted; or

Given the Wishes and the Behavior, the Resistance may be quite accurately deduced.

21.12

John Dollard   Leonard W. Doob

(born 1900)   (born 1909)

Neal E. Miller   O. Hobart Mowrer

(born 1909)   (born 1907)

AND

Robert R. Sears

(born 1908)

Aside from its direct contribution to theory and its importance as a starting point for experimental studies, in many of which the name of Neal Miller has figured, this book is historically memorable as an expression of the influence which social events, accompanying the economic depression of the early thirties, exercised on the thinking of psychologists. Indeed, the collaborative nature of this work is itself one expression of the turn to social rather than individual thinking. Despite the disclaimer regarding a possible genetic basis for the frustration-aggression sequence, the many followers of this thesis have almost invariably interpreted it as implying that there is no genetic basis for aggression sans frustration.

Dollard, the oldest member of this remarkable group, had formulated the general principle in Freudian terms in his Caste and class in a southern town (1937). This book expresses the effort of the period to achieve a compatible fusion of Freud and Pavlov.

Frustration and aggression. New Haven: Yale University Press, 1939. [Pp. 1–2, 10–11, 53–54.]

The problem of aggression has many facets. The individual experiences difficulty in controlling his own temper and often sees others carrying on an unwitting struggle with their hostilities. . . . Children are often expert at annoying their elders by sly mischief or a sudden tantrum. Helpless minorities are persecuted. The lynching mob has a grimness and cruelty not to be expected from people who are so gentle and kind in other situations. Primitive tribesmen slay one another and even civilized people are frightened by the prospect of new and increasingly destructive wars. This book represents an attempt to bring a degree of systematic order into such apparently chaotic phenomena.

This study takes as its point of departure the assumption that aggression is always a consequence of frustration. More specifically the proposition is that the occurrence of aggressive behavior always presupposes the existence of frustration and, contrariwise, that the existence of frustration always leads to some form of aggression. From the point of view of daily observation, it does not seem unreasonable to assume that aggressive behavior of the usually recognized varieties is always traceable to and produced by some form of frustration. But it is by no means so immediately evident that, whenever frustration occurs, aggression of some kind and in some degree will inevitably result. In many adults and even children, frustration may be followed so promptly by an apparent acceptance of the situation and readjustment thereto that one looks in vain for the relatively gross criteria ordinarily thought of as characterizing aggressive action. It must be kept in mind, however, that one of the earliest lessons human beings learn as a result of social living is to suppress and restrain their overtly aggressive reactions. This does not mean, however, that such reaction tendencies are thereby annihilated; rather it has been found that, although these reactions may be temporally compressed, delayed, disguised, displaced, or otherwise deflected from their immediate and logical goal, they are not destroyed.
. . .

Aggression is not always manifested in overt movements but may exist as the content of a phantasy or dream or even a well thought-out plan of revenge. It may be directed at the object which is perceived as causing the frustration or it may be displaced to some altogether innocent source or even toward the self, as in masochism, martyrdom, and suicide. . . .

Although the frustration-aggression hypothesis assumes a universal causal relation between frustration and aggression, it is important to note that the two concepts have been defined *independently* as well as *dependently*. The dependent definition of aggression is that *response which follows frustration, reduces only the secondary, frustration-produced instigation, and leaves the strength of the original instigation unaffected.* Frustration is independently defined as *that condition which exists when a goal-response suffers interference*. Aggression is dependently defined as *an act whose goal response is injury to an organism* (or *organism-surrogate*).

It is not necessary for the purpose of this discussion to take the position that frustration originally (in a genetic sense) produces aggressive behavior. Frustration is possible as soon as unlearned or learned reaction sequences are in operation in the child. . . . The first reactions to frustration may indeed be of a random character and may lack that destructiveness which is here posited for aggression. It may also be that out of a battery of random responses to frustration certain ones are learned as effective in reducing the strength of the frustration-induced instigation (though not the strength of the original instigation) and that these later appear as aggression. Whether the relationship be learned or innate, when the curtain rises on the theoretical scene which is surveyed in this volume, frustration and aggression are already joined as response sequences. . . .

. . . The expression of any act of aggression is a catharsis that reduces the instigation to all other acts of aggression. From this and the principle of displacement it follows that, with the level of original frustration held constant, there should be an inverse relationship between the expression of various forms of aggression.

21.13

James Olds AND Peter Milner

(born 1922)   (born 1919)

W. R. Hess (10.10) introduced the use of permanently implanted electrodes to study the localization of functions in the diencephalon. Olds ingeniously arranged to have the animal subject control its own stimulation, and thus showed that direct stimulation of the brain can have motivational effects, which are also localizable.

Stimuli have eliciting and reinforcing functions. In studying the former, one concentrates on the responses which come after the stimulus. In studying the latter, one looks mainly at the responses which precede it. In its reinforcing capacity, a stimulus increases, decreases, or leaves unchanged the frequency of preceding responses, and accordingly it is called a reward, a punishment, or a neutral stimulus.

Previous studies using chronic implantations of electrodes have tended to focus on the eliciting functions of electrical stimuli delivered to the

Positive reinforcement produced by electrical stimulation of septal area and other regions of rat brain. *Journal of Comparative and Physiological Psychology* 47 (1954): 419–427. [Pp. 419, 421, 425–426.]

brain. The present study, on the other hand, has been concerned with the reinforcing function of the electrical stimulation.

[Method.] Stimulation was carried out by means of chronically implanted electrodes which did not interfere with the health or free behavior of Ss to any appreciable extent. The Ss were 15 male hooded rats, weighing approximately 250 gm. at the start of the experiment. Each S was tested in a Skinner box which delivered alternating current to the brain so long as a lever was depressed. The current was delivered over a loose lead, suspended from the ceiling, which connected the stimulator to the rat's electrode. The S's were given a total of 6 to 12 hr. of acquisition testing, and 1 to 2 hr. of extinction testing. During acquisition, the stimulator was turned on so that a response produced electrical stimulation. . . . Each S was given a percentage score denoting the proportion of his total acquisition time given to responding. This score could be compared with the animal's extinction score to determine whether the stimulation had a positive, negative, or neutral reinforcing effect. . . .

In order to determine percentage scores, periods when the animal was responding regularly (at least one response every 30 sec.) were counted as periods of responding. . . .

[Results.] . . . The highest scores are found together in the central portion of the forebrain. Beneath the *corpus callosum* and between the two lateral ventricles . . . we find four acquisition scores varying from 75 to 92 per cent. This is the septal area. . . . Thus the electrical stimulus in the septal area has an effect which is apparently equivalent to that of a conventional primary reward as far as the maintenance of a lever-pressing response is concerned. . . .

[Discussion.] It is clear that electrical stimulation in certain parts of the brain, particularly the septal area, produces acquisition and extinction curves which compare favorably with those produced by a conventional primary reward. With other electrode placements, the stimulation appears to be neutral or punishing. . . .

As there is no evidence of a painful condition preceding the electrical stimulation, and as the animals are given free access to food and water at all times except while actually in the Skinner boxes, there is no explicitly manipulated drive to be reduced by electrical stimulation. . . . We have some evidence here for a primary rewarding effect which is not associated with the reduction of a primary drive state. It is perhaps fair in a discussion to report the "clinical impression" of the Es that the phenomenon represents strong pursuit of a positive stimulus rather than escape from some negative condition.

Should the latter interpretation prove correct, we have perhaps located a system within the brain whose peculiar function is to produce a rewarding effect on behavior. The location of such a system puts us in a position to collect information that may lead to a decision among conflicting theories of reward.

Chapter 22

MORAL SENSE

Most psychologists would agree with Hume that morality is not a subject for science but for opinion, and they would therefore exclude it from the subject matter of psychology. However, concern about moral questions has exercised conspicuous influence on psychology in times past, and continues to do so. Moral convictions guided Plato's thought, as well as that of the Stoics and Epicureans. The ancients generally agreed that reason alone should guide men in their actions, and they deplored the influence of passions on behavior as in some way infrahuman. Christianity accepted this judgment, and tried to enforce it with "mortifications" of the body and its appetites. The early history of this problem has therefore been told, in a measure, in the chapter on emotions. The present chapter begins with Aquinas, but jumps quickly to the period in which the teaching of psychology at the universities was entrusted to professors of "moral philosophy." The central theme of this chapter is the controversy as to whether moral principles are innate or acquired. Do we arrive at our conceptions of good and evil by reasoning, by induction from experience, by a sort of social contract intended to serve the common good, or does all this merely serve to reinforce universal innate awareness of differences between noble and ignoble, virtuous and sinful behavior? In the twentieth century, after being debated between Freudians and Behaviorists, between classical psychoanalysts and neo-Freudians, this question is being given a new form in controversies about the genetic determination of criminal violence.

22.1

Saint Thomas Aquinas

(1225–1274)

The problem of our chapter—whether morality depends upon innate or acquired behavioral characteristics—is considered by Saint Thomas. He also lays a basis for later discussions of "natural law" as a guide for human actions.

Whether virtue is in us by nature

. . . In like manner with regard to sciences and virtues, some held that they are wholly from within, so that all virtues and sciences would pre-exist in the soul naturally, but that the hindrance to science and virtue, which are due to the soul being weighed down by the body, are removed by study and practice, even as iron is made bright by being polished. This was the opinion of the Platonists.—Others said that they are wholly from without, being due to the inflow of the active intellect, as Avicenna maintained.—Others said that sciences and virtues are in us by nature, so far as we are adapted to them, but not in their perfection: this is the teaching of the Philosopher (*Ethic.* II), and is nearer the truth.

To make this clear, it must be observed that there are two ways in which something is said to be natural to a man; one is according to his specific nature, the other according to his individual nature. And, since each thing derives its species from its form, and its individuation from matter, and, again, since man's form is his rational soul, while his matter is his body, whatever belongs to him in respect of his rational soul, is natural to him in respect of his specific nature; while whatever belongs to him in respect of the particular temperament of his body, is natural to him in respect of his individual nature. For whatever is natural to man in respect of his body, considered as part of his species, is to be referred, in a way, to the soul, in so far as this particular body is adapted to this particular soul.

In both these ways virtue is natural to man inchoatively. This is so in respect of the specific nature, in so far as in man's reason there are to be found instilled by nature certain naturally known principles of both knowledge and action, which are the seeds of intellectual and moral

The Summa theologica of Saint Thomas Aquinas literally translated by the Fathers of the English Dominican province. New York: Benziger Bros., 1912–1925. 20 volumes. [First part of the second part: Q. 63, Art. 1; Q. 94, Art. 2; Q. 100, Art. 1.]

virtues, and in so far as there is in the will a natural appetite for good in accordance with reason. Again, this is so in respect of the individual nature, in so far as by reason of a disposition in the body, some are disposed either well or ill to certain virtues: because, to wit, certain sensitive powers are acts of certain parts of the body, according to the disposition of which these powers are helped or hindered in the exercise of their acts, and, in consequence, the rational powers also, which the aforesaid sensitive powers assist. In this way one man has a natural appetite for science, another for fortitude, another for temperance: and in these ways, both intellectual and moral virtues are in us by way of a natural aptitude, inchoatively,—but not perfectly, since nature is determined to one, while the perfection of these virtues does not depend on one particular mode of action, but on various modes, in respect of the various matters, which constitute the sphere of virtue's action, and according to various circumstances.

It is therefore evident that all virtues are in us by nature according to aptitude and inchoation, but not according to perfection, except the theological virtues, which are entirely from without.

Whether the natural law contains several precepts, or one only?

. . . All those things to which man has a natural inclination, are naturally apprehended by reason as being good, and consequently as objects of pursuit, and their contraries as evil, and objects of avoidance. Wherefore according to the order of natural inclinations, is the order of the precepts of the natural law. Because in man there is first of all an inclination to good in accordance with the nature which he has in common with all substances: inasmuch as every substance seeks the preservation of its own being, according to its nature: and by reason of this inclination, whatever is a means of preserving human life, and of warding off its obstacles, belongs to the natural law. Secondly, there is in man an inclination to things that pertain to him more specially, according to that nature which he has in common with other animals: and in virtue of this inclination, those things are said to belong to the natural law, which nature has taught to all animals (Pandect. Just. I, Tit. I), such as sexual intercourse, education of offspring and so forth. Thirdly, there is in man an inclination to good, according to the nature of his reason, which nature is proper to him: thus man has a natural inclination to know the truth about God, and to live in society: and in this respect, whatever pertains to this inclination belongs to the natural law; for instance, to shun ignorance, to avoid offending those among whom one has to live, and other such things regarding the above inclination.

Whether all the moral precepts of the old law belong to the law of nature?

. . . The moral precepts, distinct from the ceremonial and judicial precepts, are about things pertaining of their very nature to good morals. Now since human morals depend on their relation to reason, which is the proper principle of human acts, those morals are called good which accord with reason, and those are called bad which are discordant from reason. And as every judgment of the speculative reason proceeds from the natural knowledge of first principles, so every judgment of practical reason proceeds from principles known naturally, as stated above: from which principles one may proceed in various ways to judge of various matters. For some matters connected with human actions are so evident, that after very little consideration one is able at once to approve or disapprove of them by means of these general first principles: while some matters cannot be the subject of judgment without much consideration of the various circumstances, which all are not competent to do carefully, but only those who are wise: just as it is not possible for all to consider the particular conclusions of sciences, but only for those who are versed in philosophy: and lastly there are some matters of which man cannot judge unless he be helped by Divine instruction; such as the articles of faith.

It is therefore evident that since the moral precepts are about matters which concern good morals; and since good morals are such as are in accord with reason; and since also every judgment of human reason must needs be derived in some way from natural reason; it follows, of necessity, that all the moral precepts belong to the law of nature; but not all in the same way. For there are certain things which the natural reason of every man, of its own accord and at once, judges to be done or not to be done: *e.g., Honour thy father and thy mother,* and, *Thou shalt not kill, Thou shalt not steal:* and these belong to the law of nature absolutely.—And there are certain things which, after a more careful consideration, wise men deem obligatory. Such belong to the law of nature, yet so that they need to be inculcated, the wiser teaching the less wise: *e.g., Rise up before the hoary head, and honor the person of the aged man,* and the like.—And there are some things, to judge of which, human reason needs Divine instruction, whereby we are taught about the things of God: *e.g., Thou shalt not make to thyself a graven thing, nor the likeness of anything; Thou shalt not take the name of the Lord thy God in vain.*

22.2

Mathew Hale

(1609–1676)

Hale presents, with his usual thoroughness, the conventional view of his time: that man knows what is right and good by natural instinct. In this selection, he argues that reason and education cannot be the sources of such knowledge for mankind generally. It is taken from Section I, Chapter II, "Touching the excellency of the human nature in general."

3. I come now to consider of those rational Instincts as I call them, the connate Principles engraven in the humane Soul; which though they are Truths acquirable and deducible by rational consequence and argumentation, yet they seem to be inscribed in the very *crasis* and texture of the Soul antecedent to any acquisition by industry or the exercise of the discursive Faculty in Man, and therefore they may be well called anticipations, prenotions, or sentiments characterized and engraven in the Soul, born with it, and growing up with it till they receive a check by ill customs or educations, or an improvement and advancement by the due exercise of the Faculties. . . .

And if any shall say that there are or may be other means of propagation of those motions and inclinations in Men, namely, 1. A Traditional traduction of them into the World; and 2. The Exercise of the humane Intellectual Faculties upon the occurrence and observation of external Objects and Events: I answer,

1. As touching Traditional communication and traduction of those Truths that I call connatural and engraven, I do not doubt but many of those Truths have had the help of that derivation: But, first, such a Tradition possibly hath not been without interruptions by evil Education, and yet these Sentiments have obtained almost in all Ages and Places, though not without interspersion of certain corrupt additaments, obtained likewise by evil Custome or Education. But secondly, it cannot reasonably be supposed that a Tradition could so constantly and universally prevail and obtain among Mankind, unless there were some common consonancy and congruity of somewhat inherent in Nature which suits, corresponds and suffragates to that Tradition, and closeth with it, and accepts it.

2. As to the other, concerning the Exercise and Actings of our Intellectual Faculties, it must needs be agreed that those that I call Connatural Principles are in themselves highly reasonable, and deducible by a strong process of Ratiocination to be most true and most convenient; and consequently the high exercise of Ratiocination or intellective Dis-

The primitive origination of mankind. London, 1677. [Pp. 60, 62–63.]

course might evince their truth and excellency, though there were no such originally inscribed in the Mind: But this no more concludes against the supposition, than it would conclude against the supposition of implanted Instincts in Brutes; which as they are in themselves highly reasonable and useful to their ends, and evincible by true Reason to be such, as it may be any thing we know: So also many, though not all the actings of those Instincts might possibly in the Brutes themselves be elicited by a strong intention and exercise of their Phantasie and sensible Perception, Ratiocination, and Connatural Implantation, are but several means or discoveries of the same thing which in it self is most highly reasonable; only the latter is for the most part less difficult, and readier at hand. But to the Objection.

1. Let any man but duly consider how few men there are in the World that are capable in respect of the meanness of their Parts and Education, to act and improve their Intellects or Faculties to so high a strain as the eliciting of those that I call Connatural Principles by the strength of their Intellectual Operation; this requires very choice Parts, great attention of Mind, sequestration from the importunity of Secular employments, and a long advertent and deliberate connexing of Consequents; which falls not in the common road of ordinary men, but of Philosophers, Metaphysical heads, and such as have had a more refined education, which is not the thousandth part of Mankind: Other men require a more easic and familiar access to these Truths and Inclinations; and yet we see that these Sentiments are not confined to the *Literati* of mankind.

2. Again, I appeal to the most knowing men in the World that have but had the leisure to think seriously and converse with themselves; and that have kept their Minds free from the fumes of intemperance and excess, passion and perturbation; whether next under Divine Revelation their best and clearest sentiments of Morality at least have not been gathered from the due animadversion and inspection of their own Minds, and the improving of that stock of Morals that they there find, and the transcribing of that Original which they found first written there: It is true, that it is with the connatural Principles inscribed in our Minds as it is with our Faculties, they lye more torpid, and inactive, and inevident, unless they are awakened and exercised, like a spark involved in ashes; and being either suppressed or neglected they seem little better than dead, but being diligently attended, inspected and exercised, they expand and evolve themselves into more distinction and evidence of themselves. And therefore it was not without some kind of probability that some of the Ancients thought that Science was little else than Memory or Reminiscence, a discovery of what was in the Soul before. But whatever may be said of other matters, certainly the first draughts and strictures of Natural Religion and Morality are naturally in the Mind.

22.3

Pierre Bayle

(1647–1706)

A great comet, which startled all of Europe in 1680, stirred widespread fears of impending catastrophe. Bayle, one of history's great spokesmen for rationalism, took this as an opportunity to combat superstition. Here he argues against the notion that religious faith and moral conduct are necessarily related, and in doing so points to the importance of irrational determinants of behavior.

[133.] I'm at you again, Sir, and begin, by telling you that the Reason on which our Doctor insisted most, was this: What induces us to believe Atheism the most fearful State, is only a common Prejudice concerning the Dictates of Conscience, taken to be the Rule of Human Actions, merely for want of examining their true Springs. For thus the World argues: Man is naturally a reasonable Agent; he never wills without knowing; he's necessarily determin'd to a desire of Happiness, and an aversion to Misery, and to preferring the Means which seem properest for these Ends. If then he's convinc'd there's a Providence ruling the World, from whom nothing is hid, which recompenses the Vertuous with endless Felicity, and the Wicked with everlasting Pains; he can't avoid following the Ways of Vertue, and forsaking Vice, and renouncing his carnal Lusts, which he's persuaded will retribute in never-ceasing Woes for a few Moments pleasure; whereas his denying these transitory Pleasures shall be attended with eternal Enjoyments. But if ignorant of a Providence, he considers these Pleasures as his chief End, and Rule of all his Actions; he makes a Jest of what others call Honor and Vertue; he's sway'd by every Motion of Concupiscence; he gets rid of those whose Discourses are uneasy; perjures himself for a trifle; and if he climbs to a Post which sets him above Human Laws, as he's already above Remorse, there's no Crime he'l stick at. . . .

[134.] This is all very fine and right, when one considers things in their Ideas and Metaphysical Abstractions. But the Mischief is, it falls not in with Experience. I own if People of another World were left to guess at the Manners of Christians, and barely inform'd they're Creatures endu'd with Reason and good Sense, thirsting after Happiness, persuaded there's a Paradise for those who obey the Divine Law, and a Hell for such as transgress it: they of another World cou'd not doubt that Christians vy'd

Miscellaneous reflections, occasion'd by the comet which appear'd in December 1680. Chiefly tending to explode popular superstitions [1682]. Translated [anonymously] from the French. 2 volumes. London, 1708. [Vol. 1, pp. 269, 271–272, 274–275, 279.]

continually in fulfilling the Precepts of the Gospel; that the strife among
'em was only who shou'd most excel in Works of Mercy, in Prayer, in
Forgiveness of Injurys, if possible any among 'em cou'd be capable of
offering any. But whence shou'd so favorable a Judgment proceed? From
their considering a Christian by the neat Idea only: for might they consider him in the gross, and by every blind side, they'd soon retract their
good Opinion; and, did they see only one Fortnight's way of the World,
declare the People here did not walk according to the light of their
Conscience.

[135.] Here's the true way of unfolding the Mystery. When one compares the Practice of a Man pretending to Religion, with the general Idea
conceiv'd of such a Man's Manners, 'tis surprizing not to find the least
Conformity between 'em. . . . Would you know the Cause of this Contradiction? 'tis this; The Person is not determin'd to one Action rather
than another, by the general Notices of Right or Wrong, but by his private
Judgment on the matter of the present Action. Now this private Judgment
may happen to sute with the general Ideas of his Duty, but for the most
part 'tis otherwise. He almost always follows the reigning Passions of his
Soul, the Biass of his Constitution, the Force of inveterate Habits, and his
Taste and Tenderness for some Objects more than others. The poet [Ovid]
who makes *Medea* say, *I see and approve the Good, but the Evil I do,*
represents the difference exactly, between the light of Conscience, and
the particular judgment determining our Practice. . . .

[136.] You may call a Man a reasonable Creature, as long as you
please: still it's true, he hardly ever acts by fixt Principles. In matters of
Speculation, he's so far Master as not to infer wrong Consequences; for
here he errs much more thro a Facility in admitting Principles which are
false, than in drawing false Conclusions. But the Case is quite otherwise,
where the Question is concerning Morality. Giving seldom or never into
false Principles, his Conscience ever retaining the Ideas of natural Equity,
he yet almost always turns in favor of his inordinate Affections. How
comes it, pray Sir, tho there's so prodigious a Diversity of Opinions concerning the manner of serving God, and the Forms of Civil Life; yet one
finds the same Passions reign eternally in all Countrys, and in all Ages?
That Ambition, Avarice, Envy, Lust, Revenge, and all the Crimes consequent on these Passions, are so rife all the World over? . . . Whence can
this proceed, but from hence, That the true Principle of Man's Actions
(I except those in whom the Grace of the Holy Spirit operates effica-
ciously) is nothing else than the Complexion, the natural Inclination for
Pleasure, a tast for particular Objects, a desire of pleasing others, the
Turn given us by conversing with one set of Acquaintance, or some other
Disposition resulting from the Ground of our corrupt Nature, whatever
Country we are born, or whatever Principles bred in? . . .

[138.] 'Twere endless answering all the Objections which may be rais'd
against this Doctrine: for the Mind of Man being subject to infinite

Caprice and Variety, no Rule can be laid down concerning it, not liable to a thousand Exceptions. The safest is that which is for the most part true, to wit, *That Man is not determin'd in his Actions by general Notices, or Views of his Understanding, but by the present reigning Passion of his Heart.* Upon the whole, did a drunken debauch'd Christian refrain stealing, because he knows God forbids Theft; wou'd he not refrain the two other Sins, since he knows they're equally forbid? And seeing he forbears only one of the three, is it not because he fears the Infamy or Punishment, or is not of a covetous Principle; or in general, that the turn of his Fancy finds no Charms in Thieving? To conclude, if Conscience were the Cause determining Men's Actions, cou'd Christians live such wretched Lives?

22.4

Anthony Cooper,
Third Earl of Shaftesbury
(1671–1713)

Educated in his grandfather's house, under the superintendance of John Locke, Shaftesbury acquired a love of learning, but not that strong empirical bent which we associate with Locke's Essay. He conceived of men as naturally good, a view which enlisted the defense of Hutcheson, on the one hand, and provoked the irony of Mandeville (in the next selection), on the other.

The Inquiry was a youthful work and is described in the Characteristicks as having been "formerly printed from an imperfect copy: now corrected, and publish'd intire."

'Tis impossible to suppose a mere sensible Creature originally so ill-constituted, and unnatural, as that from the moment he comes to be try'd by sensible Objects, he shou'd have no one good Passion towards his Kind, no Foundation either of Pity, Love, Kindness, or social Affection. 'Tis full as impossible to conceive, that a rational Creature coming first to be try'd by rational objects, and receiving into his mind the Images or Representations of Justice, Generosity, Gratitude, or other Virtue, shou'd have no *Liking* of these, or *Dislike* of their Contrarys; but be found absolutely indifferent towards whatsoever is presented to him of this sort.

An inquiry concerning virtue or merit [1699]. In *Characteristicks of men, manners, opinions, times.* Three volumes. London, 1711. [Vol. II, pp. 43–45.]

A soul, indeed, may as well be without *Sense,* as without Admiration in the Things of which it has any knowledg. Coming therefore to a Capacity of seeing and admiring in this new way, it must needs find a Beauty and a Deformity as well in Actions, Minds, and Tempers, as in Figures, Sounds, or Colours. If there be no *real* Amiableness or Deformity in moral Acts, there is at least *an imaginary one* of full force. Tho' perhaps the thing it-self shou'd not be allow'd in Nature, the Imagination or Fancy of it must be allow'd to be from Nature alone. Nor can any thing besides Art and strong Endeavour, with long Practice and Meditation, overcome such *natural Prevention,* or *Prepossession* of the Mind, in favour of this moral Distinction.

Sense of Right and Wrong therefore being as natural to us as *natural Affection* it-self, and being a first Principle in our Constitution and Make; there is no speculative Opinion, Persuasion or belief, which is capable *immediately* or *directly* to exclude or destroy it. That which is of original and pure Nature, nothing beside contrary Habit or Custom (a second Nature) is able to displace. And this affection being *an original one* of earliest Rise in the Soul or affectionate Part; nothing but contrary Affection, by frequent check and controul, can operate upon it, so as either to diminish it in part, or destroy it in the whole.

'Tis evident in what relates to the Frame and Order of our *Bodys;* that no particular odd Mein or Gesture, which is either natural to us, and consequent to our Make, or accidental and by Habit acquir'd can possibly be overcome by our immediate Disapprobation, or the contrary Bent of our Will, ever so strongly set against it. Such a Change cannot be effected without extraordinary Means, and the Intervention of Art and Method, a strict Attention, and repeated Check. And even thus, Nature, we find, is hardly master'd; but lies sullen, and ready to revolt, on the first occasion. Much more is this *the Mind's Case* in respect of that natural Affection and anticipating Fancy, which makes the Sense of Right and Wrong. 'Tis impossible that this can instantly, or without much Force and Violence, be effac'd, or struck out of the natural Temper, even by means of the most extravagant Belief or Opinion in the World.

22.5

Bernard Mandeville

(1670–1733)

Mandeville's satiric poem, "The grumbling hive: or Knaves turn'd honest" (1705) was a reply to Shaftesbury's Inquiry which had closed with an idyllic passage describing virtue as "the prop and ornament of human affairs . . . by which countrys as well as private familys, flourish and are happy." The poem opened with an account of "a spacious hive well stock'd with bees, that liv'd in luxury and ease" though rife with corruption. When reformers succeeded in rooting out all vice and fraud, economic disaster followed, leading to the final moral: "Fools only strive to make a great an honest hive. T'enjoy the world's conveniences, be fam'd in war, yet live in ease, without great vices, is a vain Eutopia seated in the brain." It was republished in 1714 with its new title, along with "An inquiry into the origin of moral virtue." The note from which our selection is taken was added in the second (1723) edition, but there it contained several confusing typographical errors which are corrected in the third. It consists of a long gloss on the lines: "Envy itself, and vanity, were ministers of industry."

Mandeville's significance (quoting A. O. Lovejoy) was in his "insisting on the sub-rational determination of most (if not all) of our motives." But perhaps his Dutch birth helps to explain his amused view of British society.

[Note N.] Envy is that Baseness in our Nature, which makes us grieve and pine at what we conceive to be a Happiness in others. I don't believe there is a Human Creature in his Senses arrived to Maturity, that at one time or another has not been carried away by this Passion in good Earnest; and yet I never met with any one that dared own he was guilty of it, but in Jest. That we are so generally ashamed of this Vice, is owing to that strong Habit of Hypocrisy, by the Help of which, we have learned from our Cradle to hide even from ourselves the vast Extent of Self-Love, and all its different Branches. . . .

Envy then is a Compound of Grief and Anger; the Degrees of this Passion depend chiefly on the Nearness or Remoteness of the Objects as to Circumstances. If one, who is forc'd to walk on Foot envies a great Man for keeping a Coach and Six, it will never be with that Violence, or give him that Disturbance which it may to a Man, who keeps a Coach himself, but can only afford to drive with four Horses. . . .

The fable of the bees, or private vices, publick benefits. Third edition. London, 1723. [Pp. 139–147.]

22.5 Bernard Mandeville

In the rude and unpolish'd Multitude this Passion is very bare-faced; especially when they envy others for the Goods of Fortune: They rail at their Betters, rip up their Faults, and take Pains to misconstrue the most commendable Actions: They murmur at Providence, and loudly complain, that the good Things of this World are chiefly enjoy'd by those who do not deserve them. . . .

The Men of Letters labouring under this Distemper discover quite different Symptoms. When they envy a Person for his Parts and Erudition, their chief Care is industriously to conceal their Frailty, which generally is attempted by denying and depreciating the good Qualities they envy: They carefully peruse his Works, and are displeas'd at every fine Passage they meet with; they look for nothing but his Errors, and wish for no greater Feast than a gross Mistake: In their Censures they are captious as well as severe, make Mountains of Mole-hills, and will not pardon the least Shadow of a Fault, but exaggerate the most trifling Omission into a Capital Blunder.

Envy is visible in Brute-Beasts; Horses shew it in their Endeavours of out-stripping one another; and the best spirited will run themselves to Death before they'll suffer another before them. In Dogs this Passion is likewise plainly to be seen, those who are used to be caress'd will never tamely bear that Felicity in others. I have seen a Lap-Dog that would choak himself with Victuals rather than leave any thing for a Competitor of his own Kind, and we may often observe the same Behaviour in those Creatures which we daily see in Infants that are froward, and by being overfondl'd made humoursome. If out of Caprice they at any time refuse to eat what they have ask'd for, and we can but make them believe that some Body else, nay, even the Cat or the Dog is going to take it from them, they will make an end of their Oughts with Pleasure, and feed even against their Appetite.

If Envy was not rivetted in Human Nature, it would not be so common in Children, and Youth would not be so generally spurr'd on by Emulation. Those who would derive every Thing that is beneficial to the Society from a good Principle, ascribe the Effects of Emulation in School-Boys to a Virtue of the Mind; as it requires Labour and Pains; so it is evident, that they commit a Self-Denial, who act from that Disposition; but if we look narrowly into it, we shall find that this Sacrifice of Ease and Pleasure is only made to Envy, and the Love of Glory. . . .

As every Body would be happy, enjoy Pleasure and avoid Pain if he could, so Self-love bids us look on every Creature that seems satisfied, as a Rival in Happiness; and the Satisfaction we have in seeing that Felicity disturb'd, without any advantage to our selves but what springs from the Pleasure we have in beholding it, is call'd loving mischief for mischiefs sake; and the Motive of which that frailty is the result, Malice, another Offspring derived from the same Original; for if there was no Envy there could be no Malice. When the Passions lye dormant we have no apprehension of them, and often People think they have not such a Frailty in their Nature, because that Moment they are not affected with it. . . .

. . . How strangely our Passions Govern us! We envy a Man for being Rich, and then perfectly hate him: but if we come to be his Equals, we are calm, and the least Condescention in him makes us Friends; but if we become visibly Superior to him we can pity his Misfortune. The Reason why Men of true good Sense envy less than others, is because they admire themselves with less hesitation than Fools and silly People; for tho' they do not shew this to others, yet the Solidity of their thinking gives them an Assurance of their real Worth, which Men of weak understanding can never feel within, tho' they often counterfeit it.

22.6

John Gay

(1669–1745)

Gay takes the step which Hutcheson (12.4) had unaccountably omitted, and applies the principle of association to the problem of moral judgments. The author of this anonymous "preliminary dissertation" in the English translation of King's work (which first appeared in 1702 as De origine mali) might have remained unidentified if not for Hartley's reference to "the Rev. Mr. Gay" as having suggested to him "the Possibility of deducing all our intellectual Pleasures and Pains from Association." It has been called (by E. A. Burtt, The English Philosophers) "the first clear statement of the combination of associationism in psychology and utilitarianism in morals which was to exercise a controlling influence on the development of the next century and a half of English thought."

. . . I shall in the next place endeavour to answer a grand Objection to what has here been said concerning Approbations and Affections arising from a prospect of private Happiness.

The Objection is this.

The Reason or End of every Action is always known to the Agent; for nothing can move a Man but what is perceived: but the generality of Mankind love and hate, approve and disapprove, immediately, as soon as any moral Character either occurs in Life, or is proposed to them, with-

Concerning the fundamental principle of virtue or morality. In William King, *An essay on the origin of evil*. London, 1731. Pp. xi–xxxiii. [xxviii–xxxiii.]

out considering whether their private Happiness is affected with it, or no: or if they do consider any Moral Character in relation to their own Happiness, and find themselves, as to their private Happiness, unconcern'd in it, or even find their private Happiness lessen'd by it in some particular Instance, yet they still approve the Moral Character, and love the Agent; nay they cannot do otherwise. Whatever Reason may be assign'd by speculative Men why we should be grateful to a Benefactor, or pity the Distressed; yet if the grateful or compassionate Mind never thought of that Reason, it is no Reason to him. The Enquiry is not why he *ought to be* grateful, but why he *is* so. These after-reasons therefore rather shew the Wisdom and Providence of our Maker in implanting the immediate Powers of these Approbations (*i.e.* in Mr. *Hutcheson's* Language, *a Moral Sense*) and these Public Affections in us, than give any satisfactory Account of their Origin. And therefore these Public Affections, and this Moral Sense, are quite independent on private Happiness, and in reality act upon us as mere Instincts.

Answer.

The Matter of Fact contained in this Argument, in my Opinion, is not to be contested; and therefore it remains either that we make the Matter of Fact consistent with what we have before laid down, or give up the Cause.

Now, in order to shew this Consistency, I beg leave to observe, that as in the pursuit of Truth we don't always trace every Proposition whose Truth we are examining, to a first Principle or Axiom, but acquiesce, as soon as we perceive it deducible from some known or presumed Truth; so in our Conduct we do not always travel to the ultimate End of our Actions, *Happiness:* but rest contented, as soon as we perceive any Action subservient to a known or presumed *Means* of Happiness. And these presumed Truths and Means of Happiness, whether real or otherwise, always influence us after the same manner as if they were real. The undeniable Consequences of Prejudices are as firmly adhered to as the Consequences of real truths or arguments; and what is subservient to a false (but imagin'd) means of Happiness, is as industriously pursued as what is subservient to a true one.

Now every Man, both in his Pursuit after Truth, and in his Conduct, has settled and fixed a great many of these in his Mind, which he always acts upon, as upon *Principles*, without examining. And this is occasion'd by the Narrowness of our Understandings: We can consider but a few things at once; and therefore, to run every thing to the Fountain-head would be tedious, thro' a long Series of Consequences; to avoid this we choose out certain Truths and Means of Happiness, which we look upon as RESTING PLACES, which we may safely acquiesce in, in the Conduct both of our Understanding and Practice, in relation to the one, regarding them as *Axioms;* in the other, as *Ends.* And we are more easily inclined to this by imagining that we may safely rely upon what we call *Habitual* Knowledge, thinking it needless to examine what we are already satisfy'd in. And hence it is that Prejudices, both Speculative and Practical, are difficult to be rooted out, *viz.* few will examine them.

And these RESTING PLACES are so often used as Principles, that at last, letting that slip out of our Minds which first inclined us to embrace them, we are apt to imagine them, not as they really are, the *Substitutes* of Principles, but Principles themselves.

And from hence, as some Men have imagin'd *Innate Ideas,* because forgetting how they came by them; so others have set up almost as many distinct *Instincts* as there are *acquir'd Principles* of acting. And I cannot but wonder why the *Pecuniary* Sense, a Sense of *Power* and *Party, &c.* were not mention'd, as well as the *Moral,* that of *Honour, Order,* and some others.

The Case is really this. We first perceive or imagine some real Good, *i.e.* fitness to promote our Happiness, in those things which we love and approve of. Hence (as was above explain'd) we annex Pleasure to those things. Hence those things and Pleasure are so ty'd together and associated in our Minds, that one cannot present itself but the other will also occur. And the *Association* remains even after that which at first gave them the Connection is quite forgot, or perhaps does not exist, but the contrary. An Instance or two may perhaps make this clear. How many Men are there in the World who have as strong a taste for *Money* as others have for Virtue; who count so much Money, so much Happiness; nay, even sell their Happiness for Money; or to speak more properly, make the *having* Money, without any Design or Thought of using it, their ultimate End? But was this Propensity to Money born with them? or rather, did not they at first perceive a great many Advantages from being possess'd of Money, and from thence conceive a Pleasure in having it, thence desire it, thence endeavour to obtain it, thence receive an actual Pleasure in obtaining it, thence desire to preserve the Possession of it? Hence by dropping the intermediate Steps between Money and Happiness, they join Money and Happiness immediately together, and content themselves with the phantastical Pleasure of having it, and make that which at first pursued only as a *Means,* be to them a real *End,* and what their real Happiness or Misery consists in. Thus the Connection between Money and Happiness remains in the Mind; tho' it has long since ceased between the things themselves.

The same might be observ'd concerning the Thirst after Knowledge, Fame, *&c.* the delight in Reading, Building, Planting, and most of the various Exercises and Entertainments of Life. These were at first enter'd on with a view to some farther End, but at length become habitual Amusements; the Idea of Pleasure is associated with them, and leads us on still in the same eager Pursuit of them, when the first Reason is quite vanish'd, or at least out of our Minds. Nay, we find this Power of *Association* so great as not only to transport our Passions and Affections beyond their proper bounds, both as to Intenseness and Duration; as is evident from daily Instances of Avarice, Ambition, Love, Revenge, &c. but also, that it is able to transfer them to improper Objects, and such as are of a quite different Nature from those to which our Reason had at first directed them. Thus being accustom'd to resent an Injury done to our Body by a Retaliation of the like to him that offer'd it, we are apt to conceive the same kind of Resentment, and often express it in the same manner, upon receiving hurt from a Stock or Stone, whereby the hatred which we are used to place on voluntary Beings, is substituted in the Room of that Aversion which belongs to involuntary ones. The like may be observ'd in most of the other Passions above-mentioned. . . .

There is one thing more to be observed in answer to this Objection, and that is, that we do not always (and perhaps not for the most part) *make* this Association ourselves, but *learn* it from *others: i.e.* that we annex Pleasure or Pain to certain Things or Actions because we see others do it, and acquire Principles of Action by imitating those whom we admire, or whose esteem we would procure: Hence the Son too often inherits both the Vices and the Party of his Father, as well as his Estate: Hence *National* Virtues and Vices, Dispositions and Opinions: And from hence we may observe how easy it is to account for what is generally call'd the *Prejudice of Education;* how soon we catch the Temper and Affections of those whom we daily converse with; how almost insensibly we are *taught* to love, admire or hate; to be grateful, generous, compassionate or cruel, &c.

What I say then in answer to the Objection is this: "That it is necessary in order to solve the principal Actions of human Life to suppose a Moral Sense (or what is signify'd by that Name) and also publick Affections, but I deny that this Moral Sense, or these publick Affections, are innate, or *implanted* in us: they are acquired either from our own *Observation* or the *Imitation* of others."

22.7

David Hartley

(1705–1757)

Hartley was before all else a moralist. His attack on free will, clearly heretical by orthodox religious standards, was in keeping with his religious convictions about predestination, which had caused him to turn away

Observations on man, his frame, his duty, and his expectations. 2 volumes. London, 1749. [Vol. 1, pp. 371, 493–499.]

from a planned career in the church to practice medicine instead. He tells us that he was influenced by Gay and by Newton (8.9), but the deterministic system he constructed was overdetermined by the need to fit convictions already held about man's relation to divinity.

[Prop. 89] The Will appears to be nothing but a Desire or Aversion sufficiently strong to produce an Action that is not automatic primarily or secondarily. At least it appears to me, that the Substitution of these Words for the Word *Will* may be justified by the common Usage of Language. The Will is therefore the Desire or Aversion, which is strongest for the then present Time. For if any other Desire was stronger, the muscular Motion connected with it by Association would take place, and not that which proceeds from the Will, or the voluntary one, which is contrary to the Supposition. Since therefore all Love and Hatred, all Desire and Aversion, are factitious, and generated by Association; *i.e.* mechanically; it follows that the Will is mechanical also. . . .

[Prop. 99] There are certain Tempers of Mind, with the Actions flowing from them, as of Piety, Humility, Resignation, Gratitude, &c. towards God; of Benevolence, Charity, Generosity, Compassion, Humility, Gratitude, &c. towards Men; of Temperance, Patience, Contentment, &c. in respect of a Person's own private Enjoyments or Sufferings; which when he believes himself to be possessed of, and reflects upon, a pleasing Consciousness and Self-approbation rise up in his Mind, exclusively of any direct explicit Consideration of Advantage likely to accrue to himself, from his Possession of these good Qualities. . . . This is, in general, the State of the Case; but there are many particular Differences, according to the particular Education, Temper, Profession, Sex, &c. of each Person. . . .

Now both this general Resemblance, and these particular Differences, in our Ideas, and consequent Approbation or Disapprobation, seem to admit of an Analysis and Explanation from the following Particulars.

First, Children are, for the most part, instructed in the Difference and Opposition between Virtue and Vice, Duty and Sin, &c. . . .

Secondly, There are many immediate good Consequences, which attend upon Virtue, as many ill ones do upon Vice. . . .

Thirdly, The many Benefits which we receive immediately from, or which have some evident, though distant, Connexion with the Piety, Benevolence, and Temperance of others; also the contrary Mischiefs from their Vices; lead us first to the Love and Hatred of the Persons themselves by Association, as explained under the Head of Sympathy, and then by farther Associations to the Love and Hatred of the Virtues and Vices, considered abstractedly, and without any regard to our own Interest; and that whether we view them in ourselves or others. . . .

Fifthly, the Hopes and Fears which arise from the Considerations of a future State, are themselves Pleasures and Pains of a high Nature. . . .

And thus we may perceive, that all the Pleasures and Pains of Sensation, Imagination, Ambition, Self-interest, Sympathy, and Theopathy, as far as they are consistent with one another, with the Frame of our Natures, and with the Course of the World, beget in us a Moral Sense, and lead us to the Love and Approbation of Virtue, and to the Fear, Hatred, and Abhorrence of Vice. . . .

The Moral Sense or Judgment here spoken of, is sometimes considered as an Instinct, sometimes as Determinations of the Mind, grounded on the eternal Reasons and Relations of Things. Those who maintain either of these Opinions may, perhaps, explain them so as to be consistent with the foregoing Analysis of the Moral Sense from Association. . . .

. . . To me it appears, that the Instances are, as far as we can judge of them, of an opposite Nature, and favour the Deduction of all our moral Judgments, Approbations, and Disapprobations, from Association alone. However, some Associations are formed so early, repeated so often, riveted so strong, and have so close a Connexion with the common Nature of Man, and the Events of Life which happen to all, as, in a popular way of speaking, to claim the Appelation of original and natural Dispositions; and to appear like Instincts, when compared with Dispositions evidently factitious; also like Axioms, and intuitive Propositions, eternally true according to the usual Phrase, when compared with moral Reasonings of a compound Kind. But I have endeavoured to shew in these papers, that all Reasoning, as well as Affection, is the mere Result of Association.

22.8

Adolphe Quetelet

(1796–1874)

Quetelet's statistical studies of such phenomena as crime, marriages, children born out of wedlock, and suicides, led him to the view that men are not individually accountable for their actions, since the very regularity of these from year to year shows that they are determined by conditions not under the control of individual men. This emphasis on "moral statistics" not only gave a new aspect to the old problem of free will, but it also pointed to a hitherto unexploited source of data for psychology. One reflection of this influence is in the statements by Wundt, at a time when he was seeking new empirical foundations for psychology, that "it is

Traité de l'homme [1835]. Translated as Treatise on man and the development of his faculties. Edinburgh, 1842. [P. 6.]

593

statistics which first demonstrated that even love follows psychological laws" and "one can learn more from statistical information than from all the philosophers, Aristotle excepted" (Beiträge zur Theorie der Sineswahrnehmung, 1862, pp. xxiv, xxvi).

What idea should we have of the mortality of mankind by observing only individuals? Instead of the admirable laws to which it is subject, our knowledge would be limited to a series of incoherent facts, leading to a total misapprehension of the laws of nature.

The remarks we make respecting human mortality may be equally extended to man's physical and moral faculties. To attain a knowledge of the general laws regulating these latter (moral) faculties, a sufficient number of observations must be collected, in order to bring out what is constant, and to set aside what is purely accidental. If, in order to facilitate this study, all human actions could be registered, it might be supposed that their numbers would vary from year to year as widely as human caprice. But this is not what we in reality observe, at least for that class of actions of which we have succeeded in obtaining a registry. I shall quote but a single example, but it merits the attention of all philosophic minds. In everything which relates to crimes, the same numbers are reproduced so constantly, that it becomes impossible to misapprehend it—even in respect to those crimes which seem perfectly beyond human foresight, such as murders committed in general at the close of quarrels, arising without a motive, and under other circumstances to all appearance the most fortuitous and accidental: nevertheless, experience proves that murders are committed annually, not only pretty nearly to the same extent, but even that the instruments employed are in the same proportions. . . .

This remarkable constancy with which the same crimes appear annually in the same order, drawing down on their perpetrators the same punishments, in the same proportions, is a singular fact, which we owe to the statistics of the tribunals. . . . There is a *budget* which we pay with frightening regularity—it is that of prisons, dungeons, and scaffolds. Now, it is this budget which, above all, we ought to endeavour to reduce; and every year, the numbers have confirmed my previous statements to such a degree, that I might have said, perhaps with more precision, "there is a tribute which man pays with more regularity than that which he owes to nature, or to the treasure of the state, namely, that which he pays to crime." Sad condition of humanity! We might even predict annually how many individuals will stain their hands with the blood of their fellow-men, how many will be forgers, how many will deal in poison, pretty nearly in the same way as we may foretell the annual births and deaths.

Society includes within itself the germs of all the crimes committed, and at the same time the necessary facilities for their development. It is the social state, in some measure, which prepares these crimes, and the criminal is merely the instrument to execute them. Every social state supposes, then, a certain number and a certain order of crimes, these being merely the necessary consequences of its organization. . . . This observation is merely the extension of a law already well known to all who have studied the physical condition of society in a philosophic manner: it is, that so long as the same *causes* exist, we must expect a repetition of the same *effects*. What has induced some to believe that moral phenomena did not obey this law, has been the too great influence ascribed at all times to man himself over his actions: it is a remarkable fact in the history of science, that the more extended human knowledge has become, the more limited human power, in that respect, has constantly appeared. . . .

It would appear, then, that moral phenomena, when observed on a great scale, are found to resemble physical phenomena; and we thus arrive, in inquiries of this kind, at the fundamental principle, that *the greater the number of individuals observed, the more do individual peculiarities, whether physical or moral, become effaced, and leave in a prominent point of view the general facts, by virtue of which society exists and is preserved.*

22.9

Alexander Bain

(1818–1903)

The Scottish philosophers stoutly upheld the theory of innate moral dispositions; the associationists (including such men as James Mill and Bain, Scots by birth) argued for environmental influence. Here is another instance in which Bain brilliantly anticipated later developments. His account of the stages through which conscience is developed in the child is remarkably like Freud's later account of the development of the "superego." It is part of a chapter on "The ethical emotion; or, the moral sense."

21. I have purposely deferred the consideration of CONSCIENCE, as a distinct attribute or faculty, from a conviction that this portion of our constitution is moulded upon external authority as its type. I entirely dissent from Dugald Stewart and the great majority of writers on the Theory of Morals, who represent Conscience as a primitive and in-

The emotions and the will. London, 1859. [Pp. 313–316.]

dependent faculty of the mind, which would be developed in us although we never had any experience of external authority. On the contrary, I maintain that Conscience is an imitation within ourselves of the government without us; and even when differing in what it prescribes from the current morality, the mode of its action is still parallel to the archetype. I freely admit that there are primitive impulses of the mind disposing us to the performance of social duty (just as there are also other primitive impulses which dispose us to perform acts forbidden by social duty), of which the principal are the affections, sympathy, and the sense of our own dependence as well as of our interest in common with the rest of society; but the peculiar quality or attribute that we term conscience is distinct from all these, and reproduces, in the maturity of the mind a facsimile of the system of government as practised around us. The proof of this affirmation is to be met with, in observing the growth of conscience from childhood upwards, and also in examining closely its character and working generally.

22. The first lesson that the child learns as a moral agent is obedience, or acting according to the will of some other person. There can be nothing innate in the notion thus acquired of command and authority, inasmuch as it implies experience of a situation with other human beings. The child's susceptibility to pleasure and pain is made use of to bring about this obedience, and a mental association is rapidly formed between disobedience and apprehended pain, more or less magnified by fear. The peculiarity attending the kind of evil inflicted, as a deterring instrument, is the indefinite continuance, or it may be, increase of the infliction until the end is secured. The knowledge of this leaves on the mind a certain dread and awful impression, as connected with forbidden actions; which is the conscience in its earliest germ, or manifestation. . . . As the child advances in the experience of authority, the habit of acting and the dread of offending acquire increased confirmation, in other words, the sense of duty grows stronger and stronger. New elements come to be introduced to modify this acquired repugnance to whatever is prohibited by parents and teachers, and others in authority. A sentiment of love or respect, towards the person of the superior, infuses a different species of dread from what we have just supposed, the dread of giving pain to a beloved object. Sometimes this is a more powerful deterring impulse than the other. We call it a higher order of conscience to act from love than to act from fear. When the young mind is able to take notice of the use and meaning of the prohibitions imposed upon it, and to approve the end intended by them, a new motive is added, and the conscience is then a triple compound, and begirts the actions in question with a three-fold fear; the last ingredient being paramount, in the maturity of the sympathies and the reason. . . . If love, esteem, and reverence enter largely into the case, the remorse will correspond to the suffering endured from inflicting a wound on those we love, respect, or venerate.

22.10

G. Stanley Hall

(1844–1924)

After founding the early psychological laboratory at The Johns Hopkins University, Hall became the first president of Clark University and gave the department there its distinctive character as leader in child psychological research. He initiated a long series of questionnaire studies, beginning with the famous paper on "The contents of children's minds." Starting in 1894 many of these were based on printed questionnaires often widely distributed, but this study of lying by children is one of the early ones, conducted by Hall's lady friends of the Boston kindergarten. It marks a fresh pragmatic and empirical approach to problems of morality and religion, which will be developed further in Hall's book on Adolescence (1904).

Four tactful lady teachers from Mrs. Pauline A. Shaw's kindergartens in Boston examined 300 children of both sexes between 12 and 14 privately, by a carefully devised method which avoided all indelicacy to the childish conscience. The returns are divided into seven distinct species of lies, each is reported on with detail. I. *Pseudophobia,* where every deviation from painfully literal truth is alike heinous, where, "I think" or "perhaps" is silently interpolated, or "not" is said over hundreds of times to neutralize the guilt of intended and unintended falsehoods. Some even feared instant death like Ananias for even an unconscious misstatement, systematized palliatives, casuistic word-splitting, was the result. II. The *lie heroic,* which is justified as a means to noble ends. Here belong false confessions where strong children assume penalties for weaker ones. Children have a wholesome instinct for viewing moral situations as wholes, but yet are not insensitive to that eager and sometimes tragic interest which has always for all men invested those situations in both life and in literature where duties seem to conflict. . . . They declare, *e.g.,* that they would say that their mother was out when she was in, if it would save her life, giving quite a scenic setting to such a possible occurrence, adding frequently that this would not make it *exactly* right, though it would be their duty to do it, or that they would not tell a like lie to save their own lives. . . . III. *Truth for friends and lies for enemies.* With most children, as with savages, truthfulness is greatly affected by personal likes and dislikes. In many cases they could hardly be brought to see wrong in lies a parent or some kind friend had wished them to tell. Often suspected lies were long persisted in till they were asked if they would have said that to their

Children's lies. *Pedagogical Seminary* 1 (1891): 211–218.

597

mothers, when they at once weakened. Boys keep up joint or complotted lies which girls rarely do. . . . IV. *Selfishness*. Every game, especially, every exciting one, has its own temptation to cheat; and long records of miscounts in tallies, moving balls in croquet, crying out "no play" or "no fair" at critical moments to divert impending defeat . . . show how unscrupulous the all-constraining passion to excel often renders even young children. Lies of this kind, prompted by excitement, are so easily forgotten when the excitement is over that they rarely rankle, and are hard to get at, but they make boys unscrupulous and grasping. . . . Few will not give, and not many will not take prompts or peep in their books, especially if in danger of being dropped or failing of promotion. . . . Excessive emulations, penalties, opportunities, and temptations should of course be reduced, but it should be clearly seen that all these lies are at bottom, forms of self-indulgence, and should, in the great majority of cases, be treated as such, rather than dealt with directly as lies. . . . V. *Imagination and Play*. Much childish play owes its charm to partial self-deception. . . . If hit with wooden daggers in the game of war they stand aside and play they are dead. If they step on a crack in walking the floor or sidewalk, they call it they are poisoned. . . . Cagliostro found adolescent boys particularly apt for his training to subserve the exhibition of the phrenological impostures illustrating his thirty-five faculties. . . . We might almost say of children at least, somewhat as Froschamer argues of mental activity, and even of the universe itself, that all their life is imagination. Such exercise of their faculties children must have even in the most platonic school republic. Its control and not its elimination is what is to be sought in the high interest of truthfulness. . . .

VI. *Pseudomania*. The worst type of lies which may be called pathological are rare among children and are illustrated by passionate love of showing off, and false pretences, assuming new characters or going to a new place. A few children, especially girls, are honey-combed with morbid self-consciousness and affectation, and seem to have no natural character of their own, but to be always acting a part and attracting attention. Boys prefer fooling, and humbugging by tricks or lies, sometimes of almost preternatural acuteness and cleverness. This is the natural diathesis which develops girls into hysterical invalids, deceiving sometimes themselves and sometimes their relatives most, on whom faithcurers work genuine miracles, and which makes boys into charlatans and impostors of many kinds. . . .

Finally, children have many palliatives for lies that wound the conscience. If one says "really" or "truly," especially if repeated, and most solemnly of all, "I wish to drop dead this minute, if it is not so," the validity of any statement is greatly reduplicated. Only a child who is very hardened in falsehood, very fearful of consequences, or else truthful, will reiterate "it is so, anyhow," even to tears in the face of evidence he cannot rebut, while others will confess or simulate a false confession as the easiest issue. . . . To say yes, and add in whisper, "in my mind," meant no, among the children of several schools at least in one large city. To put the left hand on the right shoulder also has power, many think, to reverse a lie. . . . In short, hardly any of the sinuosities lately asserted, whether rightly or wrongly, of the earlier Jesuit confessionals, and all the elaborated pharmacopoeia of placebos they are said to have used to ease consciences outraged by falsehood, seem reproduced in the spontaneous endeavors of children to mitigate the poignancy of this sense of guilt.

In fine, some forms of the habit of lying are so prevalent among young children that all illustrations of it, like the above seem trite and commonplace. Thorough-going truthfulness comes hard and *late*, and school life is now so full of temptation to falsehood that an honest child is its rarest, as well as its noblest work.

22.11

Jean Piaget

(born 1896)

Piaget observes children at their games, questions them about the rules, learns their views about fairness and suitable punishment, and comes to the conclusion that moral judgment evolves in much the same way as their understanding of the rules that govern the physical world (see 18.9). This concept of a necessary pattern of development, guided in the one case by physical and in the other by social reality, strikes a balance between the nativist and empiricist points of view.

The analysis of the child's moral judgments has led us perforce to the discussion of the great problem of the relations of social life to the rational consciousness. The conclusion we came to was that the morality prescribed for the individual by society is not homogeneous because society itself is not just one thing. Society is the sum of social relations, and among these relations we can distinguish two extreme types: relations of constraint, whose characteristic is to impose upon the individual from outside a system of rules with obligatory content, and relations of co-operation whose characteristic is to create within people's minds the consciousness of ideal norms at the back of all rules. . . .

Le jugement moral chez l'enfant [1932]. Translated by Marjorie Gabain, as *The moral judgment of the child*. London: Routledge & Kegan Paul, 1932; Glencoe, Ill.: The Free Press, 1948. [Pp. 401–402, 404–406, 411–412.]

. . . Everyone is aware of the kinship between logical and ethical norms. Logic is the morality of thought just as morality is the logic of action. . . . It is therefore in no way surprising that the analysis of child thought should bring to the fore certain particular aspects of this general phenomenon.

One may say, to begin with, that in a certain sense neither logical nor moral norms are innate in the individual mind. We can find, no doubt, even before language, all the elements of rationality and morality. Thus sensori-motor intelligence gives rise to operations of assimilation and construction, in which it is not hard to see the functional equivalent of the logic of classes and of relations. Similarly the child's behaviour towards persons shows signs from the first of those sympathetic tendencies and affective reactions in which one can easily see the raw material of all subsequent moral behaviour. But an intelligent act can only be called logical and a good-hearted impulse moral from the moment that certain norms impress a given structure and rules of equilibrium upon this material. Logic is not co-extensive with intelligence, but consists of the sum-total of rules of control which intelligence makes use of for its own direction. Morality plays a similar part with regard to the affective life. Now there is nothing that allows us to affirm the existence of such norms in the pre-social behaviour occurring before the appearance of language. The control characteristic of sensori-motor intelligence is of external origin: it is things themselves that constrain the organism to select which steps it will take; the initial intellectual activity does actively seek for truth. Similarly, it is persons external to him who canalize the child's elementary feelings, those feelings do not tend to regulate themselves from within.

This does not mean that everything in the *a priori* view is to be rejected. Of course the *a priori* never manifests itself in the form of ready-made innate mechanisms. The *a priori* is the obligatory element, and the necessary connections only impose themselves little by little, as evolution proceeds. . . . It is neither a principle from which concrete actions can be deduced nor a structure of which the mind can become conscious as such, but it is a sum-total of functional relations implying the distinction between the existing states of disequilibrium and an ideal equilibrium yet to be realized.

How then will the mind extract norms in the true sense from this functional equilibrium? It will form structures by means of an adequate conscious realization (*prise de conscience*). To ensure that the functional search for organization exhibited by the initial sensori-motor and affective activity gives rise to rules of organization properly so called, it is sufficient that the mind should become conscious of this search and of the laws governing it, thus translating into structure what till then had been function and nothing more. . . .

. . . It is obvious that our results are as unfavourable to the method of authority as to purely individualistic methods. It is . . . absurd and even immoral to wish to impose upon the child a fully worked-out system of discipline when the social life of children amongst themselves is sufficiently developed to give rise to a discipline infinitely nearer to that inner submission which is the mark of adult morality. It is idle, again, to try and transform the child's mind from outside, when his own taste for active research and his desire for cooperation suffice to ensure a normal intellectual development. The adult must therefore be a collaborator and not a master, from this double point of view, moral and rational. But conversely, it would be unwise to rely upon biological "nature" alone to ensure the dual progress of conscience and intelligence, when we realize to what extent all moral as all logical norms are the result of cooperation. Let us therefore try to create in the school a place where individual experimentation and reflection carried out in common come to each other's aid and balance one another.

Chapter 23

CHARACTER, TEMPERAMENT, PERSONALITY

Although the epistemologically oriented psychology of the philosophers (and later of the laboratories) tended to ignore individual differences in style of behavior, these were not left wholly to the literary writer, for medical psychologists always acknowledged their importance. In general, the term character applies to a description of behavior which is oriented chiefly with regard to the social consequences of the person's behavior, while the term temperament applies to behavioral dispositions which are seen as resulting from the peculiar physiological make-up of the individual. The former tends to be literary, the latter of course medical. Character-writing has been an interesting side-show to psychology, but theories of temperament have a long, well-knit history, in which the compatibility of various systems is high enough to strongly suggest underlying validity. This continuity continues to persist into the present, though more sophisticated statistical approaches now lead us to speak of "factor loadings" and "variables" rather than of "types."

23.1

Theophrastus

(c. 372–287 B.C.)

After the death of Aristotle, Theophrastus presided over the Peripatetic school for 35 years. His major scientific work was as a botanist, but his book De Sensibus (On the senses, translated from the Greek into English by G. M. Stratton) is the chief source on early Greek theories of sense perception, and he is the probable author of the selection which will open the next chapter (24.1). Late in life, he wrote a series of character sketches which became the model for a class of literary writings that has some importance in the history of psychology. They were first translated into a modern language by La Bruyère, in 1687, but we take our selection from an eighteenth-century English translation. We give a paragraph from its introduction, and the whole of one characterization.

I have often thought, and as often wonder'd, and, perhaps, shall never cease to wonder, how it shou'd come to pass that there shou'd be so great a Diversity in our Manners, since all *Greece* lies under the same Air, and all its Inhabitants receive a like Education. As for my part, O *Polycles!* who have lived Ninety nine Years, and spent a great Part of my Time in the Contemplation of human Nature, who have convers'd with many Persons of all Sorts of Tempers, and, with much Diligence and Accuracy, compar'd both the Good and the Bad; I thought myself oblig'd to commit to Writing the respective Manners of both these Sorts of Men. And in doing this, I shall point out to you what is peculiar to each of them, in their several Ways of Living, and particularly describe their Behaviour in common Conversation. . . .

Of Mistrust

MISTRUST *is a Suspicion that all Men are Knaves.* When a mistrustful Man sends one of his Servants to Market, he never fails to dispatch another after him, to enquire what Price he gave for the Provisions which he bought. When he brings home a Sum of Money, which he has just received, he carefully tells it over every now and then in the Way, to see whether he has received his full Due. When he is in Bed, he calls his Wife to Account, and asks her if she has lock'd all her Trunks, seal'd the

The moral characters of Theophrastus. Translated from the Greek, with notes. To which is prefixed a critical essay on characteristic-writings. By Henry Gally, M.A. London, 1725. [Pp. 105–106, 240–242.]

Money-Bag, and bolted the Street-Door: And tho' she assures him that she has taken Care to do all these Things well, nevertheless this suspicious Fellow is not satisfied, but rises out of his Bed, lights a Candle, and, without having any Cloaths or Shoes on, goes about all the House, examines every Thing, and so at last, with great Difficulty, hardly gets to Sleep. When he goes to receive his Interest-Money, he always brings along with him some Witnesses, for fear that his Debtors should ever deny that they ow'd him the Principal. When his Coat wants to be scour'd, he does not send it to the best Workman in Town, but to him who gives the best Security that the Coat shall be safely return'd again. He never obliges any of his Neighbours, in lending them a Mug or a Cup at their Request, for fear that it should be broken or not return'd. A Man of this Temper is mistrustful of his own Servants to the last Degree: When he goes abroad, he orders his Footboy not to follow him, but to go before him, that so he may have an Eye upon him, and keep the Rogue from running away. When any one has agreed with him for something, and, not having ready Money enough about him, desires him to place it to Account, he immediately replies, *I wont trust you; you must either leave the Goods, or pay down the Money, for I have not Leisure to send for it.*

23.2

Galen

(131–200)

Galen's theory of temperaments, like the less elaborate earlier systems, dealt primarily with physical types resulting from imbalance of the four humors, and predisposing to certain illnesses. Among these, the syndrome called "melancholy" (or "black bile") had been prominent since early times (see 24.1). Although Galen has long been credited with describing sanguine, choleric, melancholic, and phlegmatic behavioral types, he did not actually do so. He did, however, assert that native constitution influences behavior, as in this selection.

The starting point of my entire discourse is the knowledge of the differences which can be seen in little children, and which reveal to us the faculties of the soul. Some are very sluggish, others violent; some are

Que les moeurs de l'âme sont la conséquence des temperaments du corps [That the manners of the soul are the result of the bodily temperament]. Translated (into French) by Ch. Daremberg, in *Oeuvres anatomiques, physiologiques, et médicales de Galien.* 2 volumes. Paris, 1854–1856. Vol. II, pp. 47–91. [Pp. 48–49.]

insatiable gourmands, others quite the contrary; they may be shameless, or shy; and they exhibit many other analogous differences, all of which I have enumerated elsewhere. Here it suffices for me to have demonstrated by an example that the faculties of the three species or the three parts of the soul are by nature different in little children. We can conclude from this that the nature of the soul is not the same for all; and it is evident that the word *nature* signifies, in this treatise, the same thing as the word *essence*, for if there were no difference in the essence of their souls, they would always perform the same actions, and the same emotions would be produced in them by the same causes. It is therefore plain that children differ from one another, as much by the essence of their souls as by its actions and emotions, and, since this is so, by its faculties.

23.3

Vindician

(flourished 4th century A.D.)

This is the earliest known description of a distinctive behavioral syndrome associated with each of the Hippocratic humors. This doctrine subsequently spread from the medical center at Salerno to all of Europe, and the phrases of Vindician's letter are repeated in many medieval medical manuscripts.

Daniel Le Clerc (Histoire de la médecine, 1702) says that Vindician was chief physician at the court of the emperor Valentinian and the teacher of Theodore Priscian. Augustine called him the greatest physician of his time, an endorsement which must have added to his influence in the Christian world.

Accordingly, the body of man is composed of four humors. In it there are blood, red bile, black bile, and phlegm. Each of these four humors resides in or rules in its proper place: the blood rules on the right side, in the organ which we call the liver, and the red bile rules there also; on the left side the black bile rules, in the spleen; the phlegm is in the head, and also in the bladder. The blood nevertheless rules in the heart.

In health the virtue of these same humors is, that the blood is warm, moist and sweet; the red or golden bile is bitter, dry and with a greenish fire; the black bile is acid, cold and dry; the phlegm is salty, cold and moist.

Epistula Vindiciani ad Pentadium [Vindician's letter to Pentadius]. In *Theodori Prisciani Euphoriston*, edited by Valentin Rose. Leipzig, 1894. Pp. 484–492. [Pp. 486–490.]

Each of these thrives in its own season: the blood in the springtime, from February 8 to May 8, for 91 days; red bile from May 8 to August 8; then there are 90 days of black bile, from August 8 to November 8, and 92 days of phlegm, in true winter, from November 8 to February 8.

The four humors also divide night and day among themselves. The blood rules for six hours, that is, from the ninth hour of night until the third hour of day [3 A.M. to 9 A.M.], then red bile rules from the third until the ninth hour of day, and then the black bile from the ninth hour of day until the third hour of night, and the phlegm from the third until the ninth hour of night.

They all exhale [are discharged?] through different parts of the body: the blood through the nostrils, the red bile through the ears, the black bile through the eyes, and the phlegm through the mouth.

Furthermore, these four humors are divided among the four ages, that is, the phlegm in childhood, along with the blood, from infancy until 13 years; then the red bile rules, with a portion of the blood, from youth until the twenty-fifth year; then until the forty-second year the blood is ruled for the most part by black bile; and from then until advanced age, just as in childhood, the phlegm rules, and at death they all return to their proper places.

Moreover these four humors determine the kinds of human conduct. The blood makes men of good will, open, moderate, cheerful, agreeable and energetic; red bile makes men irascible, clever, astute, capricious, lean, great squanderers and prone to dissipation; black bile makes men cunning and yet ireful, miserly, fearful, melancholy, sluggish, envious, often having black scars on their feet; phlegm makes men impassive, watchful, meditative, prone to become gray early, and of little courage. . . .

In fact it is not possible to be without these humors and they are possessed by all ages, but whenever one of them increases immoderately, then it produces a long illness, not only due to its immoderation and intemperance, but according to the particular age and the body. Each of these humors makes illnesses in different ages, when they have their increase. And the illness will be prolonged if the physician is inexperienced or negligent, and if he does not understand from which humor it arises.

23.4

Thomaso Garzoni

(1549?–1589)

One thinks of the Renaissance as fostering individuality, but a psychology of personality, as something more than the medically oriented theory of temperaments, was a product of the baroque period, when artists valued the element of surprise more than a studied harmony of the parts. Perhaps its first exponent was Garzoni, who in this work describes a large number of stereotypes, very much in the spirit of Theophrastus, poking fun at all. Garzoni writes one hundred years before La Bruyère, who is ordinarily considered the innovator of this class of literature.

Garzoni says that he will leave it to philosophers and physicians to speak of the brain as "the most important part of the body, the source of human life, the abode of the rational soul, the instrument and source of all animal faculties." He will use the word in a popular sense, as standing for a style of behavior. He describes 55 styles, classifying them as only the Italian language permits, into cervellini, cerveluzzi, cervelletti, cervelloni, cervellazzi. Our selection deals with one variety of the cervelletti, or petty brains. The immediately preceding chapter dealt with "petty brains who are vainglorious but most proper." They are masters of all social graces, know the manual of conversation by heart, take infinite pride in their special little collections and trivial distinctions. They are well pleased with themselves—but not so much as those to whom he turns next.

Of Petty Brains That Are Vainglorious and Pretentious

Surely there are not so many crickets on the earth, nor so many buzz-flies in the air, nor so many moths going to the light, as there are of these swaggerers, who today pretentiously go about in every town, in every country of the world. The number of vainglorious and pretentious petty brains was small in antiquity, compared to the moderns who now live. Caius, who placed himself among the gods, and erected so many statues to himself under the name of Jupiter Maximus—certainly he was a vainglorious and pretentious petty brain. No less vainglorious was Hanno of Carthage, who taught the birds to sing "Hanno is god." Pretentious, too, the petty brain of Varro, who believed that he could sing better than the very Muses. And Themison of Cyprus, who was pleased to have himself called Hercules. And Domitian, who in his edicts styled

Il theatro de' vari e diversi cervelli mondani [The theatre of all the different sorts of worldly brains]. Venice, 1583. [Ll. 50–51.]

himself "Our Lord and God." And above all the heretic Manes, who dared to preach that he was born of a Virgin. And sinful Nestor, who, in a speech to the people of Constantinople, promised that he personally would give paradise to all of them. In truth, these were most pretentious, but they are rare in past ages, standing well apart from one another, in their variety as well as in time. But now the sack is truly filled, the measure brimful for real with these arrogant and overly presumptuous fellows, who claim that they have good heads for everything, admiring themselves and disparaging, even deriding, everybody else. . . . Parrots do not make such a show over knowing four words, learned from their masters with such great pains, as do these fellows, bragging about the disgraceful hits they have scored on this fellow and that. An Indian cock does not put on such airs, in his fighting fury, as these fellows do in scuffles and contests to show that they have the best brain of our age. The peacock does not spread his tail so much as they spread themselves in their own praises. These petty brains ride with full sail spread to the wind of glory, any which way it blows. O how many, how many there are of this breed! One slobbers in verse, and would be Virgil. One sounds like a buzz-fly and would be Orpheus. One speaks like a clown and would be Boccaccio. An incompetent Doctor Cricket would be Galen. A legal hack would be a Bartolus in jurisprudence. A buffoon would be one of the sages of Greece. I see almost the whole theatre filled with these irrational fellows. Here the stupid ones are sitting, who would be Socrates; the ignorant who would be Aristotles and Platos; the brutish and deformed who would be Ganymedes and Narcissus; the paupered and vile who pretend to nobility. The inept who would govern, playing at being Lycurgus or Solon; the unmannerly who would be courtiers; the vain and silly ones who pretend to being brilliant; the country bumpkins who put on grand manners. God immortal, what a throng I see, how many benches are filled, how many pretentious heads there are in this theatre! One cannot distinguish them singly, one cannot count their true number; we could never reach the end of them if we would try. It would be as endless as the labyrinth of Theseus, or the chaos of Anaxagoras, or of the earth's widest sea. Rather, not to drown together with them, let us turn now to the big brains; we have spoken enough about all the sorts of petty ones.

23.5

Giovanni Battista della Porta

(*c.* 1538–1615)

*Della Porta was one of the pioneers of the scientific outlook, not himself
a discoverer but a popularizer. His work on physiognomy appeared in
four books (in Latin) in 1586, and was expanded to six books in 1591.
By 1655, it had appeared in more than thirty editions.*

*We are prone to think today of physiognomy as antiscientific, but it
was in fact a way of emphasizing the dependence of behavior on body,
a sort of physiological psychology. Some of della Porta's phrases are
borrowed from Galen (23.2). The use of animal models to explain differences in human disposition also comes down from ancient times, and was
not new with della Porta.*

[Bk. I, Ch. 1] Among all nations, and in all times, the art of divination has
been regarded as useful, illustrious, and most excellent. There has never
been a people so savage and uncivilized that it has not eagerly sought
the means of knowing future events, and how to recognize the inclinations of men, according to the various natural dispositions of the human
body. . . . From this great desire, as from a spring, there have come
forth many, many methods of divination, and among these *physiognomy*,
which is distinguished especially as the one which has its principal roots
in nature, and as being useful not only for knowing others but also for
knowing one's own failings, and how to remedy them. . . .

We turn therefore to physiognomy, which is reliable, both because of
the clarity with which it shows the inclinations of men and the utility
which can be drawn therefrom. It is indeed true, as Galen and other
physicians have said, that by relying on its principles one can recognize
the faults of others, so as to be able to change them, and of oneself, so as
to cure them. And because we are thus able, as I hope to show, to foresee future events, this rare and excellent study has been pursued, loved,
and respected by all, because from the appearance, and from sounds,
and from the shape of the parts of the body it reveals the virtues and
the vices to which we are inclined.

[Ch. 2] All our experience shows us that our soul is influenced by
whatever affects the body, and that the passions of the soul influence the
body as well. There is a great fraternity between them, sharing for good
and for ill, and mutually influencing one another. Plato says that when

Della fisonomia dell'huomo, libri sei [On human physiognomy, six books]. Padua,
1627. [Ll. 1, 3, 4, 6, 14.]

weakness comes to the body the mind also weakens, as anyone capable of reasoning will understand. Vapors arising from the coarse, discordant mucous and the bitter and choleric humors which are present in the body penetrate into the remote parts of the soul and force it to become different—bold, wild, rough and unworthy. This happens to the sensitive or corporeal part of the soul, which is attached to the bodily organs. We see also that when the soul is ill, it is cured by giving medicine to the body. Someone who is in pain and sorrow, who drinks a good deal of wine, becomes happy, and loses his cares. . . .

. . . Solomon said that a melancholy mind dries the bones, but happiness fattens them. Madness is a disease of the mind, and when a physician cures the body, he cures the soul of its madness, because the cure of the body also cures the sensitive part of the soul of its illness. Thus the dispositions of the body respond to the powers and virtues of the soul, and the soul and the body are in such correspondence with one another that either can be the cause of the other's pain or pleasure. Nature has never made an animal which has the body of one animal and the soul of another, that is, a wolf or a lamb which has the soul of a dog, or of a lion; but the wolf or the lamb always has the soul of a wolf or a lamb, and from this it necessarily follows that in a given body there must be the soul which is proper to its species. . . .

[Ch. 5] . . . That our soul is influenced by the passions of our bodies is shown by infants, who do not act as they do through intent, instruction, or imitation, but solely as nature tells them. We see that in childhood some are fearful and others fearless; some greedy and insatiable while others patiently suffer hunger; some are shy and others shameless. Seeing this, we are forced to admit either that the soul comes into the body with these same passions, or that once it is in the body it finds itself compelled to act in this manner. That the soul should come into the body already tainted, and full of such vices, is a blind, ignorant, and mad opinion, and we are persuaded of this when we see that with changes in the temperament of the body, due either to time or to medicines, the passions also change. . . .

[Ch. 15] Now we shall describe the parts, and the most notable habits, of all the best known animals, so that one who is not skilled in the natural history of animals will not have to hunt for this in many books. But first let us see what the ancients thought about this. Adamantius said that the habits of any animal can be known from its appearance, which is suited to those habits. Thus the lion is strong and prone to anger, and he has a corresponding appearance. The face of the leopard is delicate, but proud, full of deceit, and at the same time both bold and fearful, and his appearance is appropriate to his behavior. The bear is cruel, deceptive and ferocious. The wild boar has an inconsiderate rage. The ox is simple and honest; the horse fond of show, and desirous of honor. The fox is clever and insidious. The sheep is insolent, the goat

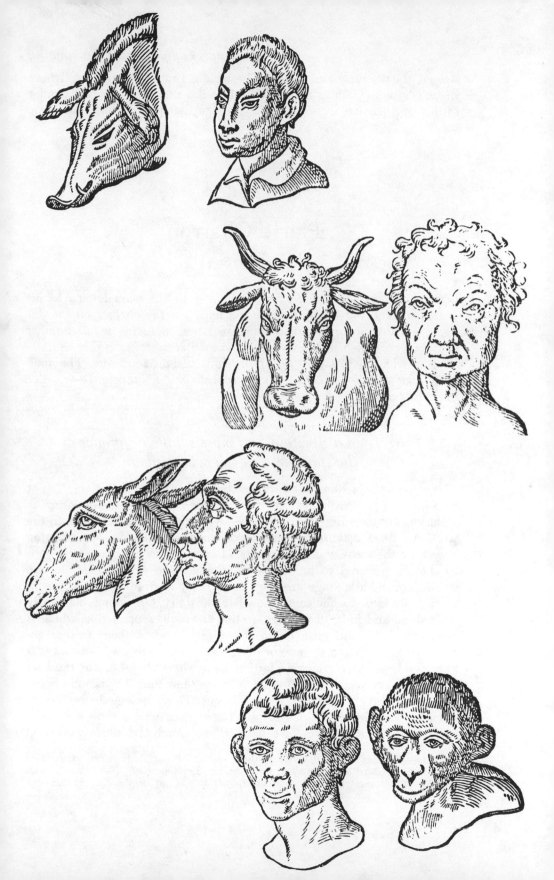

sensual, the pig dirty and greedy. The same is true of the reptiles, whose shape conforms to their habits. Therefore if a man has any part similar to that of a particular animal, this is a sign that he will have the same habits.

23.6

Pierre Charron

(1541–1603)

Charron, an avid compiler, classifies men in all the ways known to his contemporaries. For example, there is a fairly lengthy chapter on the differences between northern and southern types, including a fair number of stereotypes which still survive. But the chapter we select is one typically his own, which is to say, in the spirit of his friend Montaigne. The apologetic parenthesis—(here is nothing spoken of . . . religion)—was not in the first edition.

The second distinction, and more subtile difference of the spirits and sufficiencies of men

This second distinction which respecteth the spirit and sufficiency, is not so plain, and perceptible as the other, and comes as well from nature as atchievment; according unto which there are three sorts of people in the world, as three conditions and degrees of spirits. In the first and the lowest are the weak and plain spirits, of base and slender capacity, born to obey, serve, and to be led, who in effect are simply men. In the second and middle stage are they that are of an indifferent judgment, make profession of sufficiency, knowledg, dexterity, but do not sufficiently understand and judg themselves, resting themselves upon that which is commonly held, and given them at the first hand, without further enquiry of the truth and scource of things; yea, with a perswasion that it is not lawful; and never looking farther then where they be, but thinking that it is every where so; or ought to be so, and that if it be otherwise, they are deceived, yea they are barbarous. They subject themselves to opinions, and the municipall lawes of the place where they live, even from the time they were first hatched, not onely by observance and

De la sagesse, trois livres. [Bourdeaux, 1601; second edition, Paris, 1603]. Translated by Samson Lennard as *Of wisdom, three bookes.* London, 1658. [Ch. 43, which in the second and most later editions corresponds to Ch. 39 of the first edition. Pp. 158–160.]

custome, which all ought to do, but even from the very heart and soul, with a perswasion that that which is believed in their village is the true touchstone of truth, (here is nothing spoken of divine revealed truth, or religion) the onely, or at least the best rule to live well. These sorts of people are of the school and jurisdiction of Aristotle, affirmers, positive men, dogmatists, who respect more utility than verity, according to the use and custome of the world, then that which is good and true in it self. Of this condition there are a very great number, and divers degrees; the principal and most active amongst them govern the world, and have the command in their hand. In the third and highest stage are men indued with a quick and clear spirit, a strong, firm, and solid judgment, who are not content with a bare affirmation, nor settle themselves in common received opinions, nor suffer themselves to be wonne and preoccupated by a publick and common belief, whereof they wonder not at all, knowledg that there are many cosenages, deceits and impostures received in the world with approbation and applause, yea publick adoration and reverence: but they examine all things that are proposed, sound maturely, and seek without passion the causes, motives, and jurisdictions even to the root, loving better to doubt, and to hold in suspense their belief, then by a loose and idle facilitie or lightness, or precipitation of judgment to feed themselves with lies, and affirm or secure themselves of that thing whereof they can have no certain reason. These are but few in number, of the Schoole of *Socrates* and *Plato*, modest, sober, stayed, considering more the verity and reality of things then the utility; who if they be well born, having with that above mentioned probity and government in manners, they are truly wise, and such as here we seek after. But because they agree not with the common sort, as touching opinions, see more cleerly, pierce more deeply, and are not so facil and easie drawn to believe, they are suspected and little esteemed of others, who are far more in number, and held for phantasticks and Philosophers, a word which they use in a wrong sense, to wrong others. In the first of these three degrees or orders there is far greater number then in the second, and in the second then in the third. They of the first and last, the lowest and highest, trouble not the world, make no stir, the one for insufficiency and weakness, the other by reason of too great sufficiency, stability, and wisedom. They of the middle make all the stir, the disputations that are in the world, a presumptuous kinde of people, always stirred, and always stirring. They of the lower rank, as the bottom, the less, the sink, resemble the earth, which doth nothing but receive and suffer that which comes from above. They of the middle resemble the region of the air, wherein are formed all the meteors, thundrings, and alterations are made, which afterwards fall upon the earth. They of the higher stage resemble the firmament it self, or at least the highest region next unto heaven, pure, clear, neat and peaceable. This difference of men proceedeth partly from the nature of the first composition and temperature of the brain, which is different, moist, hot, dry, and that in many degrees, whereby the spirits and judgments are either very solid, courageous, or feeble, fearful, plain: and partly from instruction and discipline; as also from the experience and practice of the world, which serveth to put off simplicity, and to become more advised. Lastly, all these three sorts of people are found under every robe, form and condition both of good and evil men, but diversly.

2. There is another distinction of spirits and sufficiencies; for some there are that make way themselves, and are their own guides and governours. These are happy, of the higher sort, and very rare; need only a little light, it is enough if they have a guide and a torch to go before them, they will willingly and easily follow. Others there are that must be drawn, they need a spurr, and must be led by the hand. I speak not of those that either by reason of their great weakness cannot, as they are of the lower range, or the malignity of their nature will not, as they are of the middle, who are neither good to follow, nor will suffer themselves to be drawn and directed, for these are a people past all hope.

23.7

Nicholas Culpeper

(1616–1654)

Culpeper annotates Galen, giving much the longest gloss to Galen's brief account of the "signs of a cold and dry temperature." We omit paragraphs dealing with the physique, recommended diet, and exercise for each of the temperaments and give only the paragraphs describing their "conditions," that is, their typical behavior.

A Man or Woman in whose Body heat and moisture abounds, is said to be Sanguine of Complexion. . . .

As for their Conditions, they are merry cheerful Creatures, bounteful, pitiful, merciful, Courteous, bold, trusty, given much to the games of *Venus*, as thowgh they had been an Apprentice seven years To the Trade, a little thing Will make them weep, but as soon as 'tis over no further grief sticks to their Hearts. . . .

We call that Man Cholerick in whose Body heat and driness abound or is predominate. . . .

As for Conditions they are naturally quick witted, bold, no way

Galen's Art of Physick, translated into English . . . by Nich. Culpeper, Student in Physick and Astrology. London, 1657. [Pp. 84–99.]

shame-fac'd, furious, hasty, quarrelsom, fraudulent, eloquent, corragious, stout-hearted Creatures not given to sleep much, but much given to jesting, mocking, and lying. . . .

A Melancholy person is one in whose Body cold and driness predominate, and not such a one as is sad sometimes as the vulgar dream. . . .

They are naturally Covetous, Self-lovers, Cowards afraid of their own Shadows, fearful, careful, solitary, lumpish, unsociable, delighting to be alone, stubborn, ambitious, Envious, of deep cogitation, obstinate in Opinion, mistrustful, suspicious, spiteful, squemish, and yet slovenly, they retain Anger long, and aim at no smal things. . . .

Such People in whom coldness with moisture abounds are called Flegmatick. . . .

As for Conditions, they are very dull, heavy and slothful, like the Scholler that was agreat while a learning a Lesson but *Once* he had it— he had quickly forgotten it: They are drowsie, sleepy, cowardly, forgetful Creatures, as swift in motion as a Snail, they travail (and that's but seldom) as though they intended to go 15. miles in 14. daies, yet are they shamefac'd and sober. . . .

Thus much for their Complexions taken Singly by themselves without commixture one with another. . . .

I come now to their Commixture, which as far as I can find within the compass of my *Pia Mater,* are those that follow.

1. Chollerick-Melancholly.
2. Melancholly-Chollerick.
3. Melancholly-Sanguine.
4. Sanguine-Melancholly.
5. Sanguine-Flegmatick.
6. Flegmatick-Sanguine.
7. Flegmatick-Cholerick.
8. Chollerick-Flegmatick.

Let none object to me, that their may be more commixtures than these, as *Collerick-Sanguine Flegmatick-Melancholly* and the like, for I can scarce believe it and if you do but heed how and in what order the Signs of the Zodiack arise, you may happily be of my opinion, and therefore of these, and these only in order.

It is a thing very difficult if not impossible to find a man in whom two Complexions are equally predominant, but one will more or less excel, therefore where Choller exceeds in chief, and next that Melancholly, that man I call Cholerick-Melancholly. . . .

Such peopel by natural inclination are very quick Witted, excellent Students, yet will they begin many businesses ere they finish one, they are bold, furious, quarrelsom, something fraudulent, prodigal and eloquent they are not so unconstant and scornful as Chollerick men are, but more suspitious, and fretful, more solitary and studious after Curiosities, and retain their anger longer than Cholerick men do. . . .

[Melancholly-Cholerick:] As for Conditions they are very gentle and sober, willing to do good, admirable students, delighting to be alone, very shamefac'd and bashful, somewhat fretful, constant to their Friends, and true in all their actions. . . .

[Melancholly-Sanguine:] They are more liberal, and merrier than Melancholly persons are, as also less cowardly, not so pensive nor solitary, neither are they troubled with such fearful conceits, but are gentle, sober, patient, trusty, affable, courteous, studious to do others good. . . .

[Sanguine-Melancholly:] Their Conditions are much like the Conditions of a Sanguine Man, but that they are not altogether so merry nor so liberal, a spice of a Melancholly temper being inherent in them. . . .

[Sanguine-Flegmatick:] As for Conditions they are less liberal and not so much addicted to the Sports of *Venus* as Sanguine are, neither are their spirits so bold, nor their Bodies so hairy. . . .

[Flegmatick-Sanguine:] Their Conditions are so-so, between Flegmatick and Sanguine; neither very liberal nor very covetous, neither very idle nor much imployed, neither very merry nor very sad; rather fearful of the two than valiant. . . .

[Flegmatick-Cholerick:] They are not such drowsie, lazy, sleepy Creatures as Flegmatick folks are, but are nimbler, bolder, and kinder, merrier, and quicker witted. . . .

[Colerick-Flegmatick:] Their Conditions are not much different from those of Chollerick men, only the Vices of Choller is moderated by Flegm, therefore a Chollerick-Flegmatick man is nothing so vicious as one purely Chollerick; neither doth any Humour set a stop to the unbridled passions of Choller, so as Flegm doth, because 'tis so contrary to it; judg the like by the rest.

23.8

Johann Kaspar Lavater

(1741–1801)

Lavater was a man of religion and an inspirational poet, who wrote his physiognomic essays almost as sermons. His works were fashionable rather than profound, and it is said that they owed their success to the sump-

Physiognomische Fragmente zur Beförderung der Menschenkenntnis und Menschenliebe. 4 volumes. Leipzig and Winterthur, 1775–1778. Translated (from the French!) by Henry Hunter, as *Essays on Physiognomy, designed to promote the knowledge and love of mankind.* Illustrated by Thomas Holloway. 3 volumes in 5. London, 1789–1798. [Vol. III, pp. 391–393.]

tuous manner in which they were published. The edition from which we take this selection consists of five elegant folio volumes, luxuriously printed and handsomely bound, with more than 800 engravings, and a list of subscribers which reads like a social registry of Britain. Lavater cannot be dismissed as merely popular, because he had great influence. The time when this work appeared coincided with the years in which the young Gall, as he later related, studied the facial structure of his fellow students and found there [not in Lavater?] the indications for his future work. Lavater created some stereotypes and perpetuated others, and doubtless was responsible for the great vogue of silhouette portraiture in the nineteenth century.

The Cheeks

The cheeks, properly speaking, are not parts of the face. We must consider them as the ground of the other parts, or rather as the ground of the sensitive and vivified organs of the face. They are the feeling of the physiognomy.

Fleshy cheeks indicate, in general, humidity of temperament, and sensual appetite; lean and shrivelled, they announce dryness of humours, and privation of enjoyment. Chagrin hollows them—rudeness and brutality impress on them gross ridges—wisdom, experience, and ingenuity, intersect them with traces slight and gently undulated. The difference of the physical, moral, and intellectual character of man, depends on the smoothing or swelling of the muscles, on their sinking and contraction, on their appearance or imperceptibility, finally on their undulation, or rather on that of the small wrinkles or clefts, which are determined by the specific nature of the muscles. Shew to an experienced, and happily organized Physionomist, the simple contour of the section which extends from the wing of the nose to the chin; shew him this muscle in a state of rest and in a state of motion; shew it him especially at the moment when it is agitated by laughter or by tears, by a sense of pleasure or of pain, by pity or indignation—and this trait will supply a text for important observations. This trait, when it is marked by slight contours, gently shaded and intersected, becomes of infinite expression: it conveys the finest emotions of the soul; and this trait, carefully studied, will be sufficient to inspire you with the most profound veneration, and the most tender affection. Painters almost always neglect it, and their portraits favour very disadvantageously this neglect, from an insipid and trivial air perceptible in them.

Certain hollows, more or less triangular, which may sometimes be remarked in the cheeks, are the infallible signs of envy or of jealousy.

A cheek naturally graceful, agitated by a gentle transport which raises it towards the eyes, is the pledge of a heart sensible, generous, incapable of the least meanness. Trust not too far to a man who never smiles agreeably. A gracefulness in smiling may serve as a barometer to goodness of heart, and dignity of character.

The Chin

Long experience has demonstrated to me, that an advancing chin always announced something positive; whereas the signification of a retreating chin is always negative. Frequently the character of energy in the individual, or the want of energy, is manifested by the chin alone.

A deep incision in the middle of the chin seems to indicate, beyond contradiction, a man judicious, staid, and resolute, unless this trait is belied by other contradictory traits. We shall presently verify this assertion by examples.

A pointed chin usually passes for the sign of cunning. I have, however, met with this form in persons the most honourable: in them, cunning was only a more refined goodness.

A double chin soft, and fleshy, is, for the most part, the mark and the effect of sensuality. Angular chins are scarcely ever seen but in persons sensible, firm, and benevolent. Flat chins suppose coldness and dryness of temperament. The small characterize timidity. The round, with a dimple, may be considered as the pledge of goodness.

I establish three general classes for the different forms of chin.

In the first I rank chins which retreat. In the second, those which in profile are in a perpendicular line with the under lip. In the third, such as project beyond the under lip, or in other words, pointed chins. The retreating chin—which we may confidently call the feminine chin, as we find it in almost all persons of that sex—always excited in me a suspicion of some weak side. Chins of the second class inspire me with confidence. Those of the third support, in my judgment, the idea of a mind active and acute, provided they do not present the form of a handle, for this exaggerated form usually leads to pusillanimity and avarice.

23.9

Francis Galton

(1822–1911)

Galton had hoped that visual imagery might be a useful index of mental power generally. Disappointed in this, he went on to study differences by age, sex, profession, and just individual disposition. Aside from providing

Inquiries into human faculty and its development. London, 1883. [Pp. 83–88, 92–93.]

one of the earliest examples of questionnaire research, he created an important tool for quantitative study of qualitatively varying responses: a rating scale based on selection of strategically situated instances from the ordered arrangement of all the responses of a standardizing population.

Anecdotes find their way into print, from time to time, of persons whose visual memory is so clear and sharp as to present mental pictures that may be scrutinized with nearly as much ease and prolonged attention as if they were real objects. I became interested in the subject and made a rather extensive inquiry into the mode of visual presentation in different persons, so far as could be gathered from their respective statements. It seemed to me that the results might illustrate the essential differences between the mental operations of different men, that they might give some clue to the origin of visions, and that the course of the inquiry might reveal some previously unnoticed facts. . . .

. . . After the inquiry had been fairly stated it took the form of submitting a certain number of printed questions to a large number of persons. . . .

The first group of the rather long series of queries related to the illumination, definition, and colouring of the mental image, and were framed thus:—

> "Before addressing yourself to any of the Questions on the opposite page, think of some definite object—suppose it is your breakfast-table as you sat down to it this morning—and consider carefully the picture that rises before your mind's eye.
>
> 1. *Illumination.*—Is the image dim or fairly clear? Is its brightness comparable to that of the actual scene?
>
> 2. *Definition.*—Are all the objects pretty well defined at the same time, or is the place of sharpest definition at any one moment more contracted than it is in a real scene?
>
> 3. *Colouring.*—Are the colours of the china, of the toast, bread-crust, mustard, meat, parsley, or whatever may have been on the table, quite distinct and natural?"

The earliest results of my inquiry amazed me. I had begun by questioning friends in the scientific world, as they were the most likely class of men to give accurate answers. . . .

To my astonishment, I found that the great majority of the men of science to whom I first applied protested that mental imagery was unknown to them, and they looked on me as fanciful and fantastic in supposing that the words "mental imagery" really expressed what I believed everybody supposed them to mean. They had no more notion of its true nature than a colour-blind man, who has not discerned his defect, has of the nature of colour. They had a mental deficiency of which they were unaware, and naturally enough supposed that those who affirmed they possessed it, were romancing. . . .

On the other hand, when I spoke to persons whom I met in general society, I found an entirely different disposition to prevail. Many men and a yet larger number of women, and many boys and girls, declared that they habitually saw mental imagery, and that it was perfectly distinct to them and full of colour. The more I pressed and cross-questioned them, professing myself to be incredulous, the more obvious was the truth of their first assertions. . . .

Here, then, are two rather notable results: the one is the proved facility of obtaining statistical insight into the processes of other persons' minds, what ever *à priori* objection may have been made as to its possibility; and the other is that scientific men, as a class, have feeble powers of visual representation. There is no doubt whatever on the latter point, however it may be accounted for. My own conclusion is, that an over-ready perception of sharp mental pictures is antagonistic to the acquirement of highly-generalized and abstract thought, especially when the steps of reasoning are carried on by words as symbols, and that if the faculty of seeing the pictures was ever possessed by men who think hard, it is very apt to be lost by disuse. . . .

The facts I am now about to relate are obtained from the returns of 100 adult men, of whom 19 are Fellows of the Royal Society, mostly of very high repute, and at least twice, and I think I may say three times, as many more are persons of distinction in various kinds of intellectual work. . . .

. . . I cannot procure a strictly haphazard series for comparison . . . (but) the general result is that the above returns may be accepted as a fair representation of the visualising powers of Englishmen. Treating these according to the method described in the chapter of statistics, we have the following results, in which, as a matter of interest, I have also recorded the highest and the lowest of the series:—

Highest.—Brilliant, distinct, never blotchy.

First Suboctile.—The image once seen is perfectly clear and bright.

First Octile.—I can see my breakfast-table or any equally familiar thing with my mind's eye quite as well in all particulars as I can do if the reality is before me.

First Quartile.—Fairly clear; illumination of actual scene is fairly represented. Well defined. Parts do not obtrude themselves, but attention has to be directed to different points in succession to call up the whole.

Middlemost.—Fairly clear. Brightness probably at least from one-half to two-thirds of the original. Definition varies very much, one or two objects being much more distinct than the others, but the latter come out clearly if attention be paid to them.

Last Quartile.—Dim, certainly not comparable to the actual scene. I have to think separately of the several things on the table to bring them clearly before the mind's eye, and when I think of some things the others fade away in confusion.

Last Octile.—Dim and not comparable in brightness to the real scene. Badly defined with blotches of light; very incomplete; very little of one object is seen at one time.

Last Suboctile.—I am very rarely able to recall any object whatever with any sort of distinctness. Very occasionally an object or image will recall itself, but even then it is more a generalised image than an individual one. I seem to be almost destitute of visualising power as under control.

Lowest.—My powers are zero. To my consciousness there is almost no association of memory with objective visual impressions. I recollect the table, but do not see it.

23.10

Sigmund Freud

(1859–1939)

The Three essays on sexuality (18.6) dealt respectively with (a) universal dispositions to "perverse" sexual expressions, (b) infantile sexuality, and (c) transformations of sexual instincts occurring in puberty. The implications of this whole complex of startling ideas for the personality development of individuals, normal as well as neurotic, in the course of psychosexual development, were developed in the short paper on anal erotism published three years later. This is the starting point for the psychoanalytic theory of character types.

Among those whom one tries to help by means of psycho-analytic treatment, one very often meets with a type of character in which certain traits are strongly marked, while at the same time one's attention is arrested by the behaviour of these persons in regard to a certain bodily function and of the organ connected with it during their childhood. I can no longer say on what precise occasions I first received the impression that a systematic relationship exists between this type of character and the activities of this organ, but I can assure the reader that no theoretical anticipations of mine played any part in its production.

My belief in such a relationship has been so much strengthened by accumulated experience that I venture to make it the subject of a communication.

The persons whom I am about to describe are remarkable for a regular combination of the three following peculiarities: they are exceptionally *orderly, parsimonious,* and *obstinate.* Each of these words really covers a small group or series of traits which are related to one another. 'Orderly' comprises both bodily cleanliness and reliability and conscientiousness in the performance of petty duties: the opposite of it would be 'untidy' and

Charakter und Analerotik. *Psychiatrische und neurologische Wochenschrift* 9 (1908): 465–467. Translated by R. C. McWatters, as Character and anal erotism, in *Collected Papers,* Vol. II. New York, Basic Books, 1959. Pp. 45–50.

'negligent'. 'Parsimony' may be exaggerated up to the point of avarice; and obstinacy may amount to defiance, with which irascibility and vindictiveness may easily be associated. The two latter qualities—parsimony and obstinacy—hang together more closely than the third, orderliness; they are, too, the more constant element in the whole complex. It seems to me, however, incontestable that all three in some way belong together.

From the history of the early childhood of these persons one easily learns that they took a long time to overcome the infantile *incontinentia alvi*, and that even in later childhood they had to complain of isolated accidents relating to this function. As infants they seem to have been among those who refuse to empty the bowel when placed on the chamber, because they derive an incidental pleasure from the act of defaecation; for they assert that even in somewhat later years they have found a pleasure in holding back their stools, and they remember, though more readily of their brothers and sisters than of themselves, all sorts of unseemly performances with the stools when passed. From these indications we infer that the erotogenic significance of the anal zone is intensified in the innate sexual constitution of these persons; but since none of these weaknesses and peculiarities are to be found in them once childhood has been passed, we must conclude that the anal zone has lost its erotogenic significance in the course of their development, and that the constant appearance of this triad of peculiarities in their character may be brought into relation with the disappearance of their anal erotism.

I know that no one feels inclined to accept a proposition which appears unintelligible, and for which no explanation can be offered, but we can find the basis of such an explanation in the postulates I have formulated in my {*Three essays on the theory of sexuality*}. I there attempt to show that . . . the peripheral stimulation of certain specialized parts (genitals, mouth, anus, urethra), which may be called erotogenic zones, furnishes important contributions to the production of sexual excitation, but the fate of the stimuli arising in these areas varies according to their source and according to the age of the person concerned. Generally speaking, only a part of them finds a place in the sexual life; another part is deflected from a sexual aim and is directed to other purposes, a process which may be called sublimation. During the period of life which may be distinguished as the 'sexual latency period', *i.e.* from the end of the fourth year to the first manifestations of puberty at about eleven, reaction-formations, such as shame, disgust, and morality, are formed in the mental economy at the expense of the excitations proceeding from the erotogenic zones, and these reaction-formations erect themselves as barriers against the later activity of the sexual instinct. Now anal erotism is one of those components of the instinct which in the course of evolution and in accordance with our present civilizing education has become useless for sexual aims; it would therefore be no very surprising result if these traits of orderliness, parsimony, and obstinacy, which are so prominent in persons who were formerly anal erotics, turned out to be the first and most constant results of the sublimation of anal erotism.

The inherent necessity for this relationship is naturally not clear even to myself, but I can make some suggestions which help towards an understanding of it. The cleanliness, orderliness, and reliability give exactly the impression of a reaction-formation against an interest in things that are unclean and intrusive and ought not to be on the body. . . . To bring obstinacy into relation with interest in defaecation seems no easy task, but it should be remembered that infants can very early behave with great self-will about parting with their stools (see above), and that painful stimuli to the skin of the buttocks (which is connected with the anal erotogenic zone) are an instrument in the education of the child designed to break his self-will and make him submissive. . . .

The connections which exist between the two complexes of interest in money and of defaecation, which seem so dissimilar, appear to be the most far-reaching. . . . In reality, wherever archaic modes of thought predominate or have persisted—in ancient civilization, in myth, fairy-tale and superstition, in unconscious thoughts and dreams, and in the neuroses—money comes into the closest relation with excrement. . . .

If there is any reality in the relation described here between anal erotism and this triad of character-traits, one may expect to find but little of 'anal character' in persons who have retained the erotogenic quality of the anal zone into adult life, as for example certain homo-sexuals. Unless I am greatly mistaken experience on the whole is fully in accord with this anticipation.

One ought to consider whether other types of character do not also show a connection with the excitability of particular erotogenic zones. As yet I am aware only of the intense, 'burning' ambition of those who formerly suffered from enuresis. At any rate, one can give a formula for the formation of the ultimate character from the constituent char-acter-traits: the permanent character-traits are either unchanged per-petuations of the original impulses, sublimations of them, or reaction-formations against them.

Carl Gustav Jung

(1875–1961)

While academic psychology still looked askance at Freud, Jung influenced the experimental study of personality, first by his early studies of word association, which drew attention to the possibilities of this method as a diagnostic tool, and later by his theory of types. This selection gives no hint of the finer distinctions between feeling, thinking, and intuitive types, nor of Jung's emphasis on the compensatory opposition of unconscious to conscious attitudes. But these features of the theory attracted little interest outside Jungian circles, whereas the contrast of introvert and extravert (paralleling a distinction often made under other names, as by William James in his description of the "tough-minded" and the "tender-minded") has come over into everyday speech, and it directly inspired many early efforts to use questionnaire devices for the measurement of personality traits. In many of these, introvert traits became the indices of neurotic tendency.

[559] . . . There are in nature two fundamentally different modes of adaptation which ensure the continued existence of the living organism. The one consists in a high rate of fertility, with low powers of defence and short duration of life for the single individual; the other consists in equipping the individual with numerous means of self-preservation plus a low fertility rate. This biological difference, it seems to me, is not merely analogous to, but the actual foundation of, our two psychological modes of adaptation. I must content myself with this broad hint. It is sufficient to note that the peculiar nature of the extravert constantly urges him to expend and propagate himself in every way, while the tendency of the introvert is to defend himself against all demands from outside, to conserve his energy by withdrawing it from objects, thereby consolidating his own position. . . .

[563] Although it is true that everyone orients himself in accordance with the data supplied by the outside world, we see every day that the data in themselves are only relatively decisive. The fact that it is cold out-

Psychological types, or The psychology of individuation [1920]. *The Collected works of C. G. Jung,* ed. by G. Adler, M. Fordham, H. Read, trans. by R. F. C. Hull, Bollingen Series XX, vol. 6. A revision by R. F. C. Hull of the translation by H. G. Baynes. London: Routledge & Kegan Paul, Ltd., and Princeton: Princeton University Press, 1971. (Copyright © 1971 by Princeton University Press.) Reprinted by permission of Princeton University Press and Routledge & Kegan Paul. [Pars. 559, 563, 566, 621, 623, 625.]

side prompts one man to put on his overcoat, while another, who wants to get hardened, finds this superfluous. One man admires the latest tenor because everybody else does, another refuses to do so, not because he dislikes him, but because in his view the subject of universal admiration is far from having been proved admirable. . . .

Now, when orientation by the object predominates in such a way that decisions and actions are determined not by subjective views but by objective conditions, we speak of an extraverted attitude. When this is habitual, we speak of an extraverted type. If a man thinks, feels, acts, and actually lives in a way that is *directly* correlated with the objective conditions and their demands, he is extraverted. His life makes it perfectly clear that it is the object and not his subjective view that plays the determining role in his consciousness. Naturally he has subjective views too, but their determining value is less than that of the objective conditions. Consequently, he never expects to find any absolute factors in his own inner life, since the only ones he knows are outside himself. . . .

[566] Hysteria is, in my view, by far the most frequent neurosis of the extraverted type. The hallmark of classic hysteria is an exaggerated rapport with persons in the immediate environment and an adjustment to surrounding conditions that amounts to imitation. A constant tendency to make himself interesting and to produce an impression is a basic feature of the hysteric. The corollary of this is his proverbial suggestibility, his proneness to another person's influence. . . .

[621] Although the introverted consciousness is naturally aware of external conditions, it selects the subjective determinants as the decisive ones. It is therefore oriented by the factor in perception and cognition which responds to the sense stimulus in accordance with the individual's subjective disposition. For example, two people see the same object, but they never see it in such a way that the images they receive are absolutely identical. Quite apart from the variable acuteness of the sense organs and the personal equation, there often exists a radical difference, both in kind and in degree, in the psychic assimilation of the perceptual image. Whereas the extravert continually appeals to what comes to him from the object, the introvert relies principally on what the sense impression constellates in the subject. . . .

[623] The introverted attitude is normally oriented by the psychic structure, which is in principle hereditary and is inborn in the subject. This must not be assumed, however, to be simply identical with the subject's ego. . . . The really fundamental subject, the self, is far more comprehensive than the ego, since the former includes the unconscious whereas the latter is essentially the focal point of consciousness. Were the ego identical with the self, it would be inconceivable how we could sometimes see ourselves in dreams in quite different forms and with entirely different meanings. But it is a characteristic peculiarity of the introvert, which is as much in keeping with his own inclinations as

with the general bias, to confuse his ego with the self, and to exalt it as the subject of the psychic process, thus bringing about the aforementioned subjectivization of consciousness which alienates him from the object. . . .

[625] . . . Should he become neurotic, it is the sign of an almost complete identity of the ego with the self; the importance of the self is reduced to nil, while the ego is inflated beyond measure. The whole world-creating force of the subjective factor becomes concentrated in the ego, producing a boundless power-complex and a fatuous egocentricity. Every psychology which reduces the essence of man to the unconscious power drive springs from this kind of disposition.

23.12

Ernst Kretschmer

(1888–1964)

Among modern typologies, that of Kretschmer, building upon the psychiatric classification of Kraepelin and Bleuler, has been most influential. The schizothyme-cyclothyme classification is prominent in the extensive experimental work of H. J. Eysenck and his collaborators.

. . . Three ever-recurring types of physique have emerged from our clinical material, which we will call 'asthenic', 'athletic', and 'pyknic'. . . . The way, however, in which these three types are correlated with the schizophrene and circular categories, is very varied and remarkable. Among healthy people we come across these types on every side; they have no foundation in disease, but they indicate certain normal biological tendencies of which only a small proportion comes to pathological culmination. . . .

Cycloid men are simple and uncomplicated beings, whose feelings rise directly, naturally, and undisguised to the surface, so that everyone can soon get a correct judgment of them. Schizoid men have a surface and a depth. Cuttingly brutal, dull and sulky, bitingly sarcastic, or timidly retiring, like a mollusc without a shell—that is the surface. Or else the surface is just nothing: we see a man who stands in our way like a question mark, we feel that we are in contact with something flavourless, boring, and yet with a certain problematic quality about it. What is there

Körperbau und Character . . . [1921]. Translated by W. J. H. Sprott as *Physique and character. An investigation of the nature of constitution and of the theory of temperament.* Second edition, revised. London: Kegan Paul, Trench, Trübner & Co., Ltd., 1936. [Pp. 20–21, 150, 214, 265, 267–268.]

in the deep under all these masks? Perhaps there is a nothing, a dark, hollow-eyed nothing—affective anaemia. Behind an ever-silent façade, which twitches uncertainly with every expiring whim—nothing but broken pieces, black rubbish heaps, yawning emotional emptiness, or the cold breath of an arctic soullessness. But from the façade we cannot see what lurks behind. Many schizoid folk are like Roman houses and villas which have closed their shutters before the rays of the burning sun; perhaps in the subdued interior light there are festivities. . . .

. . . We call the members of that large constitution-class from which the schizophrenes are recruited, "*schizothymes*", and those corresponding to the circular psychotics are called "*cyclothymes*". One may for convenience call the transitional stages between illness and health, or the abortive pathological forms, "schizoid" and "cycloid", as we have already done. We must, accordingly, make it clear from the outset, that the notions "schizothyme" and "cyclothyme" have nothing to do with the question: pathological or healthy; but that they are inclusive terms for large general bio-types, which include the great mass of healthy individuals with the few cases of corresponding psychoses which are scattered among them. The words do not indicate that the majority of scizothymes must have psychic clefts, and that the majority of cyclothymes must have periodical emotional disturbances; we are only using for the sake of convenience a designation for the healthy coresponding to that type which is already applied to psychopaths of the same type. . . .

. . . Inside the two main groups there is a further dual division, according as the cyclothymic temperament is habitually more on the gay or the sad side, and according as the schizothymic temperament tends towards the sensitive or the cold pole. An indefinite number of individual temperamental shades emerge from the psychaesthetic and diathetic proportions, *i.e.*, from the manner in which in the same type of temperament, the polar opponents displace one another, overlay one another, or relieve one another in alternation. Besides asking about the proportions of any given temperament, we must at the same time ask about its admixture, *i.e.*, about the tone which the particular type of temperament which dominates has got from inherited ingredients of other types. . . .

In their complex attitudes and reactions to environment the cyclothymics are in the main men with a tendency to throw themselves into the world about them and the present, of open, sociable, spirited, kind-hearted, and 'naturally-immediate' natures, whether they seem at one time more jolly, or at another cautious, phlegmatic, and melancholic. There emerges from them, among others, the everyday type of energetic practical man, and the sensual enjoyer of life. Among the more gifted members of the class, we find the broad expansive realists and the good-natured, hearty humorists, when we come to artistic style; the type of observant, describing, and fingering empiricist, and the man who wants to popularize science for the laity, when we come to scientific mode of thought; and in practical life the well-meaning, understanding conciliator, the energetic organizer on a large scale, and the tough, strongminded whole-hogger.

The attitude towards life of the schizoid temperament, on the other hand, has a tendency to autism, to a life inside oneself, to the construction of a narrowly-defined individual zone, of an inner world of dreams and principles which is set up against things as they really are, to an acute opposition of 'I' and 'the world', a tendency to an indifferent or sensitive withdrawal from the mass of one's fellow-men, or a cold flitting about among them with regard to them and without *rapport* with them. Among them we find, in the first place, an enormous number of defective types, or sulky eccentrics, egoists, unstable idlers, and criminals; among the socially valuable types we have the sensitive enthusiast, the world-hostile idealist, the simultaneously tender and cold, formal aristocrat. In art and poetry we find them as stylistically pure, formal artists and classicists, as romanticists fleeing the world, as sentimental idyllists, as tragic 'pathetics', and so on to the extremes of expressionism and pessimistic naturalism, and finally as witty ironists and sarcastics. In their scientific method of thought we find a preference for academic formalism or philosophical reflexion, for mystical metaphysics, and exact schematism. And, lastly, of the types which are suitable for active life, the schizothymes seem to produce in particular the tenacious energetics, the inflexible devotees of principle and logic, the masterful natures, the heroic moralists, the pure idealists, the fanatics and despots, and the diplomatic, supple, cold calculators.

23.13

Hermann Rorschach

(1884–1922)

Rorschach's ink blot test is probably the most widely used clinical instrument, and it has given rise to an enormous literature and much controversy. Needless to say, our excerpts omit mention of most of the dimensions on which it is scored, and this characterization of what may be called a hypernormal individual can only suggest the breadth of the diagnoses which are commonly based on this single instrument. Aside

Psychodiagnostik: Methodik und Ergebnisse eines Wahrnehmungsdiagnostischen Experiments (Deutenlassen von Zufallsformen) [1921]. Translated by P. Lemkau, as *Psychodiagnostics. A diagnostic tool based on perception.* Berne: Verlag Hans Huber, 1942. [Pp. 15–16, 36–37, 41.]

from its wide clinical use, it has great historic interest as the forerunner of many other projective tests of personality—tests which seek to penetrate the defenses of the individual by analysis of response to unstructured materials.

The experiment consists in the *interpretation of accidental forms,* that is, of non-specific forms. . . .

The production of such accidental forms is very simple: a few large ink blots are thrown on a piece of paper, the paper folded, and the ink spread between the two halves of the sheet. Not all figures so obtained can be used, for those used must fulfill certain conditions. . . .

The subject is given one plate after the other and asked, "What might this be?" He holds the plate in his hand and may turn it about as much as he likes. . . .

Almost all subjects regard the experiment as a test of imagination. . . . Nevertheless, the interpretation of the figures actually has little to do with imagination, and it is unnecessary to consider imagination a prerequisite. . . .

The interpretation of the chance forms falls in the field of perception and apperception rather than imagination. . . .

The normal subject goes at the experiment in somewhat the following manner. He first tries to interpret a given plate as a whole, searching his store of visual memories for something which coincides as far as possible with the entire figure on the plate. If his search is successful, we have a "Whole Answer," hereafter designated as W. This done, he goes on to the separate parts of the figure. He keeps to those parts which are most prominent because of their arrangement. We then have one or more "Detail Answers" (D). When the most striking details are exhausted, he goes on to the smallest details of the figure and gives, perhaps, one or more interpretations of these "Small Detail Answers" (Dd). The next figure is treated in the same way and the sequence W-D-Dd is repeated, and so on through the entire series as regularly as possible. A normal subject interpreting the plates in this schematic manner would give, perhaps, ten whole answers, twenty detail answers, and thirty small detail answers; a total of about sixty interpretations. Every plate would be conceived in the sequence *W-D-Dd.*

If there were a subject who would react exactly in this way, he would be so "normal" that he could no longer be considered normal at all in any practical sense. Among my many subjects not one has reacted in this "normal" manner. It is possible that some day such a subject will turn up. Basing my conclusions on observations of subjects most closely approaching the fictitious "normal," this man would have a psychological make-up something like this:—He would be a know all, have a large store of available associations, and would show a logic far beyond the range of anything that might be called healthy common sense. He would constantly impress one as tyrannical, grumbling, impatient and pedantic. He would also be very proud of his power and stamina of thinking, especially of his logical reasoning ability, but he would show no originality of reasoning nor sense for practical things. He would be original only in his desire to know and do everything. He would have almost no capacity to form rapport, would be empty of any temperament, but full of self-righteousness and pride. In fine, he would be a proud but sterile technician of logic and memory. Such would be the "normal" individual.

Actually the problem is more complicated. There are many associative and emotional factors which tend to modify this fictitious normal type. . . .

A series of *apperceptive types* may be differentiated according to the relationship of W, D, and Dd to each other as they occur in the protocols. . . .

23.14

Gordon Willard Allport

(1897–1967)

In most of its history and most of its branches, psychology has been a "nomothetic" science, dealing usually with a norm or even an ideal, occasionally with "types," but very rarely with individuals, unless they have been frankly regarded as abnormal. The individualized person has been a subject of art, not science. Allport calls for a new orientation, in which the focus of interest will be the individual's "unique" characteristics.

Somewhere in the interstices of its nomothetic laws psychology has lost the human person as we know him in everyday life. To rescue him and to reinstate him as a psychological datum in his own right is the avowed purpose of the psychology of personality. . . .

. . . To this end particular stress has been given to the following somewhat novel principles.

1. The proposition that psychology seeks laws has not been denied, but it has been shown that *a general law may be a law that tells how uniqueness comes about.* Part II of this volume is especially devoted to a discussion of laws of this order, the central one being the principle of

Personality: a psychological interpretation. New York: Holt, Rinehart & Winston, Inc. 1937. [Pp. 558–560, 562, 565–566.] Copyright © 1937 by Holt, Rinehart & Winston, Inc.; copyright © 1965 by Gordon W. Allport. Reprinted by permission of Holt, Rinehart & Winston, Inc.

the functional autonomy of motives. This law—altogether basic for the psychology of personality—accounts, as no other principle of dynamic psychology is able to do, for the concrete impulses that lie at the root of personal behavior.

In still another sense the psychology of personality deals with laws. One may say (with penetrating accuracy) that each personality is a law unto itself, meaning that each single life, if fully understood, would reveal its own orderly and necessary process of growth. The course of each life is a lawful event, even though it is unlike all others of its class. Lawfulness does not depend upon frequency nor upon uniformity, but upon necessity. There is a necessary patterning in each life, separate from every other life. . . .

3. . . . Biosocial impressions are like reflecting mirrors in an amusement park. Each distorts the face and figure in a different way . . . while still keeping some sort of likeness. But all the while there is only *one* person present; he remains single however much the reflecting images may multiply. The psychology of personality proceeds from the point of view of the person himself. It asks what *he* is like in his essential nature. . . . He himself is the datum; he *is* something and *does* something (or if one prefers, he is *many* things and does *many* things); but we can still find out what they are, viewed from *within*, from the person's *own* point of view.

4. Having accepted the biophysical conception it is vital to follow it up with the principle that *the analysis of personality shall proceed at significant levels only*. What are its natural units or substructures? They are certainly not specific habits nor identical elements, nor are they abstract dimensions gleaned from a comparison of mind with mind. The units of personality are complex neuropsychic dispositions, in this volume generically called *traits*. They are internally generalized, flexible, interdependent dispositions, attuned to a range of equivalent stimuli and issuing into an equivalent range of responses. It is their function to guarantee stability and economy in personal life. . . .

5. What is true of substructures is true likewise of total structure. The problem of the *unity* of personality is as much a subject for psychological concern as are its elements. . . . To be sure unity is never perfect, but only "high level" concepts of consistency are capable of depicting adequately such unity as exists. The common devices of correlation and other measures of correspondence are not sufficient. To express total organization new and more adequate formulations are needed. . . .

9. Another somewhat novel principle is the *empirical-intuitive theory of understanding*. . . . Its special significance lies in the fact that it does for the level of impression what the remainder of the book does for the objective level of study. Existentially considered, personality is a many-sided structure. It is also *perceived* as such (within certain limitations imposed by the process of judgment). To equate in this way the objective

and subjective representations of personality is a step toward the conceptual unification of the field as a whole. . . .

Thus there are many ways to study man psychologically. Yet to study him most fully is to take him as an individual. He is more than a bundle of habits; more than a nexus of abstract dimensions; more too than a representative of his species. He is more than a citizen of the state, and more than a mere incident in the gigantic movements of mankind. He transcends them all. The individual, striving ever for his own integrity, has existed under many forms of social life—forms as varied as the nomadic, feudal, and capitalistic. He struggles on even under oppression, always hoping and planning for a more perfect democracy where the dignity and growth of each personality will be prized above all else.

Chapter 24

MENTAL ILLNESS

The study and treatment of mental illness plays a large part in the history of psychology and perhaps occupies an even larger relative position in the interests of the typical student of psychology. To adequately represent the history of this field within the scope of a general source book seems an impossible task. Fortunately, there already exists an excellent anthology covering a large part of the field, in Hunter and Macalpine's Three Hundred Years of Psychiatry (Oxford University Press, 1963). This chapter is designed to supplement that fine work, rather than in any way to substitute for it. Our selections give an overview of the development of thought regarding mental illness from ancient times to the present. But for the monumental contribution of Freud, the reader is referred to selections 18.6, 19.9, and 23.10.

24.1

Theophrastus

(*c.* 372–287 B.C.)

Although traditionally attributed to Aristotle, modern scholarship has assigned the authorship of this so-called "monograph on black bile" to his successor, Theophrastus. It raises a question which has often intrigued critics of the arts: Is there a natural affinity between madness and genius?

Why is it that all those who have become eminent in philosophy or politics or poetry or the arts are clearly melancholic, and some of them to such an extent as to be affected by diseases caused by black bile? . . .

In order to find out the reason, we must begin by making use of an analogy: Wine in large quantities produces in men much the same characteristics which we attribute to the melancholic, and as it is being drunk it fashions various characters, for instance irritable, benevolent, compassionate or reckless ones. . . . Now, even as one individual who is drinking changes his character according to the quantity of wine he consumes, so there is for each character a class of men who represent it. For as one man is momentarily, while drunk, another is by nature: one man is loquacious, another emotional, another easily moved to tears; for this effect, too, wine has on some people. . . .

. . . Wine makes a man abnormal, not for long, but for a short time only, but a man's natural constitution does it permanently, for his whole lifetime; for some are bold, others taciturn, others compassionate and others cowardly by nature. It is therefore clear that it is the same agent that produces character both in the case of wine and of the individual nature, for all processes are governed by heat. Now melancholy, both the humour and the temperament, produce air; wherefore the physicians say that flatulence and abdominal disorders are due to black bile. Now wine too has the quality of generating air, so wine and the melancholy temperament are of a similar nature. . . .

It is for this reason that wine excites sexual desire, and Dionysus and Aphrodite are rightly said to belong together, and most melancholy persons are lustful. For the sexual act is connected with the generation of air, as is shown by the fact that the virile organ quickly increases from a small size by inflation. . . .

. . . To most people the bile engendered from their daily nutriment

"Problem 30 (1)." Translated in R. Klibansky, F. Saxl, and E. Panofsky, *Saturn and melancholia: Studies in the history of natural philosophy, religion, and art.* Sunbury-On-Thames, Middlesex, England: Thomas Nelson & Sons, Ltd., 1964. [Pp. 18–21, 23–26, 28–29.]

does not give a distinctive character but merely results in some atra-bilious disease. But among those who constitutionally possess this tem-perament there is straight away the greatest variety of characters, each according to his individual mixture. For example, those who possess much cold black bile become dull and stupid, whereas those who pos-sess much hot bile are elated and brilliant or erotic or easily moved to anger and desire, while some become more loquacious. Many too are subject to fits of exaltation and ecstasy, because this heat is located near the seat of the intellect; and this is how Sibyls and soothsayers arise and all that are divinely inspired, when they become such not by illness but by natural temperament. . . .

So too with the despondency which occurs in everyday life, for we are often in a state of grieving, but could not say why, while at other times we feel cheerful without apparent reason. To such affections and to those mentioned before we are all subject in some small degree, for a little of the stuff which causes them is mixed in with everybody. But with people in whom this quality goes deep, it determines the character. . . . For if their melancholy habitus is quite undiluted they are too melancholy; but if it is somewhat tempered they are outstanding. . . .

To sum up: The action of black bile is variable, melancholics are variable, for the black bile becomes very hot and very cold. And as it determines the character (for heat and cold are the factors in our bodies most important for determining the character): like wine introduced in a larger or smaller quantity into the body, it makes us persons of such and such a character. And both wine and bile contain air. Since it is possible for this variable mixture to be well tempered and well adjusted in a cer-tain respect—that is to say, to be now in a warmer and then again a colder condition, or vice versa, just as required, owing to its tendency to extremes—therefore all melancholy persons are out of the ordinary, not owing to illness, but from their natural constitution.

24.2

Aulus Cornelius Celsus

(flourished 1st Century A.D.)

Very little is known about Celsus, who has been called both "the Roman Hippocrates" and "the Cicero of physicians." Most likely he was not a physician at all, but an encyclopedist who compiled compendia of knowl-

De medecina. Translated by W. G. Spencer. Cambridge, Mass.: Harvard University Press, Loeb Classical Library, 1935. [Pp. 289–291, 295, 299–303.] Reprinted by per-mission of the publisher and the Loeb Classical Library.

edge in several fields, of which medicine was but one. Probably he borrowed freely from Greek authors since lost, and he gives us a good picture of the state of medical practice in the period just before Galen. The prescription for "certain tortures" as beneficial is one which was still followed by many psychiatrists with a decidedly humane outlook, including the American Benjamin Rush, well into the nineteenth century. But it was not widely generalized, and Celsus does differentiate between classes of madmen as to treatment and prognosis.

[Book III] 18. The regimen of fevers has now been expounded; there are, however, other affections of the body which follow upon this, among which I subjoin in the first place those which cannot be assigned to any definite part.

I shall begin with insanity, and first that form of it which is both acute and found in fever. The Greeks call it phrenesis. Before all things it should be recognized, that at times, during the paroxysm of a fever, patients are delirious and talk nonsense. . . . This form of the malady does not require other remedy than that prescribed for the curing of the fever. But insanity is really there when a continuous dementia begins, when the patient, although up till then in his senses, yet entertains certain vain imaginings; the insanity becomes established when the mind becomes at the mercy of such imaginings. But there are several sorts of insanity; for some among insane persons are sad, others hilarious; some are more readily controlled and rave in words only, others are rebellious and act with violence; and of these latter, some only do harm by impulse, others are artful too, and show the most complete appearance of sanity whilst seizing occasion for mischief, but they are detected by the result of their acts. Now that those who merely rave in their talk, or who make but trifling misuse of their hands, should be coerced with the severer forms of constraint is superfluous; but those who conduct themselves more violently it is expedient to fetter, lest they should do harm either to themselves or to others. Anyone so fettered, although he talks rationally and pitifully when he wants his fetters removed, is not to be trusted, for that is a madman's trick. . . . But in dealing with the spirits of all patients suffering from this type of insanity, it is necessary to proceed according to the nature of each case. Some need to have empty fears relieved, as was done for a wealthy man in dread of starvation, to whom pretended legacies were from time to time announced. Others need to have their violence restrained as is done in the case of those who are controlled even by flogging. In some also untimely laughter has to be put a stop to by reproof and threats; in others, melancholy thoughts are to be dissipated, for which purpose music, cymbals, and noises are of use. More often, however, the patient is to be agreed with rather than opposed, and his mind slowly and imperceptibly is to be turned from the irrational talk to something better. At times also his interest should be awakened; as may be done in the case of men fond of literature, to whom a book may be read, correctly when they are pleased by it, or incorrectly if that very thing annoys them; for by making corrections they begin to divert their mind. Moreover, they should be pressed to recite anything they can remember. . . .

There is another sort of insanity, of longer duration because it generally begins without fever, but later excites a slight feverishness. It consists in depression which seems caused by black bile. Bloodletting is here of service; but if anything prohibits this, then comes firstly abstinence, secondly, a clearance by white hellebore and a vomit. After either, rubbing twice a day is to be adopted; if the patient is strong, frequent exercise as well: vomiting on an empty stomach. Food of the middle class should be given without wine; but as often as I indicate this class of food, it should be understood that some of the weakest class of food also may be given, provided that this is not used alone; and that it is only the strongest class of food which is excluded. In addition to the above: the motions are to be kept very soft, causes of fright excluded, good hope rather put forward; entertainment sought by story-telling, and by games, especially by those with which the patient was wont to be attracted when sane; work of his, if there is any, should be praised, and set out before his eyes; his depression should be gently reproved as being without cause; he should have it pointed out to him now and again how in the very things which trouble him there may be cause of rejoicing rather than of solicitude. When there is fever besides, it is to be treated like other fevers.

The third kind of insanity is of all the most prolonged whilst it does not shorten life, for usually the patient is robust. Now of this sort there are two species: some are duped not by their mind but by phantoms, such as the poets say Ajax saw when mad or Orestes; some become foolish in spirit.

If phantoms mislead, we must note in the first place whether the patients are depressed or hilarious. For depression black hellebore should be given as a purge, for hilarity white hellebore as an emetic; and if the patient will not take the hellebore in a draught, it should be put into his bread to deceive him the more easily; for if he has well purged himself, he will in great measure relieve himself of his malady. Therefore even if one dose of the hellebore has little effect, after an interval another should be given. It should be known that a madman's illness is less serious when accompanied by laughter than by gravity. This also is an invariable precept in all disease, that when a person is to be purged downward, his belly is to be loosened beforehand, but confined when he is to be purged upwards.

If however it is the mind that deceives the madman, he is best treated by certain tortures. When he says or does anything wrong, he is to be coerced by starvation, fetters and flogging. He is to be forced both to fix his attention and to learn something and to memorize it; for thus it will be brought about that little by little he will be forced by fear to consider what he is doing. To be terrified suddenly and to be thoroughly frightened is beneficial in this illness and so, in general, is anything which strongly agitates the spirit. For it is possible that some change may be effected when the mind has been withdrawn from its previous state. It also makes a difference, whether from time to time without cause the patient laughs, or is sad and dejected: for the hilarity of madness is better treated by those terrors I have mentioned above. If there is excessive depression light and prolonged rubbing twice a day is beneficial, as well as cold water poured over the head, and immersion of the body in water and oil. The following are general rules: the insane should be put to fatiguing exercise, and submitted to prolonged rubbing, and given neither fat meat nor wine: after the clearance the lightest food of the middle class is to be used; they should not be left alone or among those they do not know, or among those whom either they despise or disregard; they ought to have a change of scene, and if the mind returns, they should undergo the tossing incident to travel, once a year.

Rarely, yet now and then, however, delirium is the product of fright; this class of insanity, has similar sub-divisions, and is to be treated by the same species of dietetic regimen, except that, in this form of insaneness alone, wine is properly given.

24.3

Michael Constantine Psellus

(c. 1018–1080)

Psellus was a Byzantine Platonist who wrote prolifically in many fields, and this work, a dialogue, is one of the major sources used by Stanley in his account of the Chaldean doctrines. Though this is a third-hand account, it gives a vivid picture of the hosts of evil demons who found their place in Christian lore as well and who provide the basis for theories of mental illness as caused by demonic "possession." The conflict between priestly and medical theories ("Possession" versus "acrid humors") continued in this form down to early modern times, and its aftereffect persists in the conflict of mentalistic and somatic theories of psychosis and neurosis.

Peri energeias daimonon [On the works of the demons. c. 1050.] Abstracted by Thomas Stanley, in *The history of the Chaldaick philosophy* [1662]. London, 1701. [Pp. 14–15.]

Of Material Daemons

Of Daemons, as we said, they asserted two kinds, some good, others ill; the good, light, the ill dark. . . . Of the first we have treated already; of the latter *Psellus* in his Discourse upon this Subject, gives a large account from one *Marcus* of *Mesopotamia*, who having been of this Religion, and well acquainted with their Institutions, was afterwards converted to Christianity: What he relates, as well from the Doctrine it self, as from the place, sufficiently appears to be of the *Chaldaick* Tradition. It is to this effect.

These Daemons are of many kinds, and various sorts, both as to their Figures and Bodies, insomuch that the Air is full of them, as well that which is above us, as that which is round about us. The Earth likewise is full, and the Sea, and the most retired Cavities and Depths.

There are six general kinds of these Daemons. The first named *Leliurius*, which signifies Fiery. This kind dwelleth in the Air that is above us: for from the places next about the Moon, as being Sacred, all kinds of Daemons, as being Prophane, are expelled. The second kind is that which wandreth in the Air contiguous to us, and is by many peculiarly called Aereal. The third, Terrestrial. The fourth, Watery and Marine. The fifth, Subterraneous. The sixth, Lucifugous, and hardly sensible.

All these kinds of Daemons are haters of God, and Enemies of Man. Moreover, of these ill Daemons, some are worse than others. Aquatile, and Subterraneous, and Lucifugous, are extreamly malicious and pernicious: For these do not hurt Souls by Phantasms and Delusions, but by Assault, like the most Savage Beasts, accelerate the Destruction of Men. The Watery Drown those who are Sailing upon the Water. The Subterraneous and Lucifugous, insinuating into the Entrails, cause Epilepsies and Frenzy. The Aereal and Terrestrial circumvent Men by Art and Subtilty, and deceive the Minds of Men, and draw them to absurd and illegal Passions.

They effect these things not as having Dominion over us, and carrying us as their Slaves whithersoever they please, but by Suggestion; for applying themselves to the phantastick Spirit, which is within us, they themselves being Spirits also, they instil Discourses of Affections and Pleasures, not by Voice verberating the Air, but by whisper, insinuating their Discourse.

Nor is it impossible that they should speak without voice, if we consider that he who speaks, being a far off, is forced to use a greater sound; being near, he speaks softly into the ear of the Hearer, and if he could get into the Spirit of the Soul, he would not need any Sound, but what discourse soever he pleaseth, would, by a way without sound, arrive there where it is to be received, which they say is likewise in Souls, when they are out of the Body, for they discourse with one another without noise. After this manner the Daemons converse with us, privately, so that we are not sensible which way the War comes upon us.

Neither can this be doubted, if we observe what happens to the Air. For, when the Sun shineth it assumeth several colours and forms, transmitting them to other things, as we may see in Looking-glasses. In like manner the Daemons, assuming Figures and Colours, and whatever Forms they please, transmit them into our animal Spirit, and by that means afford us much business, suggesting Counsels, representing Figures, resuscitating the remembrance of pleasures, exciting the images of passions, as well when we sleep, as when we wake, and sometimes, titillating the genital parts, inflame us with frantick and unlawful desires, especially if they take, co-operating with them the hot humidities which are in us.

The rest of the Daemons know nothing that is subtile, nor how to breed disturbance, yet are they hurtful and abominable, hurting in the same manner as the spirit or vapour in *Charon*'s Cave: For as that is reported to kill whatsoever approacheth it, whether Beast, Man, or Bird; in like manner these Daemons destroy those upon whom they chance to fall, overthrowing their Souls and Bodies, and their natural Habits, and sometimes by Fire, or Water, or Precipice, they destroy not Men only, but some irrational Creatures.

The Daemons assault Irrational Creatures, not out of Hate, or wishing them ill, but out of the love they have of their Animal heat: For dwelling in the most remote Cavities, which are extreamly cold and dry, they contract much coldness, wherewith being afflicted, they affect the humid and animal heat, and, to enjoy it, they insinuate themselves into irrational Creatures, and go into Baths and Pits; for they hate the heat of Fire and of the Sun, because it burns and drieth up.

But they most delight in the heat of Animals, as being temperate, and mixt with moisture, especially that of men, being best tempered, into which insinuating themselves, they cause infinite disturbance, stopping up the pores in which the Animal Spirit is inherent, and streightning and compressing the Spirit, by reason of the grossness of the Bodies with which they are indued. Whence it happeneth, that the Bodies are disorder'd, and their principal Faculties distemper'd, and their Motions become dull and heavy.

Now if the insinuating Daemon be one of the Subterraneous kind, he distorteth the possess'd Person, and speaketh by him, making use of the Spirit of the patient, as if it were his own Organ. But if any of those who are called Lucifugous, get privately into a Man, he causeth relaxation of the Limbs, and stoppeth the Voice, and maketh the possessed person in all respects like one that is dead. For this being the last of Daemons is more Earthly, and extreamly Cold and Dry, and into whomsoever it insinuates, it hebetates and makes dull all the Faculties of his Soul.

And because it is Irrational, void of all Intellectual Contemplation, and is guided by irrational Phantasie, like the more Savage kind of Beasts, hence it comes to pass, that it stands not in aw of Menaces, and for that reason most Persons aptly call it Dumb and Deaf, nor can they who are possessed with it by any other means be freed from it, but by the Divine Favour obtained by Fasting and Prayer.

That Physicians endeavour to perswade us, that these Passions proceed not from Daemons, but from humours, and Spirits ill affected, and therefore go about to cure them, not by incantations and Expiations, but by Medicines and Diet, is nothing strange, since they know nothing beyond Sense, and are wholly addicted to Study the Body. And perhaps not without reason are some things ascribed to ill affected Humours, as Lethargies, Melancholies, Frenzies, which they take away and cure, either by evacuating the Humours, or by replenishing the Body, if it be empty, or by outward applications. But as for Enthusiasms, ragings, and unclean Spirits, with which whosoever is possessed is not able to act any thing, neither by Intellect, Speech, Phantasie nor Sense; or else there is some other thing that moves them unknown to the Person Possessed, which sometimes fortelleth future Events; how can we call these the Motions of depraved Matter?

24.4

Johann Weyer

(1515–1588)

Weyer was personal physician to the Duke of Clêves. He expressed a bold new point of view on the nature of witchcraft, according to which its practitioners were often to be regarded as helpless victims of the devil, somewhat in line with the theory of possession, rather than his willing cohorts, as they were depicted by the church's inquisitors.

The characterization of witches as melancholics is taken from the preface; it is of course stated much more fully in the work, along with many fascinating tales and case histories. The discussion of the physician's role, and the collaboration which should exist between him and the spiritual counselor, is taken from the fifth book.

I distinguish between . . . magicians and witches. The latter are unstable because of their sex, insecure in faith, and not sufficiently settled in mind

[*De prestigiis daemonum*, . . . 1563.] *Histoires, disputes et discours des illusions et impostures des diables* [An account and discussion of the illusions and impostures of devils. 2 volumes. 1579]. Reprinted, Paris, 1885. [Vol. I, pp. xxxii–xxxiv; vol. II, pp. 151–153.]

because of their age, and therefore they are more subject to the deceits of the devil, who insinuates himself into their imaginations whether they are asleep or awake, and makes them fantasy all sorts of shapes and apparitions, stirring their humors and their vital spirits with such skill and address, in order to accomplish his ends, that they know no better than to confess that they themselves have done things that were rather done by the devil, in accordance with God's permission and will; and that they were the cause of calamities which befell men and beasts, of premeditated crimes, or of misfortunes which occurred by natural means —just as we see, in those whose brains are confused by melancholy or by its vapors, that the spirit is wounded and troubled and filled with various fantasies and apparitions. The witches have no books, no exorcisms, signs, or like monstrosities, as infamous magicians do; and they have no other teachers or instructors than their own minds, which have been impaired by the devil, and their corrupted imaginations. For these reasons anyone can easily see that they are very different from the infamous magicians, for magicians are usually people who are educated and sophisticated, but curious, and often they make long voyages to learn the art of magic, so that they will be able to pride themselves on tricks and impostures which go beyond the order of nature. Witches are ordinary old women, in their dotage, staying at home; the devil, being a spirit, can easily glide into their fantasies, which are as if benumbed, and which are a convenient organ and seat suitable for his work, especially if they are ill with melancholy, or if they are saddened and in extreme danger. He does not so much deceive them by his impostures as to impress on their fantasies that they are the cause of all the misfortunes of men, of deaths and calamities, and this he does with such vehemence that, as I have said, they become of the opinion that they have caused all these wicked things, as great as they are, although in fact they were far from them, and not at all guilty. . . .

First of all, immediately upon recognizing any illness which is against the order of nature, one should (according to the law of God) turn to the one who is well known, by doctrine, profession, and custom, to have an understanding of ailments, their differences, their signs and their causes: that is, to a physician of good conscience. This is because sometimes such strange things happen in sicknesses, even when they conform to the force and the impulse of nature, that uneducated men who do not understand natural things, and who are of wavering faith, immediately attribute them to witchcraft—as we have seen in different sorts of convulsions and contractions of nerves, in melancholy, epilepsy, congestion of the liver, putrefaction of the semen, and a number of other effects of poisons and venoms. But the prudent and informed physician will distinguish the ailment, its symptoms and its accidents, and when he has carefully considered them, and made a diligent inquiry into natural things, he will decide as well as he can whether it passes beyond the limits of nature. If he recognizes in it the actions of Satan, who is a spirit, he will turn the charge of the patient over to the spiritual doctor, that is, to a minister of the church. The latter should be a man of good and healthy doctrine, keeping the mystery of the faith with pure conscience; one who is known to live an innocent life, not given to wine, nor to dishonest gain, and for whom honest folk will bear good witness. Nevertheless, it is necessary to remember that there are some things which do not come from witchcraft, but from some hidden natural cause which is unknown to physicians. For just as there are things which have secret powers to help and do good, so there are some which have such powers to do ill, and which the physician nevertheless does not always know.

In any case, the physician can help by seeing whether by nature, or from the illness, or for any other reason, the patient has an excess of melancholic humor, in which the devil gladly meddles, because he finds it a convenient basis for his deceits. If so, he can purge the patient thoroughly. . . . For people commonly suffer from double maladies, one physical, from the melancholic humor, and the other spiritual, in which the sworn enemy of mankind belabors them with madness, sorrow, fear, distaste for living, and despair, by which they are tormented day and night. . . .

There was at Burg a melancholic girl who . . . after long conjuring confessed that she was possessed by the spirit of Vergil. . . . After the conjurors had lost their time, a physician cured her by the grace of God, using first, as prescribed by the art, medicines to purge the melancholy, and then others which restore strength and give comfort. After the body is purged in this manner, the minister of the church can more easily use his means to drive away the evil spirit, for the natural barriers are removed, and he can readily undertake the rest of the cure. [The rest of the cure, as described, consists of religious and moral instruction, but this is to be based on careful inquiry into the patient's prior conduct.]

24.5

Jean Bodin

(1530–1596)

Jean Bodin has been called the greatest scholar of his age. He was primarily a jurist, and his chief contributions were to political theory. His attack against Weyer (Wier) seems inconsistent with his general character, and convinces us how deeply entrenched was the belief in witchcraft, even among educated men. (On the other hand, Montaigne expressed a quite sceptical view in his Essays, about the same time.)

Just as Bodin had completed this work on sorcery, based in part on his participation in the trial of a confessed witch, he read a minor work by Weyer, De lamiis (On witches), 1577. It provoked Bodin into an eighty-page refutation, which has a place in the history of psychology as an explicit statement of the controversy over criminal responsibility of the insane.

When we read Bodin's argument that women are not melancholy, we are reminded that Freud was told by his teacher, Meynert, that men cannot be hysterics, because hysteria (the name of which is derived from the Greek word for uterus) is obviously a disease only of women.

. . . If one reads all the books written about witchcraft, one will find that there are 50 female witches or demoniacs for every male. . . . In my opinion this does not happen because of the weakness of the sex: in most cases we see an unmistakeable stubbornness, and they often withstand the sufferings of the inquisition better than men. . . . Satan addresses himself primarily to women because it was through her that man was seduced. Furthermore, I think that God wanted to restrict and weaken Satan, and therefore gave him power in the ordinary course primarily over less worthy creatures, like serpents and flies and other beasts which are called unclean in God's law; then over other beasts rather than over the human species, over women rather than men, and over men who live like beasts rather than over the others. Granted too that Satan uses women to draw men and children in tow. Therefore the judgment of God's law remains, that the witch should be quickly put to death, and Wier's calumny against that law and against the magistrates who enforce its commands must be rejected. For Wier agrees that the witches have communication and pacts with the devil, and that they do much evil by his help; and nevertheless in the book *On witches* he sometimes says that there is no pact, sometimes that it cannot be proved, sometimes that we should

De la démonomanie des sorciers [On the demonomania of sorcerers.] Paris, 1582. [Ll. 225a–227a, 238ab.]

not believe the confessions of witches, that they deceive themselves into thinking that they do the things they say and that this is due to the illness of melancholy, from which they suffer. This is a camouflage which either the witches or the ignorant have assumed in order to provide an escape for their kind and to make the kingdom of Satan grow. Hitherto, those who have attributed this to melancholy did not believe in demons, or perhaps even in angels, or in any God. But Wier admits that there is a God (as the devils also admit it, and tremble before his power, as we read in Scripture) and he admits in all his writings that there are good and evil spirits who possess intelligence, and form pacts with men. Nevertheless he attributes the transportation of witches, their misdeeds, and their strange actions to melancholy; he makes out that women are melancholics, although it was mentioned in antiquity as a remarkable fact that women never die of melancholy, nor men of happiness, whereas on the contrary women do die of extreme happiness. Since Wier is a physician, he cannot be ignorant of the fact that the feminine humor is quite the opposite of that parched melancholy from which madness comes; for physicians all agree that it comes *à bile flava adusta, aut à succo melancholico* [from a scorched yellow bile, or a melancholic humor]. For both arise, as Galen says in his book *De atrabile,* from heat and excessive dryness. Now women are by nature cold and moist, as the same author says, and all of the Greeks, Latins and Arabs agree. That is why Galen also says that men, because they have a hot and dry temperament, fall prey to melancholic illnesses in hot and dry climates. Nevertheless, Olaus Magnus [16th cent. Swedish historian], Gaspar Peucerus [German physician, 1525–1602], Saxo Grammaticus [12th cent. Danish historian], and Jean Wier himself agree with all the inquisitors of Germany that the Arctic region, or Sea of Ice, Germany, the Alps, and the Savoy are all full of witches. Now it is certain that these northern peoples have as little melancholy as those of Africa have phlegm. For all the northern people are fair, with green eyes, straight blond hair, rosy cheeks, happy and ready chatterers, all things which are contrary to the melancholic humor. Furthermore, Hippocrates . . . and Galen . . . both state that women generally are healthier than men, because their menstrual flow protects them from a thousand ailments. . . . Therefore Wier must confess that it is a remarkable incongruity and a very gross ignorance (but it is not ignorance) that he, a physician, should attribute to women melancholic ailments which are no more fitting to them than would be the praiseworthy effects of that tempered melancholic humor which renders men wise, sedate, and contemplative (as all the ancient philosophers and physicians have remarked)—qualities which are as incompatible with women as fire is with water. . . .

. . . As to the other argument by which Wier concludes (as he does throughout) that witches do not deserve to be punished because Satan sets them to work, this is full of sophistry, as well as being impious. For if this argument were allowed, all the great impieties that men commit would remain unpunished, because although men are sometimes impelled to strike someone by a desire for vengeance, or to violate another's modesty by the force of brutal desire, still the greatest crimes are not this sort of merchandise: those who lie in wait to kill (like all the killings and poisonings performed by witches), the murders of children, parricides, and other such crimes done by persons who are not witches—these also are directed by Satan, and would also go unpunished. In short, if the sophistry of Wier and the fine doctors from whom he has drawn his arguments were allowed, then robbers and brigands would always have recourse to a guarantee against the devil, against whom the defenders of justice have neither jurisdiction nor power. . . .

24.6

Thomas Willis

(1621–1675)

In his chapter "Of Madness," Willis presents a detailed somatic account of its causes, but he acknowledges that when the somatic predisposition exists, the immediate initiating cause may be some frustrating experience.

After *Melancholy, Madness* is next to be treated of, both which are so much akin, that these Distempers often change, and pass from one into the other; for the *Melancholick* disposition growing worse, brings on *Fury;* and *Fury* or *Madness* growing less hot, oftentimes ends in a *Melancholick* disposition. These two, like smoke and flame, mutually receive and give place one to another. And indeed, if in *Melancholy* the Brain and Animal Spirits are said to be darkned with fume, and a thick obscurity; In *Madness,* they seem to be all as it were of an open burning or flame. But indeed, for that as we have already shewn, that the Animal Spirits being inkindled or inflamed do excite a *Phrensie* with a *Feavour,* which is wanting in *Madness,* their affection will be better illustrated in this Disease, as well as in *Melancholy,* by the Analogy of *Chymical Liquors.*

Whenever therefore *Madness* without a *Feavour* being excited, with a remarkable hurt of the animal Function, is wont to be permanent, and

[De anima brutorum, 1672.] *Two discourses concerning the soul of brutes, which is that of the vital and sensitive of man.* Englished by S. Pordage. London, 1683. [Pp. 201, 203–205.]

646

continue long, its next and immediate subject are the Animal Spirits; which acting not by consent, nor from any force from another, but of themselves, are habitually distemper'd, and depart from their proper and genuine nature, to wit, a *Spiritual-saline,* into a *Sulphureous-saline* disposition, like to *Stygian-water,* as we have shewed above; therefore they perform only inordinate acts, and so persist a long while to act amiss or evilly. To this vice of theirs, perhaps the Brain, or the Blood, or other parts may contribute somewhat, but the Spirits themselves are first and chiefly in fault.

It is observed in *Mad men,* that these three things are almost common to all: *viz.* First, That their *Phantasies* or Imaginations are perpetually busied with a storm of impetuous thoughts, so that night and day they are muttering to themselves various things, or declare them by crying out, or by bauling out aloud. Secondly, That their notions or conceptions are either incongruous, or represented to them under a false or erroneous image. Thirdly, To their *Delirium* is most often joyned Audaciousness and Fury, contrary to *Melancholicks,* who are always infected with Fear and Sadness. These primary *symptoms* of *Madness* in the Animal Spirits, indued with the nature of *Stygian*-Water, may be thence most aptly deduced as appears clearly by what follows. . . .

. . . The depravation of the Animal Spirits, together with the juice watering the Brain, or the disposition of Madness, is wont to arise after various ways and for diverse causes; but truly, for the most part this Distemper (as we have observed of *Melancholy*) begins either from the Spirits themselves, or else from the Blood.

First, *Madness* beginning from the Spirits, arises sometimes from an evident solitary cause, as a violent Passion; sometimes also it proceeds from a foregoing cause lying in the Brain, as when it comes upon *Melancholy* or a *Phrensie.* We shall a little weigh the reasons of either case, and the various manner of their being made.

1. As to the former, when a vehement affection puts any one besides himself, that happens to be made thus; either because the Animal Spirits are too much overthrown, and hurried into confusion; or because they are elevated above measure, and endeavour to stretch themselves forth beyond their sphere.

First, The Spirits are wont to be cast down by a violent and terrible Passion; so it often happens, that some being struck with a panick fear, by seeing a true or an imaginary Spectre or Ghost, afterwards fall into a perpetual Madness. Further, some by reason of some notable disgrace or repulse, others by reason of their hopes of obtaining their Love being suddenly and unthought of frustrated, and others by reason of a rash breaking their oaths or vows, and violated Conscience, being first highly troubled in mind, anon become Mad. The reason of which is, because the Animal Spirits being driven beyond their orders and wonted passages, and put into confusion, do make for themselves new and devious ways, which entring into, immediately they bring forth delirious *Phantasms;* in the mean time, the *Saline* Particles of the nervous juice, the spirituous being depressed, depart from their volatileness; and suffering a flux, assume to themselves the *Sulphureous* little bodies poured forth from the Blood, into the then weak and open Brain; From whence this Liquor, being most sharp like *Stygian* Water, and the Animal Spirits being fierce and very much incited, become furious.

Secondly, Sometimes the Animal Spirits, whilst they are too much elevated, almost after the same manner induce both to themselves, and the nervous juice, the mad disposition. Hence Ambition, Pride, and Emulation, have made some mad; the reason of which is, because whilst the Corporeal Soul swelling up with an opinion and pride of its own excellency, lifts up it self, and endeavours on every side to expand or stretch it self forth most amply, beyond the border or sphere of its body, the Animal Spirits being tumultuarily called into the Head, will not be contained within their wonted bounds, but being there broken and diversly reflected, by reason of their too much excretion, are compelled into new and plainly devious tracts; wherefore, both they being thrust forth from the course of their proper emanation, and also from the nervous Liquor, do quickly acquire a sharp and incitative Disposition, as was said but now, for that reason Madness follows.

This much concerning Madness, excited by reason of a solitary evident cause; but this Disease doth also arise from a *Procatartick* cause, pre-existing in the Brain, and chiefly from *Melancholy* or the *Phrensie* going before; in that the Animal Spirits with the nervous juice being a little more exalted, and in this a little more depressed, acquire the disposition of Madness. As to the former, it is a vulgar observation, that sudden and great *Melancholy* is for the most part next to Madness: the reason of which is, because, when the Animal Spirits, together with the nervous liquor, degenerate into a sourness, are perverted, there only wants the accession of *Sulphur*, by which they afterwards getting a *Stygian* nature; may induce *Madness;* (as when an acid Liquor distilled out of *Vitriol* or Salt, by the addition of *Sal Nitrosus*, becomes *Aqua fortis*) but indeed, in a great passion of *Melancholy*, because the Spirits being disturbed, the passages of the Brain are too open, the *Sulphureous* Particles carried from the Bilious and Rancid Blood, find an easie entrance, and so the former sour or acid disposition, turns into a *Stygian* or Maddish. Hence it is observed, if anyone of a more hot temperament, falls into a *Melancholic Delirium*, with fear and sadness, forasmuch as the *Sulphureous* Particles in its humors, are joyned to the Salts being depressed into a flux, that sadness and thinking at the beginning, very readily a short time after becomes madness. Secondly, for that also a *Phrensie* often ends in *Madness*, the reason is almost the same with the former, but inverted; to wit, because in a *Phrensie* the Spirits and the nervous Liquor becoming *Sulphureous*, and too much inflamed, afterwards burning forth, get to themselves *Saline* Particles, and so in like matter get a most sharp and as it were a *Stygian* nature; wherefore the *Feavour* then ceasing, the Fury becomes fixed and continual.

2. The disposition of *Madness*, hath no less frequently its roots in the bloody Mass, and is at length produced into act, to wit, when as the Blood being depraved, and becomes *Nitro-Sulphureous*, it either perverts the nervous Liquor, as also the Animal Spirits, or supplies them but evilly. Which kind of taint of the Blood is either hereditary or acquired. First, It is a common observation, that men born of Parents that use sometimes to be mad, are obnoxious to the same disease, and though they have lived above thirty of forty years prudent and sober; yet afterwards without any occasion or evident cause, they have fallen into Madness. The reason of which is, for that the Blood at that time bending from its due temper, by degrees into a *Nitro sulphureous*, affords to the Head Animal Spirits, and also the nervous juice, participating (as hath been said) of a most sharp nature. We have formerly shewn, that in our Complexion, Elementary Particles do persist during life, apart from the secondary, afforded by nutrition, and have their times of crudity, maturity, and defection; wherefore we suppose, the morbid seeds do ripen into fruit, according to the periods of Ages. Further, we take notice, that oftentimes the fruits of Diseases of this kind, do remain ripening for a long time, or perpetually as long as life; yet sometimes falling off as it were of their own accord, do wither away; then sometimes in another tract of time, from the infection being left, new fruits do spring up, and by little and little rise up to their height. Wherefore, *Hereditary Madness* is sometimes continual, and sometimes intermitting; its fits are wont sometimes to come again after a shorter time, and sometimes after a longer interval.

Secondly, As the foregoing Cause of Madness sticking in the Blood, is oftentimes innate or original, so sometimes the same is by degrees begotten, either by an evil manner of diet, or by the suppression of usual evacuations, or by reason of a Feavour going before, or for some other causes, and at length being brought to maturity, breaks forth into *Madness*. It is an usual thing in great want of sustenance, that some poor people, being constrained to feed only on very disagreeing meats, and of ill digestion, become at first sad, with an horrid aspect, louring and dark, and a little after Mad. . . .

Thirdly, Venomous Ferments being insinuated to the Blood and nervous juice, as first of all from the biting of mad Animals, or by the taking of some poisons, are wont to stir up Madness. . . .

Thus much for the formal Reason, and Causes of *Madness*. The *primary Symptoms* of it, we have mentioned to be a *Delirium* and a *Fury*; the reasons of which appear clear enough from what has been already said. To these we may moreover add Boldness, Strength, and that they are still unwearied with any labours, and suffer pains unhurt, of which we will speak briefly.

24.7

William Battie

(1703–1776)

Battie was a full-time psychiatrist and a governor of Bethlem Hospital. Hunter and Macalpine say that he was perhaps the first to teach psychiatry as a specialty. His distinction between "original" and "consequential" forms of mental illness is forerunner of the long regnant differentiation between "organic" and "functional" disturbances.

The Causes of Madness

Whoever is satisfied with our account of the seat and causes of natural and true Sensation, will acknowledge that the one immediate necessary and sufficient cause of the praeternatural and false perception of objects, which either do not exist, or which do not in this instance excite such sensation, must be some disorder of that substance which is medullary and strictly nervous. And moreover, as he cannot discover the natural and internal constitution of this medullary substance, which renders it fit for the proper perception of real and external impulse or rather of the ideas thereby excited; he must for the same reason own that he is unable to discover wherein consists that praeternatural and internal state of the same nervous matter, which disposes it to be without any such impulse affected by those very ideas, that would have been presented to the imagination, if the same nervous matter had been acted upon by something external. Or, to speak more technically, forasmuch as the one immediate necessary and sufficient cause of the perception of real objects is unknown, we must likewise remain entirely ignorant of the one immediate necessary and sufficient cause of the perception of Chimaeras, which exist no where except in the brain of a Madman.

But, altho' the immediate and internal cause of delusive as well as of true Sensation is absolutely hid, many remoter and external causes thereof frequently discover themselves to the by-stander, notwithstanding that the idea thus excited is not by the patient himself referred to

A *treatise of madness.* London, 1758. [Pp. 41–44, 59–61.]

any one of those true causes, but to something else, which may or may not exist, and which certainly does not in this particular case act upon the affected organ.

Thus, to instance a very common accident, the eye that is violently struck immediately sees flames flash before it; which idea of fire presented to the imagination plainly shews that those material particles which constitute the medullary substance of the optic nerve are affected by such blow exactly in the same manner, as they are when real fire acts upon the eye of a man awake and in his senses with force sufficient to provoke his attention. Thus variety of sounds disturb the ear that is shocked by the pulsation of vessels, by the inflammation or other obstruction of those membranes which line the *meatus auditorius*, by the intrusion of water, and in short by any material force external to the medullary portion of the seventh pair of nerves; which force hath no connection with any sonorous body, that by its elastic vibration communicates an undulatory motion to the intermediate air.

Now suppose that any one perfectly awake without the accident of such a blow sees fire, or without the pulsation of vessels, inflammation, or any obstruction in the *meatus auditorius*, &c. hears sounds; or suppose that the idea of flames really excited by a blow is by him referred to an house on fire, or the idea of sound excited by the pulsation of vessels, &c. is referred to a musical instrument, which is not near enough to be heard, or is not really played upon; the man who is so mistaken, and who cannot be set right either upon his own recollection or the information of those about him, is in the apprehension of all sober persons a Lunatic.

From whence we may collect that Madness with respect to its cause is distinguishable into two species. The first is solely owing to an internal disorder of the nervous substance: the second is likewise owing to the same nervous substance being indeed in like manner disordered, but disordered *ab extra*; and therefore is chiefly to be attributed to some remote and accidental cause. The first species, until a better name can be found, may be called *Original*, the second may be called *Consequential Madness*.

The internal disorder of the medullary substance, or the cause of Original Madness, for the same reason as the immediate necessary and sufficient cause of true Sensation, can be but one: but the external and accidental causes of Consequential Madness, as well as of true Sensation, may be many. . . .

The Diagnostic Signs of Original and Consequential Madness; and the Prognostic arising therefrom

Having in the two preceding Sections discovered most of the causes of Madness that deserve our attention, and thereby divided this disorder into two species, *viz. Original and Consequential:* It will be necessary to mention some particular circumstances attending either species, which will enable the Physician not only to distinguish Original Madness from Consequential, but also the better to settle his prognostic and method of cure.

First then, there is some reason to fear that Madness is Original, when it neither follows nor accompanies any accident, which may justly be deemed its external and remoter cause.

Secondly, there is more reason to fear that, whenever this disorder is haereditary, it is Original. For, altho' even in such case it may now and then be excited by some external and known cause, yet the striking oddities that characterise whole families derived from Lunatic ancestors, and the frequent breaking forth of real Madness in the offspring of such illconcerted alliances, and that from little or no provocation, strongly intimate that the nerves or instruments of Sensation in such persons are not originally formed perfect and like the nerves of other men.

Thirdly, we may with the greatest degree of probability affirm that Madness is Original, when it both ceases and appears afresh without any assignable cause. For, although we cannot guess why this disease of the nerves is ever relieved without the real assistance of art, or why it attacks the patient again without any new provocation, any more than we can account for the spontaneous intermission of convulsion, fever, head-ach, and such like spasmodic disorders of the muscles; it is however impossible that any one effect whatever can perfectly cease, so long as that cause which was capable of producing it continues to act upon the same subject and in the same manner. And it is as impossible that the effect of any action can after a total discontinuance arise again, without its being regenerated by the same or at least by a similar action. Therefore that disorder, be it muscular or nervous, be it convulsion or Madness, which spontaneously ceases and as spontaneously invades again, cannot be consequential to any external cause, which always exists, and whose action always continueth the same.

Original Madness, whether it be haereditary or intermitting, is not removable by any method, which the science of Physick in its present imperfect state is able to suggest.

24.8

Johann Christian Reil

(1759–1813)

*Crusty, curmudgeony Reil, always bluntly outspoken, explains in the pref-
ace of this volume that he wrote it on the invitation of H. B. Wagnitz, a
Lutheran preacher who was a pioneer advocate of reform in the treatment
of the insane. It was intended for serial publication in Wagnitz's magazine,
but he rejected it as too lengthy, so Reil published it anonymously as a
book, dedicated to Wagnitz.*

*Many today would cheer Reil's call for a special medical degree in
psychotherapy!*

It is an extraordinary sensation, to suddenly step from the tumult of a
large city into its madhouse. Here is the city once more, but set before us
in vaudeville style, although this society of fools also has a special
quality of its own. The madhouse has its usurpers, its tyrants, its slaves,
its wantons and its defenseless sufferers, fools that laugh without reason
and fools that torment themselves without reason. Pride, egoism, vanity,
greed—all the human faults run their course in this eddying bywater, as
in the ocean of the great world outside. However, the fools in Bedlam
and Bicêtre are more candid and less harmful than those in the madhouse of the world. Here an avenger may command lightning bolts from
heaven, and an imaginary general with a foolhardy plan may believe that
his sword lays waste half the world. But no villages burn, no people moan
and bleed.

What must we feel when we see this horde of irrational creatures,
some of whom might once have stood by the side of a Newton, a Leibnitz, or a Sterne? What remains of our belief in our ethereal origins, in
the immateriality and independence of our souls, and other hyperboles
of poetic talent, which have been invented in the pressure of conflict
between hopes and fears? How can this same energy work so differently
in these perverted creatures? How, if activity is its essence, can it slumber
years on end in the cretin? How can it change with the moon, like a
fever alternating with chills, to rave in one phase and be rational in
another? How can an irrational animal lose the reason it never possessed,
becoming stupid, mad and foolish in the same way as a man, because
some wheel in its mechanism breaks down? A part of the soul can be

Rhapsodien über die Anwendung der psychischen Curmethode auf Geisteszerrütungen
[Rhapsodies on the application of psychic methods of treatment to mental distur-
bances]. Halle, 1803. [Pp. 7–12, 22, 25–27.]

amputated with each limb, with each sense organ. A flood of ideas in the archives of literature: the delicate play of wit, the most genial discoveries, the most tender feelings, the most ardent fantasies, the most impetuous yearnings—these products which rush ceaselessly from the soul into action—they would be nonexistent, if that part of the body which generates each of them did not exist. A fiber in the brain grows numb, and the divine spark that dwells within us becomes only a fairy-tale. . . .

Another reflection. Does our behavior toward these unfortunate fellow men conform to the dictates of reason? Alas, no! Laziness, greed, selfishness, intrigue, and cold barbarity are hidden in the background here, as everywhere, and under their whitewash they spew out the rules which govern the reciprocal relationships of groups of men. This way of behaving is not only in conflict with the duties which we owe to other men, but it is even against our own interests. The insane, who cannot rightly guide their own conduct and are unable to match one deceit with another, suffer from a weakness which has its basis in human nature—one to which we are all exposed and from which neither reason nor rank nor riches can protect us. Either moral or physical forces—an attack of high fever, or some unavoidable turn of fate, such as may overtake either a single family or a whole state—can put any of us into the madhouse forever. Fortune plays its game with men in wondrous ways. It may place a coronet on a man's brow, and then plant upon it this extremity of misfortune, as readily as on a beggar's cowl. It is like a snake in which the head and tail are joined. It was only in 1772, says Langerman [1797], when the capacity of the public institutions for madmen in Torgau and Waldheim was doubled, but twenty years later they were again inadequate to accommodate all the insane of Kursaxony who sought admission. . . . Nature has planted in us as many seeds of madness as divine dispositions to lofty and noble deeds: the quest for fame and for perfection, strength for self-determination and resoluteness, and passions which by their turbulence insure a fatal lethargy. We come closer to the madhouse with each step we take along the road of material and intellectual civilization. . . .

Public madhouses have two essentially different purposes, and they must be correspondingly different in their construction if both purposes are to be realized. On one hand they are institutions for the safe keeping of those lunatics who are incurable. These institutions must be constructed according to the following principles: (1) to protect the lunatics from hurting themselves or others; (2) to offer them all means for the happy enjoyment of their existence, in keeping with their position; (3) finally, insofar as possible, to keep them occupied. For lunatics also have organic and moral natural strength, which a good administrator should not allow to go unused. . . . A second purpose which we seek to attain through madhouses is *to liberate subjective-curable lunatics from their sickness.* The institution for safe-keeping has need only for active and upright persons of benevolent disposition. If the therapeutic institution is to attain its purpose, it needs a quite different personnel, including physicians, preachers and philosophers who are trained for its purposes, and many sorts of special equipment. . . .

What are *psychic methods of treatment?* . . .

. . . [Means of treatment] work either by virtue of their *chemical* or by virtue of their *physical-mechanical* characteristics. The latter include surgical means, the former foods and medicines. Usually the chain is closed there, but too soon. For there are other things which are means of treatment, because they relieve sickness; but they do not work either chemically or mechanically, but *psychically.* These forces, which work psychically, also lie within the bounds of instruction in therapy. . . .

[They work] by bringing about changes in the organization, through which its sickness is cured, by giving a definite direction to the soul's faculties, ideas, feelings and desires. Until now, the tools of this art have never been brought together into a system. . . .

. . . Now the changes which therapeutic means produce in the organization are *progressive,* and their *final* product may be of a different nature from the therapeutic means itself. The therapeutic means initiate a change, the organization completes it. Madder-root works chemically, but it straightens the crooked bones of rachitic children, and thus *finally* produces a *mechanical* result. Furthermore it is probable that the final effects of all therapeutic means, even the psychic, consist in a change in matter and its structure. This brings new difficulties in setting up a system, but I leave this question aside, because it belongs to the philosophy of pharmacology and general therapeutics.

Therefore if general medical science, to which this investigation belongs, sets up two methods of therapy, the surgical and the medical (which includes dietetics as one part), depending on the nature of the means which is applied and its manner of operation, then, if it is to be consistent, it must also add a *third* method, the *psychical.* It is true that this is still an unworked field, but by cultivation it can be raised to the same and perhaps even a higher effectiveness than that possessed by the other therapeutic methods. A significant increase indeed, which extends the borders of medical science by a third! This opens a new sphere of activity for the application of the physician's industry, and one which offers him the most interesting material for elaboration. After this new acquisition the medical faculties will have to add a third degree to the two which now exist, namely the *doctorate in psychic therapeutics.*

24.9

Wilhelm Griesinger

(1817–1868)

Griesinger proclaims the uncompromisingly somatic orientation of German psychiatry which would endure until challenged by Freud in the late years of the nineteenth century.

§ 81. After extensive observation and comparison we find that the etiology of insanity is in general none other than that of any other cerebral or nervous disease. In particular, the etiology of epilepsy and of the states of chronic irritation of the spinal cord offer instructive analogies as well in regard to predisposition as to the more immediate causes. Excluding the predisposing circumstances (period of life, hereditary predisposition, certain errors in education), we find that in all these diseases two distinct modes of origin may be recognised: in the first place, an origin (idiopathic) from influences working directly on the brain—shock, injury, excessive fatigue and exhaustion of the brain and entire nervous system, alcoholics, narcotics, excessive mental irritation through emotion, and the like; in the second place, an origin (symptomatic) resulting from other further morbid changes in the organism through which the function of the brain becomes affected. These different morbid states now appear to act upon the brain principally in three different ways: in the first place, by generating or favouring anomalies in the circulation (hyperaemia, anaemia) within the cranium (disease of the heart and arteries); in the second place, by nervous irritation of the brain, which we can scarcely otherwise account for than by communication and transmission of peripheral irritation of certain nerves to the central organ, occurring to a certain extent in a reflex manner (injury of a peripheral nerve, influence of the sexual organs, &c.); in the third place, by deficient nutrition and excitation of the brain in consequence of dyscrasia (general anaemia, &c.). . . .

§ 110. A classification of mental diseases according to their nature—that is, according to the anatomical changes of the brain which lie at their foundation—is, at the present time, impossible. But, as the whole classification of mental diseases is merely a symptomatological one . . . we must adopt the functional, the physiological; and this is . . . also

Pathologie und Therapie der psychischen Krankheiten [1845]. Translated by C. L. Robertson and J. Rutherford, from the second (1861) German edition, as *Mental pathology and therapeutics*. London, 1867. [Pp. 131–132, 206–208.]

a psychological basis. Insanity is, therefore, to be divided according to the form and nature of the psychical anomalies. . . .

The analysis of observations leads to the conclusion that there are two grand groups or fundamental states of mental anomalies, which represent the two most essential varieties of insanity. In the one, the insanity consists in the morbid production, governing, and persistence of *emotions* and *emotional states,* under the influence of which the whole mental life suffers according to their nature and form. In the other, the insanity consists in disorders of the intellect and will, which do *not* (any longer) proceed from a ruling emotional state, but exhibit, without profound emotional excitement, an *independent,* tranquil, *false mode of thought* and of *will* (usually with the predominant character of mental weakness). Observation shows, further, that in the great majority of cases, those conditions which form the first leading group *precede* those of the second group; that the latter generally appear only as consequences and *terminations* of the first, when the cerebral affection has not been cured. There is, moreover, again presented within the first group, in a great proportion of cases, a certain definite *succession* of the various forms of emotional states, whence there results a method of viewing insanity which recognises in the different *forms,* different *stages* of one morbid process; which may, indeed, be modified, interrupted, or transformed by the most varied intercurrent pathological circumstances, but which, on the whole, pursues a constantly progressive course, which may proceed even to complete destruction of the mental life. . . .

Pathological anatomy shows us, even at present, that in the first group, or in the first stages of insanity, it is rare to find important organic alterations, or such as are not capable of complete removal; whilst in the second group, or in the terminal stages, very often there exist palpable organic changes which are incapable of cure—particularly atrophy of the brain more or less extensive, with oedema of the membranes, and chronic hydrocephalus. We may say, then, that those cerebral lesions which give rise to the first stages of insanity . . . have this in common, that they terminate in very many cases in those characteristic consecutive changes in the brain which we have spoken of as a stage of permanent anatomical lesion.

Consequently, the simple symptomatological, the psychologico-analytical method, and the anatomical manner of investigation, come all to the same practically important conclusion, that insanity is a *curable* disease only so long as it is confined to the first group of *primitive* (emotional) mental disorders, and that it becomes *incurable* with the development of the secondary lesions which constitute the second group. That first series includes the forms of melancholy, mania, and monomania, the second, the forms of chronic mania and dementia.

24.10

Johannes Lange

(1891–1938)

Many kinds of criminal behavior, though of course not all, must be regarded as forms or at least symptoms of mental illness. Lange's study demonstrated conclusively the importance of genetic factors in predisposing individuals to criminal behavior "under our present social conditions." F. J. Kallman's similar studies (The genetics of schizophrenia, 1938) are far more extensive and sophisticated. Current research on the frequency of XYY-trisomy among tall men prone to criminal violence continues the same trend. For a variety of reasons, some moralistic and some utopian, many persons find the implications of such research unacceptable, but there can be no doubt of its importance historically.

In the first part of these investigations we applied the Twin method with regard to criminals in a purely statistical manner. With the help of the records we ascertained in the case of all available twins whether they themselves and their fellow-twins had come into conflict with the law or not. In every single case we also endeavoured to find out conclusively whether we were dealing with monozygotic twins, i.e., those with the same heredity, or dizygotic pairs, i.e., those with different heredity. In addition we confined ourselves exclusively to those of the same sex and such pairs of whom at least one partner had been sentenced.

Largely with the help of the Bavarian Minister of Justice and the Institute of Criminal Biology at Straubing Prison we found thirty pairs of twins, of whom thirteen were monozygotics and seventeen were dizygotics. Of the thirteen monozygotic pairs, both twins had been sentenced in ten cases, and in three cases only one twin had come in conflict with the law while the other had not done so. Of the seventeen dizygotic pairs, both twins had only been sentenced in two cases, whilst in all the rest only one twin had come before the courts whilst the other had not. In addition, a comparison between the criminality of dizygotic twins with that reckoned out of a large material of the criminality of ordinary brothers and sisters showed that both of a pair of dizygotic twins were not sentenced more frequently than was to be expected.

Even allowing for all necessary restrictions . . . these facts show quite definitely that under our present social conditions heredity does play a

Verbrechen als Schicksal; Studien an kriminellen Zwillengen. Leipzig: Georg Thieme Verlag, 1929. Translated by Charlotte Haldane, as *Crime as destiny; A study of criminal twins.* London: George Allen & Unwin, 1931. [Pp. 172–173, 175.]

rôle of paramount importance in making the criminal; certainly a far greater rôle than many are prepared to admit.

Our rough figures also permit the conclusion that heredity alone is not exclusively a cause of criminality, but that one must also allow a certain amount for environmental influences. Even our monozygotic pairs did not by any means show complete agreement in their attitudes to crime. The fact that in about one-quarter of the cases only one of the monozygotic twins was sentenced must be interpreted as showing that in these cases some environmental influence or other determined the criminal behaviour. . . .

The estimation of the extent of the influence of environmental causes of crime should be greatly assisted by a study of the discordant monozygotic couples. If we assume the same innate characteristics, as we may do in these cases, they should only have a subordinate influence in determining the criminality of one of the pair. The chief part should be due to external influences, and the life-histories of the twins should clearly reveal this fact. But our observations contradicted most definitely our expectations of finding social and mental factors chiefly responsible for their criminality. In at least two out of three cases the criminal twins, and they alone, had suffered serious brain lesions; it is possible to conclude that the crimes in question were actually among the consequences of these lesions.

24.11

Harry Stack Sullivan

(1892–1949)

Sullivan's emphasis on mental illness as the outgrowth of the same processes by which the personalities of healthy persons are shaped expresses the increasing preference of psychiatrists for an approach based on the recognition of environmental rather than organic determinants. It encouraged the development of "intensive" psychotherapeutic techniques applied to schizophrenics and other psychotics as well as to neurotics. The particular line of thought presented in this selection leads to placing on parents a heavy burden of guilt for the maladjustments of their children.

Conceptions of modern psychiatry. London: Tavistock Publications, Ltd., and New York: W. W. Norton & Co., 1953. [Pp. 15, 18–23.] Reprinted by permission of the publishers. First appeared in *Psychiatry* 3 (1940): 1–117. Copyright 1940, 1945, 1947, and 1953 by the William Alanson White Psychiatric Foundation.

659

. . . If this series of lectures is to be reasonably successful, it will finally have demonstrated that there is nothing unique in the phenomena of the gravest functional illness. The most peculiar behavior of the acutely schizophrenic patient, I hope to demonstrate, is made up of interpersonal processes with which each one of us is or historically has been familiar. . . . In most general terms, we are all much more simply human than otherwise, be we happy and successful, contented and detached, miserable and mentally disordered, or whatever. . . .

Childhood includes a rapid acculturation, but not alone in the basic acquisition of language, which is itself an enormous cultural entity. By this I mean that in childhood the peculiar mindlessness of the infant which seems to be assumed by most parents passes off and they begin to regard the little one as in need of training, as being justifiably an object of education; and what they train the child in consists of select excerpts from the cultural heritage, from that surviving of past people, incorporated in the personality of the parent. . . .

Along with learning of language, the child is experiencing many restraints on the freedom which it had enjoyed up till now. Restraints have to be used in the teaching of some of the personal habits that the culture requires everyone should show, and from these restraints there comes the evolution of the self system—an extremely important part of the personality—with a brand-new tool so important that I must give you its technical name, which unhappily coincides with a word of common speech which may mean to you anything. I refer to *anxiety.*

With the appearance of the self system or the self dynamism, the child picks up a new piece of equipment which we technically call anxiety. Of the very unpleasant experiences which the infant can have we may say that there are generically two, pain and fear. Now comes the third. . . .

As one proceeds into childhood, disapproval, dissatisfaction with one's performances becomes more and more the tool of the significant adult in educating the infant in the folk ways, the tradition, the culture in which he is expected to live. This disapproval is felt by the child through the same empathic linkage which has been so conspicuous in infancy. Gradually he comes to perceive disapproving expressions of the mother, let us say; gradually he comes to understand disapproving statements; but before this perception and understanding he has felt the disapproval which he was not able to comprehend through the ordinary sensory channels.

This process, coupled with the prohibitions and the privations that he must suffer in his education, sets off the experiences that he has in this education and gives them a peculiar coloring of discomfort, neither pain nor fear but discomfort of another kind. . . . The peculiar discomfort is the basis of what we ultimately refer to as anxiety.

The self dynamism is built up out of this experience of approbation and disapproval, of reward and punishment. . . .

Needless to say, the self is extremely important in psychiatry and in everyday life. Not only does anxiety function to discipline attention, but it gradually restricts personal awareness. The facilitations and deprivations by the parents and significant others are the source of the material which is built into the self dynamism. Out of all that happens to the infant and child, only this 'marked' experience is incorporated into the self, because through the control of personal awareness the self itself from the beginning facilitates and restricts its further growth. In other words, it is self-perpetuating, if you please, tends very strongly to maintain the direction and characteristics which it was given in infancy and childhood.

For the expression of all things in the personality other than those which were approved and disapproved by the parent and other significant persons, the self refuses awareness, so to speak. It does not accord awareness, it does not notice; and these impulses, desires, and needs come to exist disassociated from the self. . . .

Needless to say, limitations and peculiarities of the self may interfere with the pursuit of biologically necessary satisfactions. When this happens, the person is to that extent mentally ill. Similarly, they may interfere with security, and to that extent also the person is mentally ill.

The self may be said to be made up of reflected appraisals. If these were chiefly derogatory, as in the case of an unwanted child who was never loved, of a child who has fallen into the hands of foster parents who have no real interest in him as a child; as I say, if the self dynamism is made up of experience which is chiefly derogatory, then the self dynamism will itself be chiefly derogatory. It will facilitate hostile, disparaging appraisals of other people and it will entertain disparaging and hostile appraisals of itself. . . .

Let us rest this matter here for the time being, and review what has been said. We have seen something of the origin and organization of the self and of its marked tendency to stabilize the course of its development. We have seen that if, for example, it is a self that arose through derogatory experience, hostility toward the child, disapproval, dissatisfaction with the child, then this self more or less like a microscope tends to preclude one's learning anything better, to cause one's continuing to feel a sort of limitation in oneself, and while this can not be expressed clearly, while the child or the adult that came from the child does not express openly self-depreciatory trends, he does have a depreciatory attitude toward everyone else, and this really represents a depreciatory attitude toward the self.

24.12

Carl Ransom Rogers

(born 1902)

Quite apart from its theoretical contribution, which is considerable, Rogers' sponsorship of what was at first called "non-directive" and subsequently "client-centered" methods of therapy—eschewing the probing question, the learned interpretation, and the quieting reassurance which was often more comforting to therapist than to patient—produced a decisive change in the work-methods of therapists of all schools and stimulated a flood of research into the relative effectiveness of different sorts of therapist-behaviors. "Relationship," which had been a recognized but subordinate aspect of the patient-therapist interaction, became its principal and for many its exclusive focus. Aside from this influence on therapeutic method, the influence of Rogers also accelerated acceptance of psychologists as therapists, even when not practicing the techniques he recommended or limiting themselves to the range of problems with which "client-centered" therapists customarily dealt.

Although a great deal of counseling is being carried on, although members of several professions regard it as one of their major functions, it is a process to which very little adequate study has been given. We know much less about the outcomes of counseling of students, for example, than we do about the results of foster-home placement for children. The process of counseling has been much less adequately described than the methods of play therapy, although the latter is applicable only to a relatively small group of clients. We have much less understanding of what makes counseling effective or ineffective than we do of other approaches.

So vast is our ignorance on this whole subject that it is evident that we are by no means professionally ready to develop a definitive or final account of any aspect of psychotherapy. What is needed, it would seem, are some hypothetical formulations, based on counseling experience, which may then be put to the test. Scientific advance can be made only as we have hypotheses which may be experimentally tried, tested, and improved. The field of counseling has not been rich in fruitful hypotheses. It has rather been a field where good intentions and a desire to be of assistance have been accepted as substitutes for the careful formulation of the principles involved. . . .

Counseling and psychotherapy: newer concepts in practice. Boston: Houghton Mifflin, 1942. [Pp. 16, 18, 28, 173, 216.]

The Basic Hypothesis. . . . Effective counseling consists of a definitely structured, permissive relationship which allows the client to gain an understanding of himself to a degree which enables him to take positive steps in the light of his new orientation. This hypothesis has a natural corollary, that all the techniques used should aim toward developing this free and permissive relationship, this understanding of self in the counseling and other relationships, and this tendency toward positive, self-initiated action. . . .

This newer approach differs from the older one in that it has a genuinely different goal. It aims directly toward the greater independence and integration of the individual rather than hoping that such results will accrue if the counselor assists in solving the problem. The individual and not the problem is the focus. The aim is not to solve one particular problem, but to assist the individual to *grow,* so that he can cope with the present problem and with later problems in a better-integrated fashion. . . .

In effective counseling and psychotherapy one of the major purposes of the counselor is to help the client to express freely the emotionalized attitudes which are basic to his adjustment problems and conflicts. In carrying out this purpose, the counselor adopts various methods which enable the client to release his feelings without inhibition. Primarily the counselor endeavors to respond to, and verbally recognize, the feeling content, rather than the intellectual content, of the client's expression. This principle holds, no matter what the type of emotionalized attitude— negative attitudes of hostility, discouragement, and fear, positive attitudes of affection and courage and self-confidence, or ambivalent and contradictory attitudes. This approach is sound whether the client's feelings are directed toward himself, toward others, or toward the counselor and the counseling situation. In each case, the counselor aims to recognize and respond to the feeling expressed, openly accepting it as an element in the problem and in the counseling relationship. He avoids the verbal recognition of repressed attitudes which the client has not yet been able to express.

In this process the client finds emotional release from feelings heretofore repressed, increasing awareness of the basic elements in his own situation, and increased ability to recognize his own feelings openly and without fear. . . .

The free release of the client's feelings and emotionalized attitudes in an accepting type of counseling relationship leads inevitably to insight. This development of insight comes for the most part spontaneously, though cautious and intelligent use of interpretive techniques can increase the scope and the clarity of such self-understanding.

The client's insight tends to develop gradually, and proceeds in general from less to more significant understandings. It involves the new

663

perception of relationships previously unrecognized, a willingness to accept all aspects of the self, and a choice of goals, now clearly perceived for the first time.

Following these new perceptions of self, and this new choice of goals, come self-initiated actions which move toward achieving the new goals. These steps are of the most significant sort for growth, though they may relate only to minor issues. They create new confidence and independence in the client, and thus reinforce the new orientation which has come about through increased insight.

Chapter 25

THE MATHEMATICAL HURDLE

To earn a place among the sciences, psychology had to meet criteria which Hume succinctly stated in the closing sentences of his Enquiry concerning human understanding (1748):

> If we take in our hands any volume, of divinity or school metaphysics, for instance; let us ask, *Does it contain any abstract reasoning concerning quantity or number?* No. *Does it contain any experimental reasoning concerning matter of fact and existence?* No. Commit it then to the flame: For it can contain nothing but sophistry and illusion.

Psychology has amply met the first criterion by the building of mathematical models, and the statistical overlay of its "experimental reasoning" has become so heavy that it is now more often criticized for being overly mathematical than the contrary. In Pearson's phrase, it has mastered "the grammar of science."

25.1

Francis Hutcheson

(1694–1746)

Note the change in subtitle (see 12.4) after the favorable reception to the first edition. We take this selection from the second edition because of its first paragraph, an important addition. (Other changes are minimal.) In it, Hutcheson anticipates the concept of fortune morale, stated in 1738 by Daniel Bernoulli (1708–1782) in relation to the psychological magnitude of a given win or loss at the gambling table, for a rich man or a poor man. The reverend·Hutcheson applies the concept to philanthropy.

Although Hutcheson's views are predominantly nativist, he invents the very phrase, "the greatest happiness for the greatest numbers," which was to become the banner for empirically minded utilitarians.

The selection is from Section III of the second treatise, which deals, in part, with "The Manner of computing the Morality of Actions." What a pity that Reid's refutation (the next selection) did not come until after Hutcheson's death, depriving us of Hutcheson's reply!

VI. . . . Wherever a Regard to *my self,* tends as much to the good of the *Whole,* as Regard to *another;* or where the *Evil* to my self, is equal to the *Good* obtain'd for another; tho by acting, in such Cases, for the good of *another,* I really shew a very amiable Disposition; yet by acting in the contrary manner, from Regard to *my self,* I evidence no evil Disposition, nor any want of the most extensive *Benevolence;* since the *Moment* of Good to the *Whole* is, in both Cases, exactly equal. And let it be here observ'd, that this does not supersede the necessity of *Liberality,* or *gratuitous Gifts,* altho in such Actions the Giver loses as much as the other receives; since the *Moment* of Good to any Person, in any given Case, is in a *compound Ratio* of the *Quantity* of the Good it self, and the *Indigence* of the Person. Hence it appears, that a Gift may make a much greater *Addition* to the happiness of the *Receiver,* than the *Diminution* it occasions in the happiness of the *Giver:* And that the most useful and important Gifts are those from the *Wealthy* to the *Indigent.* . . .

VIII. In comparing the *moral Qualitys* of Actions, in order to regulate our *Election* among various Actions propos'd, or to find which of them has the greatest *moral Excellency,* we are led by *our moral Sense* of

An inquiry into the original of our ideas of beauty and virtue. In two treatises. I. Concerning Beauty, Order, Harmony, Design. II. Concerning Moral Good and Evil. The second edition, corrected and enlarged. London, 1726. [Pp. 174–175, 177–178, 182–185, 190, 194–195.]

Virtue to judge thus; that in *equal Degrees* of Happiness, expected to proceed from the Action, the *Virtue* is in proportion to the *Number* of Persons to whom the Happiness shall extend: (and here the *Dignity,* or *moral Importance* of Persons, may compensate Numbers) and in equal *Numbers,* the *Virtue* is as the *Quantity* of the Happiness, or natural *Good;* or that the *Virtue* is in a *compound Ratio* of the *Quantity* of Good, and *Number* of Enjoyers. In the same manner, the *moral Evil,* or *Vice,* is as the *Degree* of Misery, and *Number* of Sufferers; so that, *that Action is best,* which procures the *greatest Happiness* for the *greatest Numbers;* and *that, worst,* which, in *like manner,* occasions *Misery.* . . .

XI. To find a *universal Canon* to compare the *Morality* of any Actions, with all their Circumstances, when we *judge* of the Actions done by our selves, or by others, we must observe the following *Propositions,* or *Axioms.*

1. The *moral Importance* of any *Agent,* or the *Quality* of *publick Good* produc'd by him, is in a *Compound Ratio* of his *Benevolence* and *Abilitys:* or (by substituting the initial Letters for the Words, as $M = $ *Moment* of *Good,* and $\mu = Moment$ of *Evil*) $M = B \times A$.

2. In like manner, the *Moment* of *private Good,* or *Interest* produc'd by any Person to himself, is in a *compound Ratio* of his *Self-Love,* and *Abilitys:* or (substituting the initial Letters) $I = S \times A$.

3. When in comparing the *Virtue* of two Actions, the *Abilitys* of the *Agents* are equal; the *Moment* of *publick Good* produc'd by them in like Circumstances, is as the *Benevolence:* or $M = B \times 1$.

4. When *Benevolence* in two *Agents* is equal, and other Circumstances alike, the *Moment* of *publick Good* is as the *Abilitys:* or $M = A \times 1$.

5. The *Virtue* then of *Agents,* or their *Benevolence,* is always *directly* as the *Moment* of *Good* produc'd in like Circumstances, and *inversly* as their *Abilitys:* or $B = \dfrac{M}{A}$.

6. But as the natural Consequences of our Actions are various, some *good* to our selves, and *evil* to the Publick; and others *evil* to our selves, and *good* to the Publick or either *useful* both to our selves and others, or *pernicious* to both; the entire Motive to good Actions is not always *Benevolence alone;* or, Motive to Evil, *Malice alone;* (nay, this last is seldom any Motive at all) but in most Actions we must look upon *Self-Love* as another Force, sometimes conspiring with *Benevolence,* and assisting it, when we are excited by Views of *private Interest,* as well as *publick Good;* and sometimes opposing *Benevolence,* when the good Action is any way *difficult* or *painful* in the Performance, or *detrimental* in its Consequences to the *Agent.* . . .

These *selfish Motives* shall be hereafter more fully explain'd; here we may in general denote them by the Word *Interest:* which when it concurs with *Benevolence,* in any Action capable of Increase, or Diminution, must produce a greater Quantity of *Good,* than *Benevolence* alone in the same *Abilitys;* and therefore when the *Moment* of *Good,* in an Action partly intended for the *Good* of the *Agent,* is but equal to the *Moment* of *Good* in the Action of *another Agent,* influenc'd only by *Benevolence,* the former is less *virtuous;* and in this Case the *Interest* must be deducted to find the true Effect of the *Benevolence,* or *Virtue.* In the same manner, when *Interest* is opposite to *Benevolence,* and yet is surmounted by it; this *Interest* must be added to the *Moment,* to increase the *Virtue* of the Action, or the Strength of the *Benevolence.* . . .

XIII. From Axiom the *5th,* we may form almost a demonstrative Conclusion, "that we have a *Sense* of *Goodness* and *moral Beauty* in Actions, distinct from *Advantage;*" for had we no other Foundation of Approbation of Actions, but the *Advantage* which might arise to us from them, if they were done toward our selves, we should make no Account of the *Abilitys* of the *Agent,* but would barely esteem them according to their *Moment.* The Abilitys come in only to shew the Degree of *Benevolence,* which supposes *Benevolence* necessarily *amiable.* . . .

XV. . . . The applying a *mathematical Calculation* to moral *Subjects,* will appear perhaps at first *extravagant* and *wild;* but some Corollarys, which are easily and certainly deduc'd below, may shew the Conveniency of this Attempt, if it could be further pursu'd. At present, we shall only draw this one, which seems the most joyful imaginable, even to the lowest Rank of Mankind, *viz.* "That no external Circumstances of Fortune, no involuntary Disadvantages, can exclude any Mortal from the *most heroick Virtue.*" For how small soever the *Moment of publick* Good be, which any one can accomplish, yet if his *Abilitys* are proportionably small, the *Quotient,* which expresses the Degree of *Virtue,* may be as great as any whatsoever.

25.2

Thomas Reid

(1710–1796)

This reply to Hutcheson is Reid's first published work, and it already shows him anticipating certain aspects of Kantian philosophy. Although Reid does not flatly state that feelings and sensations must be forever recalcitrant to measurement, he certainly implies it. Kant also took the view (see the next selection) that psychology could not become a science because it

An essay on quantity; occasioned by reading a treatise, in which simple and compound ratio's are applied to virtue and merit. *Philosophical Transactions* 45 (1748): 505–520. [Pp. 505–510, 512–513.]

could not measure the things it dealt with. But these very protests by Reid and Kant are testimony to the existence of a new trend, which is pushing men to apply mathematics in all fields.

It is interesting to study parallels between this discussion and Fechner's steps in developing a rationale for the measurement of sensation, later in this chapter.

Since mathematical Demonstration is thought to carry a peculiar Evidence along with it, which leaves no Room for further Dispute; it may be of some Use, or Entertainment at least, to inquire to what Subjects this kind of Proof may be applied.

Mathematics contain properly the Doctrine of Measure; and the Object of this Science is commonly said to be Quantity; therefore Quantity ought to be defined, What may be measured. Those who have defined Quantity to be whatever is capable of More or Less, have given too wide a Notion of it, which I apprehend has led some Persons to apply mathematical Reasoning to Subjects that do not admit of it.

Pain and Pleasure admit of various Degrees, but who can pretend to measure them? Had this been possible, it is not to be doubted but we should have had as distinct Names for their various Degrees, as we have for Measures of Length or Capacity; and a Patient should have been able to describe the Quantity of his Pain, as well as the Time it began, or the Part it affected. To talk intelligibly of the Quantity of Pain, we should have some Standard to measure it by; some known Degree of it so well ascertained, that all Men, when they talked of it, should mean the same thing; we should also be able to compare other Degrees of Pain with this, so as to perceive distinctly, not only whether they exceed or fall short of it, but how far, or in what proportion; whether by an half, a fifth, or a tenth.

Whatever has Quantity, or is measurable, must be made up of Parts, which bear Proportion to one another, and to the Whole; so that it may be increased by Addition of like Parts, and diminished by Subtraction, may be multiplied and divided, and in a Word, may bear any Proportion to another Quantity of the same kind, that one Line or Number can bear to another. That this is essential to all mathematical Quantity, is evident from the first Elements of Algebra, which treats of Quantity in general, or of those Relationships and Properties which are common to all Kinds of Quantity. Every algebraical Quantity is supposed capable not only of being increased and diminished, but of being exactly doubled, tripled, halfed, or of bearing any assignable Proportion to another Quantity of the same kind. This then is the Characteristic of Quantity; whatever has this Property may be adopted into Mathematics; and its Quantity and Relations may be measured with mathematical Accuracy and Certainty. . . .

I call that *Proper* Quantity which is measured by its own Kind; or which of its own Nature is capable of being doubled or tripled, without taking in any Quantity of a different Kind of a Measure of it. . . .

Improper Quantity is that which cannot be measured of its own Kind; but to which we assign a Measure by the means of some proper Quantity that is related to it. Thus Velocity of Motion, when we consider it by itself, cannot be measured. We may perceive one Body to move faster, another slower; but we can have no distinct Idea of a Proportion or *Ratio* between their Velocities, without taking in some Quantity of another Kind to measure them by. Having therefore observed, that by a greater Velocity a greater Space is passed over in the same time, by a less Velocity a less Space, and by an equal Velocity an equal Space; we hence learn to measure Velocity by the Space passed over in a given Time, and to reckon it to be in exact Proportion to that Space. And having once assigned this Measure to it, we can then, and not till then, conceive one Velocity to be exactly double, or half, or in any other Proportion to another; we may then introduce it into mathematical Reasoning without Danger of Confusion, or Error, and may also use it as a Measure of other Improper Quantities. . . .

It is not easy to say how many Kinds of improper Quantity, may in time, be introduced into Mathematics, or to what new Subjects Measures may be applied: But this I think we may conclude, that there is no Foundation in Nature for, nor can any valuable End be served by applying Measure to any thing but what has these two Properties. First it must admit of Degrees of greater and less. Secondly, it must be associated with, or related to something that has proper Quantity, so as that when one is increased the other is increased, when one is diminished, the other is diminished also; and every Degree of the one must have a determinate Magnitude or Quantity of the other corresponding to it. . . .

There are many Things capable of More or Less, which perhaps are not capable of Mensuration. Tastes, Smells, the Sensations of Heat and Cold, Beauty, Pleasure, all the Affections and Appetites of the Mind, Wisdom, Folly, and most Kinds of Probability, with many other Things too tedious to enumerate, admit of Degrees, but have not yet been reduced to Measure, nor, as I apprehend, ever can be. I say, most Kinds of Probability, because one Kind of it, *viz.* the Probability of Chances is properly measurable by Number, as is above observed.

Altho' Attempts have been made to apply mathematical Reasoning to some of these Things, and the Quantity of Virtue and Merit in Actions has been measured by simple and compound *Ratio's;* yet I do not think that any real Knowledge has been struck out this Way: It may perhaps, if discretely used, be a Help to Discourse on these Subjects, by pleasing the Imagination, and illustrating what is already known; but until our Affections and Appetites shall themselves be reduced to Quantity, and exact Measures of their various Degrees be assigned, in vain shall we essay to measure Virtue and Merit by them. This is only to ring

Changes upon Words, and to make a Shew of mathematical Reasoning, without advancing one Step in real Knowledge.

25.3

Immanuel Kant

(1724–1804)

In the preface to this work on the foundations of science, Kant dismisses the possibility that psychology might fall within its scope. He sees some hope for chemistry, but he regards psychological phenomena as intrinsically incapable of measurement, or even of proper experimental manipulation.

That only can be called science (*wissenschaft*) *proper* whose certainty is apodictic: cognition that can merely contain empirical certainty is only improperly called science. A whole of cognition which is systematic is for this reason called *science,* and, when the connection of cognition in this system is a system of causes and effects, *rational* science. But when the grounds or principles it contains are in the last resort merely empirical, as, for instance, in chemistry, and the laws from which the reason explains the given facts are merely empirical laws, they then carry no consciousness of their *necessity* with them (they are not apodictically certain), and thus the whole does not in strictness deserve the name of science; chemistry indeed should be rather termed systematic art than science. . . .

Thus all natural science *proper* requires a *pure* portion, upon which the apodictic certainty required of it by the reason can be based; and inasmuch as this is in its principles wholly heterogeneous from those which are merely empirical, it is at once a matter of the utmost importance . . . to expound this part separately and unmixed with the other, and as far as possible in its completeness; in order that we may be able to determine precisely what the reason can accomplish for itself, and where its capacity begins to require the assistance of empirical principles. . . .

. . . But I maintain that in every special natural doctrine only so much science *proper* is to be met with as mathematics; for, in accordance with the foregoing, science proper, especially [science] of nature, requires a pure portion, lying at the foundation of the empirical, and based upon

Metaphysische Anfangsgründe der Naturwissenschaft [1786]. Translated by Ernest Belfort Bax as *Kant's Prolegomena and Metaphysical foundations of natural science.* London, 1883. [Pp. 138–142.]

an *à priori* knowledge of natural things. Now to cognise anything *à priori* is to cognise it from its mere possibility; but the possibility of determinate natural things cannot be known from mere conceptions; for from these the possibility of the thought (that it does not contradict itself) can indeed be known, but not of the object, as natural thing which can be given (as existent) outside the thought. Hence, to the possibility of a determinate natural thing, and therefore to cognise it *à priori*, is further requisite that the *intuition* corresponding *à priori* to the conception should be given; in other words, that the conception should be constructed. But cognition of the reason through construction of conceptions is mathematical. A pure philosophy of nature in general, namely, one that only investigates what constitutes a nature in general, may thus be possible without mathematics; but a pure doctrine of nature respecting *determinate* natural things (corporeal doctrine and mental doctrine), is only possible by means of mathematics; and as in every natural doctrine only so much science proper is to be met with therein as there is cognition *à priori*, a doctrine of nature can only contain so much science proper as there is in it of applied mathematics.

So long, therefore, as no conception is discovered for the chemical effects of substances on one another, which admits of being constructed, that is, no law of the approach or retreat of the parts can be stated . . . chemistry will be nothing more than a systematic art or experimental doctrine, but never science proper, its principles being merely empirical and not admitting of any presentation *à priori*. . . .

But still farther even than chemistry must empirical psychology be removed from the rank of what may be termed a natural science proper; firstly, because mathematics is inapplicable to the phenomena of the internal sense and its laws, unless indeed we consider merely the *law of permanence* in the flow of its internal changes; but this would be an extension of cognition, bearing much the same relation to that procured by the mathematics of corporeal knowledge, as the doctrine of the properties of the straight line does to the whole of geometry; for the pure internal intuition in which psychical phenomena are constructed in time, which has only one dimension. But not even as a systematic art of analysis, or experimental doctrine, can it ever approach chemistry, because in it the manifold of internal observation is only separated in thought, but cannot be kept separate and be connected again at pleasure; still less is another thinking subject amenable to investigations of this kind, and even the observation itself, alters and distorts the state of the object observed. It can never therefore be anything more than an historical, and as such, as far as possible systematic natural doctrine of the internal sense, i.e. a natural description of the soul, but not a science of the soul, nor even a psychological experimental doctrine.

25.4

Johann Friedrich Herbart

(1776–1841)

Herbart's technical writings are not easily understood even without the barrier of translation. Instead of selecting one of those passages which commonly serve only to convince most present-day readers that Herbart's use of mathematics was unrealistic and unproductive, we prefer to give his own attempt at a nontechnical justification, in a lecture before a sceptical audience of his own time. It is too easy to dismiss Herbart's formulas for the "sum of arrests" and "remainders" as mere speculation. He was in fact a pioneer in the use of mathematical models for psychological theory, and from his model he deduced the necessity for inhibition. It has taken us 150 years to catch up to this insight!

We add [B] a few sentences in his more metaphysical manner, which concisely state the need for inhibitory interaction among mental phenomena.

[A]

. . . Socrates has been praised through the centuries because he brought philosophy from heaven down to earth, and applied it to people. If he were to appear again today, and was fully informed as to the status of our sciences, and if he looked again toward the heavens to see what benefit he might draw from them for mankind, what he would see there is not philosophy, but mathematics, busily at work and being rewarded for its efforts by the happiest and most brilliant successes. And it might well occur to him to say, "Tell me, excellent sirs, what is of more worth: physical things, or the soul? What is more important to you—the nutation of the earth's axis or the vacillations of your own opinions and motives? . . . And if mathematics is such an excellent tool for your research, why don't you try to apply it to the things which are most important and most necessary to you?" . . . Would you perhaps reply that mathematics is being put to work inside our prisons, and before the walls of our cities under siege? That it teaches us not only how to advance human industry,

[A] Ueber die Möglichkeit und Nothwendigkeit, Mathematik auf Psychologie anzuwenden [On the possibility and necessity of applying mathematics to psychology. 1822]. In *Sämmtliche Werke*, edited by G. Hartenstein. Volume VII, Leipzig, 1851. Pp. 129–172. [Pp. 134–145, 147–148.]
[B] *Psychologie als Wissenschaft neu gegründet auf Erfahrung, Metaphysik, und Mathematik* [Psychology as science, newly founded on experience, metaphysics, and mathematics. 1824–1825.] In *Sämttliche Werke*, Vols. V and VI. Leipzig, 1850. [Vol. V, pp. 24, 96, 98.]

but also how to destroy it? We would not dare to reply in this manner, and expose ourselves to his ridicule. . . . I at least shall not do so, particularly since I am more concerned with another matter. . . . I have in fact been aware that surprise has been expressed about my efforts to put mathematics to work in psychology, and that quite recently this surprise was stirred up again by my article on the general conditions of attention and its measurement. . . . So I have decided for once to give a short report on my efforts in a language other than that of algebraic symbols. . . . I shall speak first of the apparent reasons for this surprise; only after answering those arguments can I hope to gain a receptive audience for the proof that the application of mathematics to psychology is *possible*, and that it is *necessary*. . . .

The first apparent reason brought against me is really nothing but an old habit, although it is put into words as an assertion which is completely untrue. No one has ever heard of applying mathematics except to objects which are either spatial in themselves, or can at least be spatially represented. For example, forces which increase or decrease with distance, and the effects of which are measured or accurately observed. But what yardstick can we use to measure and compare our mental experiences, the changes taking place in our ideas, feelings and desires? Our thoughts are swifter than lightning—how shall we observe and describe their path? Human fancies are as flighty as the winds, our moods as uncertain as the weather—who can find measures for them, to bring them under the rule of mathematical laws? *Where measurement is not possible, neither is calculation;* consequently it is not possible to make use of mathematics in psychological investigation. So goes the syllogism which is put together by clinging to habit, and adding an obvious untruth. For it is quite false . . . to say that we can only calculate after we have taken measurements. Quite the contrary! Any hypothetical law dealing with relationships between magnitudes, even if it is recognized as incorrect, can be the basis for a calculation; and in dealing with matters which are important but quite obscure we *must* try out different hypotheses, accurately calculating the consequences which follow from them, until we discover which hypothesis coincides with experience. In this way the ancient astronomers *tried out* eccentric circles, and Kepler *tried out* the ellipse . . . ; Newton likewise *tried out* whether gravitation, inversely as the square of the distance, would suffice to keep the moon in its path around the earth; if this assumption had not sufficed he would have tried another power, such as the cube or the fourth or fifth power of the distance, and calculated the consequences, in order to compare them with experience. For it is the great merit of mathematics that long before we have sufficiently definite experience, we can survey the possibilities within which reality must lie; and therefore we can utilize very imperfect intimations of experience, in order to free ourselves at least from the worst mistakes. . . . It is true that measurements invite calculation, and any easily noticed regularity among certain magnitudes is a stimulus to mathematical investigation. Conversely, the less symmetry there is in phenomena, the more will the appearance of scientific effort be delayed. If the heavenly bodies moved in a medium which offered noticeable resistance, or if their masses were not so small in respect to their distance, astronomy might have got no farther than psychology is today, nor would it then be in a position to hope, as psychology may, to make up by the number of observations what they lack in precision.

A second objection is based on the fact that mathematics deals only with *quantities,* but psychology deals with states and activities which differ *greatly* in quality. If I wanted to refute this pretended reason in thorough fashion, I would start out with a metaphysical proof that the true . . . qualities of things are completely hidden from us, and they do not constitute the subject matter of our investigations. When in our ordinary experience we think we are perceiving qualities, their basis is often merely quantitative. For example, we hear different tones . . . merely because longer or shorter strings are vibrating faster or slower. . . . For the present it will be enough to say that no matter how many imagined qualities someone thinks he can distinguish in his mind, he still cannot deny that there is also an infinite number of quantitative determinants of mental experience. Our ideas are stronger, weaker, clearer, dimmer; their coming and going is quicker or slower, their number at any moment greater or less; our sensitivity to sensations, our responsiveness to feelings and emotions, ceaselessly wavers, between more and less. . . . Everyone knows what sleep is: that it consists in the suppression of our ideas, which is quite complete in deep sleep, incomplete during dreams. But very few stop to think that even in times of the brightest wakefulness very few of our ideas are present in a single instant; the others occupy us no more than they do in sleep; or, to express the same thing more definitely, most of our ideas are *latent,* and very few are *free* at any moment. I ask you to think for a moment of physics, and to recall what latent and free heat are. What was physics, before this distinction had been made and taken into account? That is the status of psychology today. . . .

Still further objections are based on current opinions about the so-called higher mental faculties, and I know quite well . . . that here I come up against the strongest prejudices of all, prejudices which are invincible because we do not *want* to give them up. . . . What shall I say about *freedom?* First, that I am tired of talking about it. . . . Still, all the difficulties of the doctrine of freedom would disappear if we did not have the strangest ideas about the "will" which is left over when the confession of freedom is removed. If someone says: "I cannot conceive of a will that is not necessarily free," we can answer him: "Keep your freedom, because it really does exist in the sense which you give to the word." The human mind is no puppet theatre; our desires and decisions are no marionettes; no conjuror stands behind them. Our own true life is in what we will, and this life has rules that are not external to itself, but of itself; it has its own, purely mental laws, which are in no sense borrowed from the physical world. But these laws are fixed and sure, and because they are so definite they have more resemblance to the laws of pushing and pulling (to which they are otherwise so foreign) than to the miracles of a pretended inconceivable freedom.

Now, in order to prove that it is possible to apply mathematics to psychology, I must first of all distinguish between *material* and *formal* possibility. The first relates to the actual things which present themselves to psychologists for measurement; the latter, to the procedure which must be followed in research. . . . Consider first the form of procedure. . . . It is true that mathematics can do nothing without magnitudes, but it is amazing with what skill it takes hold of these, wherever it meets them. . . . What is the heavenly sphere? Is it a real vault, a true hollow sphere, on which we can draw spherical triangles? No! It is a useful fiction. . . . What is a center of gravity? . . . Why do we speak, in statics, about mathematical levers which do not exist in nature? Or in mechanics, about the movement of points and simple pendula and bodies falling in a vacuum? . . . In a word, why do we use so many fictional magnitudes; why don't we calculate immediately in terms of things that happen in the real world? The answer is . . . (that) these fictions are real helps: if we are to make the real magnitudes accessible, either precisely or approximately, we will first have to relate them to such assumed magnitudes. . . . Therefore, insofar as mental states and activities really depend on quantities, we can foresee that the calculation of these quantities will be based on relating them to more convenient fictional magnitudes. . . .

Now we can point out more precisely those magnitudes which offer themselves for calculation. We must start with the simplest, leaving aside at first all connections among ideas. This leaves only two magnitudes to which we must give attention: the *strength of individual ideas,* and the *degree of inhibition among them.* . . .

The calculations based on the strengths of two ideas and the degree of inhibition between them are very simple; they become more complicated if we also take into account a third factor, the *degree of connectedness* between the ideas. . . . Then a fourth factor enters, namely, the *number* of connected ideas. Particularly noteworthy are the *long and short chains* which arise as a result of *incomplete connections,* when one idea is connected to a second, the second to a third, the third to a fourth, all in different degrees, while the first and third, or the second and fourth, etc., do not blend at all, or only in a very slight degree. Such chains of ideas are like the threads or fibers of which our larger mental organs are composed. Their excitation is governed by very definite laws, and a more exact knowledge of these is very important. There are some remote but highly inadequate intimations of this in what has long been called the association of ideas, but more definite knowledge must be based on calculation, and this will have the most important consequences not only for the theory of memory, fantasy, and understanding, but also for the study of feelings, desires and emotions. I see no reason why I should not say without restraint that mathematics here exposes the boundless ignorance of psychology until the present. Even our ideas of space and time have their seat and origin in this, and not in supposed basic forms of sensibility. . . .

. . . It is not only possible, but also necessary to apply mathematics to psychology. The reason for this necessity lies, in a word, in the fact that otherwise we can never attain the goal of all speculation, which is conviction. . . . Mathematics is the ruling science of our time. Its conquests grow daily, though without any clamor. If we do not have mathematics *with* us, we will one day have it *against* us.

[B]

[§ 7] If we think how changeable is the spectacle which planned introspection meets, but cannot hold still in any state, and besides this of the changes taking place among the states of feeling which flow into one another, and which make up the stuff of our real life story—all this appears as coming and going, as rising and waning; in a word, as becoming *stronger* or *weaker*.

Each of these expressions includes a *quantitative concept*. Therefore, either there is no exact regularity in the facts of consciousness, or that regularity is of a *mathematical* kind, and we must try to understand it mathematically. . . .

[§ 29] Another very important step is essential before we can give a new direction, and at the same time a new impetus, to our observations.

The several objects (not *real* things, of course, but merely those things which are ideated, as such) which together are supposed to do what they cannot do separately, that is, to prepare a base for the *self-identity* which has no basis, are obviously no better suited to do this as a mere sum or aggregate than when taken separately. They must mutually modify one another; that much we already know. But how they are to modify one another must still be indicated in a more precise manner. . . .

Now it is a contradiction to suppose that any given idea A should itself be able to alter or diminish the act of ideating A. In that case A would have to be opposed to itself.

Since therefore no idea taken by itself, such as a given idea A, or B, or C, and so forth, can free us *of itself*, the only possibility which remains is that different ideas, insofar as this may be determined by their different content as this and as that, shall mutually diminish one another; that *one* idea shall free us from *another*.

Therefore the multiplex ideas must naturally terminate one another, if self-identity is to be a possibility.

25.5

Ernst Heinrich Weber

(1795–1878)

Weber's careful quantitative studies of sensory discrimination were seen by him as part of his work as a physiologist. On the other hand, he commends to the attention of psychologists a possible method for the experimental study of memory. But it was the method he devised for studying sensory discrimination, the method of "just noticeable differences," which became of great significance to psychology as an experimental science. He points out that in each sensory modality this "just noticeable difference" is not a fixed quantity, but takes different values according to a ratio law.

The theory of the senses is a point at which, some time in the future, the research of physiologists, psychologists and physicists must converge. For it is to be foreseen that when natural forces are properly defined, and the laws by which they work have been discovered, there will be a very pressing need to understand how the movements that occur in nature take effect on our sense organs and how they produce in us the ideas we have of phenomena in the world.

However, it is the sense of touch which lends itself exceptionally well to showing, through a series of experiments, how we reach those ideas which we owe to it. Its organ is so widely distributed over the surface of the body, and experiments are so noninjurious, that one can carry out many experiments which cannot be performed on other sense organs. Some of the things we discover in this way . . . can be applied to the other senses with some degree of probability.

The following observation gave me the first incentive to this investigation: if one touches a person on the back at two places simultaneously, *e.g.* with the two rounded points of a compass, then the points seem to him to lie very close together even when they are 1 to 1½ inches apart. There are many places on the skin where compass points which are separated by as much as that produce only the sensation of a single contact. . . . But even when the two impressions begin to merge and to be perceived as a single impression, if this merger is not quite complete one can still perceive a difference from which one can at least judge the

Ueber den Tastsinn [On the sense of touch]. *Archiv für Anatomie, Physiologie, und wissenschaftliche Medicin*, 1835: 152–159. [152–158.]

[relative] position of the corresponding points on the body: for the point then seems to us, when both impressions are not completely merged, to be somewhat stretched out, having its longer diameter in the direction of the imaginary line connecting the two points of the compass. Now, if one touches a person simultaneously with the two rounded points of the compass, without his watching, and if one changes the distance between the points until he feels both contacts as one and is no longer able to determine whether the imaginary line connecting the compass points runs lengthwise or across the body part which is being touched, one has a means of determining experimentally how fine the sense of touch is on different parts of the body, and whether the same relationships obtain in this regard for different people. I have carried out a great many such experiments on myself and on others, and I have found that for me the impressions begin to be distinguished as two when the separation of the compass points is as follows:

at the tip of the tongue	½ ligne
at the finger tips	1 "
on the red part of the lips	2 lignes
on the forehead	10 "
on the middle of the upper arm	30 "

[In the original, values are given for 27 locations. The French *ligne* was one-twelfth of a *pouce*, or inch.]. . . .

If one separates the compass points by about an inch and a quarter, and touches the face just in front of the ear, in such a way that one point lies directly over the other, and then moves the compass . . . to the lips and from them to the other ear, they will at first (because the skin near the ear is less sensitive) appear to lie close together, but the closer one comes to the more sensitive lower and upper lips, the farther they seem to separate from one another; and in the same manner, as they are moved toward the ear on the other side of the face, they seem to come closer together. One even believes, as the compass moves, that he perceives the form of the curved line along which each point of the compass seems to move. In order to explain this phenomenon, I assume that through frequent contact we have acquired an obscure consciousness of the existence of all the sensitive points of the skin. The interval seems greater to us if many sensitive points lie between two points that are touched, and smaller if fewer such points lie between them. . . .

I have also performed similar experiments . . . on the perception and comparison of the pressure of two weights, and of the temperature of two objects coming into contact with the skin. . . .

Under the most favorable circumstances, one can still perceive a difference between two weights which is only $\frac{1}{30}$ [of their combined weights] or $\frac{1}{15}$ of one of the weights, *i.e.*, if one weight is 15 and the other 14 ounces, *loths*, or drams, for what matters here is not the *absolute*, but the *relative* magnitude of the difference in weight. This last observation merits the attention of psychologists and physiologists, for it is also true of other senses. I have shown . . . that one can still perceive a difference between two lines when one is 100 millimeters long and the other 101, so that the difference is $\frac{1}{100}$ of the length of the constant line, but that the lines seem to be equal if the difference is still less, *e.g.* when one line is 100 millimeters and the other $100\frac{1}{2}$. Under these circumstances one does not perceive the $\frac{1}{2}$ millimeter by which one line is longer than the other. But under other circumstances, *e.g.* if one line is 4 millimeters long and the other $4\frac{1}{2}$, one perceives the difference of $\frac{1}{2}$ millimeter very clearly. From this we see that with lengths, just as with weights, we perceive in comparison not the absolute but the relative difference—a fact which can also be confirmed in hearing, and from which one can draw a number of conclusions as to how we go about comparing two magnitudes by means of our senses. . . .

Differences in weights are more accurately perceived when we place first one weight on the hand and then, after removing it, the other, rather than simultaneously placing the weights on both hands or on one hand. Likewise one discriminates differences in the temperature of substances coming into contact with the hand more accurately if first one object is touched and then the other. . . .

It is in any case surprising that one can better compare an ongoing impression with one that has just ended, than two simultaneous impressions to which one can direct one's attention alternately. For in the former case we are required to compare a present impression with an idea in fantasy, with an impression that is being repeated in memory, which would seem to be very difficult; and yet that is the case. The comparison is most perfect when one impression has just ended and the second impression follows the first immediately. . . . One can determine experimentally how the clarity of the idea of an impression falls off, during intervals of 3, 4, 5, 6, 8, 10, 20 or more seconds. . . . One can do the same with several lines that are equally thick and black, by first presenting one of them and then, after a shorter or longer interval, the other. . . . In this way one can really make measurements on the decline in strength from impressions that have been received.

25.6

Adolphe Quetelet

(1796–1874)

Quetelet, mathematician and astronomer by profession, became the father of social and psychological statistics when he began applying statistical methodology to the study of social phenomena. His approach was to measure man only in the mass, but his doctrines of the "average man" and "moral statistics" (22.8) came to exercise great influence. His techniques influenced Galton (11.7, 17.10).

Where the translator of the first selection writes "appreciate," he might better have written "evaluate" or "estimate."

[A]

Certain moral qualities are very analogous to physical ones; and we may appreciate them, by admitting that they are proportioned to the effects which they produce. Thus, we cannot hesitate to say that one operative has twice or thrice the activity of another, if, all things being equal, he performs double or triple the amount of labour which the other one does. Here the effects are purely physical, and . . . we have only to admit the hypothesis that causes are proportioned to the effects produced by them. But in a great number of cases, this appreciation becomes impracticable. When the activity of man is exerted on immaterial labours, for example, what standard can we adopt, except the works, such as books, statues, or paintings, produced? for how can we obtain the value of the researches and thought which these works have required? The number of the works can alone give an idea of the productive power of the author, as the number of children brought into the world gives us the fecundity of a female, without taking into account the value of the work produced.

If, like the fecundity of females, the different qualities of men were manifested by deeds to which we could assign a value, we conceive that these qualities might be appreciated and compared with each other. Thus, we should not be astounded at hearing, that one man has twice the courage of another, but only one-third the genius; but, since such an appreciation has nothing definite and exact, we confine ourselves to saying that a certain individual has courage, or has not courage, or is even a

[A] *Traité de l'homme* [Paris and Brussels, 1835]. Translated as *A treatise of man and the development of his faculties.* Edinburgh, 1842. [Pp. 73, 96.]
[B] *Anthropométrie, ou mésure des differentes facultés de l'homme* [Anthropometry, or the measurement of different faculties in man]. Brussels, 1871. [Pp. 413–414.]

coward; which in mathematical language would be expressed by saying that his courage is *positive, zero,* or *negative.* We say that one man has more courage than another. . . . It might also be considered absurd in anyone to attempt to express by numbers the relative courage, genius, prudence, or evil propensities of two individuals. Yet, let us examine such an expression more narrowly; let us try to find out why it is absurd; and see if the ratio for which we contend may not be laid down in some cases.

Let us suppose that two individuals are every day placed in circumstances inclining to acts of bravery, and that each one has the same readiness to seize them: moreover, let us suppose that each year we enumerate, pretty constantly, 500 acts of the one, and 300 of the other: moreover, these acts, though more or less remarkable, may be considered collectively, as having each the same value, because they are generally produced under the same circumstances. This being admitted, and considering causes as proportioned to their effects, we should have no difficulty in saying that the bravery of these two individuals is as 500 to 300, or 5 to 3. . . . Here, then, the absurdity only proceeds from the *impossibility,* in the first place, of placing two men in equally favourable circumstances to display their bravery and courage; in the second place, of enumerating each of these acts; and, lastly, of collecting a sufficient number of them, in order that the conclusion we form may be as little removed from truth as possible. . . . However, let us suppose . . . that one of them represents the generality of men between 21 and 25 years of age, and the other the generality between 35 and 40: moreover, instead of courageous acts, let us substitute thefts, of such a nature as come under the power of the criminal tribunals, and all the rest will be realised, in such a manner that we may consider it as very probable that in France, the inclination to theft is almost as five to three, in men between 21 and 25, and 35 and 40. . . .

Now, let us suppose that society, in a more perfect state than its present and real one, takes the opportunity some day to register and appreciate courageous and virtuous actions, as crimes are now done, will there not be some means of measuring the relative degrees of courage or virtue at different ages? Therefore the absurdity which is now attached to an endeavour to appreciate this virtue for the average man, is more apparent than real, and is owing to the impossibility which still exists, in the actual state of society, of procuring the necessary elements of the calculation.

It appears to me that it will always be impossible to estimate the absolute degree of courage, &c., of any one particular individual: for what must be adopted as unity?—shall we be able to observe this individual long enough, and with sufficient closeness, to have a record of all his actions, whereby to estimate the value of the courageous ones; and will these actions be numerous enough to deduce any satisfactory conclusions from them? Who will guarantee that the dispositions of this individual may not be altered during the course of the observations? When we operate on a great number of individuals, these difficulties almost entirely disappear, especially if we only want to determine the ratios, and not the absolute values. . . .

This determination of the average man is not merely a matter of speculative curiosity; it may be of the utmost service to the science of man and the general system. It ought necessarily to precede every other inquiry into social physics, since it is, as it were, the basis. The average man, indeed, is in a nation what the centre of gravity is in a body; it is by having this central point in view that we arrive at the apprehension of all the phenomena of equilibrium and motion.

[B]

Take men of the same age—I mean those that have been born in the same year—thirty years of age, for example; measure them in height, in weight, in strength, or for any other physical quality whatever, or even for an intellectual or moral quality, and you will see these men array themselves, unknown to them and in a manner depending on the units of measurement, in the most regular manner. No matter in what order one takes them, in every age they will fall into numerical classes like the ordinates of the same curve. This law is uniform, and the curve, which I have called *binomial*, is always the same; it is perfectly regular, no matter what test one wishes to apply to human nature. In passing from one year to the next, one passes from one binomial curve for all the individuals of that age, to another similar curve for the age which follows. This has always been lost sight of, and it may be difficult to be completely convinced of it.

This observation is of great importance: it gives, in a way, the answer to the most interesting problem in the theory of man. It tells us in effect that he is a single species; and that these variations take place around a single constant, according to the law which demonstrates this unity, and which is one of the most remarkable laws, I will not say for man, but for nature generally.

25.7

Gustav Theodor Fechner

(1801–1887)

Physicist and mystic, Fechner blended his philosophy and his experimental talent to demonstrate what he considered to be a functional relationship between mind and body. In so doing, he dispelled forever the notion that psychology could not become a science because it could not measure mental contents. His achievement was a brilliant generalization of what Weber had already learned, and a solid methodological basis which provided countless future psychologists with endless problems.

We give two selections: One, from Chapter 7, presents the rationale for his methodology, and the other, from Chapter 10, deals with the problem of the threshold. How directly Fechner builds on Herbart is apparent in comparing the first paragraph of these selections with the previous selection from Herbart. The threshold problem is of course common to Leibniz (in his "petites perceptions"), Herbart, and Fechner.

The first volume of this two-volume work has been translated into English by Helmut E. Adler (Holt, Rinehart and Winston, 1966). However, the following selections from it are independently translated.

It must be conceded in advance, as a general proposition, that mental phenomena do after all provide a foundation for [the appearance of] quantitative relationships. Not only can we speak of the greater or lesser intensity of sensations, but impulses also differ in strength, and there are greater and lesser degrees of attention, of vividness in memory images and in fantasy, or of clarity in consciousness as a whole, as well as in the intensity of individual thoughts. Consciousness may be extinguished altogether in sleep, or raised to the highest level in deep meditation. Individual thoughts and ideas wax and wane in their ordinary course. Thus, higher mental activity is no less subject to quantitative determination than is sensory activity, and the activity of the mind as a whole no less than in specific details.

But in all these relationships what we form at first, and directly, is only a judgment as to more or less or equal, not as to *how many times*. That is what is required for true measurement, and what we shall try to attain. Without as yet having a real measure of sensation—and we will limit ourselves from here on to pursue this problem with respect to sensation only—we are able to say: this pain is stronger than that, this sensation

Elemente der Psychophysik [Elements of psychophysics]. Leipzig, 1860. [Pp. 55–60, 64, 246–248.]

of brightness is stronger than that. But if we could measure sensation we would be able to say that this sensation is twice or three times or just so many times more intense than that other, and who before now has been able to say this? We are quite able to judge equality in respect to sensations: all our methods for measuring sensitivity, which we will later discuss in detail, and all our photometric procedures, are based on this. But with all this, we still have no measure of sensation.

We have no measure thereby, but we do have a foundation for measurement, which requires that we be able to count equal units, and therefore, first of all, that we shall be able to judge equality among sensations. It will in fact appear that psychic measurement, like physical, comes to nothing more than the summation of so-and-so-many equal parts. . . .

Just as, in order to measure space, we need a physical yardstick which is contained in space, so, in order to measure the psychic, we will need something physical which underlies it. But insofar as we cannot directly observe the psychophysical activity which does directly underlie it, the stimulus which evokes that activity, and with which it waxes and wanes in regular fashion, will be able to serve in place of the yardstick.

This would be very simple if the magnitude of the sensation were directly proportional to the magnitude of the stimulus. Then we would assume twice as great a sensation, when the effective stimulus is twice as great. But this is not the case. On one hand, there is no justification for assuming proportionality, and on the other, that measure once attained will not confirm it. So we cannot simply lay the stimulus against the sensation, as we lay a corporeal yardstick against a corporeal distance. But now the insight arrives, that any other functional relationship between stimulus and sensation will serve just as well as direct proportionality to mediate a measurement of sensation that is based on the quantitative characteristics of the stimulus if only we derive that relationship without presupposing a measure of sensation. For once we have expressed y as a function of x in an equation, we can find the value of y from x or x from y even though the way in which one varies with the other is something quite different from a proportional increase. The problem therefore is only to express the value of the stimulus and the value of the sensation in this manner, as functions of one another, regardless of what sort of function this might be, in order to be able to find one value from the other. It must, however, be a function which is based on reality, if we are to be able to apply it to reality. . . .

The difference between one stimulus intensity and another can always be regarded as a positive or negative increment to one or the other of these, and, from a mathematical point of view, a total stimulus can be regarded as built up of positive increments starting from zero, thinking of each increment as being added to the sum of the earlier increments, until the full stimulus is reached. In the same way, a difference between sensations can be regarded from a mathematical point of view as a positive increment to one sensation, or a negative increment to the other, and a total sensation would be regarded as built up to its full strength by positive increments from zero. If we know the functional relationship between the sum of stimulus increments, starting from zero, and the sum of the corresponding increments of sensation, we would know thereby the relationship between the total stimulus and the total sensation which it evokes.

Three methods for measuring sensitivity to differences will be explained in the next chapter. [To Weber's method of just noticeable differences, Fechner will add the method of right and wrong cases and the method of average error.] All alike show . . . that the increase in the stimulus which is needed to produce a given increase in sensation, or to increase sensation at a constant rate, does not remain the same when it is added to a weak stimulus or to a strong one. Rather, this difference grows as the stimulus grows. That is, the increment to a strong stimulus must be more than to a weak one, if it is to be just noticeable, or equally noticeable, as an increment. If an increment of half an ounce gives a just noticeable increment to the pound's weight, then when added to two pounds it will no longer do this, but a considerably greater increment of weight will be necessary, and with three pounds as much again, and so forth. Exact investigation by the methods mentioned leads to a general law concerning the dependence on stimulus magnitude of the variable stimulus increments which will always produce the *same* increment of sensation. . . .

In principle, therefore, our measure of sensation comes to this: every sensation must be analyzed into equal parts, that is, into the equal increments by which it has been built up from zero, and we must think of the number of these parts as determined by the corresponding variable stimulus increments (which will serve like the inches of a yardstick) which are capable of producing equal increments of sensation. It is just so that we measure a piece of cloth, counting how many equal parts it has by how many yardsticks are needed to cover its length; except that in our case *producing* takes the place of *covering.* In short, we determine the magnitude of the sensation, which we cannot determine directly, by counting how many equal parts there are contained within it, and this we can determine directly. But we do not read this number from the sensation, but from the stimulus which evokes the sensation, where it can be read more easily. Finally, in place of this enumeration of an infinite number of infinitesimal increments, which we have only set up in principle and which could never be carried out in reality, we will use the infinitesimal calculus, which will give us the results of this summation without having to carry it out in detail. . . .

The law that larger stimulus increments are needed in higher parts of the stimulus scale than in lower parts, in order to produce an equal intensification of the sensation, has been known for a long time, because it is a matter of daily experience.

We hear a neighbor's words clearly when things are quiet, or amid the usual mild noises, but on the other hand, if things are very noisy, we cannot hear our own words, as the saying goes—that is, we find the increment which they produce imperceptible.

The same difference which is clearly felt between small weights, is imperceptible between large weights.

Lights of equal intensity, which are very considerably different photometrically, still seem almost equally bright to the eye. A light which is seen in a mirror seems almost as bright as the same light outside it, despite the fact that a considerable loss of light takes place in reflection.

Analogous examples can easily be found in all fields of sensation. But this general fact did not suffice as a basis for psychic measurement. The more *exact* statement, that the magnitude of a stimulus increment, if it is to have a constant effect in increasing sensation, must increase precisely in proportion to the magnitude which the stimulus itself has already reached, was first made by E. H. Weber, and demonstrated by his experiments. I therefore call it *Weber's Law.* . . .

There is a certain paradox inherent in the fact of the threshold. A stimulus, or stimulus-difference, can be increased up to a certain limit without being detected; above a certain limit it is detected, and its further increase as well. How can something which has no effect in consciousness when it is weak, begin to take effect when it is strengthened? It seems as if the summation of null effects can add up to something in effectiveness. But even if this may make some difficulty for a metaphysician, it makes none from a mathematical point of view, and perhaps this points to the fact that the mathematical point of view, according to which the magnitude of a sensation can be regarded as a function of the magnitude of the stimulus (or of the internal movements which the latter releases), is also the correct metaphysical point of view. For if y is a function of x, then y may vanish, or assume negative or imaginary values, but when x exceeds a certain value we will see y assume positive values again. . . .

If in a given experiment the difference between weights, or more generally speaking between stimuli, is so small that it falls below the limit at which it can be detected by consciousness, the question arises whether it will have any influence whatever on the number of right and wrong cases; whether the effect in this regard is not the same as if there were no difference at all, until the difference passes the limit at which it is detectable as such, and whether its influence from that point on should not depend, not on the absolute magnitude of the difference, but on its difference from the value at which it first begins to become detectable.

This seems obvious at first, for how can a difference which does not affect our consciousness influence our judgment? Nevertheless, we cannot accept this conclusion unless we discard as invalid the principles on which our measurement procedure is founded, including the principles according to which the probability of an error can be calculated from its magnitude, which is an essential basis for this particular procedure. Furthermore, a closer look into this apparently obvious conclusion leads to quite opposite results. Despite the fact that a difference is not perceptible in itself, in a sufficient number of comparisons it will nevertheless result in a preponderance of right judgments in favor of the heavier weight, or more generally speaking of the greater stimulus.

For we must take into consideration that accidental influences are at work along with the difference which is to be perceived; when the weights are equal, they influence the judgment on the average just as often in favor of one weight as the other. But now the difference is added to those influences which favor one of the weights. In part, it makes those influences which would not have been noticeable become noticeable, in favor of this direction; in part, it strengthens already noticeable influences and makes them outweigh the opposing influences by this little bit more. There will still be many cases in which the influences of this excess of weight, together with the disturbances that are present at the time, will remain below what is noticeable, and in that case the judgment will be ambiguous. Such cases occur very often in trials of this sort, but in principle they can be reduced to the other cases by classifying them as half right, and half wrong.

25.8

Julius Bernstein

(1839–1917)

As Wundt expressed it, the relation which Fechner had defined might have a physiological, a psychological, or a psycho-physical explanation. (Wundt himself opted for a purely psychological explanation, in terms of subjective contrast.) Bernstein, a physiologist who is remembered best for his demonstration that the nerve current is attended by a wave of negative electricity, offered a brilliant physiological hypothesis. In reading it, one should remember that the neuron theory and the concept of the synapse are more than 30 years in the future, and that Heidenhain's demonstration of local

Zur Theorie des Fechner'schen Gesetzes der Empfindung [On the theory of Fechner's law of sensation]. *Archiv für Anatomie, Physiologie, und wissenschaftliche Medicin,* 1868, pp. 388–393. [388–392.]

cortical inhibition (see 9.12), which itself attracted little attention, would not come for thirteen years. Details aside, there can be little question today that Bernstein had hit on the essential explanation of Fechner's phenomenon: that the increasing mobilization of central inhibition explains the decreasing relative effectiveness of stronger stimuli—a necessary arrangement in any organism if it is to be capable of graduated response to a wide range of stimulus intensities.

It is well known that Fechner's law states that the strength of a sensation is not proportional to the strength of the stimulus, but to its natural logarithm. . . .

Thus the process in the central organ of our nervous system, where the judgment about the strength of a sensation is formed, bears a relationship to the peripheral process of stimulation which, though not altogether simple, can be given expression as a law. We must therefore ask the question whether we can conceive of a mechanism that will satisfy this law of sensation, and will conform to the most likely assumptions based on our present state of knowledge. . . .

A number of reflex phenomena make it highly probable that the conduction of excitation throughout the central portions of the nervous system must overcome a certain resistance. . . .

This assumption is in agreement with Sechenov's observations on the operation of inhibitory centers. . . .

Conversely, the effect of certain poisons, such as strychnine, is to reduce resistance in the reflex centers, so that even the weakest stimuli release powerful contractions.

Second, we know that the spread of conduction in the centers is less than in the peripheral nerves. . . .

Finally, Fechner's discovery of the "threshold" also speaks for this assumption. It is well known that the threshold is that stimulus which is just sufficient to evoke a sensation. Weaker stimuli are quite ineffectual, because they are immediately extinguished by a resistance. . . .

It is now permissible to make what would appear to be the simplest assumptions regarding the nature of this resistance.

In mechanics, resistance means in general any cause which effects a reduction in the velocity of a moving body. In our case, we must give a different definition of resistance, because we are not dealing with a moving body but with an advancing process.

An example which is closer to our case is the propagation of a sound wave, which undergoes resistance due to the friction of the particles of air. This effects a loss of momentum, and it can therefore be expressed as a reduction in intensity of the sound wave.

If we therefore assume that the resistance which the centers offer to the excitatory process results in a decrease of its intensity, this decrease must bear some relation to the decline which the excitation suffers at

689

every point in its path. The simplest case would be that in which the resistance at any moment is proportional to the intensity of excitation.

. . . The threshold represents a strength of excitation which is not able to penetrate the sensory centers, nor to propagate itself within them. Therefore when the initial excitation, β, reaches this threshold value, b, no further propagation will take place.

If x stands for the distance traversed, and y for the strength of the excitatory process at any time, the following relationship holds:

$$dy/dx = -k \cdot y, \text{ where } k \text{ is a constant.}$$

If the value of x equals 0 for the initial strength of y, and if p [the distance traversed until the threshold intensity, b, is reached] equals s, then:

$$\int_b^\beta dy/d = -k \int_s^0 dx$$

and we obtain

$$\log_n \beta/_b = k \cdot s$$

It follows that the distance which the excitation traverses in the sensory center is proportional to the natural logarithm of β/b. Therefore it is obvious that only one more step is needed to reach the end result of our derivation.

Space is the measure we apply to the intensity of any force. We measure the force of gravity by distance of fall in a second. We measure heat by the expansion which a heated body undergoes. The strength of an electric current by the deflection of a magnetic needle from its resting position. We have no direct measure of intensity.

It is equally inconceivable that we should directly perceive the intensity of a sensation as such. In that case we would arrive at the absurd conclusion that we have an innate sense for natural logarithms, just as for the series of natural numbers.

Since, therefore, no measure other than space remains for us, we are led to the fairly obvious assumption that we estimate the intensity of a sensation according to [the length of] the path which it traverses in the center. . . .

The simplest assumption, therefore, is to set the intensity of the sensation equal to the length of the path traversed by the excitation in the center. Let

$$\gamma = a \cdot s$$

where γ stands for the sensation and a is a constant; we then obtain:

$$\gamma = K \log_n \frac{\beta}{b}$$

which is the formula expressing Fechner's law.

[Subsequently, in his book *Untersuchungen über den Erregungsvorgang im Nerven-Und Muskelsystem*, 1871, Bernstein showed that the same result would obtain if propagation is thought of as taking place simultaneously in all directions of a complex network, rather than on a linear path.]

25.9

Harry Helson

(born 1898)

Work based on the principle here enunciated has been summed up in Helson's book, Adaptation-level theory (Harper & Row, 1964). J. P. Guilford, himself a distinguished contributor to mathematical aspects of psychology, has called this "one of the great books" in psychology, and stated that "Psychology has achieved very few principles that have such great scope, at least principles that can be experimentally demonstrated." He notes that the applications are made "over a very great range of psychological topics, from sensation and simple conditioning to personality and social interaction [Contemporary Psychology, 1965, 10, 241–242]."

The theory of adaptation-level originated as a short-hand description and explanation of certain fundamental phenomena in vision. It provided a unitary theory for such superficially diverse phenomena as constancy, contrast, and adaptation. Since phenomena of level, contrast, and so-called central tendency in the field of psychophysics are analogous to, if not identified with, adaptation, contrast, and constancy in vision it seems natural to attempt an extension of the theory to psychophysical data. Fundamental to the theory is the assumption that effects of stimulation form a spatio-temporal configuration in which order prevails. For every excitation-response configuration there is assumed a stimulus which represents the pooled effect of all the stimuli and to which the organism may be said to be attuned or adapted. Stimuli near this value fail to elicit any response from the organism or bring forth such neutral responses as indifferent, neutral, doubtful, equal, or the like, depending upon the context of stimulation. Such stimuli are said to be at adaptation-level. Conversely, adaptation-level may be quantitatively specified by giving a value of stimulus eliciting the neutral response.

Stimuli above the adaptation level (AL) are assumed to establish positive gradients with responses of one kind, and stimuli below establish negative gradients with responses of an opposite kind. Positive or

Adaptation-level as frame of reference for prediction of psychophysical data. *American Journal of Psychology* 60 (1947): 1–29. [Pp. 2–3, 28.]

negative enhancement occurs as stimuli are above or below the *AL;* which may be high, medium, or low, depending upon a number of factors in the stimulus-configuration like background in vision, comparison-stimulus in psychophysical judgments, and in the organism which may be 'set' at a given level due to effects of previous stimulation. A stimulus far above the stimulus-range may raise the *AL* so high that most of the stimuli will be below the *AL* and the majority of the judgments will be of the 'negative' sort while the opposite will be the case with a stimulus far below the range. . . .

The concept of adaptation-level (*AL*) must not be restricted to the effects of prolonged adaptation to more or less constant stimulation with greatly reduced capacity for response as a final end-state. There is an *AL* for every moment of stimulation, changing in time and with varying conditions of stimulation. It is a function of *all* the stimuli acting upon the organism at any given moment as well as in the past. To arrive at a quantitative value for the *AL* it is necessary to weigh all factors in the situation confronting the organism as well as factors within the organism. Practically only a small number of primary factors can be handled in a mathematical formulation and a good first approximation to the *AL* in vision was obtained by taking a weighted logarithmic mean of all stimuli and background in the field times a constant. Choice of a logarithmic function is in keeping with the well-established Weber-Fechner law governing stimulus-response relationships over a fairly wide range as well as the law of diminishing returns operative in the wider field of social and economic behavior. The formula found adequate in vision proved to be:

$$AL = K \, (A_o{}^3 \bar{A})^{1/4}$$

where *K* is a fractional constant, A_o is the brightness of the background, and $\bar{A}$ is the logarithmic mean of the brightnesses of the samples on the background. From this formula it is seen that the *AL* is a weighted geometric mean in which background is loaded three times as heavily as the log mean of all samples in the field. . . .

. . . Having shown that this method can clarify problems in psychophysics it would be fruitful to apply it to judgments of higher order where physical measurements are out of the question. In this realm the fundamental ideas of level as pooled effect and response as gradient from level may be treated quantitatively perhaps only by statistical theory. The structure of such a theory should, however, mirror the properties of the organism much more truly than statistical constructs which take no account of the fundamental basis of the phenomena with which they are dealing.

The method of mathematical description advocated here has hardly been tried in psychology. Too often it is assumed that if purely rational equations cannot be formulated no mathematical understanding at all is possible and as a result many who would welcome this type of attack prefer to wait until enough is known to write sets of postulates from which all can be strictly deduced. The time when this can be done may, however, be so far off as to be practically unrealizable and in the meantime the advantages of mathematical formulation are lost. Semi-empirical equations can yield a considerable amount of new information and can serve as very useful tools as we have tried to show in this study.

# Chapter 26

THE REACTION
EXPERIMENT

The reaction experiment has a peculiarly important place in the history of experimental psychology. An outgrowth of the astronomer's interest in the "personal equation," it was the first laboratory procedure in which data were collected on a somatic response to stimulation. (Dynamometric measurements had been taken earlier.) It was conceived at first as a method permitting more controlled study of the subjective response, but interest shifted rapidly to the response as such, and it was obvious that the protocols were often superfluous. On the other hand, it was within the framework of the reaction experiment that the Würzburg school (see 16.9) conducted those "systematic" introspections which finally demonstrated the hopeless inadequacy of introspection as a way to analyze the process of thinking. The gadgetry which surrounded the experiment, above all the famous Hipp gravity chronoscope which was the most essential piece of apparatus in any well-equipped laboratory of its era, helped give "brass instrument psychology" its name. Speed of reaction, and speed of perception in tachistoscopic studies, remain indispensable techniques in experimental psychology, pure and applied.

26.1

Wilhelm Wundt

(1832–1920)

*William James once remarked that it is impossible to criticize Wundt suc-
cessfully, because he is always changing his views, going off in new directions like a worm cut into parts. There is probably no single important
factual contribution we owe to Wundt, but his influence in stimulating
research was immense, and there is no way to study him except to view
the confusing sequence of his ideas on various subjects. With respect to
the measure of mind, we offer three selections, all from what may be called
his early period, before he was recognized as "Mr. Psychology." The first
is from a book based on research largely completed during the period when
he was assistant to Helmholtz, without however establishing a close working relationship with him. Here Wundt proclaims the importance of experiment for psychology, and he refers to his own most recent work, as
yet unpublished, on what came to be called the complication experiment.
He proudly states that he has discovered the natural unit of time, the
minimal time required for a thought, and that incidentally he has given
experimental proof of the unity of perception, in the fact that the mind
can entertain only one perception at a time. The second selection, from the
Lectures issued the following year, describes this experiment in greater
detail. The claims he makes for its significance will not be repeated in
future writings. The third selection is from the first edition of the Physiological Psychology, the book which brought him worldwide recognition
and won him a chair at Leipzig; by this time he is aware that he had been
rushing to unwarranted conclusions. He does not openly retract but simply
goes off in another direction, in the typical fashion which James has described.*

*One of the interesting aspects of the first selection is the emphasis on
the unconscious element in thinking, which reflects the influence of Helmholtz. Another is the reference to the use of experimentation for the study
of the higher thought processes. Later he denied that psychology should
deal with anything but the content of consciousness, and he rejected the
possibility that higher thought processes can be studied experimentally.*

Meanwhile, the growth of "brass instrument psychology" is illustrated

[A] *Beiträge zur Theorie der Sinneswahrnehmung* [Contributions to the theory of
sense perception]. Leipzig and Heidelberg, 1862. [Pp. xxvi–xxviii.]
[B] *Vorlesungen über die Menschen- und Thierseele* [Lectures on the human and
animal mind]. Leipzig, 1863. [Pp. 30–31, 38–39.]
[C] *Grundzüge der physiologischen Psychologie* [Principles of physiological psychol-
ogy]. Leipzig, 1874. [P. 753.]

by the contrast in the early and late forms of the apparatus used for the complication experiment. The description of this piece of apparatus runs for three pages of small type in the Physiological Psychology!

[A]

Until now two methods have been used almost exclusively in psychology: introspection and the derivation of the phenomena of mental life from metaphysical hypotheses. The first of these methods is defective because it only embraces a small part of the phenomena, and the second is to be rejected on principle.

All psychology begins with introspection, and this always remains an indispensable aid in arriving at judgments regarding psychic phenomena existing outside ourselves. But introspection is almost completely inadequate for dealing with the origins and causes of the phenomena. It can never pass beyond the facts of consciousness, and therefore a science that is based on introspection begins where it ought to end. For the phenomena of consciousness are complex products of the unconscious mind, and from their composition, after they have entered into consciousness in completed form, we can rarely draw direct conclusions about the manner of their formation. The psychology which is based on introspection, and which likes to call itself *empirical* psychology, must therefore limit itself to an unordered accumulation of the facts of consciousness, and because it can find no inner connections among them, things that belong together are split up into a mass of unrelated details. This is how empirical psychology came to look upon each manifestation of mental activity as the expression of a special mental *faculty*. The differentiation between faculties is the true expression of the state of a science in which the whole is completely dissolved into its parts, and in which external partitioning of unconnected facts takes the place of system.

This confusion of empirical psychology was countered with great success by philosophic schools [such as Herbartianism], which made it their task to derive mental phenomena from definite metaphysical hypotheses. . . .

The only auxiliary method which has been used until now, to supplement the observation of the single individual, was the study of history. But this gave no greater certainty. . . . The situation is quite different when, with the help of statistics, the *natural history* of men is used to supplement psychological observation. . . . The statistician, by seeking as many cases as possible, is doing the same thing as the natural scientist, who gives sufficient certainty to his results by the accumulation of observations or experiments, and in this respect the statistical method is closely related to the second method which we regard as essential for psychological investigation.

26.1 Wilhelm Wundt

This second auxiliary method consists in the widespread application of experimentation. The importance which experimentation will come to have for psychology can hardly as yet be appreciated. We do already possess many noteworthy beginnings in physiological research, but experimental psychology as a connected science still awaits its founding. Those beginnings relate primarily to the areas in which psychology and physiology are in close contact, in the area of sensation and perception. The view has been advanced that the application of the experimental method is possible there because physiological factors always come into play, but that it would be a vain effort to try to make progress along the experimental road in the field of the higher mental activities. This is surely a prejudice. As soon as we look upon the mind as a natural phenomenon, and the study of mind as a natural science, the experimental method must find its full application to this science. In fact we do already possess experimental investigations which are outside the area of psychophysics, and which have as their subject matter purely psychic events, insofar as any such exist.

The last article in this volume makes reference to the *personal differences* which have been observed by astronomers, and can only be explained by the fact that the process of perception and thinking requires a certain amount of time. Recently I have tried to determine this time with greater accuracy, experimentally. I let a pendulum swing along a circular scale; at a certain point in its path it strikes a [hidden] lever. We can then compare the true position on the scale at the moment when the sound was produced with the position where it seemed to be when the sound was heard. A constant scale difference was found, and from this and the speed of the pendulum the time elapsed between the auditory and visual perceptions was calculated. This time is found to be, on the average, 1/8 second, and this difference may be either positive or negative, that is, the Observer might first see and then hear, or first hear and then see.

I believe that this investigation of the speed of perception can be called *purely* psychological, even though sensory excitations are used in it, for they are in no sense essential and are used only as auxiliary aids, and it cannot be doubted that perception and thought take place following the same laws and in the same time intervals quite independently of these external stimuli. The contrary assumption is so unlikely that it is not necessary to give it special consideration: it would assume a double consciousness, by asserting that the consciousness for reproduced ideas is something quite different from that for those ideas which are directly excited by external impressions.

These measurements not only made it possible to determine a definite psychic constant, which was heretofore completely unknown, but they also gave rise to certain general conclusions about the nature of consciousness, which seem to me very noteworthy. Here for the first time

697

the psychological view of the *unity* of perception was clearly demonstrated. This had indeed been made very probable by the observations of the astronomers, but it did not perhaps have sufficient certainty because of the complication of seeing and hearing with a third activity, the counting of the strokes of the pendulum.

[B]

. . . The *swiftest thought* is the natural unit of time, and my mind knows nothing swifter than *swift as thought.* . . .

How is it possible to measure the time taken by the *swiftest thought?* I have discovered a method by which this measurement can be carried out easily and in very short time. It makes use of a large metal or wooden pendulum, at the bottom of which there is a pointer *e,* which passes in front of a graduated arc. The fulcrum of the pendulum, *m,* is approximately at its midpoint, and a perpendicular metal rod is attached to it at this place. When the pendulum swings toward *l,* this rod strikes against a brass lever, *h,* which is knocked over, making a clearly perceptible sound as the rod strikes it. . . .

This leads to the remarkable result that at the moment of the sound the pointer on the pendulum, which is swinging in front of the graduated arc, is never seen to be at the place which it is really passing when the lever is struck, but always at a distance of several scale divisions from it. In relaxed observations I usually see the pointer before I hear the sound, that is, the pointer seems to be at *e'* on the scale, which corresponds to a position of the rod, *ab,* which is still considerably before striking the lever. But if I direct my attention primarily to the sound and wait expectantly for it, in order to be able to read off the position of the pointer at the moment when the sound occurs, then I first perceive the pointer after hearing the sound, and indeed approximately as long *after* as I had previously seen it *before.* . . . So it is merely a question of how the attention is composed, whether one sees first and then hears, or hears first and then sees, and if one has learned to direct his attention voluntarily he is able to produce a significant difference between his own observations.

Observations of the swinging pendulum give directly the absolute magnitude of the time which the swiftest thought requires to arise and vanish, since the speed of the pendulum in any part of its path can be very easily calculated . . . (and thence) the time elapsed between becoming conscious of the sound impression and becoming conscious of the visual impression, or conversely. This however is a direct measure of the shortest time within which two perceptions can follow one another, or the time of the swiftest thought. . . .

Experiments conducted in the manner described show that 1/8 second may be regarded as the average space of time for the *swiftest thought*. This is somewhat less than the time for very fast counting, for in counting very fast each number takes about 1/5 second, but it is considerably greater than the time we require to discriminate between impressions of the same sense.

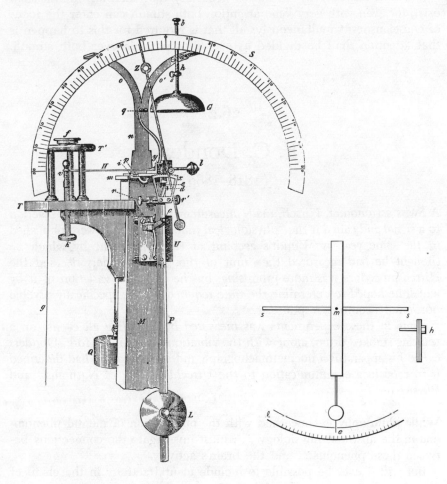

[C]

. . . Our attention needs a certain time to move from one stimulus to another. As long as the first stimulus lasts, the whole strain of attention is directed to it; therefore it cannot prepare itself to grasp the second stimulus at the very moment when it takes effect. Therefore a certain interim time elapses during which the first stimulus still has some after-effect, and the second stimulus is working against it. This time generally appears to us in consciousness as a gap of time which is empty, or at least not definitely filled, between two clear ideas, but under some circumstances, it can become nil, so that the stimuli seem simultaneous, or it can even assume a negative value, so that the later stimulus is placed first.

. . . It is however by no means necessary that such an interim shall exist, for even with very keen attention both stimuli can enter the focus of consciousness simultaneously: all that is required for this to happen is that attention shall be divided as *evenly* as possible over both stimuli.

26.2

F. C. Donders

(1818–1889)

A Swiss astronomer, Hirsch, made measurements of the speed of reaction to a signal and called it the "physiological time." His results were published in the same year as Wundt's account of the experiment by which he thought he had measured the "unit of thought." Donders decided the Hirsch procedure was more promising, but he devised a variation of it by which he hoped to determine the time required for the specifically psychic portion of a complex response.

Time in these experiments was measured by recording all events on a rotating smoked drum, along with the vibrations of a tuning fork. Donders called his apparatus a noematotachograph and states that he had described it in 1866 in a communication to the Utrecht Society of Naturalists and Physicians.

While philosophy is concerned with the observation of mental phenomena in the abstract, physiology . . . must investigate the connections between these phenomena and the brain's activity. . . .

But will it ever be possible to include mental activity in the chain of energies which are transformed one into another? As far as we can see, there is not the slightest prospect of this. . . .

But is every quantitative treatment of mental processes therefore excluded? By no means! One important factor seems accessible to measurement: I mean the time that is required for simple mental processes. The determination of this time seems not without importance for a resolution of the question whether we are justified in applying to specific cases the general relationship that has been established; in other words,

Die Schnelligkeit psychischer Processe. Erster Artikel. [The speed of mental processes. First article.] *Archiv für Anatomie, Physiologie, und wissenschaftliche Medicin*, 1868, pp. 657–681. [Pp. 657–666, 671–672.]

whether we may assume that the distinctiveness of each special feeling, each special idea, each instance of volition, is associated with an absolutely corresponding distinctive brain activity. . . .

Scarcely 25 years ago, the time required for activity in a stimulated nerve to reach the brain, and for the brain to deliver its command to the muscles, was regarded as "infinitesimal." Johannes Müller, who held first place among the physiologists of his time, not only said that the speed of conduction in the nerves was unknown, but went so far as to prophesy that we would forever be denied the means to determine it. Yet behold, soon thereafter, in 1845, duBois-Reymond sketched in outline how this might be done, and by 1850 Helmholtz had achieved it. . . .

This result was obtained with frogs. The method was not applicable to warm-blooded animals, and particularly to humans. Here Helmholtz took a different path. He stimulated the skin successively at two points, one a short distance from the brain and the other a greater distance, and in both cases reacted to the stimulus as quickly as possible with a specific signal, for example, a movement of the hand. Having thus established the elapsed time between the stimulus and the signal, for both cases, the difference is the time required for conduction along the sensory nerves for a distance equal to the separation of the two points, since aside from this difference the two trials seemed to be perfectly identical. In this way the speed of conduction in humans was calculated as approximately 200 feet a second, that is, almost twice as fast as in the frog.

One can easily see that this method of investigation is not unobjectionable. . . . Recently the speed of conduction in human motor nerves has been determined in a manner as simple and direct as for the frog, that is, completely excluding mental processes in the brain. Again it is Helmholtz who has shown the way. At his instigation, Baxt [1867] stimulated the nerve to the ball of the thumb, either at the wrist or above the elbow, while the hand, forearm and elbow were held motionless in a plaster cast. The muscle twitched in both cases, and the moment of twitching could be registered on the myograph. . . . The speed of conduction is found to be 33 meters a second, with very slight variations, that is, only slightly greater than in the frog. . . .

Thus the speed of nerve conduction has become known, and Johannes Müller's prophecy has been given the lie in a brilliant manner. It is noteworthy that the courage to undertake the solution of what had been called an unsolvable problem came from theory. The theoretical concept that the conduction should not be regarded as a movement or as a spread of energy, but rather as a chemical process which renews itself at each point, and an electromotor process allied to that—this is what led to the supposition that nerve conduction is not so extraordinarily swift, and that the short length of the nerves is therefore no absolute obstacle to its empirical determination.

I.

Then may it not also be the case that thought does not have that infinite quickness which we used to ascribe to it, and that it may be possible to determine the time required to form an idea or a volition?

This question has long concerned me. I have described, above, the method used to study the speed of conduction in the nerves for the sense of touch. The time elapsed in these experiments, between the stimulus and the signal, also includes a mental process. The same thing holds for experiments in which the stimulus acts on any other sense organ. The first comparative experiments of this kind were carried out by Hirsch, the well known astronomer at Neuchâtel. He called the elapsed time between stimulus and signal the physiological time, and using the same signal (for example, a movement of the hand) he found that this time was shortest for stimulation of the skin (naturally in the vicinity of the brain), longer for an auditory stimulus, longer still for a visual stimulus. This result has in general been confirmed by later investigators. From all these experiments, including those by myself and my students, I calculate that the physiological times for touch, hearing and vision are, respectively, 1/7, 1/6, and 1/5 second.

But how much of this belongs to the actual mental process? About this we are completely unsure. A good deal must take place in this short time. . . . [Twelve supposed segments of the physiological process are specified.] The time required for the various segments of this process cannot be stated. We can calculate, approximately, only the speed of conduction in the nerve, and this brings us to the conclusion that the mental process of ideation and decision lasts less than 1/10 second, but it does not even permit us to assert that it lasts longer than 0. The truth is that these experiments instruct us only as to the maximal limit, and tell us nothing about the minimum.

It occurred to me to interpolate additional terms of mental activity into the physiological time process. Then if I studied how much the physiological time was lengthened thereby, I would know, I decided, the duration of the interpolated act.

In the first series of trials, similar electrodes were attached to both feet. . . . These experiments were carried on in two ways: (*a*) with foreknowledge of which foot would be stimulated, the signal to be given with the hand on the same side; (*b*) without foreknowledge of which foot would be stimulated, and with the signal to be given by the hand on the stimulated side. More time was required in the latter case than in the former, and this difference represented the time needed to form an idea of which side was stimulated, and to direct the volitional action to the right or the left, in conformity with this idea. In other respects the entire process was the same in both cases. The result was that this interpolated mental activity lasted 1/15 of a second, as calculated from mean values. It had been found earlier that it takes 0.009 seconds longer to respond with the left hand than with the right, and this difference was taken into account.

This was the first determination of the duration of a mental process which was well circumscribed, which seems to me not to have been the case in Wundt's experiments. It concerned the decision of a dilemma, and a voluntary act conforming to that decision.

The same investigation was carried out with stimulation of the visual apparatus. The physiological time was determined for simple reaction to light and for a differential reaction to red light and white light. In these experiments the signal had to be performed with the right hand for red light, and with the left hand for white. The decision of this dilemma and the performance of the corresponding signal required more time than in the previous experiments: the average for five persons was 0.154 seconds. . . .

. . . Later I set up a series of experiments in which the stimulus was a letter of the alphabet either exposed or suddenly illuminated by the spark of an induction coil, and the signal consisted in speaking the sound. In this case the interpolated mental process took 0.166 (1/6 second) calculated from mean values, and 0.124 (1/8 second) calculated from minimal values.—This method permitted experiments in which it was required to recognize not one out of two, but one out of five vowel signs, which then had to be uttered as a sound. I ran no less than five series of experiments of this sort, on different days, with the result that somewhat more time was required to make a choice out of five than out of two, namely, 0.170 seconds calculated from the means, and 0.163 seconds calculated from the minima. . . .

After measuring the combined time needed both for discrimination among two or more impressions and for the corresponding volitional determination, the question arose whether it would be possible to establish the time for each part of this process separately.

It seemed to me that we could approach the solution of this problem by setting up this condition: that the signal should be given only to one stimulus, and omitted for all the others.

Vowel sounds were used as stimuli, without any other indication, but a response was to be given only to one of them, for example to *i*, and no response to the others. One tensed oneself, therefore, for recognizing *i*, and held the mouth and the vocal apparatus completely ready so that, on recognizing *i*, it was only necessary to expel the breath in order to produce the corresponding sound, just the same as when reacting with *i* to the sound *i* with foreknowledge that only that sound would be heard. Therefore no choice of a signal is demanded in this experimental procedure; only the differentiation, the recognition of *i*, is interpolated into the usual procedure. And the outcome in fact was that this required less time than answering to each vowel with its corresponding sound. Of the many experiments which I performed in this way I want to give the results of only three series, which were carried out on the same evening, in an order such that any fatigue which may have entered was equally distributed over all three types of experiment:

a. with reaction to a known sound;
b.   ”   ”   ” unknown sounds;
c.   ”   ”   ” *one* of the unknown sounds.

For each type the mean and minimal times were determined, in thousandths of a second:

For *a*, mean duration was 201, minimal duration 170.5
   b,   ”   ”   ” 284,   ”   ” 237.5
   c,   ”   ”   ” 237,   ”   ” 212.6

We then calculate:

	from means	*from minima*	*on the average*
$b - a =$	83	67	75
$c - a =$	36	42	39

Therefore in these experiments the ideation of a given sound (as shown by the longer duration with method c than with method a) took only an ample half of the time needed for ideation along with the corresponding volitional determination. In my case, the development of the ideation required 0.039, that is, almost 1/25 of a second; the determination of the volition required less time, about 1/28 of a second.

26.3

James McKeen Cattell

(1860–1944)

In one of many brilliant innovations, Cattell controls the time of exposure to the stimulus, and tests capacity for an intellectual response. We skip rapidly through earlier parts of this article, giving our attention especially to the problem of "limits of consciousness," or, as it was also called, "span of attention." Characteristically, Cattell attacks a problem of great theoretical interest, but his discussion points the way toward practical applications. The emphasis on individual differences, so alien to the spirit of the Leipzig laboratory from which this report is made, will lead him very soon to propose a series of "mental tests and measurements" for assessment of individual capacities.

The inertia of the eye and brain. *Brain* 8 (1885–86): 295–312. [295, 297–299, 304, 306, 308, 310–312.]

26.3 James McKeen Cattell

Inertia is a property of our sense organs. . . . In the case of sight, the lasting of the motion in the retina, and consequently of the sensation, after the stimulus ceases has long been known, and the phenomena of rotating discs and after-images have been carefully investigated. Less attention has been paid to inertia in the retina and in the brain when the sensation is excited. . . .

The apparatus I used, which may be called a gravity chronometer, is quite simple. It consists of two heavy brass columns, 30 cm. high and 10 cm. apart. . . . Wedge-shaped grooves are worked into the columns, and in these a heavy soft-iron screen slides without appreciable friction. The screen is 13 c. high, and has an opening 5 cm. wide, placed 5 cm. from the bottom. This screen is held up by an electro-magnet. . . . The object to be seen is fixed on a card, 15 × 3 cm., and this card is held in position on the columns by two springs, so that it is hid from the observer by the screen. A grey spot on the black screen exactly covers the object to be seen, the spot being 3 mm. in front of the object. . . . The observer fixates the grey spot on the screen, and by breaking the current which had been flowing through the spiral of the electro-magnet, lets the screen fall. . . . The object was in view the time desired, at the point fixated, and illumined with a light to which the eye was adapted, and the observer found himself looking at a black surface, an impression having been made by the object on the retina. . . .

I find that the time a coloured light must work upon the retina, in order that the colour may be seen, is different for the several colours. . . .

Substantially the same method as for colours was used to determine the time the light reflected from a letter or word must work on the retina in order that the letter or word may be distinguished. . . .

In the foregoing section we . . . found that some alphabets are harder to see than others. In this section it will be shown that the different letters of the same alphabet are not equally legible. These are both circumstances of the greatest practical importance. . . .

. . . Certain letters were usually correctly read, whereas others were usually misread or not seen at all. . . . Out of [270] trials, W was seen 241 times, E only 63 times. . . .

. . . Out of a hundred trials, d was read correctly 87 times, s only 28 times. . . .

There is not only a threshold of sensation, but also a maximum intensity of the sensation beyond which an increase in the strength of the stimulus does not increase the intensity of the sensation; analogous to this is a limit to the number of objects, or complexity of the object, consciousness can at one time attend to.

Whether the mind can attend to more than one thing at a time was a disputed question in the scholastic philosophy . . . and the subject has been discussed by a number of modern philosophers. As the several philosophers reached their results chiefly through theoretical considerations, we need not be surprised that the number of ideas consciousness can hold at one time has been placed at from one to an indefinitely large number. . . . Special experiments have been made by Wundt and his pupils, from which it seems that when twelve to sixteen beats follow one another at intervals of .2 to .3 s. the number can be correctly judged, the separate beats not having been counted. In this case, however, it is probable that the beats are combined into groups, so that not sixteen simple, but fewer slightly complex impressions are at the same time present in consciousness. I have made experiments which show that the number cannot be correctly judged when more than four or five sound-impressions follow one another with great rapidity.

Experiments on the limits of consciousness can, however, be made to better advantage through the sense of sight. I have shown in a previous paper that from three to five (varying with the person) letters can be considered by consciousness at one time. This result is confirmed by an extended series of experiments I have made with the aid of the gravity chronometer above described. In the first of these experiments, short perpendicular lines, 2 m. apart, were printed on a card, and . . . were allowed to be seen for .01 s. Eleven cards were used, containing from four to fifteen lines, and the observer tried to give the number of lines on the card he had seen. The determination was carefully made on eight persons, and it was found that two could judge the number of lines correctly up to six, two up to five, three four, and one not four. This gives the number of simple impressions consciousness can at one time attend to. When the number of lines is larger than consciousness can grasp, it is estimated, those persons who can grasp the largest number estimate, as a rule, the most accurately. . . . Practice does not seem to improve the accuracy of the judgment.

In the same manner numbers, letters, words and sentences were exposed to view for .01 s., and it was determined how much consciousness can attend to at one time. . . . The determinations made on eight individuals show a considerable personal difference, but on an average consciousness can at one time grasp four numbers, three to four letters, two words, or a sentence composed of four words. The letters are slightly more difficult to grasp than the numbers, every combination of numbers making a number that gives "sense." Not as many words as letters can be grasped at one time, but three times as many letters when they make words as when they have no connection. Twice as many words can be grasped when they make a sentence as when they have no connection. The sentence is taken up as a whole; if it is not grasped, scarcely any of the words are read; if it is grasped, the words appear very distinct; this is also the case when the observer constructs an imaginary sentence from the traces he has taken up.

In making these experiments I notice that the impressions crowd simultaneously into my consciousness, but, beyond a certain number, leave traces too faint for me to grasp. Though unable to give the impression, I can often tell, if asked, whether a certain one was present or not. This is especially marked in the case of long sentences; I have a curious feeling of having known the sentence and having forgotten it. The traces of impressions beyond the limits of consciousness seem very similar to those left by dreams.

The individual difference is a matter of special interest. *B.* out of forty trials read correctly five times a card containing seven numbers, and could always read five numbers correctly. He could grasp six letters, four disconnected words, or a sentence of seven words, whereas others could grasp but three letters, two words, or a sentence of four words. The latter numbers are the limits for one of the four students experimented on, and for the two women, one an educated young lady, the other the wife of a mechanic. The limit for a boy nine years old was somewhat higher. I tried to make the determinations on two rather obtuse porters, but their consciousness did not seem able to take up at all such delicate impression. They required three times as long as educated people to read a letter or word.

26.4

Ludwig Lange

(1863–1936)

Lange's distinction between muscular and sensorial reactions was decisive in ending the effort to use reaction times as a means to investigate the time taken for the "psychic" portion of the reaction. Wundt decided that the faster "muscular" reaction should be designated as "incomplete," and he considered that well-trained observers would make "complete" responses, of longer duration! He firmly rejected the tendency of some psychologists, particularly Baldwin in America, to see the difference as related to individual types. The reader will note that Lange himself was evidently disposed in this direction, although in deference to his teacher he gives his principal attention, including a long physiological speculation which we omit, to the "incompleteness" of the muscular response.

For Wundt, typically, this finding became an opportunity to throw doubt on the validity of research in other laboratories, which had reported shorter reaction times. They were dealing with "incomplete" reactions, not a proper basis for psychological investigation!

Neue Experimente über den Vorgang der einfachen Reaction auf Sinneseindrücke [New experiments on the process of the simple reaction to sensory stimuli]. *Philosophische Studien* 4 (1888): 479–510. [Pp. 479–480, 487–488, 490, 496–498, 510.]

The experimental investigation whose results are published below started out from a special question, namely, what influence the state of anticipation exercises on the apperception of a sensory stimulus. From the outset it seemed hardly to be doubted that the apperceptive grasp of a stimulus takes place more quickly when it is more tensely anticipated, but we can hope to form a clear picture of the objective significance of this influence of anticipation only with the help of experimentation.

Reaction time measurements, which have already served so often for similar purposes, seemed to offer the most convenient path for such an investigation. It could indeed be supposed that as the apperceptive time was increased or reduced by circumstances, this would find expression in a parallel increase or reduction of the reaction times. Thus we could hope that even if it is not possible to obtain the values of the apperception times themselves, we might at least obtain the difference between them.

How to determine the degree of tension in anticipation seemed to present more difficulties than the comparative measurement of the reaction times. . . .

. . . While we were engaged in our first practice trials, a question forced itself upon us, the exact solution of which seemed to be a prior condition for secure progress.

. . . The supposition arose that it would have some influence on the speed of reaction whether anticipation were concentrated basically more on the sensory stimulus [sound] which was to be perceived or more on the reactive movement which was to be performed. Further experience did in fact show us the following:

1) On the one hand, one can get reactions in which one *does not think at all* about the sensory stimulus which is to occur, but rather prepares the innervation of the reactive movement which is to be performed, in as lively a manner as possible.

2) On the other hand, while completely avoiding any preparatory motor innervation, we can direct our whole preparatory tension toward the stimulus which is to be anticipated—at the same time, however, undertaking to let the motor impulse follow immediately upon the perception of the stimulus without needlessly lingering over the latter. Reactions which are obtained under these circumstances are completely different from those of the first kind, in their psychological significance as well as in their duration.

It seems best to adopt designations for these two kinds of response which will express as aptly as possible the *purely factual characteristics* of the response conditions. In this sense, reactions of the first type can be designated as "extreme muscular responses" . . . [and those] of the second type . . . as "extreme sensorial responses." . . .

. . . It is almost obvious that one can also take a middle road between these two extreme methods, by dividing the tension in any proportions whatever between, so to say, the hand and the ear. . . .

With respect to the extreme methods, however, we must always keep in mind that the degree of strained expectancy is entirely the same in both cases, and only the direction in which the anticipation is strained is different. . . .

[Results for three subjects show that the extreme sensorial reaction to sound is about 85σ to 110σ longer than the extreme muscular reaction; it is also more variable. Results with other, less practised subjects show a difference in the same direction.]

If a number of individuals who are as yet quite unexperienced in psychology are given the task of carrying out a series of reactions, while they are still purposely left in ignorance of the difference between the two methods, some will give predominantly muscular, and others will give predominantly sensorial responses. With increasing practice, most of them will finally approach the muscular type of response because in their effort to give the fastest reaction possible they will unconsciously find that it helps them achieve this. But what form of response an individual prefers *at the outset* is probably a matter of temperament. Those with exceptional motor energy will immediately react almost in the extreme muscular manner, while those who are of a contemplative nature will in general be inclined to a more sensorial manner of response. . . .

To my knowledge, no previous observer has pointed out that there are two essentially different kinds of simple reaction. One does indeed find intimations that as a result of "practice" the reaction takes on an ever increasing automatic character; but the increasing concentration of attention is regarded as a sufficient basis for this phenomenon, and no mention is made that the *direction* of attention is the decisive thing, indeed, that in order to obtain a reaction of the most automatic character the reagent's anticipation must *not* be turned *toward the sensory stimulus*. In other words, a difference which is really qualitative has been regarded as merely quantitative. . . .

Donders had already attempted to analyze the simple reaction into its essential components. Wundt soon after set up a simpler schema, emphasizing certain elements from a predominantly psychological standpoint and condensing others whose separation did not seem essential. Five subdivisions of the process were distinguished:

1) Centripetal conduction from the sense organ to the brain.
2) Perception, or entry into the field of consciousness (probably coincidental with excitation of the central cerebral sensory areas).
3) Apperception, or entry into the focus of consciousness.
4) Volitional arousal and central release of the movement that is being recorded.
5) Centrifugal conduction from the center to the reacting muscles, and the build-up of energy therein.

Since then, this schema has been essentially retained by psychometric experimenters in the Leipzig Laboratory. . . .

Briefly summing up the principal results, . . . they lead to this:

1) In the sensorial reaction, which follows *preparatory attention,* perception and apperception apparently coincide; that is, active apperception presumably has zero duration.

2) The muscular reaction includes no apperception at all, and no act of volition. It rather represents an involuntary, reflex movement, or at any rate one which takes place under the influence of the aftereffect of an *earlier* volitional impulse. The cerebellum may with a certain degree of probability be regarded as the mediating organ for this brain reflex.

26.5

Robert Sessions Woodworth

(1869–1962)

Wundt had found the hurried muscular response, without clear apperception of the stimulus, "incomplete." Here now is a leisurely, hesitant response—without the motor image which generations of psychologists had assumed as the basis of the volitional act. (Compare for example Hartley, 13.8.) Still using the experimental paradigm of the reaction experiment, Woodworth finds that the image is epiphenomenal and dispensable. He obtains evidence of "imageless thinking" by a method quite different from that of the Würzburg psychologists (see 16.9).

It is interesting to speculate on the influence of personal habits or dispositions to imagery on the theoretical views of different psychologists. Compare the sparse imagery of Woodworth, who says he "has almost none but auditory imagery," to the rich and varied imagery of Titchener (3.8), who refuses to accept the concept of "imageless thought." Compare also the work by Galton (11.7), which he would not have commenced if he did not himself have fairly vivid visual imagery, something quite uncommon, as he discovered, among his scientist friends.

. . . What is the immediate conscious antecedent of the innervation of the muscles; or since there may be present in the complexity of a mental state various elements, . . . what is the really effective factor in the

The cause of a voluntary movement. *Studies in philosophy and psychology, by former students of Charles Edward Garman,* ed. J. H. Tufts et al. Boston, 1906. Pp. 351–392. [Pp. 351–352, 354–357, 376–378, 388–389, 391–392.]

consciousness immediately preceding a movement, that gives it its motor power?

A purely schematic psychology finds a ready answer to this question. Voluntary movement, it would say, is clearly movement that is foreseen and intended. There must therefore be in the mind an idea of the movement, and as such an idea could result only from previous experience of the movement, it will consist of reproduced sensations, sensations originally produced by the movement. Therefore the cue of a voluntary movement consists of a sensorial image of the movement. . . .

. . . Wundt's formula is that voluntary movement, considered as a phenomenon of consciousness, "consists simply in the apperception of an idea of movement." For Münsterberg an idea of the result to be gained is an essential factor in voluntary action, but the anticipating idea need by no means contain the same elements as the actual perception of the accomplished result. . . .

We find then in current psychological literature a broader and a narrower conception of the mechanism of voluntary movement. According to the narrower view, the mental content directly concerned in causing the movement is always a kinesthetic image, a picture in "muscular" and perhaps also tactile terms of how the movement is going to feel; other ideas operate to cause movement only by first, through association, calling up the kinesthetic image. . . . The broader conception is that any sort of image of the results to be gained by the movement may become associated with the movement and constitute its only cue. . . .

The experimental observations which I am about to report have convinced me that neither the narrower nor the broader of these conceptions is correct. . . .

These experiments were simple in character. The "subject" was required to make a given movement with some preliminary hesitation, and to note the condition of mind that preceded the movement. He was to note particularly what imagery appeared; and in case of motor images he was asked to compare them with the sensations resulting immediately afterwards from the actual movement. Care was then taken to avoid as far as possible any confusion of centrally produced images with sensations of peripheral origin. The movement was required to be hesitant, in the belief that imagery would thus be more apt to crop up; prompt movements were, however, also made, and were, in fact, preceded by less imagery than the hesitant movement. Some of the movements made, such as opening the mouth, wagging the jaw, winking, opening the closed eyes, flexing or separating the fingers, and flexing the foot, were "free" in the sense that motion was not communicated to any external object; in other cases, some instrument, such as scissors, forceps, or the dynamometer, was manipulated. Sometimes a choice of movements was allowed: the hand was to touch any part of the body; or it was to touch any object in the seen foreground; or the fingers were to be either flexed or extended; or a reaction to a sound was to be made with either hand or either foot. . . .

. . . In a large proportion of cases, no image whatever could be reported by my subjects as occurring in anticipation of a movement. Individuals differ, some having visual images frequently, if not regularly, as they are preparing to move, and some seldom having images of any kind. Where imagery is lacking, peripheral sensations are sometimes present in the field of attention, but after these cases are subtracted, there still remain a good share of the whole number—about one fifth in my observations—in which no sensorial content could be detected.

The first reaction of a psychologist to the statement of this result is apt to take the form of insisting that there clearly must have been present some image of the movement or of its result, otherwise the movement was not voluntary, since it could not have been foreshadowed in consciousness. How could a particular movement be determined upon, unless there was present some image representing and identifying the movement? In spite of the feeling that there "must be" an image present, it is worth while finding out whether there actually is always one there. There is not. . . . In my own case, I am perfectly certain that no sensorial image appears in anticipation of most of my movements. . . . How is a man who has almost none but auditory images to obtain images of most of his movements? . . . If I open a penknife I have no preliminary feeling of opening it or of its appearance with the blade open. If I start to walk into the next room, I have no preliminary feeling of a rhythmical motion of my legs, nor preliminary vision of the next room. . . . Such being my own experience, I am inclined to give entire credence to the statements of my subjects, when they report no image of the desired result to be present as a preliminary to movement. . . .

The discussion so far has led us to two negations: we have rejected first the kinesthetic image, and second any image at all, as the adequate determinant of voluntary movement. But there is still a third and more radical negation to which we are forced by the introspective evidence. Not only is the image inadequate, but the very thought, the field of attention just prior to the movement, is often inadequate as a distinguishing mark of the movement. It would not serve to identify the act among all the acts that can be intended and executed. The intention is not always present, and is seldom fully present, in the field of attention at the moment just preceding the innervation of the movement. . . .

The complete determinant of a voluntary motor act—that which specifies exactly what act it shall be—is nothing less than the total set of the nervous system at the moment. The set is determined partly by factors of long standing, instincts and habits, partly by the sensations of the moment, partly by recent perceptions of the situation and by other thoughts lately present in consciousness; at the moment, however, these factors, though they contribute essentially to the set of the system, are for the most part present in consciousness only as a background or "fringe" if at all, while the attention is occupied by the thought of some particular change to be effected in the situation. The thought may be clothed in sensorial images,—rags and tatters, or gorgeous raiment,—but these are after all only clothes, and a naked thought can perfectly well perform its function of starting the motor machinery in action and determining the point and object of its application.

Chapter 27

SOCIAL PSYCHOLOGY

Previous chapters should have made it clear that modern psychology was shaped in important respects by the political theories which developed during the seventeenth and eighteenth centuries. What these theories fostered, however, was emphasis on the individual and on the rational element in control of behavior. It was the nineteenth century's steadily increasing concern with irrational determinants which promoted the development of a social psychology. In one way or another, almost all research in social psychology continues to be concerned chiefly with nonrational aspects of behavior.

The inclusion of two studies of animal behavior will seem an unwarranted intrusion to many social psychologists, but both have important implications for students of human social interaction. Münsterberg's early contribution to industrial psychology easily gains entry because it is not many years since courses in "social and industrial psychology" were offered in leading American universities. If this chapter is less cohesive than most others, that only reflects the state of affairs and the past course of development, in the field it represents.

27.1

Heymann Steinthal

(1823–1899)

Steinthal and his coworker Moritz Lazarus were pioneers in the new science of comparative linguistics. When Wundt came to write the ten-volume "folk psychology" which occupied almost the whole of the last twenty years of his life, he was greatly influenced by them. Here also is the root of Wundt's conviction that the higher thought processes must be studied through their social products, not in the laboratory.

Steinthal's emphasis on the importance of language as a social bond, and the existence of multilingual national entities, makes it impossible to translate Volk as nation, but in reading this selection one should hold in mind that the English word folk must be interpreted in a now archaic sense, and implies something like a "true" national entity, rather than an administrative one.

In our introductory remarks, we have already said that it is not only as a mental activity, like other such activities, that language is an object of psychological observation, but that besides this the proof of how it came into being, its essential nature, its position in the development and activity of the mind, constitute a peculiar and essential portion of psychology. We were on psychological territory throughout our discussion of language and of grammar, including that of the reality of different languages. Nor do we leave this territory in dealing with the differences among languages; we only leave one of its provinces, to which as it happens psychology is presently restricted, but we enter into another province which is no less a part of it, although until now it has been worked only incidentally. For contemporary psychology is *individual* psychology, that is, it takes as its object the mental individual, as it manifests itself in all creatures with mind, not only in humans but, up to a certain point, in animals as well. It is however an essential attribute of the human mind that it does not stand by itself as an individual but that it belongs to a society, and first of all, in body and soul, to a folk. Therefore individual psychology calls quite essentially for its extension through *folk psychology.* A man belongs by birth to a folk, and this determines his mental development in many respects. Therefore the individual cannot even as such be fully understood without

Grammatik, Logik, und Psychologie, ihre Prinzipien und ihr Verhältnis zueinander. [Grammar, logic, and psychology: their principles and their interrelationships]. Berlin, 1855. [Pp. 387–388, 390–392.]

taking into account the mental totality within which he arises and lives.
. . .

We cannot think of a man otherwise than as possessing speech, and hence as the member of a folk community; consequently, we cannot think of mankind otherwise than as divided into folks and races. Any other conception, which takes man as he was before the development of folks and of languages, can be a necessary scientific fiction, like a mathematical line, a mathematical point, or falling in empty space; but it does not grasp him as he really is. Folk psychology transports us immediately into the reality of human living, with the differentiation of people according to folks as well as the smaller communities within them.

Now every folk constitutes a closed entity, an individual manifestation of the human essence; and all the individual members of the same folk carry the impress of this individual folk nature in their bodies and in their minds. On the bodily side, this resemblance derives from similarity of blood, that is, from inheritance, as well as from the external influences of nature and the style of life; but resemblance in mental development is based on living together, that is, thinking together. Originally thinking takes place only in society; each person joins his thoughts to those of someone else in his stock, and the new thought shaped in this way belongs just as much to the other person as to him, just as a child belongs to its father and mother. The same body, and the same external stimuli, produce similar feelings, tendencies, desires, and these in turn produce similar thoughts, similar speech. That we can think of people only as living in a folk means as well that we can think of a man only as similar to many individuals—that is, that we can think of a man conceptually only in terms of various folk units, each of which embraces many harmoniously disposed individuals.

The effect of bodily influences on the mind is to cause certain tendencies, dispositions, sets, mental qualities, and since these occur in the same way in all individuals they all possess the same folk mind. This folk mind shows itself first of all in language, then in customs and mores, institutions and behaviors, traditions and songs: these are the products of the folk mind. . . .

The most important part in all of these considerations belongs to the investigation of language, and linguistic science is the most direct path into folk psychology. Indeed, just as the development of the general nature of language is virtually a chapter of individual psychology, so the investigation of different languages (as special forms of actualization of language generally, and as special homogeneous systems of an instinctive world view, each possessing its own special principle) is a chapter of mental ethnology. If it has been necessary to trace the origin and development of language generally in the individual mind (although even in this we have already come up against man as a social being), now we must ask, when we consider the actual, existing, and individual language, *To whom does it belong? Who created it?* Not the individual person by himself, but the individual person speaking in society. And while he created language in his speech, it was being understood; consequently, what one person spoke, and how he spoke it, already existed in the mind of the listener. Thus the speaker created language simultaneously out of his own mind and that of his listener, and the spoken word does not belong only to him, but also to the other person.

Language is therefore essentially a product of society, of the folk. We called language an instinctive self-consciousness, an instinctive world view and logic. This implies that it is *the self-consciousness, the world view and the logic of a folk mind.*

How bright a light must language therefore throw upon the principles of folk psychology! The unity of individuals in a folk is mirrored in their common language; the special individuality of the folk soul can never express itself more clearly than in the individual forms of language; the cooperation of the individual person and his folk rests primarily upon the language in which and through which he thinks, but which belongs to the folk. The history of the language and the historical development of the folk mind, the creation of new folks and new languages, and on the other hand the refined development of their internal form, are among the most important points for recognition of the particular folk mind.

27.2

Gabriel Tarde

(1843–1904)

David Hume in his Treatise had declared that "No quality of human nature is more remarkable, both in itself and in its consequences, than that propensity we have to sympathise with others, and to receive by communication their inclinations and sentiments, however different from, or even contrary to, our own [Book II, Part I, Sect. 11]." His friend Adam Smith made this disposition to sympathy a basis of his Theory of moral sentiments (1759). But the time seemed not yet ripe for the development of a social psychology. Tarde found a new way to emphasize this direct and irrational influence of men on each other, linking it up with the currently exciting topic of hypnotic influence.

Les lois de l'imitation [1890]. Translated from the second French edition by Else Clews Parsons, as *The laws of imitation*. New York: Holt, 1903. [Pp. 74–79, 83, 87–88.]

... I began by asking: What is society? I have answered: Society is imitation. We have still to ask: What is imitation? Here the sociologist should yield to the psychologist.

1. Taine sums up the thought of the most eminent physiologists when he happily remarks that the brain is a *repeating* organ for the senses and is itself made up of elements which repeat one another. In fact, the sight of such a congery of like cells and fibres makes any other idea impossible. . . .

2. What is the essential nature of the suggestion which passes from one cerebral cell to another and which constitutes mental life? We do not know. Do we know anything more about the essence of the suggestion which passes from one person to another and which constitutes social life? We do not; for if we take this phenomenon in itself, in its higher state of purity and intensity, we find it related to one of the most mysterious of facts, a fact which is being studied with intense curiosity by the baffled philosophic alienists of the day, *i.e.*, somnambulism {hypnotism}. If you re-read contemporaneous works on this subject, especially those of Richet, Binet and Féré, Beaunis, Bernheim, Delboeuf, I shall not seem fanciful in thinking of the social man as a veritable somnambulist. I think, on the contrary, that I am conforming to the most rigorous scientific method in endeavoring to explain the complex by the simple, the compound by the element, and to throw light upon the mixed and complicated social tie, as we know it, by means of a social tie which is very pure, which is reduced to its simplest expression, and which is so happily realised for the edification of the sociologist in a state of somnambulism. Let us take the hypothetical case of a man who has been removed from every extra-social influence, from the direct view of natural objects, and from the instinctive obsessions of his different senses, and who has communication only with those like himself, or, more especially, to simplify the question, with one person like himself. Is not such an ideal subject the proper one through which to study by experiment and observation the really essential characteristics of social relations, set free in this way from all complicating influences of a natural or physical order? But are not hypnotism and somnambulism the exact realisation of this hypothesis? . . .

The social like the hypnotic state is only a form of dream, a dream of action. Both the somnambulist and the social man are possessed by the illusion that their ideas, all of which have been suggested to them, are spontaneous. To appreciate the truth of this sociological point of view, we must not take ourselves into consideration, for should we admit this truth about ourselves, we would then be escaping from the blindness which it affirms; and in this way a counter argument might be made out. Let us call to mind some ancient people whose civilisation differs widely from our own, the Egyptians, or Spartans, or Hebrews. Did not that people think, like us, that they were autonomous, although, in reality, they were but the unconscious puppets whose strings were pulled by their ancestors or political leaders or prophets, when they were not being pulled by their own contemporaries? What distinguishes us modern Europeans from these alien and primitive societies is the fact that the magnetisation has become mutual, so to speak, at least to a certain extent; and because we, in our democratic pride, a little exaggerate this reciprocity, because, moreover, forgetting that in becoming mutual, this magnetisation, the source of all faith and obedience, has become general, we err in flattering ourselves that we have become less credulous and docile, less imitative, in short, than our ancestors. This is a fallacy, and we shall have to rid ourselves of it. But even if the aforesaid notion were true, it would nevertheless be clear that before the relations of model and copyist, of master and subject, of apostle and neophyte, had become reciprocal or alternative, as we ordinarily see them in our democratic society, they must of necessity have begun by being one-sided and irreversible. Hence castes. Even in the most democratic societies, the one-sidedness and irreversibility in question always exists at the basis of social imitations, *i.e.*, in the family. For the father is and always will be his son's first master, priest, and model. Every society, even at present, begins in this way.

Therefore, in the beginning of every old society, there must have been, *a fortiori*, a great display of authority exercised by certain supremely imperious and positive individuals. Did they rule through terror and imposture, as alleged? This explanation is obviously inadequate. They ruled through their *prestige*. The example of the magnetiser alone can make us realise the profound meaning of this word. The magnetiser does not need to lie or terrorise to secure the blind belief and the passive obedience of his magnetised subject. He has the prestige—that tells the story. That means, I think, that there is in the magnetised subject a certain potential force of belief and desire which is anchored in all kinds of slooping but unforgotten memories, and that this force seeks expression just as the water of a lake seeks an outlet. The magnetiser alone is able through a chain of singular circumstances to open the necessary outlet to this force. All forms of prestige are alike; they differ only in degree. We have prestige in the eyes of anyone in so far as we answer his need of affirming or of willing some given thing. Nor is it necessary for the magnetiser to speak in order to be believed and obeyed. He need only act; an almost imperceptible gesture is sufficient.

This movement, together with the thought and feeling which it expresses, is immediately reproduced. Maudsley says that he is not sure that the somnambulist is not enabled to read unconsciously what is in the mind through "an *unconscious* imitation of the attitude and expression of the person whose *exact* muscular contractions are *instinctively copied*." Let us observe that the magnetised subject imitates the magnetiser, but that the latter does not imitate the former. *Mutual imitation,* mutual prestige or *sympathy*, in the meaning of Adam Smith, is produced only in our so-called waking life and among people who seem to exercise no magnetic influence over one another. If, then, I have put prestige, and not sympathy, at the foundation and origin of society, it is because, as I have said before, the unilateral must have preceded the reciprocal. Without an age of authority, however surprising this fact may be, an age of comparative fraternity would never have existed. But, to return, why should we really marvel at the one-sided, passive imitation of the somnambulist? Any act of any one of our fellows inspires us who are lookers-on with the more or less irrational idea of imitation. If we at times resist this tendency, it is because it is neutralised by some antagonistic suggestions of memory or perception. Since the somnambulist is for the time being deprived of this power of resistance, he can illustrate for us the imitative quiescence of the social being in so far as he is social, *i.e.*, in so far as he has relations exclusively with his fellows and, especially, with one of his fellows. . . .

We should also observe, however, that as the suggestions of example become more numerous and diversified around an individual, each of them loses in intensity, and the individual becomes freer to determine his choice according to the preference of his own character, on the one hand, and on the other, according to certain logical laws which I will discuss elsewhere. Thus it is certain that the progress of civilisation renders subjection to imitation at once more *personal* and more *rational*. We are just as much enslaved as our ancestors by the examples of our environment, but we make a better choice of them through our more logical and more individual choice, one adapted to our own ends and to our particular nature. And yet, as we shall see, this does not keep extra-logical and prestigeful influences from always playing a very considerable part. . . .

. . . I hope that I have at least made my reader feel that to thoroughly understand the essential social fact, as I perceive it, knowledge of the infinitely subtle facts of mind is necessary, and that the roots of even what seems to be the simplest and most superficial kind of sociology strike far down into the depths of the most inward and hidden parts of psychology and physiology. *Society is imitation and imitation is a kind of somnambulism.* As for the second part of the proposition, I beg the reader's indulgence for any exaggeration I may have been guilty of. I must also remove a possible objection. It may be urged that submission to some ascendency does not always mean following the example of the person whom we trust and obey. But does not belief in anyone always mean belief in that which he believes or seems to believe? Does not obedience to someone mean that we will that which he wills or seems to will? *Inventions are not made to order*, nor are discoveries undertaken as a result of persuasive suggestion. Consequently, to be credulous and docile, and to be so as pre-eminently as the somnambulist and the social man, is to be, primarily, imitative. To innovate, to discover, to awake for an instant from his dream of home and country, the individual must escape, for the time being, from his social surroundings. Such unusual audacity makes him super-social rather than social.

27.3

Scipio Sighele

(1868–1914)

Sighele's theory of crowd behavior was written in the framework of the Italian anthropological school of criminology, as expressed primarily by Lombroso, and was influenced also by Tarde's emphasis on the importance of suggestion in determining behavior. He published it first in 1891, that is, at the age of 23. There was a French edition in the following year. Several years later (in 1895), Georges Le Bon published his Psychology of the crowd, which was to have uncounted editions in all modern languages. Le Bon at that time was 54. There is little reason to question that the "credit" for this theory, if credit it is, belongs to the younger man, and while it is not impossible for both authors to have arrived at it independently, it is unlikely that Le Bon was unacquainted with Sighele's earlier work in the French translation.

I have been unable to obtain either the original Italian edition or a copy of the first French edition (Paris: Baillière). I judge that my selection derives wholly from the first edition by comparison with a German translation (Psychologie des Auflaufs und der Massenverbrechen, translated by Hans Kurella, Dresden, 1897).

But, it will be said, all that you have said up to this point [about imitation, suggestion, etc.] may suffice to explain certain movements and actions of a crowd, but not all. It explains why when one person applauds, all applaud; why when one runs away, they all run; why the anger which is felt by a single individual is reflected immediately in every face. But it does not explain why this anger leads to evil actions, to murder; it does not suffice to explain how a crowd reaches the extremes of assassination and massacre, of nameless atrocities, of which the French revolution gave us perhaps the most terrible examples. Your theory— that an emotion is transmitted to an entire crowd by suggestions, merely from the sight of this emotion in one individual—is insufficient in cases

La foule criminelle [The criminal crowd]. Second edition, revised. Paris: Alcan, 1901. [Pp. 56–64.]

like these. You cannot pretend that people kill merely because they see someone else who kills or who strikes a pose of killing; it takes something more than that to turn a man into a murderer.

This objection (which, we shall show, includes a basis of truth) had already occurred spontaneously to the minds of certain authors who tried to analyze the causes of the crimes that crowds commit. They felt, though confusedly, that an act of cruelty and ferocity cannot be produced solely by external circumstances, but that it must have its causes in the special characteristics of the organism of the one who perpetrates it. . . .

Certainly there is truth in what was said by Barbaste [*De l'homocide et de l'anthropophagie,* 1856] and by Lauvergne [*Les forçats, considérés sous le rapport physiologique, moral, et intellectuel,* 1841]. These distant precursors of the modern science of criminal anthropology refer a portion of the causes of human phenomena to the physiological and psychological constitution of the individual, rather than referring them all without distinction to society, as some others would do.

But before having recourse to the anthropological factor, I think it well to take account of some other considerations which, though they cannot all by themselves explain how a crowd can be led into acts of ferocity and cruelty, do explain it in large part.

We must take note first of all that crowds are in general more disposed toward evil than toward good.

Heroism, virtue, benevolence, can be the qualities of a single individual, but they are never or almost never the qualities of a large assembly of individuals. The most ordinary observation teaches us this: we always fear a multitude, but we rarely hope for anything from it. Everybody knows and feels from experience that the example of a perverse man or a fool can lead a crowd to crime; very few believe that the voice of a good or a courageous man can succeed in calming a crowd, and this does indeed happen very rarely.

Collective psychology . . . is rich in surprises, but these surprises are almost always painful: a hundred or a thousand men gathered together can commit actions which not one of the hundred or the thousand would commit alone. From a gathering of good men, you will almost never have an excellent outcome; you will often have a mediocre outcome, sometimes even a very bad one.

The crowd is a terrain on which the microbe of evil develops very easily, while the microbe of good almost always dies for lack of the conditions of life.

And why? Without speaking about the different elements which compose a crowd—in which well-intentioned men are seen alongside the cruel and the indifferent, and honest men stand beside vagrants and criminals—and limiting ourselves for the present to a general observation, we can answer by saying that in a crowd the good qualities of the individuals destroy each other, rather than uniting.

27.3 Scipio Sighele

They destroy each other, first of all, by a natural and I might say an arithmetic necessity. Just as the mean of several numbers obviously cannot be equal to the greatest of them, so an aggregation of men cannot in its behavior reflect the highest qualities belonging to those who compose it; it can only reflect those qualities which are present in all or in most of the individuals. The finest and most recently developed strata of human character, says Sergi, which civilization and education have succeeded in forming in a few privileged individuals, are eclipsed by the mediocre strata, which are part of everyone's heredity. In the grand total, the latter prevail and the former disappear.

The same thing happens in a crowd, considered from the moral point of view, which happens in all large groups considered from the intellectual point of view: in the total resultant, companionship lessens the strength both of talent and of charitable feelings. By this I do not mean to say that the crowd is incapable of every great and noble manifestation, whether of thought or sentiment. There are too many undeniable examples of collective heroism, above all those arising from love of country, and forming, so to say, from the 300 at Thermopolae down to the latest martyrs of [the Italian struggle for] independence, a *via sacra* which suffices to prove that crowds as well as individuals can rise to sublime heights of abnegation and virtue.

I only wish to state that the crowd is *predisposed*, by a fatal psychological law, more toward evil than toward good, in the same way that any gathering of men is *predisposed* to produce an intellectual resultant which is inferior to what the sum of its components should yield. There is in the crowd a hidden tendency to ferocity which, if I may so state it, constitutes the complex organic factor of its future behavior, and this factor (like the anthropological factor in the individual) can follow either a good or a bad direction according to the circumstances and according to the suggestion imposed upon it by external conditions. . . .

In the crowd, therefore, just as in the individual, every manifestation is due to two sorts of factors: the anthropological and the social. *Potentially* the crowd may be what you will, but what actually happens will be determined by the circumstances. But there is still this special difference: the circumstances, that is to say, the words or the outcry of some person, are infinitely more important for the crowd than for the single individual. The isolated individual—in the normal state, in society—always consists of stuff which is more or less non-inflammable. Touch a match to it and it will burn rather slowly, or perhaps it will extinguish itself. A crowd on the contrary is always like a heap of dry powder: if you touch a match to it, an explosion cannot fail to take place.

27.4

William McDougall

(1871–1938)

McDougall's "hormic" psychology stressed the importance of motivating forces over habit and intellect, and it led him to define psychology as "the positive science of the conduct of living creatures" as early as 1905, in his Physiological psychology. Here, a few years later, he already broadens this phrase to "the positive science of conduct or behaviour," leaving no question that he is the one who points the way for "behaviorists" to follow. But his emphasis on instinct made him in fact one of their favorite whipping-boys.

This book appeared in the same year as the Social psychology of Elwood Ross, a sociologist, based on very different principles.

. . . The department of psychology that is of primary importance for the social sciences is that which deals with the springs of human action, the impulses and motives that sustain mental and bodily activity and regulate conduct; and this, of all the departments of psychology, is the one that has remained in the most backward state, in which the greatest obscurity, vagueness, and confusion still reign. The answers to such problems as the proper classification of conscious states, the analysis of them into their elements, the nature of these elements and the laws of the compounding of them, have but little bearing upon the social sciences; the same may be said of the range of problems connected with the relations of soul and body, of psychical and physical process, of consciousness and brain processes; and also of the discussion of the more purely intellectual processes, of the way we arrive at the perception of relations of time and place or of likeness and difference, of the classification and description of the intellectual processes of ideation, conception, comparison, and abstraction, and of their relations to one another. . . . It is the mental forces, the sources of energy, which set the ends and sustain the course of all human activity—of which forces the intellectual processes are but the servants, instruments, or means—that must be clearly defined, and whose history in the race and in the individual must be made clear, before the social sciences can build upon a firm psychological foundation. Now, it is with the questions of the former classes that psychologists have chiefly concerned themselves and in regard to which they have made the most progress towards a consistent and generally

An introduction to social psychology. London: Methuen, 1908. [Pp. 2–4, 19–20, 26, 29, 42, 44.]

acceptable body of doctrine: and they have unduly neglected these more socially important problems. . . .

The human mind has certain innate or inherited tendencies which are the essential springs or motive powers of all thought and action, whether individual or collective, and are the bases from which the character and will of individuals and of nations are gradually developed under the guidance of the intellectual faculties. These primary innate tendencies have different relative strengths in the native constitutions of the individuals of different races, and they are favoured or checked in very different degrees by the very different social circumstances of men in different stages of culture; but they are probably common to the men of every race and of every age. If this view, that human nature has everywhere and at all times this common native basis, can be shown to be well founded, it will afford a much-needed basis for speculation on the history of the development of human societies and human institutions. For so long as it is possible to assume, as has often been done, that these innate tendencies of the human mind have varied greatly from age to age and from race to race, all such speculation is founded on quicksand and we cannot hope to reach views of a reasonable degree of certainty.

The evidence that the native basis of the human mind, constituted by the sum of these innate tendencies, has this stable unchanging character is afforded by comparative psychology. For we find, not only that these tendencies, in stronger or weaker degree, are present in men of all races now living on the earth, but that we may find all of them, or at least the germs of them, in most of the higher animals. Hence there can be little doubt that they played the same essential part in the minds of the primitive human stock, or stocks, and in the pre-human ancestors that bridged the great gap in the evolutionary series between man and the animal world.

These all-important and relatively unchanging tendencies, which form the basis of human character and will, are of two main classes—

(1) The specific tendencies or instincts;
(2) The general or non-specific tendencies arising out of the constitution of mind and the nature of mental process in general, when the mind and mental process attain a certain degree of complexity in the course of evolution. . . .

In treating of the instincts of animals, writers have usually described them as innate tendencies to certain kinds of action, and Herbert Spencer's widely accepted definition of instinctive action as compound reflex action takes account only of the behaviour or movements to which instincts give rise. But instincts are more than innate tendencies or dispositions to certain kinds of movement. There is every reason to believe that even the most purely instinctive action is the outcome of a distinctly mental process, one which is incapable of being described in purely mechanical terms, because it is a psycho-physical process, involving psychical as well as physical changes, and one which, like every other mental process, has, and can only be fully described in terms of, the three aspects of all mental process—the cognitive, the affective, and the conative aspects; that is to say, every instance of instinctive behaviour involves a knowing of some thing or object, a feeling in regard to it, and a striving towards or away from that object. . . .

We may, then, define an instinct as an inherited or innate psycho-physical disposition which determines its possessor to perceive, and to pay attention to, objects of a certain class, to experience an emotional excitement of a particular quality upon perceiving such an object, and to act in regard to it in a particular manner, or, at least, to experience an impulse to such action. . . .

It must be added that the conative aspect of the psychical process always retains the unique quality of an impulse to activity, even though the instinctive activity has been modified by habitual control; and this felt impulse, when it becomes conscious of its end, assumes the character of an explicit desire or aversion. . . .

. . . Directly or indirectly the instincts are the prime movers of all human activity; by the conative or impulsive force of some instinct (or some habit derived from an instinct), every train of thought, however cold and passionless it may seem, is borne along towards its end, and every bodily activity is initiated and sustained. The instinctive impulses determine the ends of all activities and supply the driving power by which all mental activities are sustained; and all the complex intellectual apparatus of the most highly developed mind is but a means towards these ends, is but the instrument by which these impulses seek their satisfactions, while pleasure and pain do but serve to guide them in their choice of the means.

Take away these instinctive dispositions with their powerful impulses, and the organism would become incapable of activity of any kind; it would lie inert and motionless like a wonderful clockwork whose mainspring had been removed or a steam-engine whose fires had been drawn. These impulses are the mental forces that maintain and shape all the life of individuals and societies, and in them we are confronted with the central mystery of life and mind and will.

27.5

Hugo Münsterberg

(1863–1916)

After several years of residence in America, Münsterberg published Psychology and life (1899). In it he argued, despite the connotations which have come to attach to the title, that psychology as a pure science must not concern itself with practical problems, and he disdainfully dismissed research into individual differences with the comment that "it is not scientific botany to find out in whose yard in the town cherries, in whose yard apples grow [p. 113]." Yet the times swept him into a new course, and soon made of him a pioneer of industrial psychology. He was not the first, but he has often been called the first because of the misleading title of that oppositely oriented book published before the end of the nineteenth century! However, in the book from which we take this selection he sees a great future for experimental psychology in the service of vocational guidance and scientific management. We select a concrete instance of service to management.

The problem of securing fit motormen for the electric railways was brought to my attention from without. The accidents which occurred through the fault, or at least not without the fault, of the motormen in street railway transportation have always aroused disquietude and even indignation in the public, and the street railway companies suffered much from the many payments of indemnity imposed by the court as they amounted to thirteen per cent of the gross earnings of some companies. Last winter the American Association for Labor Legislation . . . suggested that I undertake an inquiry into this interesting problem with the means of the psychological laboratory. . . .

It would have been quite possible to treat the functions of the motormen according to the method which resolves the complex achievement into its various elements and tests every function independently. For instance, the stopping of the car as soon as the danger of an accident threatens is evidently effective only if the movement controlling the lever is carried out with sufficient rapidity. . . . But I may say at once that I did not find characteristic differences in the rapidity of reaction of those motormen whom the company had found reliable and those who have frequent accidents. . . .

Psychology and industrial efficiency. Boston: Houghton Mifflin, 1913. [Pp. 63–66, 68–70, 72, 75, 81–82.]

For this reason, in the case of the motormen I abstracted from the study of single elementary functions and turned my attention to that mental process which after some careful observations seemed to me the really central one for the problem of accidents. I found this to be a particular complicated act of attention by which the manifoldness of objects, the pedestrians, the carriages, and the automobiles, are continuously observed with reference to their rapidity and direction in the quickly changing panorama of the street. . . .

My effort was to transplant this activity of the motormen into laboratory processes. . . .

. . . The method of examination promised to be valuable if, first, it showed good results with reliable motormen and bad results with unreliable ones; and, secondly, if it vividly aroused in all the motormen the feeling that the mental function which they were going through during the experiment had the greatest possible similarity with their experience on the front platform of the electric car. These are the true tests of a desirable experimental method, while it is not necessary that the apparatus be similar to the electric car or that the external activities in the experiment be identical with their performance in the service. After several unsatisfactory efforts, in which I worked with the complicated instruments, I finally settled on the following arrangement of the experiment which seems to me to satisfy those two demands.

The street is represented by a card 9 half-inches broad and 26 half-inches long. Two heavy lines half an inch apart go lengthwise through the centre of the card, and accordingly a space of 4 half-inches remains on either side. The whole card is divided into small half-inch squares which we consider as the unit. . . . The 26 squares which lie between the two heavy central lines are marked with the printed letters of the alphabet from A to Z. These two heavy central lines are to represent an electric railway track on a street. On either side the 4 rows of squares are filled in an irregular way with black and red figures of the three first digits. The digit 1 always represents a pedestrian who moves just one step, and that moves from one unit into the next; the digit 2 a horse, which moves twice as fast, that is, which moves 2 units; and the digit 3 an automobile which moves three times as fast, that is, 3 units. Moreover, the black digits stand for men, horses, and automobiles which move parallel to the track. . . . The red digits, on the other hand, are the dangerous ones. They move from either side toward the track. The idea is that the man to be experimented on is to find as quickly as possible those points on the track which are threatened by the red figures. . . .

. . . [He] turns the crank with his right hand, the window slips over the whole length of the card, one part of the card after another becomes visible, and then he simply has to call the letters of those units in the track at which the red figures on either side would land, if they took the number of steps indicated by the digit. . . .

. . . The results show a far-reaching correspondence between efficiency in the experiment and efficiency in the actual service.

. . . There can be no doubt that the experiments could be improved in many directions. But even in this first, not adequately tested, form, an experimental investigation of this kind which demands from each individual hardly 10 minutes would be sufficient to exclude perhaps one fourth of those who are nowadays accepted into the service as motormen. This 25 per cent of the applicants do not deserve any blame. In many other occupations they might render excellent service; they are neither careless nor reckless, and they do not act against instructions, but their psychical mechanism makes them unfit for that particular combination of attention and imagination which ought to be demanded for the special task of the motorman. If the many thousands of injury and the many hundreds of death cases could be reduced by such a test at least to a half, then the conditions of transportation would have been improved more than by any alterations in the technical apparatus, which usually are the only objects of interest in the discussion of specialists. The whole world of industry will have to learn the great lesson, that of the three great factors, material, machine, and man, the man is not the least, but the most important.

27.6

Floyd H. Allport

(born 1890)

This book is directed against the idea that the behaviors of individuals which, collectively, make up social phenomena, need any other explanation than that which falls within the scope of individual psychology. While not behaviorist, in the sense that it does not exclude introspective or subjective data, it does seek to deal with the subject entirely in terms of "the behavior viewpoint and the experimental method."

One significant concept introduced in this book but not indicated in the selection, is the "prepotent reflex" as an effort to explain innate behaviors without recourse to instinct.

Gordon Allport (1897–1967), a brother, contributed to social psychology with his studies of rumor (Allport and Postman, Psychology of rumor, 1947) and prejudice (The nature of prejudice, 1954).

Social psychology. Boston: Houghton Mifflin, 1924. [Pp. 3–4, 7–9.]

Behavior in general may be regarded as the interplay of stimulation and reaction between the individual and his environment. Social behavior comprises the stimulations and reactions arising between an individual and the *social* portion of his environment; that is, between the individual and his fellows. Examples of such behavior would be the reactions to language, gestures, and other movements of our fellow men, in contrast with our reactions toward non-social objects, such as plants, minerals, tools, and inclement weather. The significance of social behavior is exactly the same as that of non-social, namely, the correction of the individual's biological maladjustment to his environment. In and through others many of our most urgent wants are fulfilled; and our behavior toward them is based on the same fundamental needs as our reactions toward all objects, social or non-social. It is the satisfaction of these needs and the adaptation of the individual to his whole environment which constitutes the guiding principles of his interactions with his fellow men.

Impressed by the closely knit and reciprocal nature of social behavior, some writers have been led to postulate a kind of 'collective mind' or 'group consciousness' as separate from the minds of the individuals of whom the group is composed. No fallacy is more subtle and misleading than this. It has appeared in the literature under numerous guises; but has everywhere left the reader in a state of mystical confusion. Several forms of this theory will be examined shortly. The standpoint of this book may be concisely stated as follows. There is no psychology of groups which is not essentially and entirely a psychology of individuals. Social psychology must not be placed in contradistinction to the psychology of the individual; *it is a part of the psychology of the individual,* whose behavior it studies in relation to that sector of his environment comprised by his fellows. His biological needs are the ends toward which his social behavior is a developed means. Within his organism are provided all the mechanisms by which social behavior is explained. There is likewise no consciousness except that belonging to individuals. Psychology in all its branches is a science of the individual. To extend its principles to larger units is to destroy their meaning. . . .

In cases, therefore, where psychological factors are involved, it is better to use the less facile, but more exact phrase, "the *individuals* in the crowd are emotional, intolerant, immortal," and so on. This is no mere pedantry; for it lays the emphasis upon the true source to which we must look for an explanation of crowd phenomena. If we believe that it is the crowd mind rather than the individual's which exhibits the altered phases of consciousness, all explanation fades into mere description. Thus crowd behavior is explained in terms of what crowds generally do—a circular explanation, indeed! There is, moreover, according to this view no reason for one crowd to exhibit different mental characteristics from another; all are subject to the same laws of emotionality, irrationality, simple-mindedness, and the like. Against these inadequacies and fallacies we must again urge the importance of going below group phenomena to a deeper level, the individual in the group. It is only through social psychology as a science of the individual that we can avoid the superficialities of the crowd mind and collective mind theories. . . .

At every point we are thus led back to the individual as the locus of all that we may call 'mind.' Alike in crowd excitements, collective uniformities, and organized groups, the only psychological elements discoverable are in the behavior and consciousness of the specific persons involved. All theories which partake of the group fallacy have the unfortunate consequence of diverting attention from the true locus of cause and effect, namely, the behavior mechanisms of the individual. They place the group prior to this mechanism in order of study, and substitute description of social effects in place of true explanation. On the other hand, if we take care of the individuals, psychologically speaking, the groups will be found to take care of themselves.

27.7

Thorleif Schjelderup-Ebbe

(born 1894)

The concept of a "pecking order," first developed by the author in his observation of domestic fowl, opened to experimental investigation the whole range of dominance-submission behaviors which are an essential aspect of the social relationships of all birds and mammals living in groups, and these in turn have thrown new light on a broad range of problems in human interactions, both within and outside the family constellation.

. . . Between any two birds of each species, in a large number of species examined, one individual *invariably* had precedence over the other, which was thus forced into a subordinate position. . . .

. . . What are the external indications which show that a bird is despot over its fellow? This is readily answered: Both individuals display characteristic reactions. One bird, *y*, the subordinate, evinces apprehension, fear, and occasionally even terror of the other. This agitation is clearly seen in the muscle movements, which become more intense as the agitation increases. This bird does not remain in its position but endeavors

Zur Sozialpsychologie der Vögel. *Zeitschrift für Psychologie,* 1924, 95, 36–84. Adapted as "Social behavior of birds." In *Handbook of social psychology,* edited by C. Murchison. Worcester, Mass.: Clark University Press, 1935. Pp. 947–972. [Pp. 949–952, 954–955.]

to move away from the other whenever the latter appears. . . . Other signs of fear are distinctive vocalizations which are characteristic of this particular condition or agitation. Lastly, because of fear of the other individual, the plumage of the frightened bird takes on a special appearance, and certain parts of the body manifest a particular behavior. . . .

The ruling despot {z} discloses his identity by complete lack of fear toward the subordinate individual, and sometimes—strange to see— by completely ignoring the other's existence.

Furthermore, z, when it feels irritable, or whenever it wishes, endeavors to peck the other bird, in which case it may sneak up behind the other unnoticed, or it may chase y in order to deliver the peck (in this case z does not always expect to peck y, as in some cases, for example, it makes a dart sideways toward y, but not such a long dart that it will reach y, who remains stationary). The main point with z seems to be the joy of driving y away, the satisfaction of seeing y fly, swim, or run away. This joy or satisfaction z shows in various emotional expressions, for example, by the raising of certain feathers or by a rush of blood to the face or facial adornments (turkey). Finally, z may frighten or threaten y to the point of making him withdraw from the bough, twig, roosting-place, nest, or region of water, by uttering a certain peculiar, often sonorous, sound which we call the *threat-sound*. . . .

Why, in the case of birds, is one of two individuals of the same species the despot and not the other? Is it individual strength which decides? In accordance with my observations I can say: It may be possible that it is the individual strength of the two which decides the situation, but there are several other just as important factors which may prove decisive. These often have even more weight than the main factor of individual strength.

We may here introduce a third bird, with which we may make comparisons. If one observed the three birds, a, b, and c, living together, all three being of the same species, one would certainly obtain a clear view of the conditions of despotism in quite a short time. It may be observed that a pecks both b and c (that is, it is despot over the other two), and b also pecks c, while c is thus subordinate to both a and b. One cannot, in this case, directly deduce from this condition of despotism that strength is not the deciding factor. But it also happens very often that the three birds peck one another, as it were, in a "triangle": a pecks b, b pecks c, and c again pecks a. The order of despotism, in this case, has a direction which turns back upon itself, and one cannot but wonder at this most peculiar regulation of the pecking in the group. One may here clearly deduce that the order of pecking cannot possibly follow the order of individual strength. . . .

In the case of birds of the same species, which have never met before, the question of despotism is decided immediately upon meeting. Then one of the following things happens: (1) Both birds become offended at each other and prepare to fight (this case is very common). By the trial of physical strength which ensues it is decided which bird is to be the despot. The bird defeated in the fight is doomed to be the subordinate in the future. (2) One bird becomes frightened and the other not (this is also quite a typical case). Then the bird which is not frightened at the meeting becomes despot, even without a fight. This bird is then always on the offensive against the other, while the other constantly seeks to move away. (3) Both birds become mutually frightened by the sight of one another. The one which first conquers its fear directly becomes despot (as soon as the fear subsides with this individual, case number 3, as may be seen, becomes identical with case number 2). . . .

For full-grown members of the same species, meeting for the first time, the order of despotism is decided at the meeting in one of the three ways mentioned above. The conditions of despotism which then appear may last the remainder of the lives of the birds, if they are constantly together. If separated long enough, they will, upon meeting again, regard one another as strangers and a new condition of despotism is then formed. The condition of despotism continues to exist as first formed in most cases without what we may term *revolt against the despot* on the part of the subordinate. Sometimes, however, such revolts do occur. . . . The most typical result is that the despot fights with more than usual energy, as the possibility of losing a fight with a bird over whom it has for a period been despot makes it more angry than would a fight with a strange bird. It also seems as though the despot in such fights against revolting subordinates is confident of its ability to win the fight. It knows the other bird so well and has no fear of anything crafty or unexpected, as it might have in case of fighting strangers. Usually the despot wins such fights. The subordinate, on the other hand, fights with less display of energy than usual. It seems as if the spirit of the bird were dulled by a premonition of hopelessness. We have thus in the case of the subordinates examples of unconscious perseverance in regard to despotism.

27.8

Jacob L. Moreno

(born 1892)

*One may theorize about "society," but it is in the small group that quanti-
tative research on social psychological variables becomes possible. In such
research it is essential to go beyond dealing with schematic "individuals"
and "groups" and to recognize differentiation of intragroup structures and of
individual roles. The first successful means to achieve this was sociometry,
which graphically reveals such differences in the pattern of lines by which
a medley of interpersonal preferences are represented. This book reports
on research comparing 600 girls living in the cottages of a "training school,"
a group of New York City school children, and members of a government
sponsored homestead community. The method has since been used with
profit in many real life and experimental group situations.*

. . . The psychological situation of a community viewed as a whole has a
discernible ordered pattern. It presents itself in laws and tendencies
which are discoverable by means of experiment and analysis. . . .

An instrument to measure the amount of organization shown by social
groups is called *sociometric test*. The sociometric test requires an individual to choose his associates for any group of which he is or might become a member. He is expected to make his choices without restraint
and whether the individuals chosen are members of the present group
or outsiders.

This test has been made in respect to home groups, work groups, and
school groups. It determined the position of each individual in a group
in which he has a function, for instance, in which he lives or works. It
revealed that the underlying psychological structure of a group differs
widely from its social manifestations; that group structures vary directly
in relation to the age level of the members; that different criteria may
produce different groupings of the same persons or they may produce
the same groupings; that groups of different function, as, for instance,
home groups and work groups, tend towards diverse structures; that
people would group themselves differently if they could; that these
spontaneous groups and the functions that individuals act or intend to
act within them have a definite bearing upon the conduct of each individual and upon the group as a whole; and that spontaneous groupings

Who shall survive? A new approach to the problem of human interrelations. Wash-
ington, D.C.: Nervous and Mental Disease Monograph, No. 58. Beacon, N.Y.: Beacon
House Inc., 1934. [Pp. 10–11, 13–14, 16.] Used by permission of the Smith Ely
Jelliffe Trust.

and forms of groupings which are superimposed upon the former by some authority provide a potential source of conflict. It was found that chosen relations and actual relations often differ and that the position of an individual cannot be fully realized if not all the individuals and groups to which he is emotionally related are included. It disclosed that the organization of a group cannot be fully studied if all related groups or individuals are not included, that individuals and groups are often to such an extent interlocked that the whole community to which they belong has to become the scope of the sociometric test. . . .

In school groups the test had the following form. The tester entered the classroom and addressed the pupils:

"You are seated now according to directions your teacher has given you. The neighbor who sits beside you is not chosen by you. You are now given the opportunity to choose the boy or girl whom you would like to have sit on either side of you. Write down whom you would like first best; then, whom you would like second best. Look around and make up your mind. Remember that next term your friends you choose now may sit beside you." . . .

For home groups the test had to be varied. The tester called the whole population of a given community together and addressed them:

"You live now in a certain house with certain other persons according to the directions the administration has given you. The persons who live with you in the same house are not ones chosen by you and you are not one chosen by them. You are now given the opportunity to choose the persons whom you would like to live with in the same house. You can choose without restraint any individuals of this community whether they happen to live in the same house with you or not. Write down whom you would like first best, second best, third best, fourth best, and fifth best. Look around and make up your mind. Remember that the ones you choose will probably be assigned to live with you in the same house." . . .

. . . It is necessary that the subjects themselves be taken into partnership, that they become sufficiently interested in the test, that they transfer to the tester their spontaneous attitudes, thoughts and motivations in respect to the individuals concerned in the same criterion. . . . If, therefore, the inhabitants of a community are asked whom they like or dislike irrespective of any criterion this should not be called sociometric. These likes and dislikes being unrelated to a criterion are not analytically differentiated. They may relate to sexual liking, to the liking of working together, to whatever. Secondly, the individuals have no interest to express their likes and dislikes truthfully as no practical consequences for themselves are derivable from these. Similarly if children in a classroom are asked whom they like or dislike among their classmates irrespective of any criterion and without immediate purpose for them. Even if such a form of inquiry may at some age level produce similar results as the results gained through our procedure, it should not be called socio-metric testing. It does not provide a systematic basis for sociometric research.

27.9

Muzafer Sherif

(born 1906)

As a Turkish student in America, Sherif was sensitive to how much different "social norms" influence the thinking of individuals in different societies. This is an excellent example of how a social problem can be attacked by laboratory methods. Years later, the same basic method was adapted by Solomon Asch (who had been a student with Sherif at Columbia University) to devise an experimental test of leadership potential in which individuals were subjected to the pressure of patently false "social norms."

. . . In complete darkness, such as is found in a closed room that is not illuminated, or on a cloudy night in the open when there are no other lights visible, a single small light seems to move, and it may appear to move erratically in all directions. . . .

We have studied the extent of the movement experienced in two situations.

1. When alone, except for the experimenter (in order to get the reaction of the individual unaffected by other experimentally introduced social factors, and thus to gain a basic notion about the perceptual process under the circumstances).

2. When the individual is in a group situation (in order to discover modifications brought about by membership in the group). . . .

The stimulus light was a tiny point of light seen through a small hole in a metal box. The light was exposed to the subject by the opening of a suitable shutter controlled by the experimenter. The distance between the subject and the light was five meters. The observer was seated at a table on which was a telegraph key. The following instructions were given in written form: "When the room is completely dark, I shall give you the signal READY, and then show you a point of light. After a short time the light will start to move. As soon as you see it move, press the key. A few seconds later the light will disappear. Then tell me the distance it moved. Try to make your estimates as accurate as possible." . . .

The psychology of social norms. New York: Harper, 1936. [Pp. 91, 93, 95, 104–106.]

27.9 Muzafer Sherif

Certain facts stand out clearly from our results. We may summarize these facts in a few paragraphs.

When an individual faces this stimulus situation, which is unstable and not structured in itself, he establishes a range and norm (a reference point) within that range. The range and norm that are developed in each individual are peculiar to that individual. They may vary from the ranges and norms developed in other individuals in different degrees, revealing consistent and stable individual differences. . . .

When the individual, in whom a range and a norm within that range are first developed in the individual situation, is put into a group situation, together with other individuals who also come into the situation with their own ranges and norms established in their own individual sessions, the ranges and norms tend to converge. But the convergence is not so close as when they first work in the group situation, having less opportunity to set up stable individual norms.

When individuals face the same unstable, unstructured situation as members of a group for the first time, a range and a norm (standard) within that range are established, which are peculiar to the group. If, for the group, there is a rise or fall in the norms established in successive sessions, it is a group effect; the norms of the individual members rise and fall toward a common norm in each session. . . .

The fact that the norm thus established is peculiar to the group suggests that there is a factual psychological basis in the contentions of social psychologists and sociologists who maintain that new and supra-individual qualities arise in the group situations. . . .

The experiments, then, constitute a study of the formation of a norm in a simple laboratory situation. They show in a simple way the basic psychological process involved in the establishment of social norms. They are an extension into the social field of a general psychological phenomenon that we found in perception and in many other psychological fields, namely, that our experience is organized around or modified by frames of reference participating as factors in any given stimulus situation.

On the basis of this general principle considered in relation to our experimental results, we shall venture to generalize. The psychological basis of the established social norms, such as stereotypes, fashions, conventions, customs and values, is the formation of common frames of reference as a product of the contact of individuals. Once such frames of reference are established and incorporated in the individual, they enter as important factors to determine or modify his reactions to the situations that he will face later—social, and even non-social, at times, especially if the stimulus field is not well structured.

27.10

Kurt Lewin   Ronald Lippitt

(1890–1947)   (born 1914)

AND

Ralph K. White

(born 1907)

Lewin's field-theoretical approach, a quite distinctive outgrowth of the Gestalt school, exerted great influence on American psychology generally, but especially on social psychology. He also introduced the "action experiment" in which the experimental design is integrated with the real life situation of the subjects and where the experimenters enter as participant observers. We include only one of four typically Lewinian field diagrams which illustrate the lengthy theoretical discussion.

Lippitt has been associated with the Research Center for Group Dynamics which was founded by Lewin at MIT, and which moved to the University of Michigan after Lewin's untimely death. White's later work has been chiefly in evaluation of propaganda, working for such agencies as CIA and Voice of America. Together they authored a book which is a direct outcome of the study reported in this selection: Autocracy and democracy; an experimental inquiry (1960).

The present report is a preliminary summary on one phase of a series of experimental studies of group life which has as its aim a scientific approach to such questions as the following: What underlies such differing patterns of group behavior as rebellion against authority, persecution of a scapegoat, apathetic submissiveness to authoritarian domination, or attack upon an outgroup? How may differences in subgroup structure, group stratification, and potency of ego-centered and group-centered goals be utilized as criteria for predicting the social resultants of different group atmospheres? Is not democratic group life more pleasant, but authoritarianism more efficient? These are the sorts of questions to which "opinionated" answers are many and varied today, and to which scientific answers are, on that account, all the more necessary. . . .

In the first experiment Lippitt organized two clubs of 10-year-old

Patterns of aggressive behavior in experimentally created "social climates." *Journal of Social Psychology* 10 (1939): 271–299. [Pp. 271–272, 276–278, 282–284, 290, 294–295, 297.]

children, who engaged in the activity of theatrical mask-making for a period of three months. The same adult leader, changing his philosophy of leadership, led one club in an authoritarian manner and the other club in accordance with democratic techniques, while detailed observations were made by four observers. This study . . . suggested more hypotheses than answers and led to a second and more extensive series of experiments by White and Lippitt. . . . To the variables of authoritarian and democratic procedure was added a third, "*laissez-faire*" or group life without adult participation. Also the behavior of each club was studied in different "social climates." Every six weeks each group had a new leader with a different technique of leadership, each club having three leaders during the course of the five months of the experimental series. . . .

One test used systematically was for the leader to leave the room on business during the course of the club meeting, so that the "social pressure" factor could be analyzed more realistically. Another practice was for the leader to arrive a few minutes late so that the observers could record the individual and "atmospheric" differences in spontaneous work initiation and work perspective. . . .

[In the first experiment] as the club meetings progressed the authoritarian club members developed a pattern of aggressive domination toward one another, and their relation to the leader was one of submission or of persistent demands for attention. The interactions in the democratic club were more spontaneous, more fact-minded, and friendly. Relations to the leader were free and on an "equality basis." Comparing the two groups on the one item of overt hostility the authoritarian group was surprisingly more aggressive, the ratio being 40 to 1. . . .

In the second experiment . . . there were five democratic, five autocratic, and two "*laissez-faire*" atmospheres. . . .

. . . Four of the five autocracies had an extremely low level of aggression, and the fifth had an extremely high one. . . .

In the interpretation of these data it is natural to ask: Why are the results for autocracy paradoxical? Why is the reaction to autocracy sometimes very aggressive, with much rebellion or persecution of scapegoats, and sometimes very nonaggressive? Are the underlying dynamics in these two cases as different as the surface behavior? The high level of aggression in some autocracies has often been interpreted mainly in terms of tension, which presumably results from frustration of individual goals. Is it, then, an indication of nonfrustration when the aggression level in some other autocracies is found to be extremely low?

Four lines of evidence in our experiments indicate that this is not the case, and that the low level of aggression in the apathetic autocracies is not due to lack of frustration.

First of all, there are the sudden outbursts of aggression which occurred on the days of transition from a repressed autocratic atmosphere to the much freer atmosphere of democracy or *laissez-faire*. . . .

A second and very similar type of evidence can be obtained from the records on the days when the leader left the room for 10 or 15 minutes. In the three other atmospheres . . . the aggression level did not rise when the leader left the room. In the apathetic autocracies, however, the level of aggression rises very rapidly to 10 times its former level, [although not] to a level significantly above that of the other atmospheres. . . .

In the third place, there are the judgments of observers who found themselves using such terms as "dull," "lifeless," "submissive," "repressed," and "apathetic" in describing the nonaggressive reaction to autocracy. . . .

The fourth and perhaps the most convincing indication of the existence of frustration in these atmospheres is the testimony of the boys themselves. . . . With surprising unanimity the boys [in interviews] agreed in a relative dislike for their autocratic leader regardless of his individual personality. . . .

From the many theoretical problems involved we should like to discuss but one, namely, the problem of aggression and apathy. Even here we wish to show the complexity of the problem and its possible attack from a field theoretical point of view rather than to set forth a definite theory. . . .

Aggression within a group can be viewed as a process by which one part of the group sets itself in opposition to another part of the group, in this way breaking the unity of the group. Of course, this separation is only of a certain degree.

In other words, if M indicates a member or subgroup and Gr the whole group, an aggression involves a force acting on the subgroup in the direction away from the main group $(f_{M, -Gr})$ or other part of the subgroup. From this it should follow theoretically that if a subgroup can easily locomote in the direction away from the group it will do so in case this force shows any significant strength. In other words, a strong tension and an actual aggression will be built up only in case there exist forces which hinder the subgroup from leaving the group. . . .

In our experiment, autocracy provided a much more rigid social group than democracy. It was particularly difficult for the members of an autocracy to change their social status. On the other hand, in both groups the member did not like to leave the group as a whole because of the interest in the work project and the feeling of responsibility to the adult leader.

On the whole, then, the rigidity of the group will function as a restraining force against locomotion away from the group, or from the position within the group. Sufficient strength of this restraining force seems to be one of the conditions for the building up of a tension which is sufficiently high to lead to aggression.

It can be easily seen that the barriers limiting the space of free movement may have a similar function. We mentioned above, that a narrow

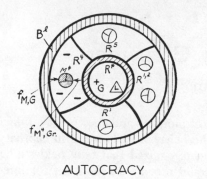
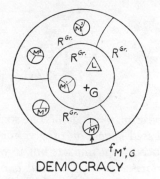

AUTOCRACY   DEMOCRACY

Rigidity of Group Structure as a Tension Factor

In autocracy where each member or subgroup (M^1, M^2 ... M^5) has a circumscribed region of activity (R^1, R^2 ... R^5), and especially where the central regions of group life (policy formation R^p) are inaccessible to most members, rigid barriers (B) to own goals (G) continually frustrate members' efforts. The member's own position in the group structure (R^4) therefore acquires a negative valence, usually creating a force away from group membership ($f_{M^4, -Gr}$). But in rigid group structures a restraining barrier (B^l) keeps members or subgroups from leaving until a very high state of tension develops.

In democracy where all group regions (R^{Gr}) are accessible to all members (M^1, M^2 ... M^5), their own goals (G) are more easily attained and no such frustrating situation develops.

space of free movment seems to be equivalent to pressure, and, in this way, creates tension. At the same time, the barriers prevent locomotion, thus providing the restraining forces necessary for building up higher tension. . . .

. . . Such a field theoretical approach seems to be rather arduous. On the other hand, only in this way will one be able to understand for instance the paradox of behavior that autocracy may lead either to aggression or to apathy. . . .

The field theoretical approach also provides indications for the circumstance under which one might generalize the results of such experimental group studies. . . . The essence of an experiment is to create a situation which shows a certain pattern. . . . This is one of the reasons why experiments are possible and worthwhile.

27.11

Clarence Ray Carpenter

(born 1905)

S. Zuckerman's study of The social life of monkeys and apes (1932), which was based largely on observations of the behavior of baboons in captivity, produced great impact, but it was soon recognized that only field studies of primates in their natural habitats could provide a valid basis for inferences regarding the biological foundations of human society. Carpenter helped open this new area of research. His field study of howling monkeys, published in 1934, was the first of a series, but observations on anthropoid apes, such as the gibbon, are of higher interest.

It should be mentioned that H. W. Nissen reported on a field study of the chimpanzee (in Western French Guinea) in a Comparative Psychology Monograph (No. 8) in 1931.

This report has given the results of prolonged observations on the gibbon *Hylobates lar* in its natural Siamese (Thailand) habitat. . . .

The smallest group observed had only 2 animals, an adult male and female, while the largest group had an adult pair and 4 immature animals which represented, as could easily be judged, a succession of births. The young ranged in stages of development from early infancy to near maturity. The size of the group, except in groups which have passed their reproductive period, may be used as a rough index of the age of the grouping. Small families are probably newly formed and large groups are at least as old as the oldest offspring in the group. This of course would not apply to a group consisting of an old non-reproducing pair.

The grouping pattern, with two exceptions [of 21], was that of a *monogamous family*. These families are inferred to be relatively stable and the budding-off, division or formation of new groups is a complex process described as apoblastosis. Mating seemingly may occur either within the family or with a suitable individual from some other group. Occasionally one finds gibbons which are presumably living temporarily solitary lives separated from the parent group. . . .

Gibbons exhibit a rather wide range of emotional expressions. In the same individual, the emotional responses may vary from extremely mild tender responses to equally extreme vicious behavior. . . .

A field study in Siam of the behavior and social relations of the gibbon (Hylobates lar). *Comparative Psychology Monographs* 16 (1940); Ser. No. 84. [Pp. 194–199.] Originally published by The Johns Hopkins Press; reprinted by permission of the Regents of the University of California, Berkeley.

27.11 Clarence Ray Carpenter

Gibbons acquire and defend sections of the forest and generally confine their activities within these possessed regions. This *territoriality* is a fundamental characteristic of the behavior of free ranging gibbons. Although in some regions the territories or ranges of groups form overlapping mosaics, in general, groups seem to have definite territories from which other groups are mainly excluded while the owner groups occupy them. Shifts in the territorial ranges of groups occur as a result of pressures from surrounding families, competition, group-splitting and shifts in the supply of food. Habituation to a given region, its food trees and trails, its lodge trees and places for rest and play are important in stabilizing the territories possessed.

This territoriality would seem to prohibit or markedly restrict migratory movements in gibbons. Territorial ranges are defended both by actual fighting and by vocalizations. These sound patterns seem to represent or substitute for actual fighting and in a measure they act as a kind of *buffer* to pugnacity. Guarding behavior is a characteristic kind of naturalistic activity seen in gibbons. Both territories and members of the group, especially attacked individuals, are protected or guarded. In gibbon groups, guarding and protective behavior seem to be almost as prominent as dominance behavior, to which it is closely related, in the organization of the families.

The coordination and control of gibbon families is carried out by complex systems of gestures and patterns of vocalizations. Learning and maturation play important roles in the communicative processes. For example, through learning, actual contact control of a mother over her infant is replaced by communicative signals or reduced movement cues and voice. Gestures may be affinitive or may produce avoiding or aggressive responses. Nevertheless, it should be noted also that there are gestures and vocal sound patterns peculiar to the species, which perseverate even with long association with other species [in captivity].

Through sound recording and other techniques, preliminary study has differentiated nine types of vocalizations. Each sound pattern has its range of communicative functions. A fairly wide range of stimulus situations evoke each particular sound pattern and these in turn stimulate in associated animals a rather wide range of response to each vocal pattern. . . .

Gibbons fight by biting, using mainly the long keen canine teeth, and by clawing with their fingers. Their fights, as observed mainly in captive animals, are sporadic, swift and often effective. When gibbons strike with their bared canines, the results are quick-felt and telling. It is inferred that fights occur in the wild mainly during processes of group-splitting and when antagonistic groups come together.

The fact that little fighting was observed in the field may be explained mainly by two things: 1, Vocalizations tend to substitute for actual fighting and 2, Gibbons in the wild have definitely structured

743

groups in which each individual has its status from which it changes only gradually.

As far as could be learned by observations, adult male and female gibbons show no striking sex difference in dominance. This may relate to their lack of anatomical secondary sex differences. It may be concluded that in this primate, though the adults are very aggressive, there is an *equivalence* of *dominance* in the sexes. However, among individuals there is a wide variation in dominance which may vary also from one type of behavior to another, e.g., the animal most dominant in feeding may not be most dominant in play or sexual behavior. . . .

The integration of primates into groups is believed to be a complex process involving mutually reciprocal patterns of naturalistic behavior which are modified and made specific by learning or conditioning. Almost every phase of behavior of which a primate is capable enters to some degree into the determination of its "gregariousness" and the qualities of its complex social behavior.

# Chapter 28

THE DEFINITION
OF A SCIENCE

Until quite recently it was thought that the earliest use of the word psychology was in a book published at Marburg in 1590, with a title including that word, freshly coined in Greek. The author was Rudolph Göckel, or Goclenius (1547–1628). Previous tracts of this nature, if not titled De anima, might be called Peri psyche, that is, On the soul. It has however recently become known that a Croatian humanist, Marko Marulič (1450–1524), wrote a Latin treatise including the word psychologia in its title, and although the work itself has not been found, he must be credited with coining the term.

It is still some distance, however, from designating a body of doctrine to defining an active science. This chapter brings together four statements which mark as many stages in defining the character of psychology.

28.1

Francis Bacon, Lord Verulam

(1561–1626)

In these "twoo bookes" Bacon first outlined his grand scheme for the re-
vitalization of the sciences. He wrote it in English, unlike the Novum
Organum (1620) and the De Augmentis Scientiarum (1623), which is an
expansion of this work. What one usually meets under the title, The ad-
vancement of learning, is one of several English translations of the latter
work. Among the sciences, Bacon sees the need for a separate science of
human nature—that is, one not ancillary either to theology or to medicine,
though maintaining communication with both.

We come therefore now to that knowledge whereunto the ancient Oracle
directeth us, which is, *the knowledge of our selves:* which deserveth the
more accurate handling, by howe much it toucheth us more neerely.
This knowledge as it is the end and Terme of Naturall Philosophy *in the*
intention of Man: So notwithstanding it is but a portion of Naturall
Philosophy *in the continent of Nature:* And generally let this be a Rule,
that all partitions of knowledges, be accepted rather for *lines & veines,*
then for *sections and separations:* and that the continuance and entire-
nes of knowledge be preserved. For the contrary here of hath made
particular Sciences, to become barren, shallow, & erronious: while they
have not bin Nourished and Maintained from the common fountaine:
So we see *Cicero* the Orator complained of *Socrates* and his Schoole,
that he was the first that separated Philosophy, and Rhetoricke, whereupon Rhetorick became an emptie & verball Art. So wee may see that
the opinion of *Copernicus* touching the rotation of the earth, which
Astronomie it self cannot correct, because it is not repugnant to any of the
Phaenomena, yet Naturall Philosophy may correct. So wee see also that
the Science of *Medicine,* if it be destituted & forsaken by *Natural Phi-*
losophy, it is not much better than an Empeirical practize: with this
reservation therefore we proceed to HUMANE PHILOSOPHY or HUMANITIE,
which hath two parts: The one considereth Man *segregate, or distribu-*
tively: the other *congregate,* or in *societie.* So as HUMANE PHILOSOPHY
is either SIMPLE and PARTICULAR, or Coniugate and Civile; HUMANITIE
PARTICULAR consisteth of the same parts, whereof Man consisteth, that
is, of KNOWLEDGES WHICH RESPECT THE BODY, & of KNOWLEDGES THAT
RESPECT THE MIND. But before we *distribute* so far, it is good to *con-*

Of the proficience and advancement of learning, divine and humane. London, 1605.
[Second Book, LL. 35–38.]

stitute. For I doe take the consideration in generall, and at large of HUMANE NATURE to be fit to be emancipate and made a knowledge by it self; Not so much in regard of those delightfull and elegant discourses, which have bin made of the dignitie of Man, of his miseries, of his state and life, and the like *Adiuncts of his common and undevided Nature*, but chiefely in regard of the knowledge concerning the SYMPATHIES AND CONCORDANCES BETWEENE THE MIND AND BODY, which being mixed, cannot be properly assigned to the sciences of either.

This knowledge hath two branches; for as all leagues and Amities consist of mutuall *Intelligence* and mutuall *Offices* So this league of mind and body, hath these two parts, *How the one discloseth the other, and how the one worketh upon the other. Discoverie, & Impression.* The former of these hath begotten two Arts, both of *Prediction* or *Prenotion* where of the one is honoured with the enquirie of *Aristotle*, & the other of *Hippocrates*. And although they have of later time beene used to be coupled with superstitous and fantasticall arts; yet being purged and restored to their true state; they have both of them a solide ground in nature, and a profitable use in life. The first is PHYSIOGNOMY, which discovereth the disposition of the mind, by the Lyneaments of the bodie. The second is the EXPOSITION OF NATURAL DREAMES, which discovereth the state of the bodie by the imaginations of the minde. . . .

The later Branch, touching IMPRESSION, hath not beene collected into Art; but hath beene handled dispersedly; and it hath the same relation or *Antistrophe*, that the former hath. For the consideration is double, EITHER HOW, AND HOW FARRE, THE HUMOURS AND AFFECTS OF THE BODIE, DO ALTER OR WORKE UPON THE MIND; or againe, HOW AND HOW FAR THE PASSIONS, OR APPREHENSIONS OF THE MINDE, DOE ALTER OR WORKE UPON THE BODIE. . . . But unto all this knowledge DE COMMUNI VINCULO, of the Concordances betweene the Mind and the bodie: that part of Enquirie is most necessarie, which considereth of the *Seates*, and *Domiciles* which the severall faculties of the minde, doe take and occupate in the Organs of the bodie, which knowledge hath been attempted, and is controverted, and deserveth to bee much better inquired. . . . So then we have constituted (as in our own wish and advise) the inquirie TOUCHING HUMANE NATURE ENTYER; as a iust portion of knowledge, to be handled apart. . . .

28.2

John Stuart Mill

(1806–1873)

More than 200 years after the death of Francis Bacon, John Mill dealt again with the problem of scientific evidence and gave an affirmative answer to the question of whether the study of human nature should hold a place among the sciences. This selection is taken from Book VI, Chapter III. The "universal laws of human nature" to which he refers in the last sentence of the selection are the laws of association. After stating these in Chapter IV (see 12.10), he went on in Chapter V to say that a science of "ethology," or the formation of character, might be based on deductions from such empirically established laws. Although experiment would be impossible, or at least unethical, these deductions could be verified by observation. In 1861, when Bain published a book On the study of character, Mill wrote to Bain that he still hoped to take up again some day the subject of ethology—but he never did.

That There Is, or May Be, a Science of Human Nature

§ 1. It is a common notion, or at least it is implied in many common modes of speech, that the thoughts, feelings, and actions of sentient beings are not a subject of science, in the same strict sense in which this is true of the objects of outward Nature. This notion seems to involve some confusion of ideas, which it is necessary to begin by clearing up.

Any facts are fitted, in themselves, to be a subject of science, which follow one another according to constant laws; although these laws may not have been discovered, nor even be discoverable by our existing resources. . . . Meteorology, therefore, not only has in itself every natural requisite for being, but actually is, a science; although, from the difficulty of observing the facts upon which the phenomena depend . . . the science is extremely imperfect; and were it perfect, might probably be of little avail in practice, since the data requisite for applying its principles to particular instances would rarely be procurable.

A case may be conceived, of an intermediate character between the perfection of science, and this its extreme imperfection. It may happen that the greater causes, those on which the principal part of a phenomenon depends, are within the reach of observation and measurement; so

A system of logic, ratiocinative and inductive, being a connected view of the principles of evidence and the methods of scientific investigation. 2 volumes. London, 1843. [Vol. II, pp. 490–491, 493–496.]

that if no other causes intervened, a complete explanation could be given not only of the phenomenon in general, but of all the variations and modifications which it admitted of. But inasmuch as other, perhaps many other causes, separately insignificant in their effects, co-operate or conflict in many or in all cases with those greater causes; the effect, accordingly, presents more or less of aberration from what would be produced by the greater causes alone. . . .

§ 2. The science of human nature is of this description. It falls far short of the standard of exactness now realized in Astronomy; but there is no reason that it should not be as much a science as Tidology is, or as Astronomy was when its calculations had only mastered the main phenomena, but not the perturbations.

The phenomena with which this science is conversant being the thoughts, feelings, and actions of human beings, it would have attained the ideal perfection of a science if it enabled us to foretel how an individual would think, feel, or act, throughout life, with the same certainty with which astronomy enables us to predict the places and the occultations of the heavenly bodies. It needs scarcely be stated that nothing approaching to this can be done. The actions of individuals could not be predicted with scientific accuracy, were it only because we cannot foresee the whole of the circumstances in which those individuals will be placed. But further, even in any given combination of (present) circumstances, no assertion, which is both precise and universally true, can be made respecting the manner in which human beings will think, feel, or act. This is not, however, because every person's modes of thinking, feeling, and acting, do not depend on causes. . . . But the impressions and actions of human beings are not solely the result of their present circumstances, but the joint result of those circumstances and of the characters of the individuals: and the agencies which determine human character are so numerous and diversified . . . that in the aggregate they are never in any two cases exactly similar. . . .

Inasmuch, however, as many of those effects which it is of most importance to render amenable to human foresight and control, are determined, like the tides, in an incomparably greater degree by general causes, than by all partial causes taken together; depending in the main on those circumstances and qualities which are common to all mankind, or common at least to large bodies of them, . . . it is evidently possible with regard to all such effects, to make predictions which will *almost* always be verified, and general propositions which are almost always true. . . .

. . . But in order to give a genuinely scientific character to the study, it is indispensable that these approximate generalizations, which in themselves would amount only to the lowest kind of empirical laws, should be connected deductively with the laws of nature from which they result . . . In other words, the science of Human Nature may be said to exist, in proportion as those approximate truths, which compose a practical knowledge of mankind, can be exhibited as corollaries from the universal laws of human nature on which they rest.

28.3

Wilhelm Wundt

(1832–1920)

Wundt, as a physiologist dealing with problems of sensory perception, issued his first call for an experimental psychology in 1862 (see 26.1). Eleven years later, his Grundzüge introduced the new science to the world. The task accepted was to study the relationships between outer and inner experience, that is, between physiological and mental events. With the passage of time Wundt's views changed, perhaps in part because he gained an acceptance as professor of philosophy at Leipzig which he had never received as professor of physiology at Heidelberg. Rewriting as always, we find him asserting that the new science is "first of all psychology" and not concerned with the relationship of the mental to the physical; it is called physiological only because it has borrowed experimental methods from the physiological laboratory. This leaves us to wonder who, if not Wundt, had "mistakenly asserted" the concern of the infant science with relating inner experiences to the attendant physiological events?

[A]

The present work shows by its very title that it is an attempt to bring together two sciences which have for a long time followed very different paths although they are concerned with almost one and the same subject matter, that is, with human life. *Physiology* informs us about those life phenomena which can be perceived through our external senses. In *psychology*, man looks at himself as it were from *within*, and he tries to explain the connections among those processes which this internal observation presents to him. But however differently the content of our external and internal life may appear, when taken as a whole, they nevertheless have many points of contact; for inner experience is constantly being influenced by external impressions, and our inner states often enter

[A] *Grundzüge der physiologischen Psychologie.* Leipzig, 1873–1874. [Pp. 1–3.]
[B] Idem. Fifth edition. 4 volumes. Leipzig, 1902–1903. Translated (in part) by E. B. Titchener, as *Principles of physiological psychology.* New York: Macmillan, 1904. [Pp. 2–3.]

decisively into the course of external events. Thus there opens up a sphere of life processes which are simultaneously accessible to both external and internal observation, a border zone which, at least so long as physiology and psychology remain separate from one another, may well be made the object of a special science standing between them. However, such a border zone offers prospects toward both sides. A science which has as its subject the points of contact between internal and external life will find occasions, from the points of view thus attained, to compare the whole scope of the two other disciplines between which it stands as mediator, and all its investigations will finally culminate in the question, how external and internal existence are ultimately related. Physiology and psychology can, each for itself, easily evade this question. Physiological psychology cannot sidestep it.

Thus we give our science this task: *first,* to investigate those life processes which, because they stand between internal and external experience, make the simultaneous application of both methods of observation, the internal and the external, essential; and *second,* using the viewpoints gained by investigations of this area, to illuminate all the life processes and thus insofar as possible to achieve a total concept of human being.

. . . Although the problems of this science lie close to those of physiology, and often overlap its actual territory, they have hitherto belonged for the most part to the domain of psychology. Nevertheless, the armament which it brings to the conquest of these problems is borrowed from both mother sciences in equal measure. Psychological introspection proceeds hand in hand with the methods of experimental physiology, and the application of the latter to the former has led to development of a special branch of experimental investigation, the psychophysical method. If principal emphasis is to be placed on methodological characteristics, our science can be called *experimental psychology* in order to distinguish it from the usual study of mind, which is based on introspection.

[B]

Physiological psychology is, therefore, first of all *psychology.* It has in view the same principal object upon which all other forms of psychological exposition are directed: *the investigation of conscious processes in the modes of connexion peculiar to them.* It is not a province of physiology; nor does it attempt, as has been mistakenly asserted, to derive or explain the phenomena of the psychical from those of the physical life. We may read this meaning into the phrase 'physiological psychology,' just as we might interpret the title 'microscopical anatomy' to mean a discussion, with illustrations from anatomy, of what has been accomplished by the microscope; but the words should be no more misleading in the one case than they are in the other. As employed in the present work, the adjective 'physiological' implies simply that our psychology will avail itself to the full of the means that modern physiology puts at its disposal for the analysis of conscious processes. . . .

There are thus two problems which are suggested by the title "physiological psychology": the problem of *method,* which involves the application of experiment, and the problem of a psychophysical *supplement,* which involves a knowledge of the bodily substrates of the mental life. For psychology itself, the former is the more essential; the second is of importance mainly for the philosophical question of the unitariness of vital processes at large.

28.4

William McDougall

(1871–1938)

Wundt's concern with inner experience did not restrain his students. Away from Leipzig, his American students especially sparked the growth of a psychology concerned (as expressed in the title of a book by one of them, E. W. Scripture) with Thinking, Feeling, Doing (1895). Galton's influence was also strong. More and more the emphasis shifted from thinking toward feeling and action. Thus there developed a science oriented increasingly toward how men (or animals) behave, that is, how they relate to others and to things outside themselves. It fell to William McDougall, who attracted much hostile criticism and few students, to define psychology as a science not of soul, not of mind, not of experience, but of conduct. He added nothing essential when, a few years later, with a happier choice of word, he called it "the positive science of behavior (Psychology: The study of behaviour, 1912)."

Psychology may be best and most comprehensively defined as the positive science of the conduct of living creatures. That is to say, it is the science which attempts to describe and explain the conduct of men and of other living creatures, and is not concerned with questions as to what their conduct ought to be. These questions it leaves to Ethics, the normative science of conduct. In adopting this definition we must understand the word conduct in the widest possible sense as denoting the sum of the activities by which any creature maintains its relations with other creatures and with the world of physical things. Psychology is more commonly defined as the science of mind, or as the science of mental or

Physiological psychology. London, 1905. [Pp. 1–2.]

psychical processes, or of consciousness, or of individual experience. Such definitions are ambiguous, and without further elaboration are not sufficiently comprehensive. They express the aims of a psychologist who relies solely upon introspection, the observation and analysis of his own experience, and who unduly neglects the manifestations of mental life afforded by the conduct of his fellow-creatures. They do not adequately define the task that modern physiological psychology sets before itself. For physiological psychology aims at describing and explaining, as far as possible, all the factors that take part in determining the conduct of all living creatures, and though conduct seems to be in great part determined by our sensations, feelings, desires, emotions and all those other varieties of states or processes of consciousness which introspection discovers and distinguishes, psychology finds itself compelled in an ever-increasing degree to recognize the co-operation in all mental process of factors that are unconscious and so cannot be introspectively observed; and though some of these may be inferred from the nature of the processes revealed by introspection, others can only be inferred from the study of movements and other bodily changes. To define psychology as the science of experience or of consciousness is therefore to exclude the study of these unconscious factors, whereas the definition stated above brings all these within the scope of psychology without excluding the study of any part of experience or element of consciousness, for all experience affects conduct.

Appendix A

A BRIEF NOTE ON VOCABULARY

Every reader recognizes that it is often impossible to translate precise shades of meaning from one language into another. Yet we all face a similar task when we read our own language as it was written two or three centuries past. Words have changed their meanings, and we may read into them connotations quite strange to their authors.

A paradoxical outcome of this situation is that the recent translation of a selection from an early French or German author will seem, in its new dress, more modern in tone than an English selection of the same date, which still retains its "quaint" forms of expression. Cleverness in translation cannot resolve this difficulty, and "modernizing" the old English texts will only complicate it further. Whether reading in the original or a translation, the reader must make the effort to think in harmony with the author's time and not leap too readily to a conclusion that the author is thinking like a twentieth-century man.

It may be helpful to indicate the principal early meanings of some conspicuously changed words which are likely to occur in psychological discussions. Fuller accounts of these words will be found in any good unabridged dictionary, but the Oxford Dictionary is undoubtedly best for this purpose because it provides such full illustrations for obsolete meanings.

A *history* is a systematic account, implying no connotation of temporal sequence or development.

Perfect means complete. A perfect animal is one with all five obvious external senses as well as memory and imagination, which are classed as internal senses.

Organization is the structural differentiation of a living creature into organs. Not before the late eighteenth century was this word transferred by analogy to social organizations, and its use in nonbiological contexts, as when we speak of the organization of a project or the organized display of materials, is very recent. Connotations based on such usage should be rejected before the latter part of the nineteenth century.

Philosopher is a word which changes its meaning as the division of

755

intellectual labor progresses. Originally it meant any learned person, and was applied more specifically to lay scholars, in later Christian times, to distinguish them from theologians. Aristotle is often alluded to as "the philosopher." As the empirical sciences develop, "natural philosophers" are distinguished as a separate group. They often write "philosophic accounts," which are so described to indicate that the accounts are scientific rather than speculative treatments of their subjects. As psychology begins to emerge as a discipline, but before there are psychologists, there are "moral philosophers" who teach "moral science."

Animal signifies, first, possessing a soul (*anima*) and, hence, being animated, be-souled. But it also signifies possession of a soul with more than nutritive power and hence implies capability for adaptive movement. It then designates functions serving an adaptive relationship to the external world. *Motion* may signify any change, while *local motion* (whence *locomotion*) signifies a change of place or position, as distinguished from *internal motion,* meaning thought or volition. A *determination* is the "motion" which leads to an overt act.

Unqualified *spirit* is the immaterial agent of intellect and sentience in man, but *animal spirit* is assumed to be just as corporeal as the stuff which escapes from an uncorked bottle of "spirits," while *vital spirit* and *natural spirit* are still more coarsely material substances active in the body.

Active and *passive* describe motions (that is, changes) which result, respectively, from internal and external causes. For an author who assumes that only mind is truly active, the bodily changes resulting from thought are *passions*. When the mind is not free to rule itself but is coerced by bodily perturbations, it also undergoes passions. This meaning is close to the Greek *pathos*—close enough for confusion and ambiguity, long before our time.

The *principle* of anything is its origin or beginning. The soul, as initiator of all motion, is an *active principle.* Eventually, the word *principle* comes to stand for "inner nature" or essence, but this is a derived meaning.

Reflex was originally synonymous with reflective and had the meanings we attach to that word today. In time it came to describe the process by which peripheral stimulation evokes peripheral muscular contraction, after going to and from a central nervous organ which serves to "reflect" it. Descartes described responses of this nature, but the word reflex was not used in that manner until long afterwards. The reader must not suppose that anything less than the highest state of consciousness is implied by "reflex thinking." What is now called a reflex was described in the seventeenth and eighteenth centuries as motion *by consent,* or *by sympathy*—two analogous words (one based on Latin roots, the other on Greek roots) implying that a "togetherness of feeling" is responsible for the coordinated action or remote parts.

756

A Brief Note on Vocabulary

To *use* means to "do customarily" or habitually. It is something one gets used to! to *discover* usually implies "to exhibit" rather than "to find out." The word *reveal* has a similar ambiguity in modern usage.

Vapors are states of mental confusion which do not involve manic behavior, but may involve delusions. Or the vaporous person may be only *melancholic,* that is, suffering the effects of an excess of black bile. The terms *neurosis* and *psychosis* do not necessarily denote pathological conditions, but may refer to states of nervous and of mental activity, respectively.

The *species* of an object is its appearance, hence its *image,* that is, whatever internal representation it has in the brain as a result of the sensory process. The *idea* or *percept* is more purely mental. For a century or more after Locke, most authors, though not all, conform to his use of *idea* to stand for any mental content whatever (so that the French sensationists came to be called *ideologists*). *Perception* means no more than sensory cognizance, unless it is specifically differentiated from sensation by the author.

Discourse originally meant orderly thinking, and only later the act of expressing thoughts in speech.

Finally, *mind.* English first, French next, and German last, felt the need to designate the totality of mental activity by a term divorced from theological dogmas about the nature of the soul. The English turned to *mind,* the original meaning of which was memory. The French adapted *l'esprit,* or spirit, a word whose many meanings require several pages of definition in a modern unabridged French dictionary. The German still stubbornly holds to *Seele,* although *Geist,* the literal equivalent of *l'esprit,* did come to represent superior mind or genius. It is not possible to establish any rule as to whether *Seele,* in later German authors, should be translated soul or mind. The choice depends on our judgment of the author's state of mind, which probably never coincides with our twentieth-century connotations for either of these words.

After these comments, the reader should consider himself warned, but only minimally informed, unless he has drawn his knowledge from a richer source. *Caveat lector.*

Appendix B

CHRONOLOGICAL SHORT-TITLE LIST OF WORKS EXCERPTED

The reader will find many reasons for browsing in this listing—one being to confirm the absence of some favorite work which is inexcusably omitted!

Dates preceded by a hyphen are dates of death for authors prior to the age of printing. Early authors for whom this information is not available are listed in probable historical sequence.

Other dates are for original editions. However, only English titles are given, even if no part of a work has previously appeared in English translation. A date followed by a hyphen is the publication date for the first volume of a multivolumed work, or for the first of several closely related articles.

Titles of journal articles, of chapters in symposia, and of addresses (but not of lecture series subsequently published in book form) are in Roman type.

B.C.

−377	Hippocrates. *On the sacred disease* (8.1).
−347	Plato. *Timaeus* (1.1); *The republic* (19.1).
−322	Aristotle. *Parts of animals* (2.1, 4.1); *On the soul* (5.1, 7.1); *On memory and recollection* (11.1); *History of animals* (14.1); *On dreams* (19.2).
−287	Theophrastus. *Problem 30* (24.1); *Moral characters* (23.1).
−270	Epicurus (see 20.2).
−258	Zeno the Stoic (see 20.1).
	Erasistratos (see 13.1).
−55	Lucretius. *On the nature of things* (5.3, 6.1, 19.3).

A.D.

−65	Seneca. *Moral epistles* (15.1).
−67	Paul of Tarsus. *Epistle to the Romans* (21.2).
−79	Pliny. *Natural history of the world* (1.2).
	Epictetus. *Handbook (Encheiridion)* (21.1).

Chronological Short-Title List of Works Excerpted

c.100   Celsus. *On medicine* (24.2).

−200   Galen. *The usefulness of the parts of the body* (4.2, 8.2, 15.2); *On muscular movement* (9.1); *On habits* (13.1); *The seats of ailments* (15.2); *Manners of the soul* (23.2).

c.200   Sextus Empiricus. *Hipotiposes* (5.2).

−270   Plotinus. *The enneads* (6.2)

c.340   Lactantius. *Epitome of the divine institutes* (1.3).

c.340   Vindician. *Letter to Pentadius* (23.3).

c.350   Nemesius. *The nature of man* (7.2).

−395   Gregory of Nyssa. *On the making of man* (4.3, 8.3, 19.4).

−430   Saint Augustine. *On the quantity of the soul* (2.2); *City of God* (3.1, 11.2); *Confessions* (18.1, 21.3).

−524   Boethius. *The consolation of philosophy* (7.3).

c.1050   Psellos. *On the works of demons* (24.3).

−1037   Avicenna. *The art of curing* (3.2).

−1204   Maimonides. *Guide for the perplexed* (1.4).

−1280   Albertus Magnus. *On animals* (14.2).

−1274   Saint Thomas Aquinas. *Summa theologia* (15.3, 22.1); *Disputation on the soul* (15.3).

−1292   Roger Bacon. *Opus majus* (6.3).

1496   Reisch. *Pearl of philosophy* (9.2, 10.1).

1537   Agrippa. *The vanity of the sciences* (11.3).

1538   Vives. *On life and the soul* (11.4, 13.3, 20.3).

1543   Vesalius. *The structure of the human body* (8.4).

1556   Leo Africanus. *Description of Africa* (13.2).

1563   Weyer (Wier). *The deceptions of demons* (24.4).

1575   Huarte. *The Examination of mens wits* (10.2, 15.4, 17.1).

1579   Rosselli. *Treasury of memory devices* (11.5).

1582   Bodin. *Demonomania of sorcerers* (24.5).

1583   Garzoni. *The theatre of . . . worldly brains* (23.4).

1591   Della Porta. *Human physiognomy* (23.5).

1601   Charron. *On wisdom* (1.5, 23.6).

1605   Francis Bacon. *Advancement of learning* (28.1).

1621   Burton. *Anatomy of melancholy* (16.1).

1622   Simone di San Paolo. *Reform of man* (9.3).

1627   Francis Bacon. *Sylva sylvarum, or a natural history* (14.3, 20.4).

1637   Descartes. *Discourse on method* (3.3, 14.4).

1641   Descartes. *Meditations on first philosophy* (3.3).

1644   Digby. *Two treatises . . . on body . . . and soul* (7.4, 13.4, 15.5, 21.4).

1645   La Chambre. *Signs of the emotions, II. The courageous emotions* (19.6, 20.5).

1647   Descartes. Letter to Canut (12.1).

1649   Descartes. *Passions of the soul* (8.5, 20.6).

1650   Hobbes. *Humane nature* (7.5, 19.5).

1651   Hobbes. *Leviathan* (12.2, 17.2).

1654   Charleton. *Physiologia Epicuro-Gassendo-Charlotoniana* (13.5, 15.6).

1655−   Stanley. *History of philosophy* (20.1, 20.2, 24.3).

1657   Comenius. *Complete pedagogy* (17.3).

759

1657   Culpeper. *Galen's art of physick* (23.7).

1662   Descartes. *On man* (6.4, 9.4).

1662   La Chambre. *Signs of the emotions, V. Of weeping, fear and despair* (20.5).

1668   Redi. *Experiments on the generation of insects* (2.4).

1669   Steno. *Discourse on anatomy of the brain* (8.6).

1672   Pardies. *Concerning the knowledge of beasts* (2.3, 7.6, 16.2).

1672   Willis. *Two discourses concerning the soul of brutes* (8.7, 13.7, 19.7, 24.6).

1674   Malebranche. *Search for truth* (6.5, 16.3, 20.7).

1676   Dilly. *The soul of beasts* (13.6).

1677   Glisson. *On the stomach* (9.5).

1677   Hale. *The primitive origination of mankind* (1.7, 3.4, 22.2).

1678   Spinoza. *A political treatise* (1.6).

1680–   Borelli. *The movement of animals* (9.6).

1680   Perrault. *On sound* (8.8).

1682   Bayle. *Reflections occasioned by the comet* (22.3).

1690   Locke. *Essay on humane understanding* (7.7, 16.4); Second edition, 1694 (21.5); Fourth edition, 1700 (12.3).

1699   d'Assigny. *The art of memory* (11.6). •

1699   Shaftesbury. *An inquiry concerning virtue or merit* (22.4).

1704   Newton. *Opticks* (7.8).

1705   Mandeville. *Fable of the bees* (22.5 [from 1723 edition]).

1709   Berkeley. *An essay towards a new theory of vision* (6.6).

1713   Newton. General Scholium added to *Principia mathematica* (8.9).

1725   Hutcheson. *An inquiry concerning the original or our ideas of beauty and virtue* (12.4, 25.1).

1731   Gay. The fundamental principle of virtue or morality (22.6).

1734   Cheyne. *The English malady* (8.10).

1739   Bougeant. *A philosophical amusement concerning the language of animals* (14.5).

1739–   Hume. *Treatise of human nature* (3.5, 12.5).

1743   Trembley. Observations and experiments upon the fresh-water polypus (2.5).

1748   Hume. *Philosophical essays concerning human understanding* (5.4).

1748   La Mettrie. *Man a machine* (1.8, 14.6).

1748   Reid. An essay on quantity (25.2).

1749   Hartley. *Observations on man* (13.8, 22.7).

1751   Diderot. *Letter on the deaf and mute* (7.9).

1751   Whytt. *An essay on the vital and other involuntary motions* (9.8).

1753   Haller. *Sensibility and irritability* (9.7).

1754   Condillac. *Treatise on sensations* (see 16.6).

1755   Condillac. *Treatise on animals* (15.7).

1756   Burke. *On the sublime and beautiful* (20.8).

1758   Battie. *Treatise on madness* (24.7).

1758   Helvetius. *On the mind* (4.4, 17.4, 21.6).

1760   Bonnet. *Analytical essay on the faculties of the mind* (16.7).

1760   Reimarus. *Observations on animal instincts* (15.8).

1762   Kames. *Elements of criticism* (12.6).

1764   Le Roy. *Letters on animals* (21.8).

Chronological Short-Title List of Works Excerpted

1764   Reid. *An inquiry into the human mind* (5.5).
1765   Leibnitz. *New essays on the human understanding* (16.5).
1768   Tucker. *The light of nature pursued* (21.7).
1774   Gerard. *An essay on genius* (12.7).
1774–   Lavater. *Physiognomical fragments* (23.8).
1774   Priestley. *An examination of Dr. Reid's inquiry* (20.9).
1781   Kant. *Critique of pure reason* (5.6).
1786   Kant. *Metaphysical foundations of science* (25.3).
1789   Bentham. *Principles of morals and legislation* (21.9).
1790–   Smellie. *Philosophy of nature* (15.9, 19.8).
1791   Galvani. *Effects of electricity on muscular motion* (8.11).
1794   Erasmus Darwin. *Zoonomia* (15.10).
1794   Condorcet. *Outline for a history of the human mind* (1.9).
1795   Cabanis. Note on execution by the guillotine (2.6).
1800   Bichat. *Physiological researches on life and death* (20.10).
1801   Itard. *The education of a savage* (17.5).
1802   Cabanis. *Relations between the body and mind of man* (8.12, 10.3, 15.11).
1803   Reil. *Psychic treatment of mental disturbances* (24.8).
1809   Gall and Spurzheim. *Researches on the nervous system* (10.4).
1811   Bell. *Idea for a new anatomy of the brain* (7.10, 9.9).
1811   Gall and Spurzheim. *On innate dispositions* (10.4, 17.6).
1812   Le Gallois. *Experiments on the principle of life* (2.7).
1820   Brown. *Lectures on the philosophy of the human mind* (12.8).
1820   Spurzheim. *A philosophical essay on the moral and intellectual nature of man* (15.12, 17.7).
1822   Herbart. On the possibility and necessity of applying mathematics to psychology (25.4).
1824   Herbart. *Psychology as science* (25.4).
1824   Flourens. *Experimental researches on the nervous system of vertebrates* (10.5).
1826   Bell. On the nervous circle which connects the voluntary muscles with the brain (9.9).
1826   Müller. *Visual phantasy phenomena* (7.11).
1829   James Mill. *Analysis of phenomena of the human mind* (12.9).
1833   Bell. *The hand . . . as evincing design* (4.5).
1835–   Comte. *Course of positive philosophy* (3.6).
1835   Quetelet. *Treatise on man* (22.8, 25.6).
1835   Weber. On the sense of touch (25.5).
1836   Dax. Lesions of the left half of the brain coinciding with loss of memory for words (10.6).
1837–   Müller. *Handbook of human physiology* (2.8).
1842   Flourens. *Examination of phrenology* (10.5).
1843   J. S. Mill. *System of logic* (12.10, 28.2).
1845   Griesinger. *Mental pathology and therapeutics* (24.9).
1846   Séguin. *Moral treatment of idiots* (17.8).
1852   Lotze. *Medical psychology* (6.7).
1853   Pflueger. *Sensory functions of the spinal column of vertebrates* (9.10).
1855   Bain. *The senses and the intellect* (12.11, 13.9).

1939   Dollard, Doob, Miller, Mowrer, and Sears. *Frustration and aggression* (21.12).

1939   Lewin, Lippitt, and White. Patterns of aggressive behavior in experimentally created "social climates" (27.10).

1940   Carpenter. A field study in Siam of the behavior and social relations of the gibbon (27.11).

1940   Sullivan, *Conceptions of modern psychiatry* (24.11).

1942   Rogers. *Counseling and psychotherapy* (24.12).

1943   Craik. *On the nature of explanation* (16.11).

1947   Helson. Adaptation-level as frame of reference for prediction of psychophysical data (25.9).

1949   Hess. *The functional organization of the diencephalon* (10.10).

1949   Spitz. The role of ecological factors in emotional development in infancy (18.10).

1950   Bard. Central nervous mechanisms for the expression of anger in animals (20.14).

1950   Lashley. In search of the engram (13.12).

1953   Skinner. *Science and human behavior* (13.13).

1953   Watson and Crick. Genetical implications of the structure of deoxyribonucleic acid (2.11).

1954   Olds and Milner. Positive reinforcement produced by electrical stimulation of septal area and other regions of rat brain (21.13).

1955   Aserinsky and Kleitman. Two types of ocular motility occurring during sleep (19.10).

1957   Walk, Gibson, and Tighe. Behavior of light- and dark-reared rats on a visual cliff (6.10).

1962   Napier. Fossil hand bones from Olduvai Gorge (4.7).

1962   Hydén and Egyházi. Nuclear RNA changes of nerve cells during a learning experiment in rats (11.10).

NAME INDEX

Numbers with decimal addends designate entire selections. Other numbers indicate pages. Not indexed are: comments on authors in the introductions to selections from their own works, editors and translators, fictional characters, historical personages whose presence in this context may be termed accidental, and cross-references without further content.

Ach, N., 425, 428
Adrian, E. D., 190, 221
Agrippa, H. C., 11.3; 260
Albertus Magnus, 14.2; 436
Albinus, B. S., 206
Alison, A., 285, 290
Allport, F. H., 27.6; 315
Allport, G. W., 23.14; 729
Amman, J. C., 345
Anaxagoras, 76, 78
Anaximines, 28
Aquinas, Saint Thomas, 15.3, 22.1; 335, 576
Aristotle, 2.1, 4.1, 5.1, 7.1, 11.1, 14.1, 19.2; 3, 54, 76, 81, 100, 103, 107, 141, 159, 193, 260, 410, 469, 503, 577, 594, 603, 613, 634, 747
Asch, S., 736
Aserinsky, E., 19.10.
Augustine, Saint, 2.2, 3.1, 11.2, 18.1, 21.3; 4, 54, 67, 196, 341, 402, 469, 549, 550, 605
Avicenna, 3.2; 67, 225, 577

Bacon, F., 14.3, 20.4, 28.1; 528, 748
Bacon, R., 6.3; 107
Bain, A., 12.11, 13.9, 20.11, 21.10, 22.9; 322, 423, 568, 748
Baldwin, J. M., 18.3; 346, 354, 477, 707
Barbaste, M., 722
Bard, P., 20.14.
Battie, W., 24.7; 147
Baxt, N., 701
Bayle, P., 22.3; 557
Beaunis, H., 718
Bekhterev, V., 216
Bell, C., 4.5, 7.10, 9.9; 82, 98, 197
Bentham, J., 21.9; 445
Berger, H., 8.13.
Berkeley, G., 6.6; 92, 96, 107, 108, 114, 116, 128, 282, 393
Bernheim, H., 718
Bernoulli, D., 666

Bernstein, J., 25.8; 190
Bichat, X., 20.10.
Bigelow, H. J., 245
Binet, A., 17.11; 464, 488, 718
Bischoff, T. L. W. von, 39
Bleuler, E., 626
Blix, M., 7.13.
Bodin, J., 24.5.
Boerhaave, H., 206
Boethius, 7.3.
Bonnet, C., 16.7; 146, 378
Borelli, G. A., 9.6; 204
Boring, E. G., 486
Bougeant, G. H., 14.5.
Bouillaud, J. B., 241
Boyle, R., 142
Brett, G. S., 120
Broca, P., 240, 242
Broussais, F., 63, 238
Broussonnet, P. M. A., 240, 241
Brown, T., 12.8; 128, 292, 295, 296, 318, 385
Bubnoff, N., 9.12.
Büchner, L., 46
Bucy, P. C., 548
Bühler, C., 492
Bühler, K., 425
Buffon, G. L. de, 146, 416
Burks, B. S., 467n
Burke, E., 20.8; 286
Burton, R., 16.1.
Burtt, E. A., 588
Bury, R. de, 77
Buschius, H., 255

Cabanis, P. J. G., 2.6, 8.12, 10.3, 15.11; 238, 242
Cagliostro, A. di, 598
Cannon, W. B., 20.13; 546
Carpenter, C. R., 27.11.
Caton, R., 190
Cattell, J. McK., 26.3.
Cattell, R. B., 465

Name Index

Spitz, R., 18.10.
Spurzheim, J. K. (or G. C.), 10.4, 15.12, 17.6, 17.7.
Stahl, G., 45, 177, 206
Stanley, T., 20.1, 20.2, 24.3.
Steinthal, H., 27.1.
Steno, N., 8.6.
Stewart, D., 285, 595
Stobeus, 516
Stratton, G. M., 6.9; 603
Sue, E., 39, 41
Sullivan, H. S., 24.11.
Sully, J., 18.4.
Swammerdam, J., 200, 386

Taine, H., 718
Tarde, G., 27.2; 721
Terman, L. M., 17.13.
Themistocles, 255
Theophrastus, 23.1, 24.1; 607
Thomas, Saint. *See* Aquinas.
Thompson, H., 492
Thorndike, E. L., 13.10; 297, 319, 354, 392
Thurstone, L. L., 465
Tighe, T. J., 6.10.
Tinbergen, N., 357
Titchener, E. B., 3.8; 710
Trembley, A., 2.5.
Tucker, A., 21.7; 285
Turpin, R. A., 457
Tyndall, J., 2.9; 48

Uexküll, J. von, 399

Verworn, M., 149
Vesalius, A., 8.4; 171, 174, 225

Vieussens, R. de, 175
Vindician, 23.3.
Vitry, J. de, 302
Vives, L., 11.4, 13.3, 20.3; 53, 53n, 260, 305, 515, 528
Vogt, C., 46, 188
Volta, A., 185

Wagnitz, H. B., 653
Wake, C. S., 474
Walk, R. D., 6.10.
Wallach, K., 104, 433
Warren, H. C., 285
Watson, J. B., 3.9; 331, 423, 445, 539
Watson, J. D., 2.11.
Watt, H., 425
Weber, E. H., 25.5; 686, 687
Wernicke, C., 219
Wertheimer, M., 16.10; 104, 486
Weyer, J., 24.4; 374, 644, 645, 646
White, R. K., 27.10.
Whitman, C. O., 399
Whyte, L., 405
Whytt, R., 9.8; 34, 193, 205, 213
Wier, J. *See* Weyer.
Wilkins, M. F. H., 49
Willis, T., 8.7, 13.7, 19.7, 24.6.
Woodworth, R. S., 26.5; 67
Wundt, W., 26.1, 28.3; 67, 295, 429, 542, 593, 688, 700, 703, 706, 707, 709, 710, 711, 715, 752

Yerkes, R. M., 72
Young, T., 153, 154

Zeno the Stoic, 20.1; 515
Zuckerman, S., 742

SUBJECT INDEX

Italic numbers refer to editorial paragraphs on those pages.

abilities, equal by nature, 442 (Hobbes)
action experiment, 738 (Lewin)
adaptation level, 691 (Helson)
admiration, see wonder
aggression: its expression cathartic, 574 (Dollard et al.); and social climate, 739 (Lewin et al.), its source in frustration, 573 (Dollard et al.)
air, see pneuma
alexia, 304 (Vives)
ambivalence, 553 (Augustine)
anal character, 621 (Freud)
anger: brain structures involved, 546 (Cannon), 547 (Bard); expression in dreams, 505 (La Chambre); increases muscular powers but lessens control, 536 (Bichat); movement of spirits in, 716 (Bacon); is omitted from primary passions, 517 (Zeno)
animal electricity, 185, 187 (Galvani)
animal magnetism, 185
animal mind: anecdotal psychology and, 354; compared to human, 334 (Albert); criterion of, 349 (Romanes); demon hypothesis of, 341 (Dougeant), estimative faculty and, 367 (Aquinas); its learning unlike human, 324 (Thorndike); limits and capabilities of, 335 (Albert); may form propositions, 313 (Willis); purpose of studying, 323 (Thorndike); research on, misdirected, 398 (Kuo); see also instinct
animal spirits: cannot serve both sense and motion, 178 (Perrault), 200 (Glisson); corporeal, 175 (Willis), 197 (Reisch); doubted, 183 (Cheyne); and electricity, 159, 185, 187 (Galvani); functions of, 169 (Vesalius), 175 (Willis); influence of Galenic doctrine, 163, 168, 171; mediate learning, 309 (Dilly), 312 (Willis); motions of, in passions, 523 (Bacon); supposed active in dissected parts, 37; and vibrations, 181; where concocted, 175 (Willis), 228 (Huarte)

anthropocentrism, of Christianity, 10 (Lactantius)
antipathies: due to sense impressions, 305 (Digby); often due to association, 282 (Locke); removed by pleasurable accompaniments, 306 (Digby); that of sheep and wolf explained, 374 (Charleton)
anxiety, its development in infant, 660 (Sullivan)
aphasics, incapable of abstract thinking, 424 (Ferrier)
apperception, as conscious thinking, 414 (Leibnitz; origin and influence of concept, 414)
apperception type, 629 (Rorschach)
appetite, is often rebellious, 405 (Burton)
aptitudes: and temperaments, 228 (Huarte); tested for industry, 727 (Münsterberg)
Arab philosophy, influence of, 11, 112, 225, 577
association of ideas: and antipathies, 282 (Locke); and diversity of tastes, 283 (Hutcheson); free and controlled, 279 (Hobbes); and errors in thinking, 281 (Locke); as habitual connections, 121 (Berkeley); importance to empiricism, 277; influence on passions exaggerated, 533 (Burke); modifying influences on, 286 (Kames); and motor learning, 315 (Hartley); origin of term, 281; principles of, 251 (Aristotle), 285 (Hume), 286 (Kames), 288 (Gerard), 295 (J. S. Mill); rarely explains progress of thinking, 430 (Wertheimer); reduced to contiguity, 293 (Mill); secondary laws of, 290 (Brown); how similarity is constructive, 297 (Bain); as train of thoughts, 279 (Hobbes); and varieties of genius, 288 (Gerard); and word association, 264 (Galton); see also memory
assuefaction, see habituation
ataraxy, freedom from opinion, 87 (Sextus)

natural law, includes all moral precepts, 579 (Aquinas)

natural theology, 80, 378

Neoplatonism, influence on Christianity, 4

nerves: circle of, 213 (Bell); conduction timed, 701 (Baxt, Helmholtz); integrative action of, 221 (Sherrington); motor and sensory distinct, 196 (Reisch), 197 (Simone), 197 (Charleton, Flemyng); nervous juice, 203 (Borelli); vibrations in, 182 (Newton), 184 (Cheyne)

neurology, origin of word, 175

opinions: passions as, 517 (Zeno); source of troubles, 551 (Epictetus); why diverse, 88 (Sextus)

pain, is precursor of pleasure, 519 (Epicurus); see also pleasure and pain

parsimony, in psychology, 354 (Morgan)

passions: all are satisfying, 531 (Malebranche); communicated by animal spirits, 375 (Charleton); disturb intellect, 166 (Gregory); how identified and measured, 561 (Helvetius); influenced by both constitution and education, 441 (Hobbes); interpretation of expressions is learned, 535 (Hartley); modified by association, 533 (Burke); not vices, 16 (Spinoza); show organic control of animal life, 536 (Bichat); physiological accounts of, 521 (Vives), 523 (Bacon), 529 (Descartes), 532 (Malebranche); root of differences in intellect, 440 (Hobbes); see also emotion

pecking order, 732 (Schjelderup-Ebbe)

perception: Gestalt theory of, 104 (Köhler); insensible perceptions, 415 (Leibnitz); and original principles of constitution, 95 (Reid); sometimes unnoticed, 406 (Pardies); its speed measured, 697 (Wundt); its subjective nature gradually appreciated, 98; types of perceptual theory, 107; its unity demonstrated, 698 (Wundt)

perseveration: as factor of intelligence, 466 (Spearman; in memory, 271 (G. E. Müller)

personal equation, 694; attempt at analysis of, 697 (Wundt)

personality: anal traits, 621 (Freud); autism, 491, 628 (Kretschmer); behavioral traits of temperamental types, 606 (Vindician), 614 (Culpeper); character writing, 603 (Theophrastus), 607 (Garzoni), 603 & 607 (La Bruyère); dispositions of young children, 604 (Galen), 610 (della Porta); functional autonomy of motives, 631 (Allport); how evidenced in cheeks and chin, 617 (Lavater); influenced by wine, 634 (Theophrastus); introvert-extravert typology, 324 (Jung); Platonic and Aristotelian types, 612 (Charron); schizothyme-cyclothyme dimension, 626 (Kretschmer); traits, 631 (Allport); uniqueness of individual, 638 (Allport)

phenomena, exist only in us, 100 (Kant)

phi phenomenon, 428

phrenes: falsely regarded as seat of mind, 161 (Hippocrates); may cause mental illness, 166 (Gregory)

phrenology: Academy report on, 231; criticism by Forichon, 236; foundations of, 232 (Gall & Spurzheim); origin of word, 28; rejects traditional faculties, 452 (Spurzheim); and Scottish faculty psychology, 452; stimulated interest in localization problem, 231

physiognomy: emphasizes dependence of behavior on body, 609; probable influence on Gall, 617; reveals mental dispositions, 610 (della Porta), 617 (Lavater), 747 (Bacon)

physiological psychology: deals with relations between external and internal existence, 751 (Wundt); does not seek to explain psychical phenomena from physical, 751 (Wundt)

physiological time, 702 (Hirsch)

pineal body: does not regulate pneuma, 163 (Galen); seat of soul, 172 (Descartes)

play, function of, 480 (Groos)

pleasure: in doing habitual acts, 304 (Vives); its role in learning, 320 (Bain); as restoration to natural state, 519 (Epicurus)

pleasure and pain: are experienced sympathetically, 22 (Condorcet); govern mankind, 568 (Bentham); are principal affections, 519 (Epicurus); men made to be happy, 21 (La Mettrie); see also motivation, sources of; pain; pleasure

pneuma: its function in brain, 161 (Hippocrates); elaborated in retiform plexus, 163 & 164 (Galen); source of life, 6, 28

pneumatology, origin of word, 28

possession: of animals by demons, 341 (Bougeant); of men by demons, 639 (Psellus); of witches by devil, 642 (Weyer); see also sacred disease

primates: apt to imitate, 338 (Bacon), 314 (Willis); behavior in captivity is